the
GRAPHIC CANON
of CRIME &
MYSTERY

VOLUME 2

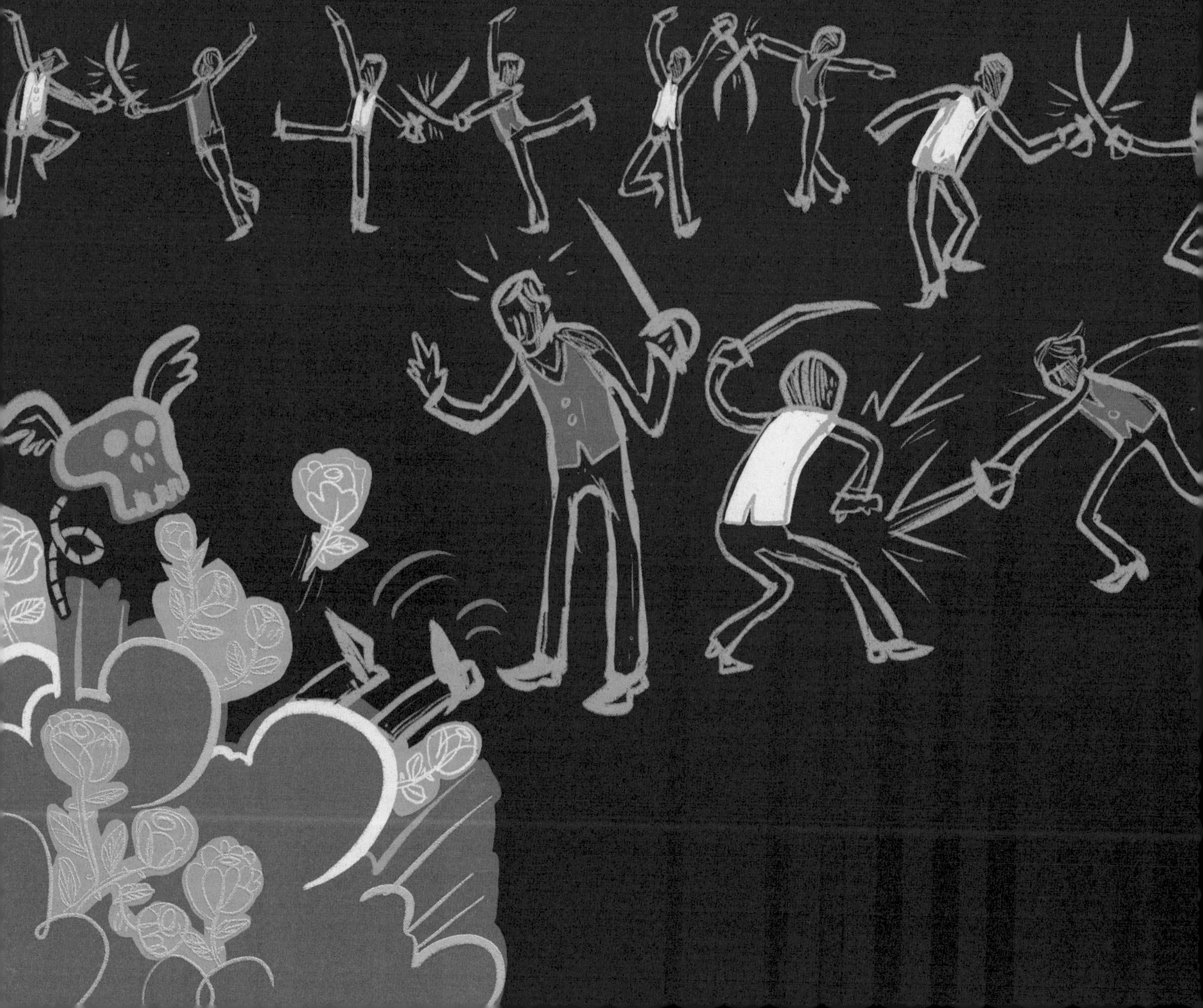

the
GRAPHIC CANON of
CRIME & MYSTERY

FROM SALOME
TO EDGAR ALLAN POE
TO *SILENCE OF THE LAMBS*

VOLUME

Edited by
RUSS KICK

SEVEN STORIES PRESS
New York • Oakland • London

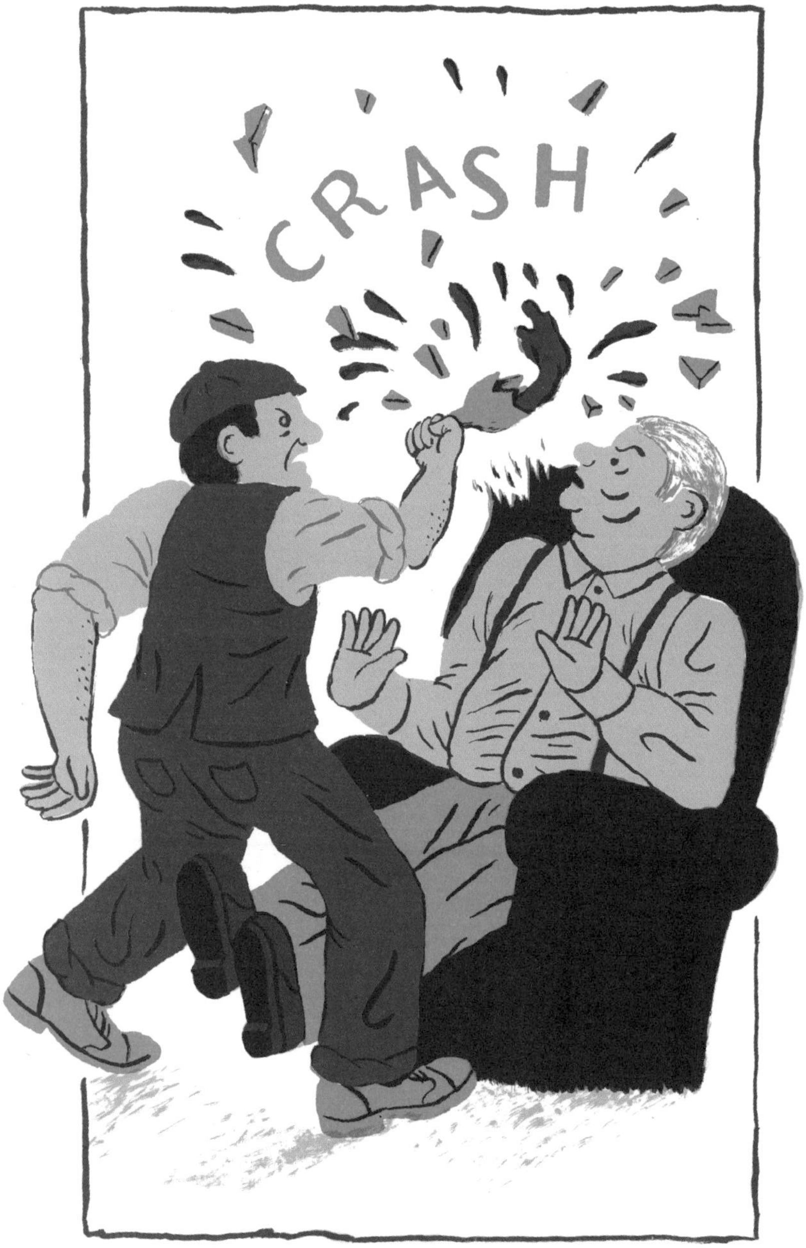
CRASH

For permissions information see page 311.

A SEVEN STORIES PRESS FIRST EDITION

SEVEN STORIES PRESS
140 Watts Street
New York, NY 10013
www.sevenstories.com

College professors and high school and middle school teachers may order free examination copies of Seven Stories Press titles. To order, visit www.sevenstories.com or send a fax on school letterhead to (212) 226-1411.

Series design: Stewart Cauley, New York
Volume design: Dror Cohen and Abigail Miller

Library of Congress Cataloging-in-Publication Data

Names: Kick, Russell, editor.
Title: The graphic canon of crime & mystery. Volume 2, From Salome to Edgar
Allan Poe to Silence of the lambs / edited by Russ Kick.
Description: A Seven Stories Press first edition. | New York : Seven Stories Press, [2020] | Series: The graphic canon | Includes index.
Identifiers: LCCN 2020007304 | ISBN 9781609808266 (trade paperback)
Subjects: LCSH: Literature--Adaptations. | Detective and mystery comic
books, strips, etc. | Graphic novels.
Classification: LCC PN6726 .G68 2020 | DDC 741.5/973--dc23
LC record available at https://lccn.loc.gov/2020007304

Printed in China

9 8 7 6 5 4 3 2 1

COVER AND INCIDENTAL ART CREDITS

Front cover: Til Lukat
Back cover: Zavka

p. i,Frank R. Stockton
p. ii and iii, Kim Clements
p. iv, Till Lukat
p. v, Zavka
p. vi, Rachel Leah Gallo
p. vii, Hila Noam
p. viii, Lara Antal and Dave Kelly--
p. 1, Hila Noam
p. 2, Frank R. Stockton
p. 3, Rachel Leah Gallo
p. 122, Anthony Ventura
p. 188, Landis Blair
p. 214, Kim Clements
p. 215, Hila Noam
p. 311, Til Luka
p. 312, Joy Kolitsky

CONTENTS

Editor's Introduction   1

Acknowledgments   2

PART ONE
Killers

CAIN AND ABEL   4
from the Book of Genesis
ART/ADAPTATION BY Zavka

"BLUEBEARD"   11
Charles Perrault
ART/ADAPTATION BY Shawn Cheng

"THE TELL-TALE HEART"   20
Edgar Allan Poe
ART/ADAPTATION BY Dame Darcy

LADY AUDLEY'S SECRET   31
Mary Elizabeth Braddon
ART/ADAPTATION BY Joy Kolitsky

MURDER BALLADS   46
ART/ADAPTATION BY John Pierard

PSYCHO   58
Robert Bloch
ART/ADAPTATION BY Rachel Leah Gallo

THE SAILOR WHO FELL FROM GRACE WITH THE SEA 79
Yukio Mishima
ART/ADAPTATION BY Andrea Montano

THE SILENCE OF THE LAMBS 88
Thomas Harris
ART/ADAPTATION BY Alice Urbino

THE BLACK DAHLIA 104
James Ellroy
ART/ADAPTATION BY Josebo Morales

I WAS DORA SUAREZ 116
Derek Raymond
ART/ADAPTATION BY Douglas Noble

PART TWO
Revenge

SALOME AND JOHN THE BAPTIST 124
from the Gospel of Matthew
ART/ADAPTATION BY Angelle Sundberg

"THE PARDONER'S TALE"
(FROM THE CANTERBURY TALES) 134
Geoffrey Chaucer
ART/ADAPTATION BY Katherine Hearst

TITUS ANDRONICUS 147
William Shakespeare
ART/ADAPTATION BY Anthony Ventura

REBECCA   **175**
Daphne du Maurier
ART/ADAPTATION BY Emily Rose Dixon

THE GODFATHER   **182**
Mario Puzo
ART/ADAPTATION BY Rachel Smythe

PART THREE
The System

"THE LADY, OR THE TIGER?"   **189**
Frank R. Stockton
ART/ADAPTATION BY Omer Hoffmann

THE TRIAL   **198**
Franz Kafka
ART/ADAPTATION BY Landis Blair

PART FOUR
Elementary

**"THE CASE OF THE WILD CAT AND THE CROWN PRINCE"
(A JUSTICE BAO MYSTERY)**   **216**
ART/ADAPTATION BY Sonia Leong

"THE SWEDISH MATCH"   **231**
Anton Chekhov
ART/ADAPTATION BY Hila Noam

"A SCANDAL IN BOHEMIA"
(A SHERLOCK HOLMES MYSTERY) 240
Arthur Conan Doyle
ART/ADAPTATION BY Lara Antal AND Dave Kelly

"THE NINESCORE MYSTERY"
(A LADY MOLLY MYSTERY) 251
Baroness Emmuska Orczy
ART/ADAPTATION BY Becky Hawkins

"THE SINS OF PRINCE SARADINE"
(A FATHER BROWN MYSTERY) 261
G.K. Chesterton
ART/ADAPTATION BY Sally Madden

THE SECRET ADVERSARY
(A TOMMY AND TUPPENCE MYSTERY) 272
Agatha Christie
ART/ADAPTATION BY Kim Clements

"THE ROAD HOME" 284
Dashiell Hammett
ART/ADAPTATION BY Teddy Goldenberg

"THE LAMP OF GOD" 296
Ellery Queen
ART/ADAPTATION BY Till Lukat

Contributor Biographies 309

Credits and Permissions 311

Index 312

EDITOR'S INTRODUCTION

WELCOME TO THE LATEST VOLUME IN our experiment to see what happens when classic works of literature are refracted through the minds and pens of some of the best contemporary comic artists using a staggering array of styles, approaches, and techniques.

This installment continues our focus on fiction and other types of writing that involve crime in some way. Be it straight-up genre fiction *a la* Dashiell Hammett and Agatha Christie. Or works of capital-L Literature such as Chaucer and Kafka. Maybe from people with a foot in both worlds like Poe and Arthur Conan Doyle. Or works that are harder to pin down: *The Godfather*, *Lady Audley's Secret*, "Ballad of Bonnie and Clyde."

The first *Crime & Mystery* volume was arranged in themed sections (unlike the first four volumes of the series, which were chronological). We continue with themes here, with the pieces in each section ordered by publication date.

Jumping right into the thick of things, the section "Killers" opens with a bloody take on the human race's first murder, followed by the first work of serial-killer fiction, rendered in fairy-tale style. From there, it's a journey through genres: Poe's confessional story, a Victorian "sensation novel," American murder ballads, British noir. Scenes from two works more familiar as movies get reimagined in ways faithful to the source material.

Revenge has been the driving force behind a lot of crime. Whether it's telling a Roman viceroy of Galilee that his marriage is illegitimate, breaking the jaw of Mafia don's son, cheating on your spouse with multiple partners, or turning your enemy's son into a human sacrifice, there are a lot of ill-advised actions that can lead to bloodshed. Of course, one of those ill-advised actions is enacting revenge, which can escalate in dramatic ways (just ask Titus and Tamora, or the creeps in "The Pardoner's Tale").

When we talk about crime, we can't ignore the justice system, which decides the fate of the accused. "The System" section contains two classic, pessimistic takes on the dispensation of justice. "The Lady, or the Tiger?" is the maddeningly ambiguous story of a justice system based entirely on chance, beautifully constructed by Omer Hoffmann, who provides his own answer to the riddle. "The Trial," presented as a choose-your-own-adventure by Landis Blair, shows that the system is an unknowable, uncaring black box that plays with our lives with no meaningful way to fight back.

In the final section, "Elementary," we enter the world of detective fiction. Sherlock is here, charmingly rendered in one of his most popular cases. Also present: Father Brown, Ellery Queen, and China's legendary Justice Bao. We get to follow the first cases of Tommy and Tuppence (Agatha Christie's classic sleuthing duo, here transformed into a cat and a rhinoceros) and the undeservedly forgotten Lady Molly of Scotland Yard. Teddy Goldenberg brings us a treat in the form of Dashiell Hammett's early short story "The Road Home," featuring manhunting detective Hagedorn. This is often credited as the first hardboiled story.

ACKNOWLEDGMENTS

DEEP THANKS TO MY FAMILY AND FRIENDS for keeping me going.

Much gratitude to Dan Simon, the founder and publisher of Seven Stories Press, who continues to publish this six-volume, 2,800-page colossus, the Ring Cycle of graphic anthologies. Endless thanks to Veronica Liu, my editor and the project manager for *The Graphic Canon*, and to Sanina Clark, who stepped in for the now-maternal Veronica, who also plays a big role helping to run the Word Up Community Bookshop in Washington Heights NYC. And many *mercis* to everyone else at Seven Stories Press, including Sam Brown, Stewart Cauley, Dror Cohen, Yves Gaston, Jon Gilbert, Lauren Hooker, Allison Paller, Silvia Stramenga, Michael Tencer, Ruth Weiner, and all the interns.

Gracias to Ann Kingman, Michael Kindness, and everyone else at Random House Distribution, as well as all the people involved in the printing, transportation, and selling of *The Graphic Canon of Crime and Mystery, Volume 2*.

Finally, the hugest thanks of all to the artists and adapters who contributed, and to the writers whose works fueled them. You all are the reason we're here.

PART ONE
Killers

JWM•712
TEXAS

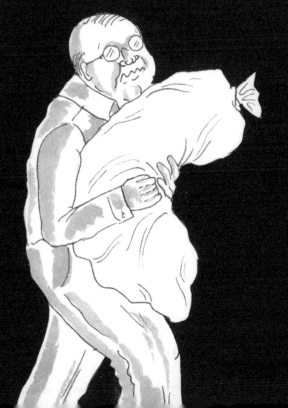

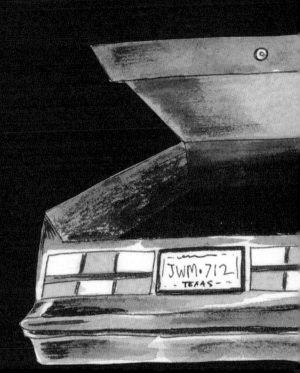

Cain and Abel

from the Book of Genesis

ART/ADAPTATION BY Zavka

IF YOU BELIEVE THAT THE BIBLE IS historically accurate, then what we have here is the world's first murder, committed by the human race's third member against its fourth. If you don't, this bit of ancient Israelite literature is still an extremely early, culturally ingrained story of homicide. Brother kills brother in a fit of jealousy. Not jealousy over a lover but because God liked Abel's meaty sacrificial offerings and disapproved of Cain's grains. (Oddly, God punishes Cain while also protecting him from murder, then allows him to marry, have a child, and found a city.)

This foundational tale of homicide, anger, jealousy, sacrifice, sibling rivalry, veganism vs. carnivorism, and a host of other themes is packed into a tight little bundle in the Book of Genesis: chapter 4, verses 1–16. The artist Zavka—who hails from Warsaw, Poland, and has published a nightmarish take on "Hansel and Gretel"—has narrowed in on the murder itself and the events immediately before and after. Her brutally primitive style offers a much-needed contrast to the defanged, literally bloodless depictions offered by most illustrated Bible stories of these two brothers.

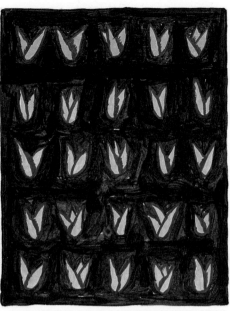

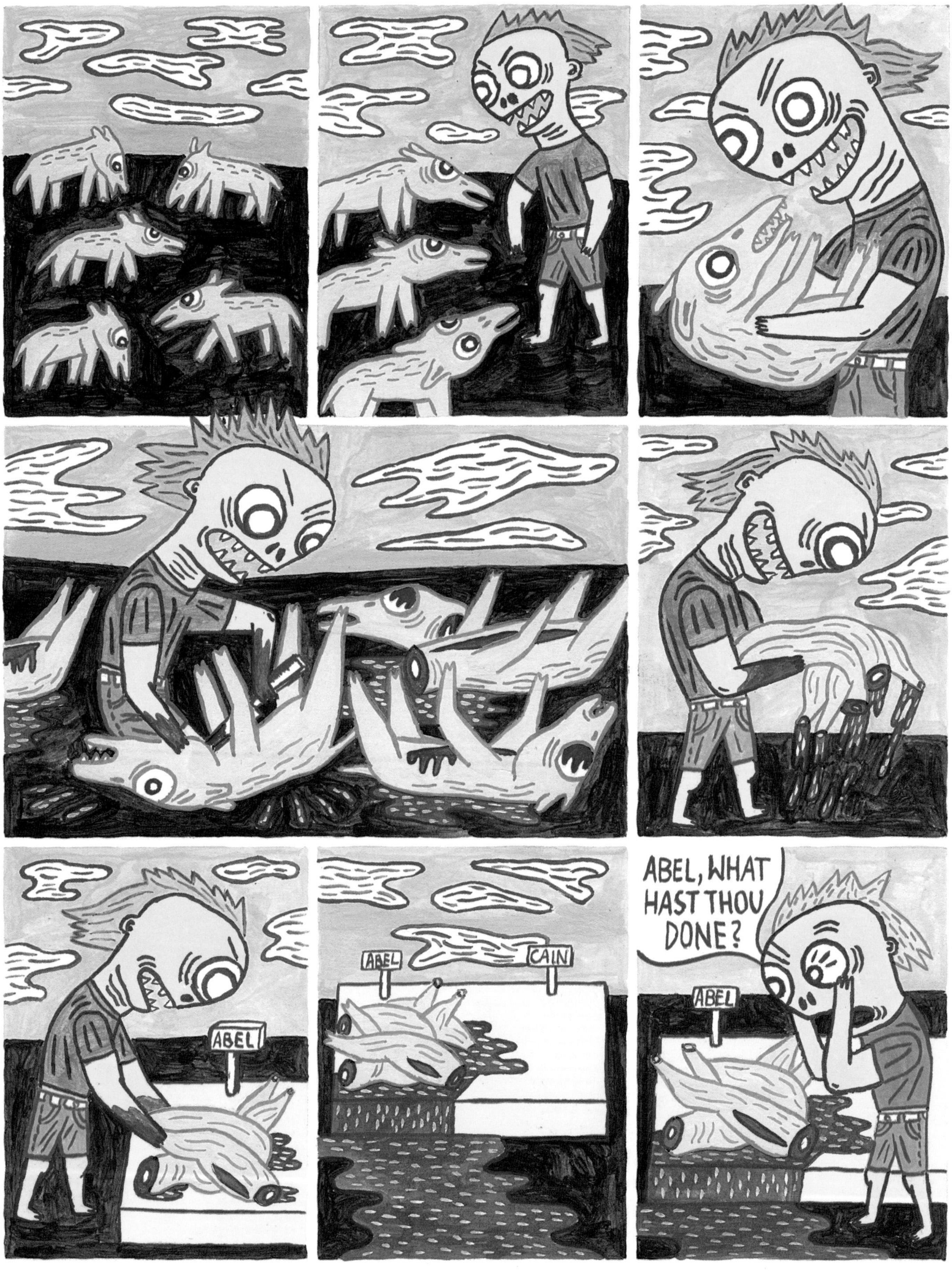
ABEL
ABEL
CAIN
ABEL, WHAT HAST THOU DONE?
ABEL

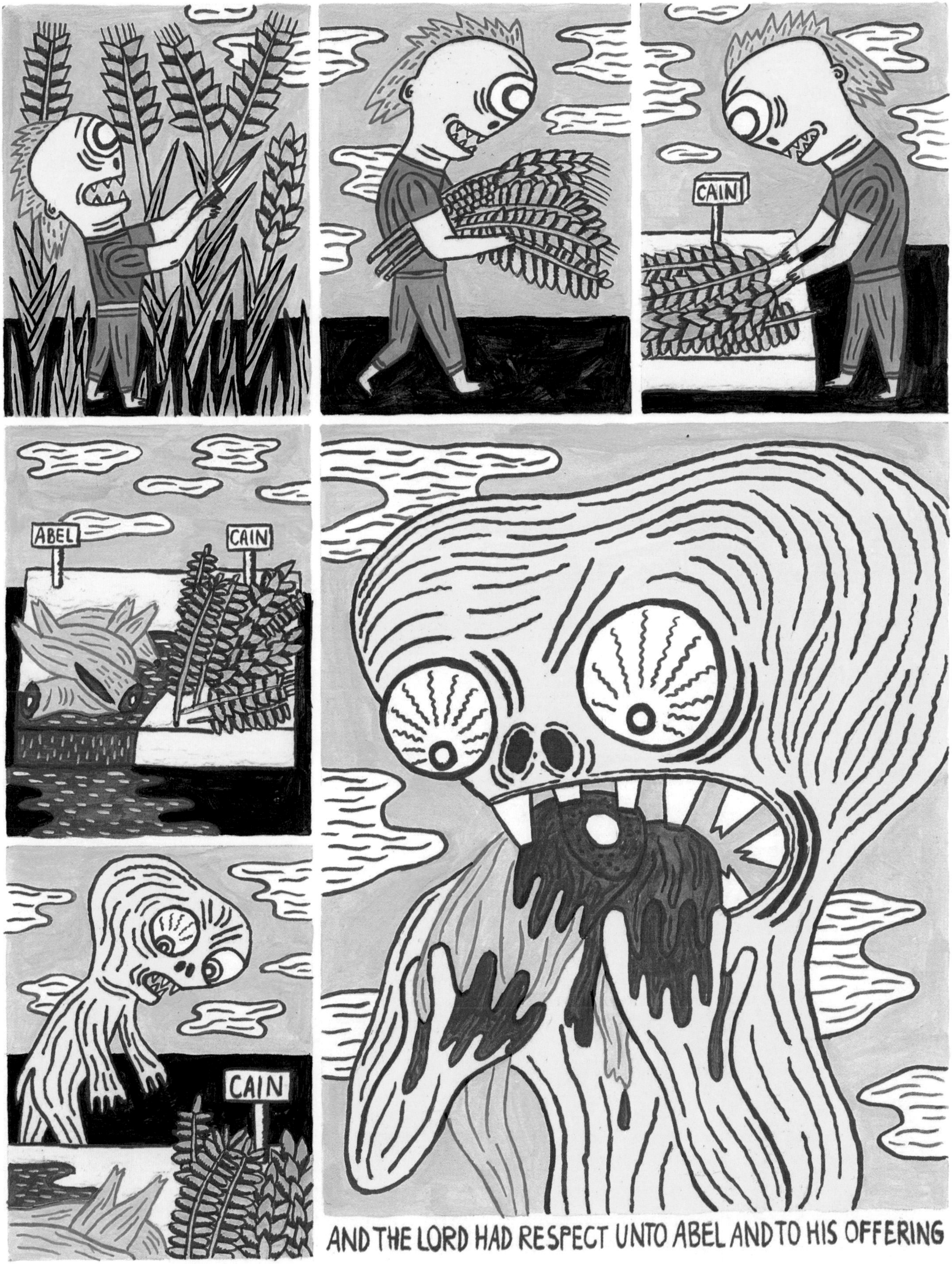
CAIN
ABEL
CAIN
CAIN
AND THE LORD HAD RESPECT UNTO ABEL AND TO HIS OFFERING

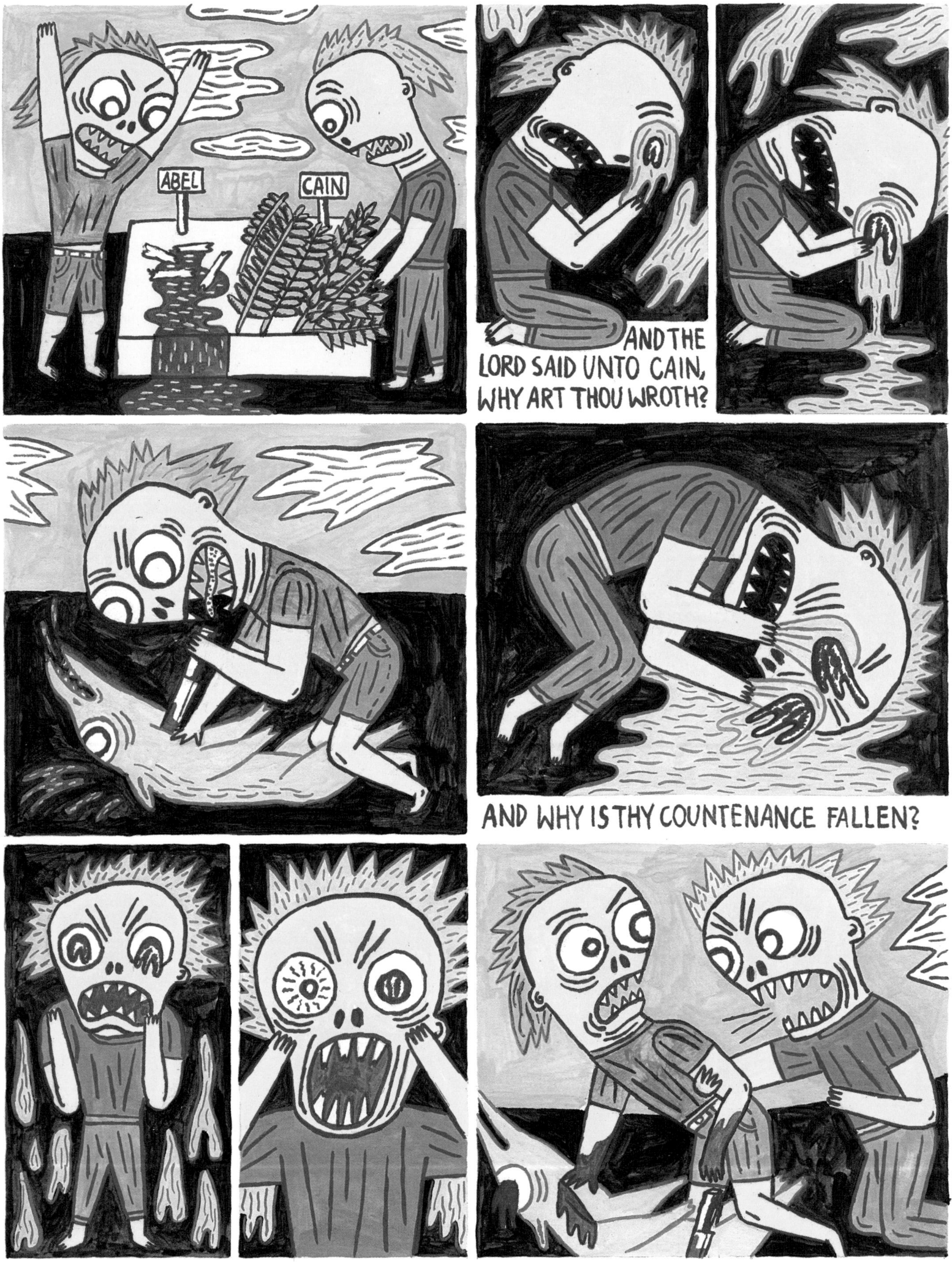
ABEL
CAIN
AND THE LORD SAID UNTO CAIN, WHY ART THOU WROTH?
AND WHY IS THY COUNTENANCE FALLEN?

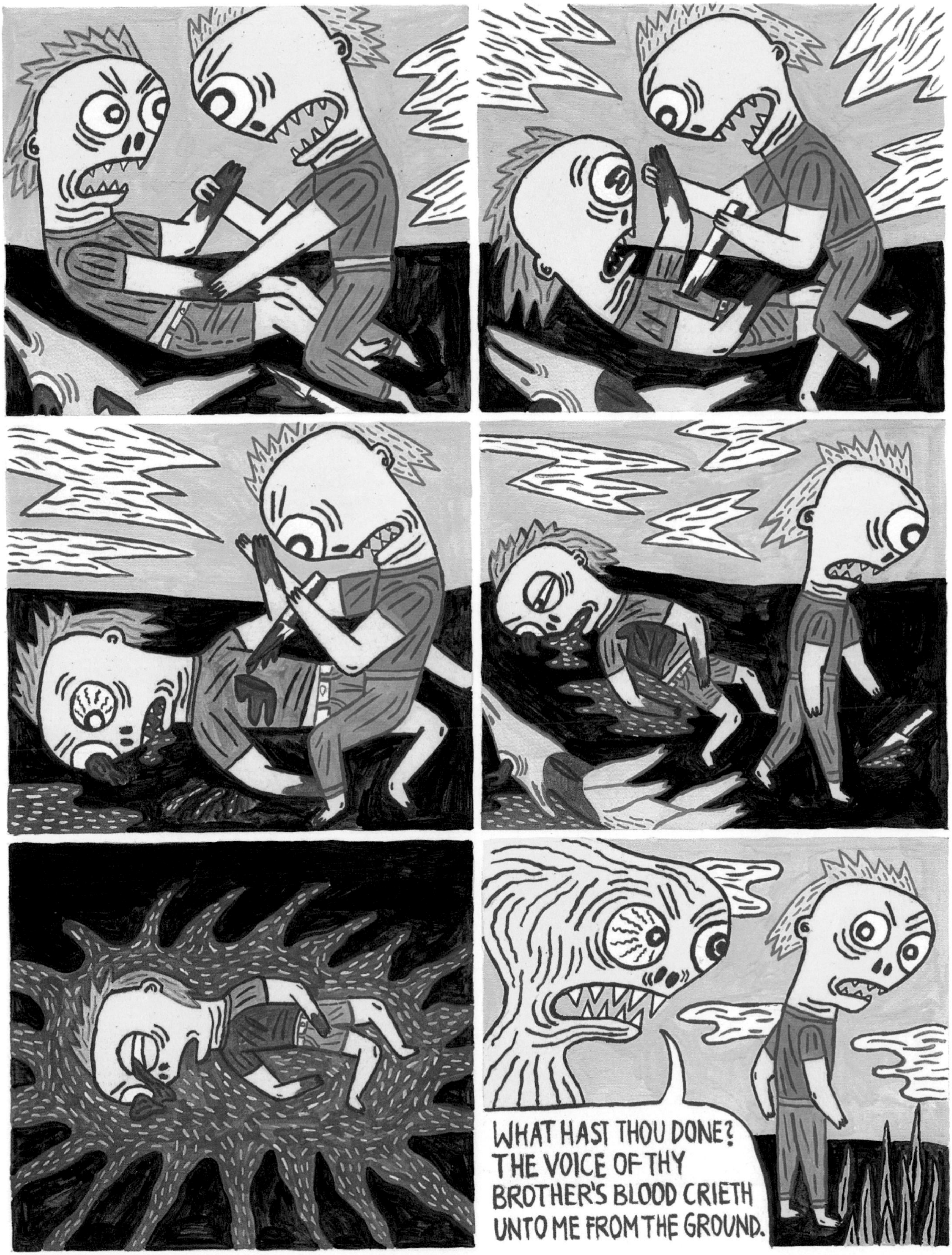
WHAT HAST THOU DONE? THE VOICE OF THY BROTHER'S BLOOD CRIETH UNTO ME FROM THE GROUND.

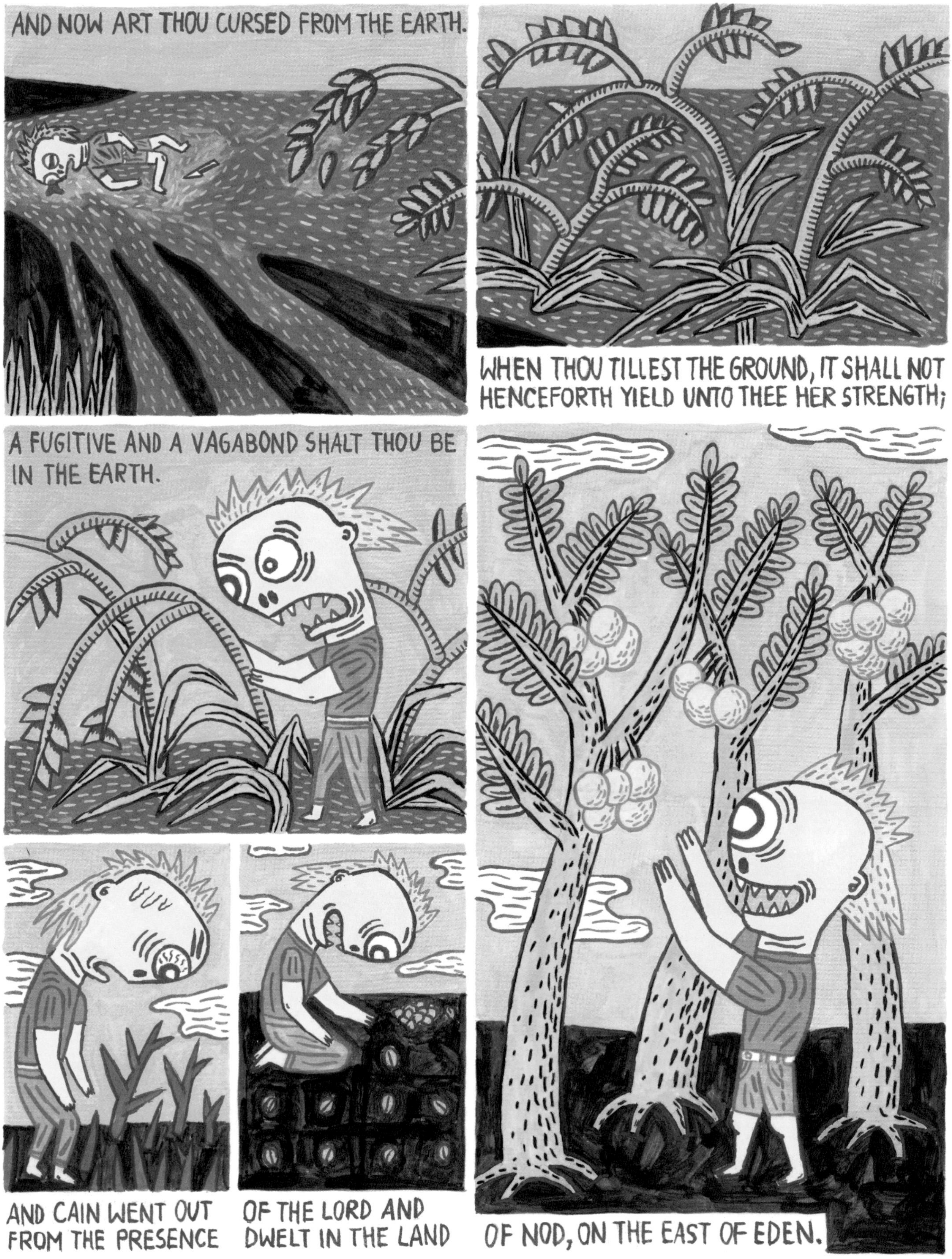
AND NOW ART THOU CURSED FROM THE EARTH.
WHEN THOU TILLEST THE GROUND, IT SHALL NOT HENCEFORTH YIELD UNTO THEE HER STRENGTH;
A FUGITIVE AND A VAGABOND SHALT THOU BE IN THE EARTH.
AND CAIN WENT OUT FROM THE PRESENCE
OF THE LORD AND DWELT IN THE LAND
OF NOD, ON THE EAST OF EDEN.

"Bluebeard"

Charles Perrault

ART/ADAPTATION BY **Shawn Cheng**

SOME OBSERVERS SAY THAT CHARLES Perrault's "Bluebeard" is the first work of serial-killer fiction. It appeared in a book subtitled *Stories of Mother Goose.*

If you've paid much attention to fairy tales, you know that they're often dark, creepy, and intensely violent. Even in this disturbing form of literature, though, "Bluebeard" stands out. The story of a nobleman who brutally kills his wives and keeps their corpses started out—like many fairy tales—as a folktale. It was then rewritten in literary style by Charles Perrault at the end of the 1600s, and he put it in his book of fairy tales

alongside "Little Red Riding Hood," "Cinderella," and "Sleeping Beauty." (As for "Bluebeard" being the earliest work of serial-killer fiction, the only earlier contenders are some of Shakespeare's plays, but those killings are motivated by politics or revenge, not as ends in themselves.)

Comics artist, painter, and printmaker Shawn Cheng has contributed to earlier *Graphic Canons*, including the children's literature volume, which included his tour-de-force adaptation of all thirteen original Oz novels by L. Frank Baum. This time, he makes the goriest fairy tale of them all look darkly beautiful.

Bluebeard

by Shawn Cheng • adapted from the folktale by Charles Perrault

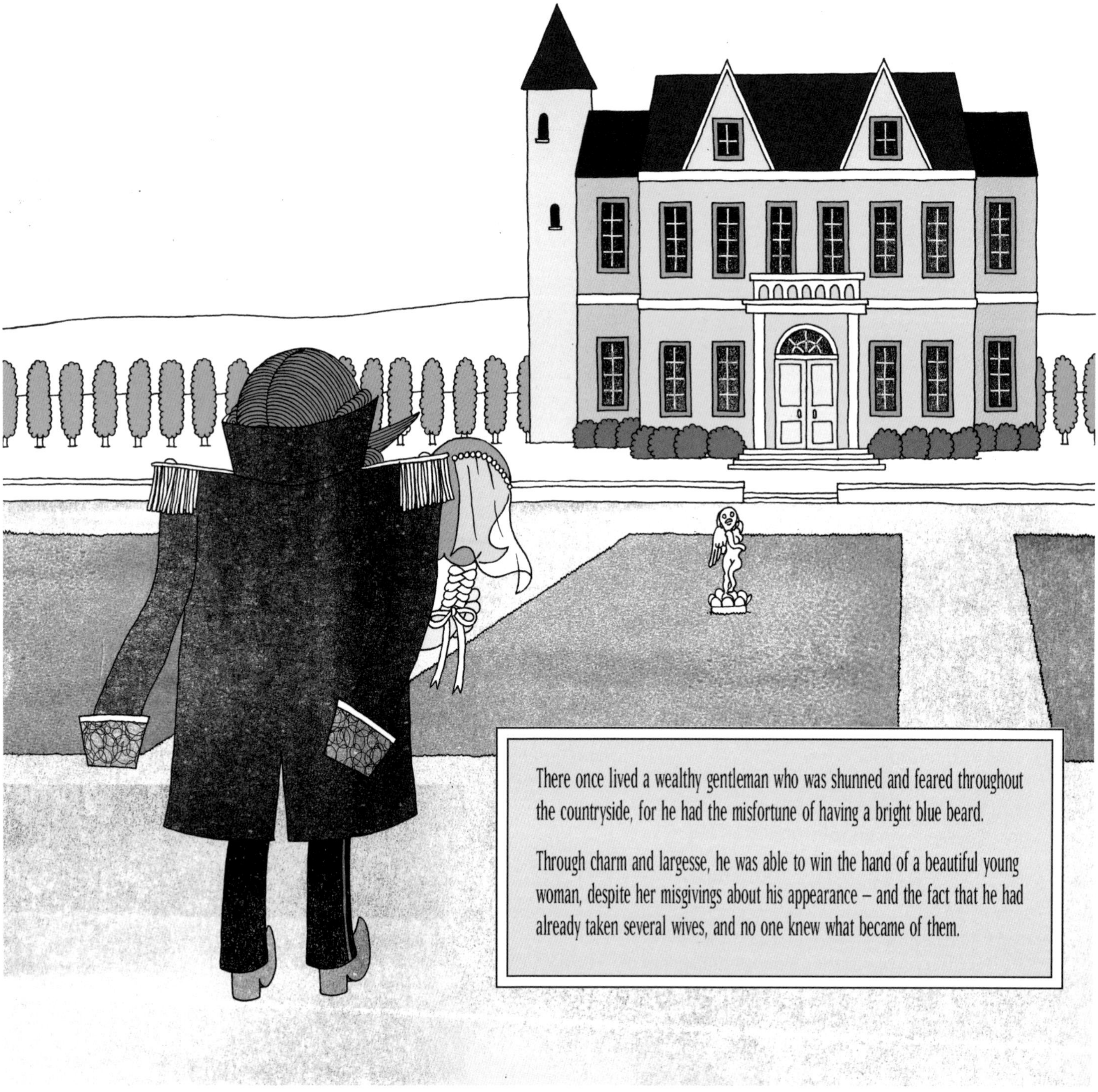
There once lived a wealthy gentleman who was shunned and feared throughout the countryside, for he had the misfortune of having a bright blue beard.
Through charm and largesse, he was able to win the hand of a beautiful young woman, despite her misgivings about his appearance – and the fact that he had already taken several wives, and no one knew what became of them.

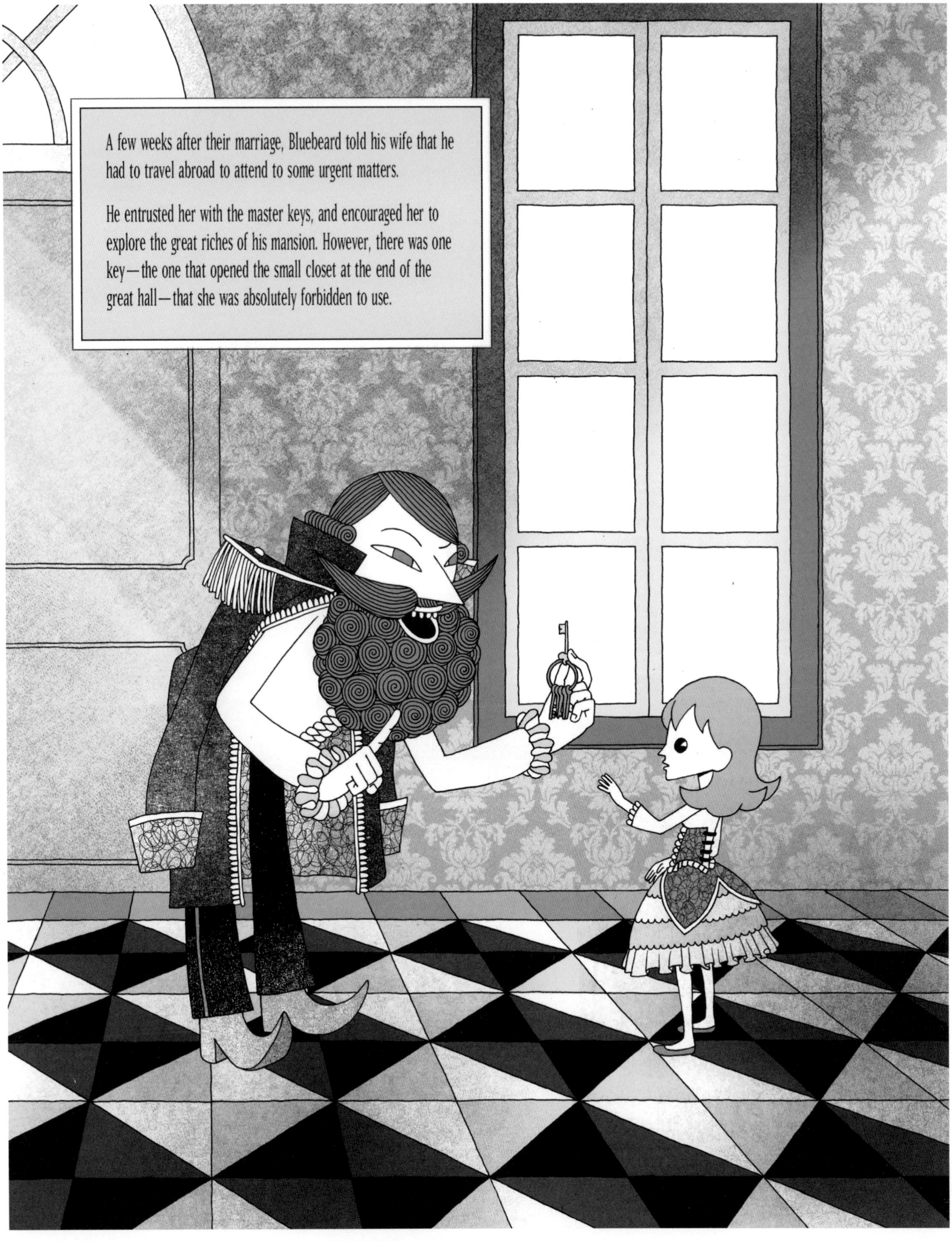
A few weeks after their marriage, Bluebeard told his wife that he had to travel abroad to attend to some urgent matters.
He entrusted her with the master keys, and encouraged her to explore the great riches of his mansion. However, there was one key—the one that opened the small closet at the end of the great hall—that she was absolutely forbidden to use.

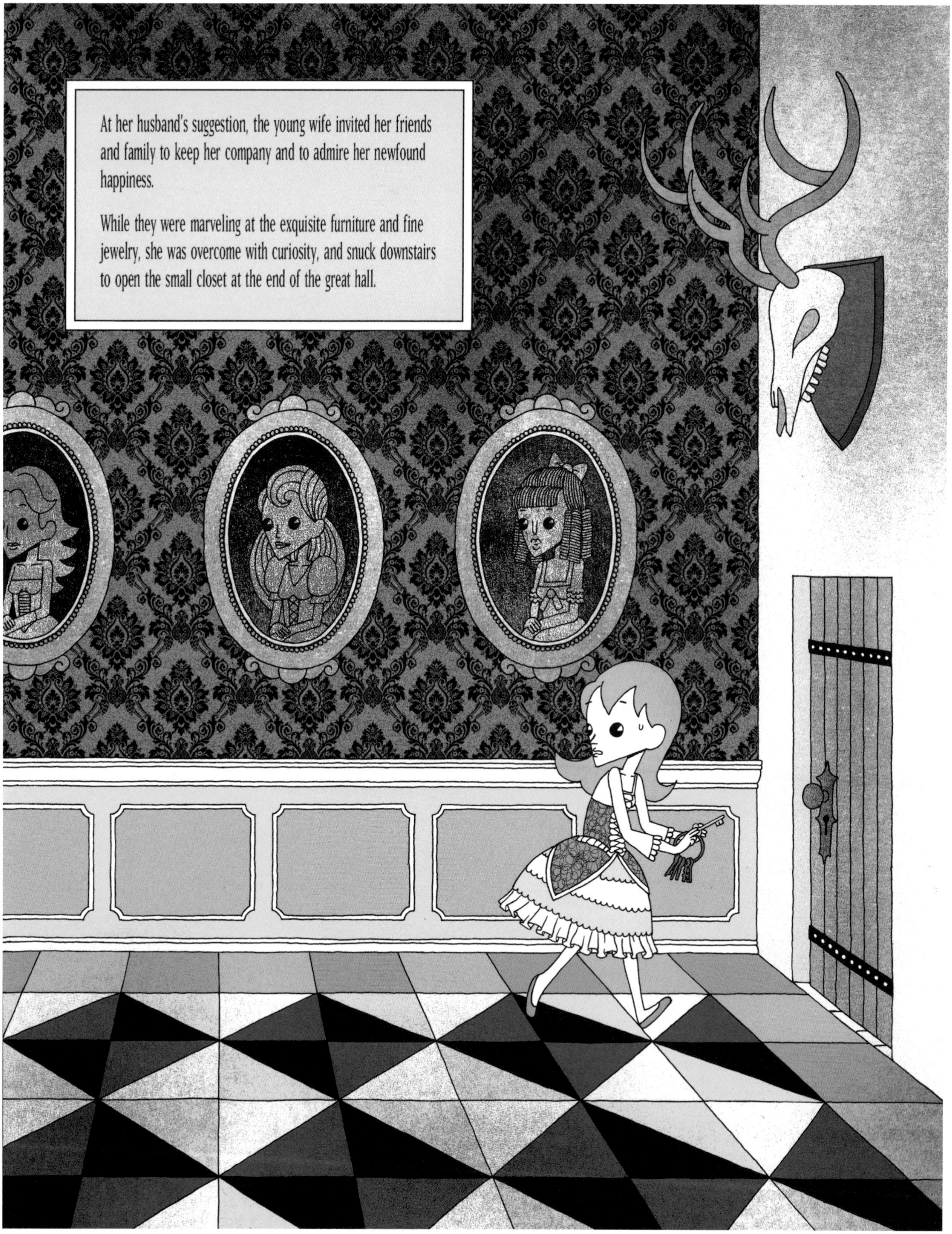
At her husband's suggestion, the young wife invited her friends and family to keep her company and to admire her newfound happiness.
While they were marveling at the exquisite furniture and fine jewelry, she was overcome with curiosity, and snuck downstairs to open the small closet at the end of the great hall.

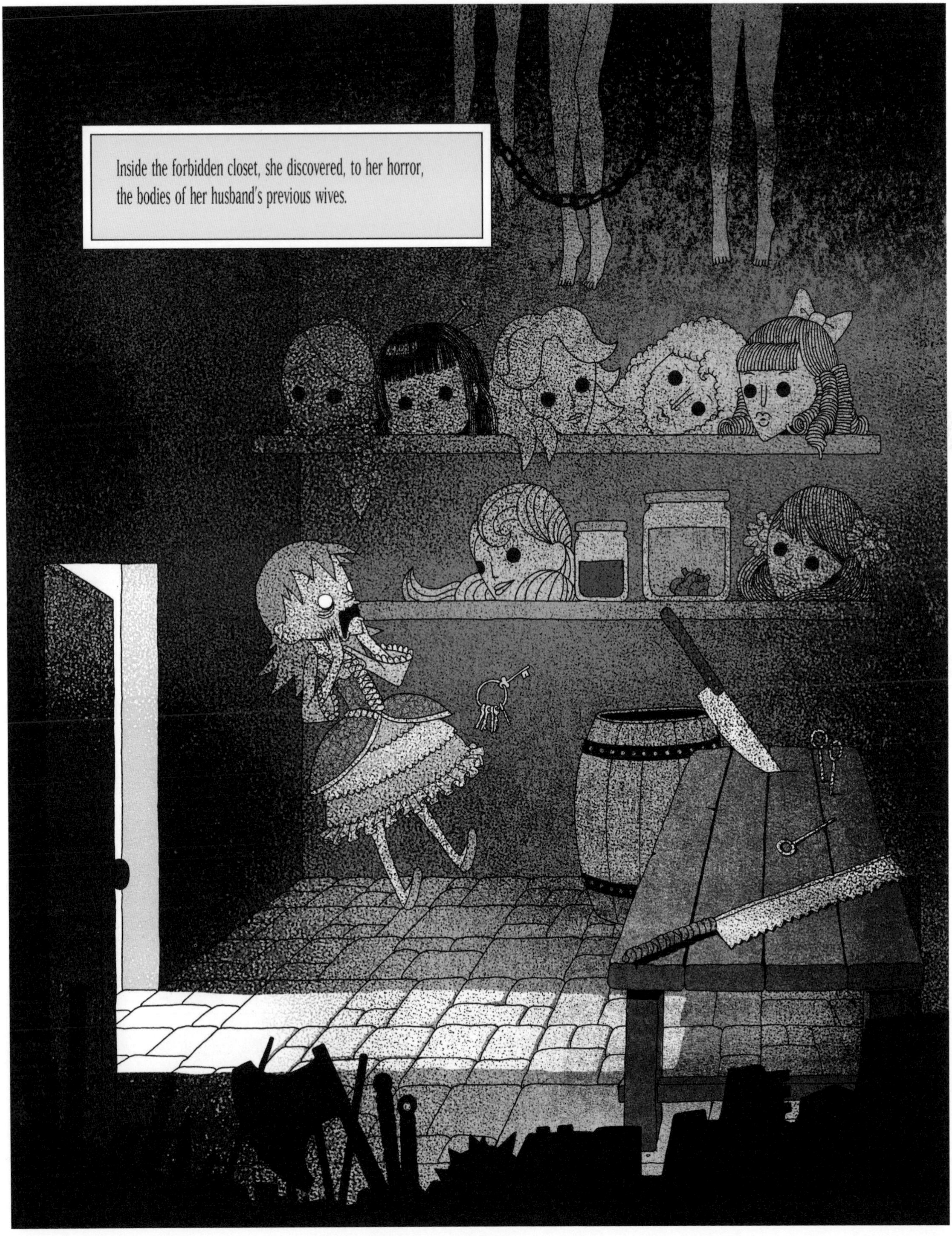
Inside the forbidden closet, she discovered, to her horror, the bodies of her husband's previous wives.

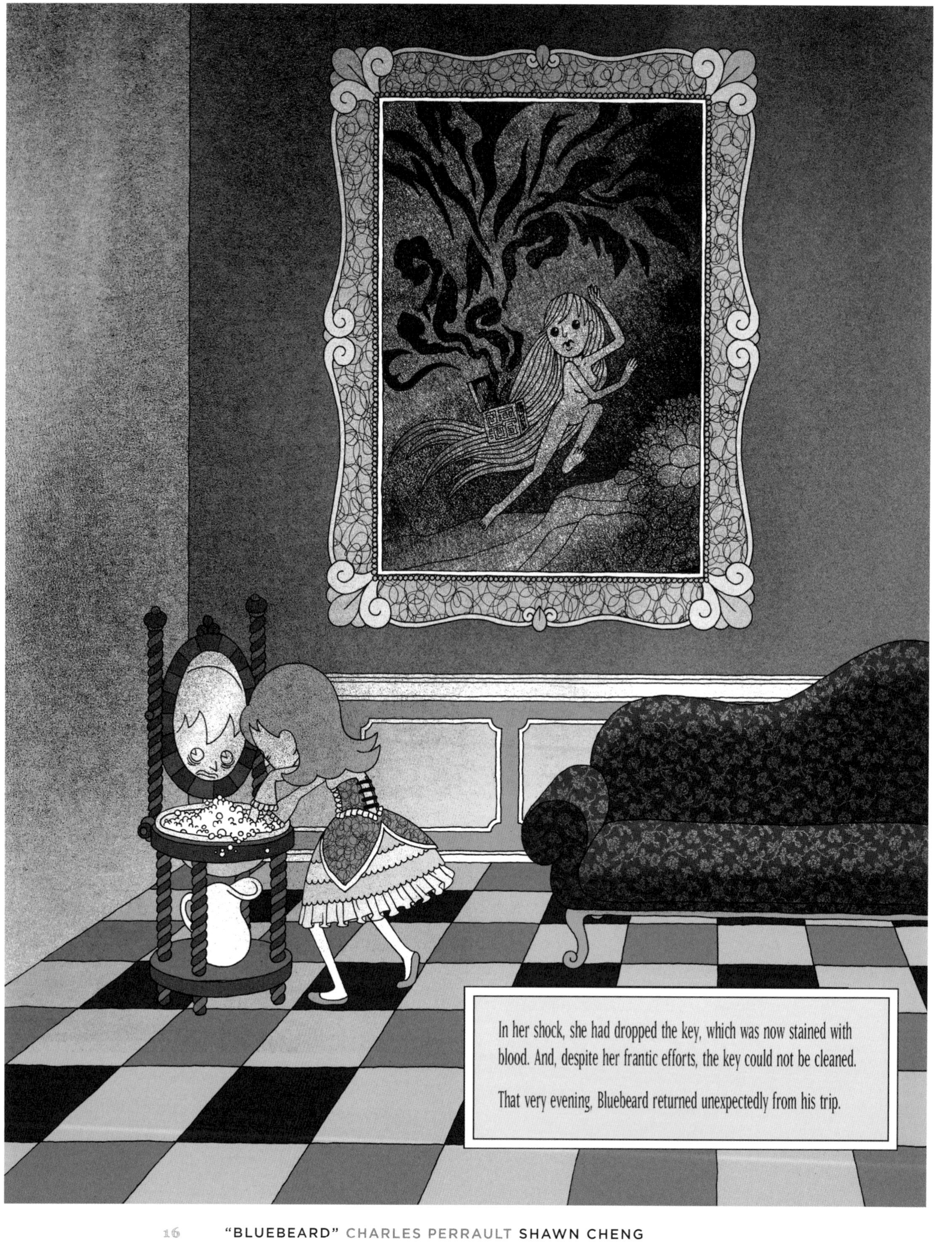
In her shock, she had dropped the key, which was now stained with blood. And, despite her frantic efforts, the key could not be cleaned.
That very evening, Bluebeard returned unexpectedly from his trip.

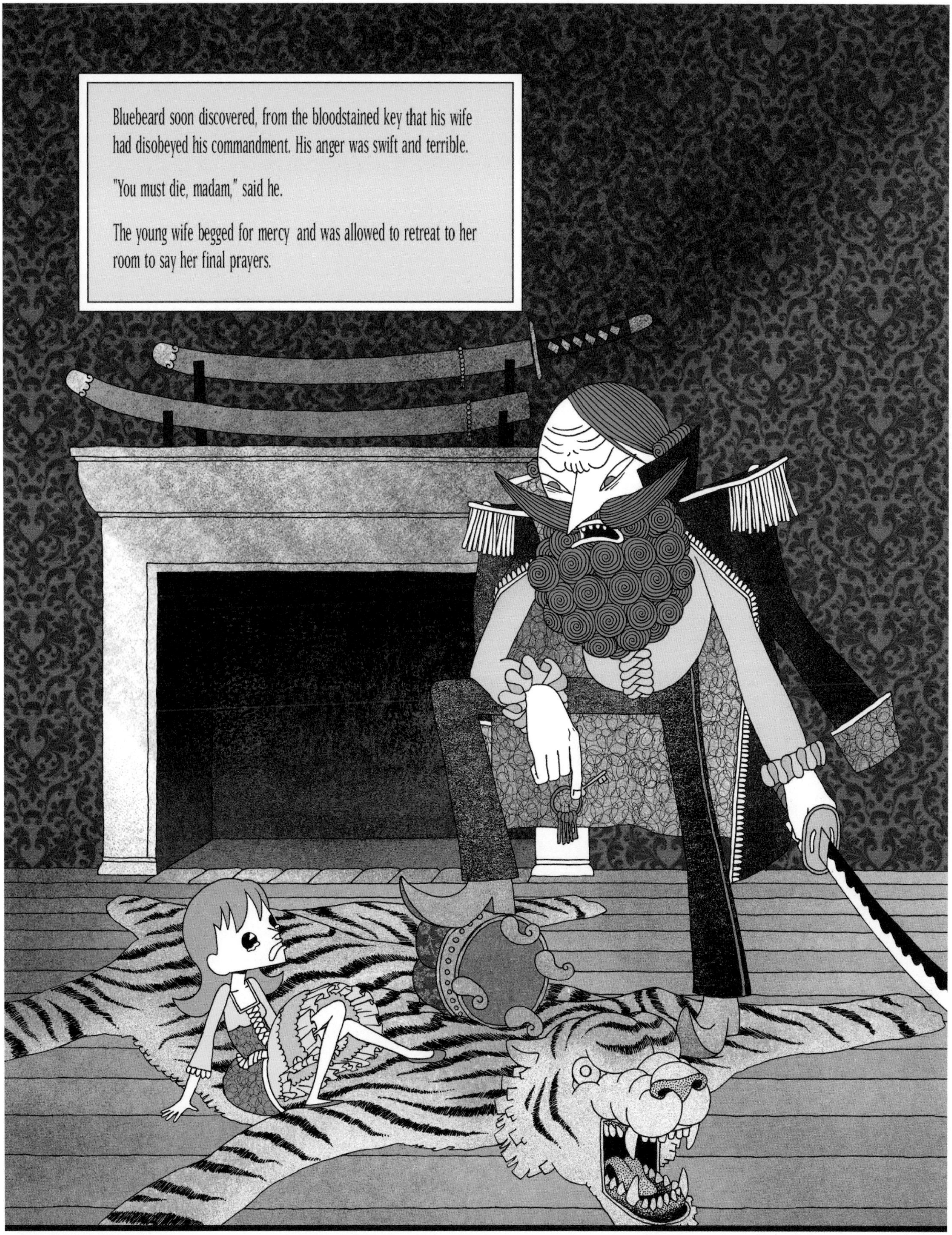
Bluebeard soon discovered, from the bloodstained key that his wife had disobeyed his commandment. His anger was swift and terrible.
"You must die, madam," said he.
The young wife begged for mercy and was allowed to retreat to her room to say her final prayers.

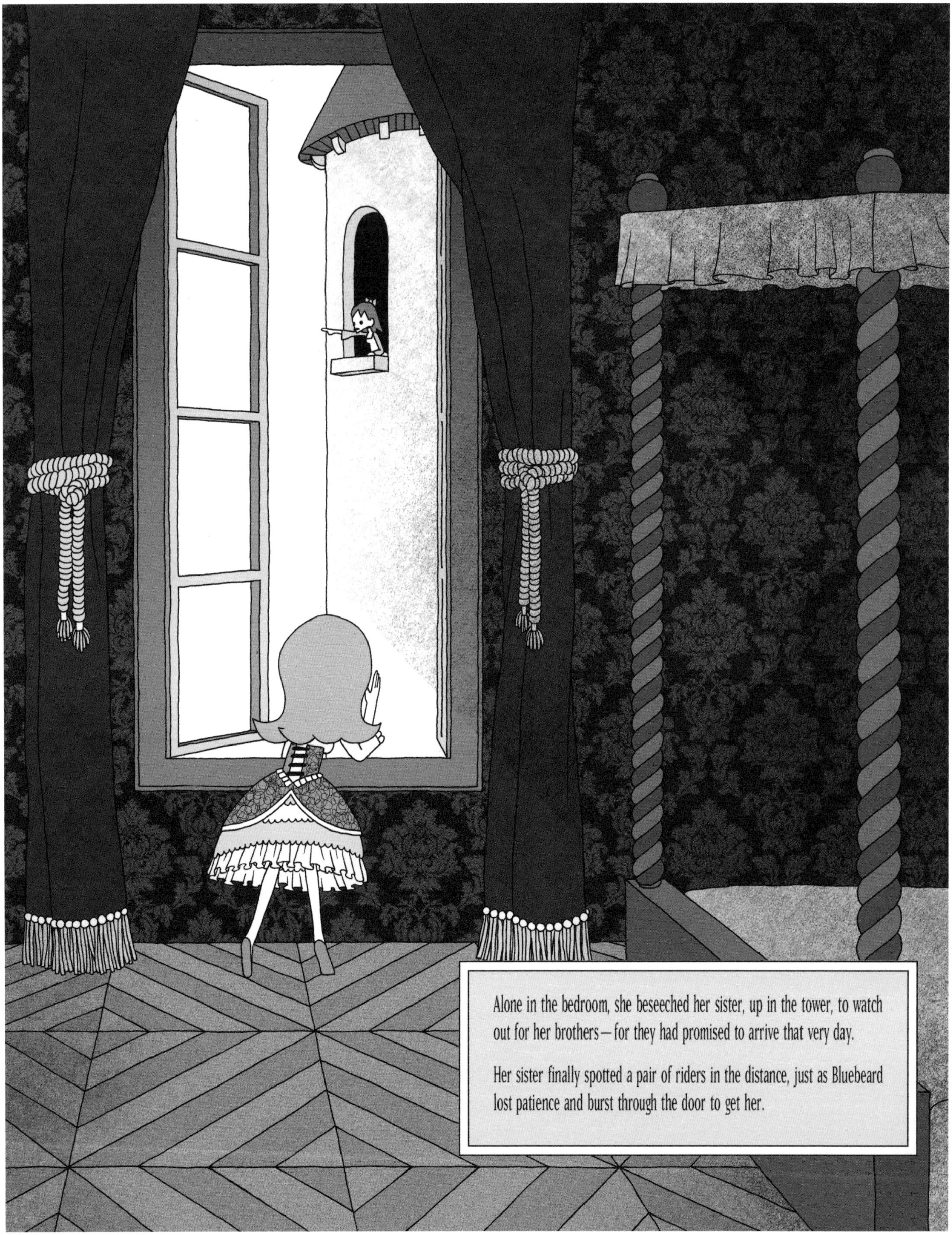
Alone in the bedroom, she beseeched her sister, up in the tower, to watch out for her brothers—for they had promised to arrive that very day.
Her sister finally spotted a pair of riders in the distance, just as Bluebeard lost patience and burst through the door to get her.

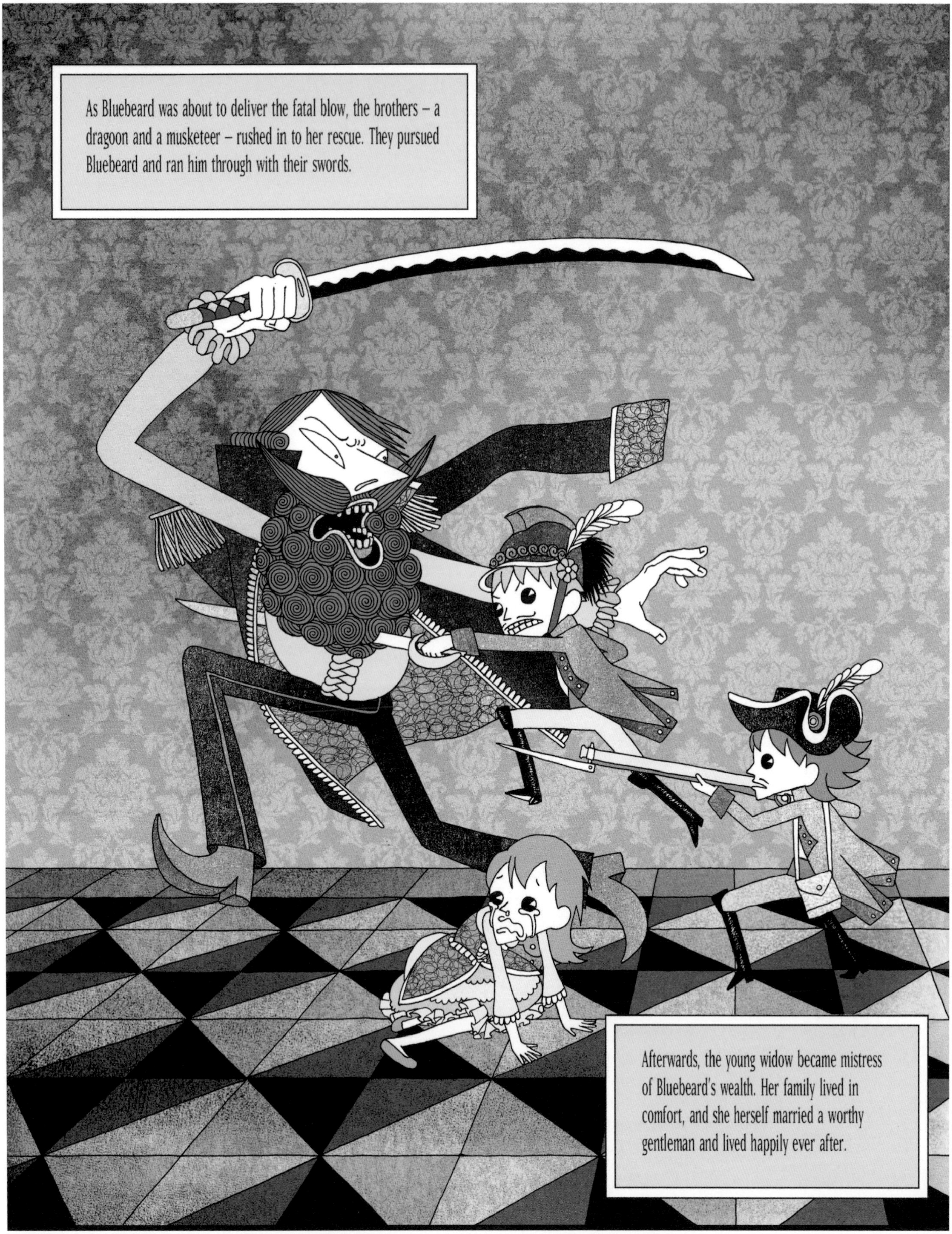
As Bluebeard was about to deliver the fatal blow, the brothers – a dragoon and a musketeer – rushed in to her rescue. They pursued Bluebeard and ran him through with their swords.
Afterwards, the young widow became mistress of Bluebeard's wealth. Her family lived in comfort, and she herself married a worthy gentleman and lived happily ever after.

"The Tell-Tale Heart"

Edgar Allan Poe

ART/ADAPTATION BY Dame Darcy

ONE OF EDGAR ALLAN POE'S MOST popular stories, "The Tell-Tale Heart" is the confession of a murderer. The narrator probably would've gotten away with it, but their guilty conscience interfered, producing a maddening auditory hallucination. However, it's also possible the overwhelming noise was made by the victim's ghost as a form of haunting. Nothing in the story points to a supernatural element, but with Poe, you never know.

That's not the only thing we're unsure about. Who is the narrator confessing to? What was the relationship between murderer and victim? Showing once again that ambiguity is a key to great literature, "The Tell-Tale Heart" leaves so many fundamental questions unanswered, yet it has become a popular, heavily studied classic that still has the power to creep us out.

Multi-modal creative Dame Darcy has been bringing her dark, neo-Victorian sensibilities to the comics world for more than 25 years now, primarily in the form of *Meat Cake*, which indirectly asks what would happen if Lewis Carroll's Wonderland were taken to its logical, twisted, Gothic extreme. For this volume, Darcy travels again to the shadiest corners of the 1800s, bringing her trademark style to one of her favorite stories.

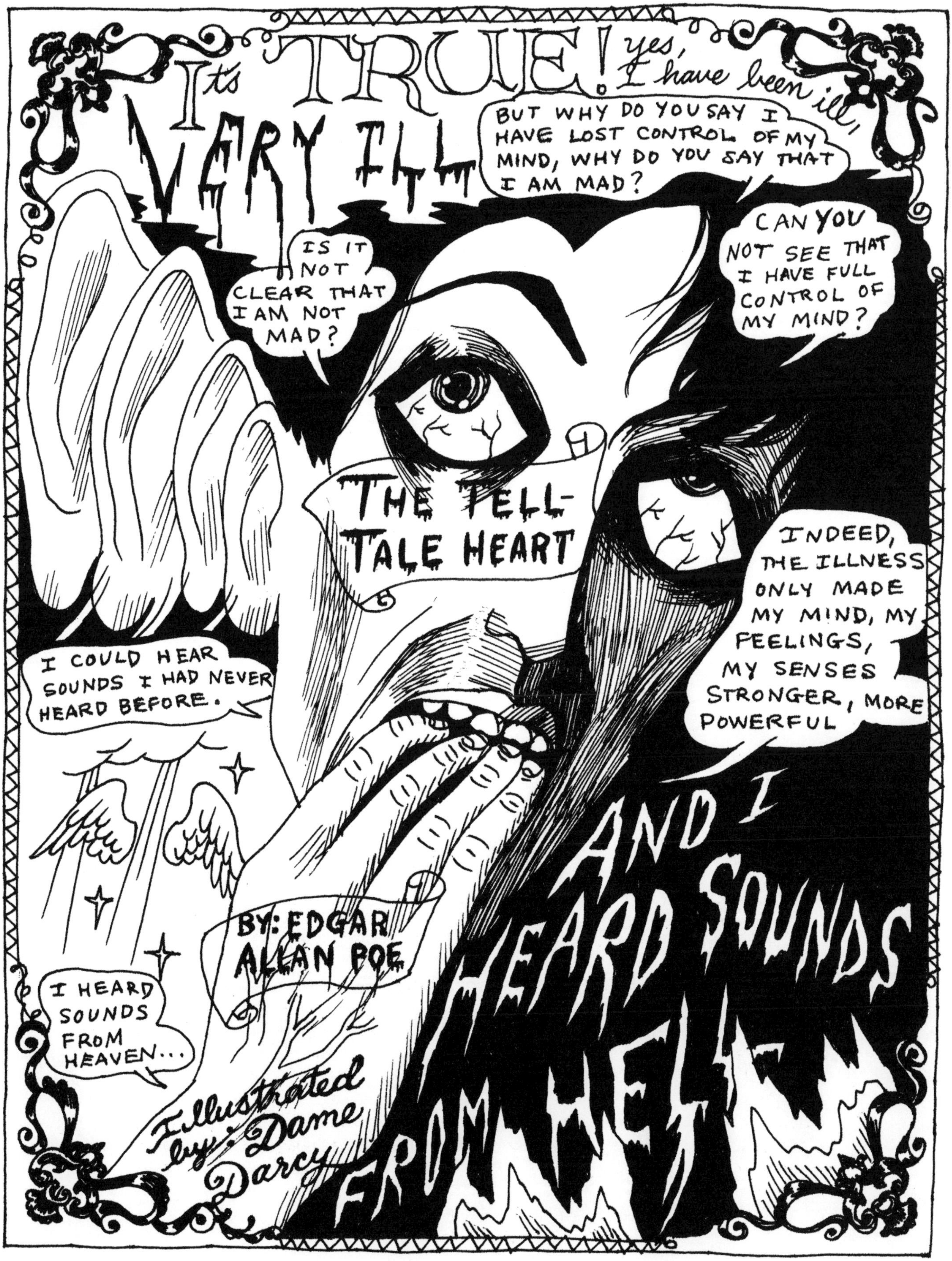
It's TRUE! yes, I have been ill,
VERY ILL
BUT WHY DO YOU SAY I HAVE LOST CONTROL OF MY MIND, WHY DO YOU SAY THAT I AM MAD?
IS IT NOT CLEAR THAT I AM NOT MAD?
CAN YOU NOT SEE THAT I HAVE FULL CONTROL OF MY MIND?
THE TELL-TALE HEART
INDEED, THE ILLNESS ONLY MADE MY MIND, MY FEELINGS, MY SENSES STRONGER, MORE POWERFUL
I COULD HEAR SOUNDS I HAD NEVER HEARD BEFORE.
BY: EDGAR ALLAN POE
I HEARD SOUNDS FROM HEAVEN...
AND I HEARD SOUNDS FROM HELL
Illustrated by: Dame Darcy

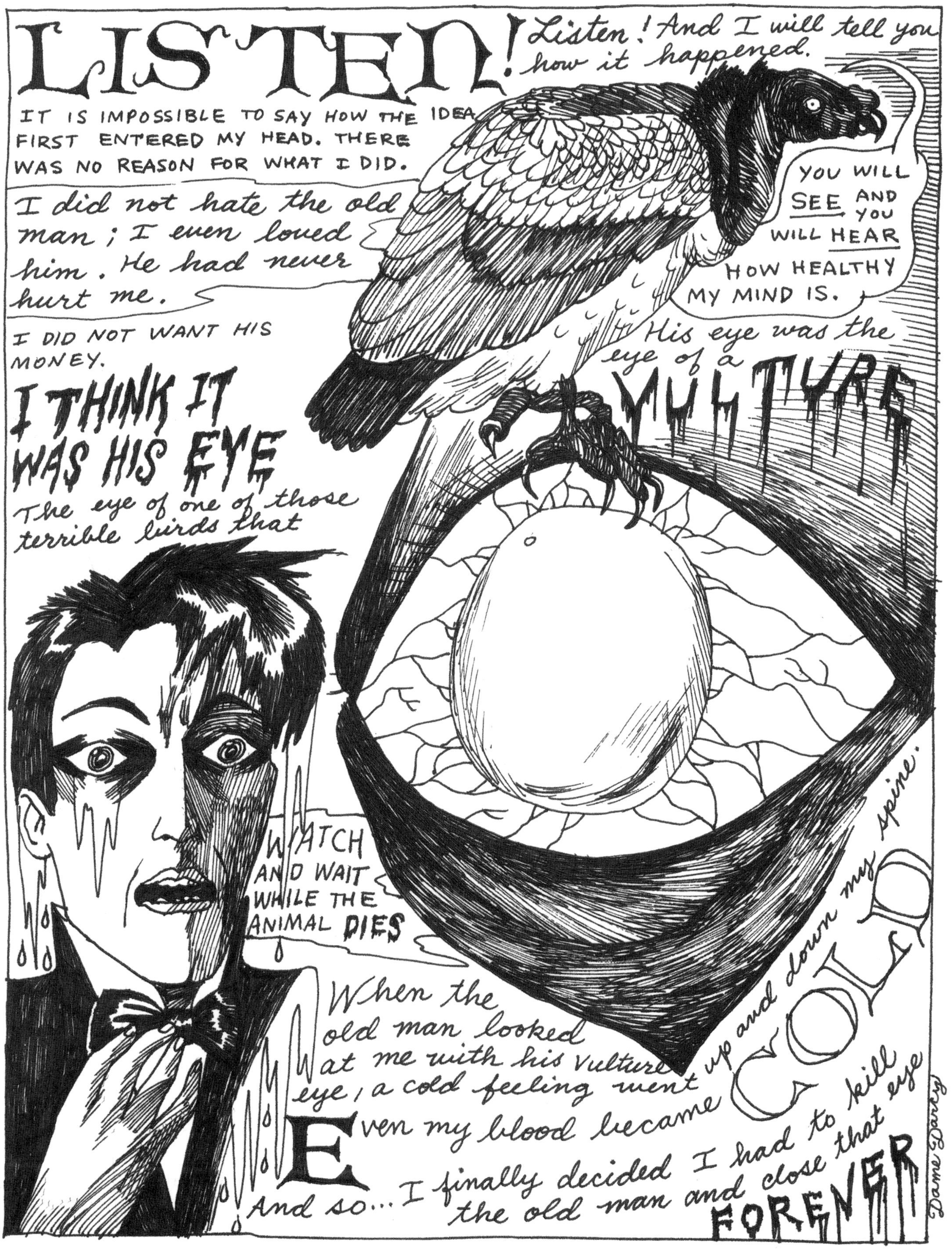

LISTEN!
Listen! And I will tell you how it happened.
IT IS IMPOSSIBLE TO SAY HOW THE IDEA FIRST ENTERED MY HEAD. THERE WAS NO REASON FOR WHAT I DID.
YOU WILL SEE AND YOU WILL HEAR HOW HEALTHY MY MIND IS.
I did not hate the old man; I even loved him. He had never hurt me.
I DID NOT WANT HIS MONEY.
I THINK IT WAS HIS EYE
The eye of one of those terrible birds that
His eye was the eye of a VULTURE
WATCH AND WAIT WHILE THE ANIMAL DIES
When the old man looked at me with his vulture eye, a cold feeling went up and down my spine.
Even my blood became COLD
And so... I finally decided I had to kill the old man and close that eye FOREVER
Dame Darcy

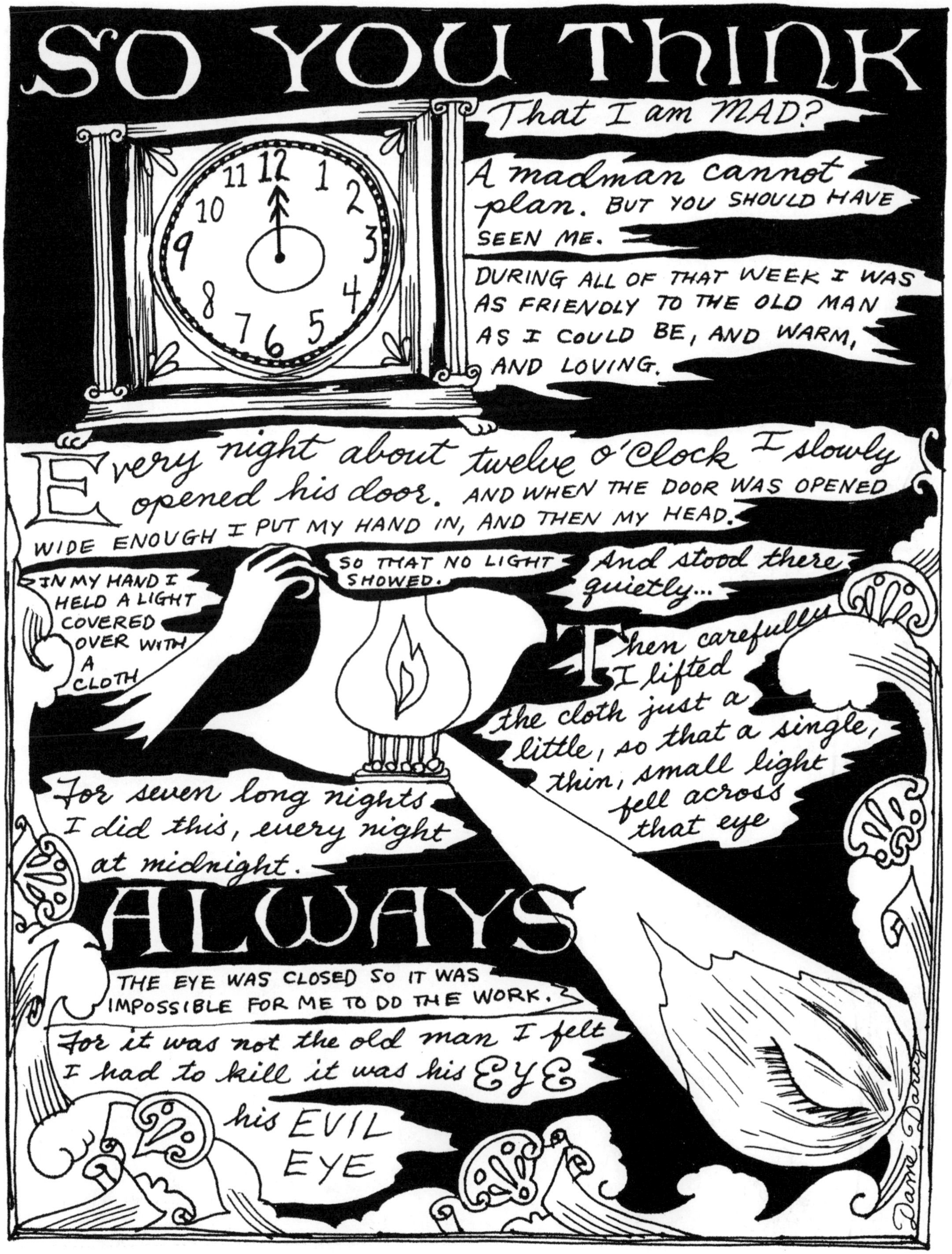
SO YOU THINK
That I am MAD?
A madman cannot plan. BUT YOU SHOULD HAVE SEEN ME.
DURING ALL OF THAT WEEK I WAS AS FRIENDLY TO THE OLD MAN AS I COULD BE, AND WARM, AND LOVING.
Every night about twelve o'clock I slowly opened his door. AND WHEN THE DOOR WAS OPENED WIDE ENOUGH I PUT MY HAND IN, AND THEN MY HEAD.
IN MY HAND I HELD A LIGHT COVERED OVER WITH A CLOTH
SO THAT NO LIGHT SHOWED.
And stood there quietly...
Then carefully I lifted the cloth just a little, so that a single, thin, small light fell across that eye
For seven long nights I did this, every night at midnight.
ALWAYS
THE EYE WAS CLOSED SO IT WAS IMPOSSIBLE FOR ME TO DO THE WORK.
For it was not the old man I felt I had to kill it was his EYE
his EVIL EYE
Dame Darcy

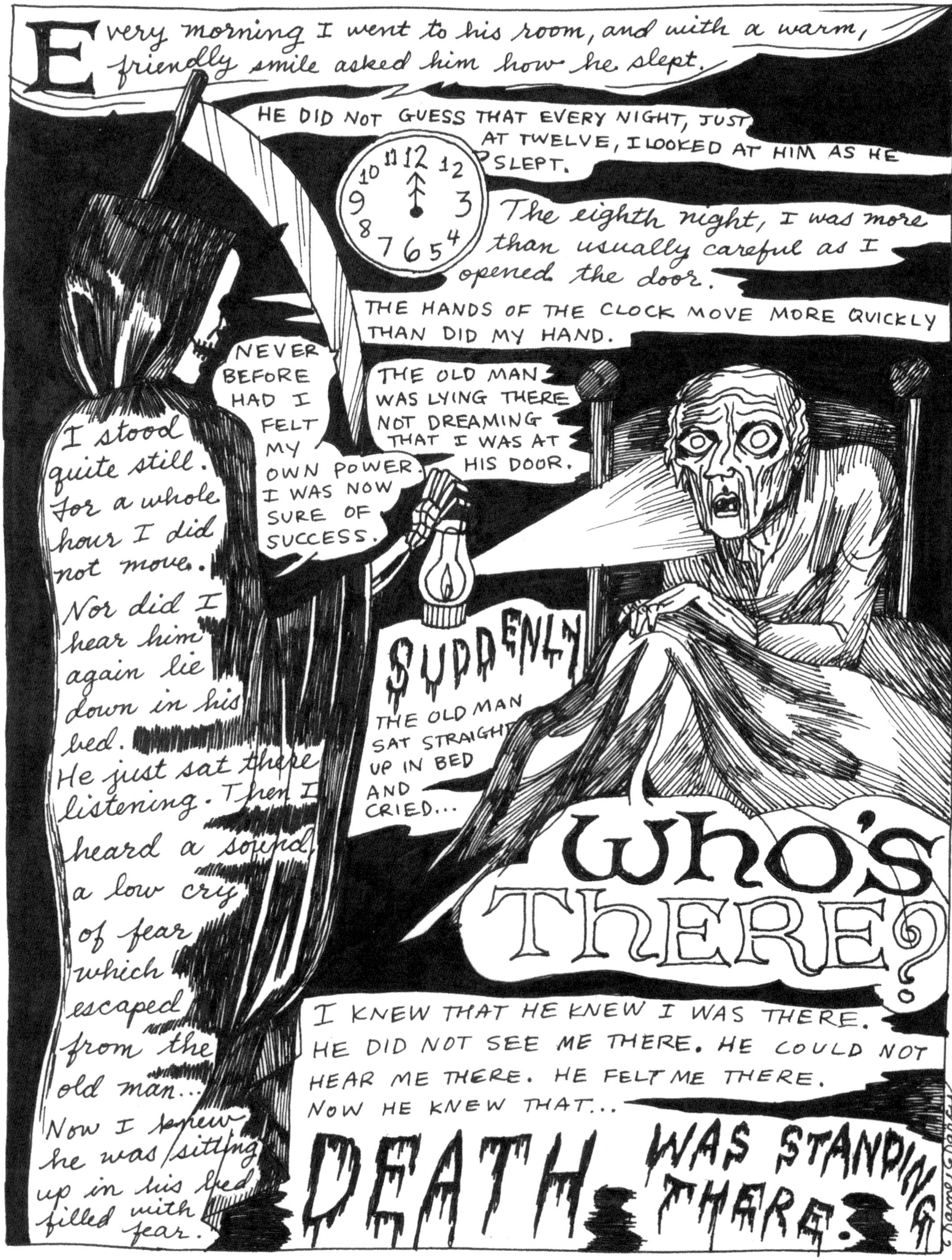
Every morning I went to his room, and with a warm, friendly smile asked him how he slept.
HE DID NOT GUESS THAT EVERY NIGHT, JUST AT TWELVE, I LOOKED AT HIM AS HE SLEPT.
The eighth night, I was more than usually careful as I opened the door.
THE HANDS OF THE CLOCK MOVE MORE QUICKLY THAN DID MY HAND.
I stood quite still. For a whole hour I did not move. Nor did I hear him again lie down in his bed. He just sat there listening. Then I heard a sound, a low cry of fear which escaped from the old man... Now I knew he was sitting up in his bed filled with fear.
NEVER BEFORE HAD I FELT MY OWN POWER. I WAS NOW SURE OF SUCCESS.
THE OLD MAN WAS LYING THERE NOT DREAMING THAT I WAS AT HIS DOOR.
SUDDENLY
THE OLD MAN SAT STRAIGHT UP IN BED AND CRIED...
WHO'S THERE?
I KNEW THAT HE KNEW I WAS THERE. HE DID NOT SEE ME THERE. HE COULD NOT HEAR ME THERE. HE FELT ME THERE. NOW HE KNEW THAT...
DEATH WAS STANDING THERE.
Dame Darcy

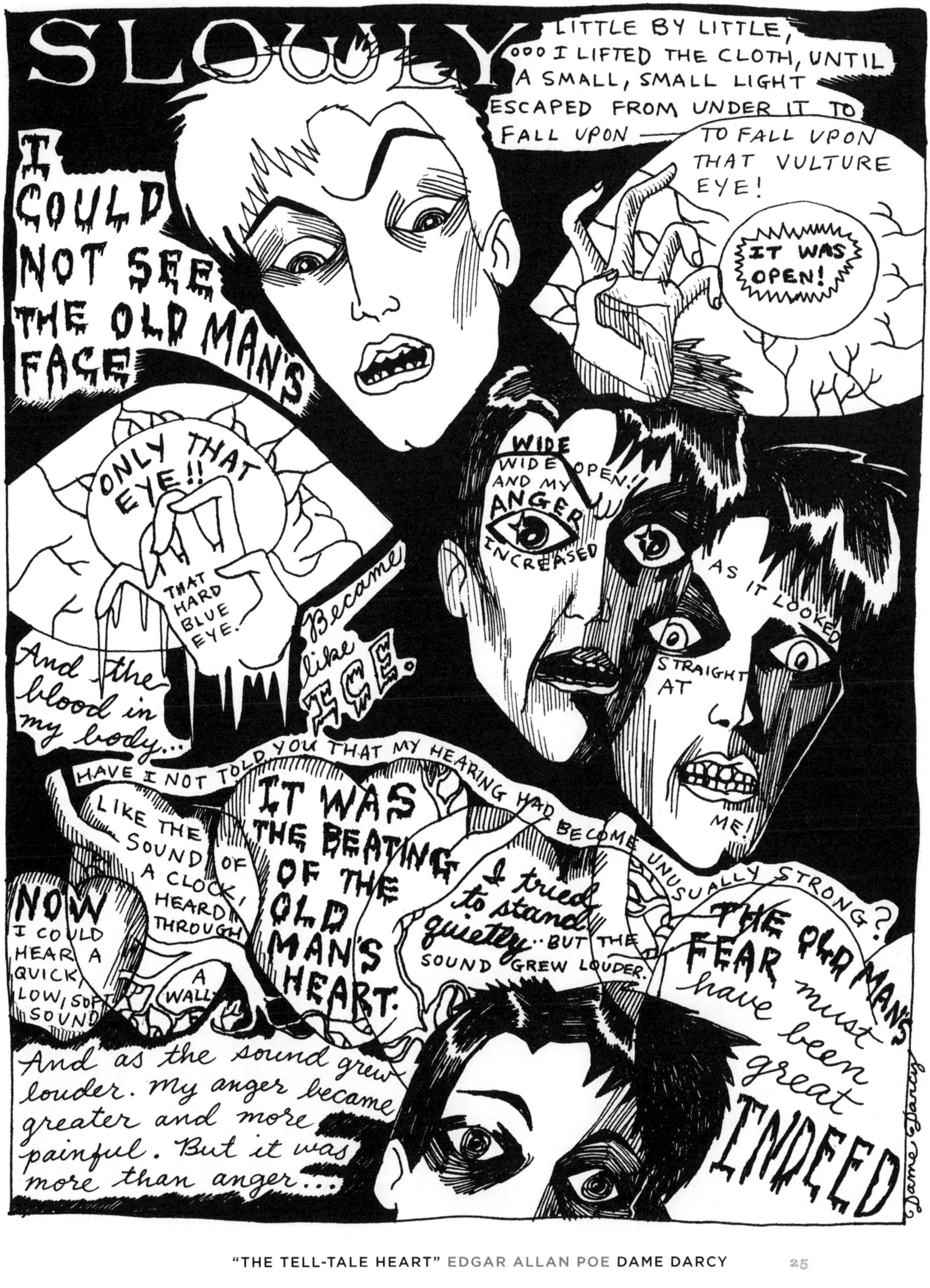

SLOWLY
LITTLE BY LITTLE, ... I LIFTED THE CLOTH, UNTIL A SMALL, SMALL LIGHT ESCAPED FROM UNDER IT TO FALL UPON — TO FALL UPON THAT VULTURE EYE!
IT WAS OPEN!
I COULD NOT SEE THE OLD MAN'S FACE
ONLY THAT EYE!!
THAT HARD BLUE EYE.
WIDE WIDE OPEN! AND MY ANGER INCREASED
AS IT LOOKED STRAIGHT AT ME!
And the blood in my body... Became like ICE.
HAVE I NOT TOLD YOU THAT MY HEARING HAD BECOME UNUSUALLY STRONG?
NOW I COULD HEAR A QUICK, LOW, SOFT SOUND
LIKE THE SOUND OF A CLOCK HEARD THROUGH A WALL
IT WAS THE BEATING OF THE OLD MAN'S HEART.
I tried to stand quietly... BUT THE SOUND GREW LOUDER.
THE OLD MAN'S FEAR must have been great INDEED
And as the sound grew louder. My anger became greater and more painful. But it was more than anger...
Dame Darcy

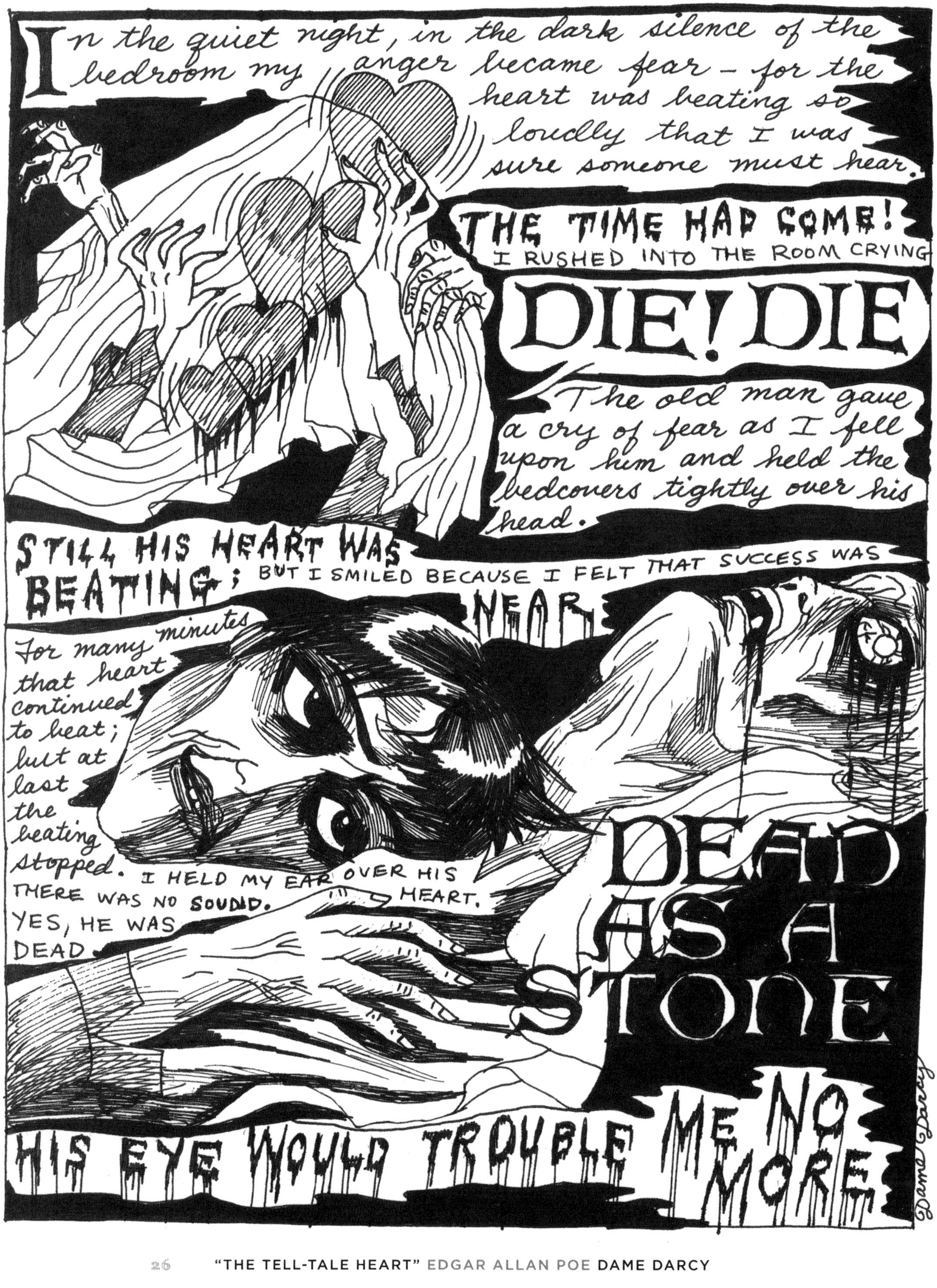
In the quiet night, in the dark silence of the bedroom my anger became fear - for the heart was beating so loudly that I was sure someone must hear.
THE TIME HAD COME!
I RUSHED INTO THE ROOM CRYING
DIE! DIE
The old man gave a cry of fear as I fell upon him and held the bedcovers tightly over his head.
STILL HIS HEART WAS BEATING; BUT I SMILED BECAUSE I FELT THAT SUCCESS WAS NEAR
For many minutes that heart continued to beat; but at last the beating stopped.
I HELD MY EAR OVER HIS HEART.
THERE WAS NO SOUND.
YES, HE WAS DEAD.
DEAD AS A STONE
HIS EYE WOULD TROUBLE ME NO MORE
Dame Darcy

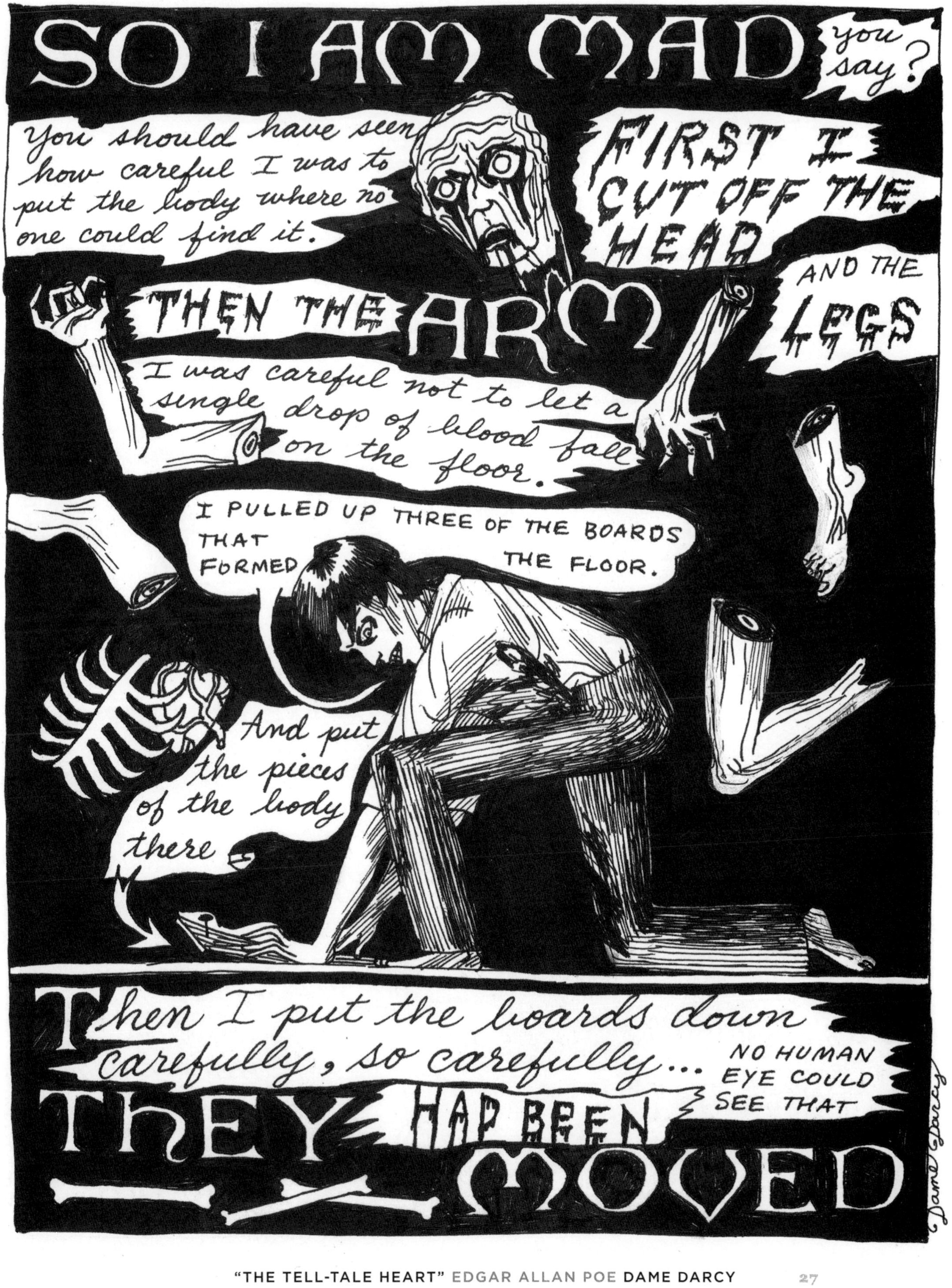
SO I AM MAD you say?
You should have seen how careful I was to put the body where no one could find it.
FIRST I CUT OFF THE HEAD
THEN THE ARM
AND THE LEGS
I was careful not to let a single drop of blood fall on the floor.
I PULLED UP THREE OF THE BOARDS THAT FORMED THE FLOOR.
And put the pieces of the body there
Then I put the boards down carefully, so carefully...
NO HUMAN EYE COULD SEE THAT
THEY HAD BEEN MOVED
Dame Darcy

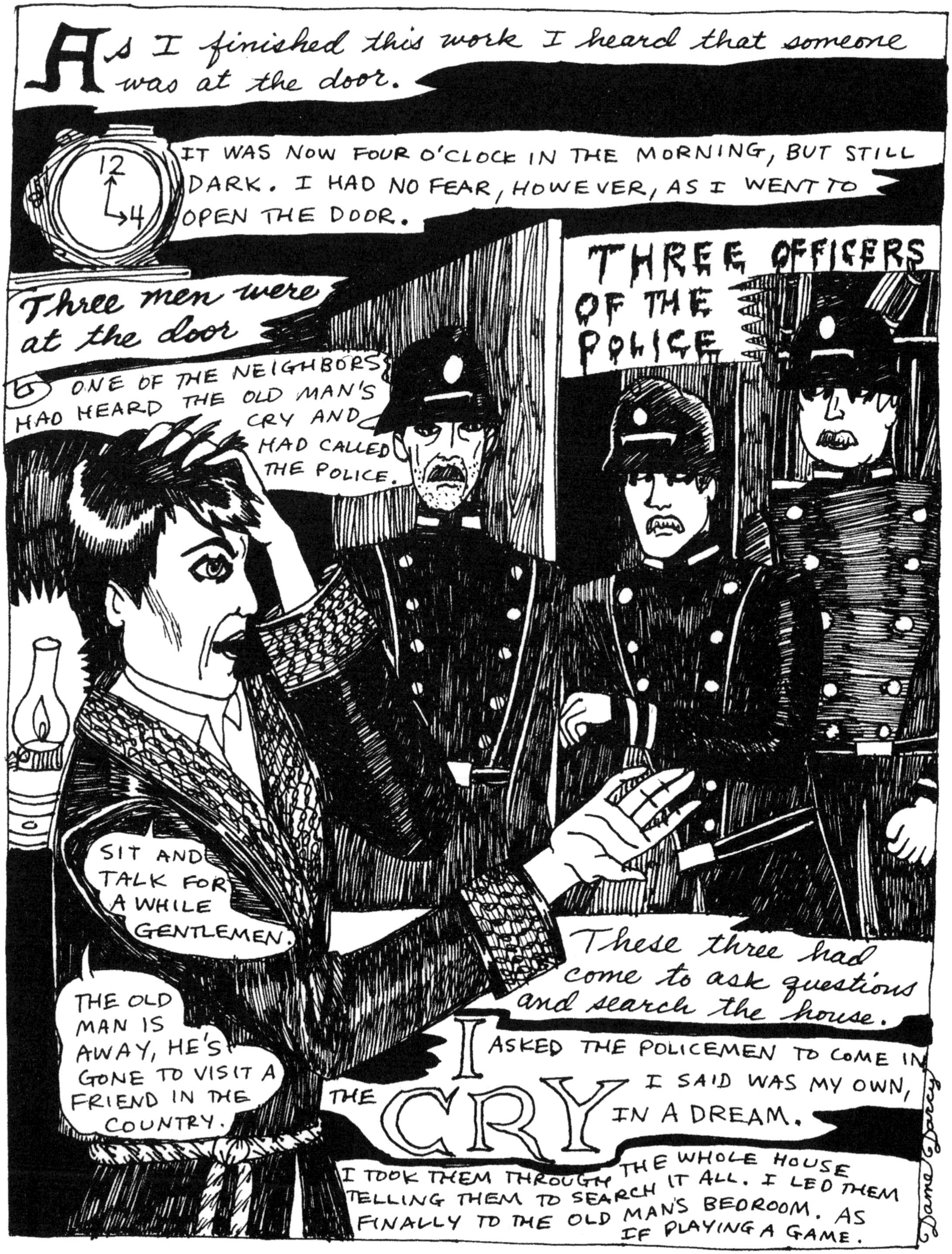
As I finished this work I heard that someone was at the door.
IT WAS NOW FOUR O'CLOCK IN THE MORNING, BUT STILL DARK. I HAD NO FEAR, HOWEVER, AS I WENT TO OPEN THE DOOR.
12
4
Three men were at the door
THREE OFFICERS OF THE POLICE
ONE OF THE NEIGHBORS HAD HEARD THE OLD MAN'S CRY AND HAD CALLED THE POLICE.
SIT AND TALK FOR A WHILE GENTLEMEN.
THE OLD MAN IS AWAY, HE'S GONE TO VISIT A FRIEND IN THE COUNTRY.
These three had come to ask questions and search the house.
I ASKED THE POLICEMEN TO COME IN
THE CRY I SAID WAS MY OWN, IN A DREAM.
I TOOK THEM THROUGH THE WHOLE HOUSE TELLING THEM TO SEARCH IT ALL. I LED THEM FINALLY TO THE OLD MAN'S BEDROOM. AS IF PLAYING A GAME.
Dame Darcy

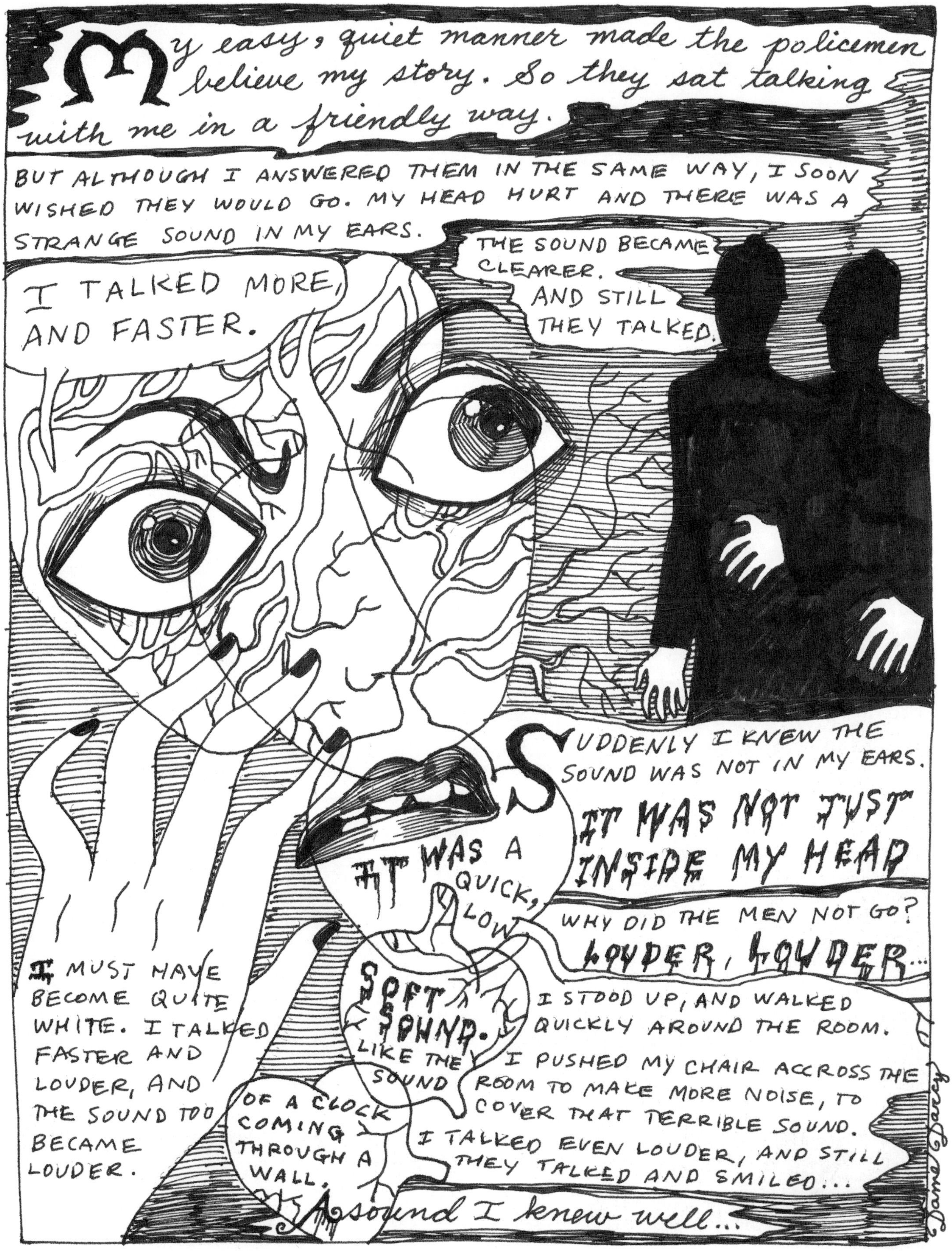
My easy, quiet manner made the policemen believe my story. So they sat talking with me in a friendly way.
BUT ALTHOUGH I ANSWERED THEM IN THE SAME WAY, I SOON WISHED THEY WOULD GO. MY HEAD HURT AND THERE WAS A STRANGE SOUND IN MY EARS.
I TALKED MORE, AND FASTER.
THE SOUND BECAME CLEARER.
AND STILL THEY TALKED.
SUDDENLY I KNEW THE SOUND WAS NOT IN MY EARS.
IT WAS NOT JUST INSIDE MY HEAD
IT WAS A QUICK, LOW
SOFT SOUND.
LIKE THE SOUND
OF A CLOCK COMING THROUGH A WALL.
A sound I knew well...
WHY DID THE MEN NOT GO?
LOUDER, LOUDER...
I MUST HAVE BECOME QUITE WHITE. I TALKED FASTER AND LOUDER, AND THE SOUND TOO BECAME LOUDER.
I STOOD UP, AND WALKED QUICKLY AROUND THE ROOM.
I PUSHED MY CHAIR ACCROSS THE ROOM TO MAKE MORE NOISE, TO COVER THAT TERRIBLE SOUND.
I TALKED EVEN LOUDER, AND STILL THEY TALKED AND SMILED...
Dame Darcy

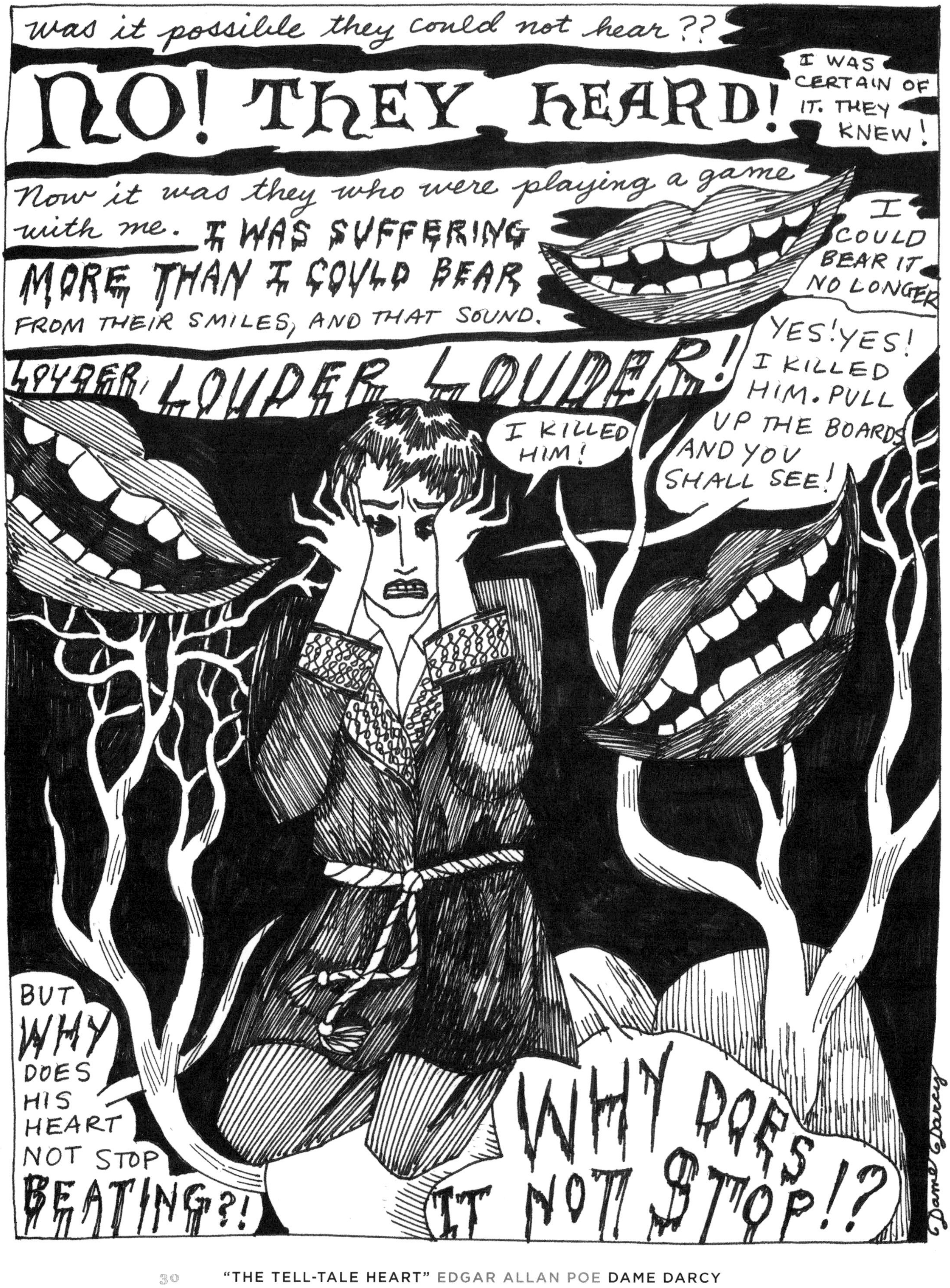

was it possible they could not hear??
NO! THEY HEARD!
I WAS CERTAIN OF IT. THEY KNEW!
Now it was they who were playing a game with me. I WAS SUFFERING MORE THAN I COULD BEAR FROM THEIR SMILES, AND THAT SOUND.
I COULD BEAR IT NO LONGER
LOUDER, LOUDER, LOUDER!
YES! YES! I KILLED HIM. PULL UP THE BOARDS AND YOU SHALL SEE!
I KILLED HIM!
BUT WHY DOES HIS HEART NOT STOP BEATING?!
WHY DOES IT NOT STOP!?
Dame Darcy

Lady Audley's Secret

Mary Elizabeth Braddon

ART/ADAPTATION BY **Joy Kolitsky**

LADY AUDLEY'S SECRET WAS ONE OF the first "sensation novels," helping ignite a genre that transfixed Britain in the 1860s. "The gripping plots of these novels involved scandalous events," according to *Oxford Bibliographies*, "including murder, adultery, bigamy, fraud, madness, and sexual deviance often perpetrated by seemingly moral and upright individuals in familiar domestic settings. The genre's popularity provoked alarm and hostility on the part of literary, political, and religious authorities who denounced sensation novels for eliciting intense physical responses from their readers."

A critic of the day, H.L. Manse, accused the books of "preaching to the nerves instead of the judgment" and said they were created "to supply the cravings of a diseased appetite" (i.e., that of readers).

Lady Audley's author was no hack, though.

Even though Mary Elizabeth Braddon wrote for the masses, she earned the respect of bigwigs. According to a PBS special on nineteenth-century female writers, "her admirers included Lord Tennyson, Charles Dickens, William Makepeace Thackeray, Henry James, and Prime Minister William Gladstone."

After their heyday, sensation novels were ignored for about a century, but we now recognize their important place in the history of crime/mystery fiction.

Joy Kolitsky has brought her exquisitely colored work to the *New York Times*, MTV, Penguin, her own line of greeting cards (Sugar Beet Press), and previous volumes of *The Graphic Canon*. For this volume, she was happy to adapt something so scandalous, and I'm delighted to see a key work of proto-genre fiction get a lovely new lease on life.

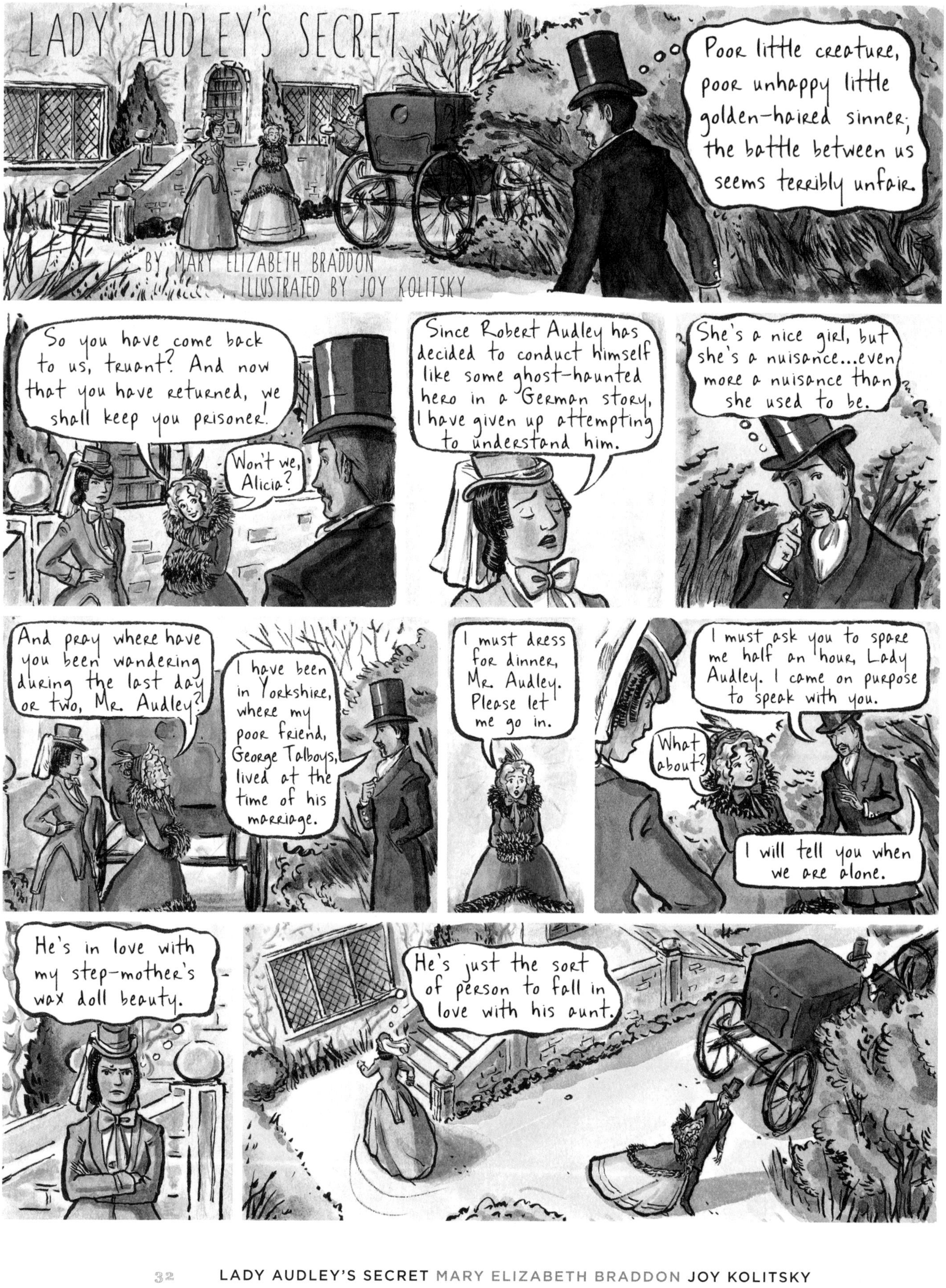
LADY AUDLEY'S SECRET
Poor little creature, poor unhappy little golden-haired sinner; the battle between us seems terribly unfair.
BY MARY ELIZABETH BRADDON
ILLUSTRATED BY JOY KOLITSKY
So you have come back to us, truant? And now that you have returned, we shall keep you prisoner!
Won't we, Alicia?
Since Robert Audley has decided to conduct himself like some ghost-haunted hero in a German story, I have given up attempting to understand him.
She's a nice girl, but she's a nuisance...even more a nuisance than she used to be.
And pray where have you been wandering during the last day or two, Mr. Audley?
I have been in Yorkshire, where my poor friend, George Talboys, lived at the time of his marriage.
I must dress for dinner, Mr. Audley. Please let me go in.
I must ask you to spare me half an hour, Lady Audley. I came on purpose to speak with you.
What about?
I will tell you when we are alone.
He's in love with my step-mother's wax doll beauty.
He's just the sort of person to fall in love with his aunt.

Shall I tell you the story of my friend, George Talboy's, disappearance as I read that story, my lady?

Very well, but pray lose no time in saying it. I haven't seen Sir Michael all day and I must dress for dinner.

When my friend returned to England the thought which was uppermost in his mind was of his wife.

Whom he deserted. At least...

I remember your telling us something to that effect earlier.

His fairest hope was of making her happy...

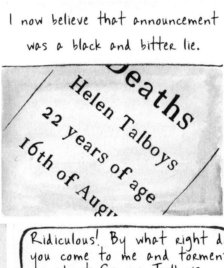

...and lavishing upon her the pittance which he had won by the force of his own strong arm in the gold-fields of Australia.

I saw him within a few hours of his reaching England, and I was witness to the joyful pride with which he looked forward to his re-union with his wife.

I was also a witness to the blow which struck him to the very heart; the announcement of his wife's death in the Times newspaper.

I now believe that announcement was a black and bitter lie.

Deaths

Helen Talboys

22 years of age

16th of Aug...

Indeed! And what reason could anyone have for announcing the death of Mrs. Talboys, if Mrs. Talboys was alive?

The lady herself might have had a reason.

What reason?

How if she had taken advantage of George's absence to win a richer husband? How if she had married again and wished to throw my poor friend off the scent?

Ridiculous! By what right do you come to me and torment me about George Talboys— by what right do you dare to say that his wife is still alive?

By the right of circumstancial evidence.

Helen Talboys disappeared on the 16th of August, 1854, and upon the 17th of that month she reappeared as you, Lucy Graham, at Mrs Vincent's school for girls.

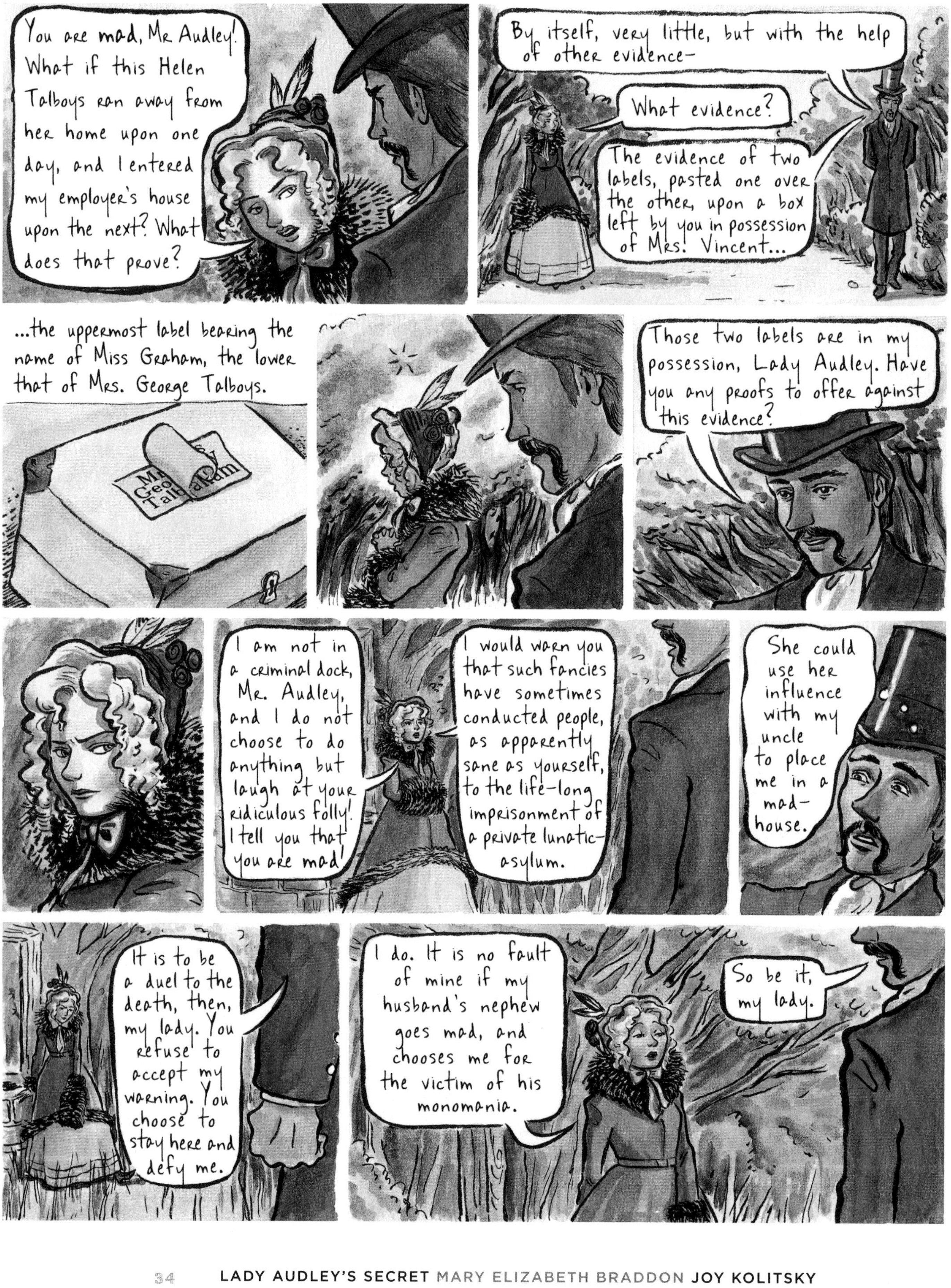
You are mad, Mr Audley! What if this Helen Talboys ran away from her home upon one day, and I entered my employer's house upon the next? What does that prove?
By itself, very little, but with the help of other evidence–
What evidence?
The evidence of two labels, pasted one over the other, upon a box left by you in possession of Mrs. Vincent...
...the uppermost label bearing the name of Miss Graham, the lower that of Mrs. George Talboys.
Those two labels are in my possession, Lady Audley. Have you any proofs to offer against this evidence?
I am not in a criminal dock, Mr. Audley, and I do not choose to do anything but laugh at your ridiculous folly! I tell you that you are mad!
I would warn you that such fancies have sometimes conducted people, as apparently sane as yourself, to the life-long imprisonment of a private lunatic-asylum.
She could use her influence with my uncle to place me in a mad-house.
It is to be a duel to the death, then, my lady. You refuse to accept my warning. You choose to stay here and defy me.
I do. It is no fault of mine if my husband's nephew goes mad, and chooses me for the victim of his monomania.
So be it, my lady.

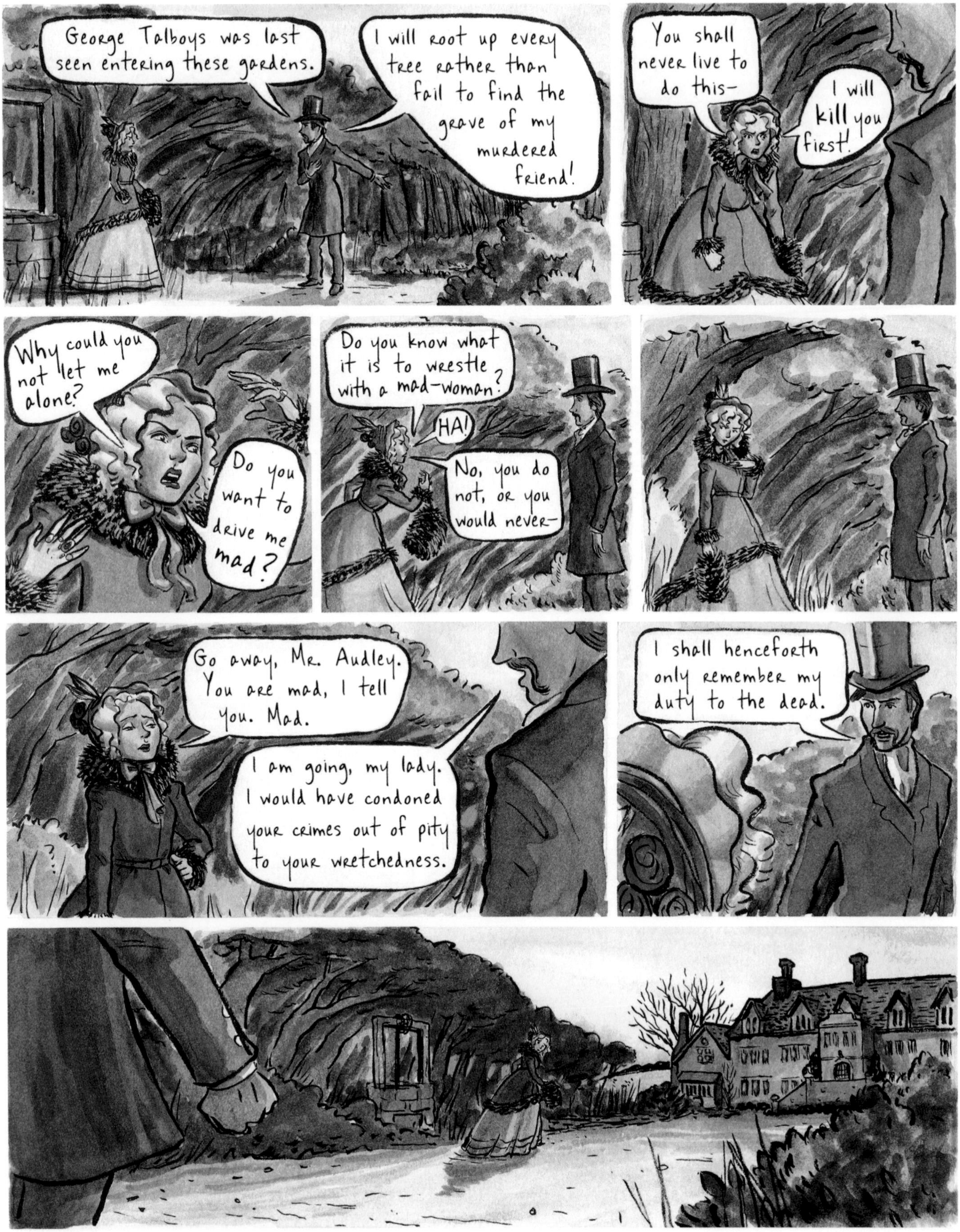
George Talboys was last seen entering these gardens.
I will root up every tree rather than fail to find the grave of my murdered friend!
You shall never live to do this-
I will kill you first!
Why could you not let me alone?
Do you want to drive me mad?
Do you know what it is to wrestle with a mad-woman?
HA!
No, you do not, or you would never-
Go away, Mr. Audley. You are mad, I tell you. Mad.
I am going, my lady. I would have condoned your crimes out of pity to your wretchedness.
I shall henceforth only remember my duty to the dead.

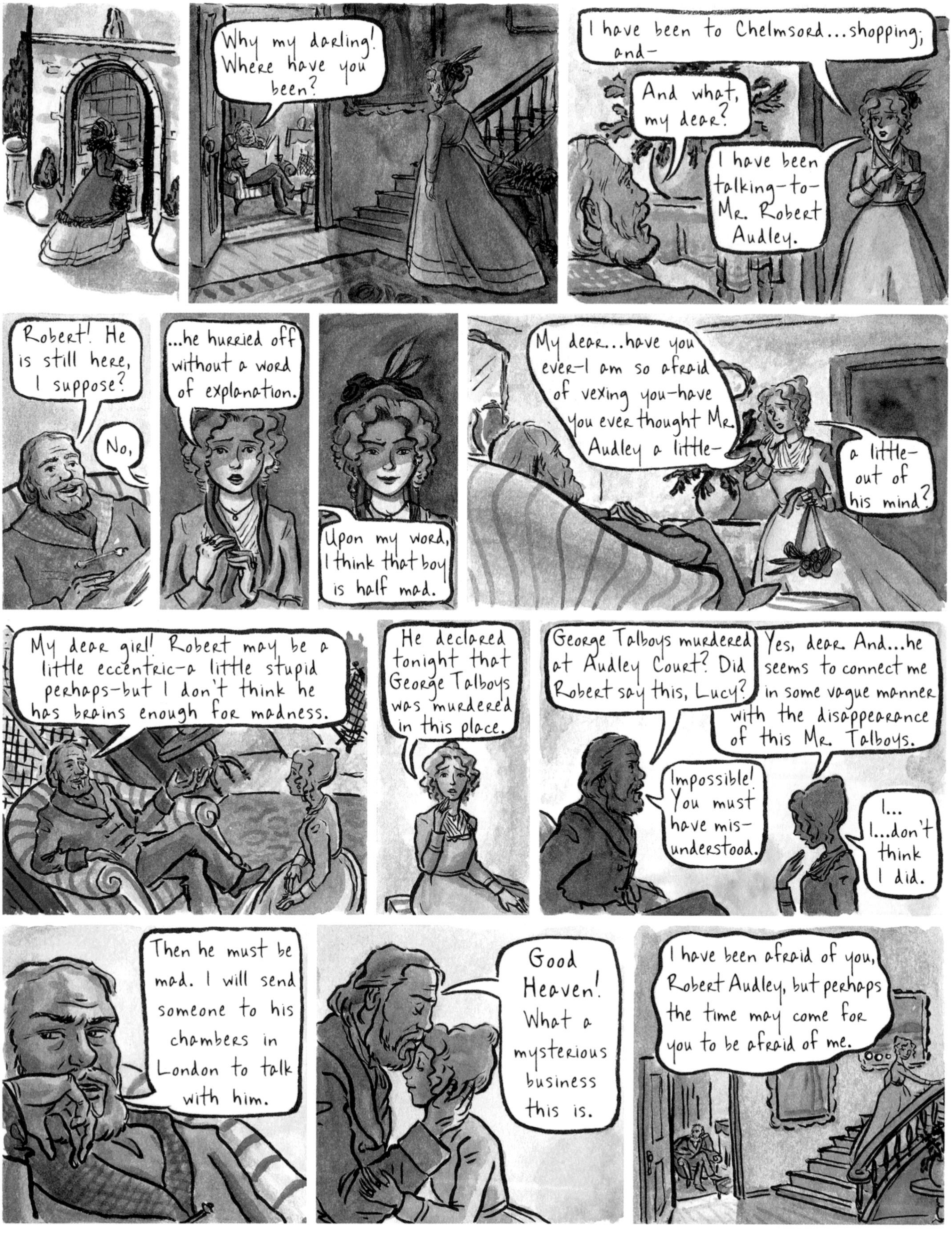
Why my darling! Where have you been?
I have been to Chelmsord...shopping; and–
And what, my dear?
I have been talking–to–Mr. Robert Audley.
Robert! He is still here, I suppose?
No,
...he hurried off without a word of explanation.
Upon my word, I think that boy is half mad.
My dear...have you ever–I am so afraid of vexing you–have you ever thought Mr. Audley a little–
a little–out of his mind?
My dear girl! Robert may be a little eccentric–a little stupid perhaps–but I don't think he has brains enough for madness.
He declared tonight that George Talboys was murdered in this place.
George Talboys murdered at Audley Court? Did Robert say this, Lucy?
Yes, dear. And...he seems to connect me in some vague manner with the disappearance of this Mr. Talboys.
Impossible! You must have mis-understood.
I... I...don't think I did.
Then he must be mad. I will send someone to his chambers in London to talk with him.
Good Heaven! What a mysterious business this is.
I have been afraid of you, Robert Audley, but perhaps the time may come for you to be afraid of me.

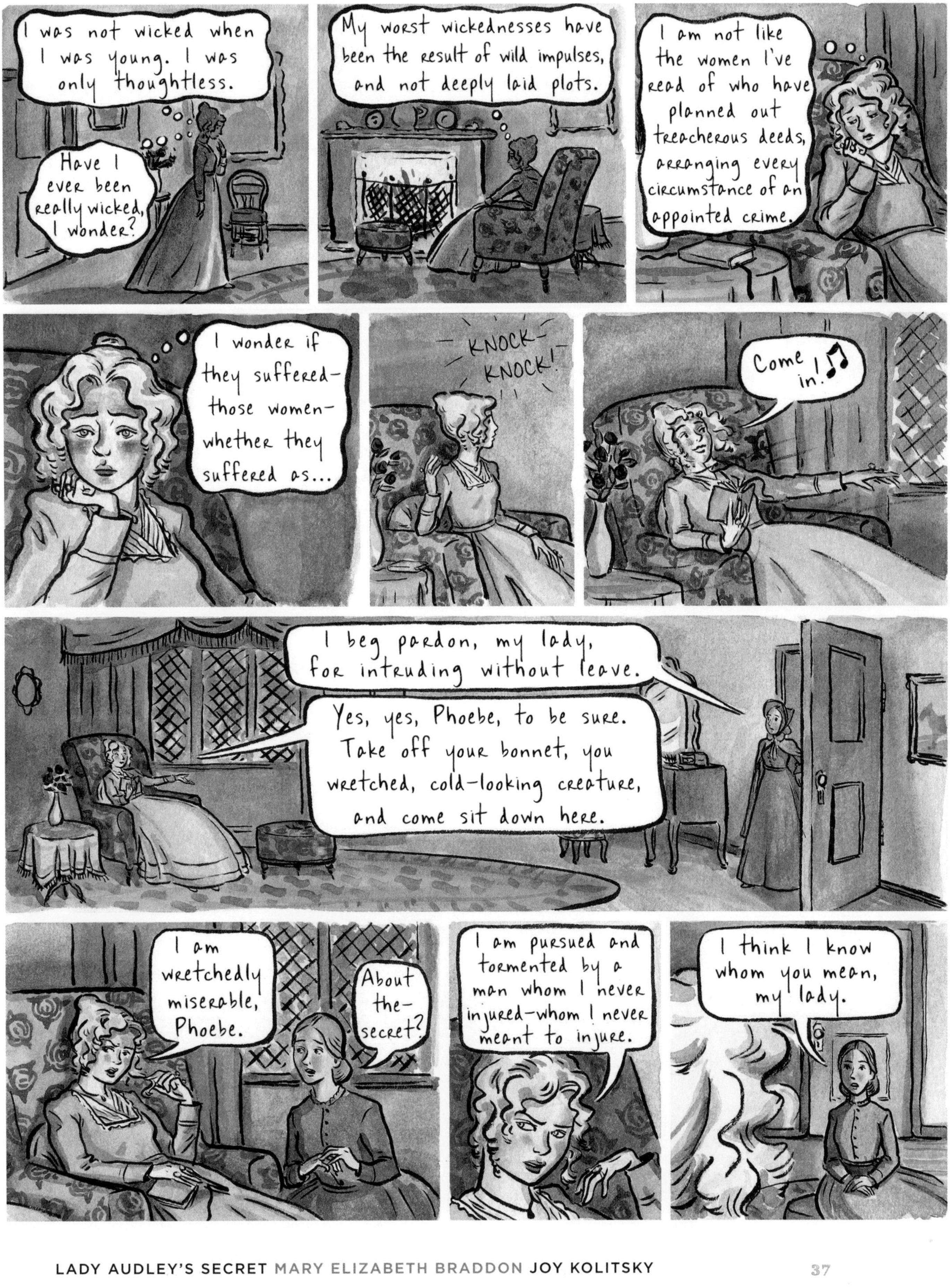
I was not wicked when I was young. I was only thoughtless.
Have I ever been really wicked, I wonder?
My worst wickednesses have been the result of wild impulses, and not deeply laid plots.
I am not like the women I've read of who have planned out treacherous deeds, arranging every circumstance of an appointed crime.
I wonder if they suffered—those women—whether they suffered as...
KNOCK KNOCK!
Come in! ♫
I beg pardon, my lady, for intruding without leave.
Yes, yes, Phoebe, to be sure. Take off your bonnet, you wretched, cold-looking creature, and come sit down here.
I am wretchedly miserable, Phoebe.
About the—secret?
I am pursued and tormented by a man whom I never injured—whom I never meant to injure.
I think I know whom you mean, my lady.

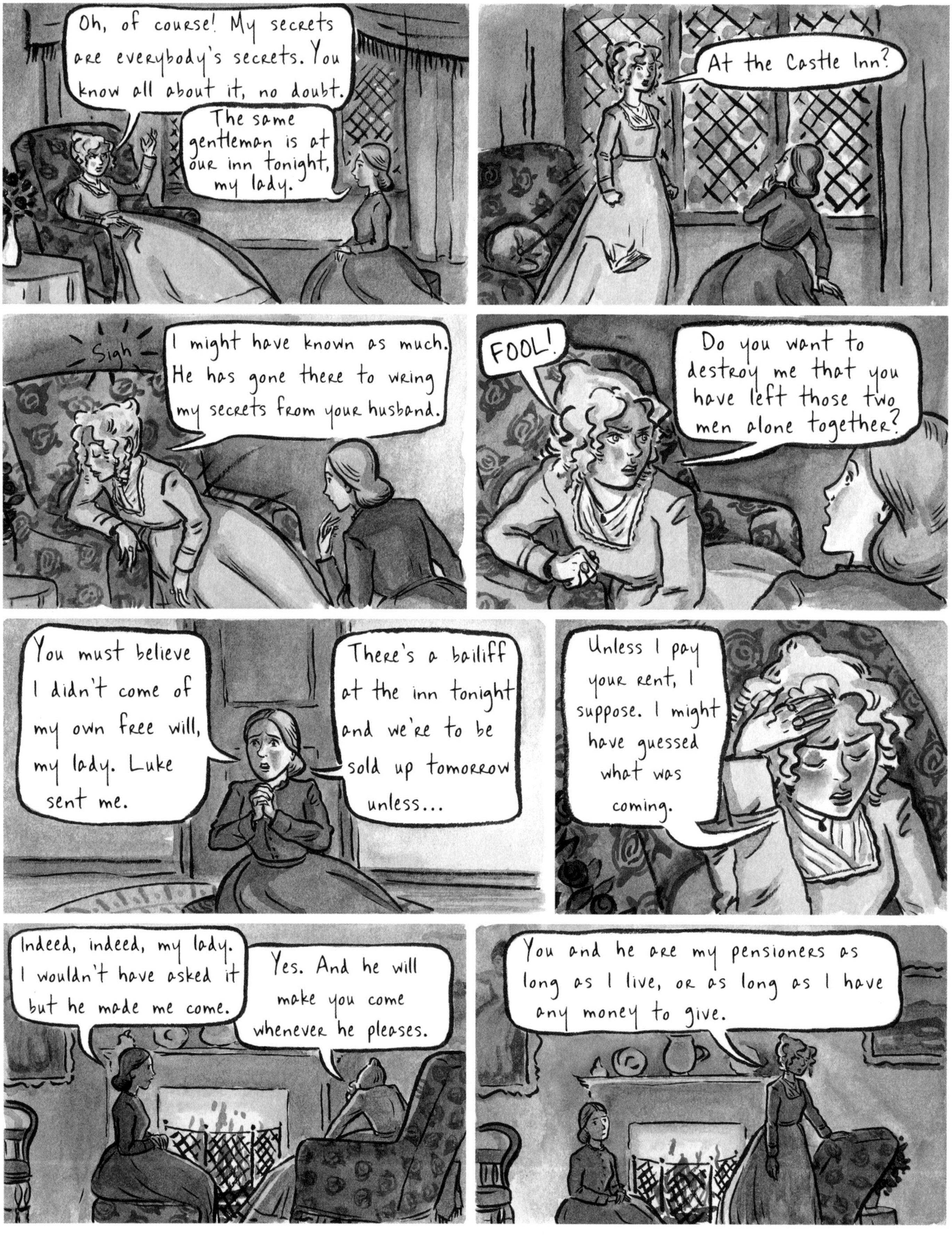

Oh, of course! My secrets are everybody's secrets. You know all about it, no doubt.
The same gentleman is at our inn tonight, my lady.
At the Castle Inn?
Sigh
I might have known as much. He has gone there to wring my secrets from your husband.
FOOL!
Do you want to destroy me that you have left those two men alone together?
You must believe I didn't come of my own free will, my lady. Luke sent me.
There's a bailiff at the inn tonight and we're to be sold up tomorrow unless...
Unless I pay your rent, I suppose. I might have guessed what was coming.
Indeed, indeed, my lady. I wouldn't have asked it but he made me come.
Yes. And he will make you come whenever he pleases.
You and he are my pensioners as long as I live, or as long as I have any money to give.

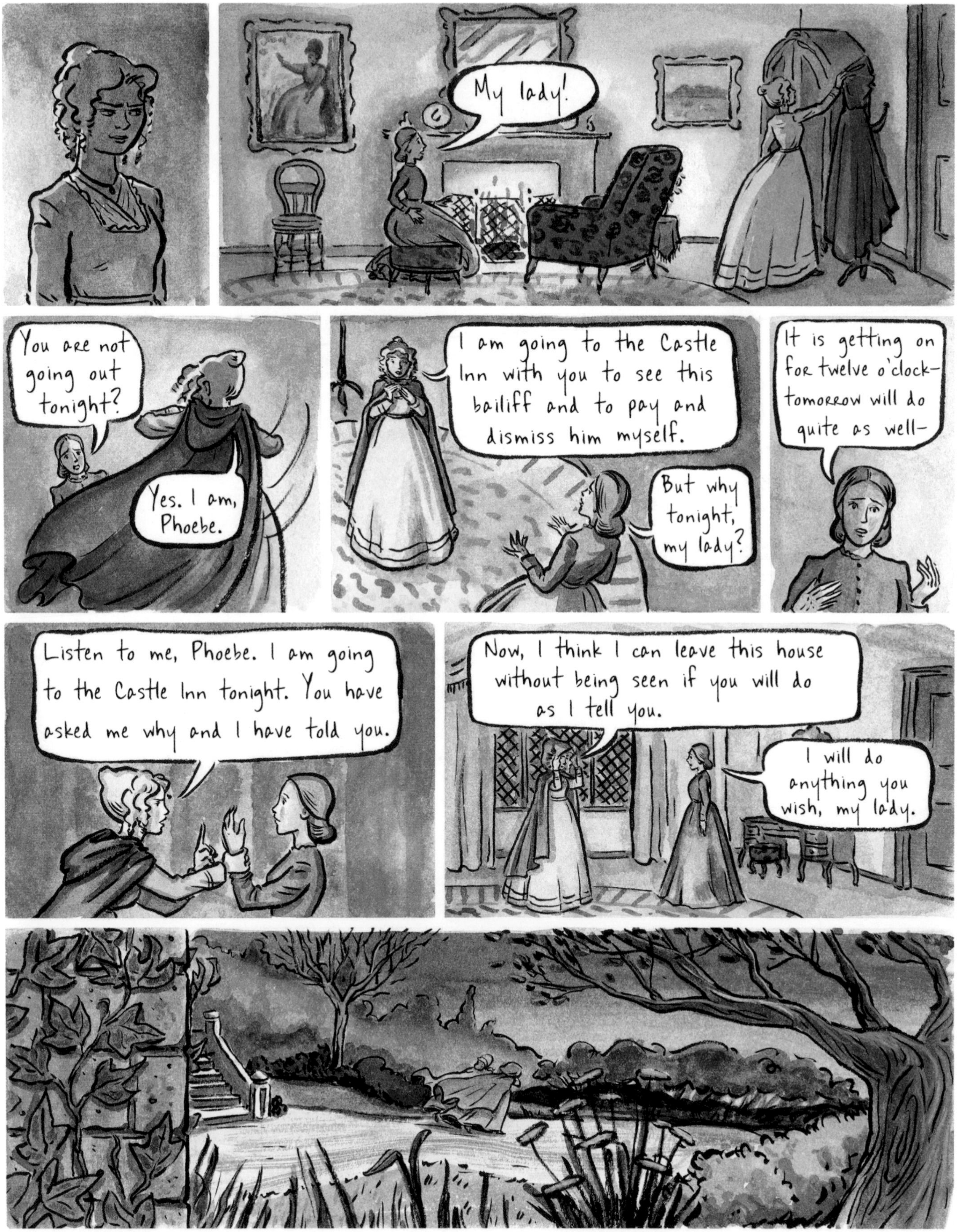
My lady!
You are not going out tonight?
Yes. I am, Phoebe.
I am going to the Castle Inn with you to see this bailiff and to pay and dismiss him myself.
But why tonight, my lady?
It is getting on for twelve o'clock— tomorrow will do quite as well—
Listen to me, Phoebe. I am going to the Castle Inn tonight. You have asked me why and I have told you.
Now, I think I can leave this house without being seen if you will do as I tell you.
I will do anything you wish, my lady.

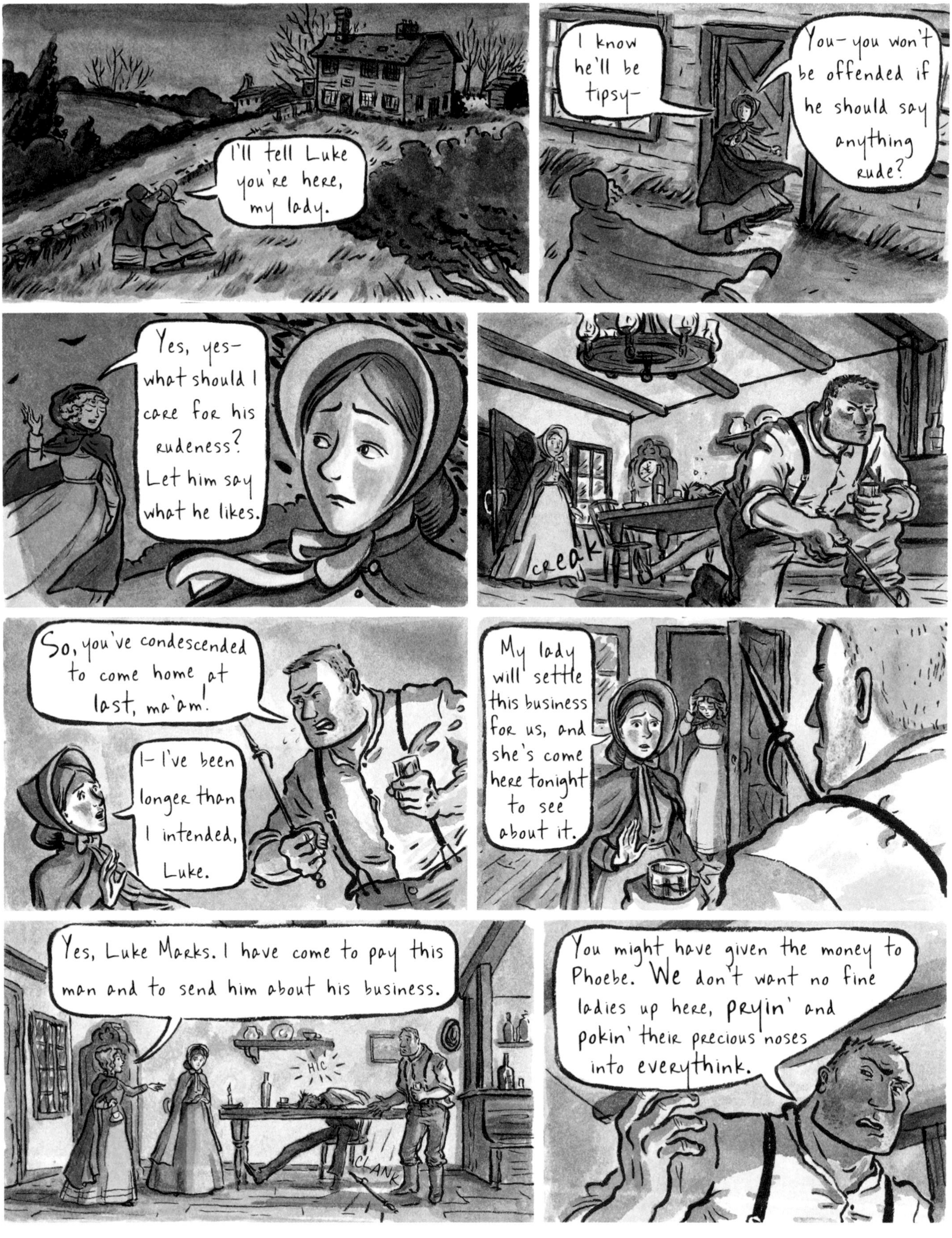
I'll tell Luke you're here, my lady.
I know he'll be tipsy–
You– you won't be offended if he should say anything rude?
Yes, yes– what should I care for his rudeness? Let him say what he likes.
creak
So, you've condescended to come home at last, ma'am!
I– I've been longer than I intended, Luke.
My lady will settle this business for us, and she's come here tonight to see about it.
Yes, Luke Marks. I have come to pay this man and to send him about his business.
HIC
CLANK
You might have given the money to Phoebe. We don't want no fine ladies up here, pryin' and pokin' their precious noses into everythink.

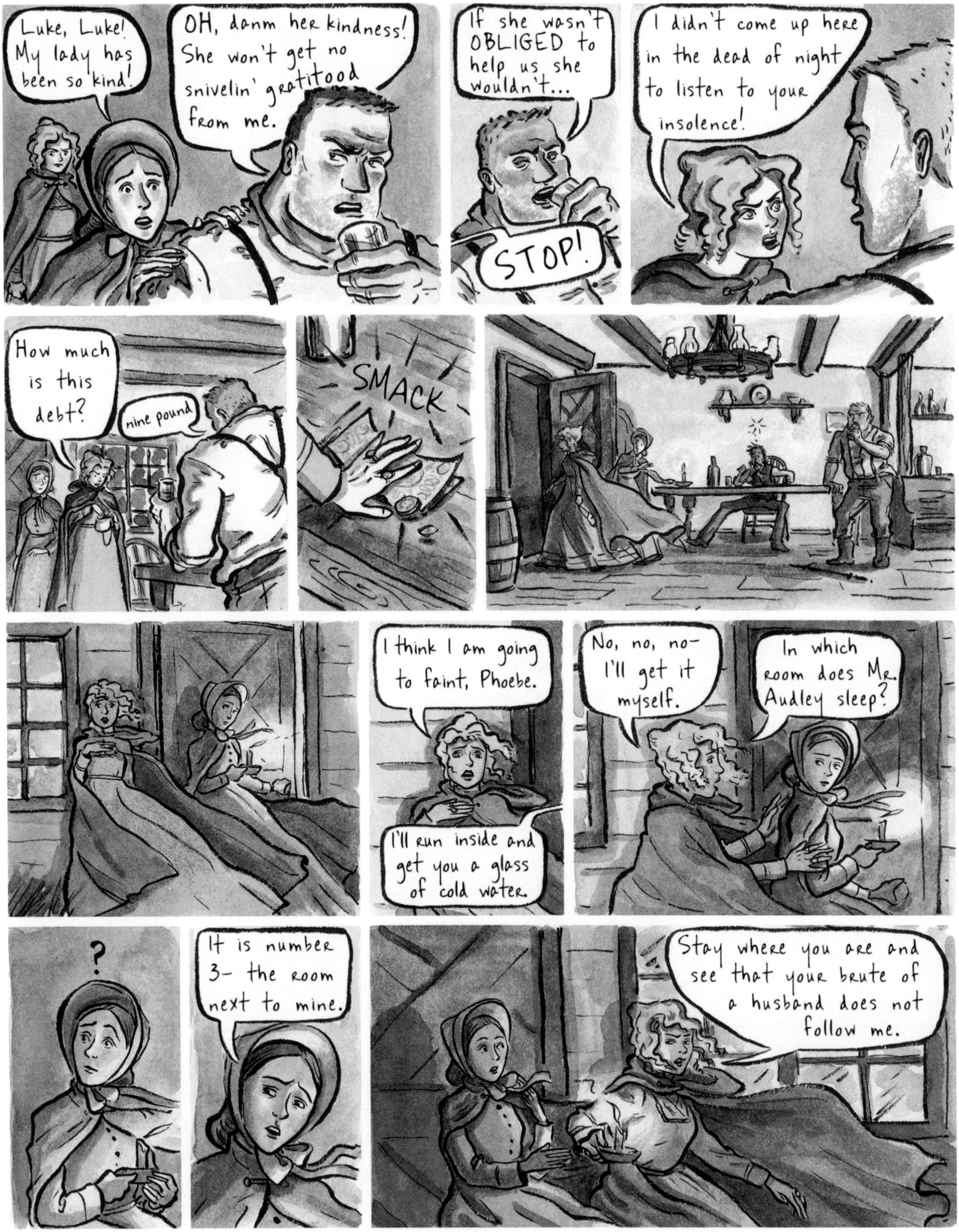
Luke, Luke! My lady has been so kind!
OH, danm her kindness! She won't get no snivelin' gratitood from me.
If she wasn't OBLIGED to help us she wouldn't...
STOP!
I didn't come up here in the dead of night to listen to your insolence!
How much is this debt?
nine pound
SMACK
I think I am going to faint, Phoebe.
I'll run inside and get you a glass of cold water.
No, no, no- I'll get it myself.
In which room does Mr. Audley sleep?
?
It is number 3- the room next to mine.
Stay where you are and see that your brute of a husband does not follow me.

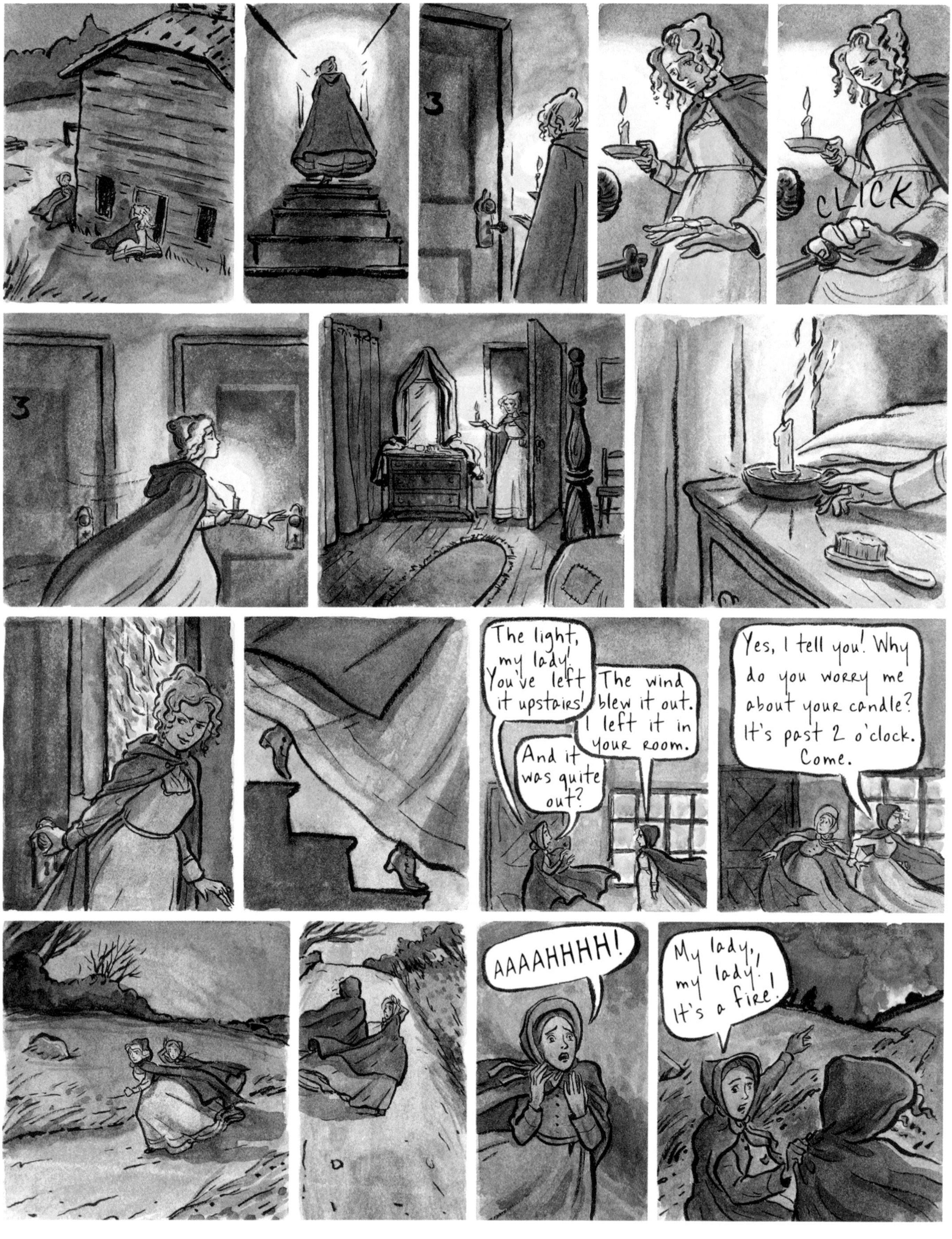
3
CLICK
3
The light, my lady! You've left it upstairs!
The wind blew it out. I left it in your room.
And it was quite out?
Yes, I tell you! Why do you worry me about your candle? It's past 2 o'clock. Come.
AAAAHHHH!
My lady, my lady! It's a fire!

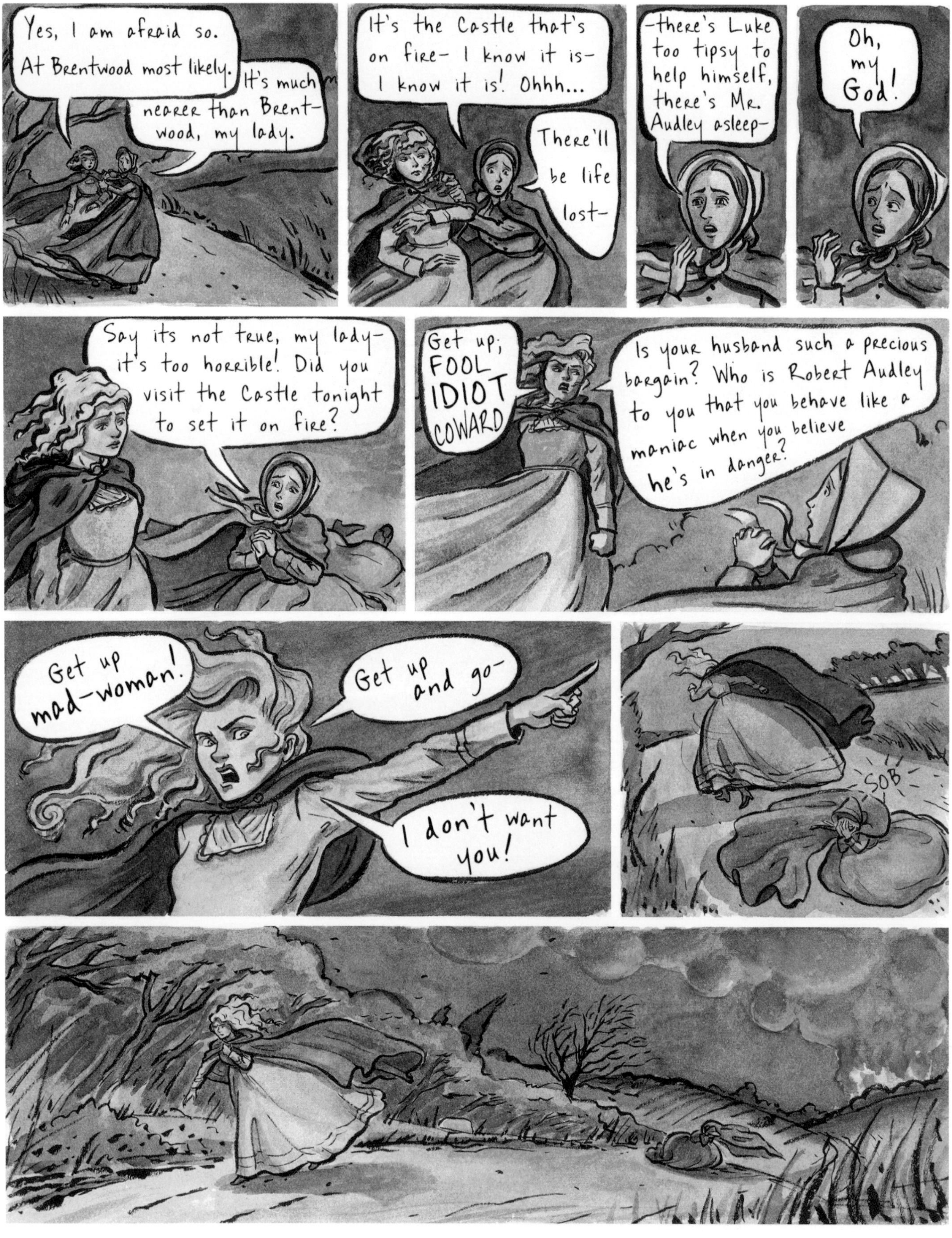
Yes, I am afraid so. At Brentwood most likely.
It's much nearer than Brentwood, my lady.
It's the Castle that's on fire- I know it is- I know it is! Ohhh...
There'll be life lost-
-there's Luke too tipsy to help himself, there's Mr. Audley asleep-
Oh, my God!
Say its not true, my lady- it's too horrible! Did you visit the Castle tonight to set it on fire?
Get up, FOOL IDIOT COWARD
Is your husband such a precious bargain? Who is Robert Audley to you that you behave like a maniac when you believe he's in danger?
Get up mad-woman!
Get up and go-
I don't want you!
SOB

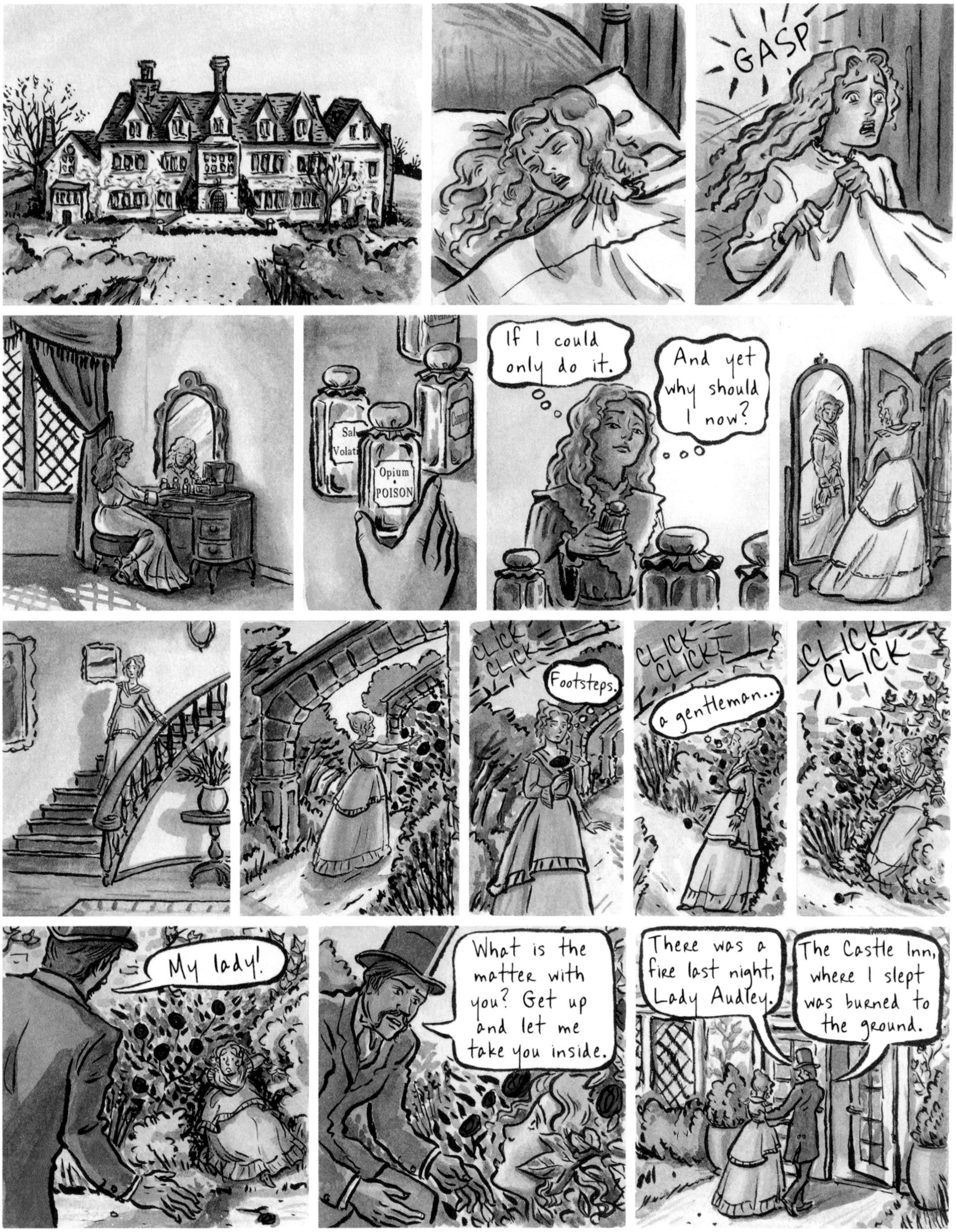
GASP
Lavender
Sal Volatile
Camphor
Opium • POISON
If I could only do it.
And yet why should I now?
CLICK CLICK
Footsteps.
CLICK CLICK
a gentleman...
CLICK CLICK
My lady!
What is the matter with you? Get up and let me take you inside.
There was a fire last night, Lady Audley.
The Castle Inn, where I slept was burned to the ground.

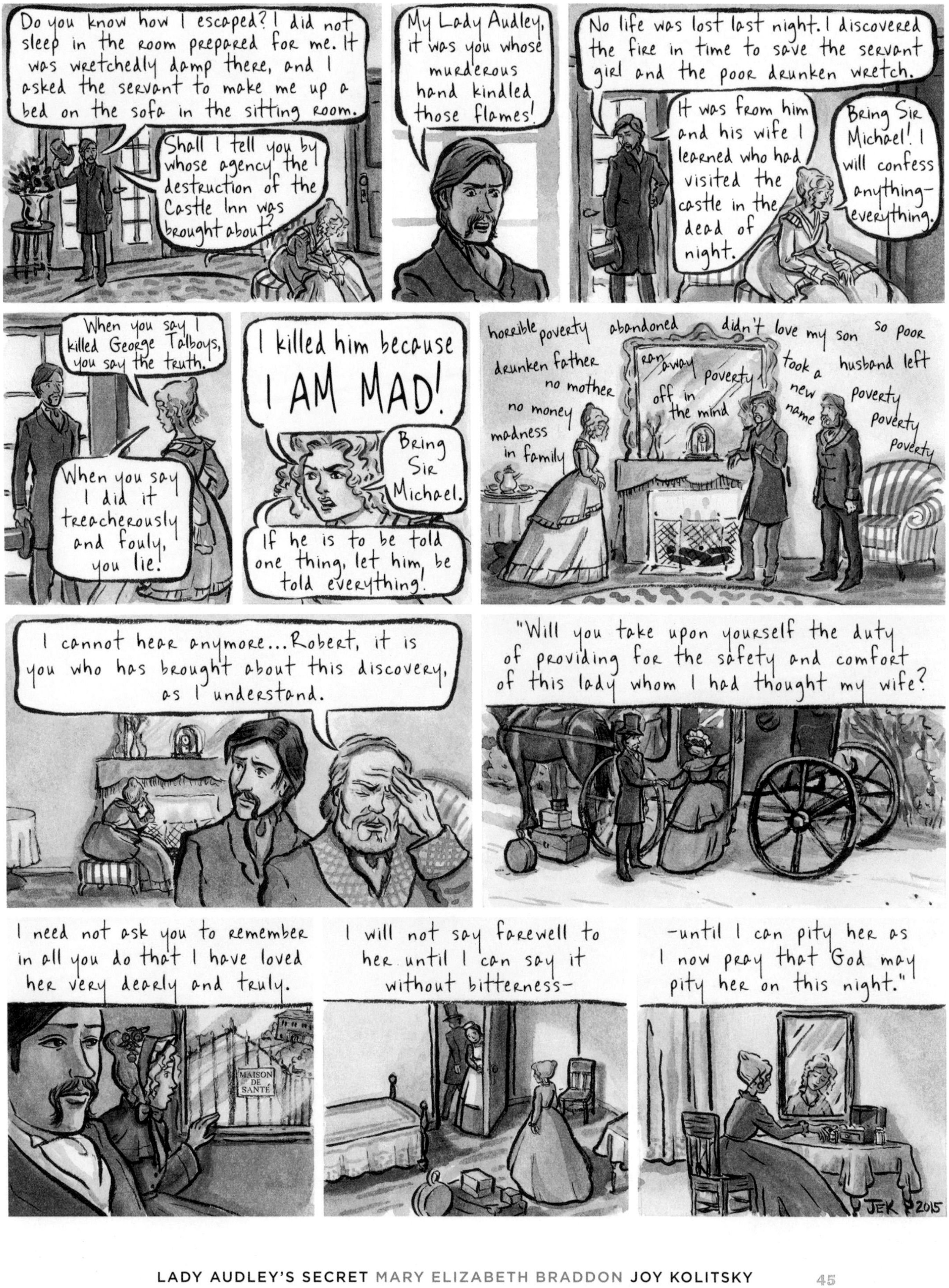
Do you know how I escaped? I did not sleep in the room prepared for me. It was wretchedly damp there, and I asked the servant to make me up a bed on the sofa in the sitting room.
Shall I tell you by whose agency the destruction of the Castle Inn was brought about?
My Lady Audley, it was you whose murderous hand kindled those flames!
No life was lost last night. I discovered the fire in time to save the servant girl and the poor drunken wretch.
It was from him and his wife I learned who had visited the castle in the dead of night.
Bring Sir Michael! I will confess anything—everything.
When you say I killed George Talboys, you say the truth.
When you say I did it treacherously and fouly, you lie.
I killed him because
I AM MAD!
Bring Sir Michael.
If he is to be told one thing, let him be told everything!
horrible
poverty
abandoned
didn't love my son
so poor
drunken father
no mother
ran away
poverty
took a new name
husband left
poverty
poverty
poverty
no money
off in the mind
madness in family
I cannot hear anymore... Robert, it is you who has brought about this discovery, as I understand.
"Will you take upon yourself the duty of providing for the safety and comfort of this lady whom I had thought my wife?
I need not ask you to remember in all you do that I have loved her very dearly and truly.
MAISON DE SANTÉ
I will not say farewell to her until I can say it without bitterness—
—until I can pity her as I now pray that God may pity her on this night."
JEK 2015

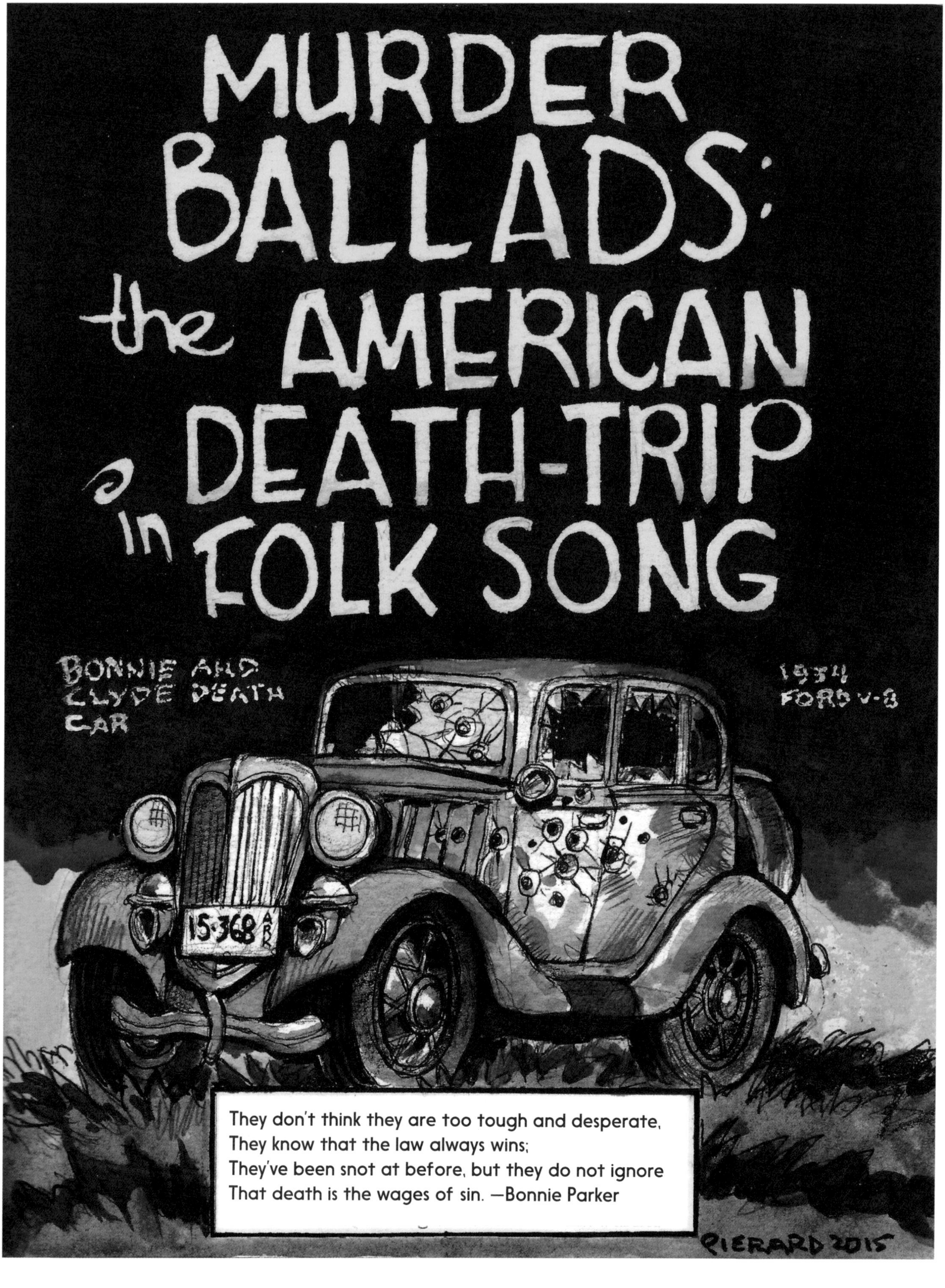
MURDER BALLADS: the AMERICAN DEATH-TRIP in FOLK SONG
BONNIE AND CLYDE DEATH CAR
1934 FORD V-8
15-368 ARK
They don't think they are too tough and desperate,
They know that the law always wins;
They've been snot at before, but they do not ignore
That death is the wages of sin. —Bonnie Parker
PIERARD 2015

Murder Ballads

ART/ADAPTATION BY **John Pierard**

IF THE TERM "FOLK SONG" MAKES YOU think of hippies strumming guitars and singing about love or the Vietnam War, you're in for a big shock. Actual folk songs are literally the songs of the people, and they've been around for centuries, even millennia. They're not meant to be recorded or sung "professionally." Like jokes, limericks, and gossip, they're picked up by family, neighbors, and passers-through, who then pass them to others.

A lot of folk songs deal with harsh realities and sensational topics. In fact, folklorists and music historians recognize an entire genre called "murder ballads." The authenticity and darkness of these homegrown tunes, which are often based on real-life incidents, inspired artist John Pierard, whose work has appeared in *Asimov's Magazine*, *Screw*, previous volumes of *The Graphic Canon*, and his series of children's books, *P.S. 13*. Several years ago, John mentioned that he'd love to adapt some murder ballads. When the theme for the current volume was chosen, we had a match.

John has chosen six murder ballads, including ones dealing with female serial killer Belle Gunness, Black folk hero Railroad Bill, and the assassination of Lincoln. "Banks of the Ohio" is an example of a ballad not based on a particular murder but employing the unfortunate trope of a male narrator relating his killing of a woman who rejected him. The song about the hugely controversial murder of Mary Phagan—which led to the probable wrongful conviction and lynching of Leo Frank—is a rare example of a murder ballad written and originally performed by a professional musician, in this case country pioneer Fiddlin' John Carson in 1915. And the ballad John opens with is another fascinating subgenre: the song written by a murderer about her own exploits, in this case "Ballad of Bonnie and Clyde" by Bonnie Parker.

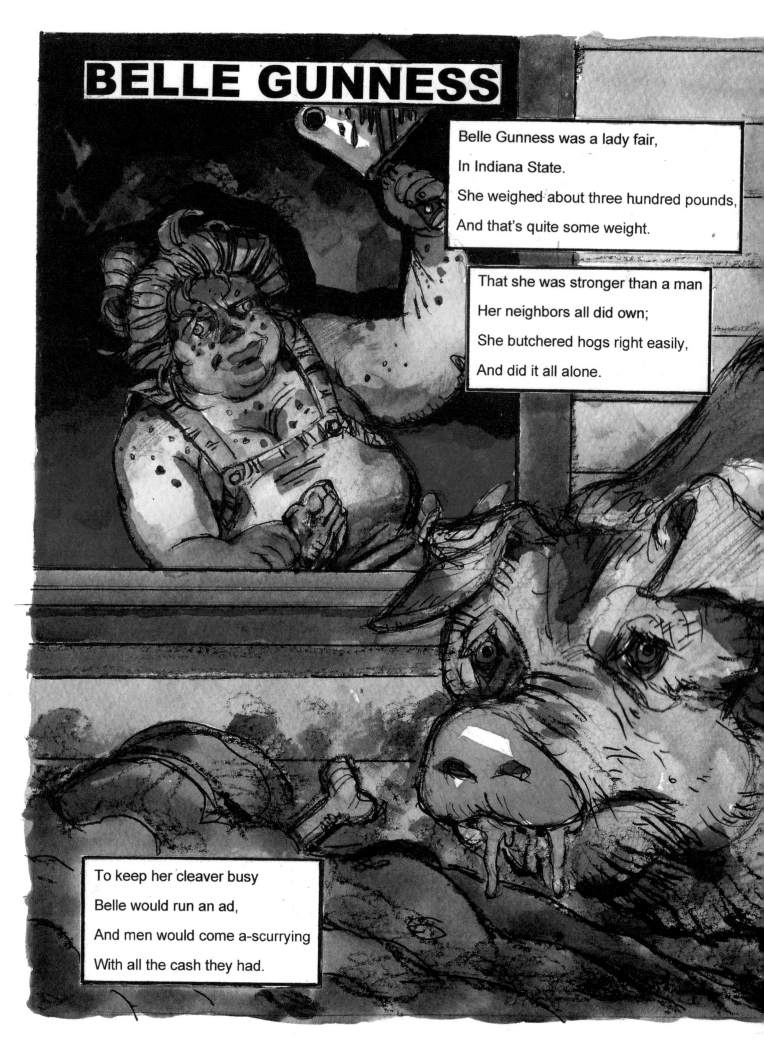

BELLE GUNNESS

Belle Gunness was a lady fair,
In Indiana State.
She weighed about three hundred pounds,
And that's quite some weight.

That she was stronger than a man
Her neighbors all did own;
She butchered hogs right easily,
And did it all alone.

To keep her cleaver busy
Belle would run an ad,
And men would come a-scurrying
With all the cash they had.

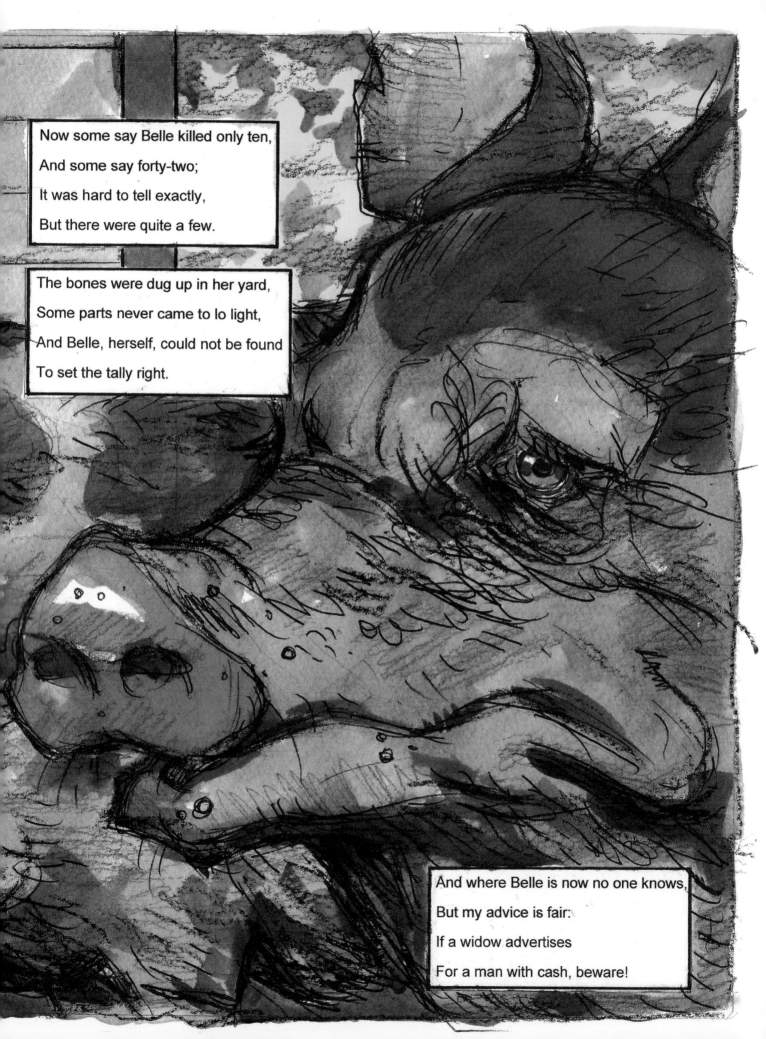

Now some say Belle killed only ten,

And some say forty-two;

It was hard to tell exactly,

But there were quite a few.

The bones were dug up in her yard,

Some parts never came to lo light,

And Belle, herself, could not be found

To set the tally right.

And where Belle is now no one knows,

But my advice is fair:

If a widow advertises

For a man with cash, beware!

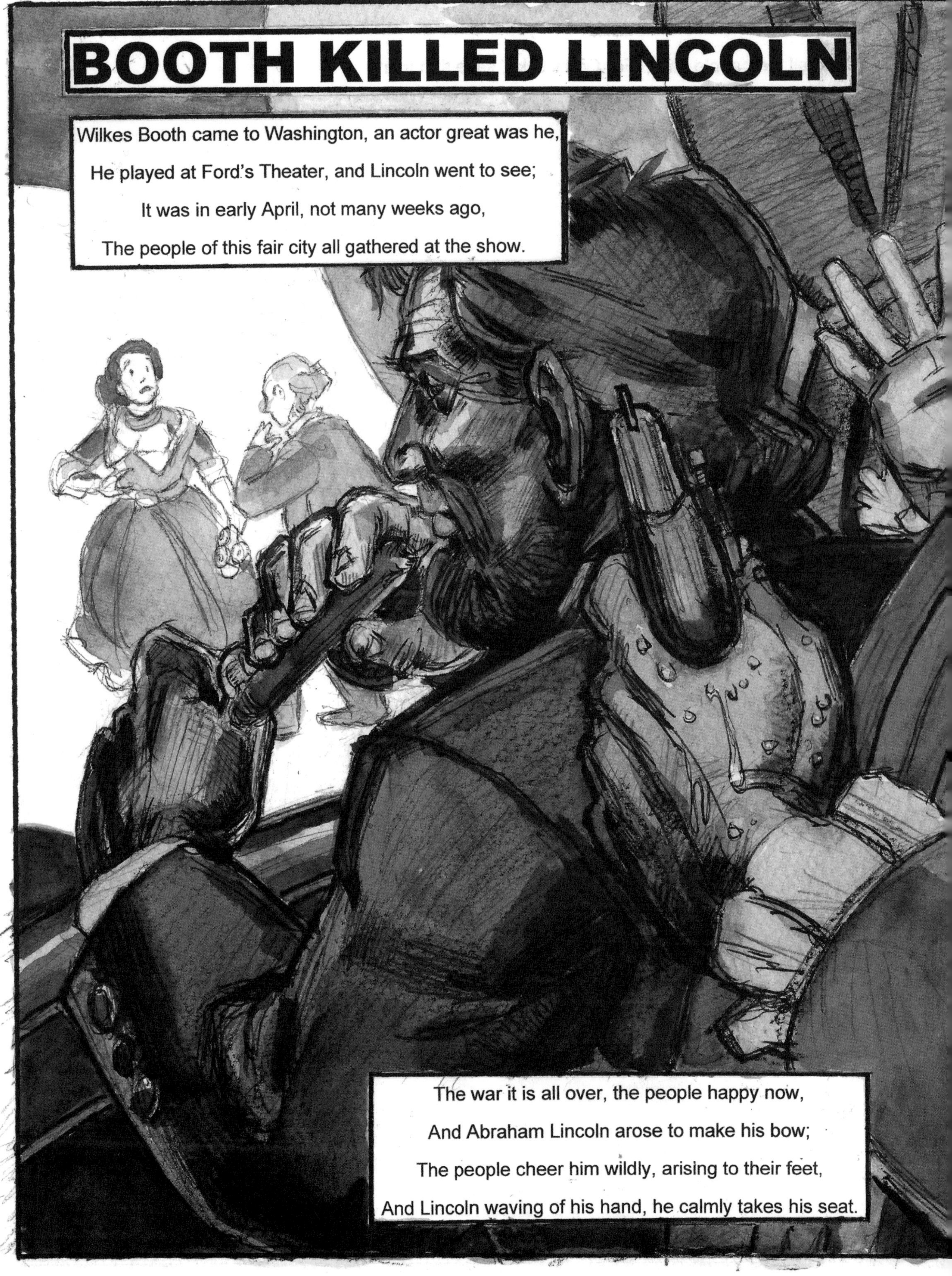
BOOTH KILLED LINCOLN
Wilkes Booth came to Washington, an actor great was he,
He played at Ford's Theater, and Lincoln went to see;
It was in early April, not many weeks ago,
The people of this fair city all gathered at the show.
The war it is all over, the people happy now,
And Abraham Lincoln arose to make his bow;
The people cheer him wildly, arising to their feet,
And Lincoln waving of his hand, he calmly takes his seat.

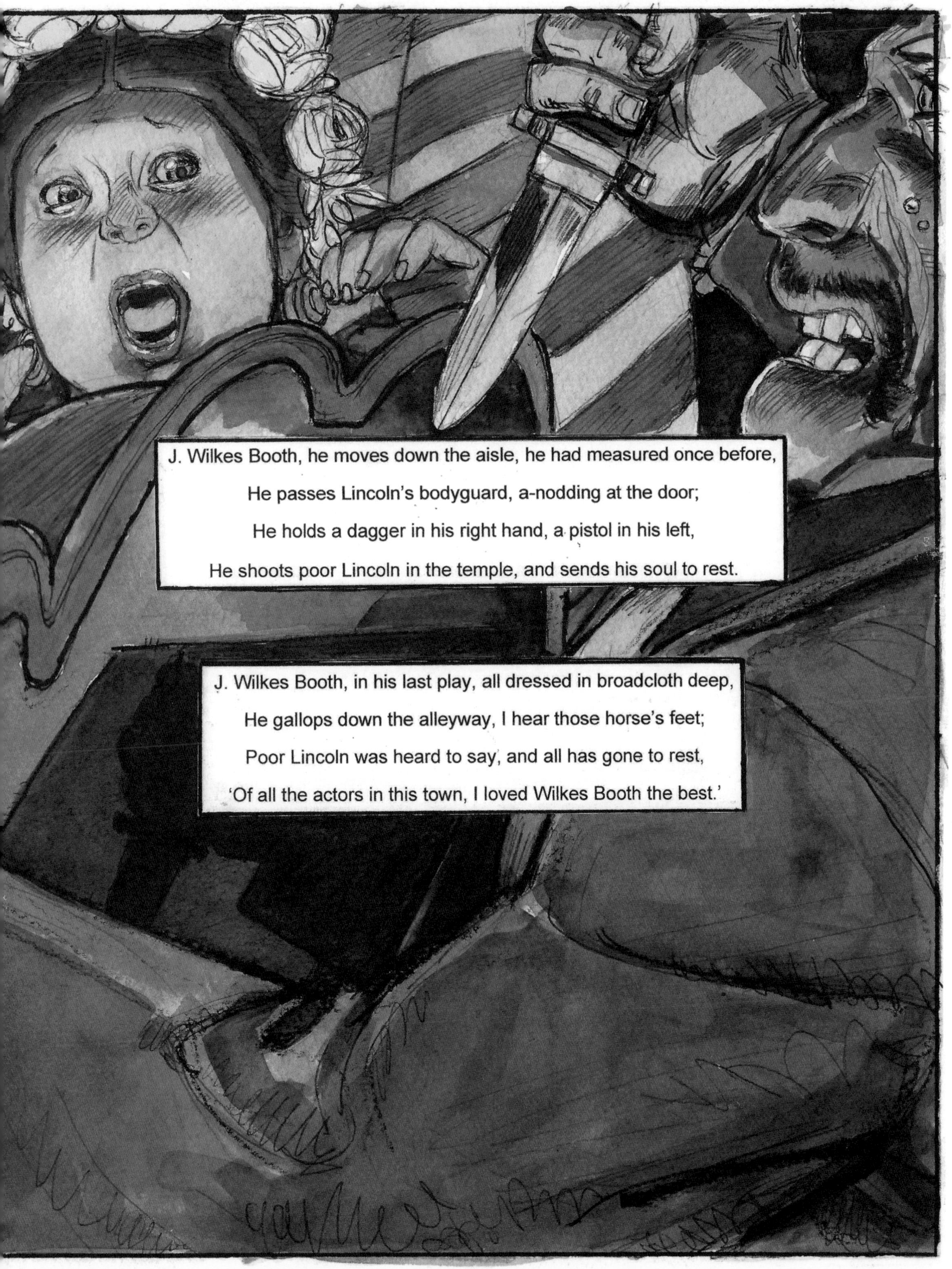
J. Wilkes Booth, he moves down the aisle, he had measured once before,
He passes Lincoln's bodyguard, a-nodding at the door;
He holds a dagger in his right hand, a pistol in his left,
He shoots poor Lincoln in the temple, and sends his soul to rest.
J. Wilkes Booth, in his last play, all dressed in broadcloth deep,
He gallops down the alleyway, I hear those horse's feet;
Poor Lincoln was heard to say, and all has gone to rest,
'Of all the actors in this town, I loved Wilkes Booth the best.'

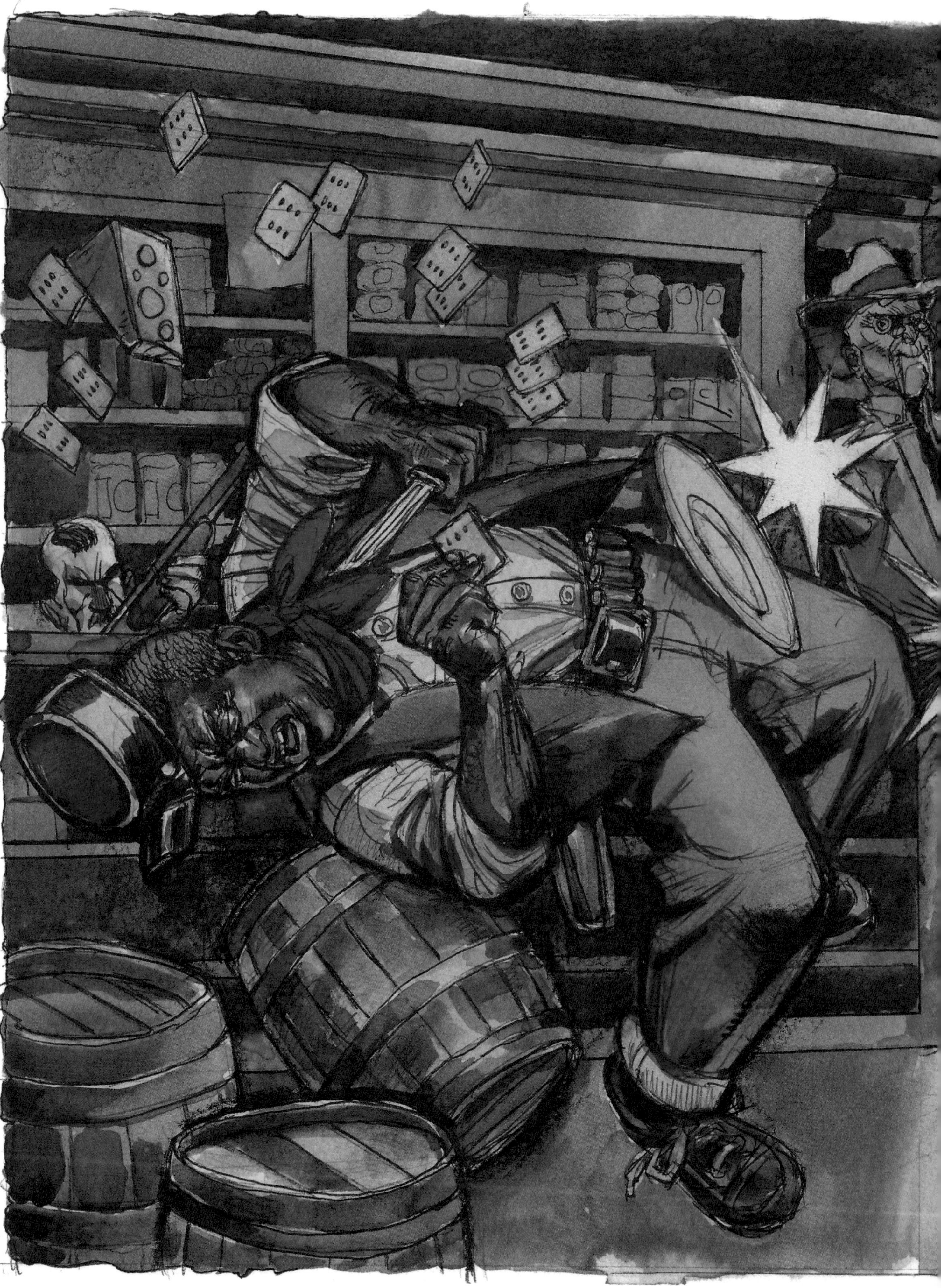

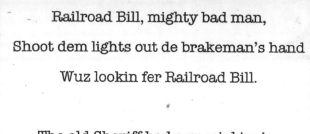

RAILROAD BILL

Railroad Bill, mighty bad man,
Shoot dem lights out de brakeman's hand
Wuz lookin fer Railroad Bill.

The old Sheriff had a special train,
When he got there, was a shower of rain,
Wuz lookin fer Railroad Bill.

Ten po-licemens all dressed in blue,
Comin' down the street, two by two,
All lookin fer Railroad Bill.

Everbody tol them they better go back,
Po-licemens comin down that railroad track
A-lookin fer Railroad Bill.

Railroad Bill might big spo't,
Shot all de buttons off de Sheriff's coat,
Wuz lookin fer Railroad Bill.

Railroad Bill eatin crackers 'n' cheese,
Long come a sheriff, chipper as you please,
Wuz lookin fer Railroad Bill.

Railroad Bill lyin on the grocery floor,
Got shot two times and two times more,
No more lookin fer Railroad Bill.

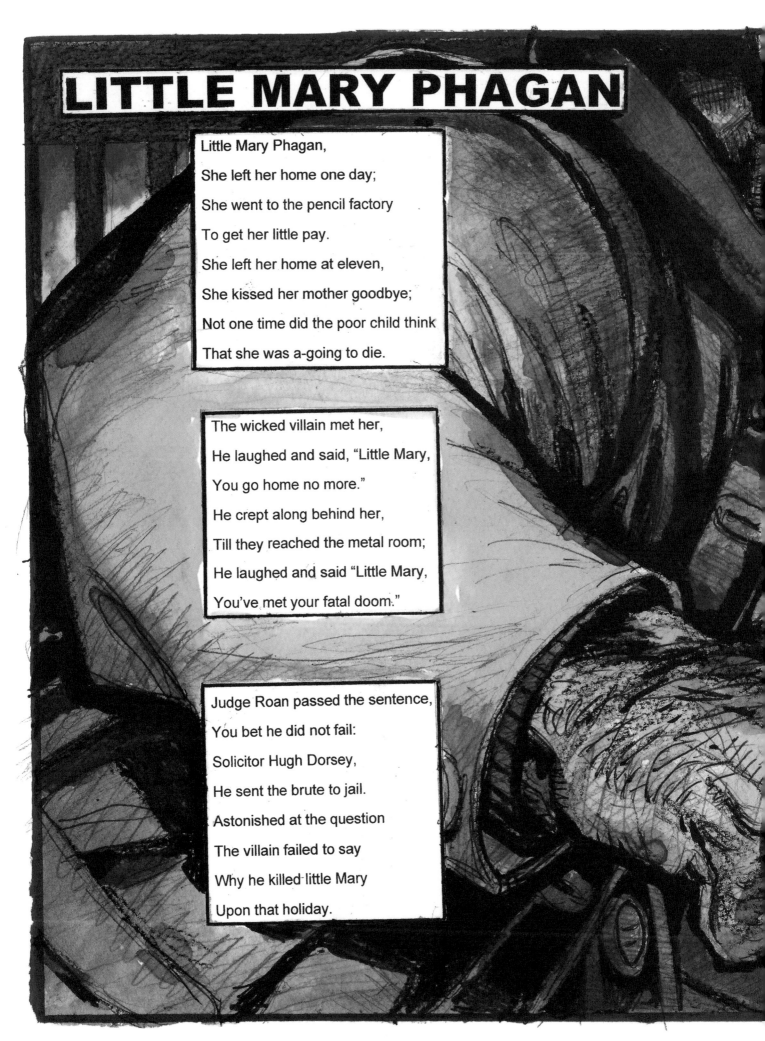

LITTLE MARY PHAGAN

Little Mary Phagan,

She left her home one day;

She went to the pencil factory

To get her little pay.

She left her home at eleven,

She kissed her mother goodbye;

Not one time did the poor child think

That she was a-going to die.

The wicked villain met her,

He laughed and said, "Little Mary,

You go home no more."

He crept along behind her,

Till they reached the metal room;

He laughed and said "Little Mary,

You've met your fatal doom."

Judge Roan passed the sentence,

You bet he did not fail:

Solicitor Hugh Dorsey,

He sent the brute to jail.

Astonished at the question

The villain failed to say

Why he killed little Mary

Upon that holiday.

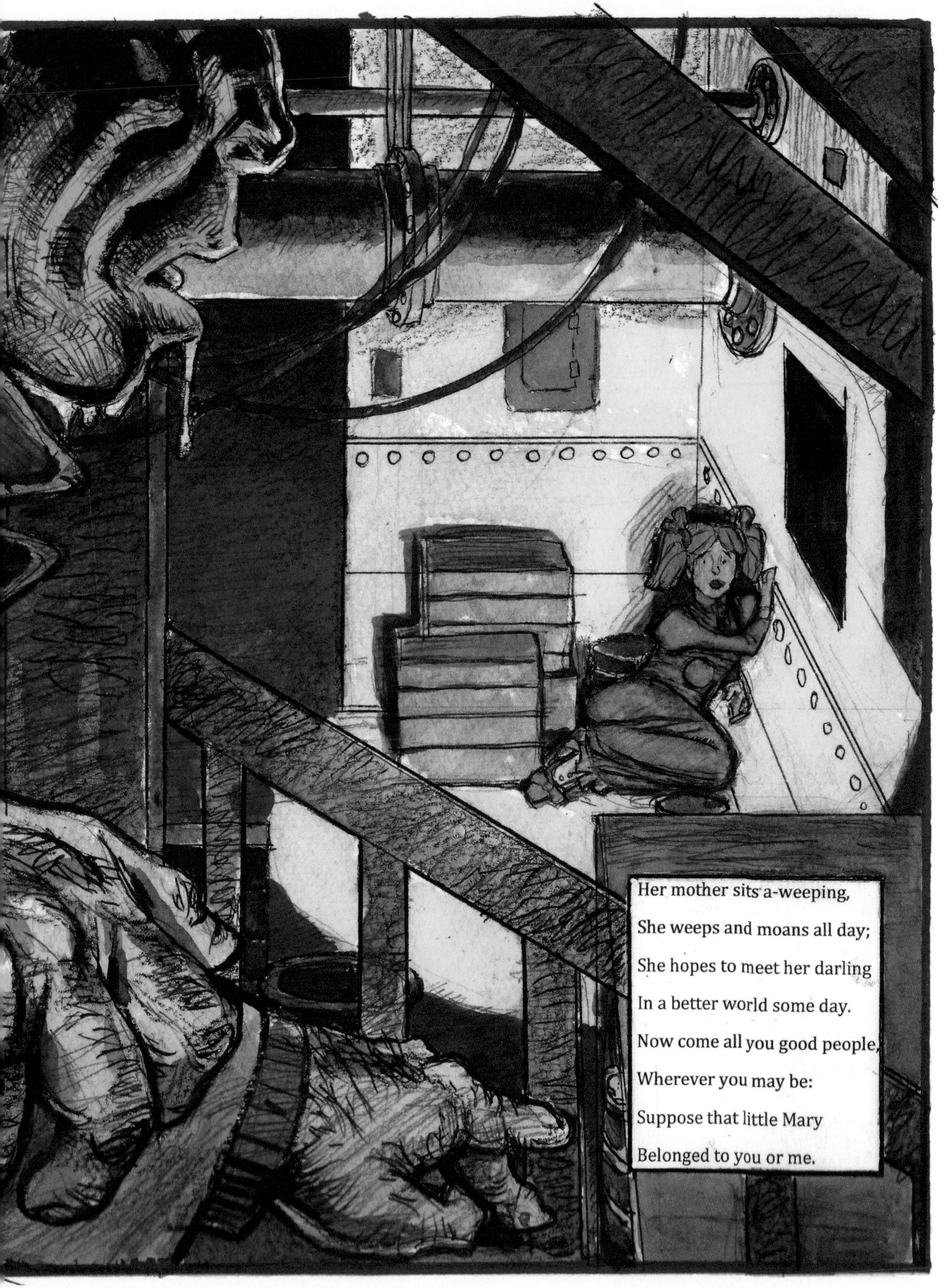
Her mother sits a-weeping,
She weeps and moans all day;
She hopes to meet her darling
In a better world some day.
Now come all you good people,
Wherever you may be:
Suppose that little Mary
Belonged to you or me.

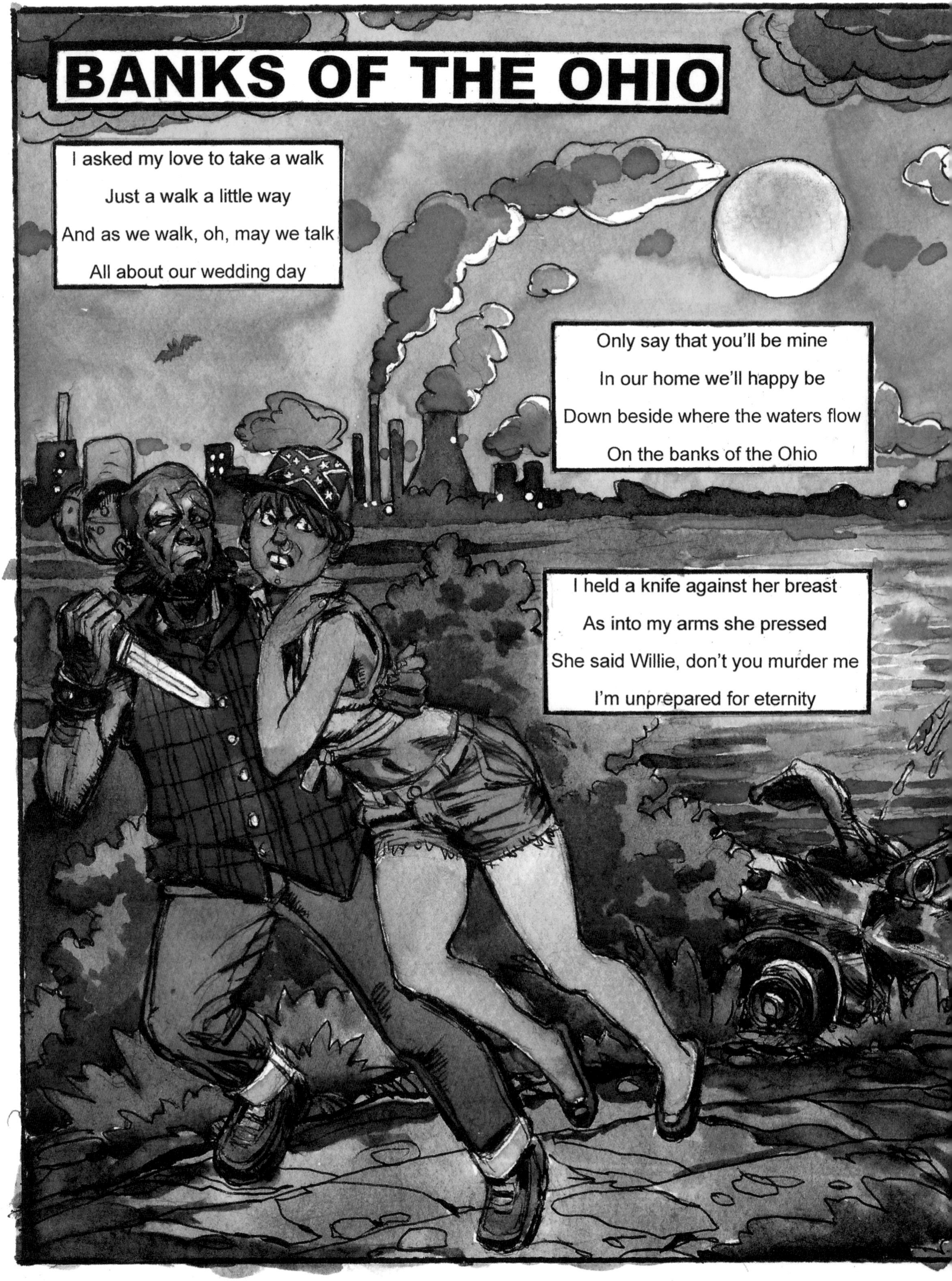
BANKS OF THE OHIO
I asked my love to take a walk
Just a walk a little way
And as we walk, oh, may we talk
All about our wedding day
Only say that you'll be mine
In our home we'll happy be
Down beside where the waters flow
On the banks of the Ohio
I held a knife against her breast
As into my arms she pressed
She said Willie, don't you murder me
I'm unprepared for eternity

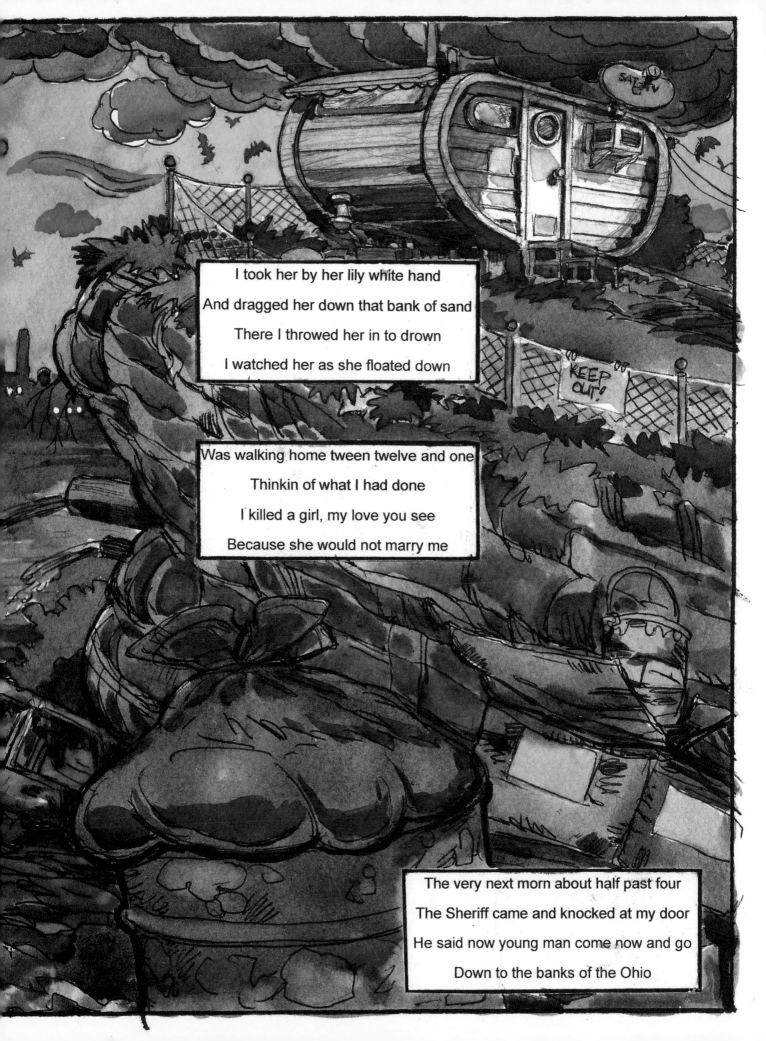

I took her by her lily white hand
And dragged her down that bank of sand
There I threwed her in to drown
I watched her as she floated down

Was walking home tween twelve and one
Thinkin of what I had done
I killed a girl, my love you see
Because she would not marry me

The very next morn about half past four
The Sheriff came and knocked at my door
He said now young man come now and go
Down to the banks of the Ohio

Psycho

Robert Bloch

ART/ADAPTATION BY **Rachel Leah Gallo**

PSYCHO IS ONE OF THOSE MOVIES THAT has eclipsed the book it's based on. Alfred Hitchcock's masterpiece (well, one of them) is not only an all-time classic of horror cinema, it's a classic of filmmaking, period. Hitch shocked everyone by casting one of the biggest stars of the day, Janet Leigh, as Norman Bates's main victim, killing her off early in one of the most important murder scenes in movie history.

So it takes a lot of artistic nerve to go back to Robert Bloch's book for a completely new look. Now, Hitchcock stayed true to the novel in most ways, but there were some divergences. Because it was a Hollywood production, the lead character just couldn't be "unattractive," so the young, tall, slim, handsome Anthony Perkins was cast despite Bloch describing Norman as "pudgy," "fat," balding, bespectacled, and forty years old. This is exactly how Philadelphia-area artist Rachel Leah, also known as RateboneInk, draws him. He's haunted, hallucinating, awkward, and angry. As far as the legendary murder scene . . . it does happen in the shower, but it ends differently than in the movie. And Rachel isn't afraid to show it.

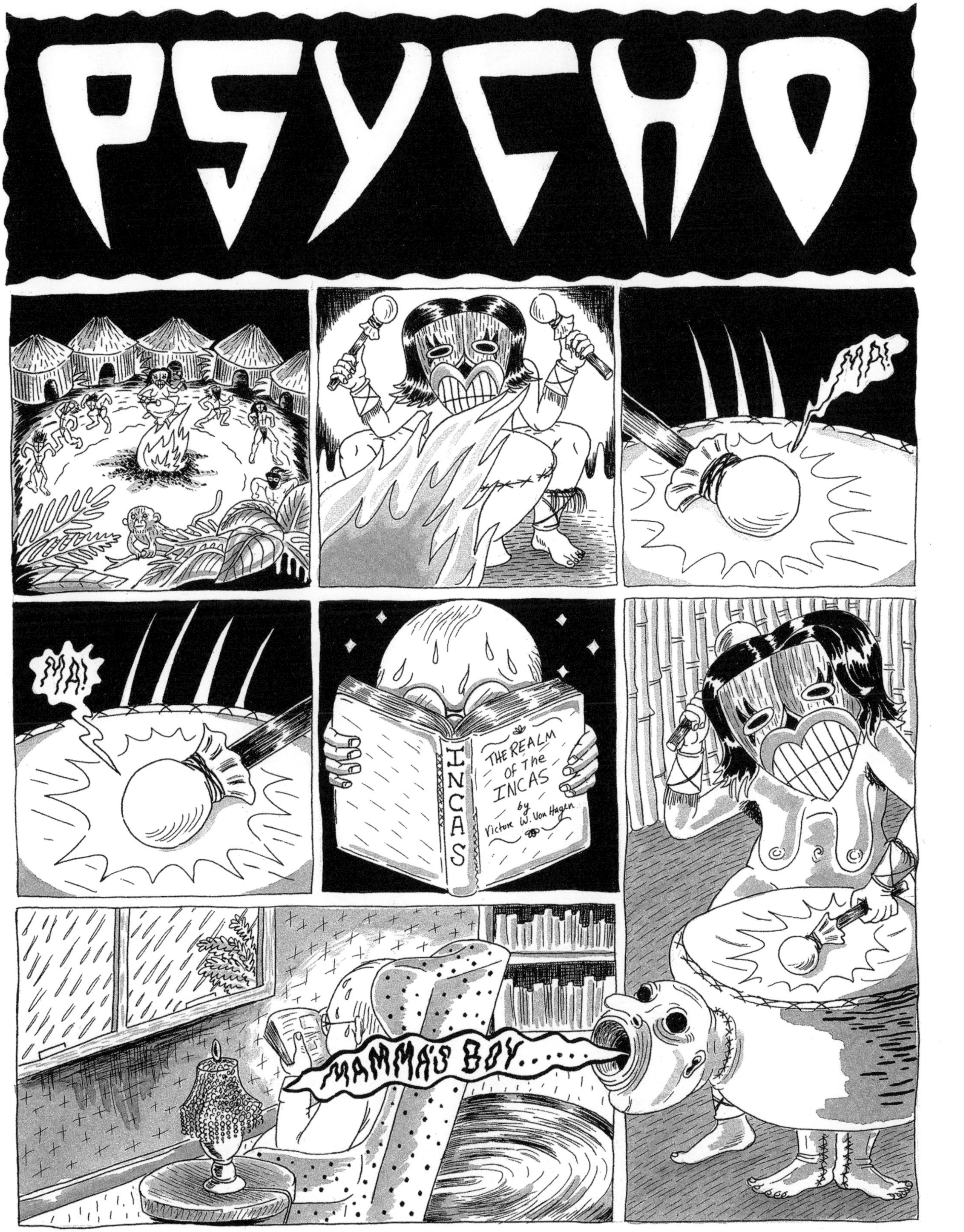
PSYCHO
MA!
MA!
THE REALM OF THE INCAS
by Victor W. Von Hagen
INCAS
MAMMA'S BOY......

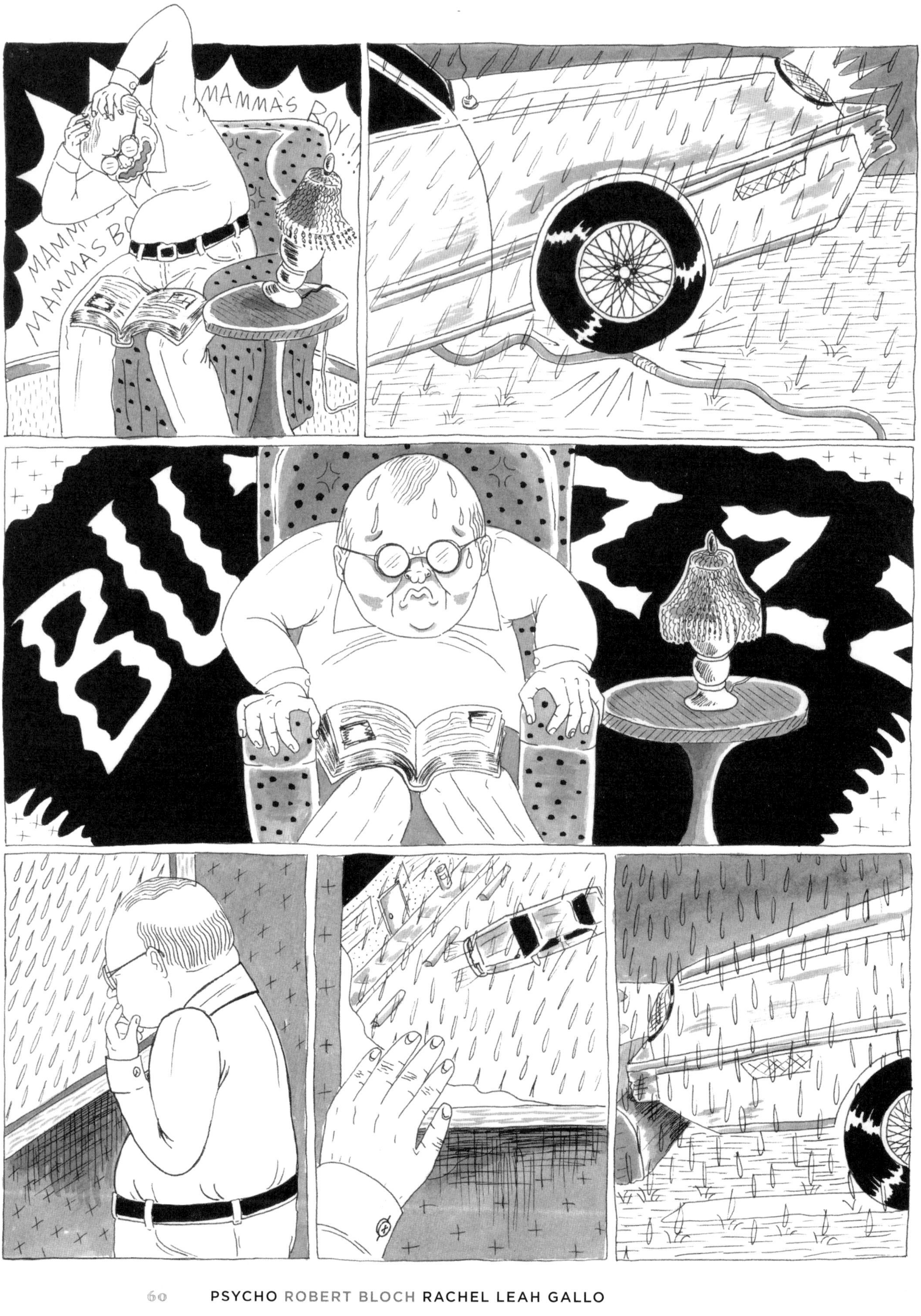
MAMMA'S BOY
MAMMA'S BO
MAMMA'S BOY

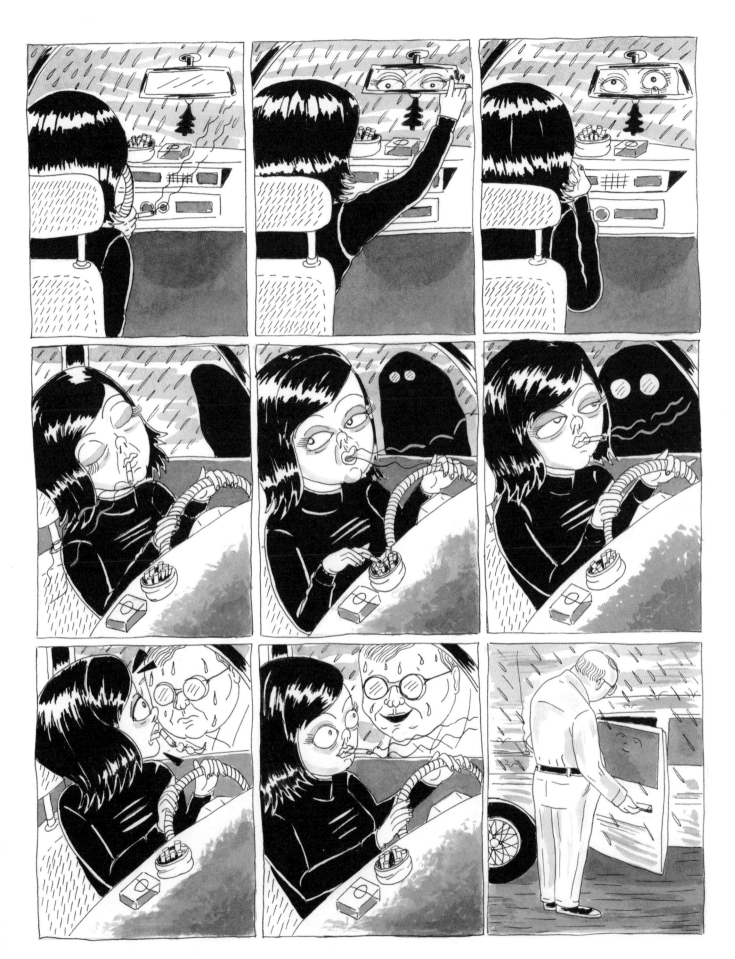

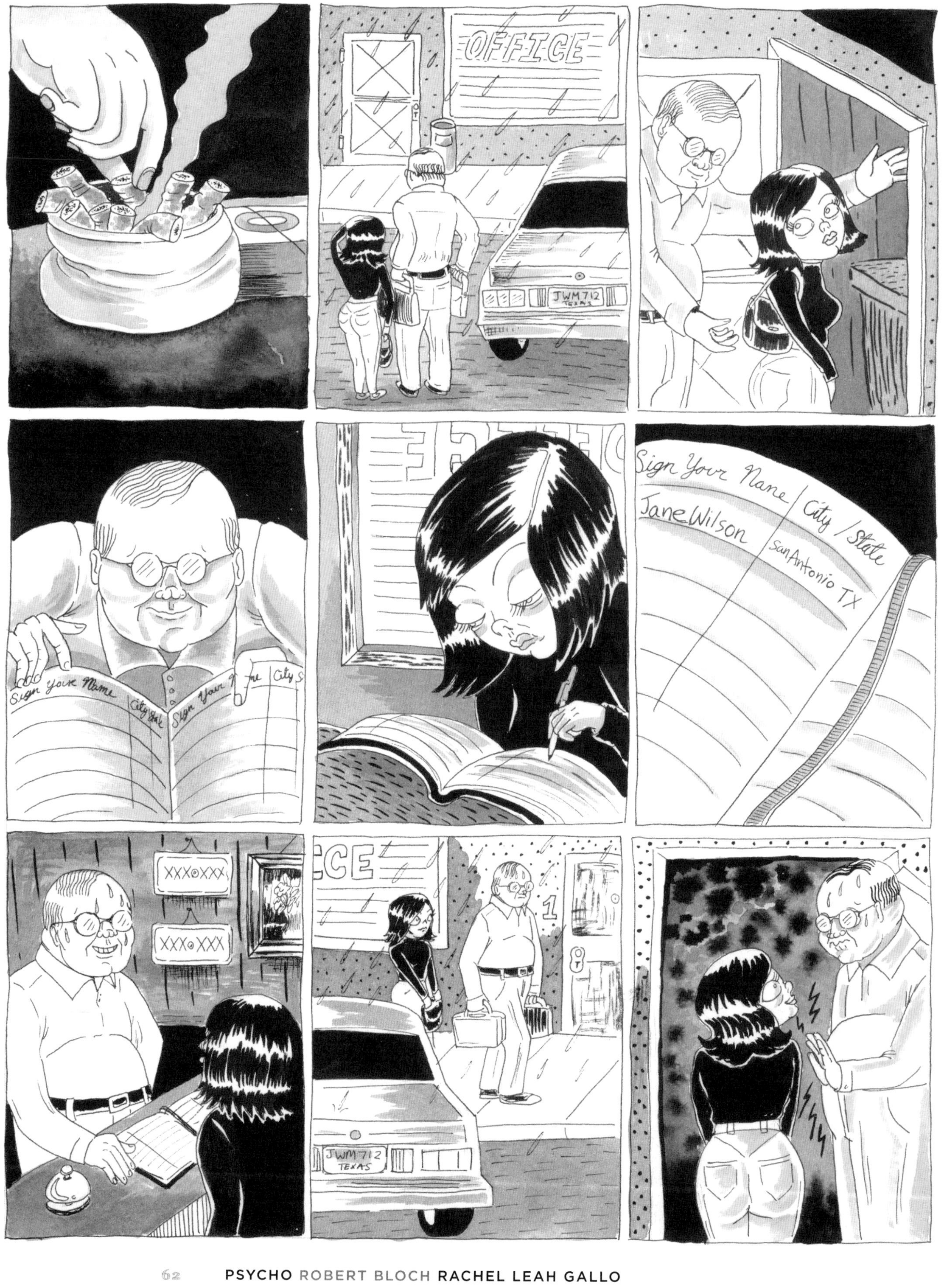
OFFICE
JWM 712
TEXAS
Sign Your Name
City/State
Sign Your Nane
City / State
Jane Wilson
San Antonio TX
XXX⊙XXX
XXX⊙XXX
CE
1
JWM 712
TEXAS

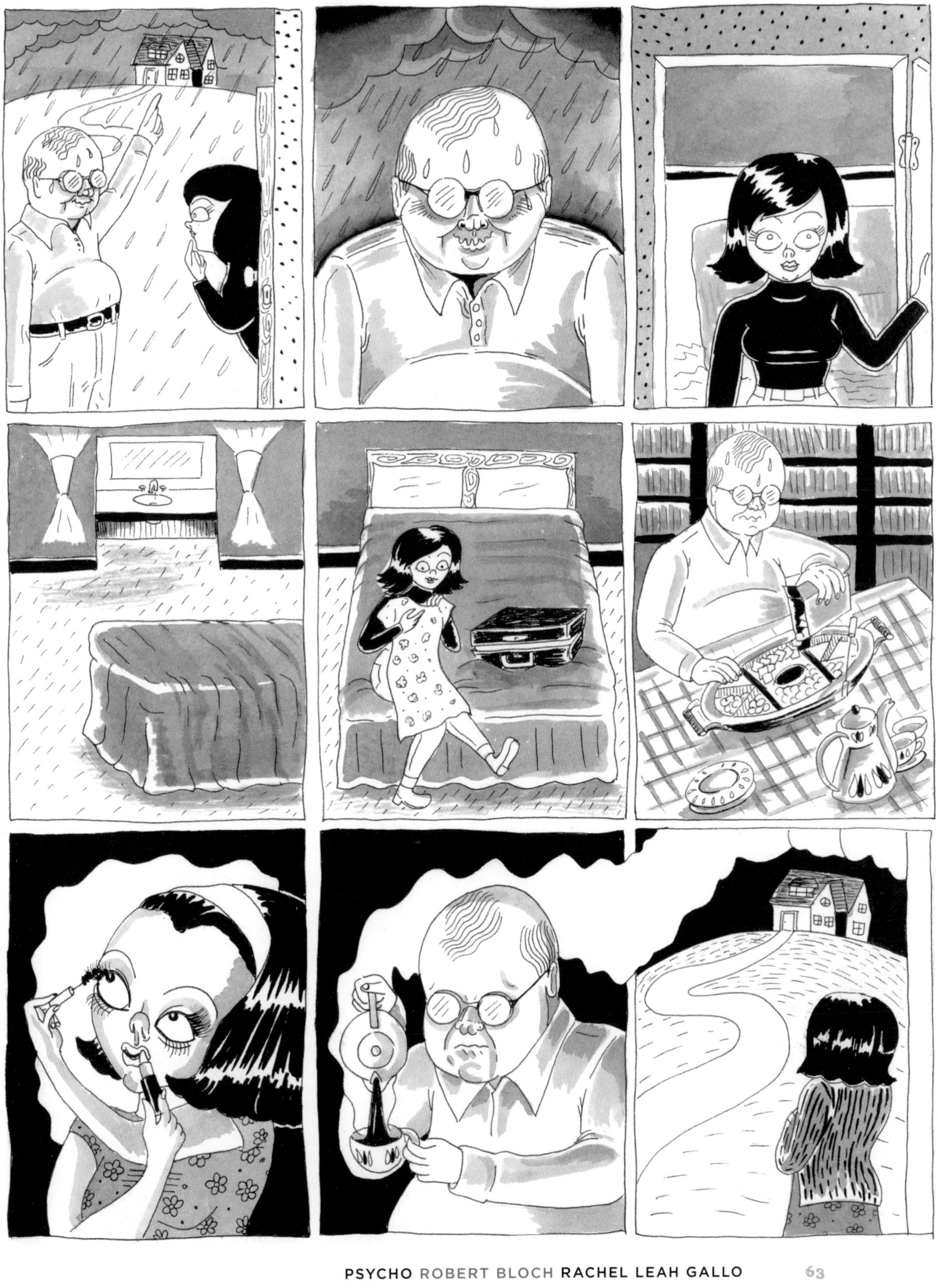

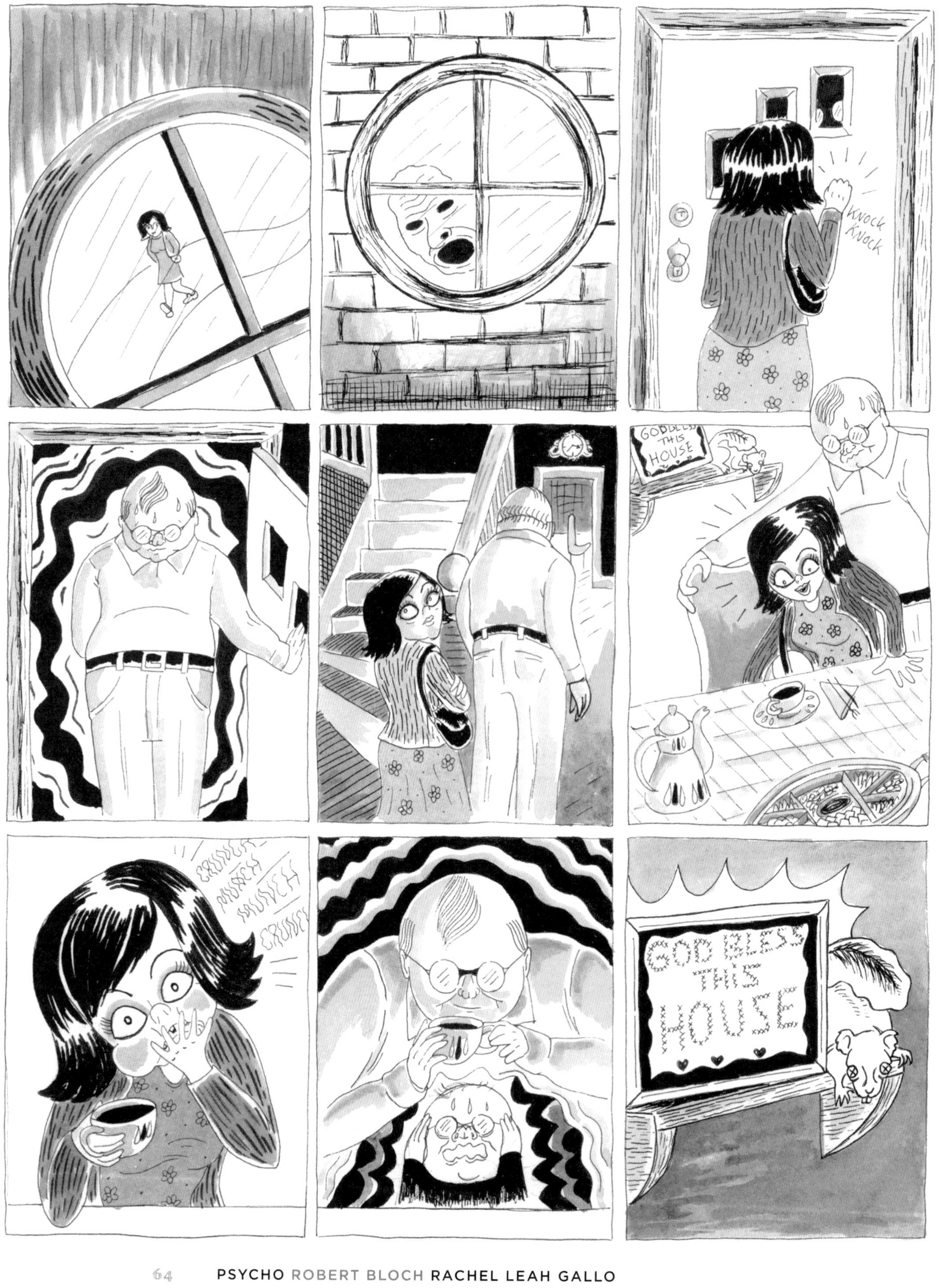
KNOCK KNOCK
GOD BLESS THIS HOUSE
CRUNCH
GOD BLESS THIS HOUSE

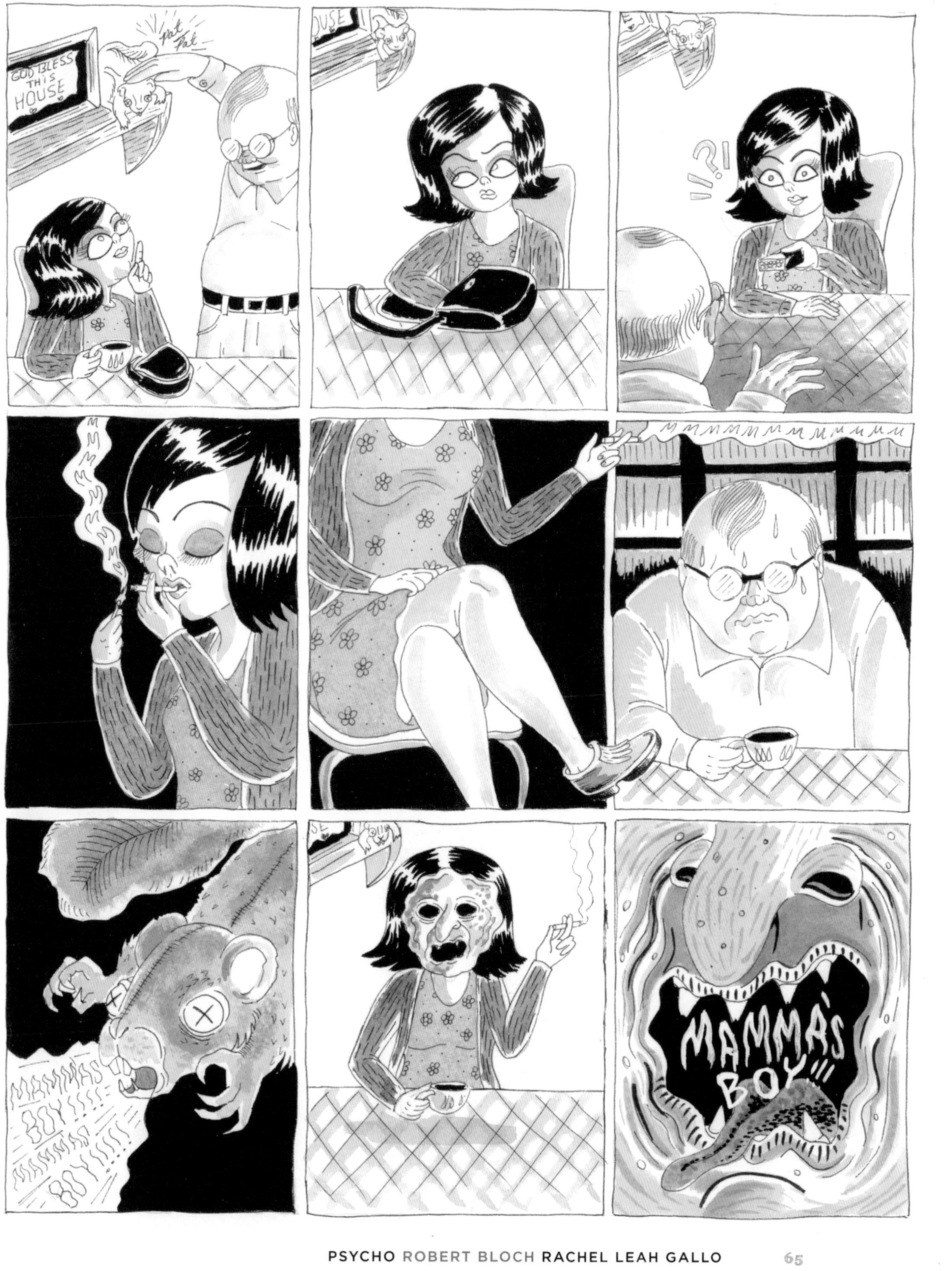
GOD BLESS THIS HOUSE
pat pat
?!
MAMMA'S BOY
MAMMA'S BOY
MAMMA'S BOY!!!

PSYCHO ROBERT BLOCH RACHEL LEAH GALLO

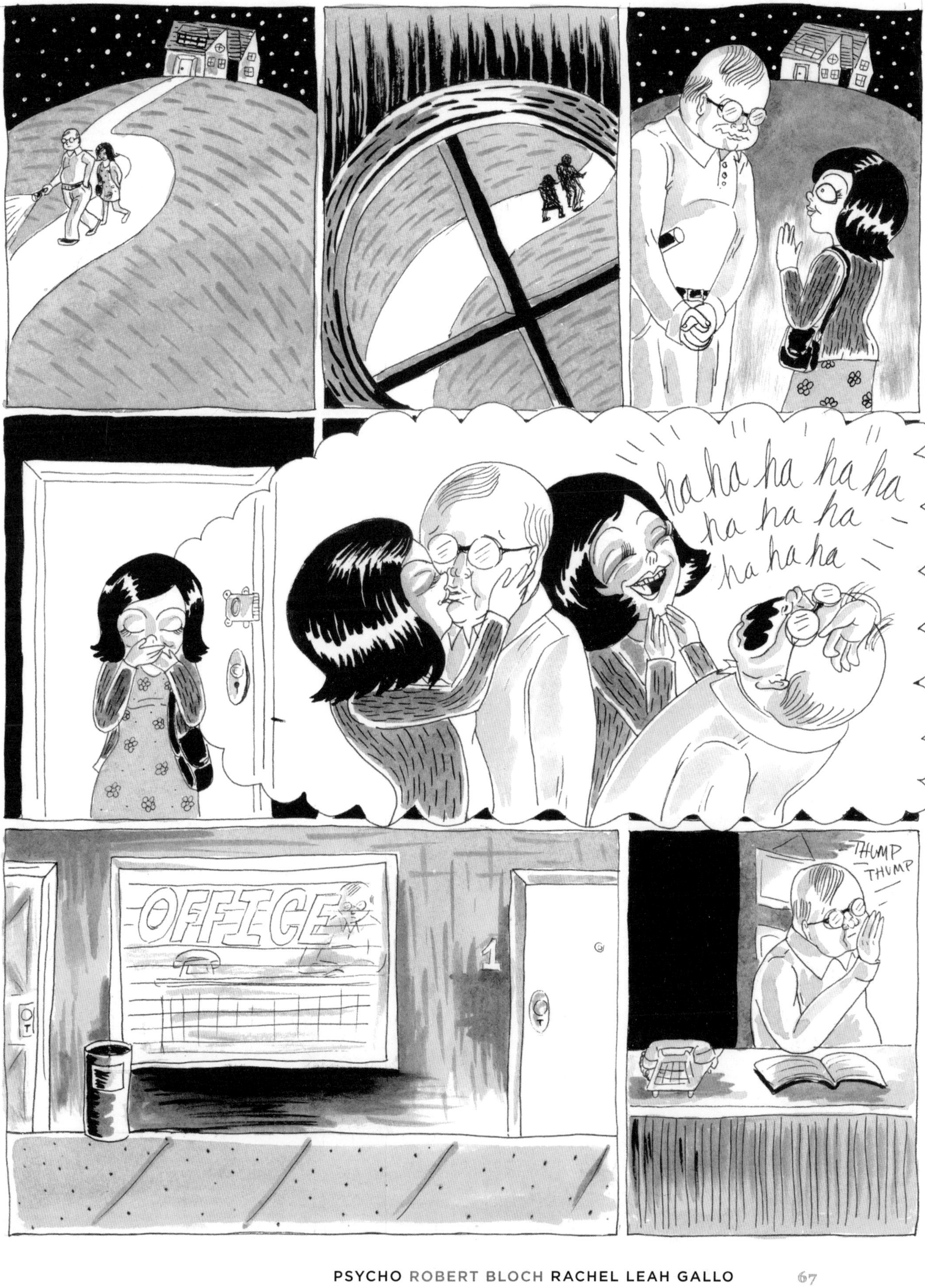
ha ha ha ha ha
ha ha ha
ha ha ha
OFFICE
1
THUMP
THUMP

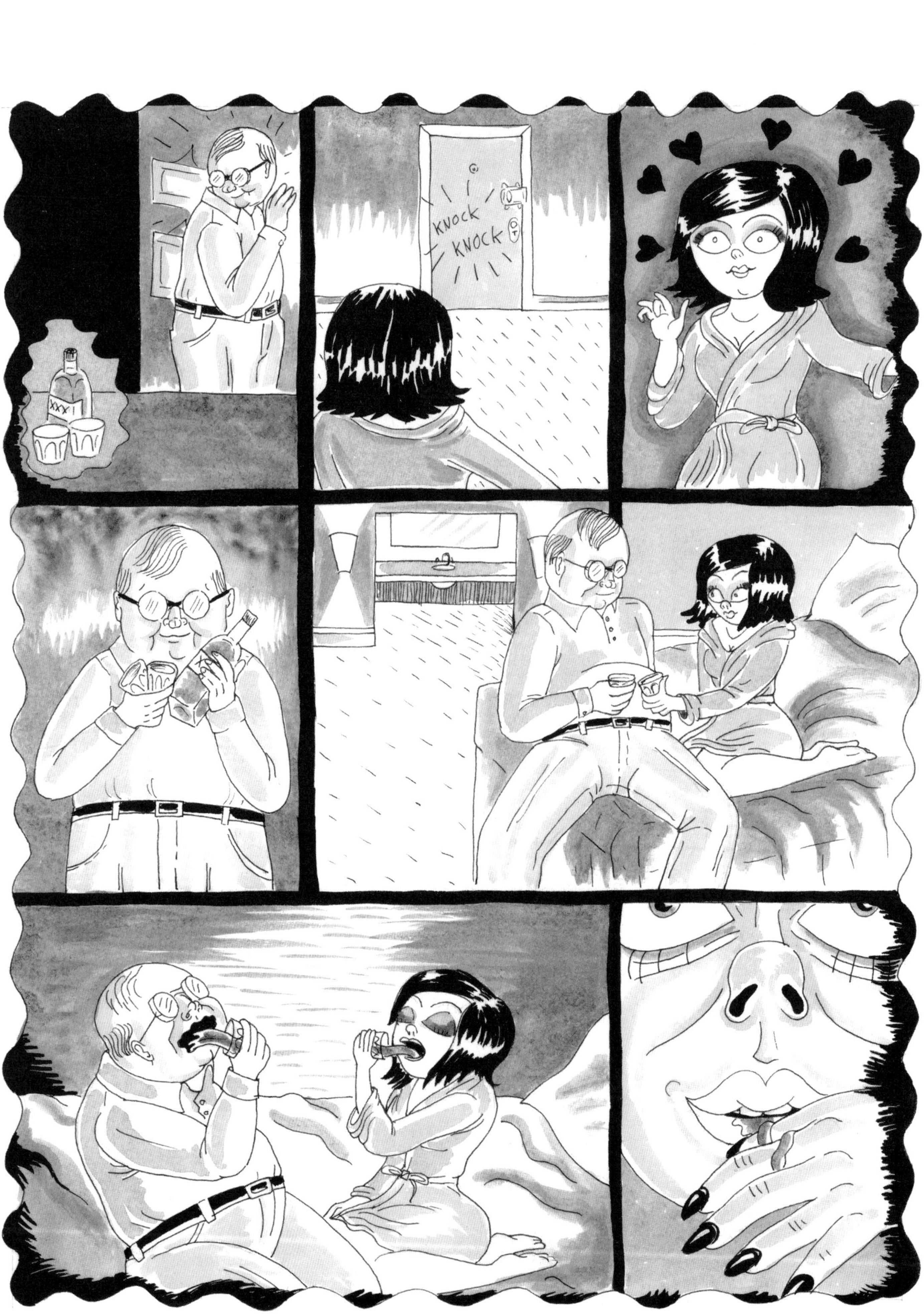
KNOCK
KNOCK

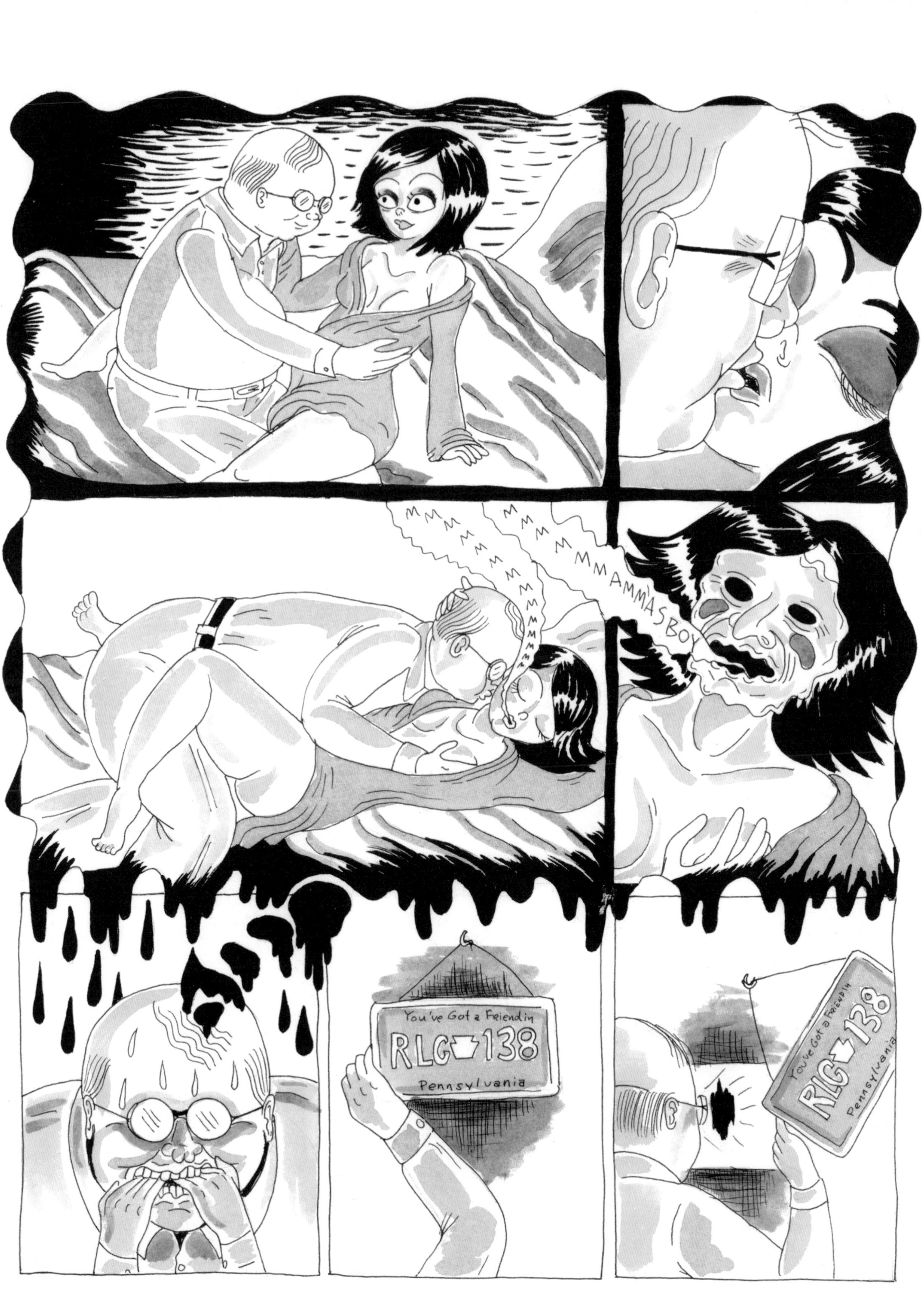
MMMMMMMMMMMMMMM
MMMMMMMAMMASBOY
You've Got a Friend in
RLG 138
Pennsylvania
You've Got a Friend in
RLG 138
Pennsylvania

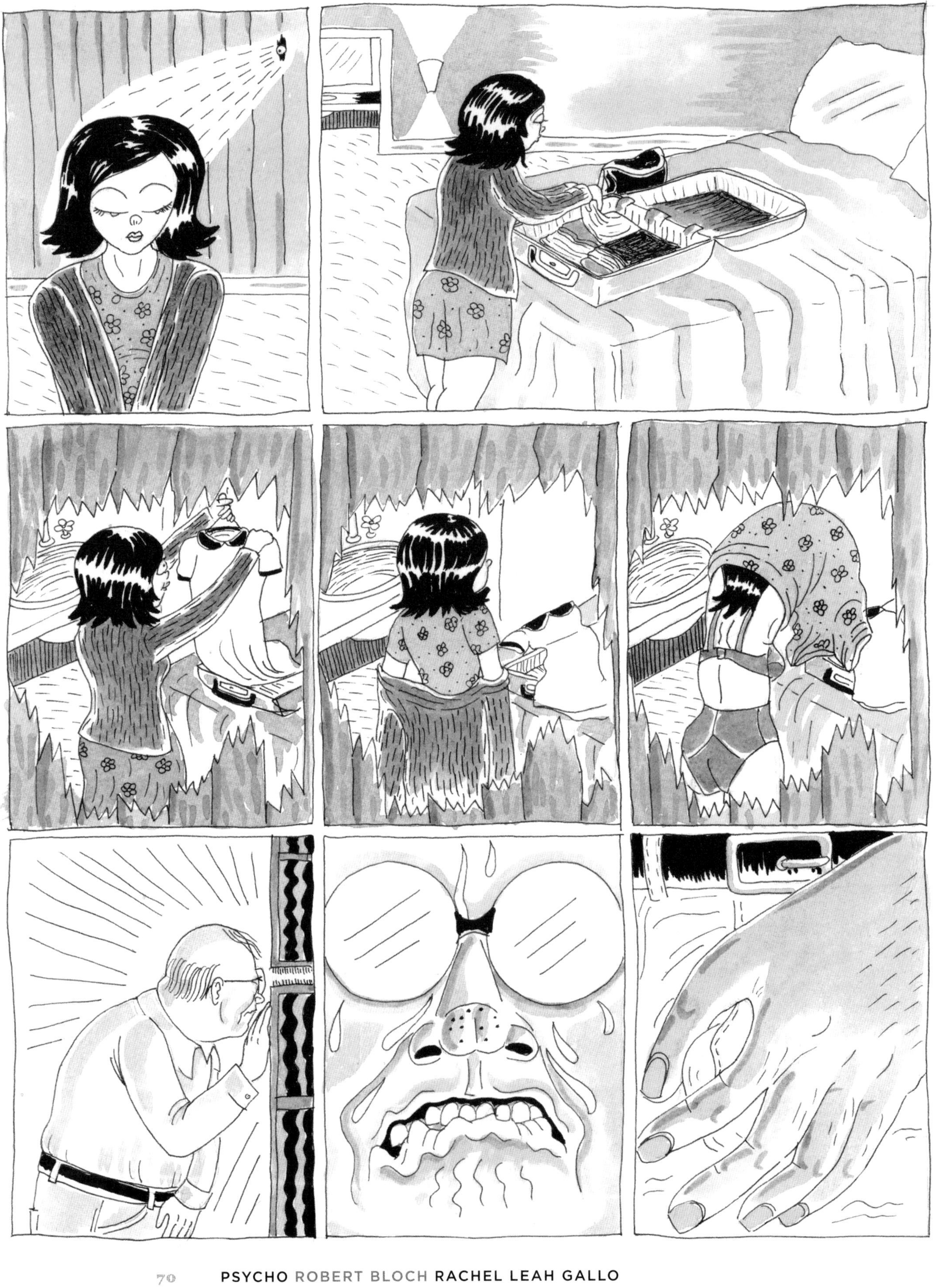

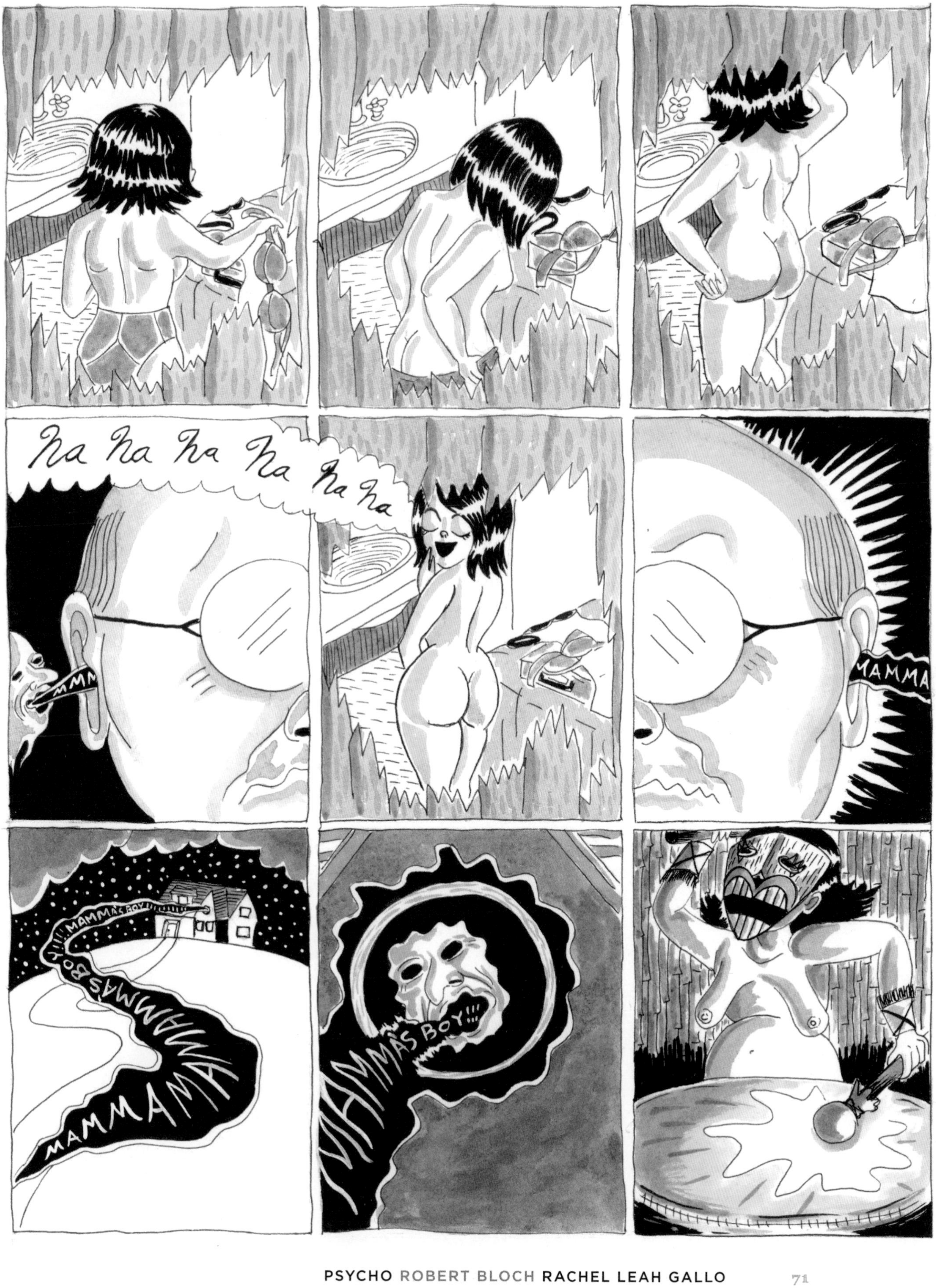
Na Na Na Na Na Na
MAMM
MAMMA
MAMMA'S BOY!!!
MAMMAMAMMAMAMMA
MAMMA'S BOY!!!

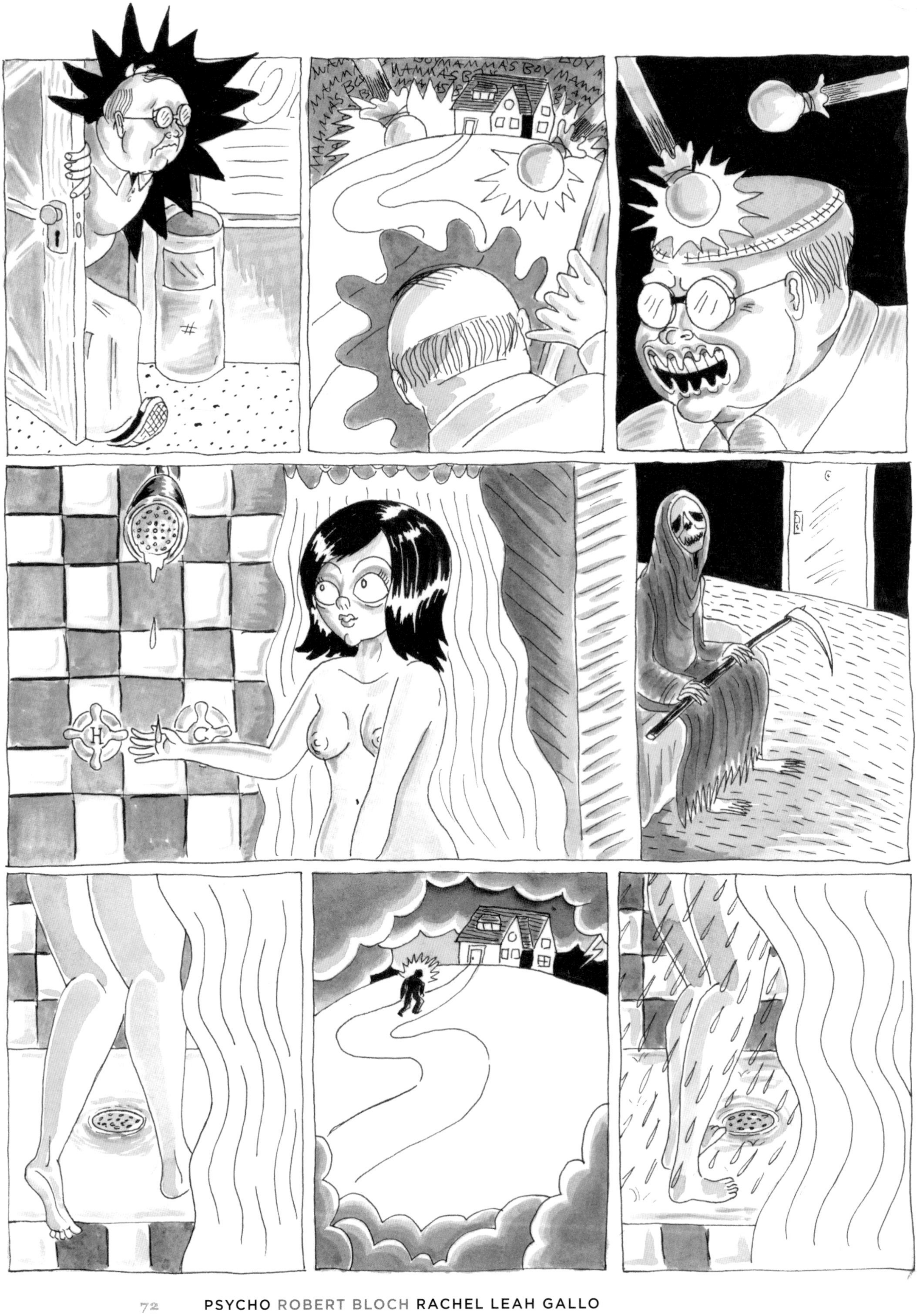
MAMMA'S BOY
H
C

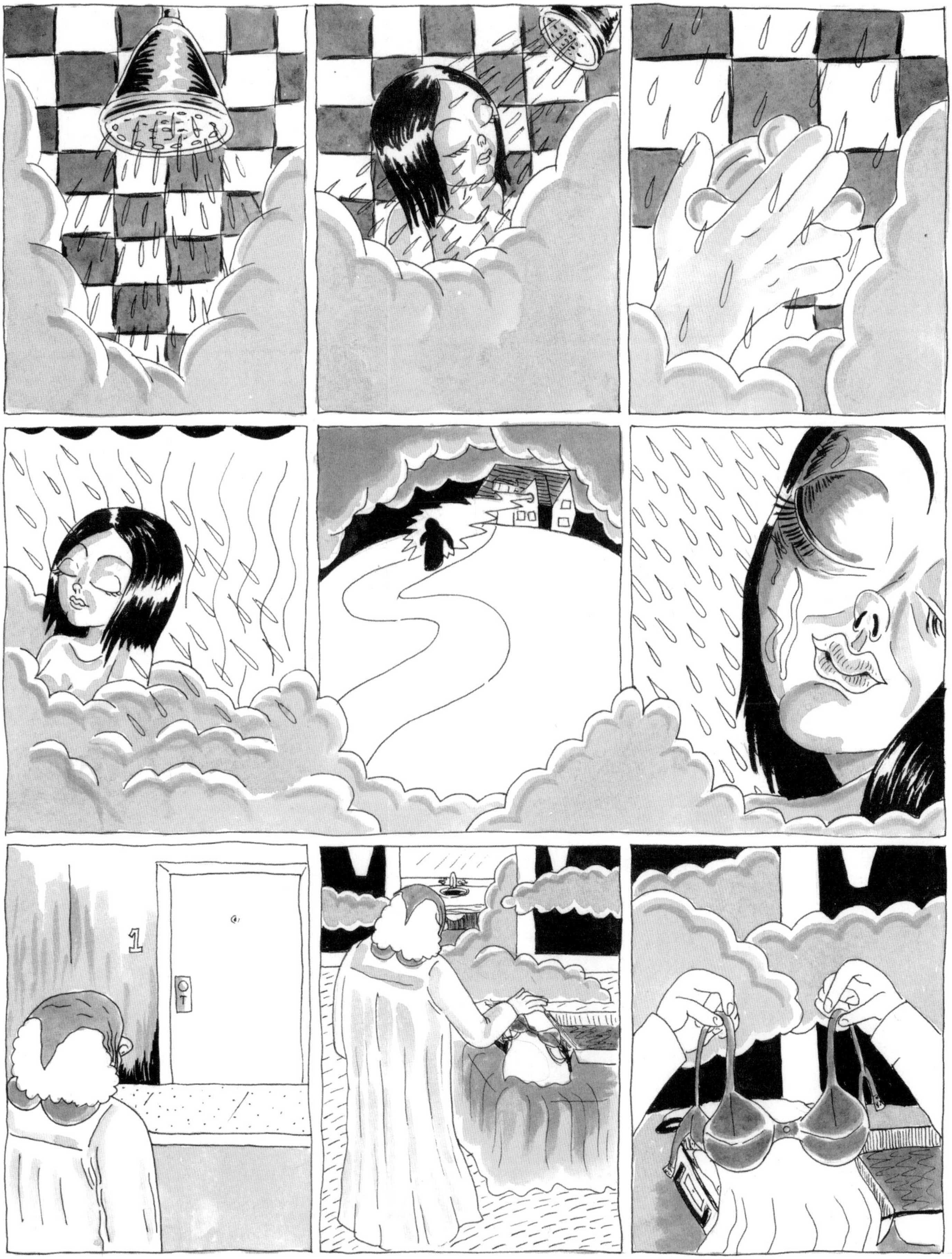
1
OT

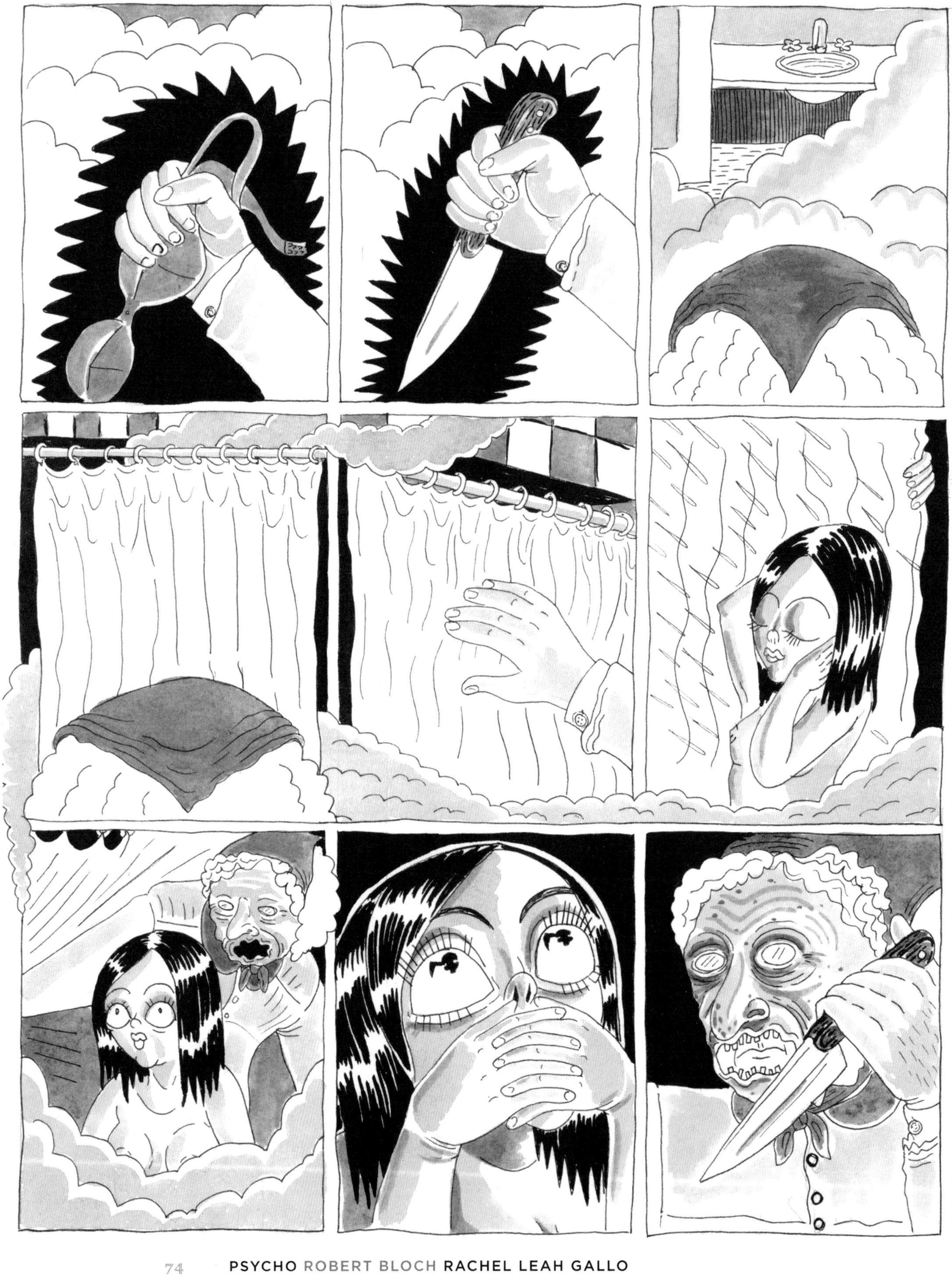

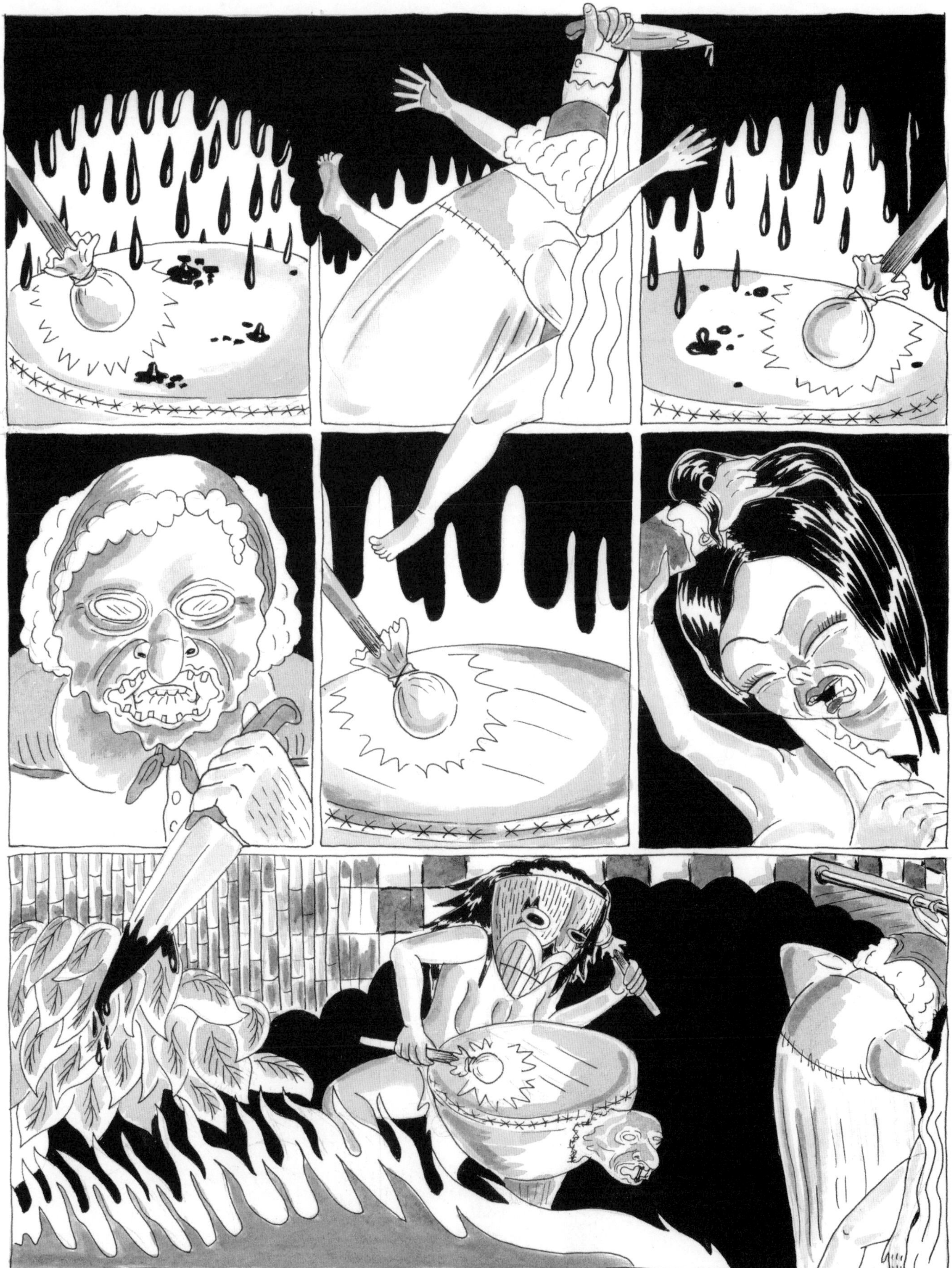

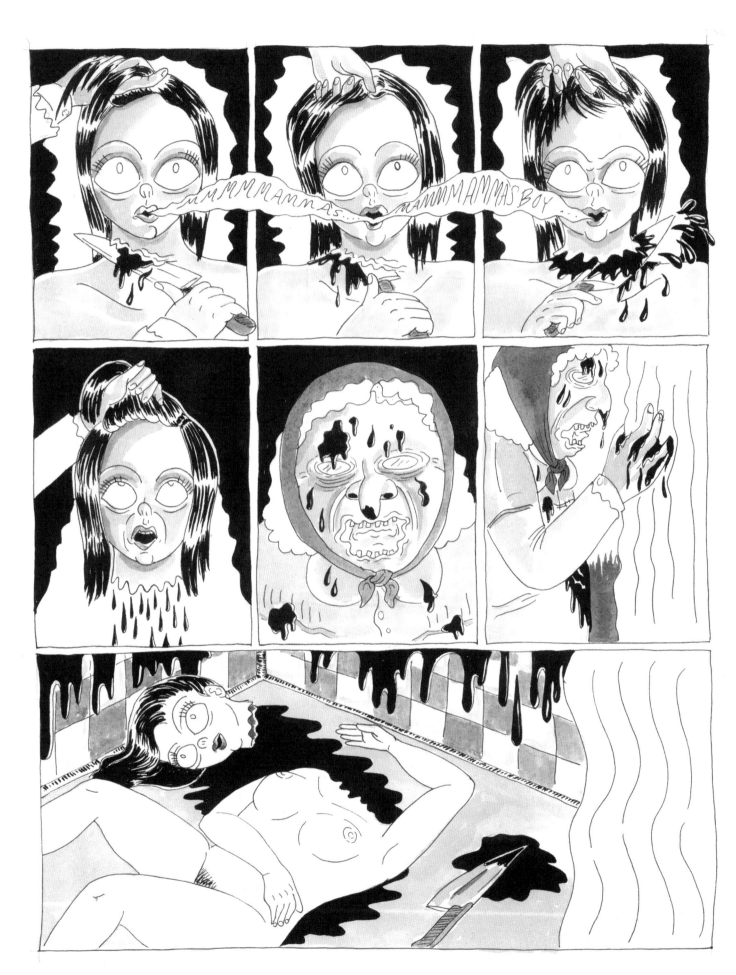

PSYCHO ROBERT BLOCH RACHEL LEAH GALLO

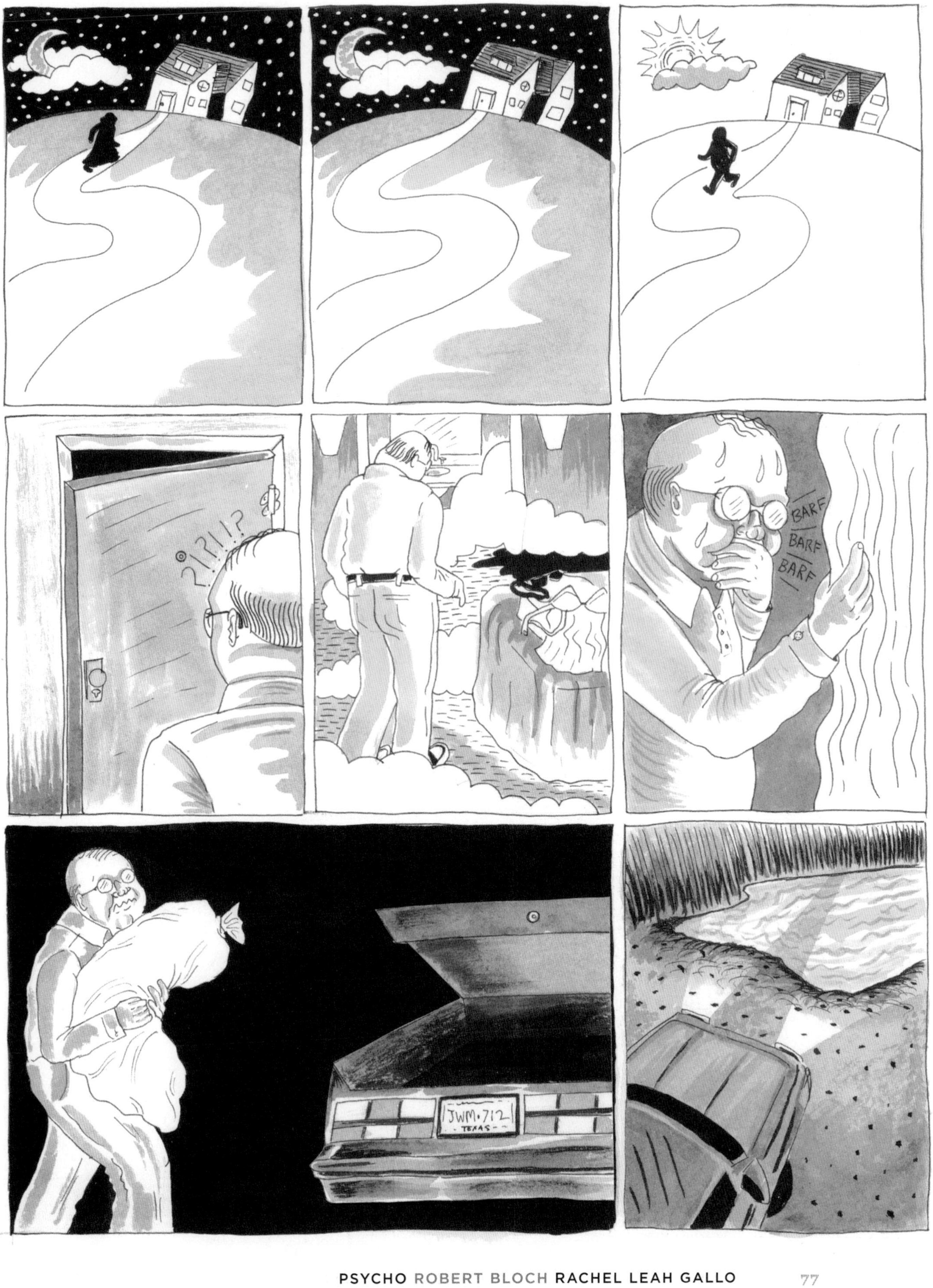
BARF
BARF
BARF
JWM•712
TEXAS

END.

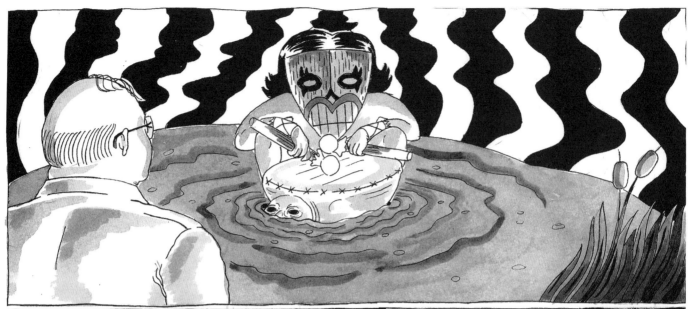

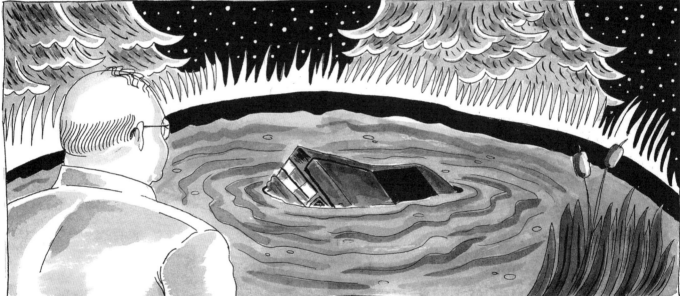

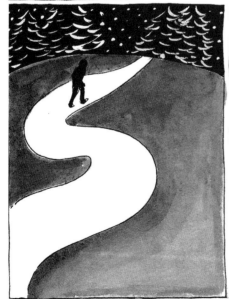

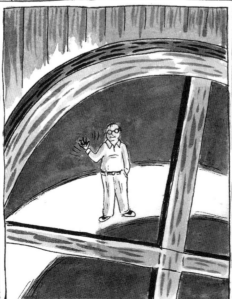

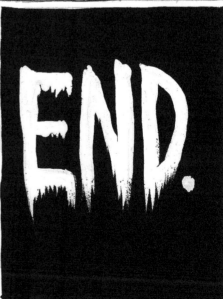

The Sailor Who Fell From Grace With the Sea

Yukio Mishima

ART/ADAPTATION BY **Andrea Montano**

NOBEL PRIZE NOMINEE YUKIO MISHIMA is one of the most important Japanese writers of the twentieth century, and several of his books are classics of world literature. Like Hemingway, Voltaire, Millay, and Aphra Behn, this is a case where the author's life is as fascinating as his works. The short version is that Mishima was an extreme right-wing militant who worshiped the Emperor and the Japan of old. He put together a small armed resistance, lamely attempted to overthrow the government, and when that didn't work, he committed ritual suicide by slicing open his abdomen with a sword. Besides a novelist, he had been a poet, playwright, actor of stage and screen, movie director, orchestra conductor, and martial artist. He also wrote about being gay, which was an extremely brave act in the 1940's. Somebody please make a graphic biography of him.

His 1963 novel, *The Sailor Who Fell From Grace With the Sea*, has one of the most beautiful titles ever, yet it contains one of the most sickening scenes in all of literature. A sailor gets into a relationship with a single mother. Her son at first admires him but then feels the sailor loses his honor when he abandons the glory of the sea for a romantic relationship. The son and his gang of brutal teenage dirtbags plan a horrifying torture-death-evisceration for him, which, in the novel's most infamous scene, they practice on a kitten.

The book ends with the sadistic hoodlums luring the sailor to a desolate hilltop and giving him tea laced with sedatives. His nauseating, ritualistic death by torture is left to our imaginations.

Comic artist and children's-book illustrator Andrea Montano chose to adapt portions of this disturbing novel, which had to have been a challenge. But Mishima's shimmering prose presented ugly subject matter in a deceptively beautiful way and Andrea's clean lines and gorgeous colors have the same effect.

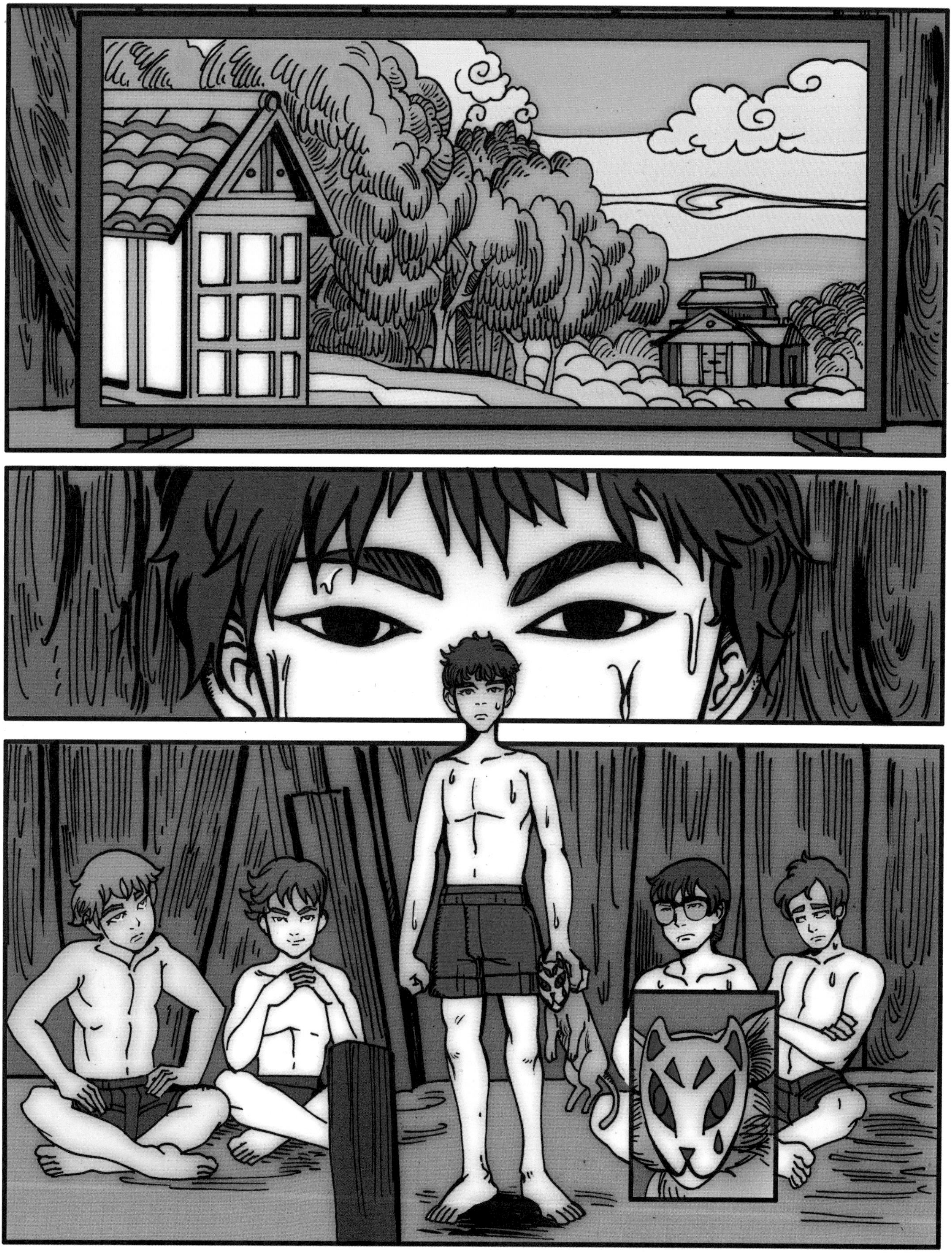

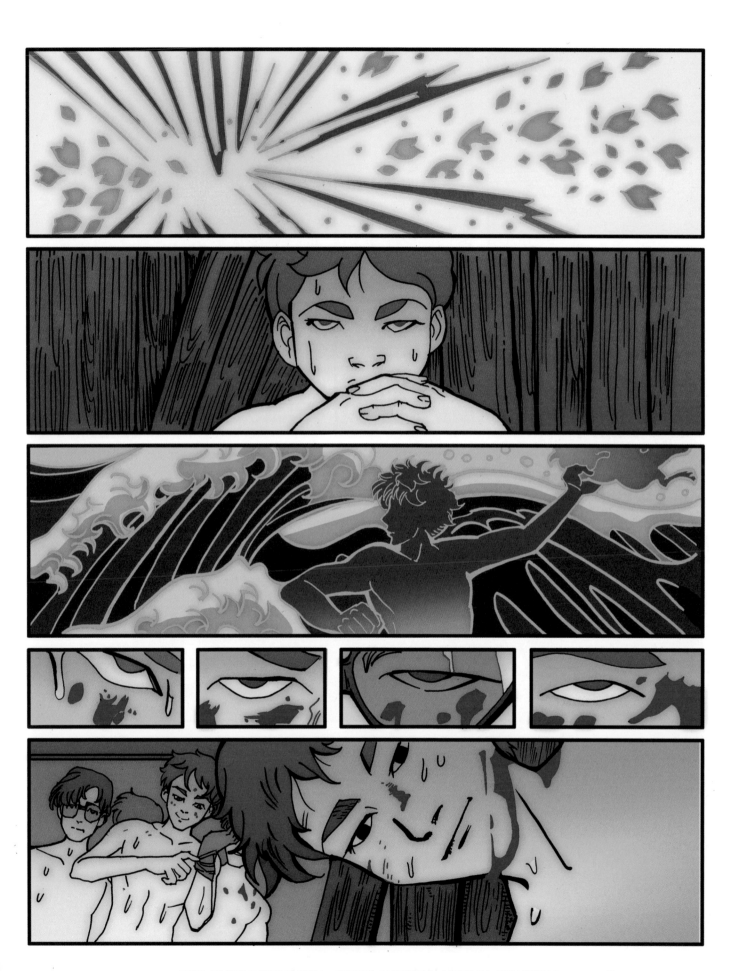

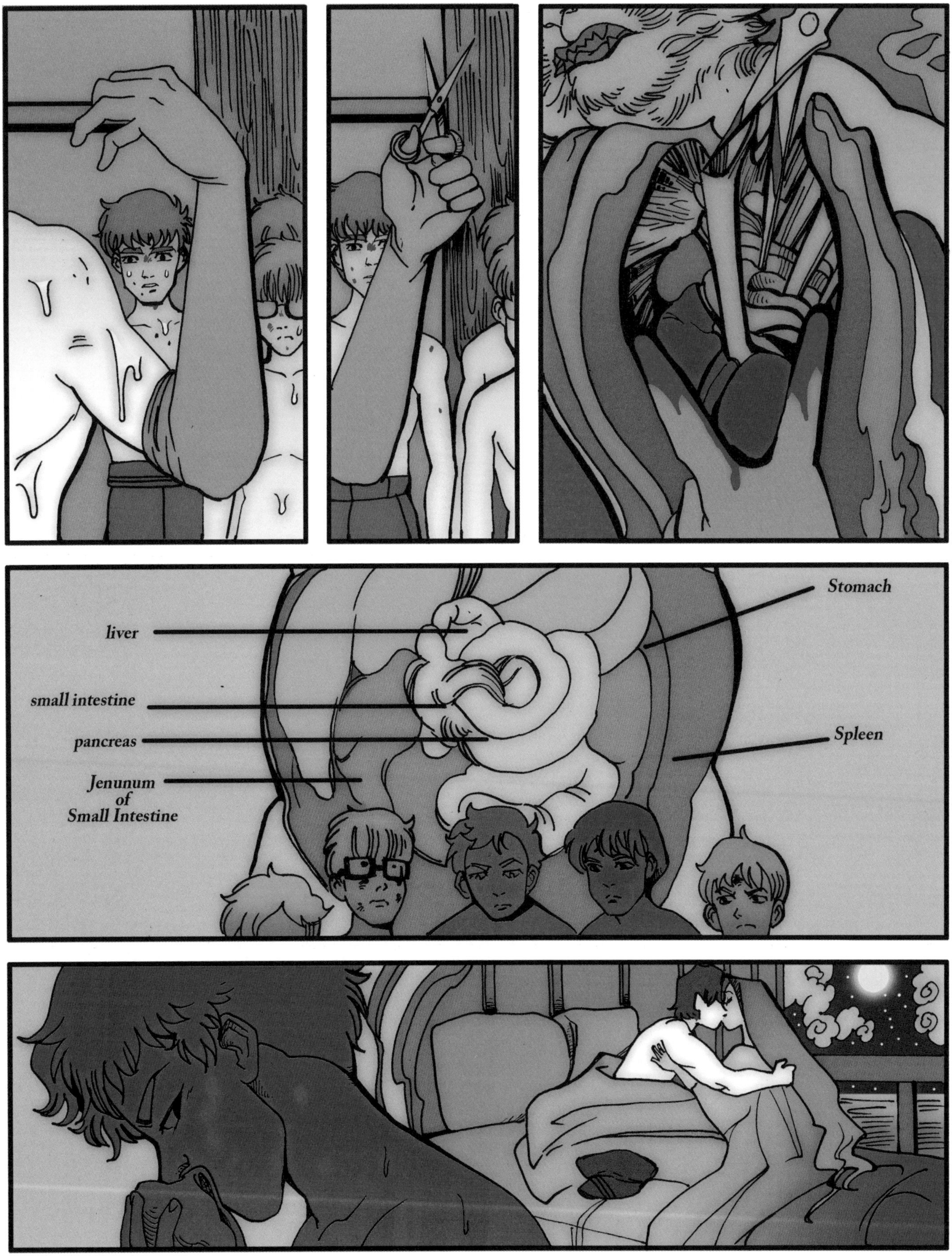
liver
small intestine
pancreas
Jenunum of Small Intestine
Stomach
Spleen

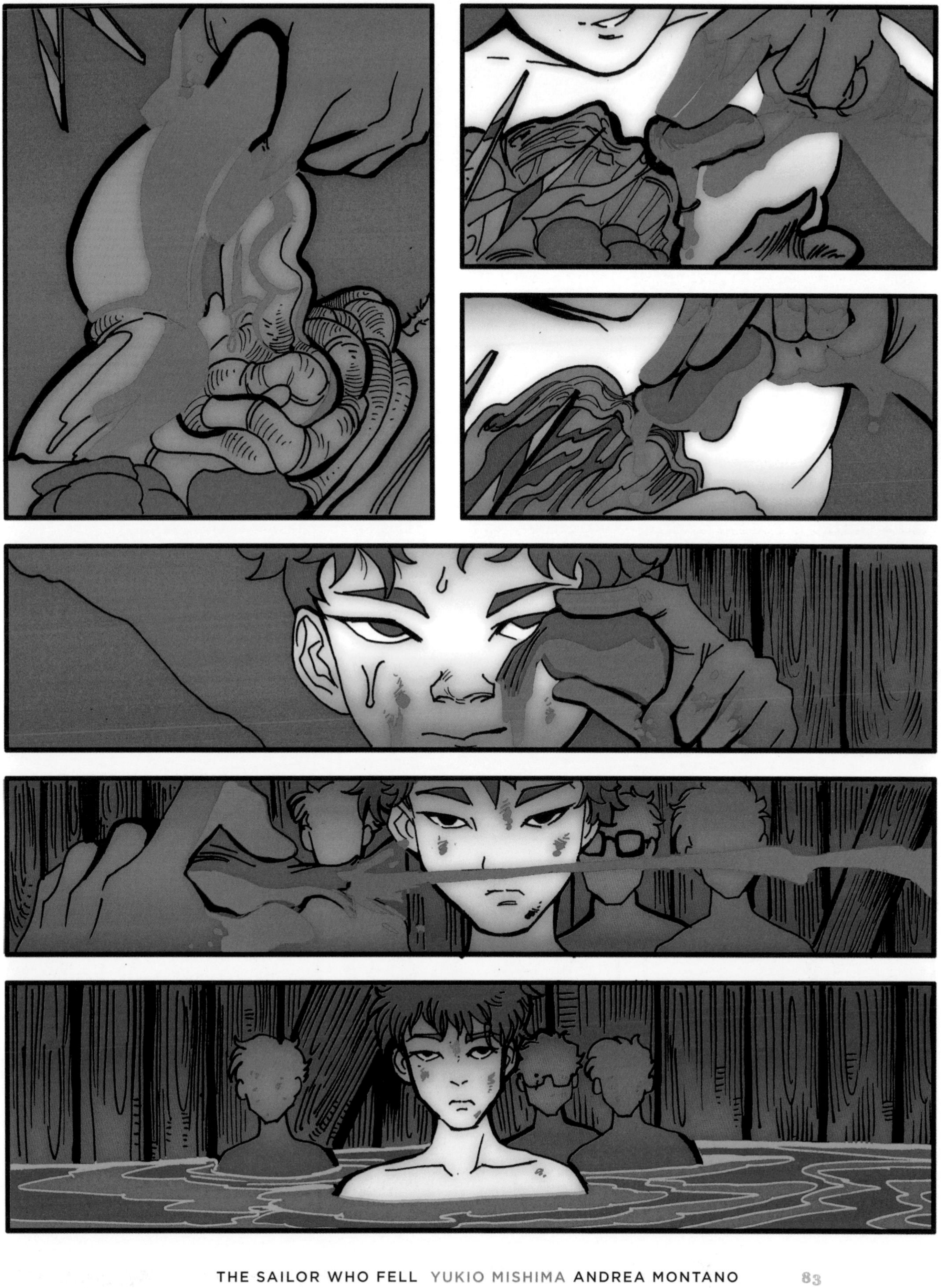

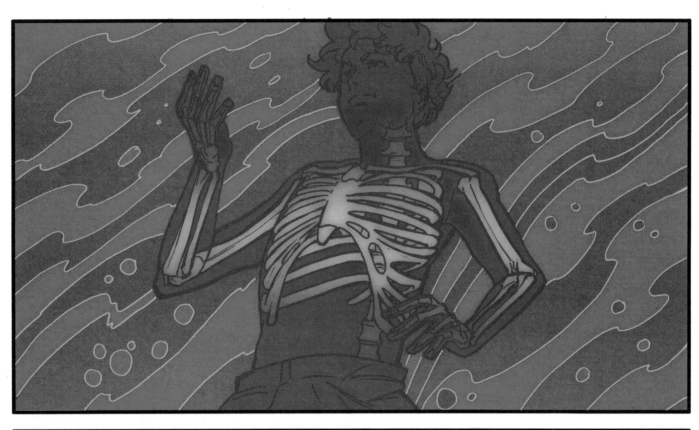

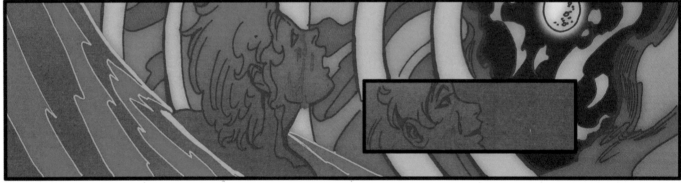

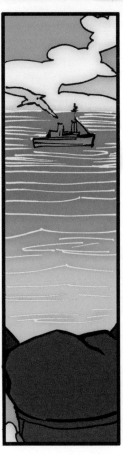

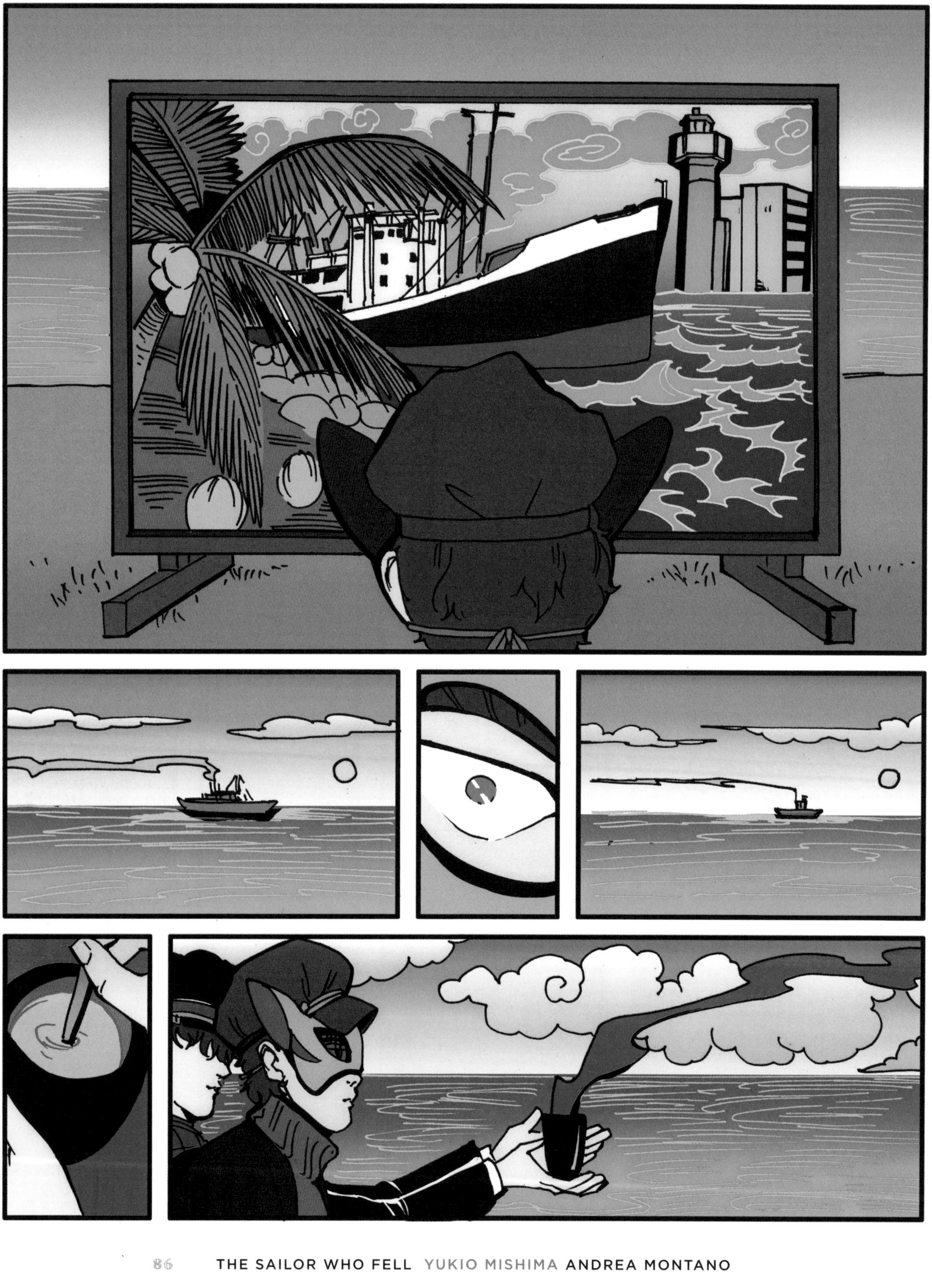

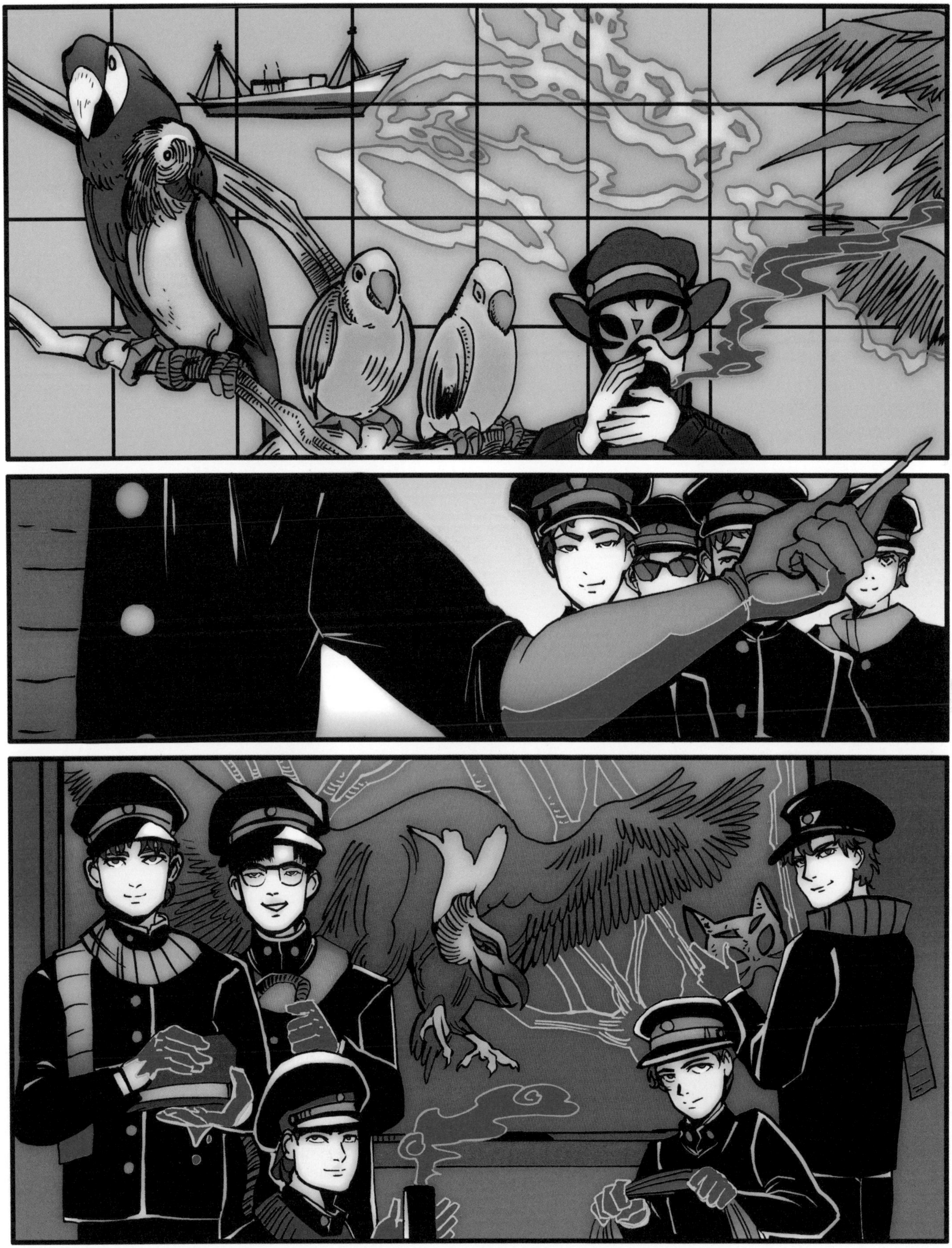

The Silence of the Lambs

Thomas Harris

ART/ADAPTATION BY **Alice Urbino**

HANNIBAL LECTER IS ONE OF FICTION'S and cinema's most unnerving, intelligent, charismatic serial killers. Who could ever unsee Anthony Hopkins's definitive portrayal of the small, slender psychiatrist with black hair and reddish eyes in *The Silence of the Lambs*? Like the similarly named Anthony Perkins as Norman Bates in the film adaptation of *Psycho*, Hopkins didn't physically resemble his killer-character. It worked for the multi-Oscar-winning movie, but still, to see the authentic Lecter—complete with six fingers on his left hand—we turn to Alice Urbino.

Alice is no stranger to disfigurement and other more subtly disquieting elements, perfect for adapting a work that contains outrageous violence yet is suffused with a quiet, lingering menace. She went back to Thomas Harris's second Lecter novel, reimagining key scenes involving the moth with her subtly distorted figures and dramatic, from-below lighting. We see the discovery of the chrysalis in a victim's body, FBI agent Clarice Starling's consultation with entomologists, and her visit to Lecter to pick his brain about the serial killer called Buffalo Bill.

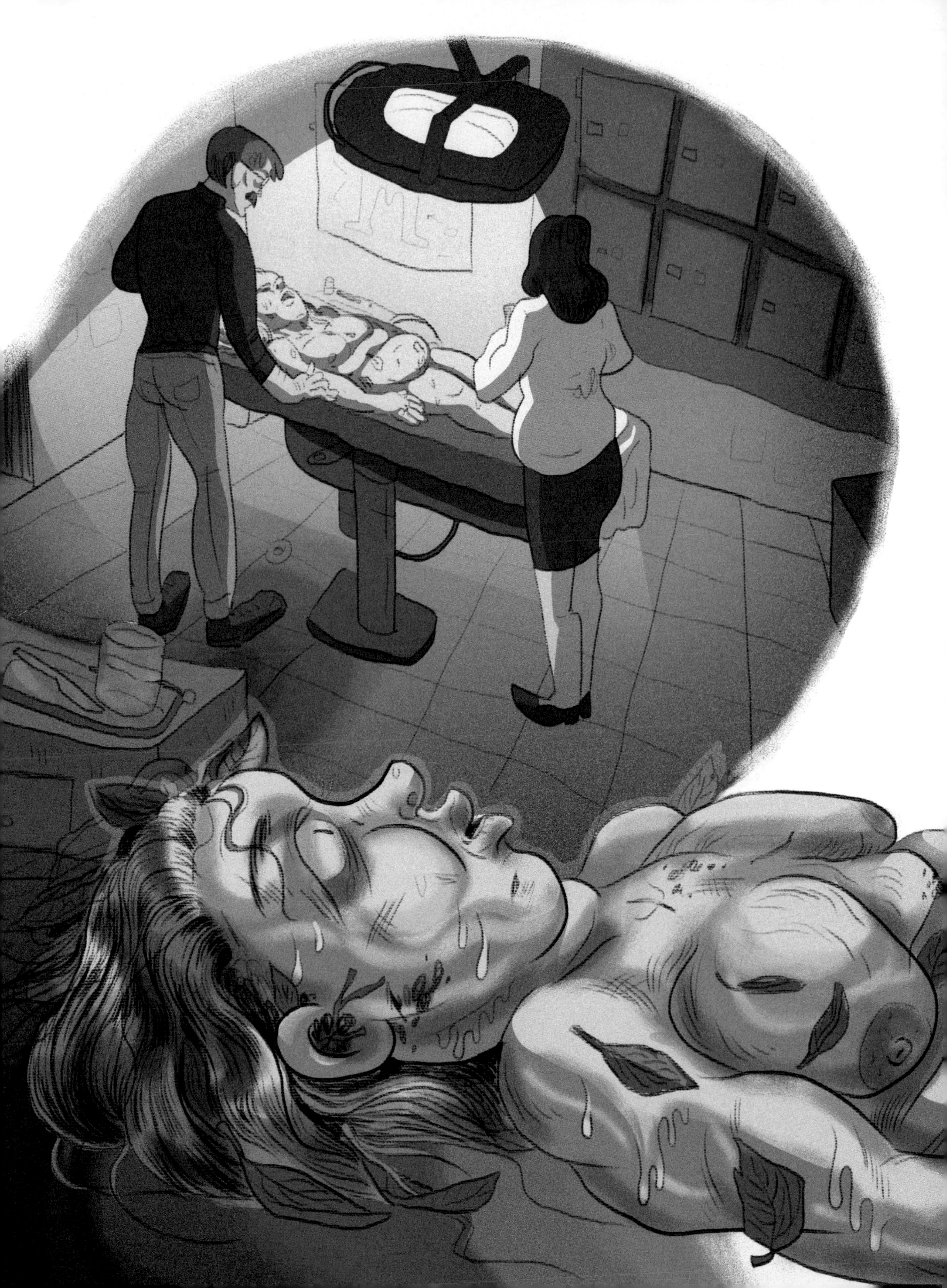

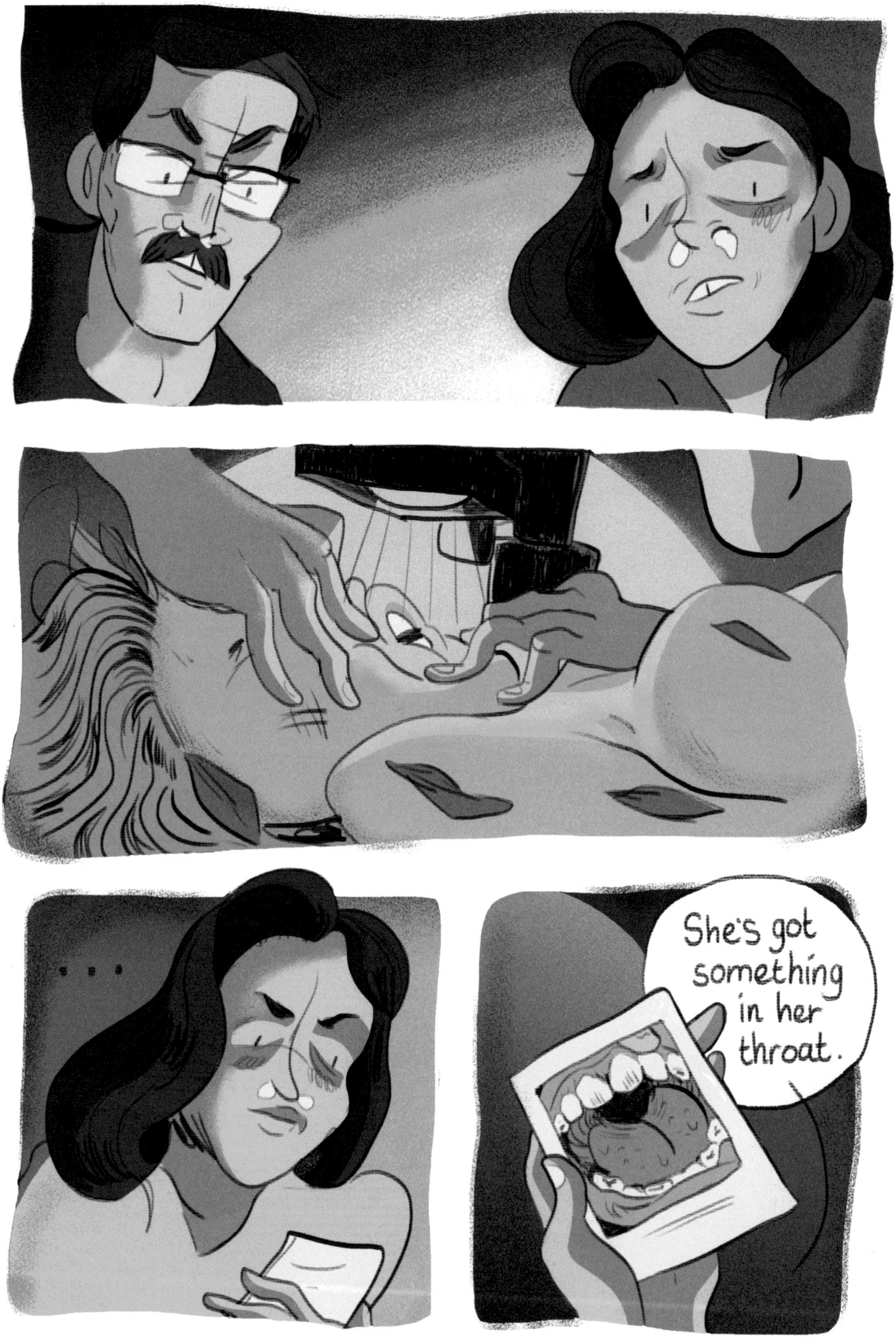
. . .
She's got something in her throat.

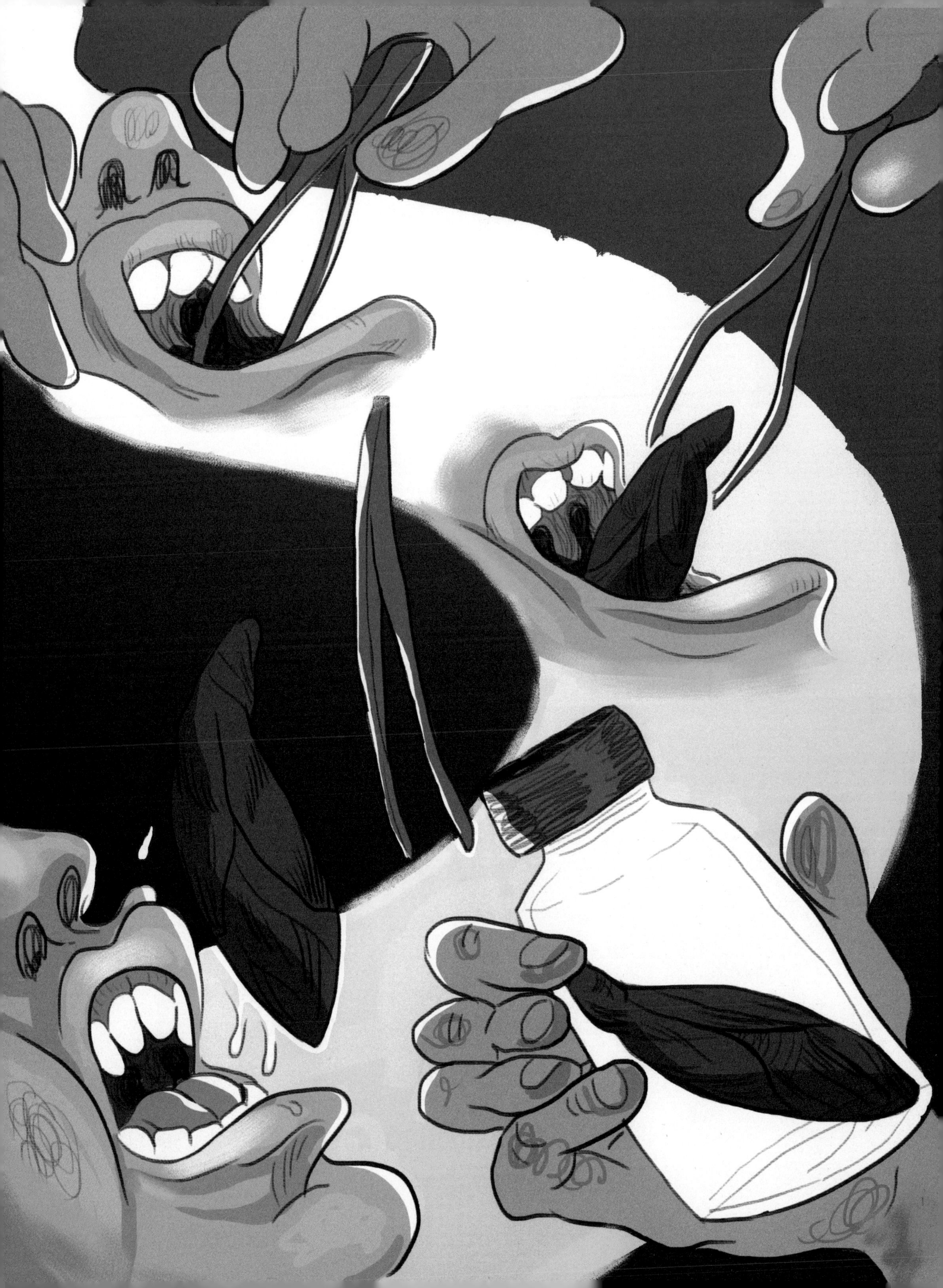

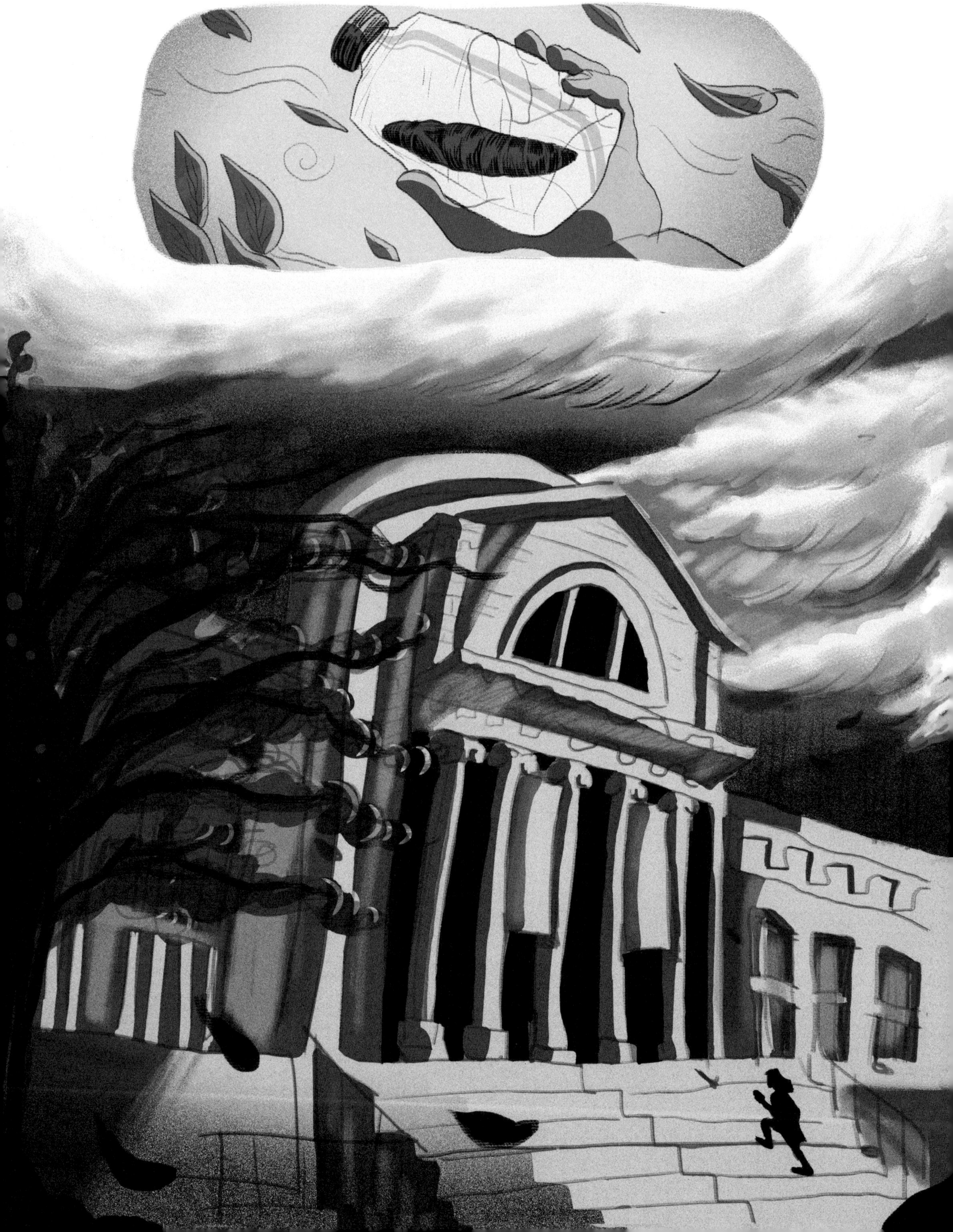

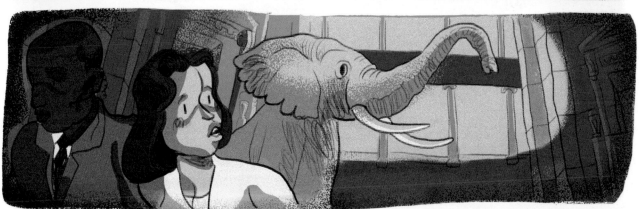

THE SILENCE OF THE LAMBS THOMAS HARRIS ALICE URBINO   93

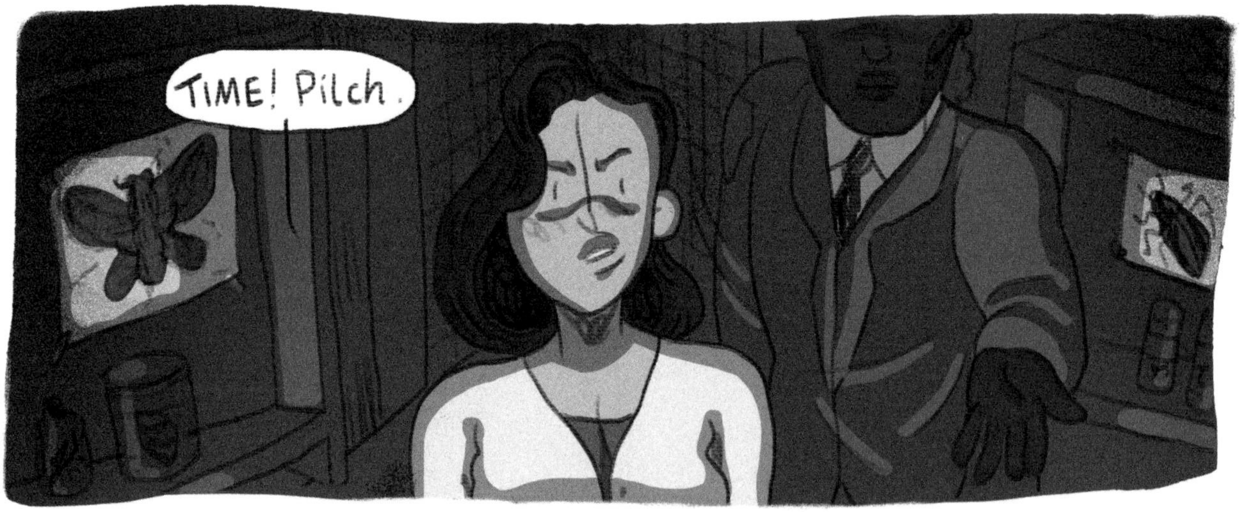
TIME! Pilch.

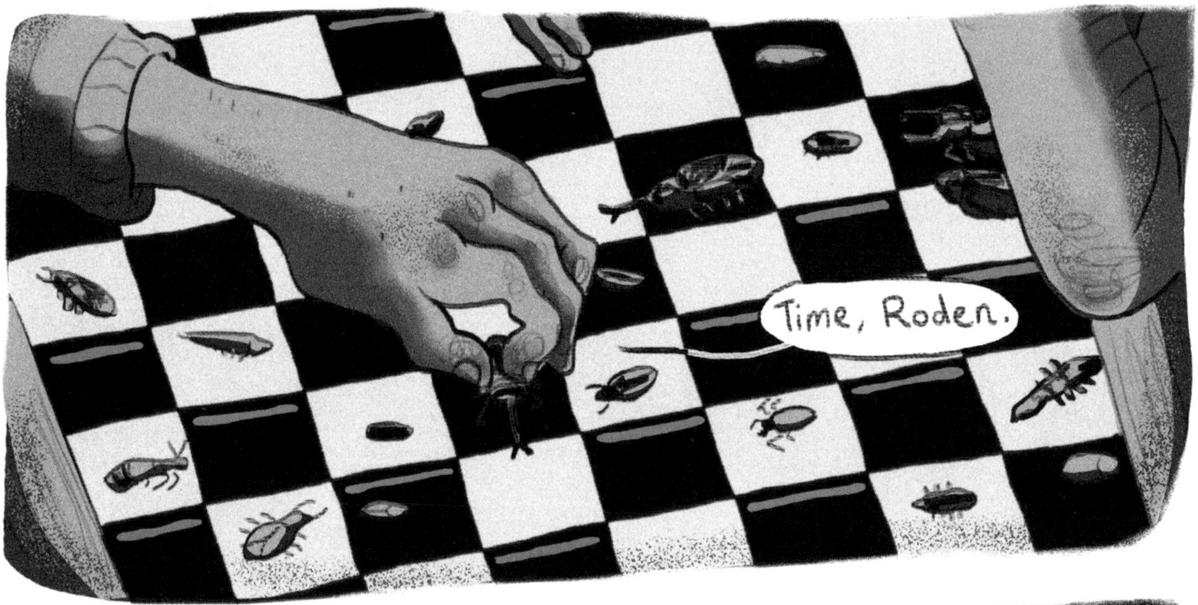
Time, Roden.

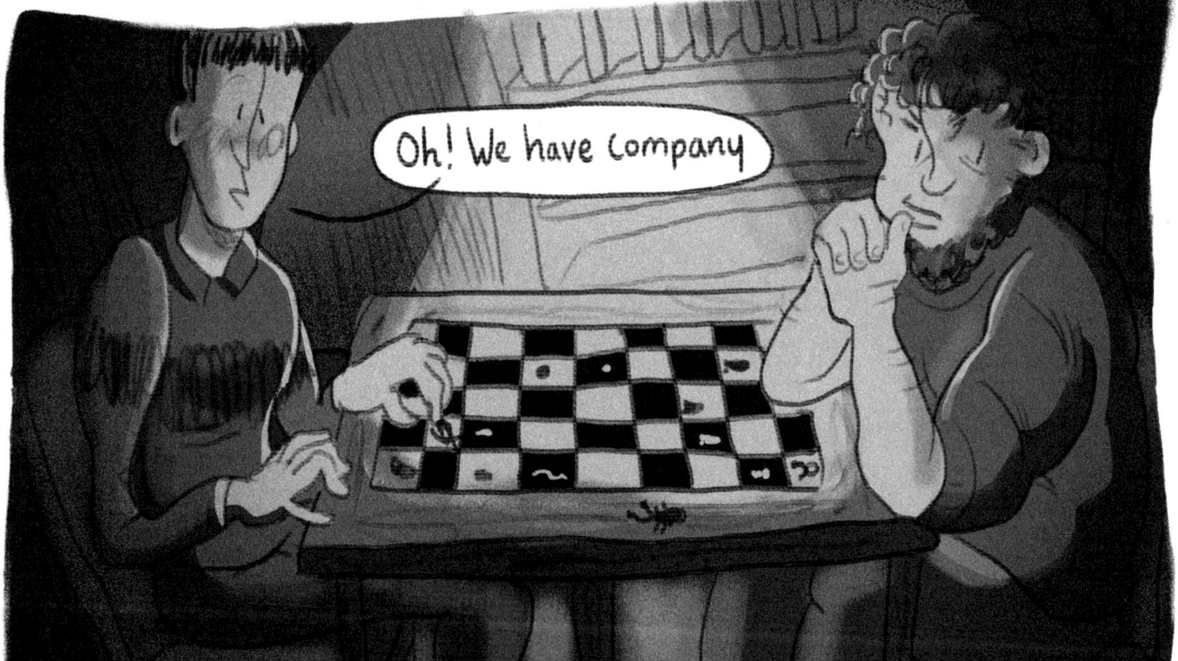
Oh! We have company

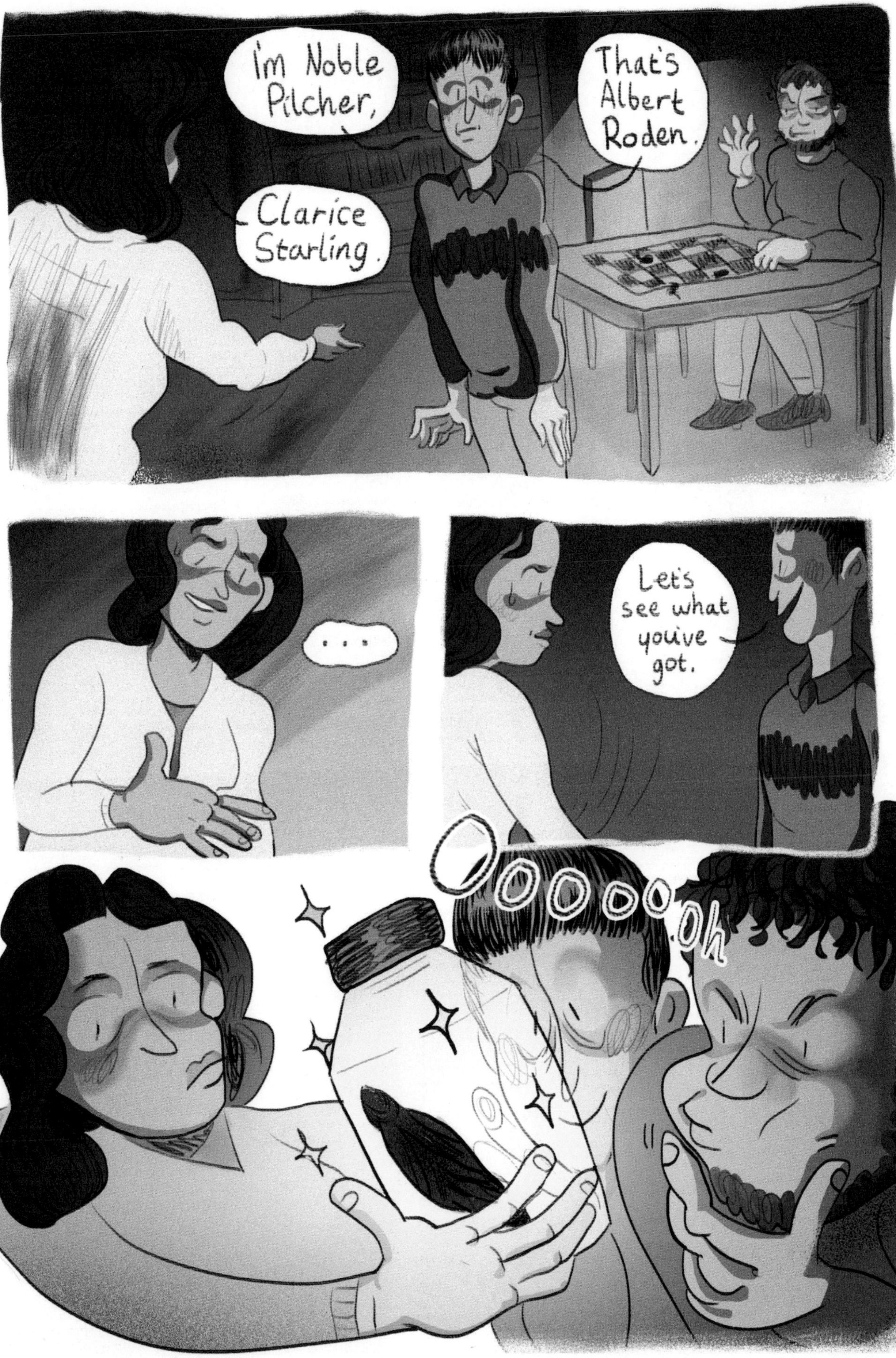
I'm Noble Pilcher,
Clarice Starling.
That's Albert Roden.
. . .
Let's see what you've got.
Ooooooh

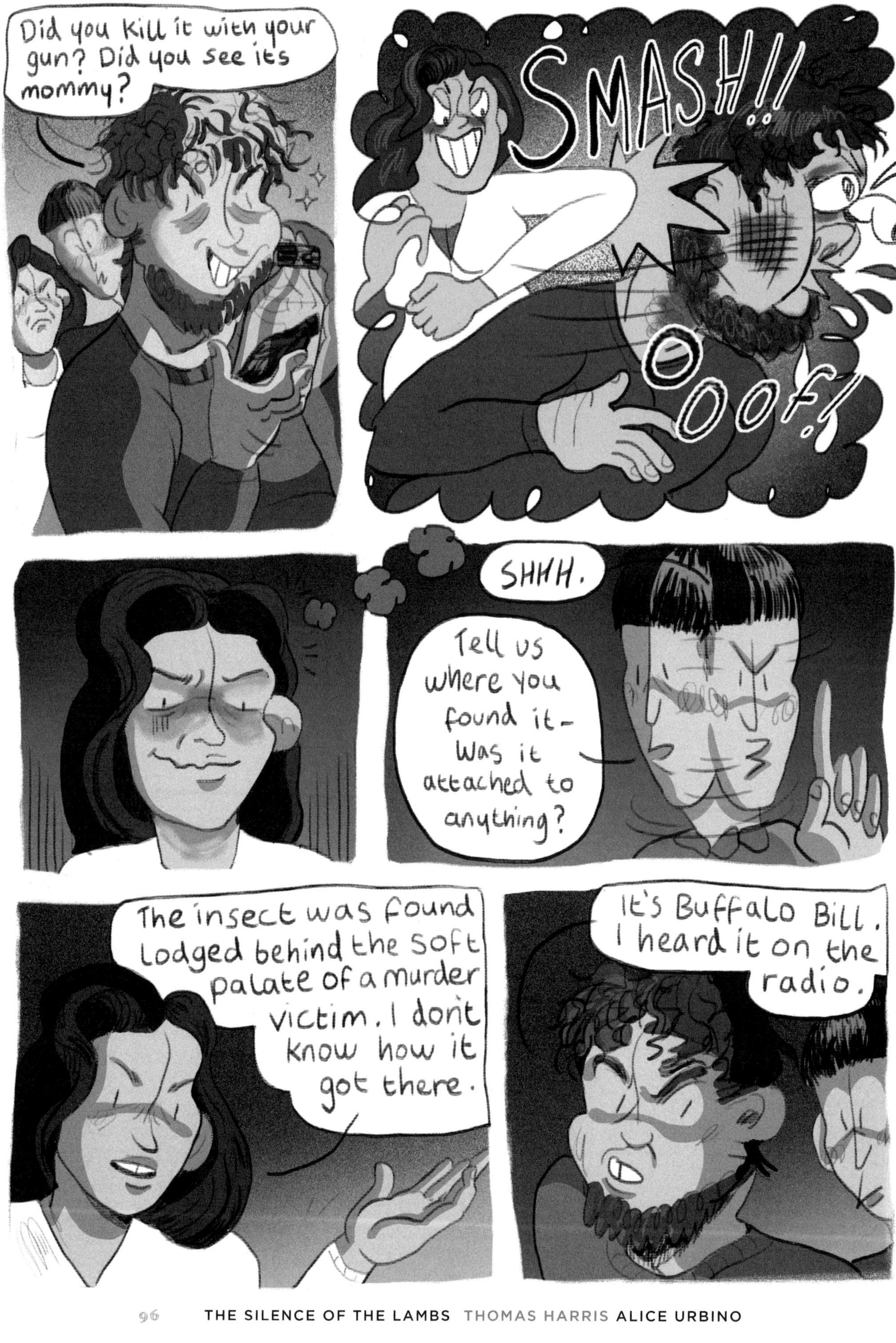
Did you Kill it with your gun? Did you see its mommy?
SMASH!!
OOOF!
SHHH.
Tell us where you found it- Was it attached to anything?
The insect was found lodged behind the soft palate of a murder victim. I dont know how it got there.
It's Buffalo Bill. I heard it on the radio.

Do you think he's holding another woman right now?

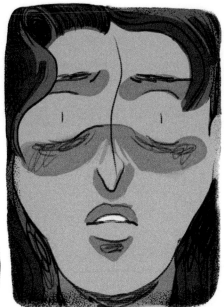

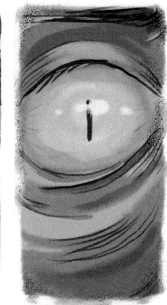

Starling?

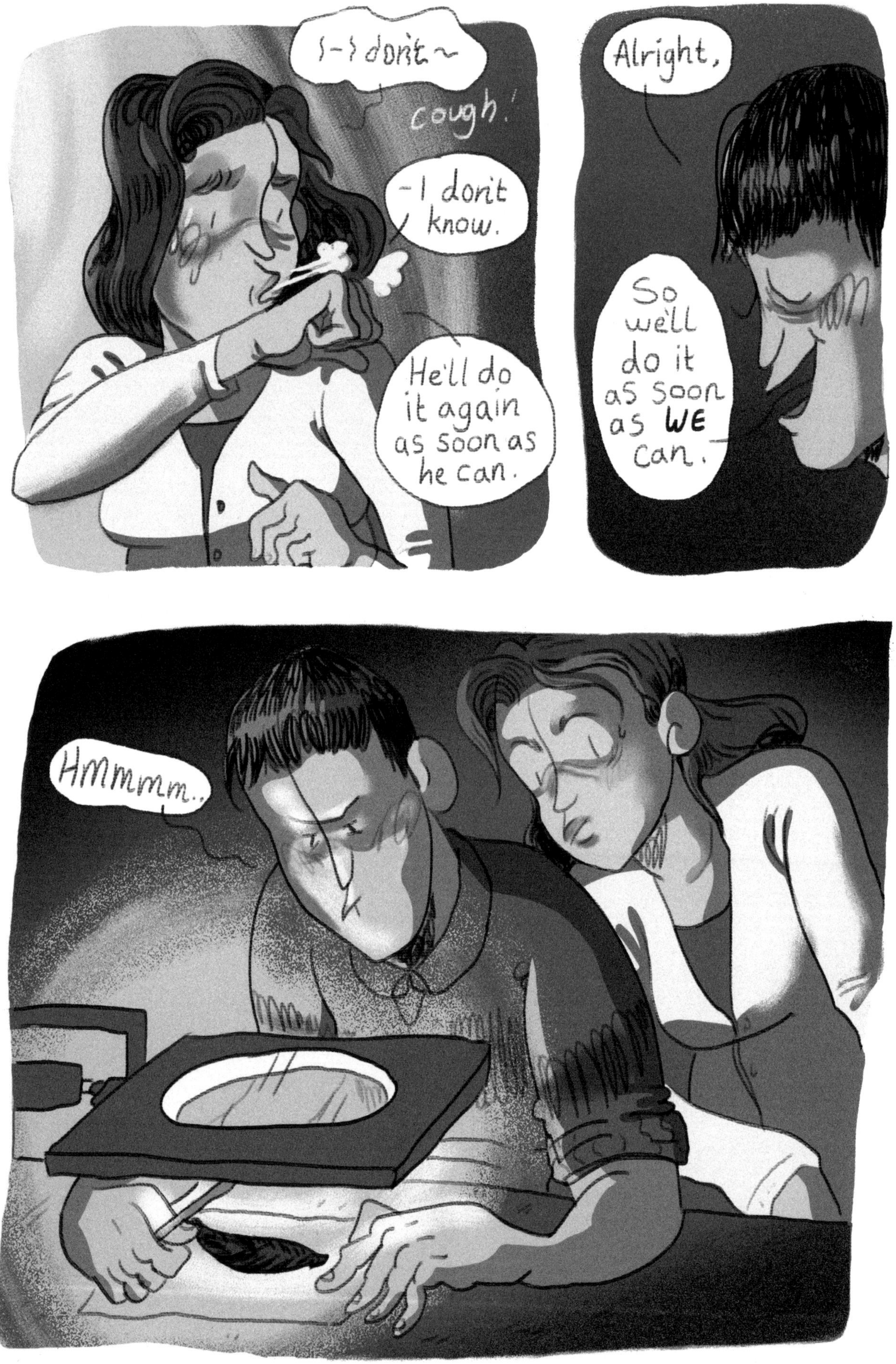
I-I don't~
cough!
-I don't know.
He'll do it again as soon as he can.
Alright,
So we'll do it as soon as WE can.
Hmmmm..

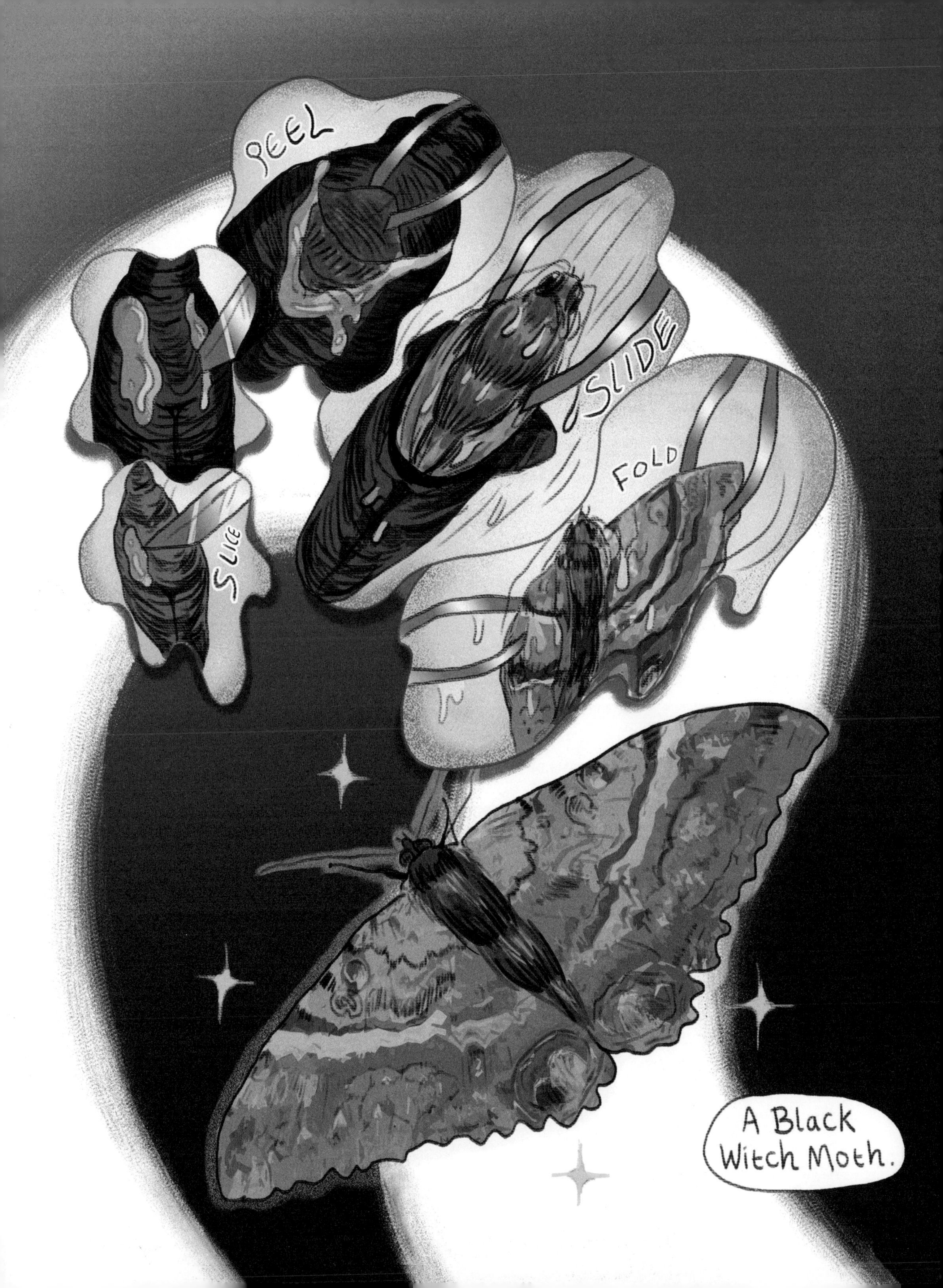
PEEL
SLIDE
FOLD
SLICE
A Black Witch Moth.

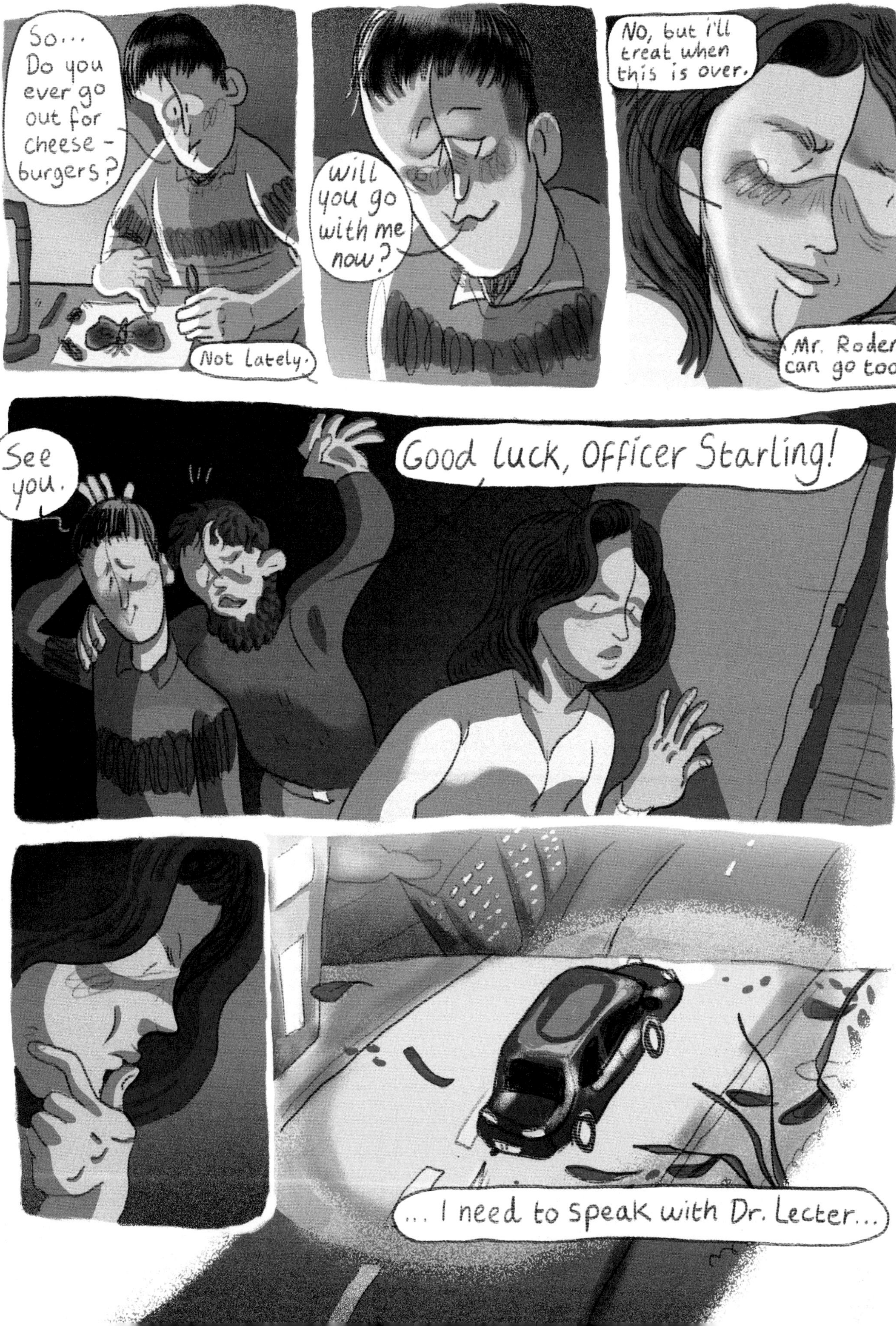
So... Do you ever go out for cheese-burgers?
Not lately.
Will you go with me now?
No, but I'll treat when this is over.
Mr. Roden can go too.
See you.
Good luck, Officer Starling!
... I need to speak with Dr. Lecter...

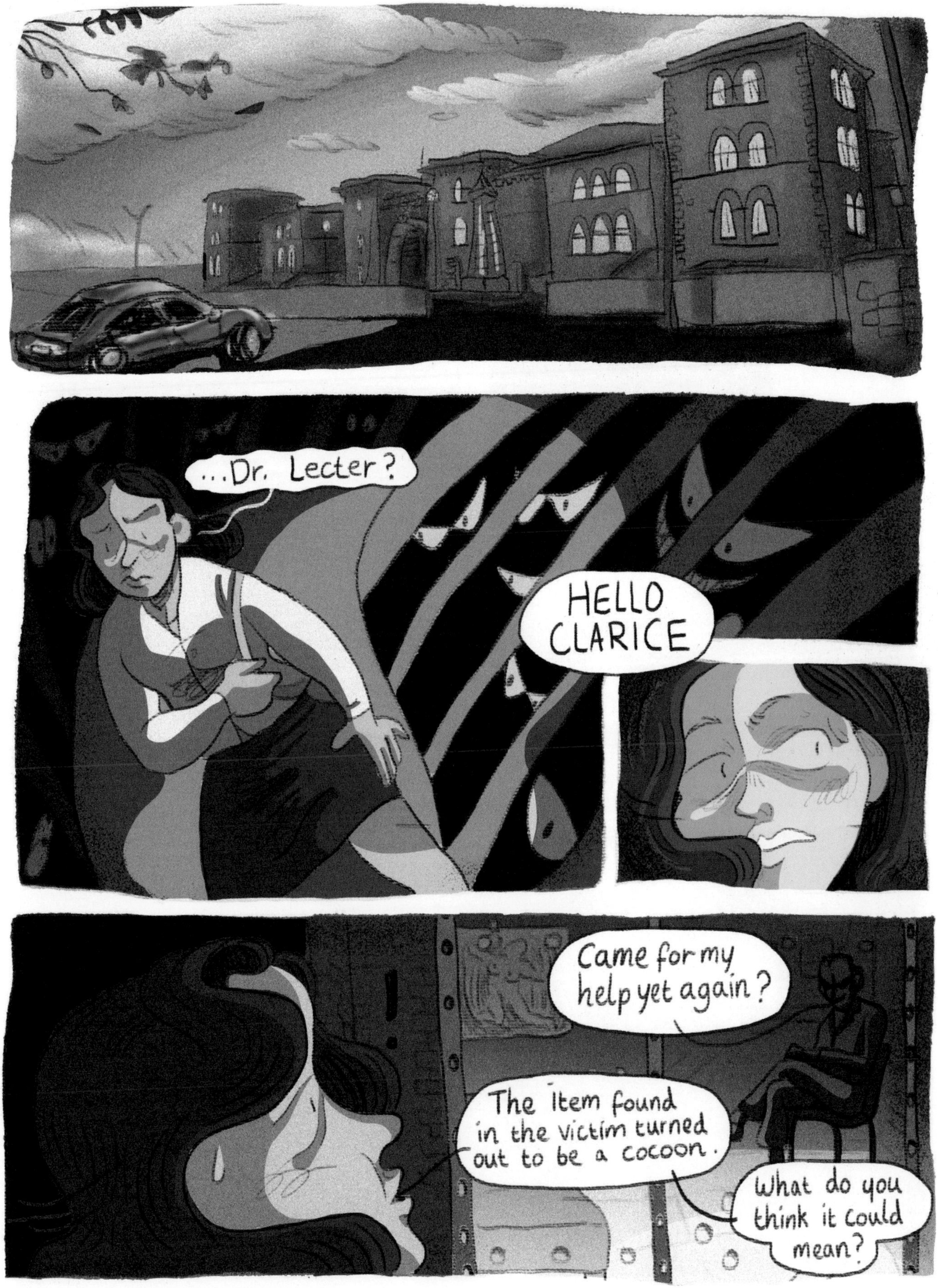
...Dr. Lecter?
HELLO CLARICE
Came for my help yet again?
The item found in the victim turned out to be a cocoon.
What do you think it could mean?

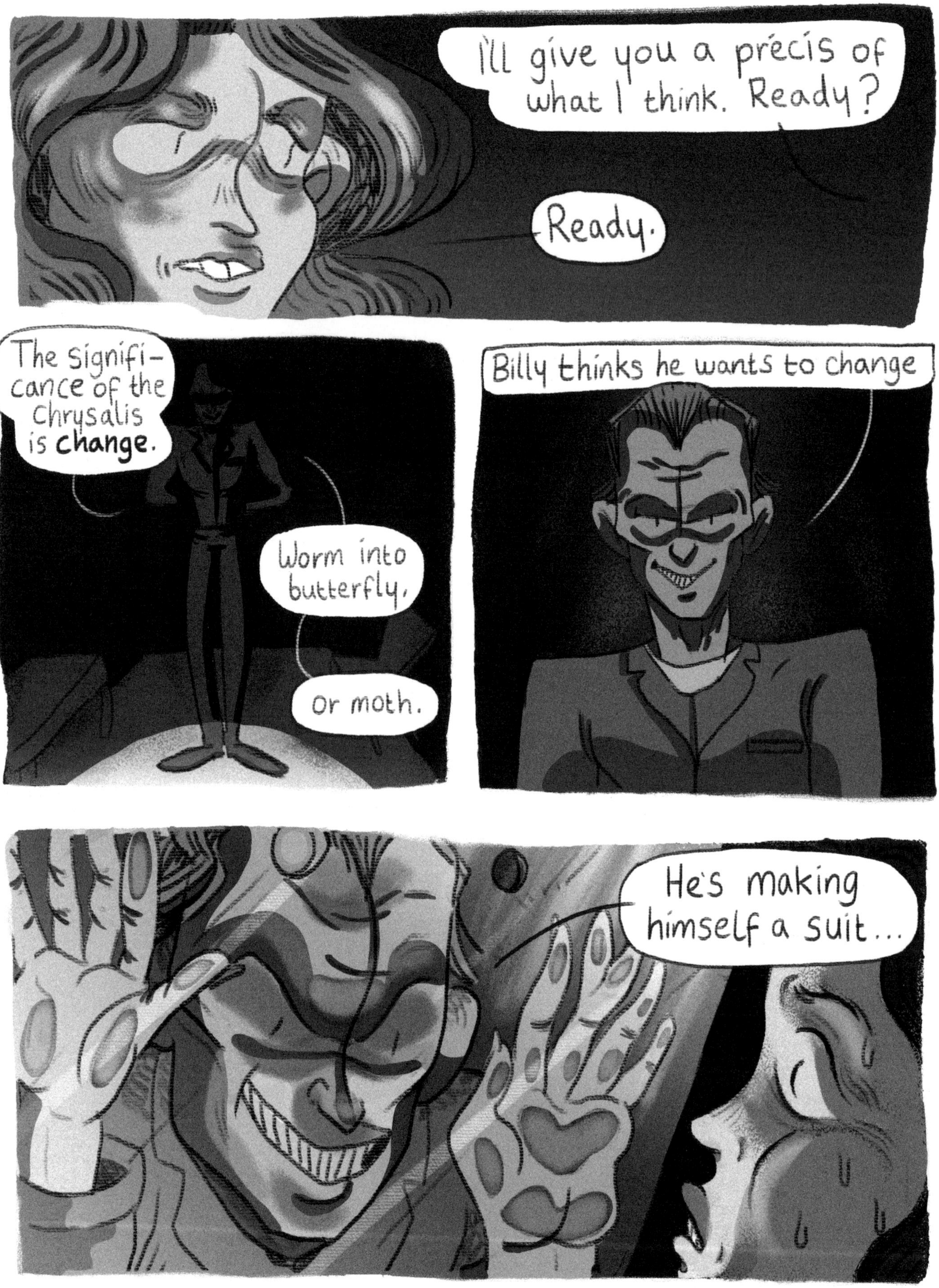
I'll give you a précis of what I think. Ready?
Ready.
The signifi-cance of the chrysalis is change.
Worm into butterfly,
or moth.
Billy thinks he wants to change
He's making himself a suit...

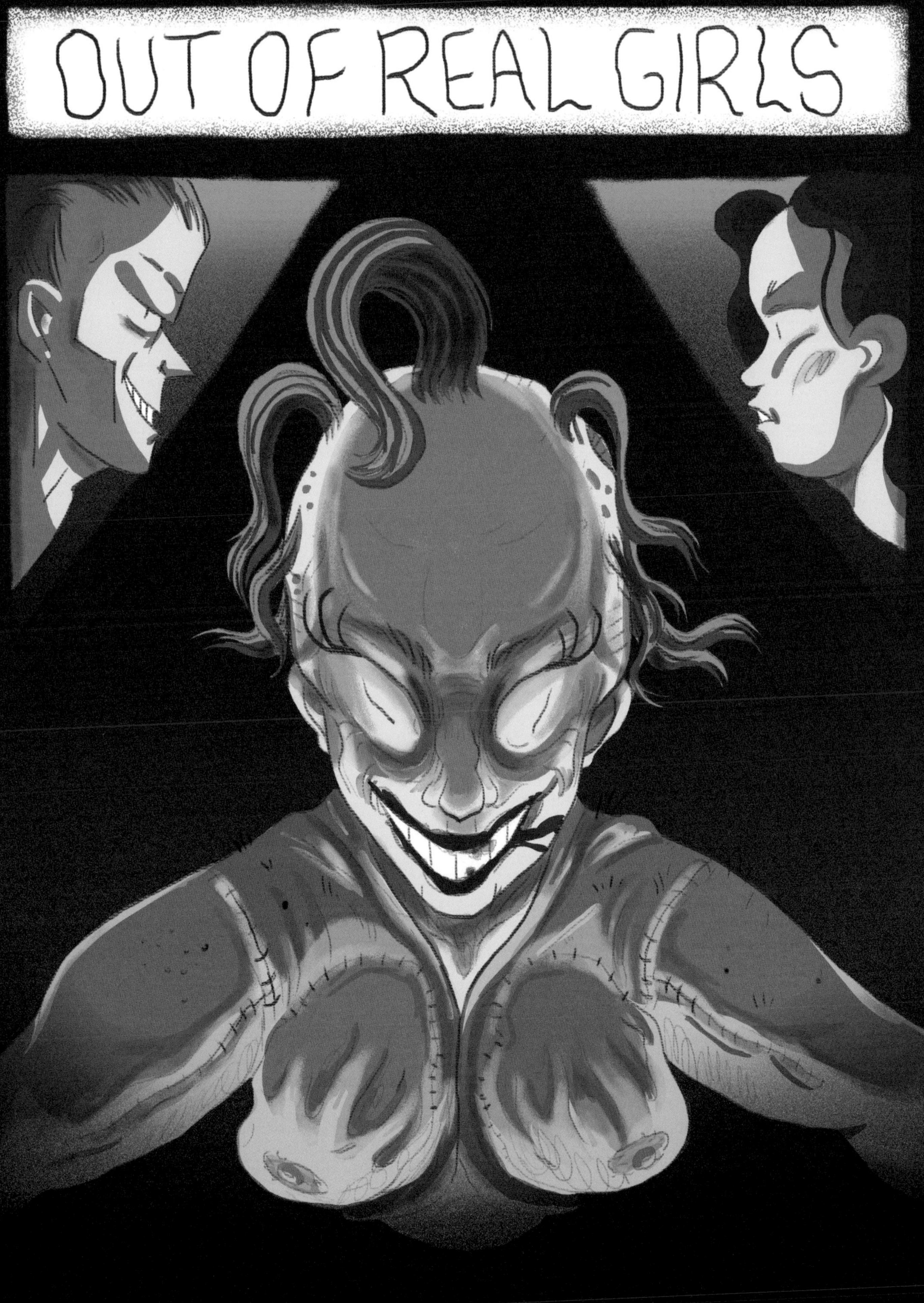
OUT OF REAL GIRLS

The Black Dahlia

James Ellroy

ART/ADAPTATION BY Josebo Morales

THE BLACK DAHLIA MURDER IS A GRUESOME lowlight of Hollywood history and one of the most well-known and much-discussed cases of unsolved murder. In early January 1947, the body of Elizabeth Short was discovered in a vacant lot in Los Angeles. The 22-year-old nomad had been cut completely in half at the waist. Bestselling author James Ellroy, who specializes in highly literary crime and mystery novels, used this slaying as the basis for his 1987 novel, *The Black Dahlia*.

Ellroy's book isn't concerned with solving the murder, though, and it veers heavily from the facts of the case. The murder provides the thread for a plot about police corruption, obsession, incest, a sort-of love triangle, and all-around seediness. Early in the book, two LAPD cops—Lee Blanchard and protagonist Bucky Bleichert—are pressured into a fundraising boxing match.

Josebo Morales has brought his clean, crisp lines to a couple of children's books, multiple horror comics anthologies (including *This Nightmare Kills Fascists*), and his ongoing webcomic *Righteous*. Here he shows the boxing match that will oddly lead to friendship between the two cops who will end up investigating the Black Dahlia murder.

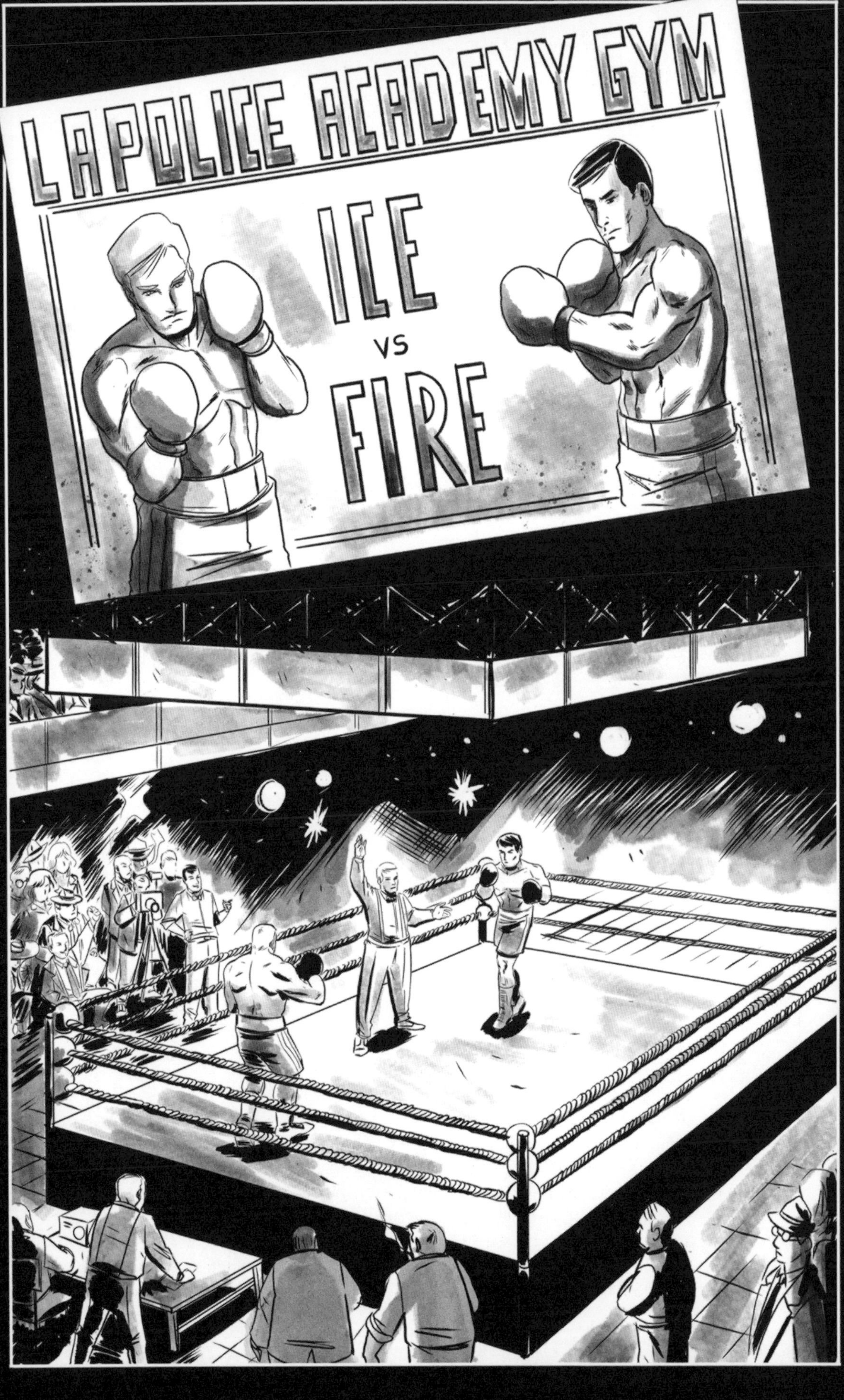
LAPOLICE ACADEMY GYM
ICE
VS
FIRE

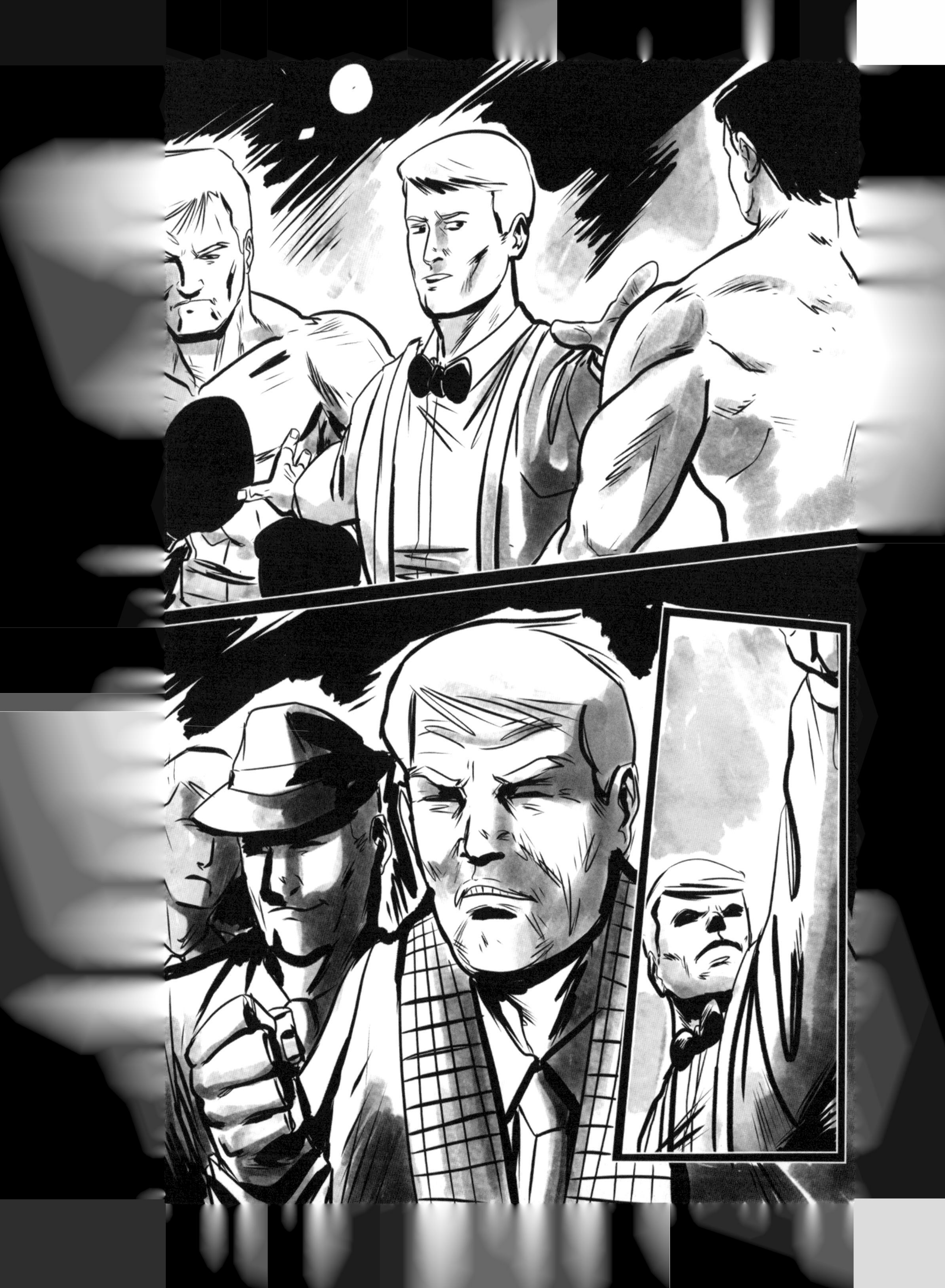

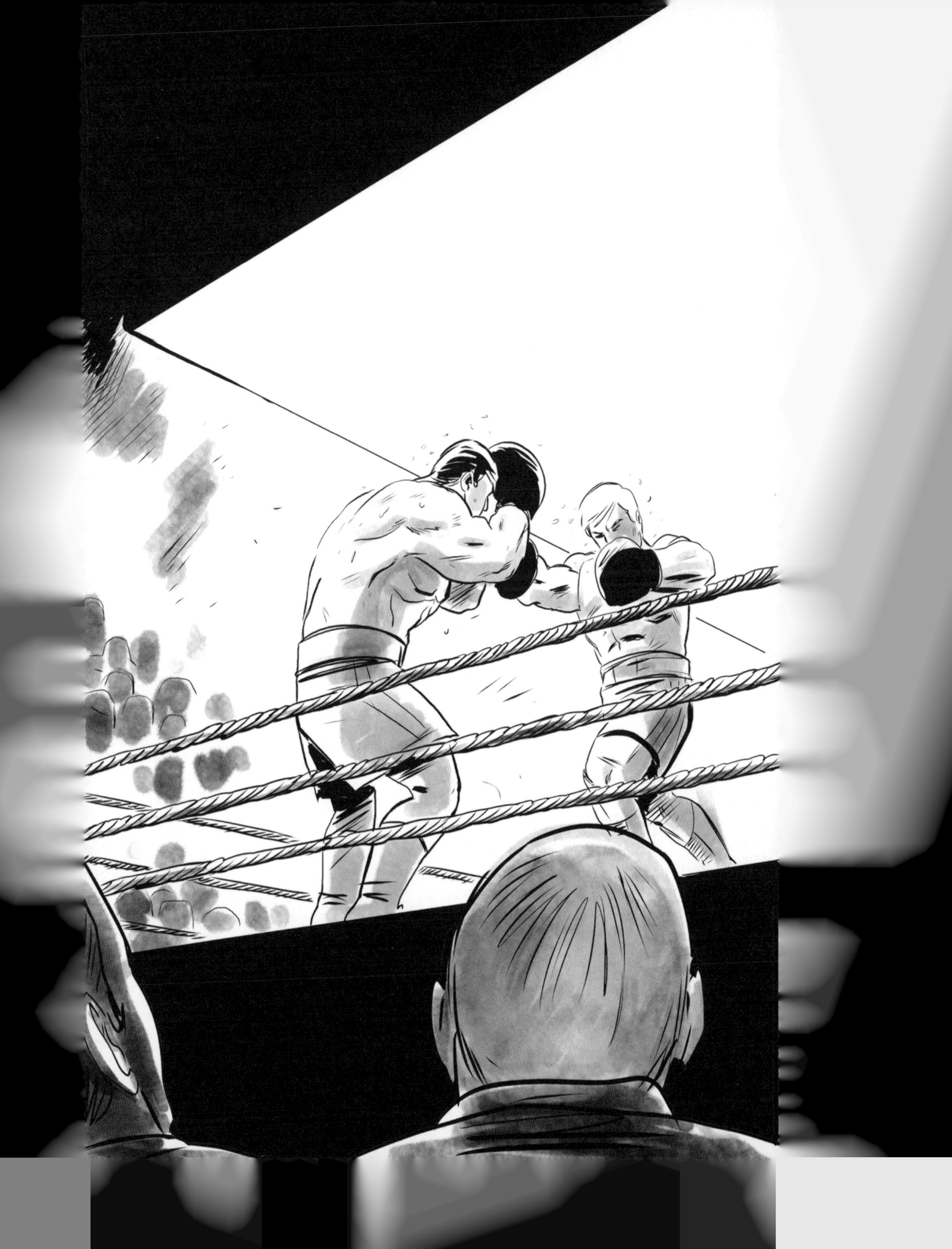

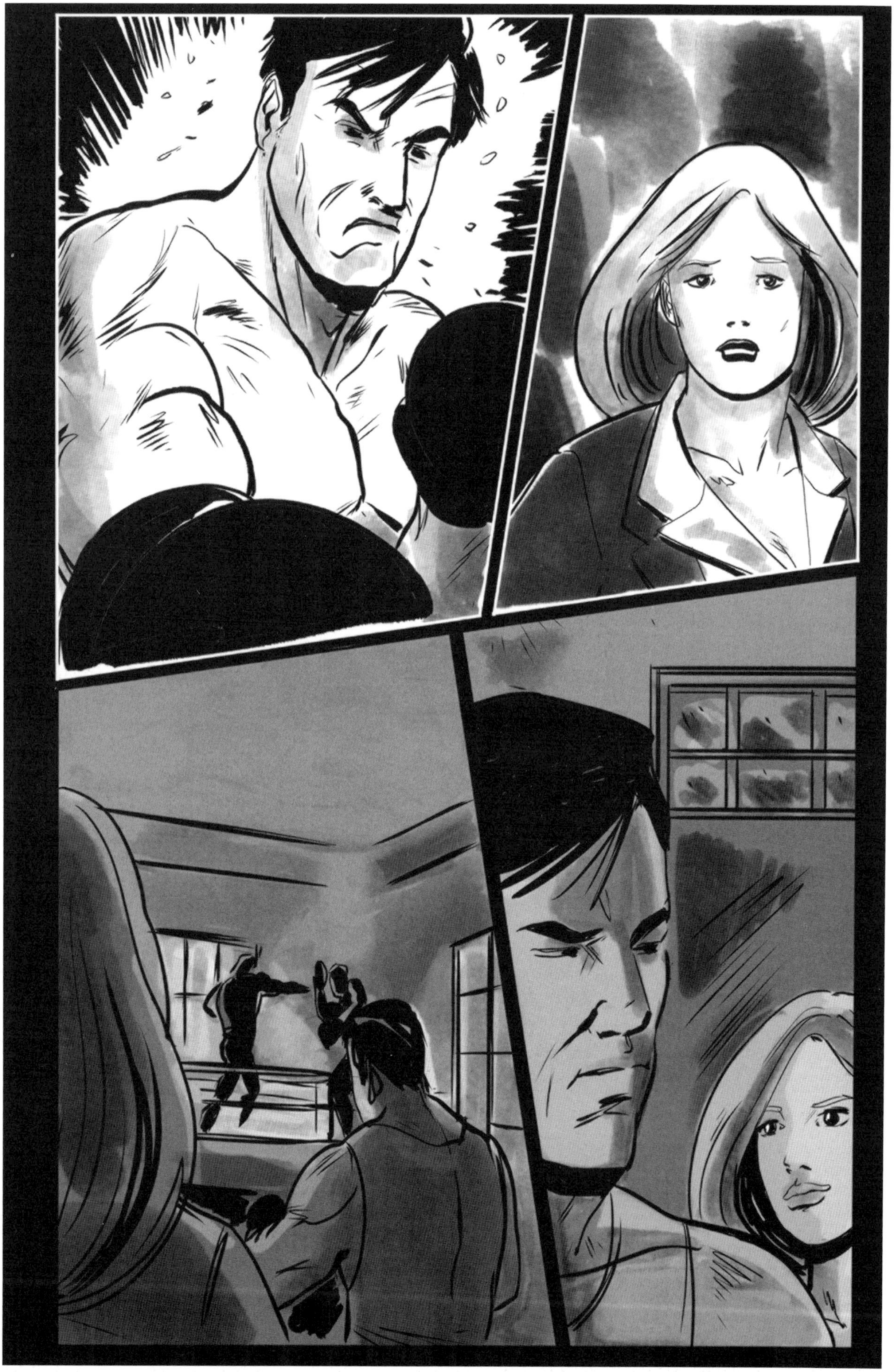

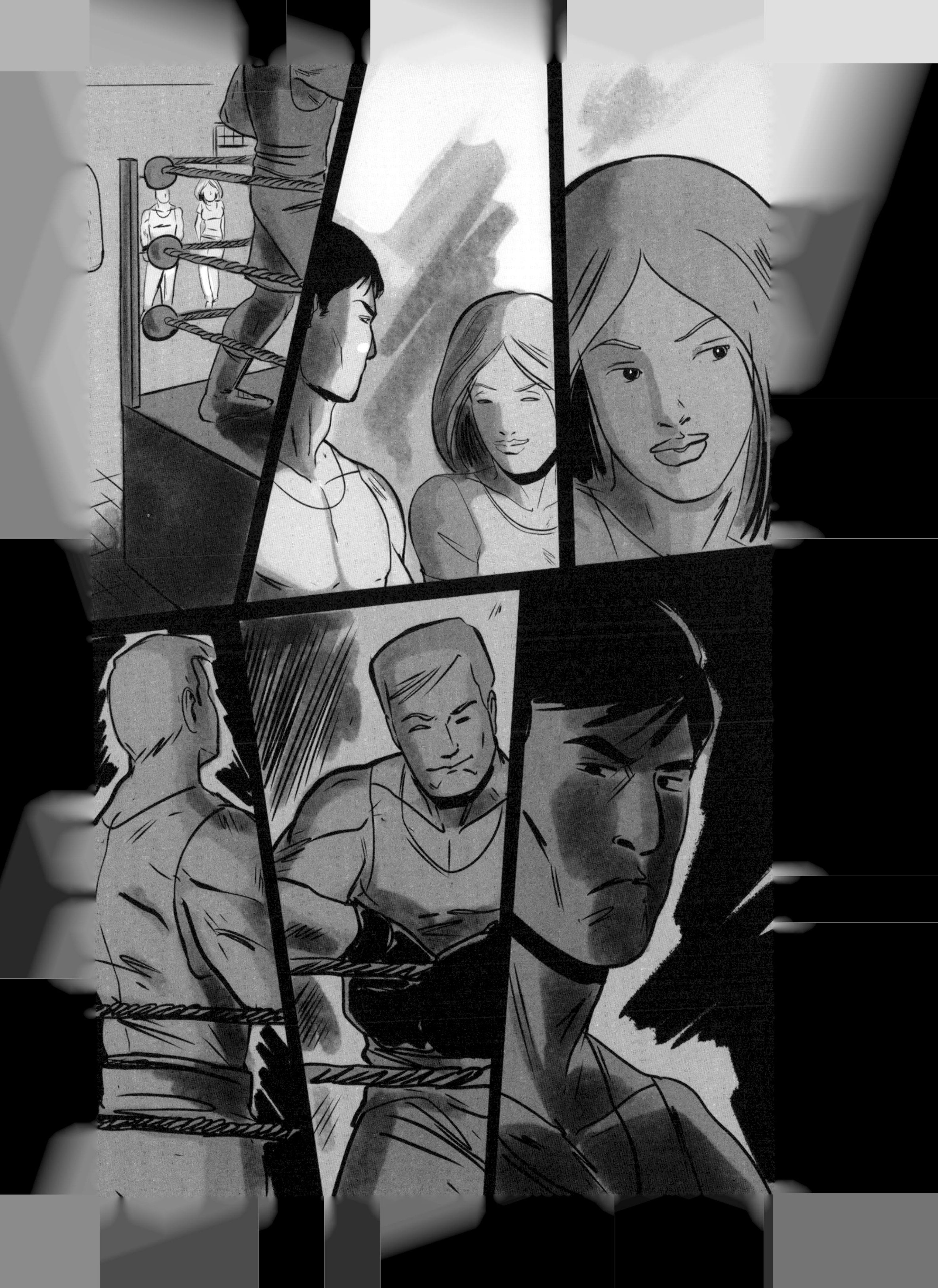

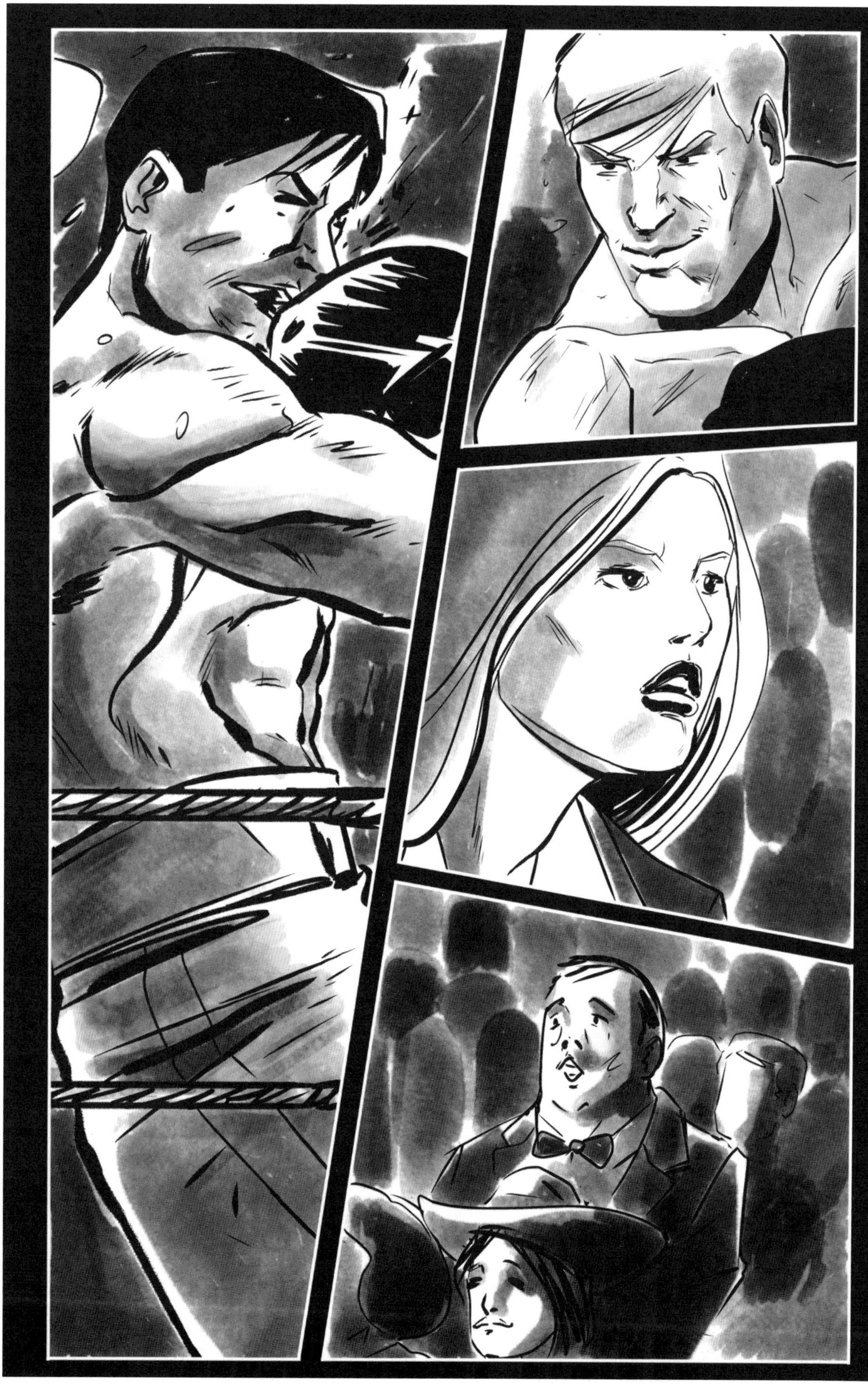

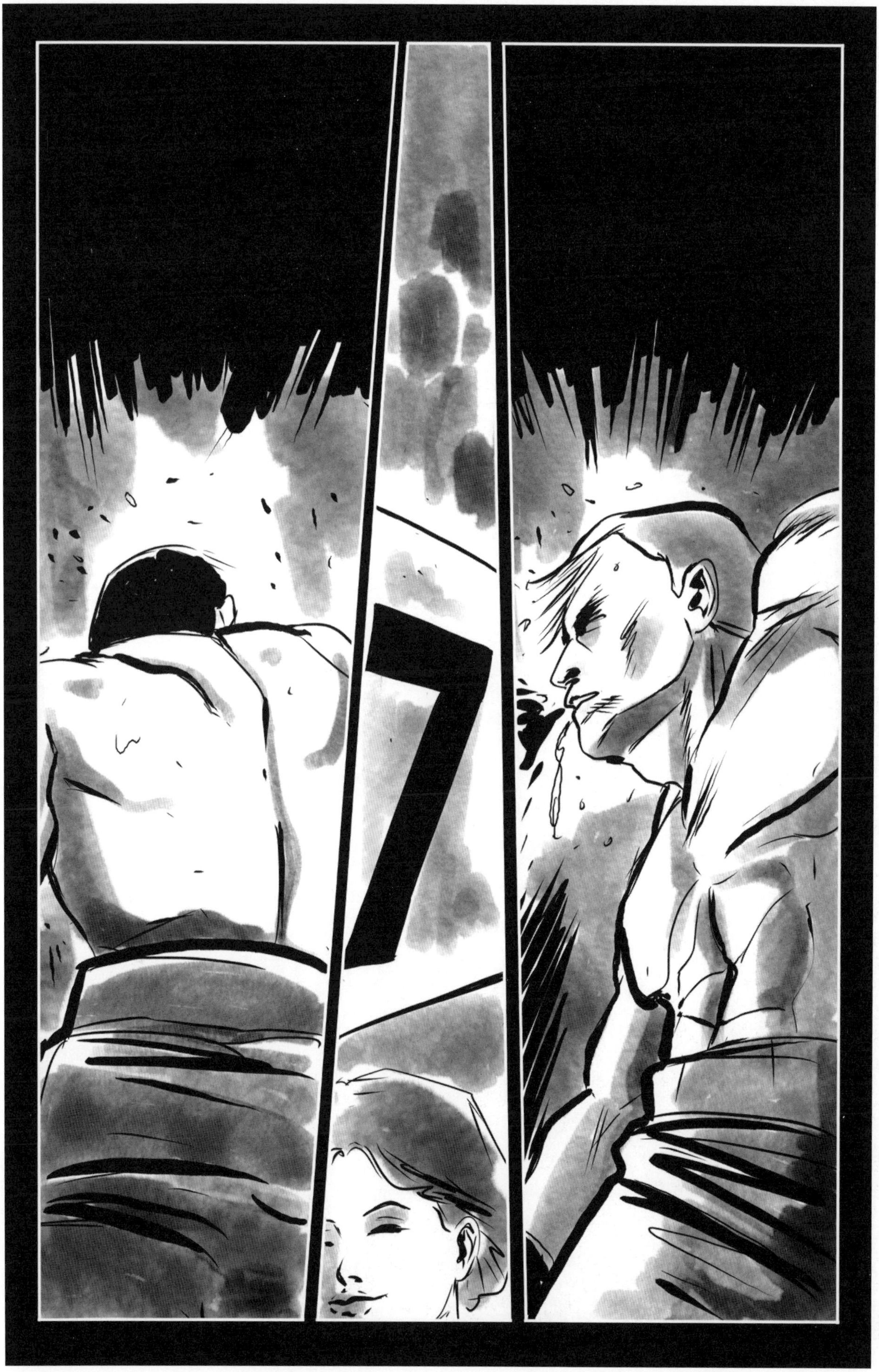
7

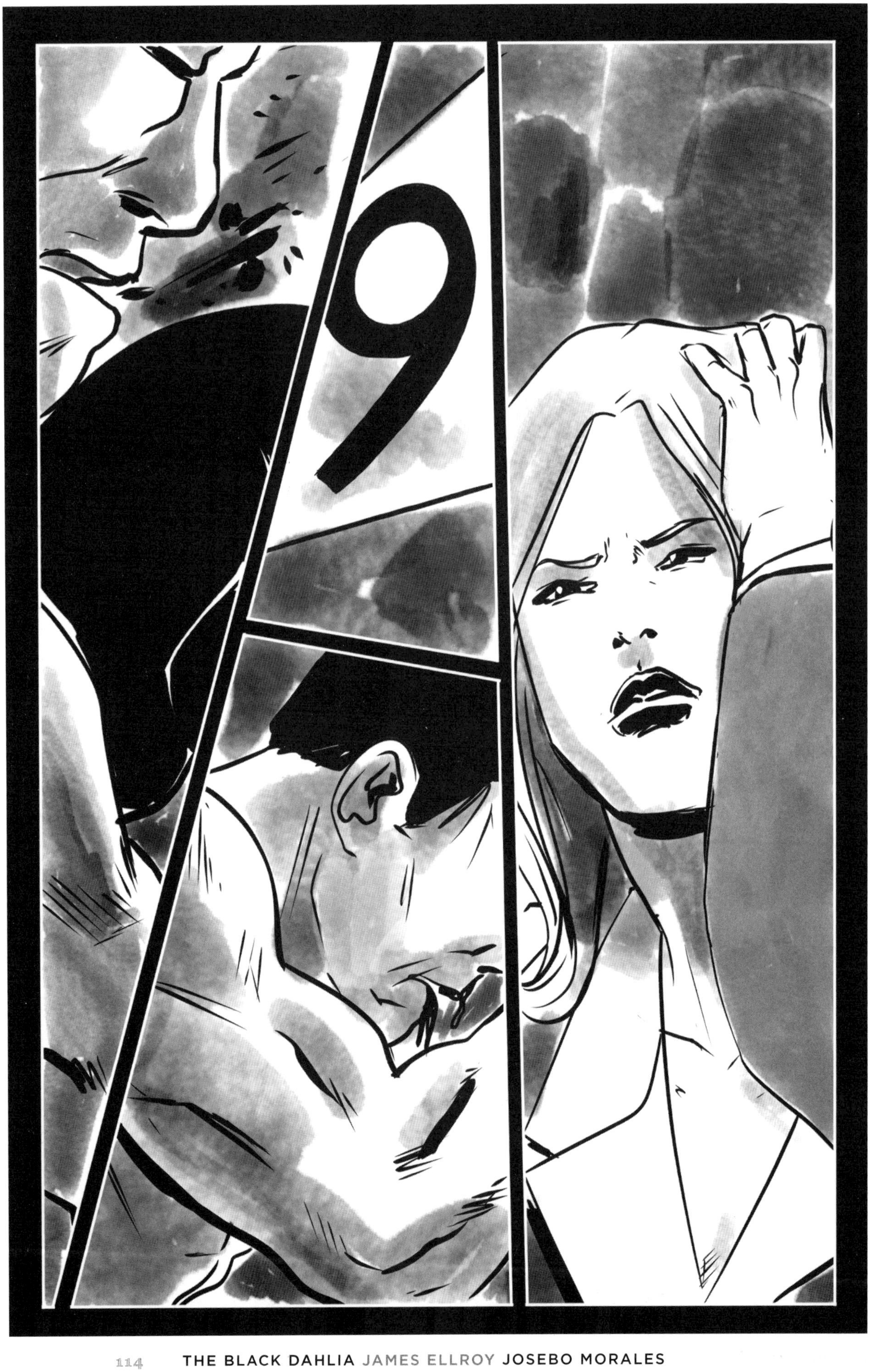
9

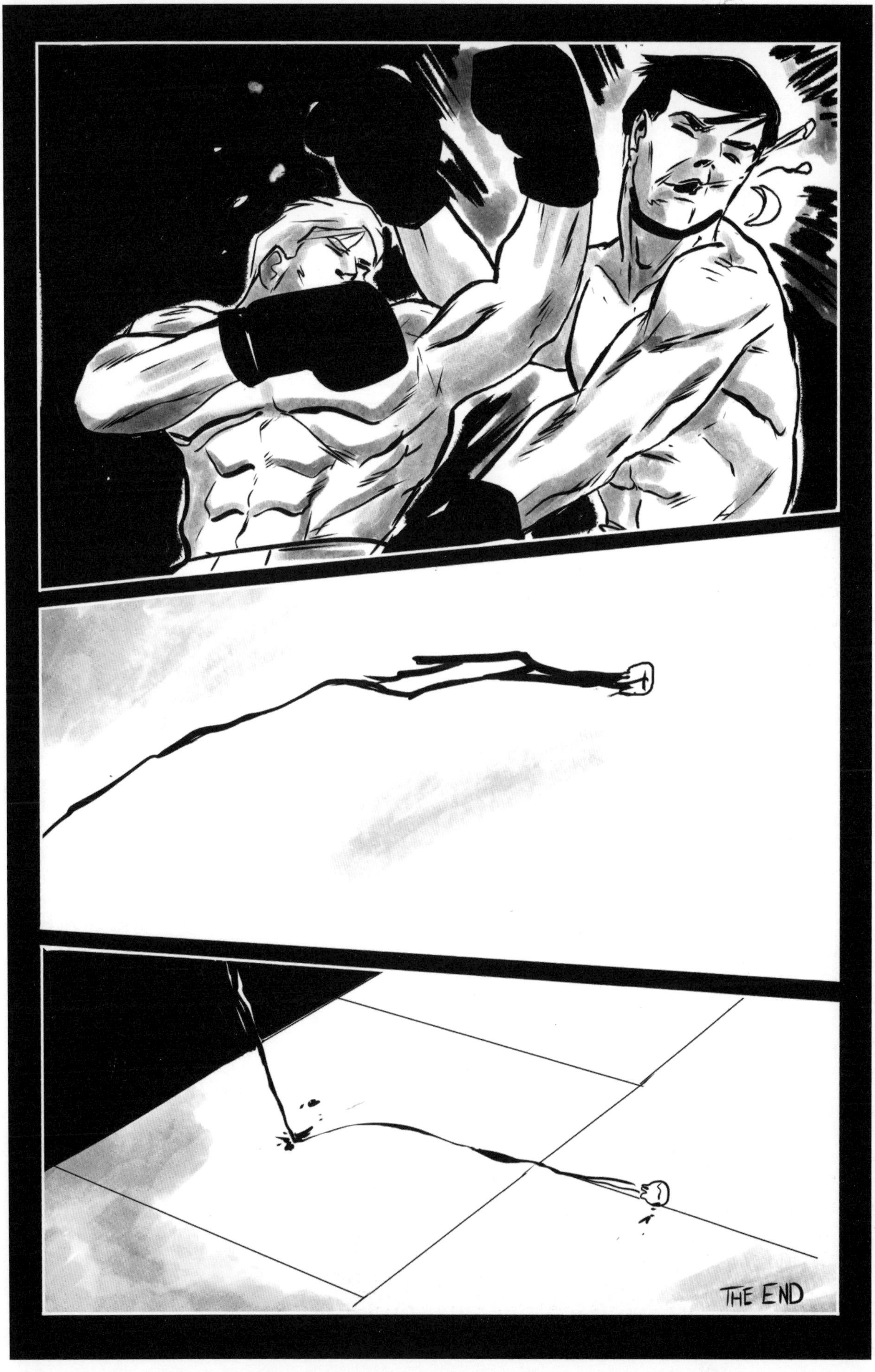
THE END

I Was Dora Suarez

Derek Raymond

ART/ADAPTATION BY **Douglas Noble**

ROBERT COOK WAS BORN INTO A LIFE OF privilege but consciously rejected it for a life of crime, then a life of quasi-legal activities involving pornography and gambling. He started writing noir crime novels in the 1960s but eventually stayed away from writing for around fifteen years. He returned with a vengeance in 1985, starting the pitch-black *Factory* series of crime novels—about an unnamed detective sergeant in the Metropolitan Police's Bureau of Unexplained Deaths—under his best-known pseudonym, Derek Raymond. He was feted in Europe, thanks mainly to French translations, which were then made into films. He achieved cult status in the US, which is still too uptight to allow such feral, disturbing books to achieve mainstream success.

Factory hit its zenith with the 1990 novel *I Was Dora Suarez*, in which the sergeant becomes obsessed with solving the horrifyingly violent murder of a young HIV-positive prostitute, a marginalized person whose killing would normally be ignored by the authorities. Legend has it that the head of Cook's publishing house literally vomited on his desk while reading the manuscript. He refused to publish it, and Cook found a new home at Scribner. In *Crimeways Magazine*, Robert Carraher wrote: "As an entry in the 'hardboiled' genre, if bounced on the floor it would chip concrete. In the 'Noir' field it is to 'black novels' what black holes are to darkness."

Artist Douglas Noble comes to us from the experimental neighborhood of the comics world, a location I'm fond of. (His self-published *Got Your Nose* is a "collection of smashed rock and broken faces" in which "24 statues tell the story of how they each came to be damaged.") He's always defying expectations regarding medium and form, often mixing unorthodox approaches. The tiles of reddish moiré work as grisly flashbacks while the inky black illustrations foreground the sergeant's first moments with Dora's body in the book that Douglas calls "a scabrous, angry howl of a thing."

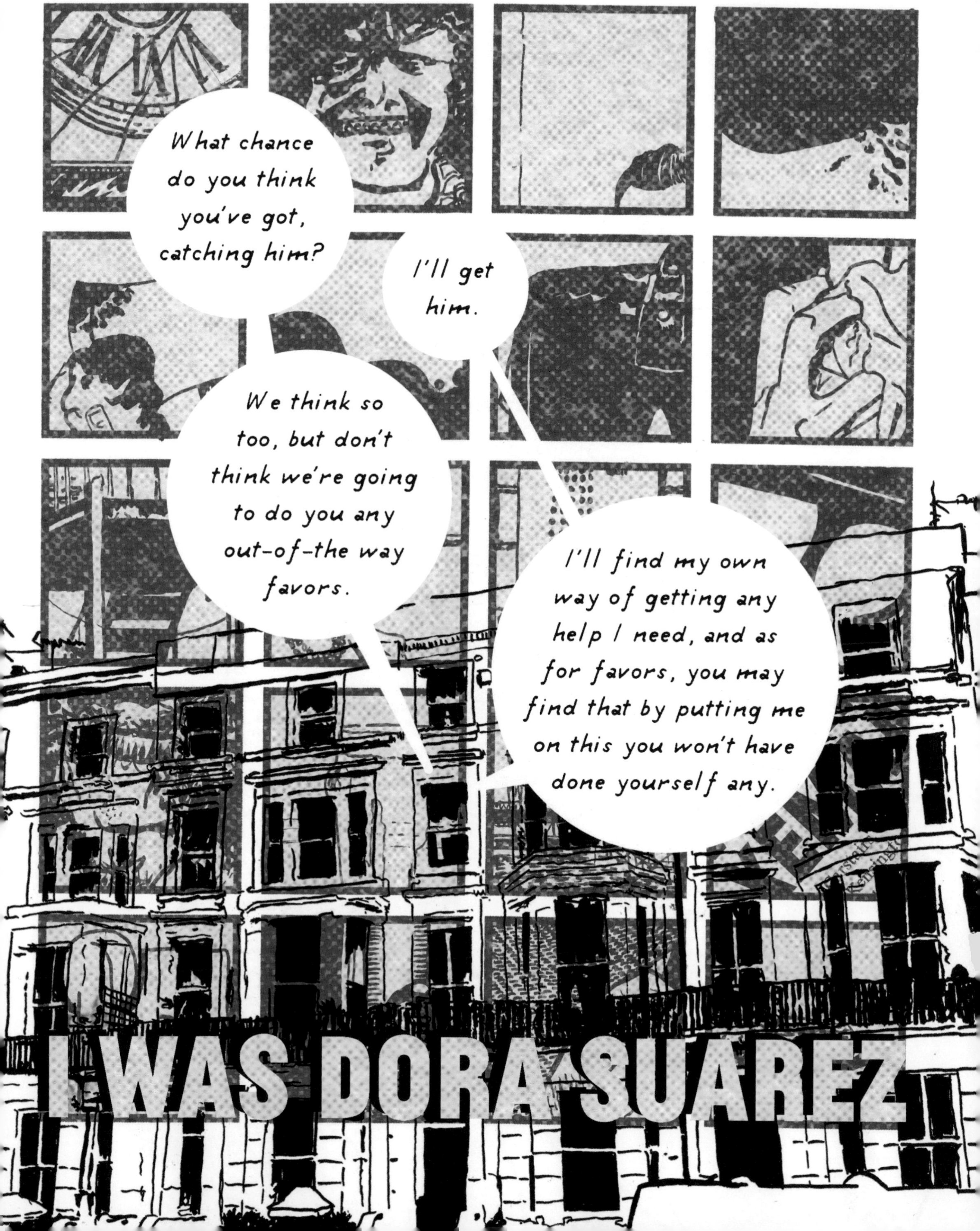
What chance do you think you've got, catching him?
I'll get him.
We think so too, but don't think we're going to do you any out-of-the way favors.
I'll find my own way of getting any help I need, and as for favors, you may find that by putting me on this you won't have done yourself any.
I WAS DORA SUAREZ

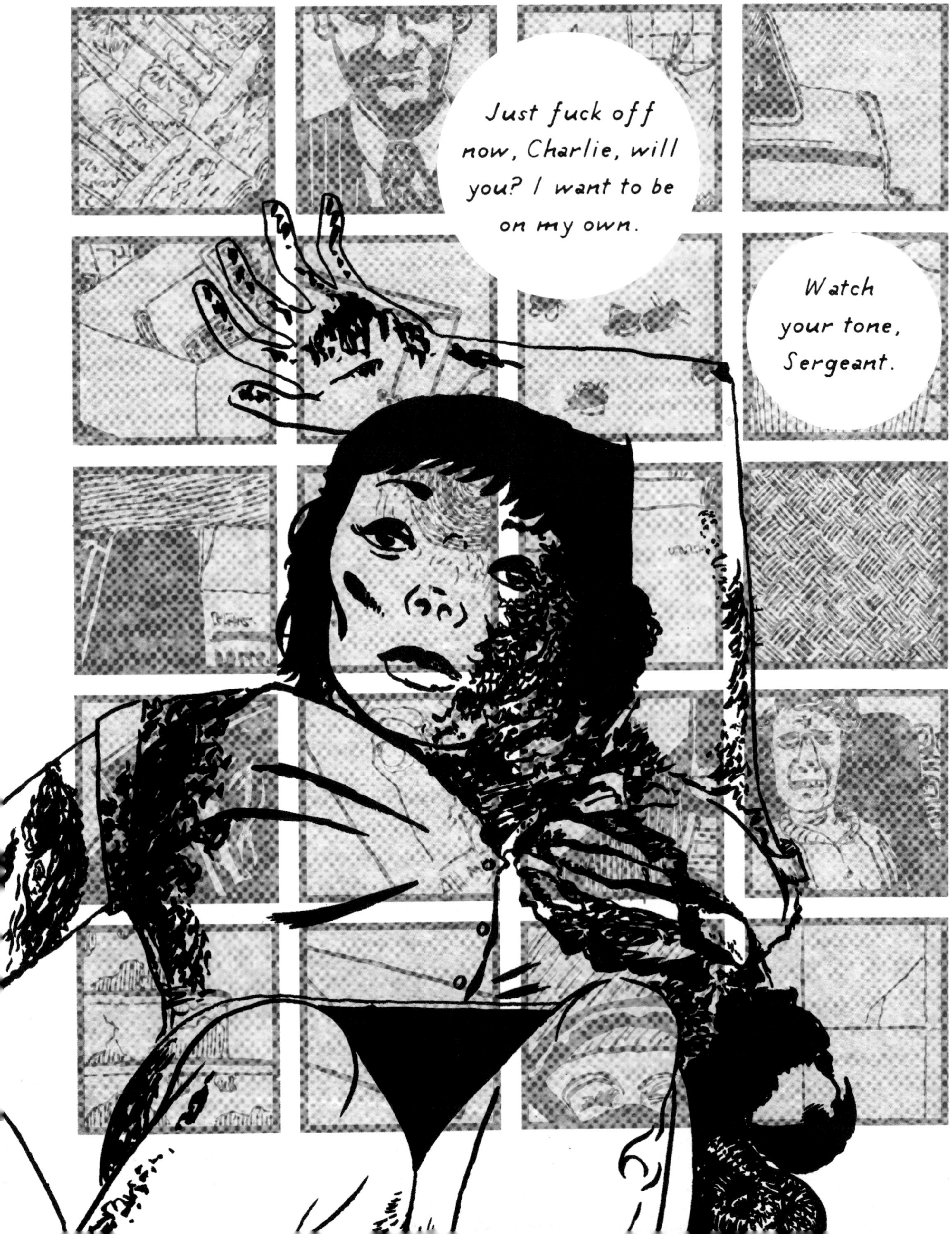
Just fuck off now, Charlie, will you? I want to be on my own.
Watch your tone, Sergeant.

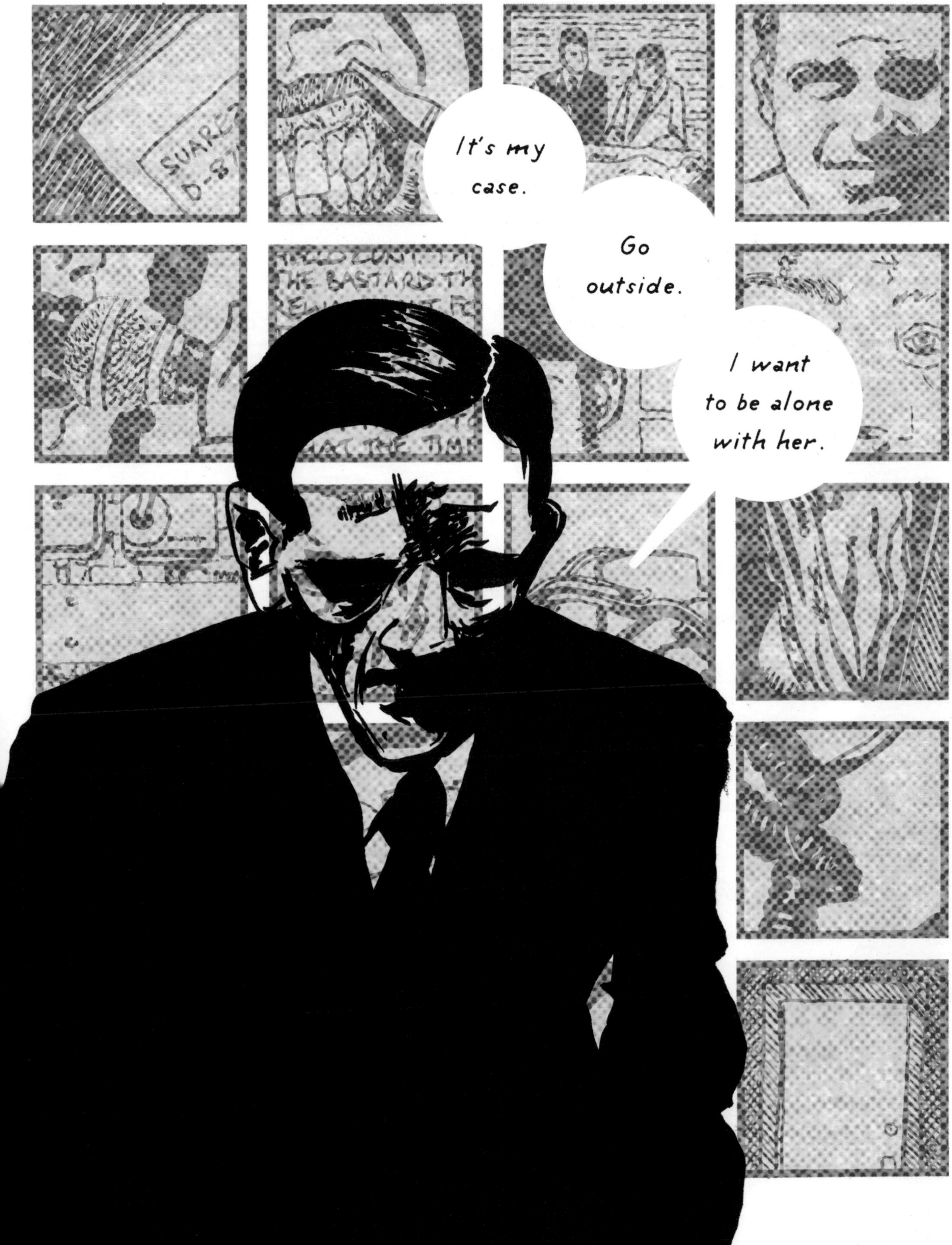

It's my case.
Go outside.
I want to be alone with her.

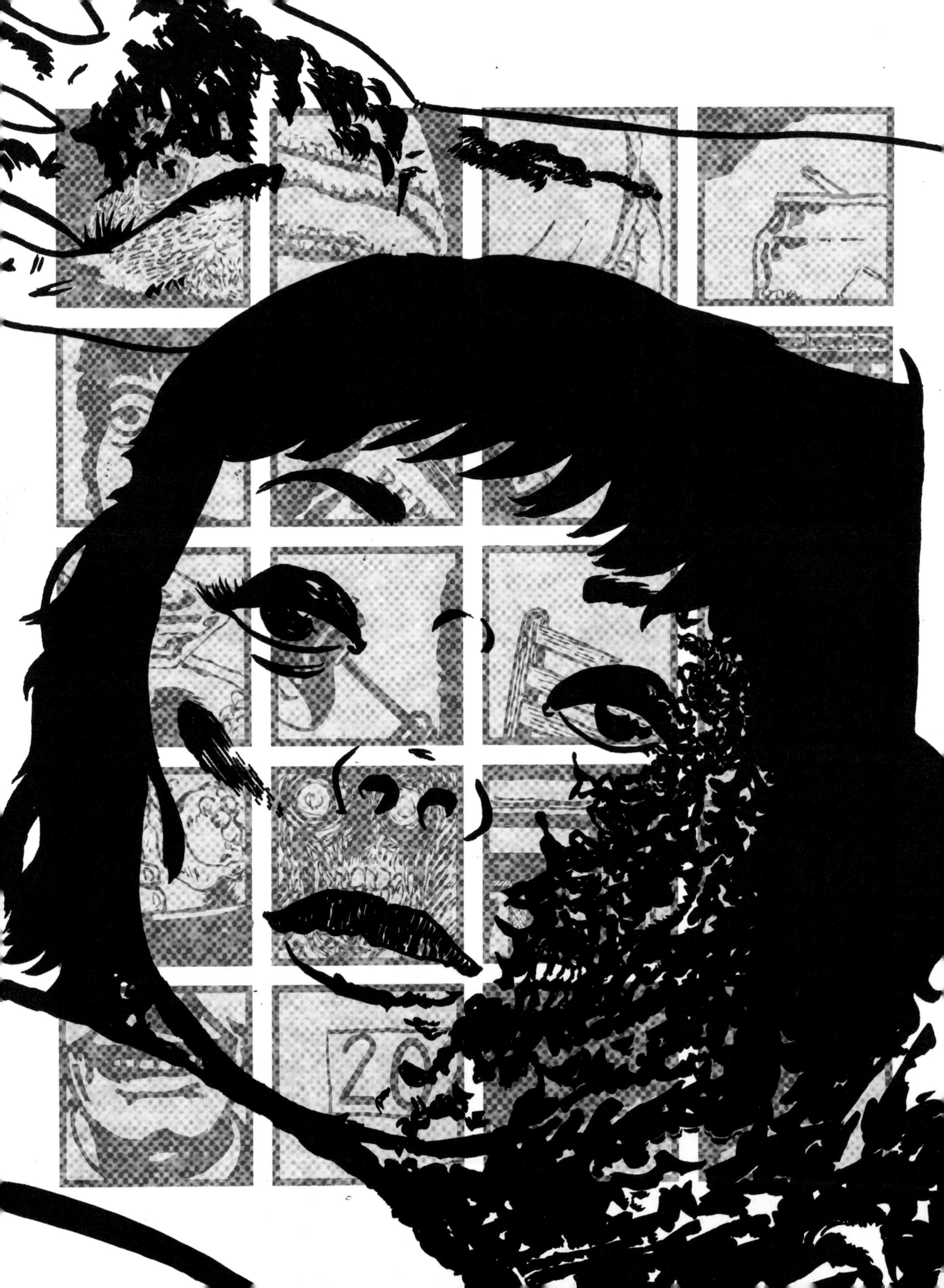
20

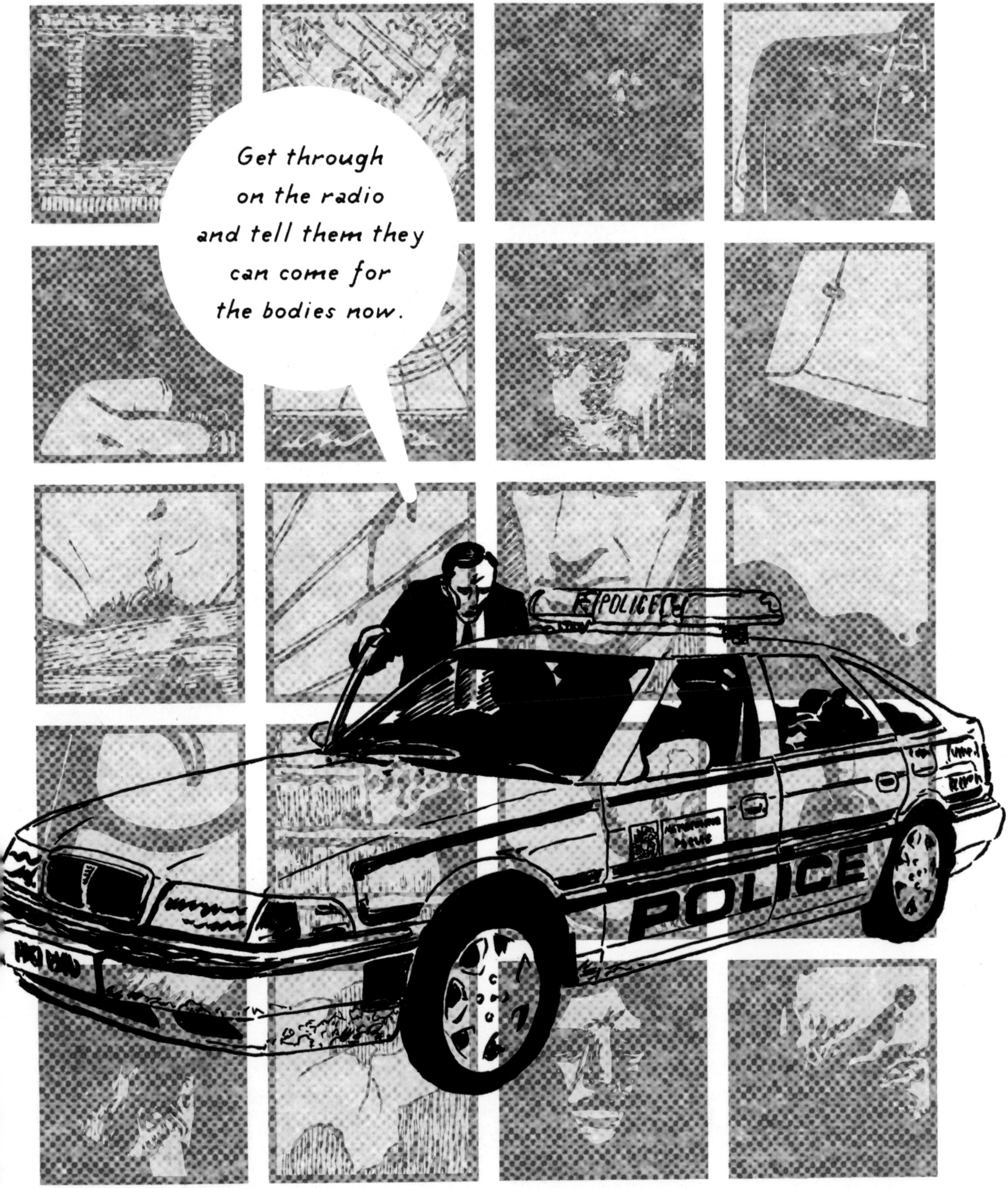
Get through on the radio and tell them they can come for the bodies now.
POLICE
POLICE

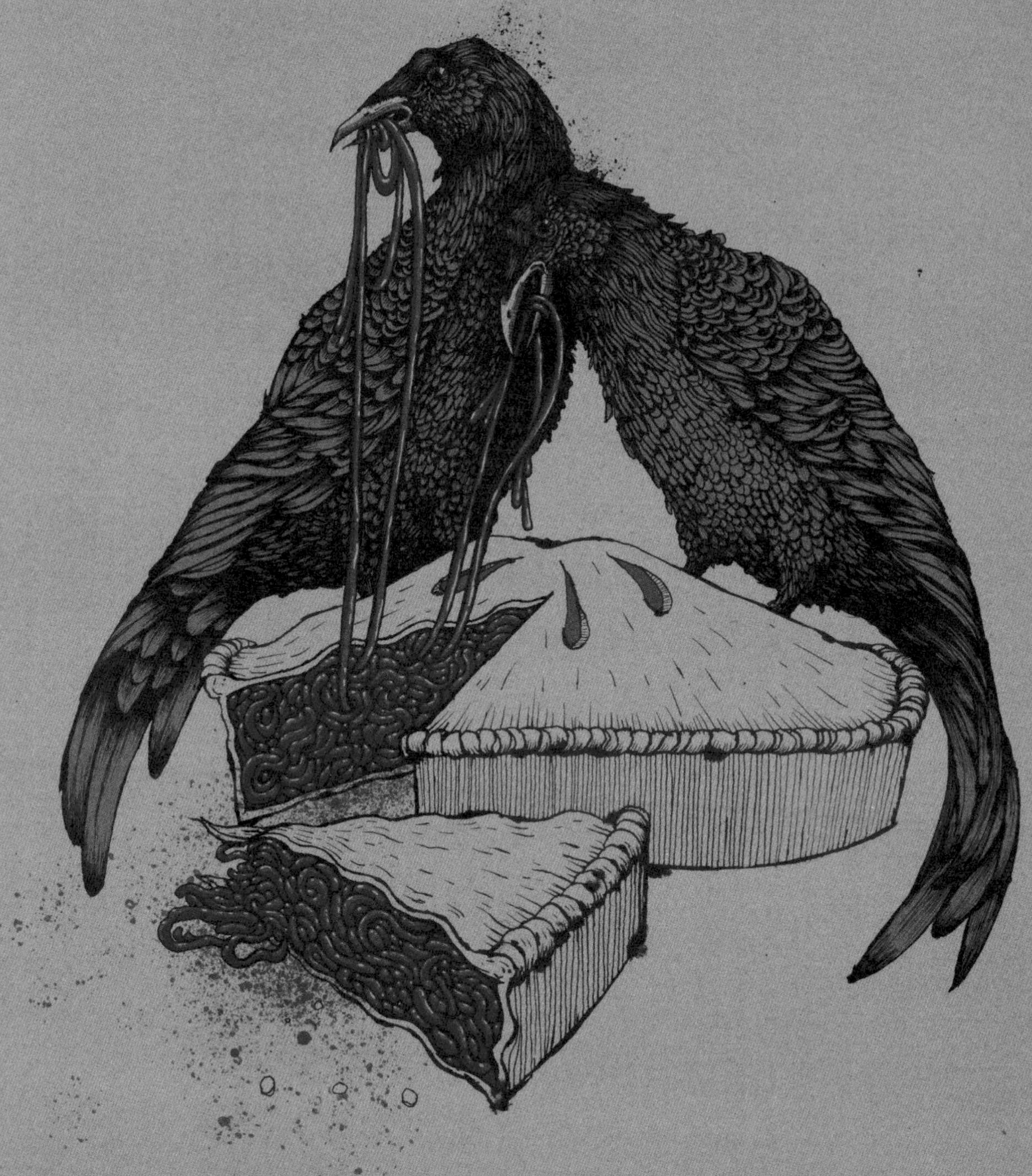

PART TWO

Revenge

Salome and John the Baptist

from the Gospel of Matthew

ART/ADAPTATION BY Angelle Sundberg

THE GRUESOME STORY OF SALOME HAS entered high culture and pop culture, often with additional elements not in the original biblical tale (for one thing, Salome's name is never given). In this adaptation, Angelle Sundberg ignores Oscar Wilde, Richard Strauss, Aubrey Beardsley, Rita Hayworth, Nick Cave, and the many others who've had their way with the tale, going back to the original telling in the Gospel of Matthew [14:1-12]. (There's a parallel telling in Mark [6:17-29].)

Herod Antipas—Rome's colonial head of Galilee—has married his half-brother's ex-wife, Herodias. Wildman preacher-prophet John the Baptist tells them that this violates Mosaic law (i.e. the laws of the Israelites, handed down by Moses via Yaweh). Herod Antipas and Herodias want him executed but are afraid to pull the trigger because of John's popularity with the people. But where there's a will . . .

Angelle Sundberg is a classically trained artist who has veered into comics and cake. As far as I know, she's the only contributor to the *Graphic Canon* series making a living in the culinary arts, creating groundbreakingly artistic pastries and cakes (I've seen the photos, which induce as much awe as hunger). She's said, "I have aspirations of bringing cake art to a gallery space, and then cutting and sharing."

Salome and John the Baptist

At that time Herod heard of the fame of Jesus and said unto his servants...

This is John the Baptist, he is risen from the dead and therefore mighty works do shew forth themselves in him.

For Herod had laid hold on John and bound him and put him in prison for Herodias's sake, his brother Philip's wife: for he had married her.

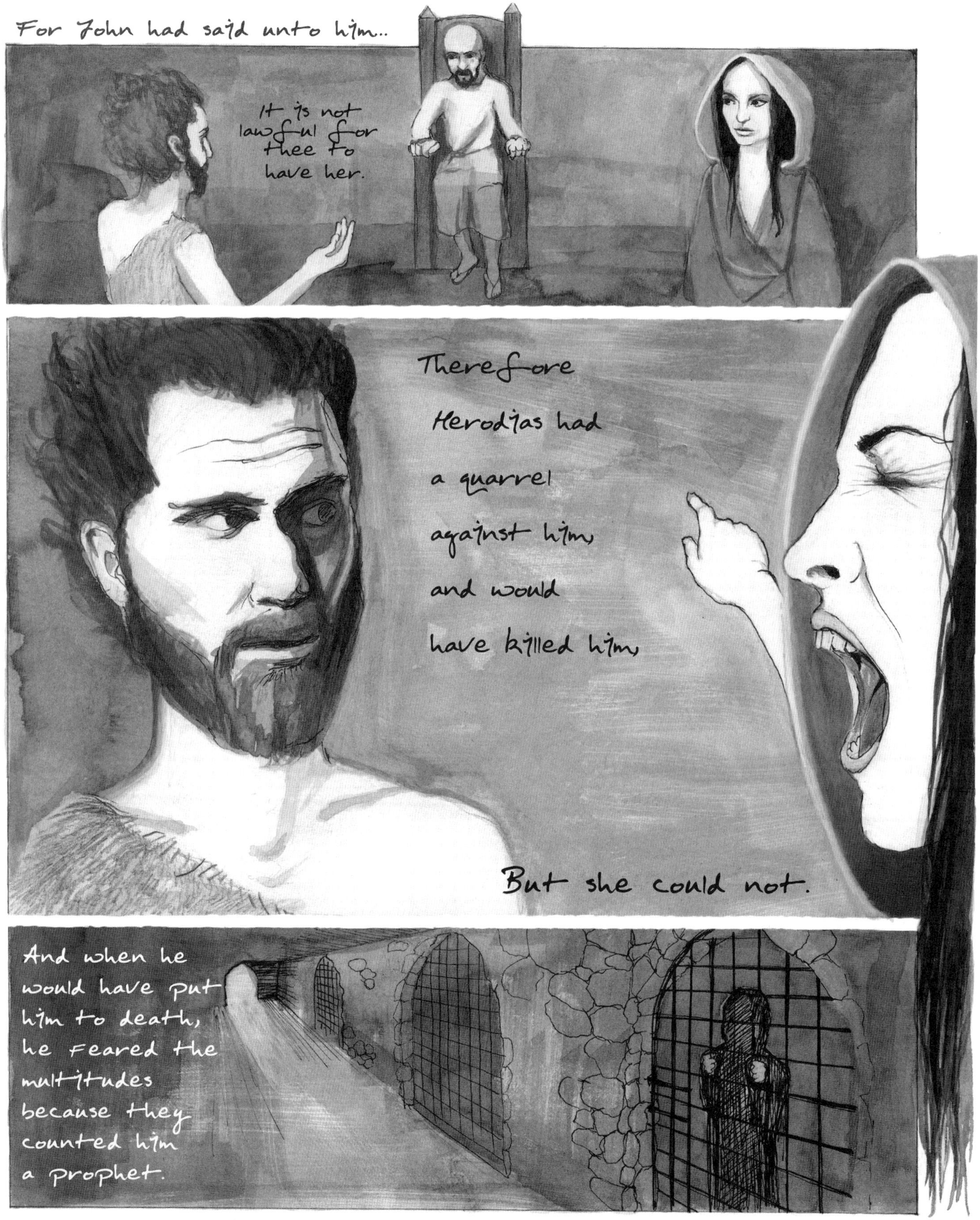
For John had said unto him...
It is not lawful for thee to have her.
Therefore Herodias had a quarrel against him, and would have killed him,
But she could not.
And when he would have put him to death, he feared the multitudes because they counted him a prophet.

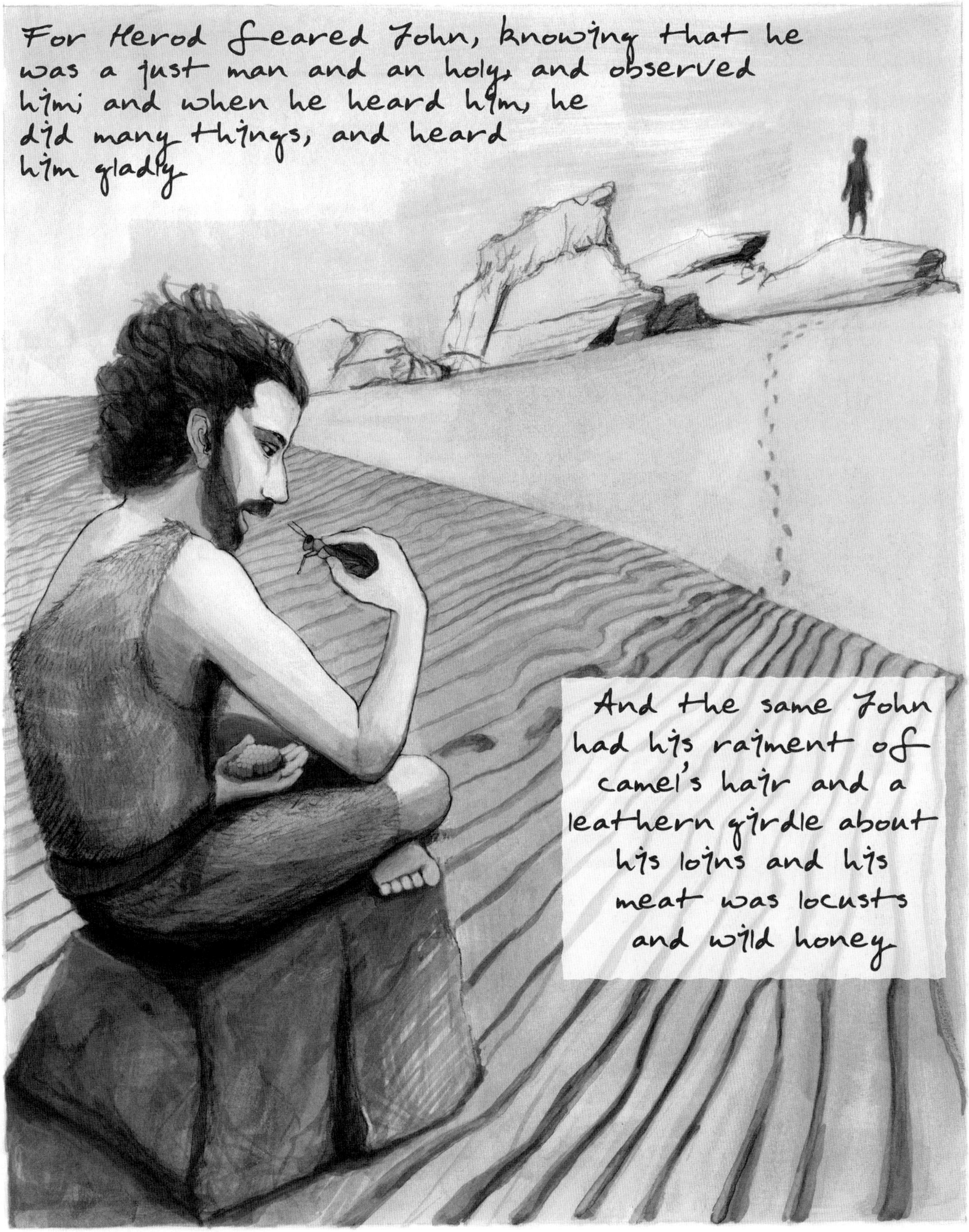
For Herod feared John, knowing that he was a just man and an holy, and observed him; and when he heard him, he did many things, and heard him gladly
And the same John had his raiment of camel's hair and a leathern girdle about his loins and his meat was locusts and wild honey

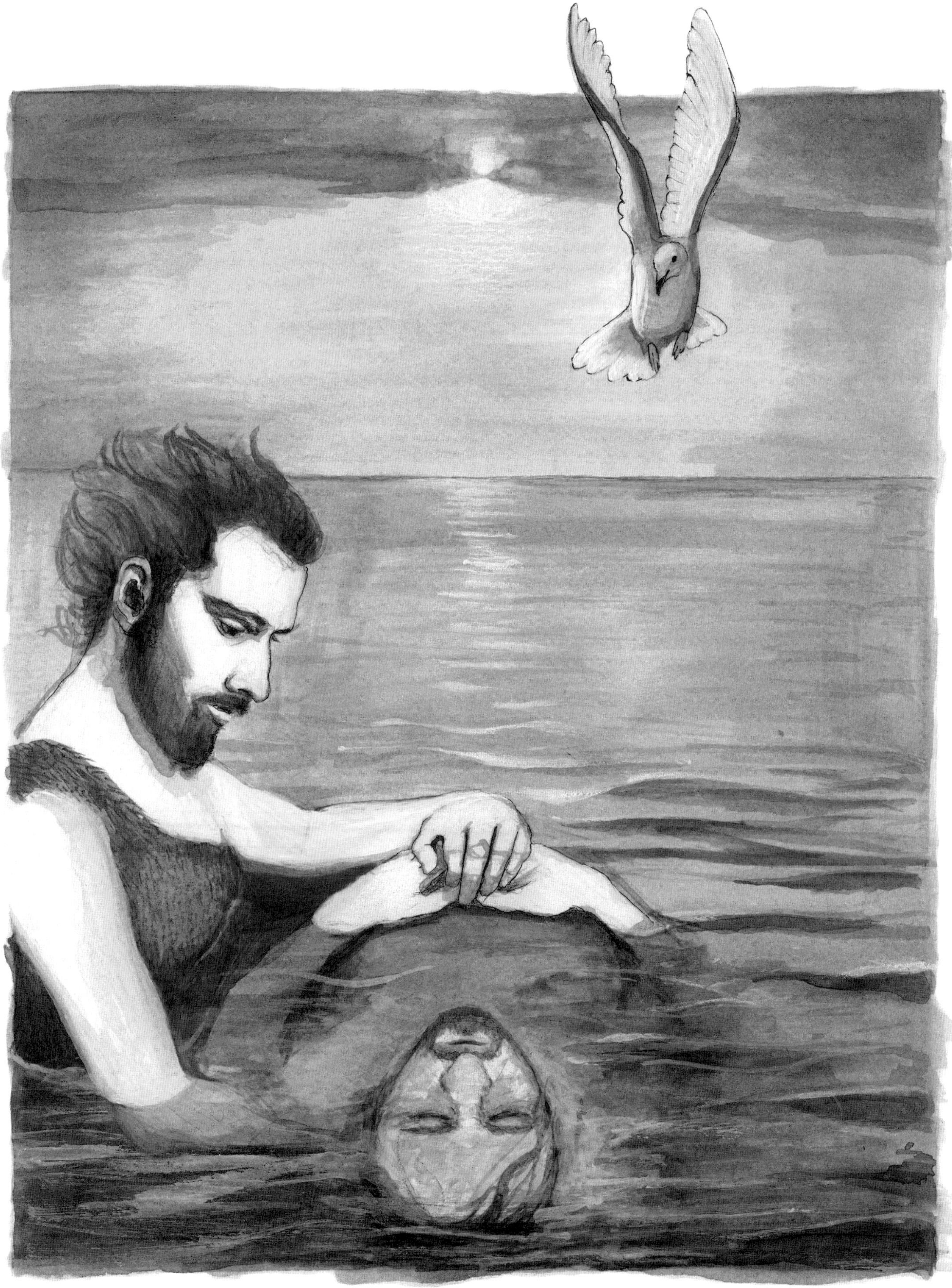

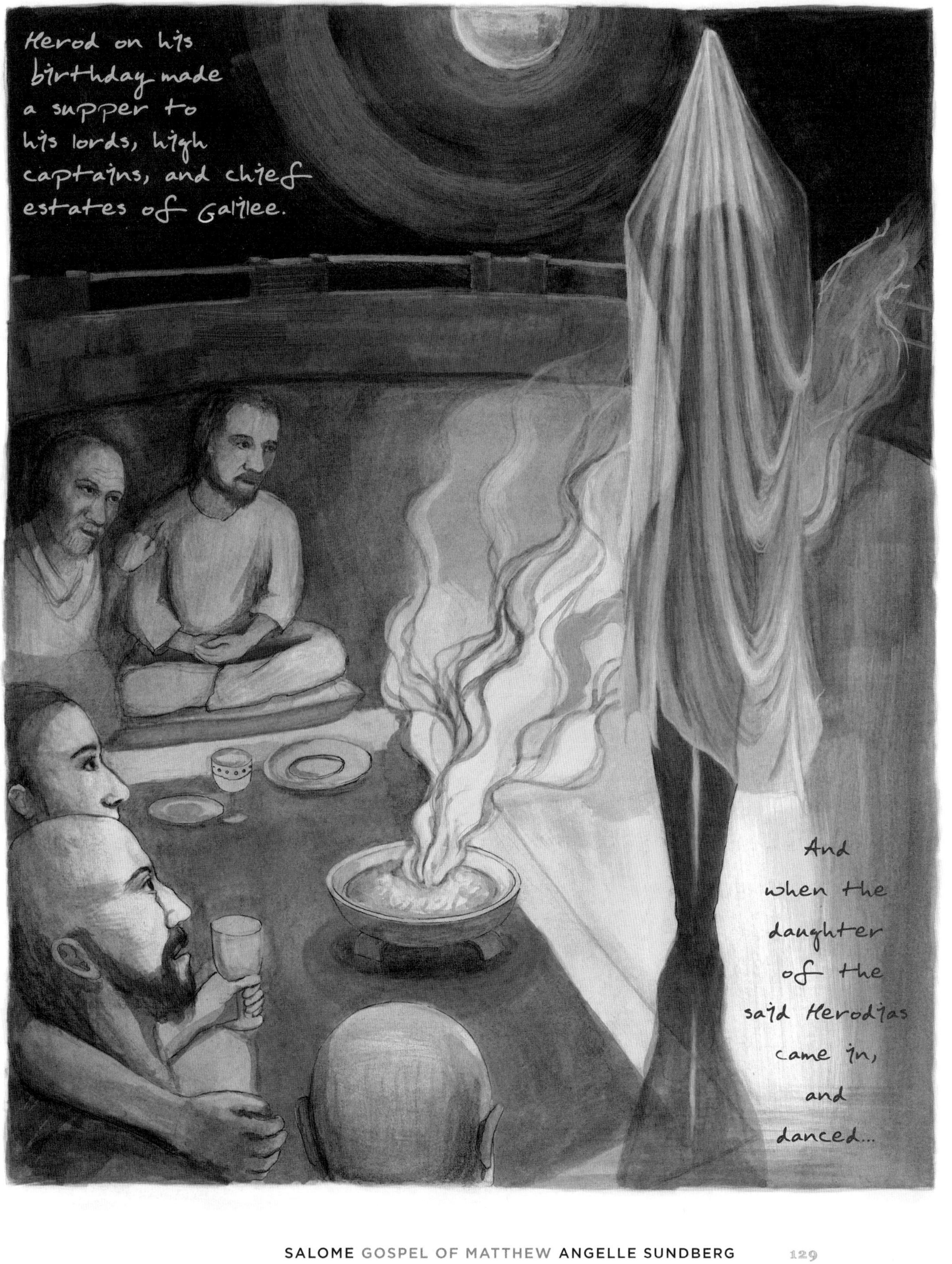
Herod on his birthday made a supper to his lords, high captains, and chief estates of Galilee.
And when the daughter of the said Herodias came in, and danced...

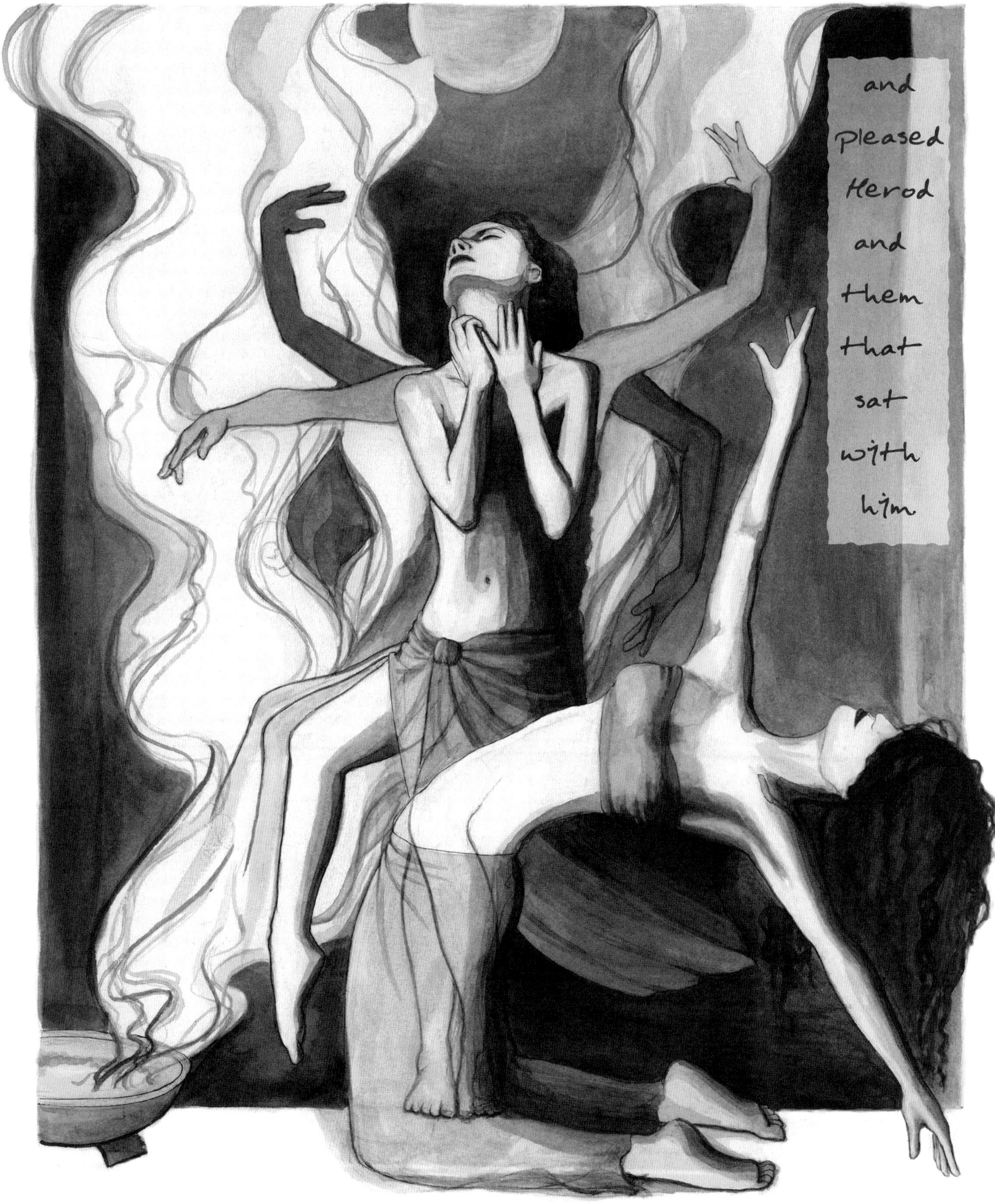
and
pleased
Herod
and
them
that
sat
with
him

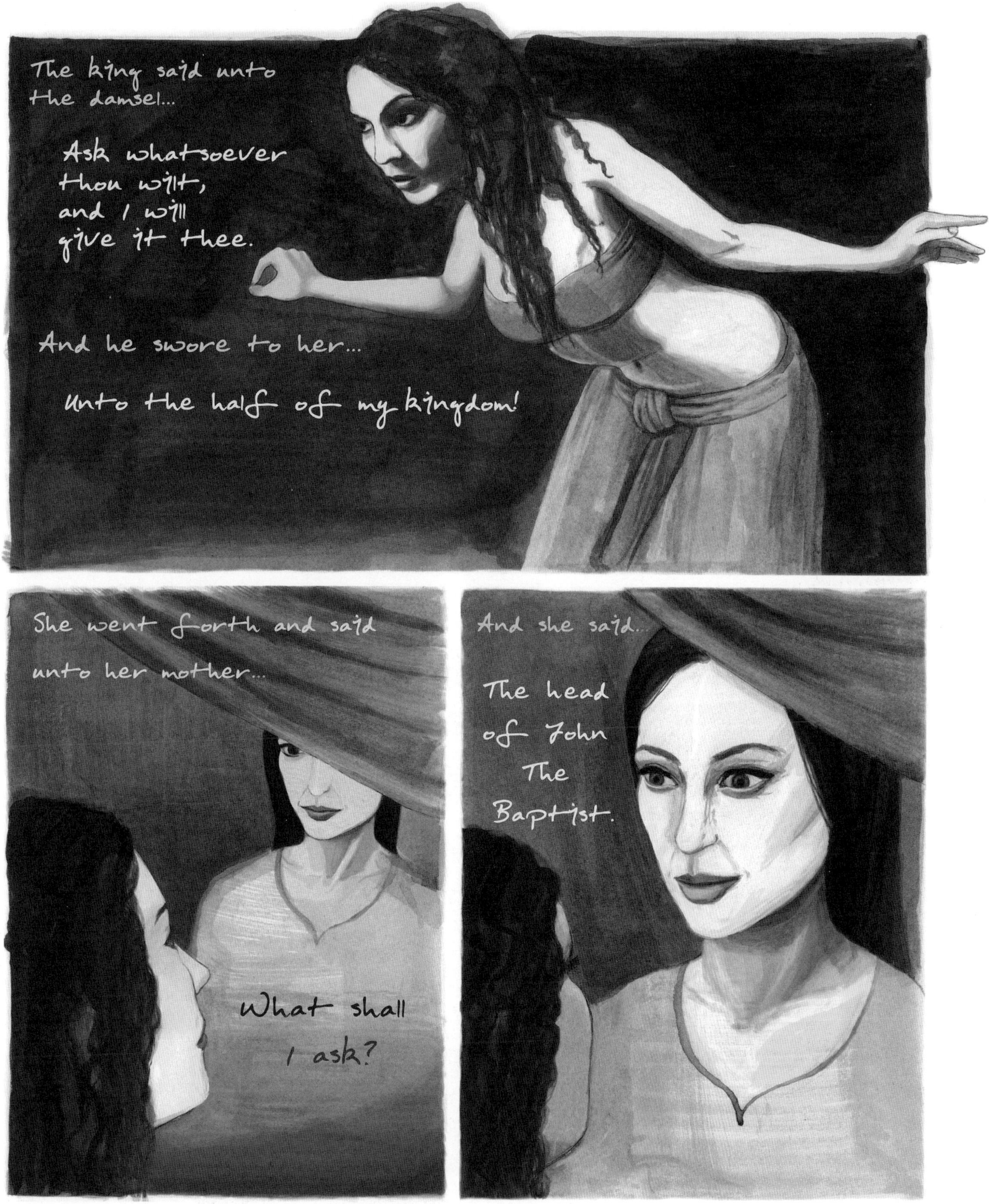
The king said unto the damsel...
Ask whatsoever thou wilt, and I will give it thee.
And he swore to her...
Unto the half of my kingdom!
She went forth and said unto her mother...
What shall I ask?
And she said...
The head of John The Baptist.

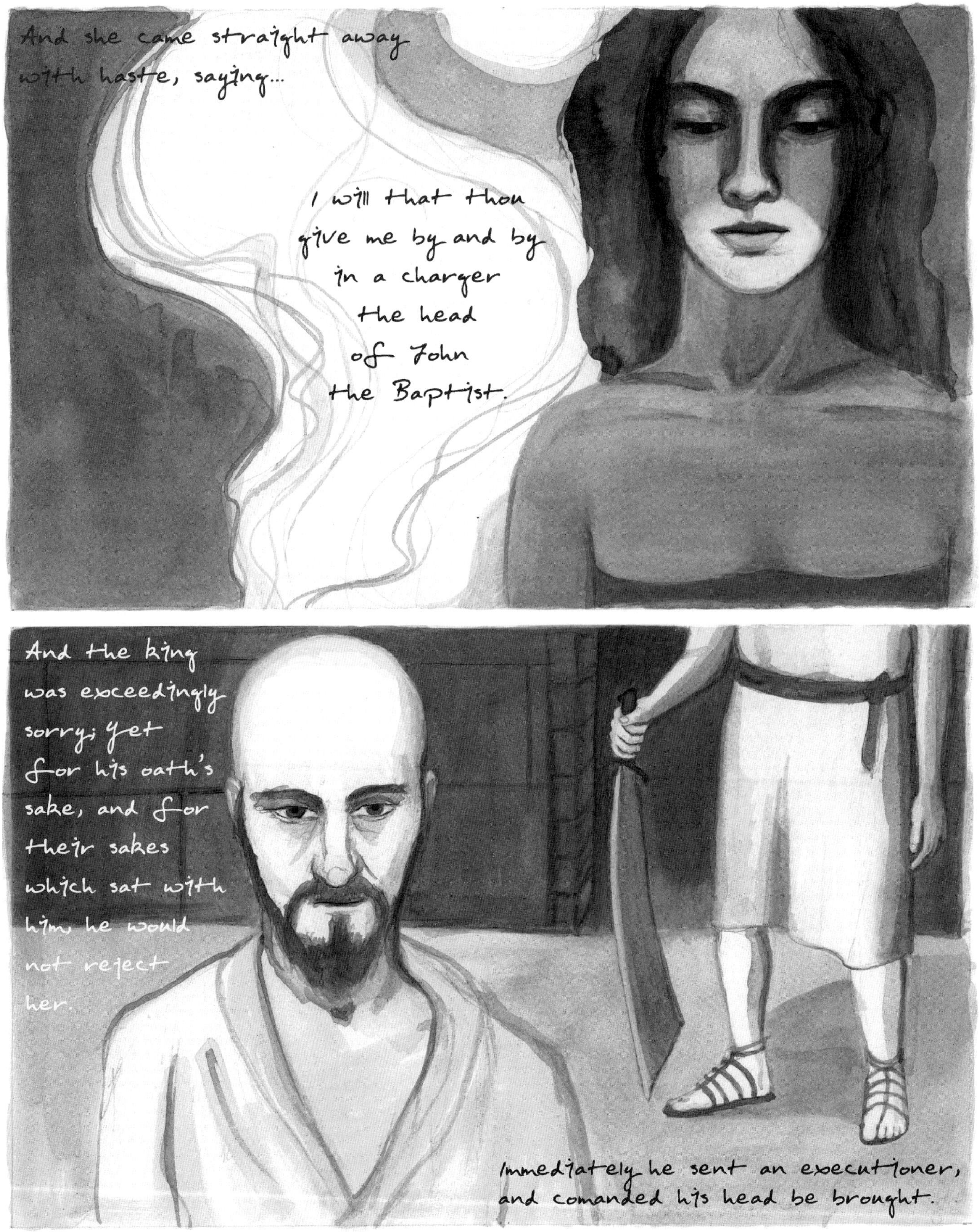
And she came straight away with haste, saying...
I will that thou give me by and by in a charger the head of John the Baptist.
And the king was exceedingly sorry; yet for his oath's sake, and for their sakes which sat with him, he would not reject her.
Immediately he sent an executioner, and comanded his head be brought.

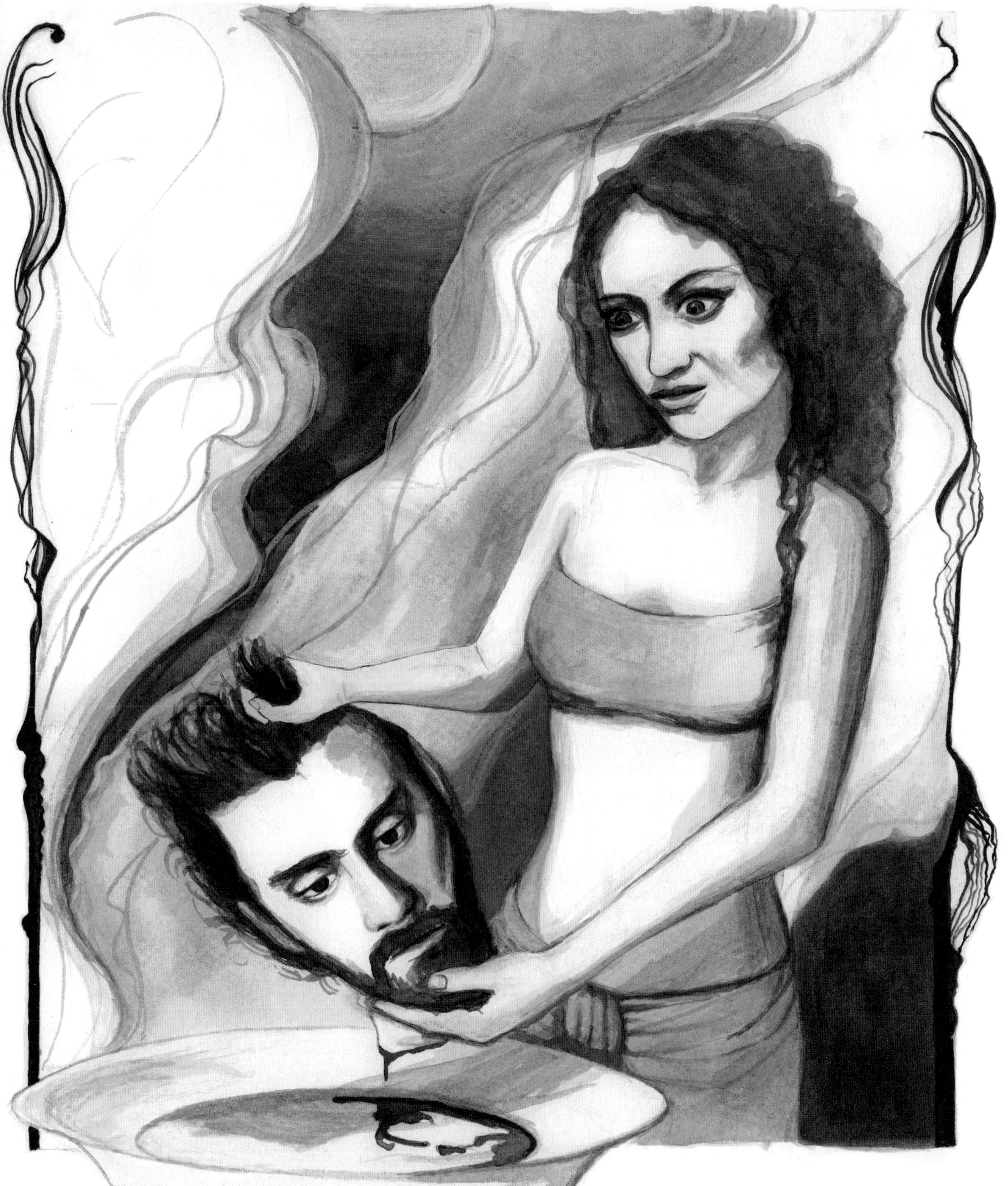

"The Pardoner's Tale"
(from The Canterbury Tales)

Geoffrey Chaucer

ART/ADAPTATION BY **Katherine Hearst**

THE CANTERBURY TALES—GEOFFREY Chaucer's fourteenth-century collection of stories told by religious pilgrims on their way to Thomas à Beckett's shrine—is filled with greed, deception, adultery, violence, thwarted love, and bathroom humor. The yarn told by the Pardoner is one of the better-known portions. The concept is irresistibly intriguing: Three lowlifes set out to kill Death because Death killed one of their friends. What happens to them is a perfect plot twist written 550 years before O. Henry.

Illustrator and animated filmmaker Katherine Hearst of London uses inks and watercolors to create an atmospheric version of this bizarre revenge tale, which doubles as a dark take on greed. She has brought her lush, complex approach to a range of stories, including "The Firebird," the Baba Yaga myth, *Peter and the Wolf*, and *Brave New World*, as well as cofounding the nonfiction graphic/comics magazine *Modern Times* ("aims to be for graphic publications what *This American Life* is to radio").

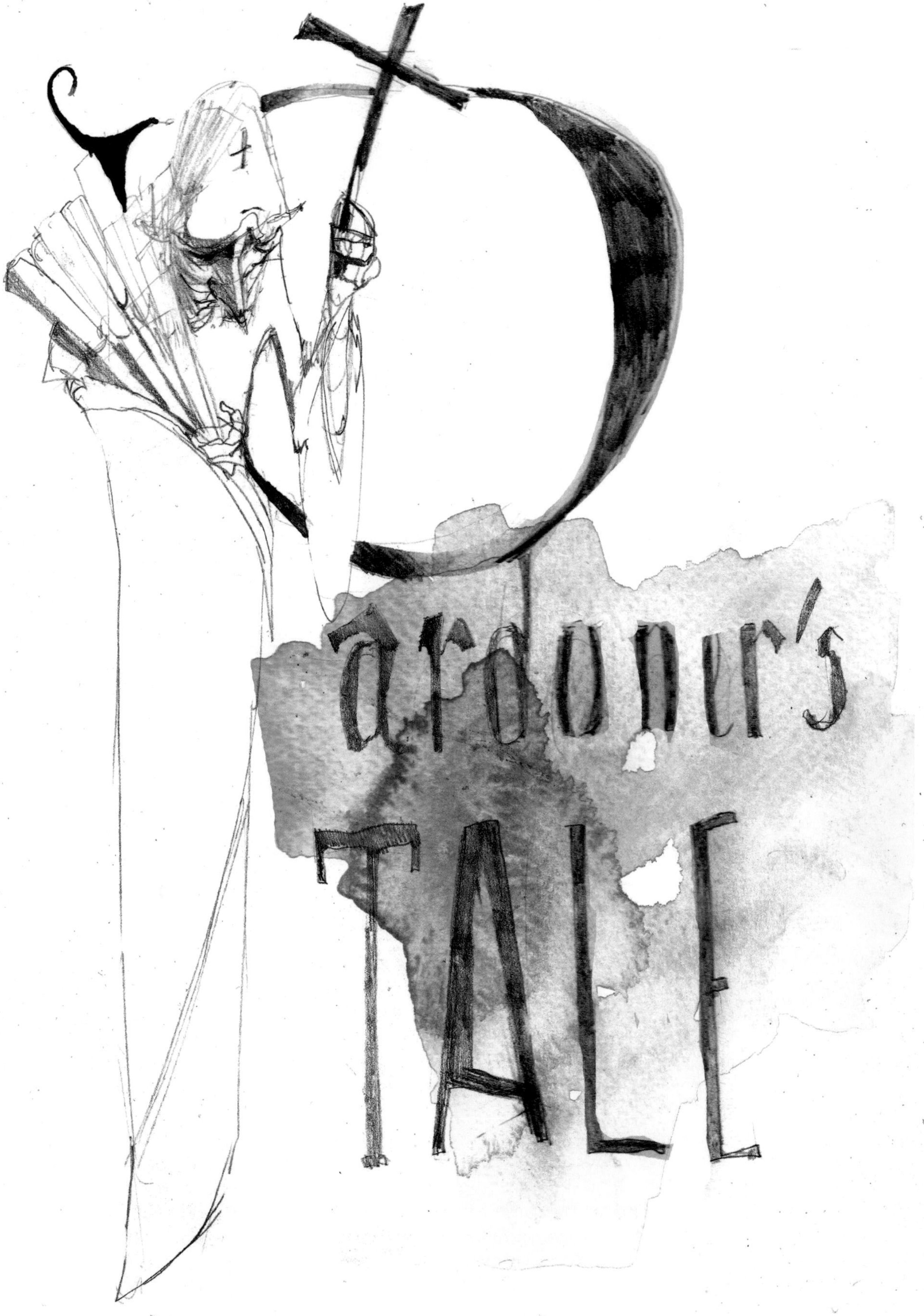
Pardoner's
TALE

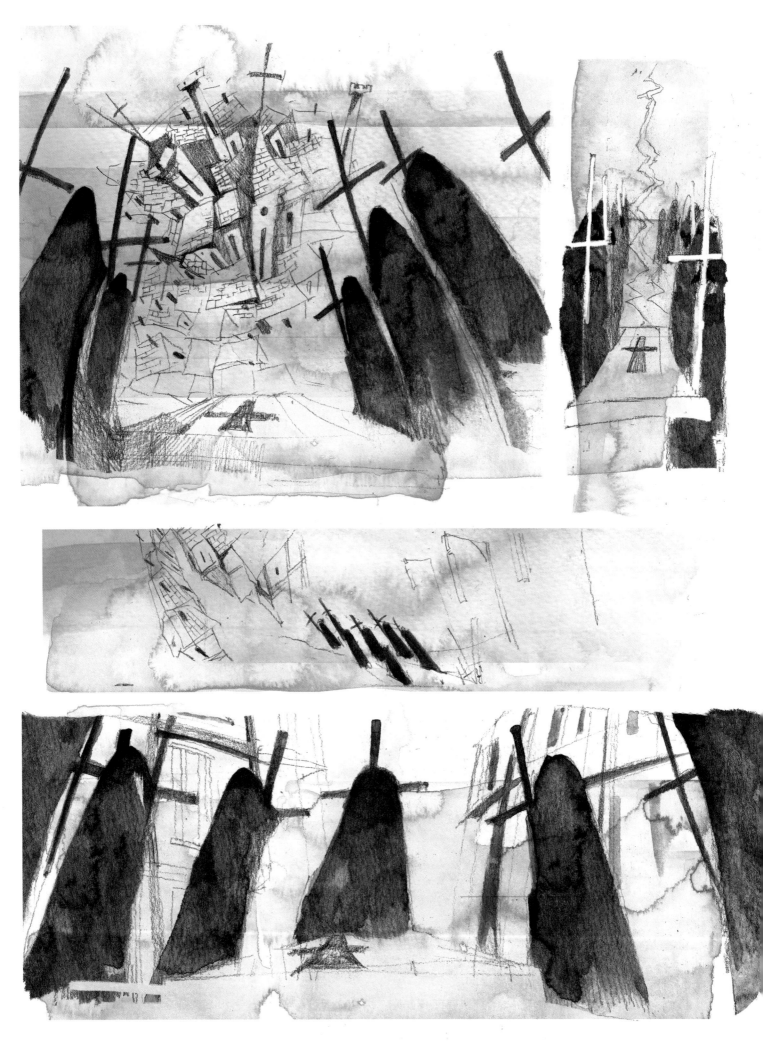

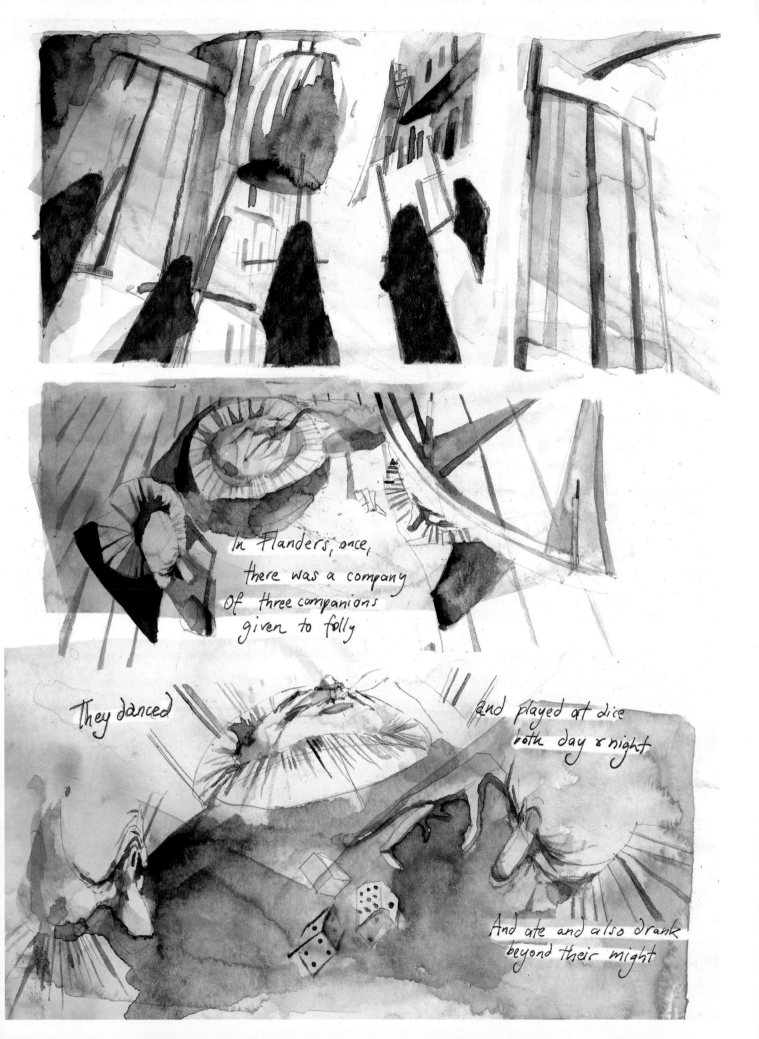

In Flanders, once,
there was a company
of three companions
given to folly

They danced

and played at dice
both day & night

And ate and also drank
beyond their might

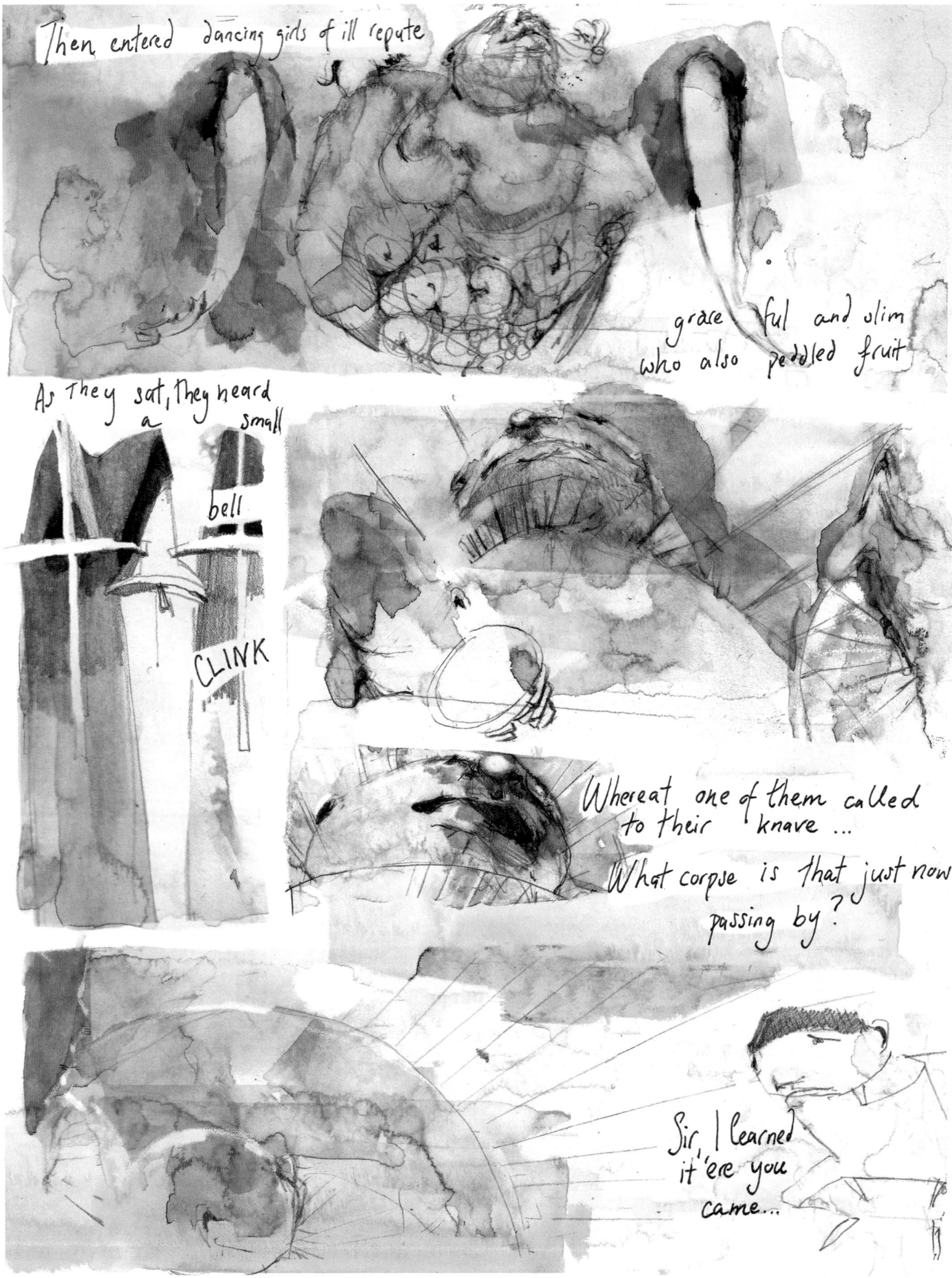
Then entered dancing girls of ill repute
graceful and slim
who also peddled fruit
As they sat, they heard a small bell
CLINK
Whereat one of them called to their knave ...
What corpse is that just now passing by?
Sir, I learned it ere you came...

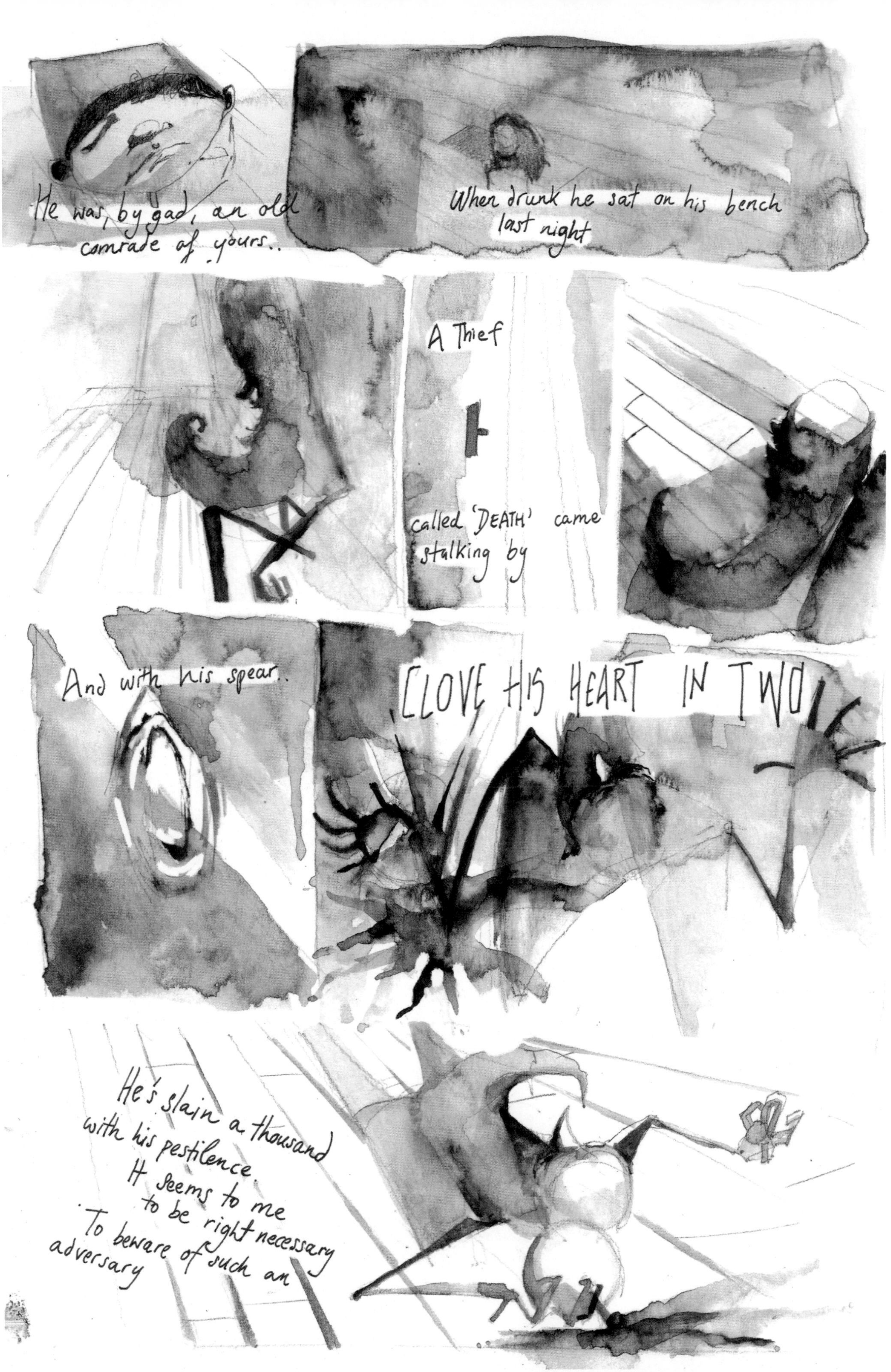
He was, by gad, an old comrade of yours..
When drunk he sat on his bench last night
A Thief
called 'DEATH' came stalking by
And with his spear..
CLOVE HIS HEART IN TWO
He's slain a thousand with his pestilence.
It seems to me to be right necessary To beware of such an adversary

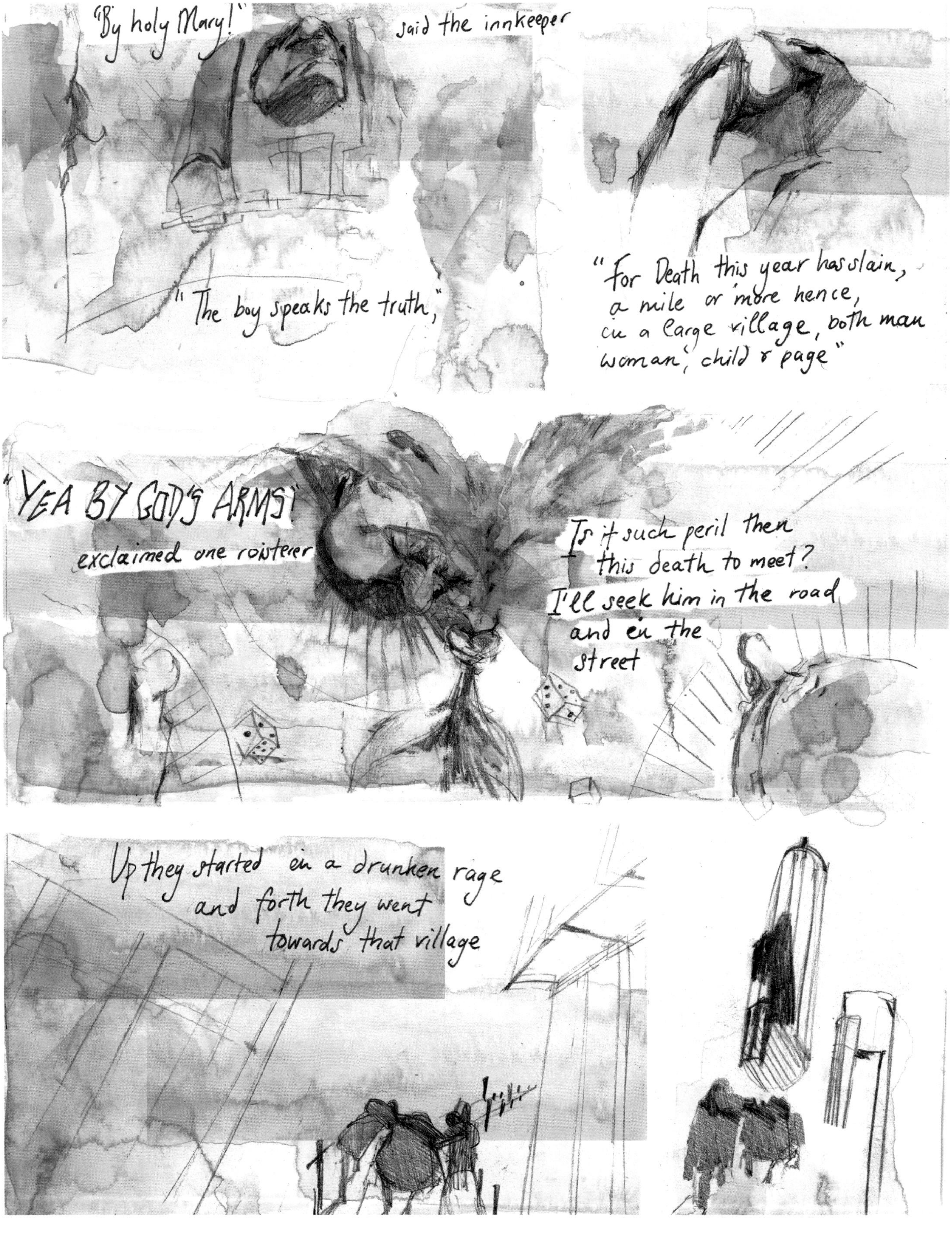
"By holy Mary!"
said the innkeeper
"The boy speaks the truth,"
"For Death this year has slain, a mile or more hence, in a large village, both man woman, child & page"
"YEA BY GOD'S ARMS!"
exclaimed one roisterer
Is it such peril then this death to meet?
I'll seek him in the road and in the street
Up they started in a drunken rage
and forth they went
towards that village

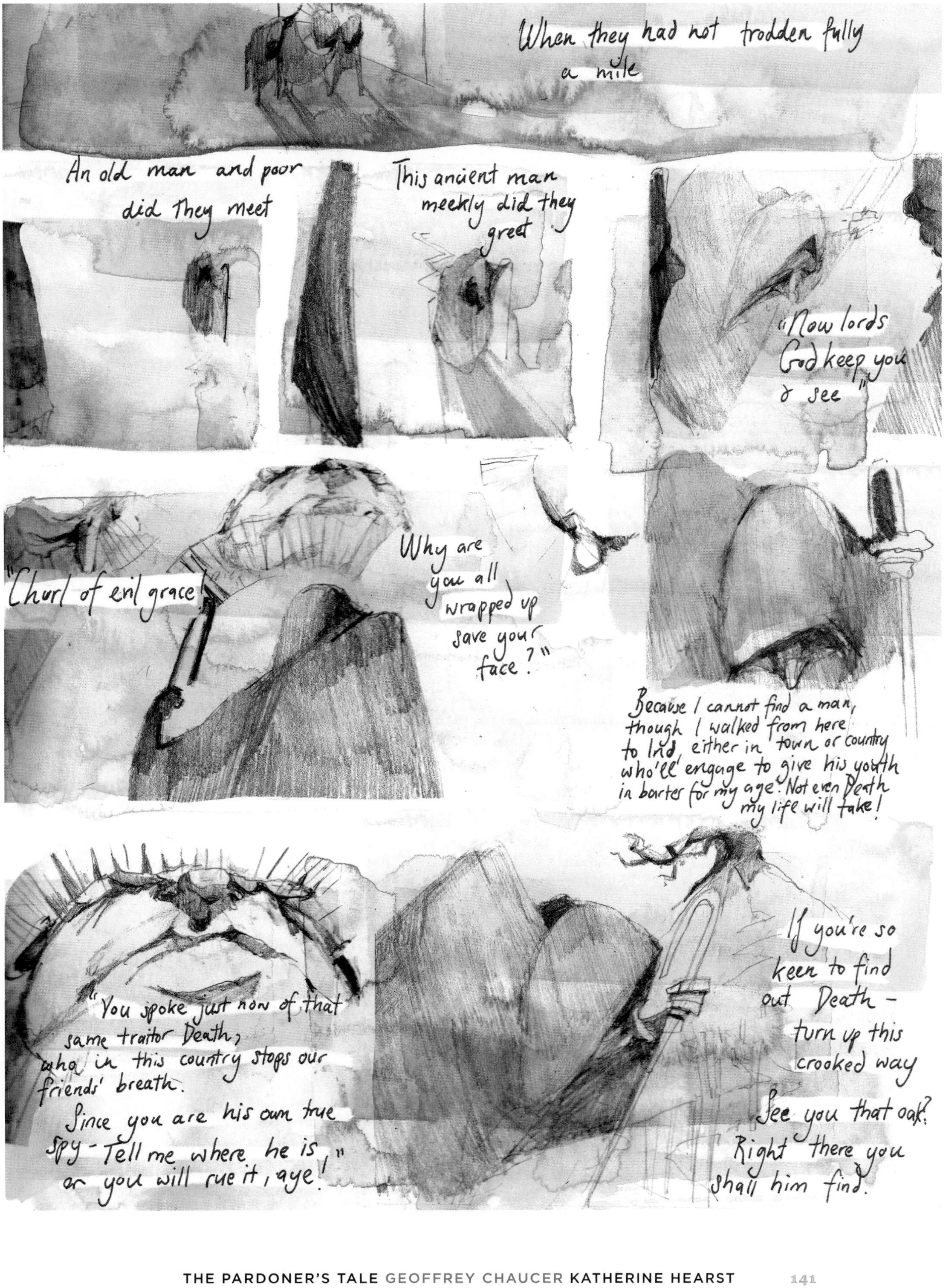
When they had not trodden fully a mile
An old man and poor did they meet
This ancient man meekly did they greet
"Now lords God keep you & see"
"Churl of evil grace!
Why are you all wrapped up save your face?"
Because I cannot find a man, though I walked from here to Ind, either in town or country who'll engage to give his youth in barter for my age. Not even Death my life will take!
"You spoke just now of that same traitor Death, who in this country stops our friends' breath.
Since you are his own true spy - Tell me where he is," or you will rue it, aye!
If you're so keen to find out Death - turn up this crooked way
See you that oak? Right there you shall him find.

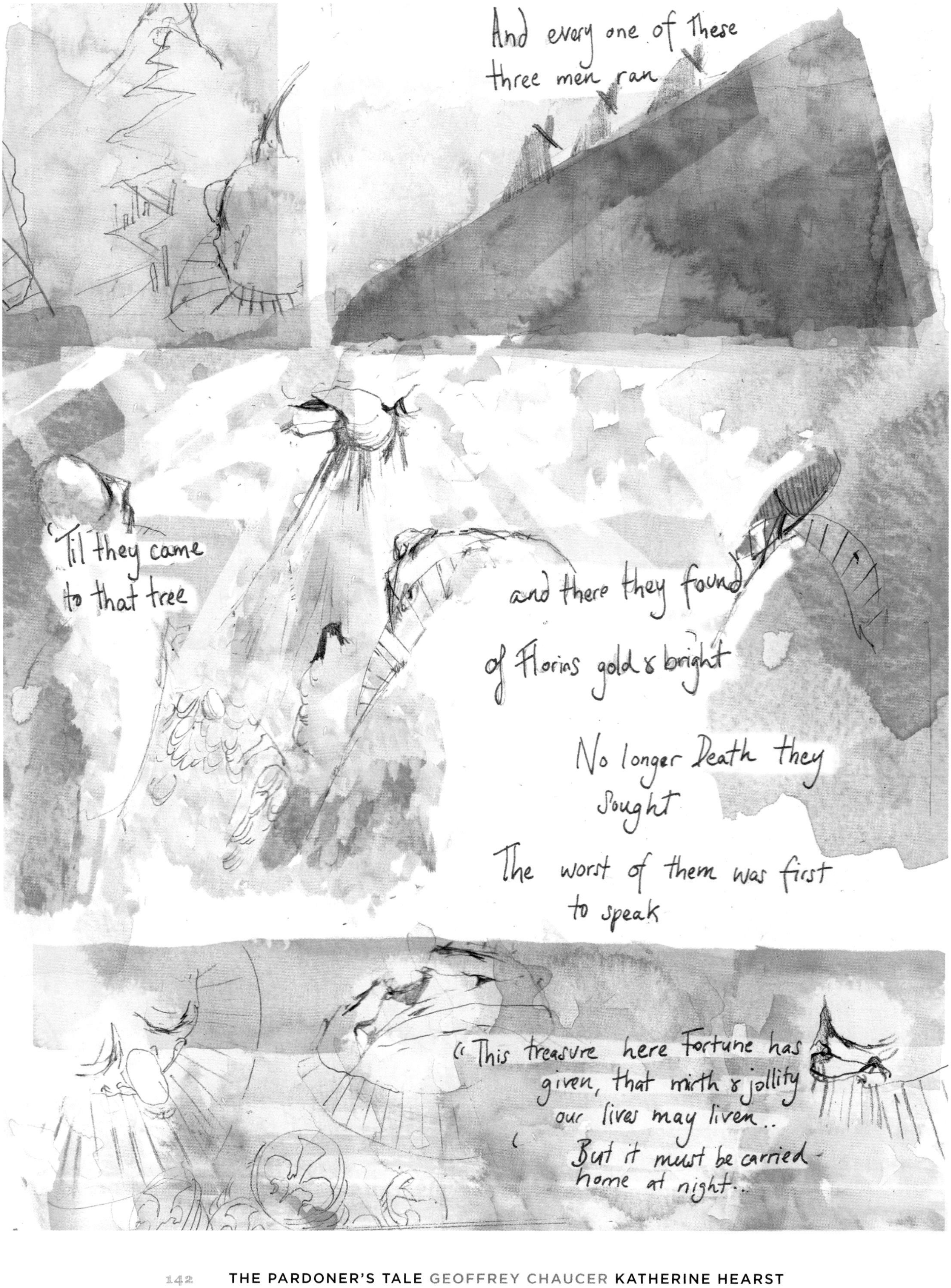
And every one of these three men ran
'Til they came to that tree
and there they found
of Florins gold & bright
No longer Death they sought
The worst of them was first to speak
"This treasure here Fortune has given, that mirth & jollity our lives may liven..
'But it must be carried home at night..

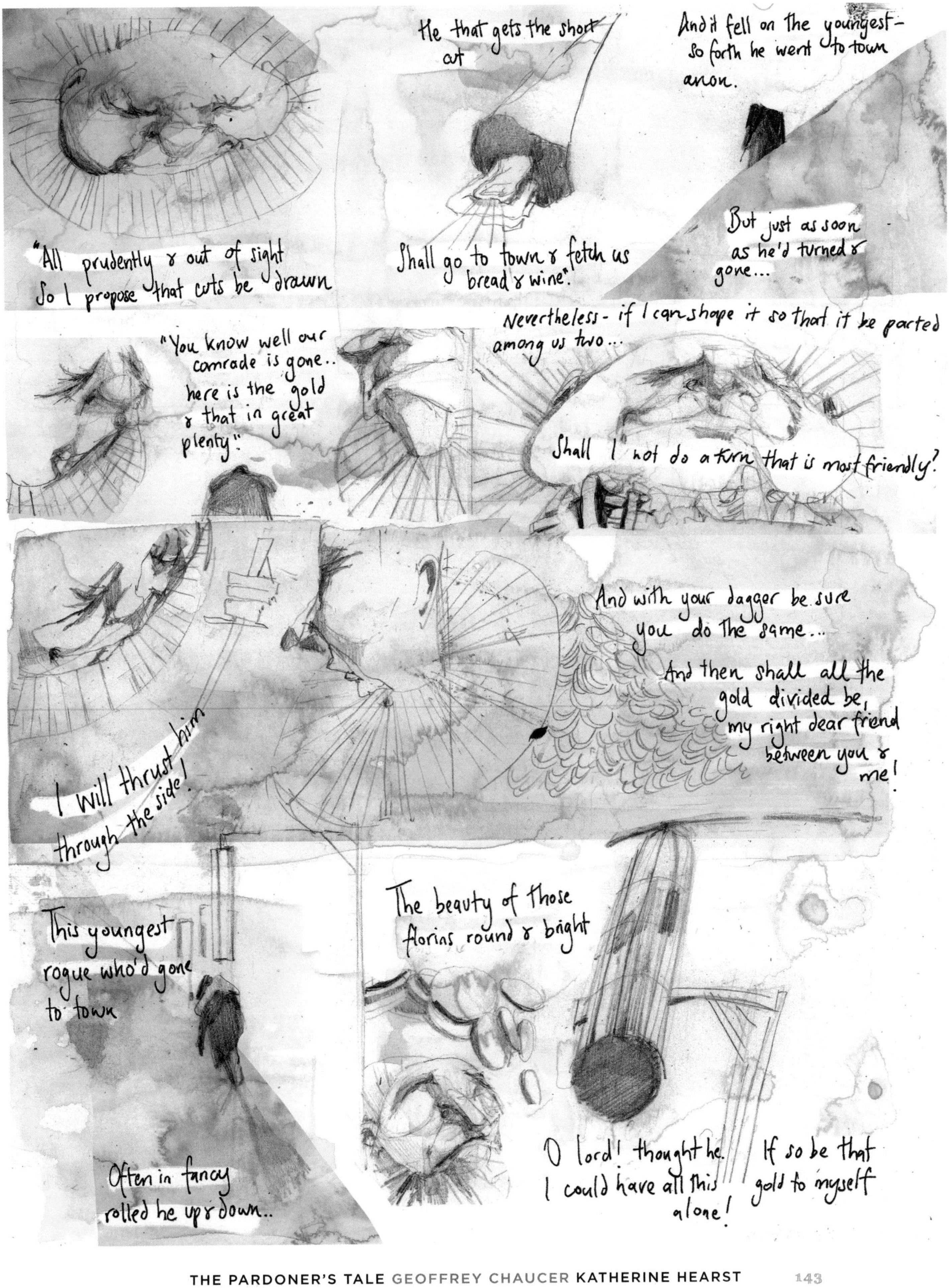
"All prudently & out of sight
So I propose that cuts be drawn
He that gets the short cut
Shall go to town & fetch us bread & wine".
And it fell on the youngest - so forth he went to town anon.
But just as soon as he'd turned & gone...
"You know well our comrade is gone.. here is the gold & that in great plenty"
Nevertheless - if I can shape it so that it be parted among us two...
Shall I not do a turn that is most friendly?
And with your dagger be sure you do the same...
And then shall all the gold divided be, my right dear friend between you & me!
I will thrust him through the side!
This youngest rogue who'd gone to town
Often in fancy rolled he up & down..
The beauty of those florins round & bright
O lord! thought he. If so be that I could have all this gold to myself alone!

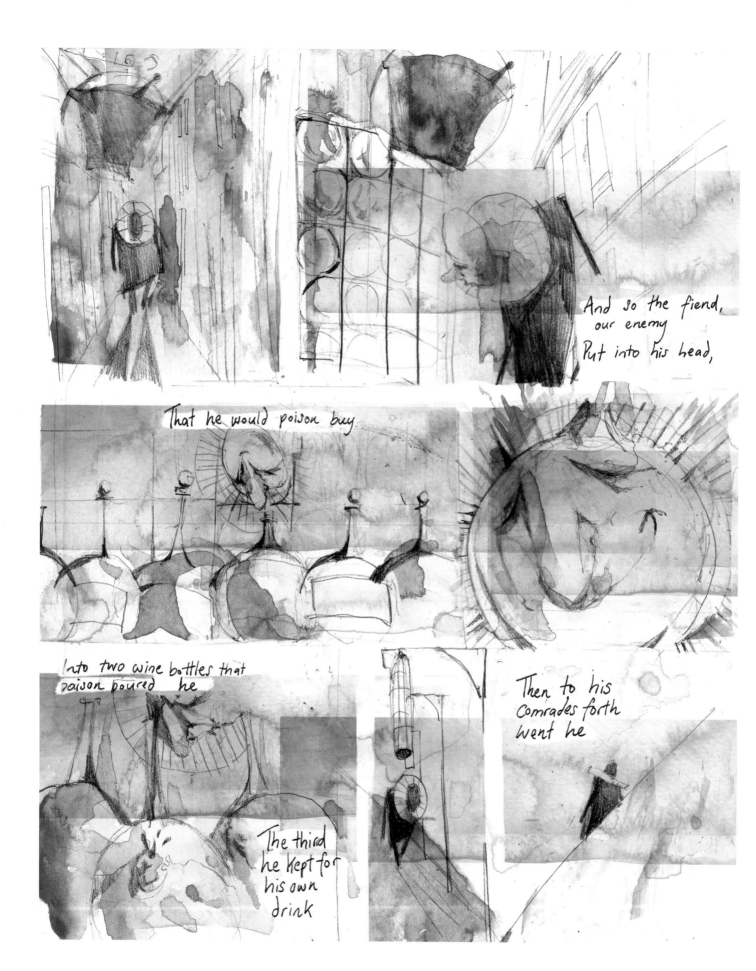

And so the fiend, our enemy
Put into his head,

That he would poison buy

Into two wine bottles that poison poured he

The third he kept for his own drink

Then to his comrades forth went he

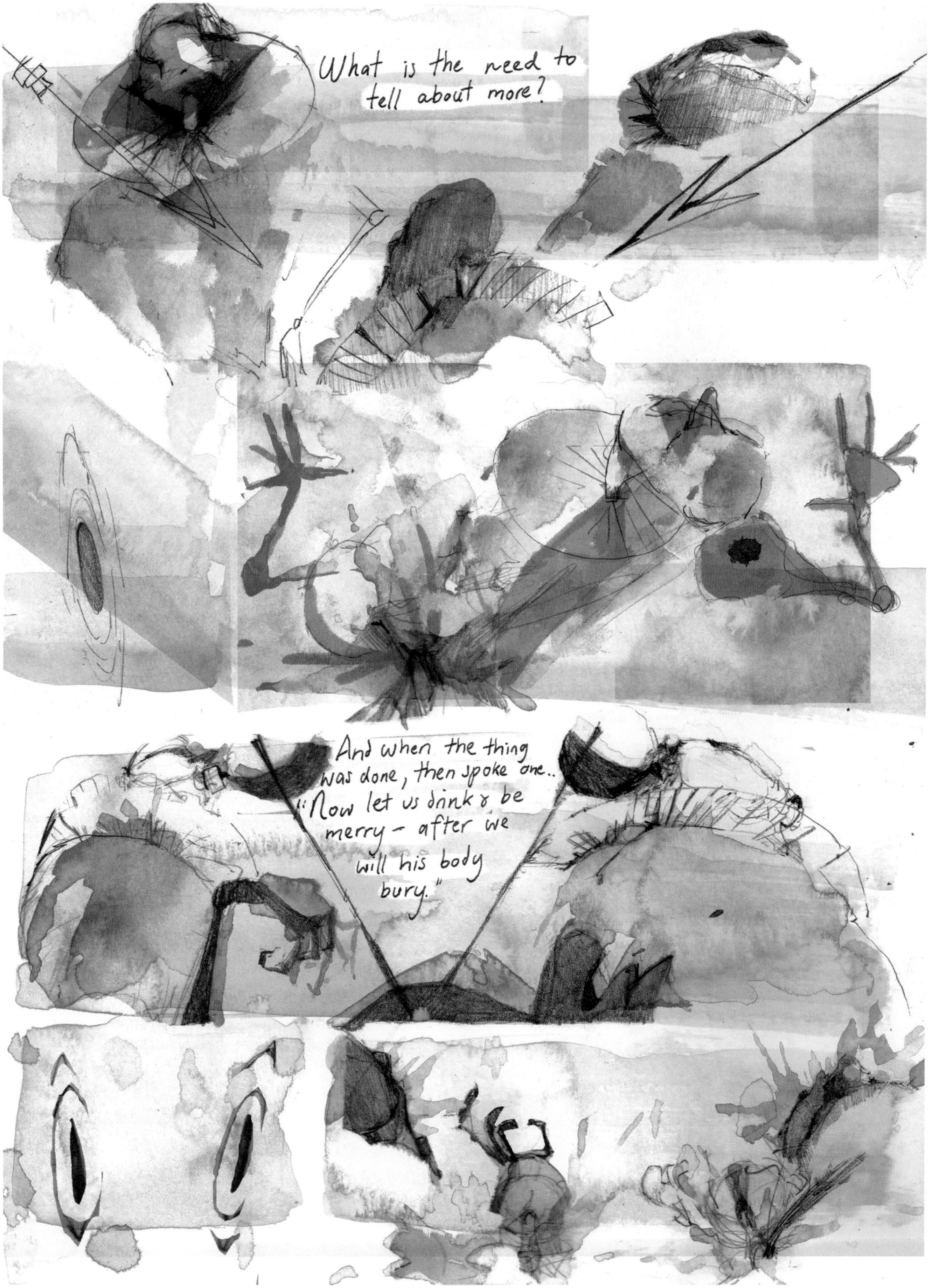
What is the need to tell about more?
And when the thing was done, then spoke one.. "Now let us drink & be merry - after we will his body bury."

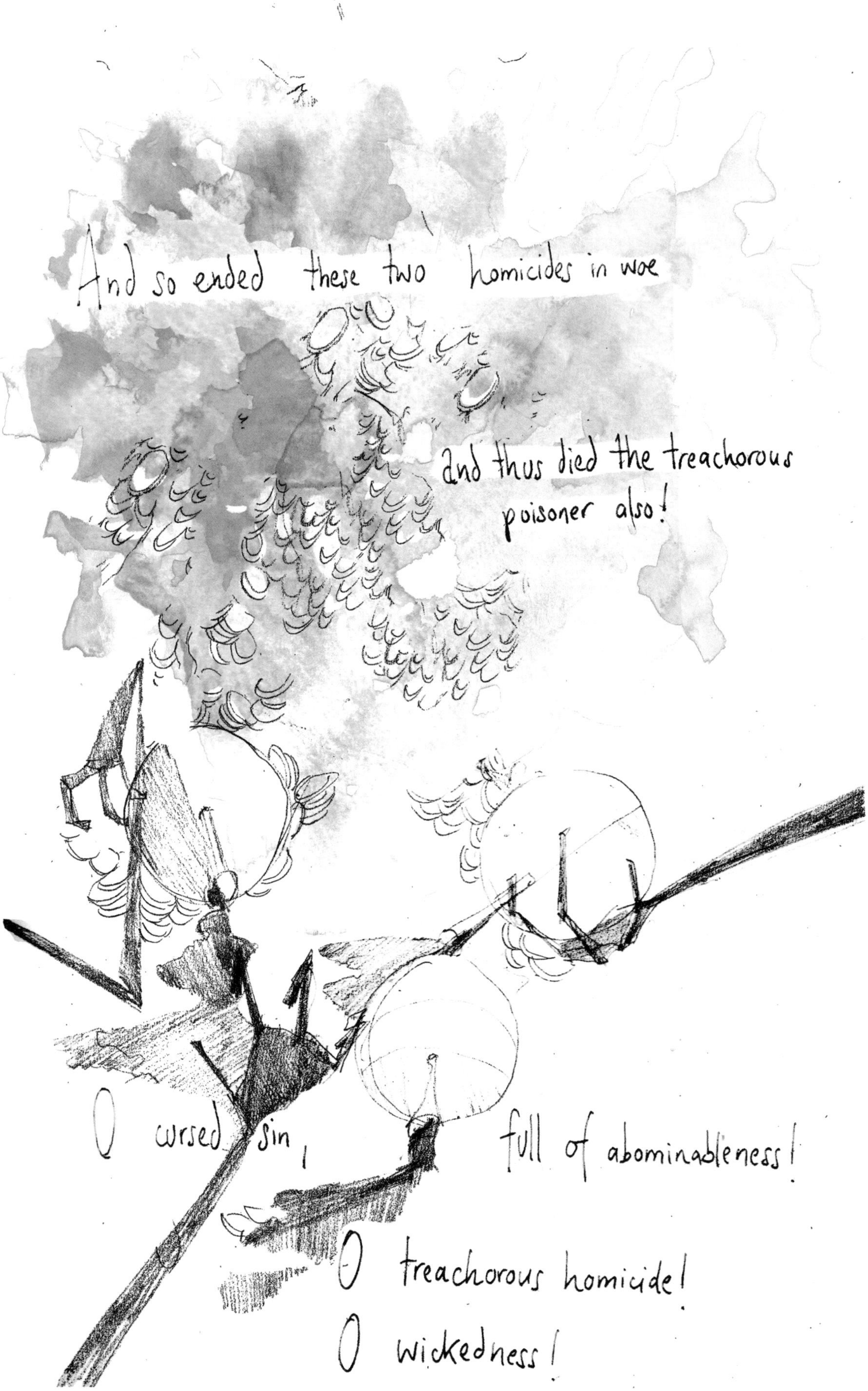
And so ended these two homicides in woe
and thus died the treachorous poisoner also!
O cursed sin, full of abominableness!
O treachorous homicide!
O wickedness!

Titus Andronicus

William Shakespeare

ART/ADAPTATION BY Anthony Ventura

***TITUS ANDRONICUS* IS SHAKESPEARE'S** most gruesome, ultraviolent play. It's wall-to-wall murder, mutilation, rape, human sacrifice, butchery, and . . . well, I don't want to give it all away, in case you're not familiar . . . most of which is depicted on-stage. It's been compared to slasher flicks and Tarantino films.

Titus is the red-headed stepchild of Shakespeare's oeuvre. Though extremely popular with original audiences in the mid-1590s, it's hardly ever performed and is rarely taught in universities outside of graduate programs in literature. Hollywood has adapted it just once. As far as I can tell, unlike many of the Bard's other plays, there is only a single full-length graphic adaptation of *Titus*, self-published by artist Alfie Griffiths.

From day one, I wanted Shakespeare's highest-body-count play to be in *The Graphic Canon of Crime and Mystery*. As a blood-soaked revenge play, this tale of escalating homicides and sexual assault fits the theme perfectly, and it's essentially terra incognita for artists.

Anthony Ventura is the perfect fit. His bold, imposing style emphasizes physicality. These characters are swimming in the corporeality of blood, severed appendages, mincemeat, and brutal loss. Anthony's work has appeared in *Rolling Stone*, *Spin*, *Time*, ESPN, and two *Graphic Canons*.

William Shakespeare's

THE LAMENTABLE TRAGEDY OF

TITUS

Andronicus

adapted and illustrated

by ANTHONY VENTURA.

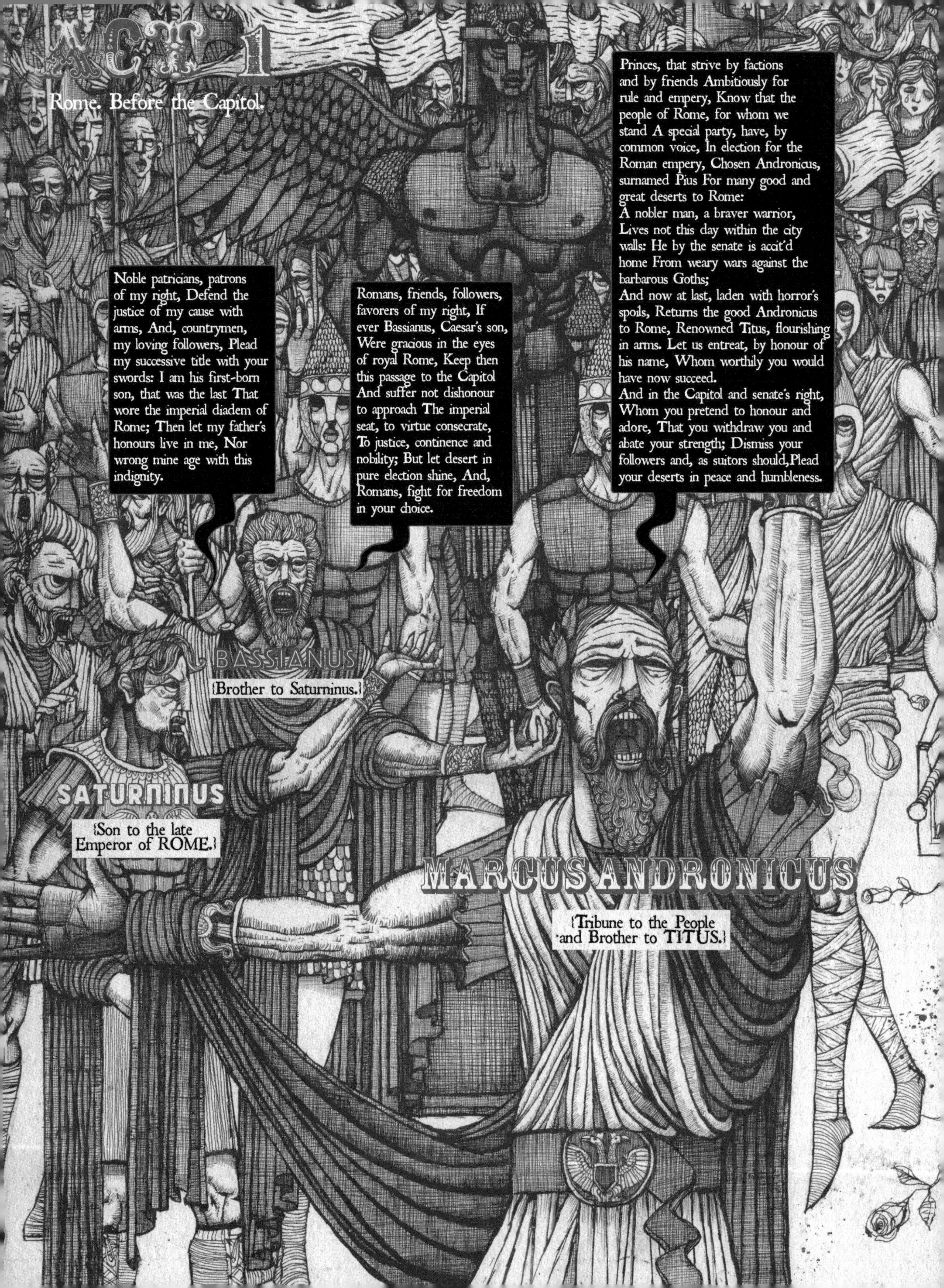
ACT 1
Rome. Before the Capitol.
Noble patricians, patrons of my right, Defend the justice of my cause with arms, And, countrymen, my loving followers, Plead my successive title with your swords: I am his first-born son, that was the last That wore the imperial diadem of Rome; Then let my father's honours live in me, Nor wrong mine age with this indignity.
Romans, friends, followers, favorers of my right, If ever Bassianus, Caesar's son, Were gracious in the eyes of royal Rome, Keep then this passage to the Capitol And suffer not dishonour to approach The imperial seat, to virtue consecrate, To justice, continence and nobility; But let desert in pure election shine, And, Romans, fight for freedom in your choice.
Princes, that strive by factions and by friends Ambitiously for rule and empery, Know that the people of Rome, for whom we stand A special party, have, by common voice, In election for the Roman empery, Chosen Andronicus, surnamed Pius For many good and great deserts to Rome: A nobler man, a braver warrior, Lives not this day within the city walls: He by the senate is accit'd home From weary wars against the barbarous Goths; And now at last, laden with horror's spoils, Returns the good Andronicus to Rome, Renowned Titus, flourishing in arms. Let us entreat, by honour of his name, Whom worthily you would have now succeed. And in the Capitol and senate's right, Whom you pretend to honour and adore, That you withdraw you and abate your strength; Dismiss your followers and, as suitors should,Plead your deserts in peace and humbleness.
BASSIANUS
{Brother to Saturninus.}
SATURNINUS
{Son to the late Emperor of ROME.}
MARCUS ANDRONICUS
{Tribune to the People and Brother to TITUS.}

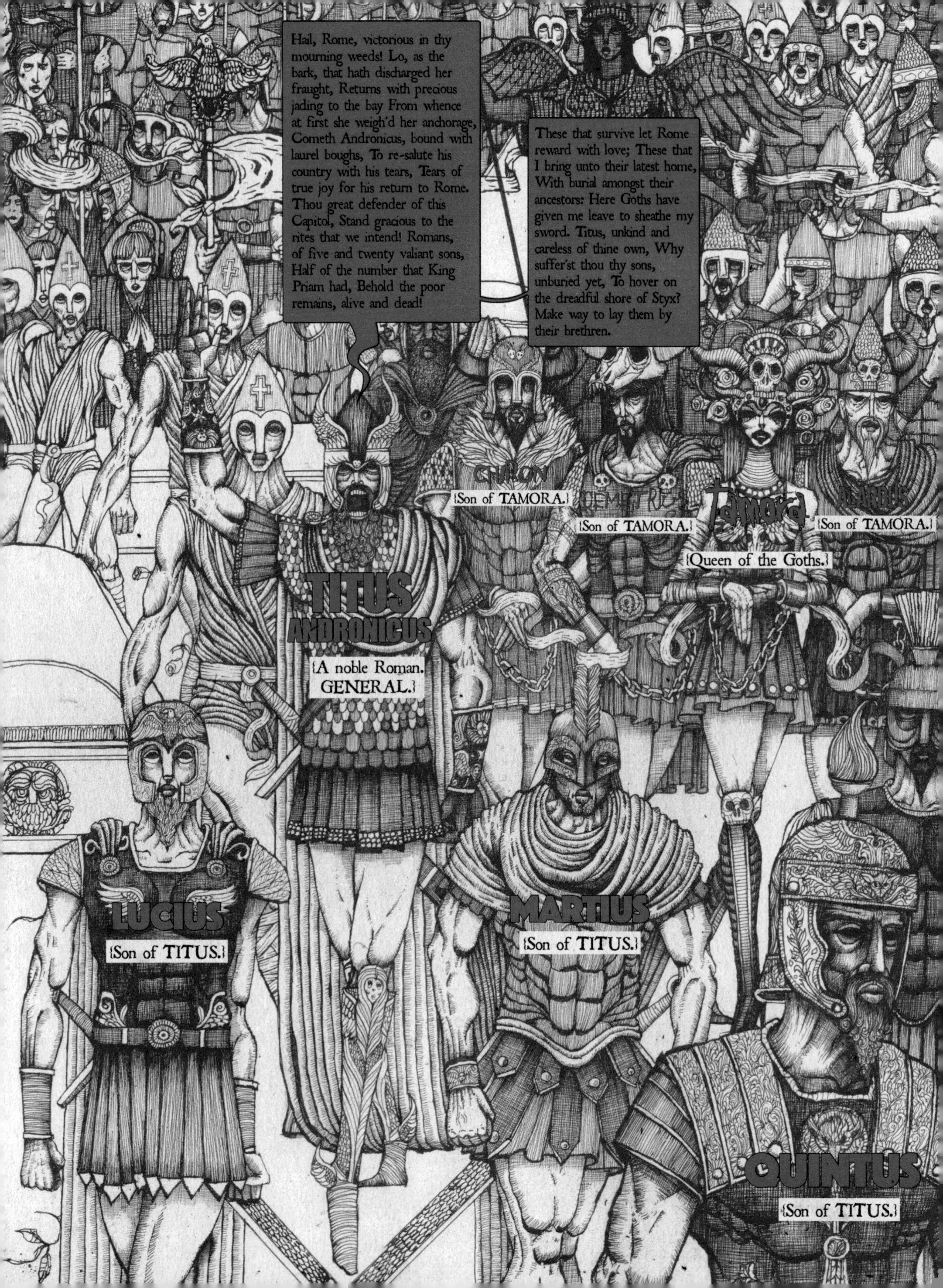

Hail, Rome, victorious in thy mourning weeds! Lo, as the bark, that hath discharged her fraught, Returns with precious jading to the bay From whence at first she weigh'd her anchorage, Cometh Andronicus, bound with laurel boughs, To re-salute his country with his tears, Tears of true joy for his return to Rome. Thou great defender of this Capitol, Stand gracious to the rites that we intend! Romans, of five and twenty valiant sons, Half of the number that King Priam had, Behold the poor remains, alive and dead!
These that survive let Rome reward with love; These that I bring unto their latest home, With burial amongst their ancestors: Here Goths have given me leave to sheathe my sword. Titus, unkind and careless of thine own, Why suffer'st thou thy sons, unburied yet, To hover on the dreadful shore of Styx? Make way to lay them by their brethren.
CHIRON
{Son of TAMORA.}
DEMETRIUS
{Son of TAMORA.}
Tamora
{Queen of the Goths.}
ALARBUS
{Son of TAMORA.}
TITUS ANDRONICUS
{A noble Roman. GENERAL.}
LUCIUS
{Son of TITUS.}
MARTIUS
{Son of TITUS.}
QUINTUS
{Son of TITUS.}

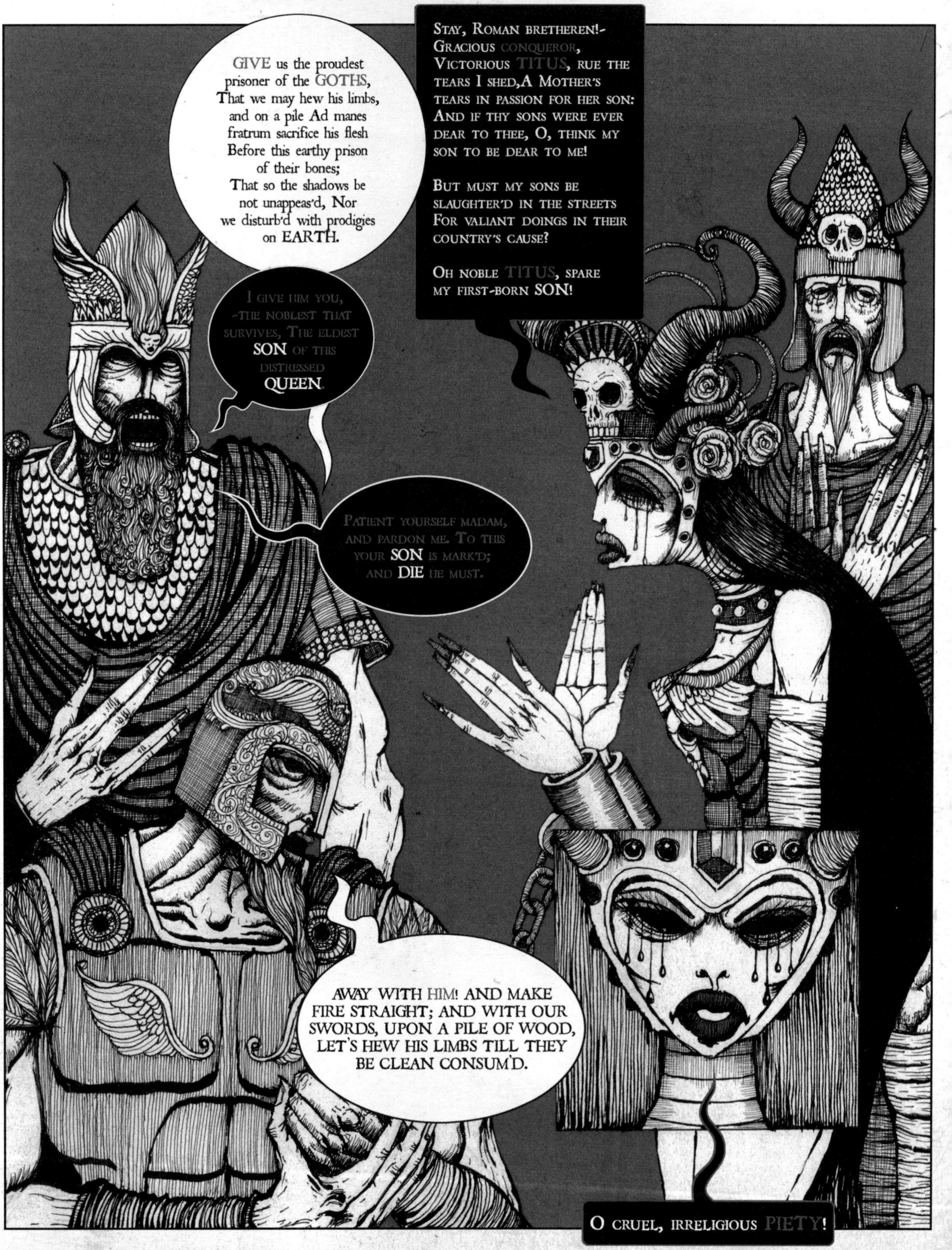
GIVE us the proudest prisoner of the GOTHS, That we may hew his limbs, and on a pile Ad manes fratrum sacrifice his flesh Before this earthy prison of their bones; That so the shadows be not unappeas'd, Nor we disturb'd with prodigies on EARTH.
I GIVE HIM YOU, -THE NOBLEST THAT SURVIVES, THE ELDEST SON OF THIS DISTRESSED QUEEN.
STAY, ROMAN BRETHEREN!- GRACIOUS CONQUEROR, VICTORIOUS TITUS, RUE THE TEARS I SHED,A MOTHER'S TEARS IN PASSION FOR HER SON: AND IF THY SONS WERE EVER DEAR TO THEE, O, THINK MY SON TO BE DEAR TO ME!
BUT MUST MY SONS BE SLAUGHTER'D IN THE STREETS FOR VALIANT DOINGS IN THEIR COUNTRY'S CAUSE?
OH NOBLE TITUS, SPARE MY FIRST-BORN SON!
PATIENT YOURSELF MADAM, AND PARDON ME. TO THIS YOUR SON IS MARK'D; AND DIE HE MUST.
AWAY WITH HIM! AND MAKE FIRE STRAIGHT; AND WITH OUR SWORDS, UPON A PILE OF WOOD, LET'S HEW HIS LIMBS TILL THEY BE CLEAN CONSUM'D.
O CRUEL, IRRELIGIOUS PIETY!

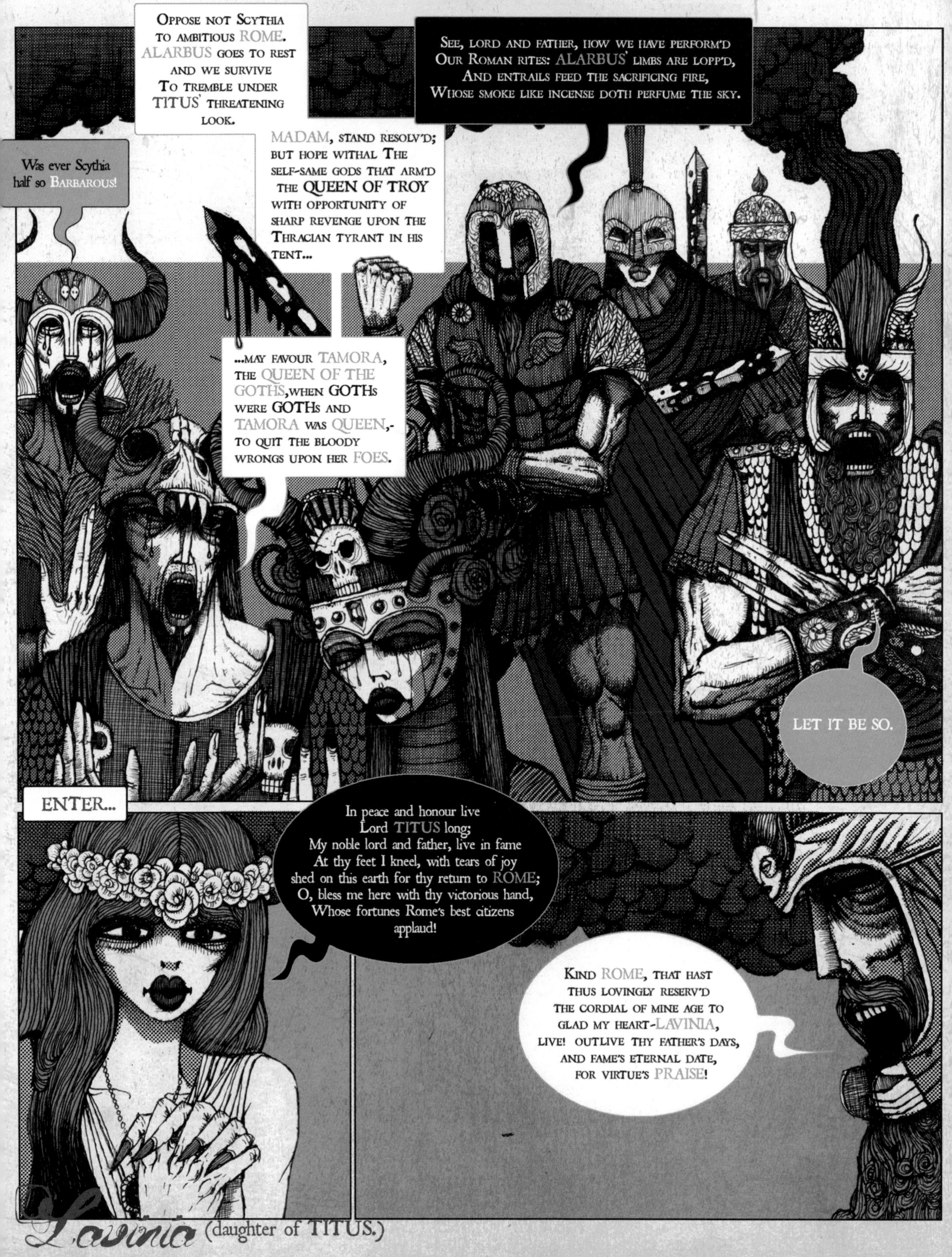
Oppose not Scythia to ambitious ROME. ALARBUS goes to rest and we survive To tremble under TITUS' threatening look.
Was ever Scythia half so Barbarous!
MADAM, stand resolv'd; but hope withal The self-same gods that arm'd the QUEEN OF TROY with opportunity of sharp revenge upon the Thracian tyrant in his tent...
...may favour TAMORA, the QUEEN OF THE GOTHS, when GOTHs were GOTHs and TAMORA was QUEEN,- to quit the bloody wrongs upon her FOES.
See, lord and father, how we have perform'd Our Roman rites: ALARBUS' limbs are lopp'd, And entrails feed the sacrificing fire, Whose smoke like incense doth perfume the sky.
LET IT BE SO.
ENTER...
In peace and honour live Lord TITUS long; My noble lord and father, live in fame At thy feet I kneel, with tears of joy shed on this earth for thy return to ROME; O, bless me here with thy victorious hand, Whose fortunes Rome's best citizens applaud!
Kind ROME, that hast thus lovingly reserv'd the cordial of mine age to glad my heart-LAVINIA, live! outlive thy father's days, and fame's eternal date, for virtue's PRAISE!
Lavinia (daughter of TITUS.)

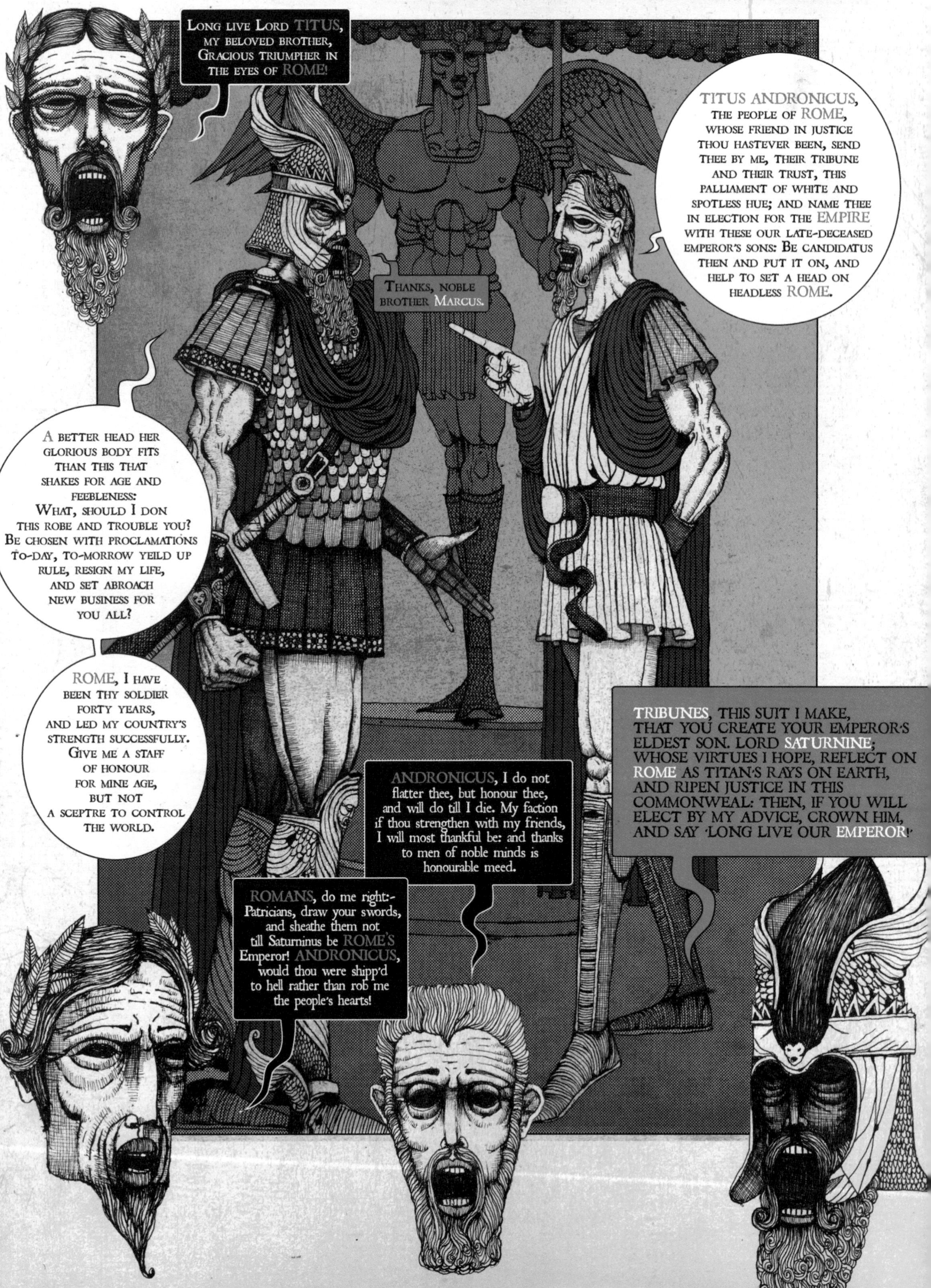

Long live Lord TITUS, my beloved brother, Gracious triumpher in the eyes of ROME!
TITUS ANDRONICUS, the people of ROME, whose friend in justice thou hastever been, send thee by me, their tribune and their trust, this palliament of white and spotless hue; and name thee in election for the EMPIRE with these our late-deceased emperor's sons: Be candidatus then and put it on, and help to set a head on headless ROME.
Thanks, noble brother Marcus.
A better head her glorious body fits than this that shakes for age and feebleness: What, should I don this robe and trouble you? Be chosen with proclamations to-day, to-morrow yeild up rule, resign my life, and set abroach new business for you all?
ROME, I have been thy soldier forty years, and led my country's strength successfully. Give me a staff of honour for mine age, but not a sceptre to control the world.
TRIBUNES, this suit I make, that you create your emperor's eldest son. Lord SATURNINE; whose virtues I hope, reflect on ROME as Titan's rays on earth, and ripen justice in this commonweal: then, if you will elect by my advice, crown him, and say 'Long live our EMPEROR!'
ANDRONICUS, I do not flatter thee, but honour thee, and will do till I die. My faction if thou strengthen with my friends, I will most thankful be: and thanks to men of noble minds is honourable meed.
ROMANS, do me right:- Patricians, draw your swords, and sheathe them not till Saturninus be ROME'S Emperor! ANDRONICUS, would thou were shipp'd to hell rather than rob me the people's hearts!

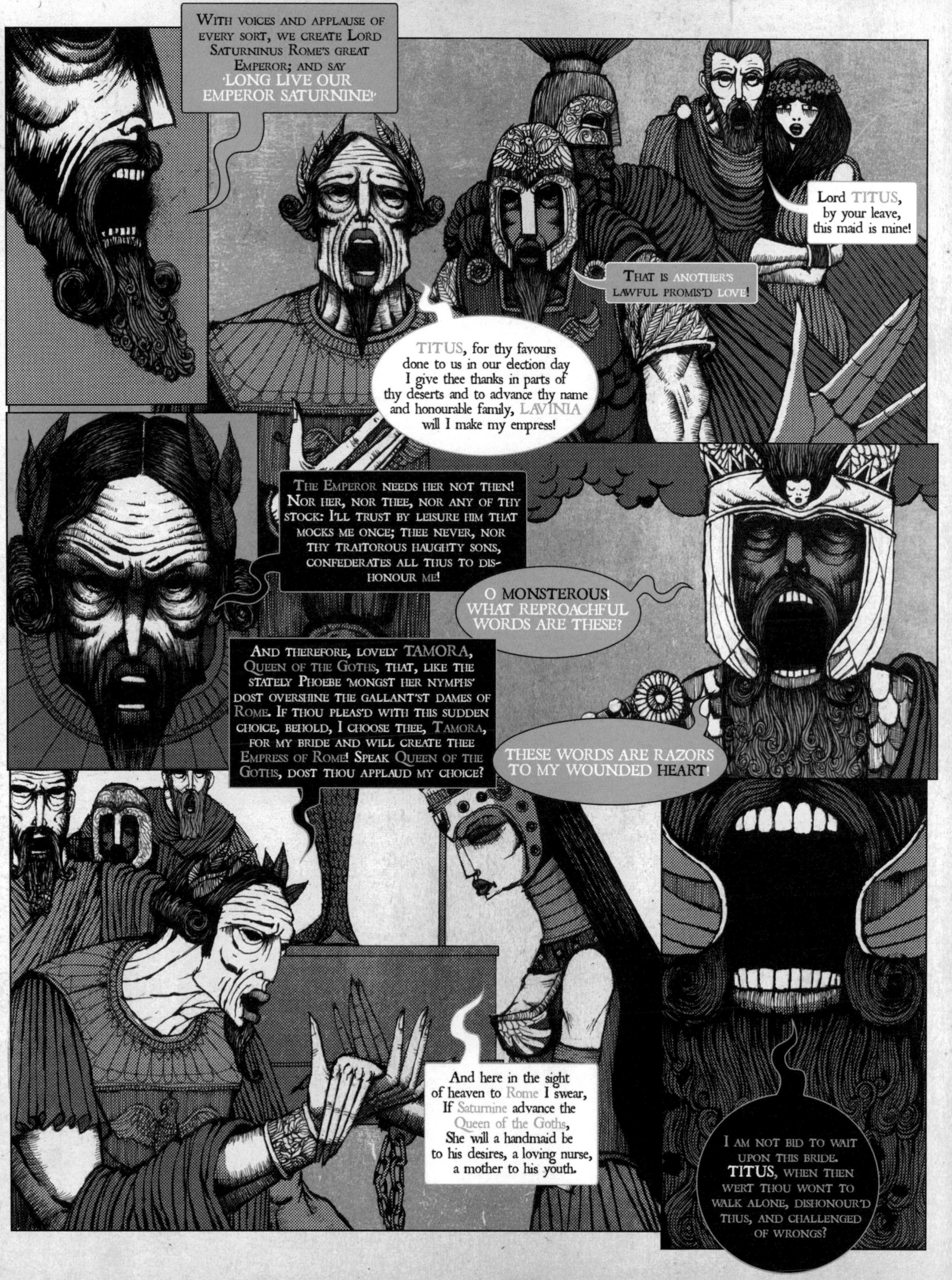
With voices and applause of every sort, we create Lord Saturninus Rome's great Emperor; and say 'LONG LIVE OUR EMPEROR SATURNINE!'
TITUS, for thy favours done to us in our election day I give thee thanks in parts of thy deserts and to advance thy name and honourable family, LAVINIA will I make my empress!
That is another's lawful promis'd love!
Lord TITUS, by your leave, this maid is mine!
The Emperor needs her not then! Nor her, nor thee, nor any of thy stock: I'll trust by leisure him that mocks me once; thee never, nor thy traitorous haughty sons, confederates all thus to dishonour me!
O MONSTEROUS! WHAT REPROACHFUL WORDS ARE THESE?
And therefore, lovely TAMORA, Queen of the Goths, that, like the stately Phoebe 'mongst her nymphs' dost overshine the gallant'st dames of Rome. If thou pleas'd with this sudden choice, behold, I choose thee, Tamora, for my bride and will create thee Empress of Rome! Speak Queen of the Goths, dost thou applaud my choice?
THESE WORDS ARE RAZORS TO MY WOUNDED HEART!
And here in the sight of heaven to Rome I swear, If Saturnine advance the Queen of the Goths, She will a handmaid be to his desires, a loving nurse, a mother to his youth.
I am not bid to wait upon this bride. TITUS, when then wert thou wont to walk alone, dishonour'd thus, and challenged of wrongs?

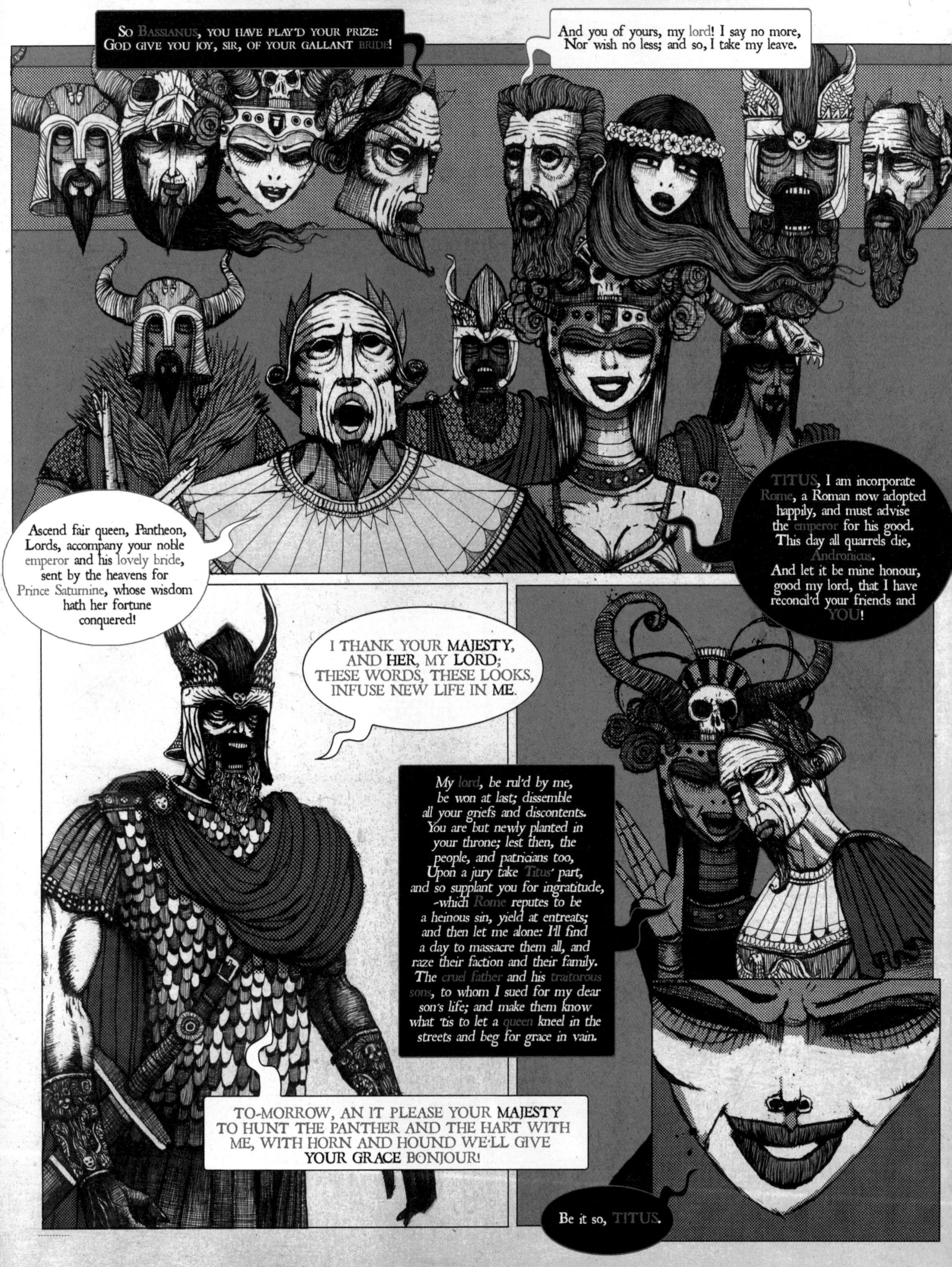
So Bassianus, you have play'd your prize: God give you joy, sir, of your gallant bride!
And you of yours, my lord! I say no more, Nor wish no less; and so, I take my leave.
Ascend fair queen, Pantheon, Lords, accompany your noble emperor and his lovely bride, sent by the heavens for Prince Saturnine, whose wisdom hath her fortune conquered!
TITUS, I am incorporate Rome, a Roman now adopted happily, and must advise the emperor for his good. This day all quarrels die, Andronicus. And let it be mine honour, good my lord, that I have reconcil'd your friends and YOU!
I THANK YOUR MAJESTY, AND HER, MY LORD; THESE WORDS, THESE LOOKS, INFUSE NEW LIFE IN ME.
My lord, be rul'd by me, be won at last; dissemble all your griefs and discontents. You are but newly planted in your throne; lest then, the people, and patricians too, Upon a jury take Titus' part, and so supplant you for ingratitude, -which Rome reputes to be a heinous sin, yield at entreats; and then let me alone: I'll find a day to massacre them all, and raze their faction and their family. The cruel father and his traitorous sons, to whom I sued for my dear son's life; and make them know what 'tis to let a queen kneel in the streets and beg for grace in vain.
TO-MORROW, AN IT PLEASE YOUR MAJESTY TO HUNT THE PANTHER AND THE HART WITH ME, WITH HORN AND HOUND WE'LL GIVE YOUR GRACE BONJOUR!
Be it so, TITUS.

ACT 2

A Forest near Rome.

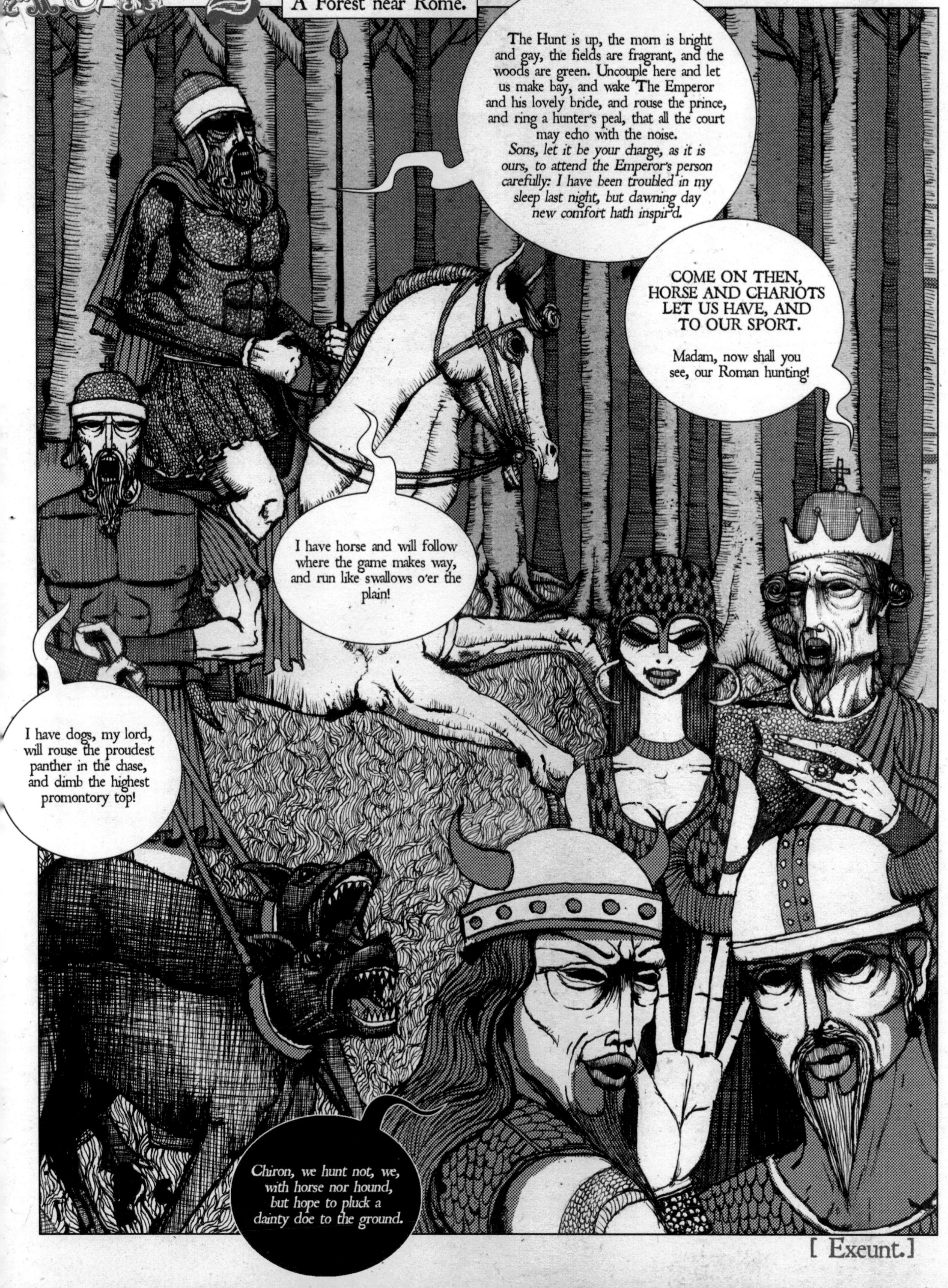
The Hunt is up, the morn is bright and gay, the fields are fragrant, and the woods are green. Uncouple here and let us make bay, and wake The Emperor and his lovely bride, and rouse the prince, and ring a hunter's peal, that all the court may echo with the noise.
Sons, let it be your charge, as it is ours, to attend the Emperor's person carefully: I have been troubled in my sleep last night, but dawning day new comfort hath inspir'd.
COME ON THEN, HORSE AND CHARIOTS LET US HAVE, AND TO OUR SPORT.
Madam, now shall you see, our Roman hunting!
I have horse and will follow where the game makes way, and run like swallows o'er the plain!
I have dogs, my lord, will rouse the proudest panther in the chase, and climb the highest promontory top!
Chiron, we hunt not, we, with horse nor hound, but hope to pluck a dainty doe to the ground.

[Exeunt.]

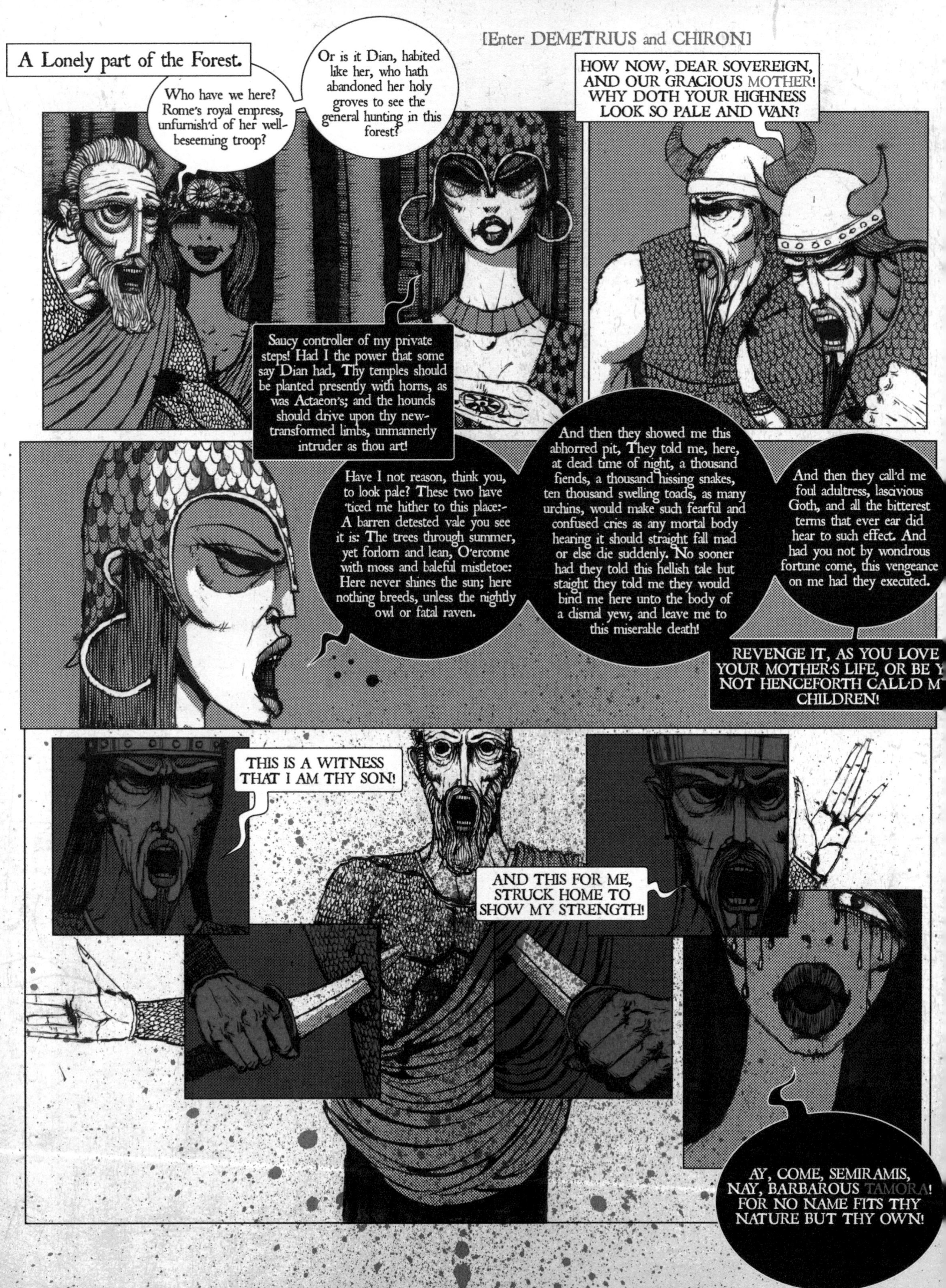

[Enter DEMETRIUS and CHIRON]
A Lonely part of the Forest.
Who have we here? Rome's royal empress, unfurnish'd of her well-beseeming troop?
Or is it Dian, habited like her, who hath abandoned her holy groves to see the general hunting in this forest?
Saucy controller of my private steps! Had I the power that some say Dian had, Thy temples should be planted presently with horns, as was Actaeon's; and the hounds should drive upon thy new-transformed limbs, unmannerly intruder as thou art!
HOW NOW, DEAR SOVEREIGN, AND OUR GRACIOUS MOTHER! WHY DOTH YOUR HIGHNESS LOOK SO PALE AND WAN?
Have I not reason, think you, to look pale? These two have 'ticed me hither to this place:- A barren detested vale you see it is: The trees through summer, yet forlorn and lean, O'ercome with moss and baleful mistletoe: Here never shines the sun; here nothing breeds, unless the nightly owl or fatal raven.
And then they showed me this abhorred pit, They told me, here, at dead time of night, a thousand fiends, a thousand hissing snakes, ten thousand swelling toads, as many urchins, would make such fearful and confused cries as any mortal body hearing it should straight fall mad or else die suddenly. No sooner had they told this hellish tale but staight they told me they would bind me here unto the body of a dismal yew, and leave me to this miserable death!
And then they call'd me foul adultress, lascivious Goth, and all the bitterest terms that ever ear did hear to such effect. And had you not by wondrous fortune come, this vengeance on me had they executed.
REVENGE IT, AS YOU LOVE YOUR MOTHER'S LIFE, OR BE Y NOT HENCEFORTH CALL'D M CHILDREN!
THIS IS A WITNESS THAT I AM THY SON!
AND THIS FOR ME, STRUCK HOME TO SHOW MY STRENGTH!
AY, COME, SEMIRAMIS, NAY, BARBAROUS TAMORA! FOR NO NAME FITS THY NATURE BUT THY OWN!

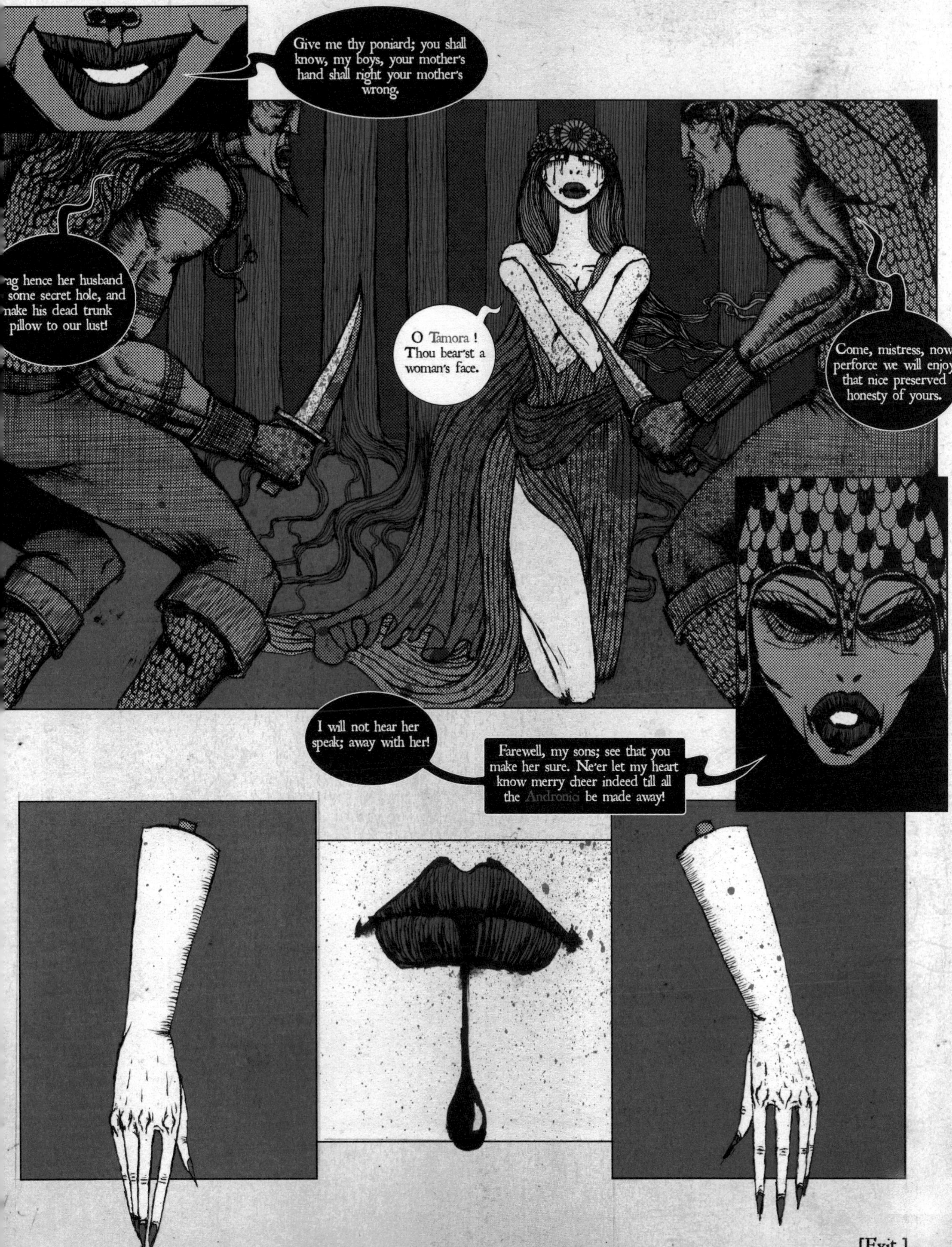
Give me thy poniard; you shall know, my boys, your mother's hand shall right your mother's wrong.
ag hence her husband some secret hole, and nake his dead trunk pillow to our lust!
O Tamora ! Thou bear'st a woman's face.
Come, mistress, now perforce we will enjoy that nice preserved honesty of yours.
I will not hear her speak; away with her!
Farewell, my sons; see that you make her sure. Ne'er let my heart know merry cheer indeed till all the Andronici be made away!

[Exit.]

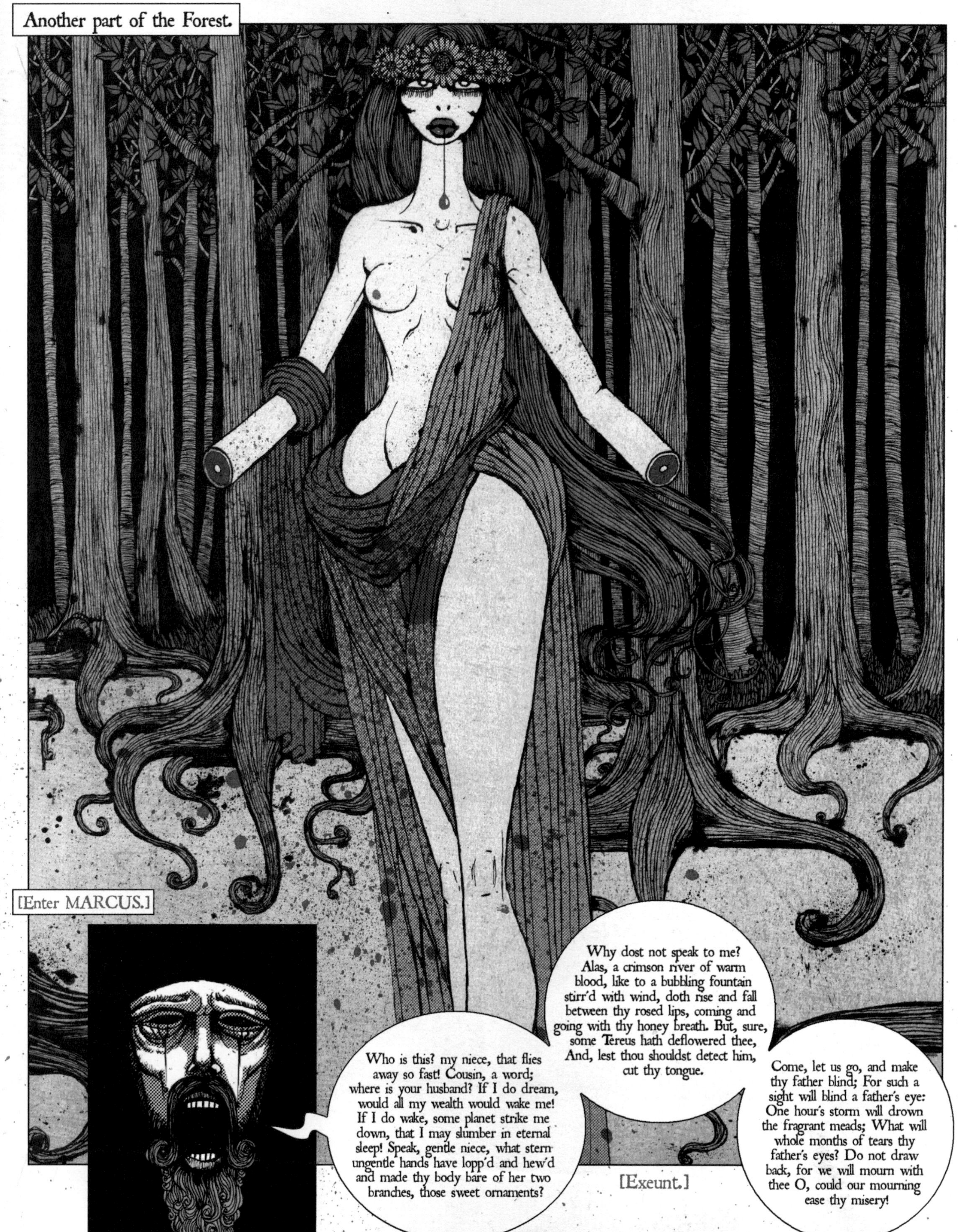
Another part of the Forest.
[Enter MARCUS.]
Who is this? my niece, that flies away so fast! Cousin, a word; where is your husband? If I do dream, would all my wealth would wake me! If I do wake, some planet strike me down, that I may slumber in eternal sleep! Speak, gentle niece, what stern ungentle hands have lopp'd and hew'd and made thy body bare of her two branches, those sweet ornaments?
Why dost not speak to me? Alas, a crimson river of warm blood, like to a bubbling fountain stirr'd with wind, doth rise and fall between thy rosed lips, coming and going with thy honey breath. But, sure, some Tereus hath deflowered thee, And, lest thou shouldst detect him, cut thy tongue.
Come, let us go, and make thy father blind; For such a sight will blind a father's eye: One hour's storm will drown the fragrant meads; What will whole months of tears thy father's eyes? Do not draw back, for we will mourn with thee O, could our mourning ease thy misery!
[Exeunt.]

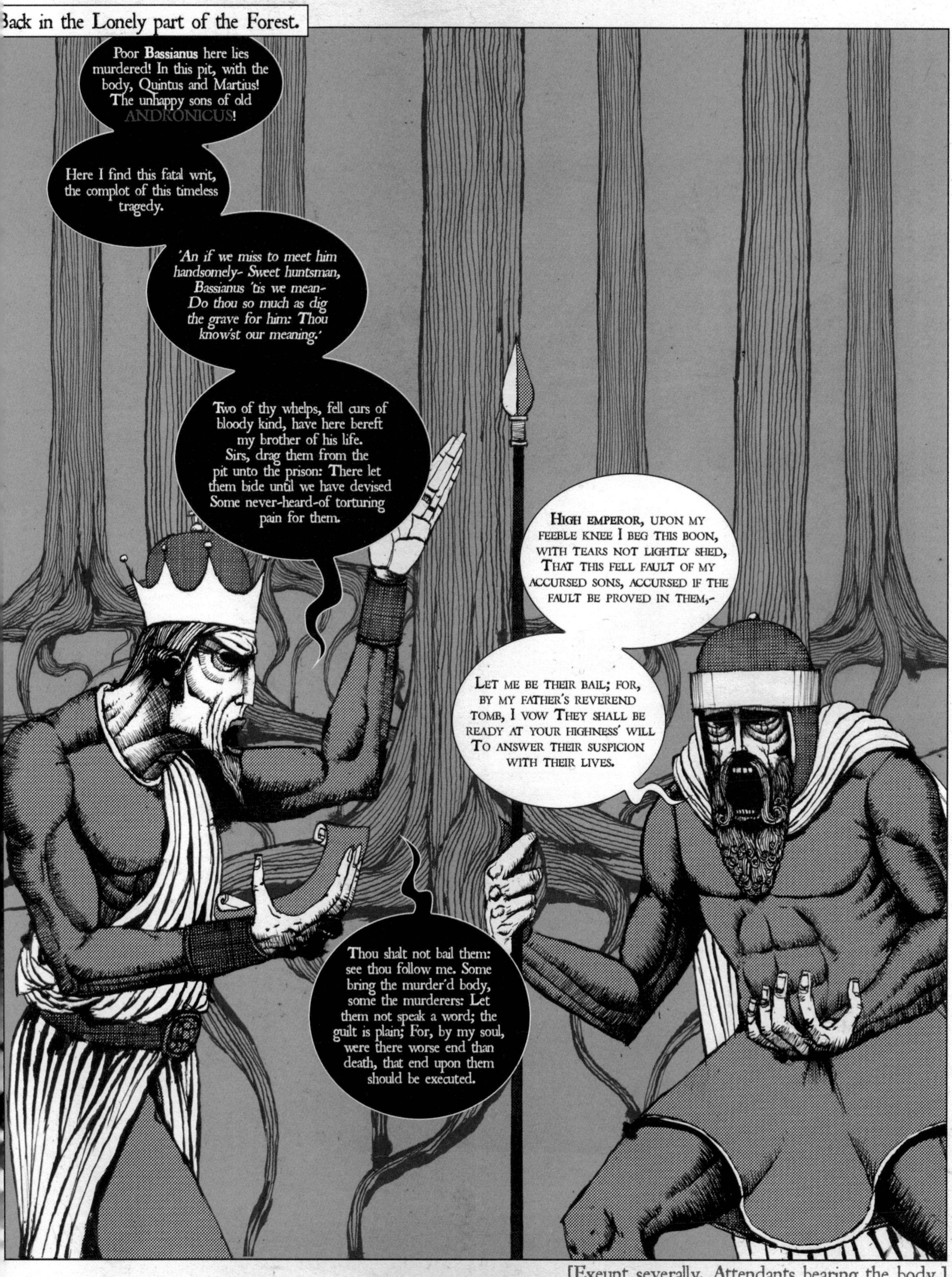
Back in the Lonely part of the Forest.
Poor Bassianus here lies murdered! In this pit, with the body, Quintus and Martius! The unhappy sons of old ANDRONICUS!
Here I find this fatal writ, the complot of this timeless tragedy.
'An if we miss to meet him handsomely- Sweet huntsman, Bassianus 'tis we mean- Do thou so much as dig the grave for him: Thou know'st our meaning.'
Two of thy whelps, fell curs of bloody kind, have here bereft my brother of his life. Sirs, drag them from the pit unto the prison: There let them bide until we have devised Some never-heard-of torturing pain for them.
HIGH EMPEROR, UPON MY FEEBLE KNEE I BEG THIS BOON, WITH TEARS NOT LIGHTLY SHED, THAT THIS FELL FAULT OF MY ACCURSED SONS, ACCURSED IF THE FAULT BE PROVED IN THEM,-
LET ME BE THEIR BAIL; FOR, BY MY FATHER'S REVEREND TOMB, I VOW THEY SHALL BE READY AT YOUR HIGHNESS' WILL TO ANSWER THEIR SUSPICION WITH THEIR LIVES.
Thou shalt not bail them: see thou follow me. Some bring the murder'd body, some the murderers: Let them not speak a word; the guilt is plain; For, by my soul, were there worse end than death, that end upon them should be executed.

[Exeunt severally. Attendants bearing the body.]

ACT 3

Rome. A Street.

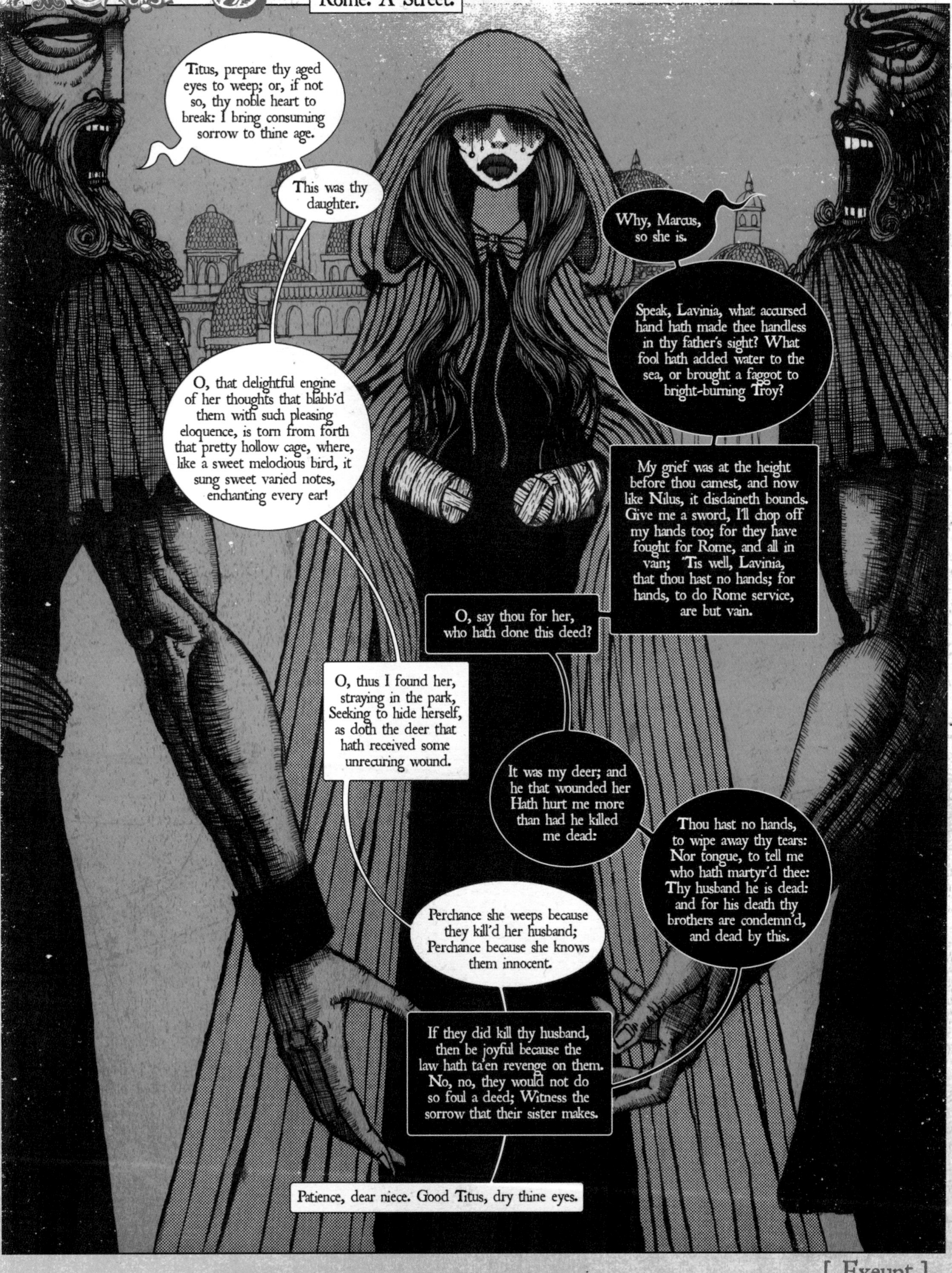
Titus, prepare thy aged eyes to weep; or, if not so, thy noble heart to break: I bring consuming sorrow to thine age.
This was thy daughter.
Why, Marcus, so she is.
Speak, Lavinia, what accursed hand hath made thee handless in thy father's sight? What fool hath added water to the sea, or brought a faggot to bright-burning Troy?
O, that delightful engine of her thoughts that blabb'd them with such pleasing eloquence, is torn from forth that pretty hollow cage, where, like a sweet melodious bird, it sung sweet varied notes, enchanting every ear!
My grief was at the height before thou camest, and now like Nilus, it disdaineth bounds. Give me a sword, I'll chop off my hands too; for they have fought for Rome, and all in vain; 'Tis well, Lavinia, that thou hast no hands; for hands, to do Rome service, are but vain.
O, say thou for her, who hath done this deed?
O, thus I found her, straying in the park, Seeking to hide herself, as doth the deer that hath received some unrecuring wound.
It was my deer; and he that wounded her Hath hurt me more than had he killed me dead:
Thou hast no hands, to wipe away thy tears: Nor tongue, to tell me who hath martyr'd thee: Thy husband he is dead: and for his death thy brothers are condemn'd, and dead by this.
Perchance she weeps because they kill'd her husband; Perchance because she knows them innocent.
If they did kill thy husband, then be joyful because the law hath ta'en revenge on them. No, no, they would not do so foul a deed; Witness the sorrow that their sister makes.
Patience, dear niece. Good Titus, dry thine eyes.

[Exeunt.]

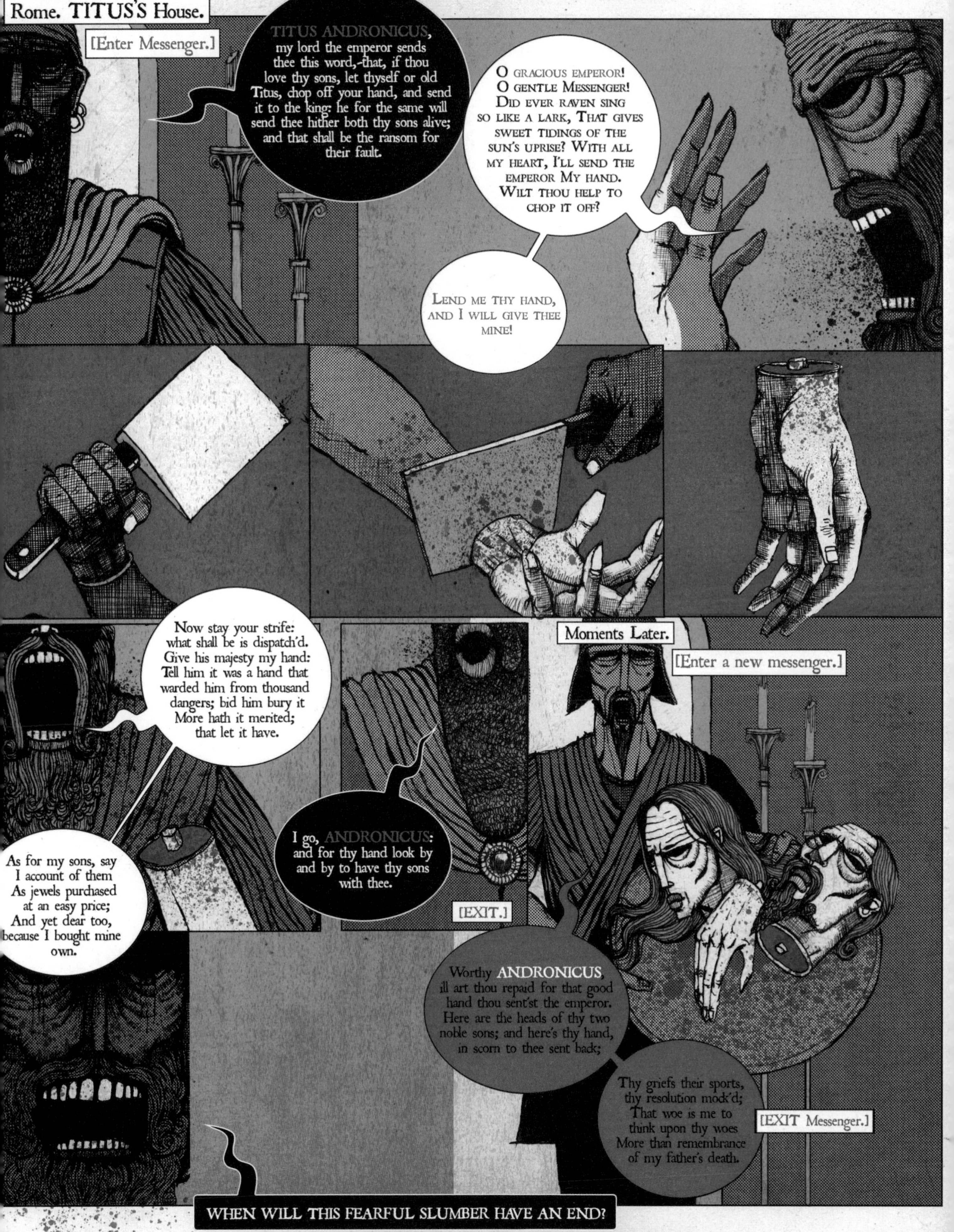

Rome. TITUS'S House.
[Enter Messenger.]
TITUS ANDRONICUS, my lord the emperor sends thee this word,-that, if thou love thy sons, let thyself or old Titus, chop off your hand, and send it to the king: he for the same will send thee hither both thy sons alive; and that shall be the ransom for their fault.
O gracious emperor! O gentle Messenger! Did ever raven sing so like a lark, That gives sweet tidings of the sun's uprise? With all my heart, I'll send the emperor My hand. Wilt thou help to chop it off?
Lend me thy hand, and I will give thee mine!
Now stay your strife: what shall be is dispatch'd. Give his majesty my hand: Tell him it was a hand that warded him from thousand dangers; bid him bury it More hath it merited; that let it have.
As for my sons, say I account of them As jewels purchased at an easy price; And yet dear too, because I bought mine own.
I go, ANDRONICUS: and for thy hand look by and by to have thy sons with thee.
[EXIT.]
Moments Later.
[Enter a new messenger.]
Worthy ANDRONICUS, ill art thou repaid for that good hand thou sent'st the emperor. Here are the heads of thy two noble sons; and here's thy hand, in scorn to thee sent back;
Thy griefs their sports, thy resolution mock'd; That woe is me to think upon thy woes More than remembrance of my father's death.
[EXIT Messenger.]
WHEN WILL THIS FEARFUL SLUMBER HAVE AN END?

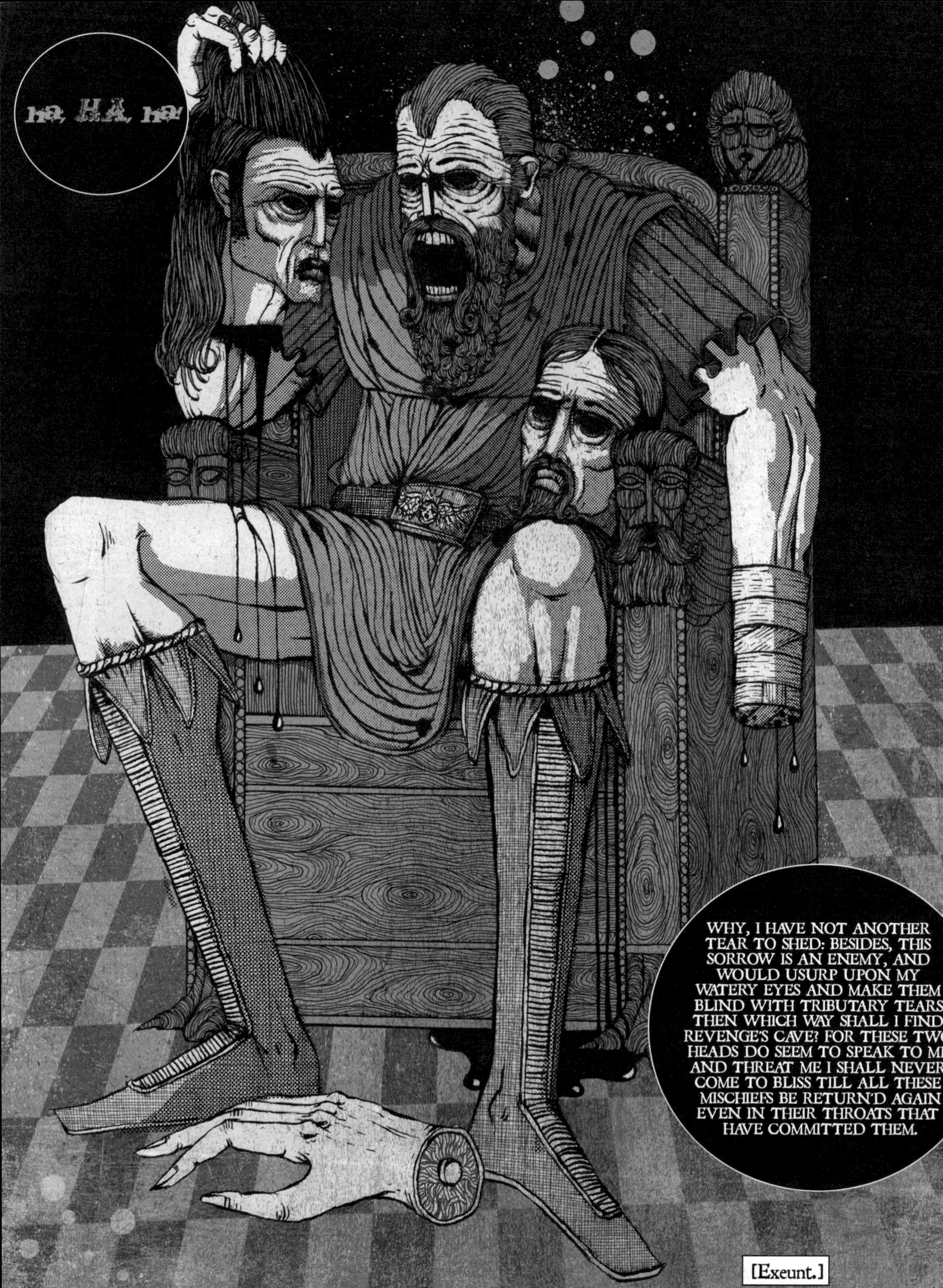
ha, HA, ha!
WHY, I HAVE NOT ANOTHER TEAR TO SHED: BESIDES, THIS SORROW IS AN ENEMY, AND WOULD USURP UPON MY WATERY EYES AND MAKE THEM BLIND WITH TRIBUTARY TEARS. THEN WHICH WAY SHALL I FIND REVENGE'S CAVE? FOR THESE TWO HEADS DO SEEM TO SPEAK TO ME AND THREAT ME I SHALL NEVER COME TO BLISS TILL ALL THESE MISCHIEFS BE RETURN'D AGAIN EVEN IN THEIR THROATS THAT HAVE COMMITTED THEM.
[Exeunt.]

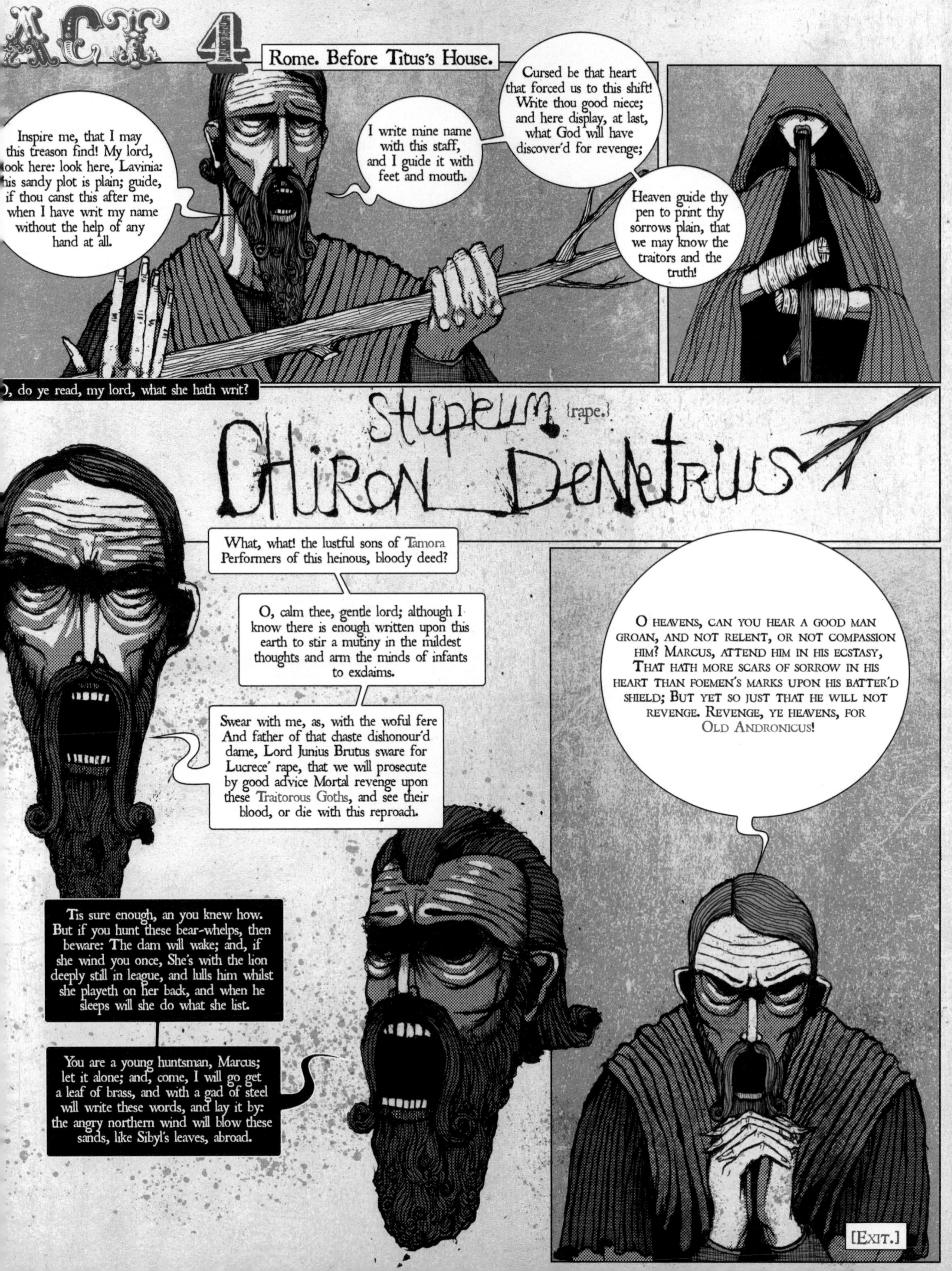
ACT 4
Rome. Before Titus's House.
Inspire me, that I may this treason find! My lord, ook here: look here, Lavinia: his sandy plot is plain; guide, if thou canst this after me, when I have writ my name without the help of any hand at all.
I write mine name with this staff, and I guide it with feet and mouth.
Cursed be that heart that forced us to this shift! Write thou good niece; and here display, at last, what God will have discover'd for revenge;
Heaven guide thy pen to print thy sorrows plain, that we may know the traitors and the truth!
), do ye read, my lord, what she hath writ?
Stuprum {rape.}
CHIRON DEMETRIUS
What, what! the lustful sons of Tamora Performers of this heinous, bloody deed?
O, calm thee, gentle lord; although I know there is enough written upon this earth to stir a mutiny in the mildest thoughts and arm the minds of infants to exclaims.
Swear with me, as, with the woful fere And father of that chaste dishonour'd dame, Lord Junius Brutus sware for Lucrece' rape, that we will prosecute by good advice Mortal revenge upon these Traitorous Goths, and see their blood, or die with this reproach.
O HEAVENS, CAN YOU HEAR A GOOD MAN GROAN, AND NOT RELENT, OR NOT COMPASSION HIM? MARCUS, ATTEND HIM IN HIS ECSTASY, THAT HATH MORE SCARS OF SORROW IN HIS HEART THAN FOEMEN'S MARKS UPON HIS BATTER'D SHIELD; BUT YET SO JUST THAT HE WILL NOT REVENGE. REVENGE, YE HEAVENS, FOR OLD ANDRONICUS!
Tis sure enough, an you knew how. But if you hunt these bear-whelps, then beware: The dam will wake; and, if she wind you once, She's with the lion deeply still in league, and lulls him whilst she playeth on her back, and when he sleeps will she do what she list.
You are a young huntsman, Marcus; let it alone; and, come, I will go get a leaf of brass, and with a gad of steel will write these words, and lay it by: the angry northern wind will blow these sands, like Sibyl's leaves, abroad.
[EXIT.]

ACT 5

Rome. Before TITUS'S House.

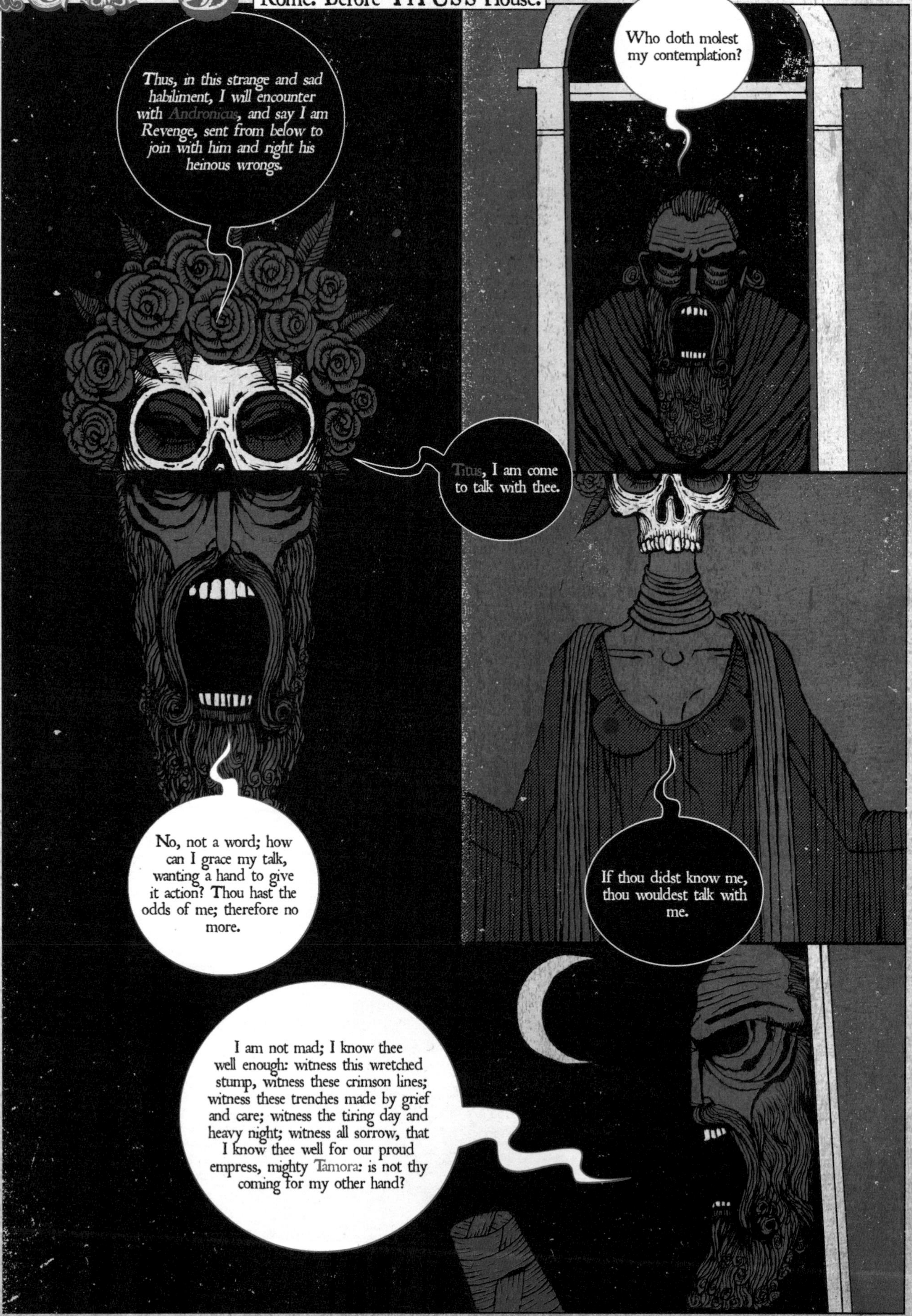
Thus, in this strange and sad habiliment, I will encounter with Andronicus, and say I am Revenge, sent from below to join with him and right his heinous wrongs.
Who doth molest my contemplation?
Titus, I am come to talk with thee.
No, not a word; how can I grace my talk, wanting a hand to give it action? Thou hast the odds of me; therefore no more.
If thou didst know me, thou wouldest talk with me.
I am not mad; I know thee well enough: witness this wretched stump, witness these crimson lines; witness these trenches made by grief and care; witness the tiring day and heavy night; witness all sorrow, that I know thee well for our proud empress, mighty Tamora: is not thy coming for my other hand?

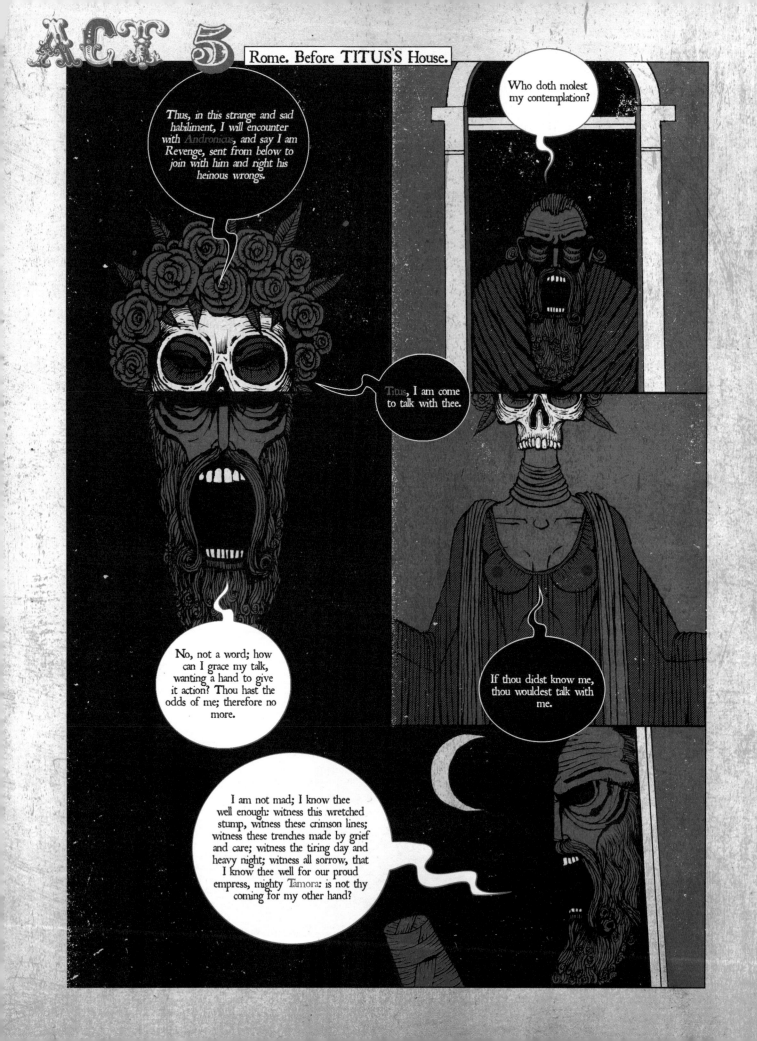

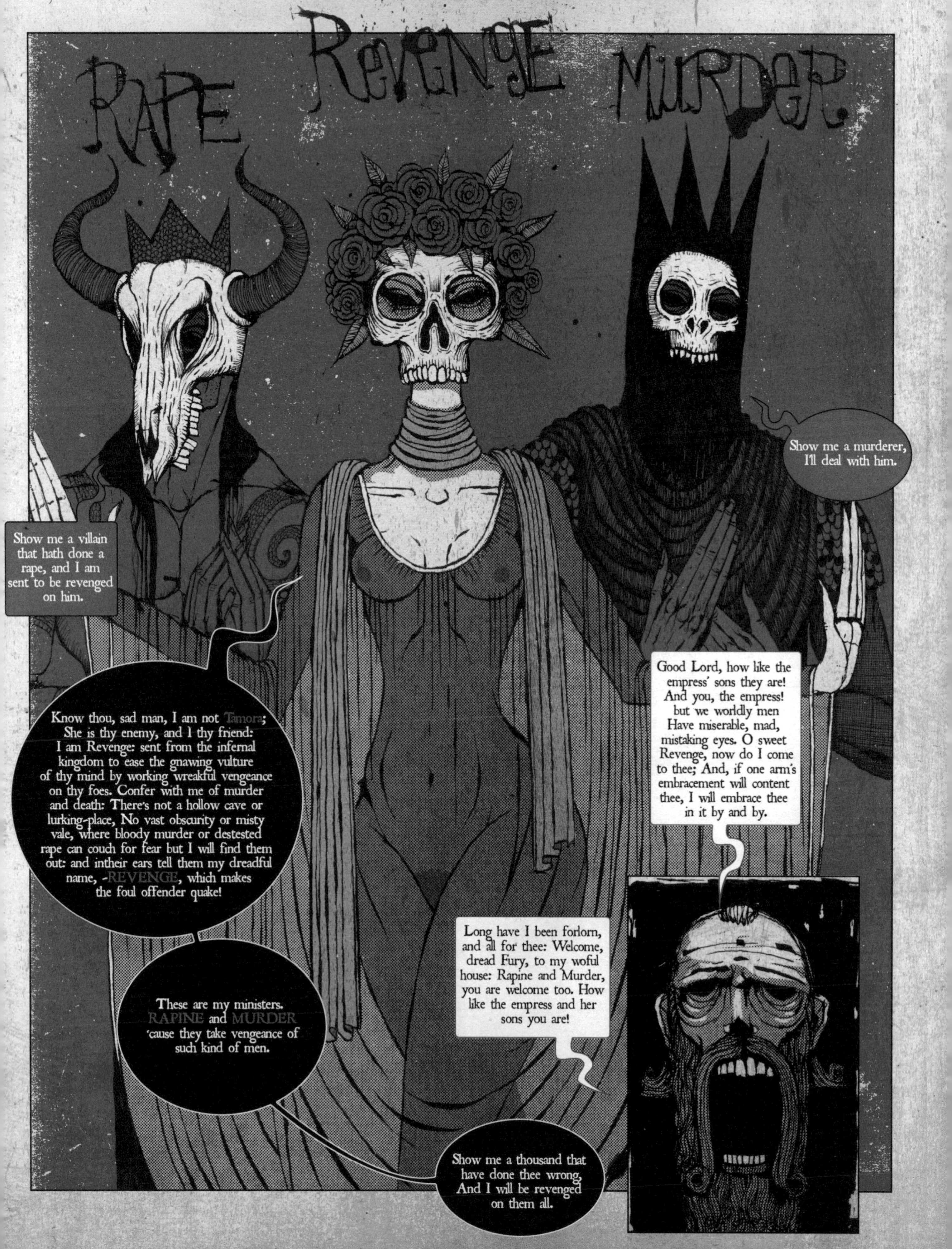
RAPE
REVENGE
MURDER
Show me a murderer, I'll deal with him.
Show me a villain that hath done a rape, and I am sent to be revenged on him.
Know thou, sad man, I am not Tamora; She is thy enemy, and I thy friend: I am Revenge: sent from the infernal kingdom to ease the gnawing vulture of thy mind by working wreakful vengeance on thy foes. Confer with me of murder and death: There's not a hollow cave or lurking-place, No vast obscurity or misty vale, where bloody murder or destested rape can couch for fear but I will find them out: and intheir ears tell them my dreadful name, -REVENGE, which makes the foul offender quake!
These are my ministers. RAPINE and MURDER 'cause they take vengeance of such kind of men.
Show me a thousand that have done thee wrong, And I will be revenged on them all.
Good Lord, how like the empress' sons they are! And you, the empress! but we worldly men Have miserable, mad, mistaking eyes. O sweet Revenge, now do I come to thee; And, if one arm's embracement will content thee, I will embrace thee in it by and by.
Long have I been forlorn, and all for thee: Welcome, dread Fury, to my woful house: Rapine and Murder, you are welcome too. How like the empress and her sons you are!

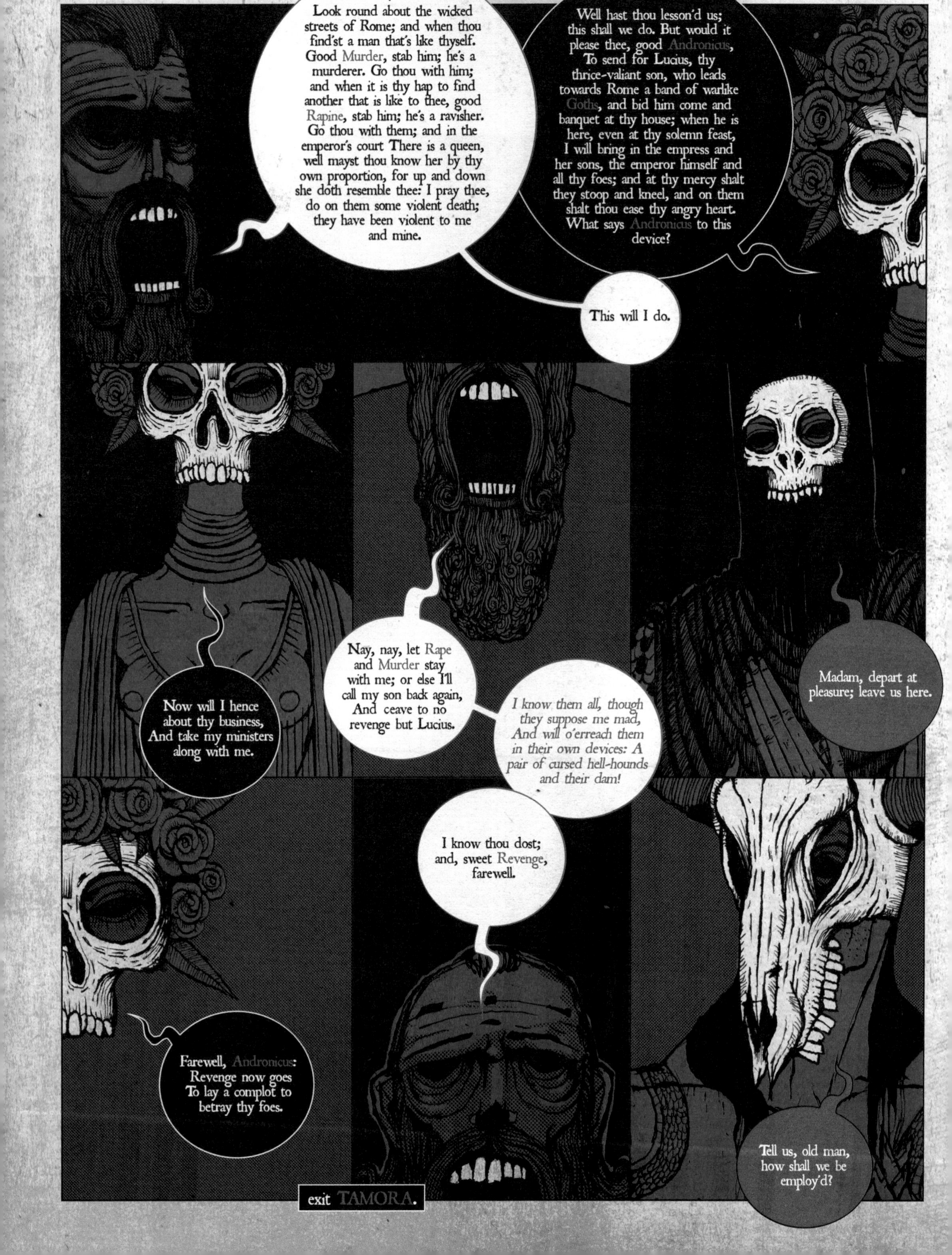

Look round about the wicked streets of Rome; and when thou find'st a man that's like thyself. Good Murder, stab him; he's a murderer. Go thou with him; and when it is thy hap to find another that is like to thee, good Rapine, stab him; he's a ravisher. Go thou with them; and in the emperor's court There is a queen, well mayst thou know her by thy own proportion, for up and down she doth resemble thee: I pray thee, do on them some violent death; they have been violent to me and mine.
Well hast thou lesson'd us; this shall we do. But would it please thee, good Andronicus, To send for Lucius, thy thrice-valiant son, who leads towards Rome a band of warlike Goths, and bid him come and banquet at thy house; when he is here, even at thy solemn feast, I will bring in the empress and her sons, the emperor himself and all thy foes; and at thy mercy shalt they stoop and kneel, and on them shalt thou ease thy angry heart. What says Andronicus to this device?
This will I do.
Now will I hence about thy business, And take my ministers along with me.
Nay, nay, let Rape and Murder stay with me; or else I'll call my son back again, And ceave to no revenge but Lucius.
I know them all, though they suppose me mad, And will o'erreach them in their own devices: A pair of cursed hell-hounds and their dam!
Madam, depart at pleasure; leave us here.
I know thou dost; and, sweet Revenge, farewell.
Farewell, Andronicus: Revenge now goes To lay a complot to betray thy foes.
exit TAMORA.
Tell us, old man, how shall we be employ'd?

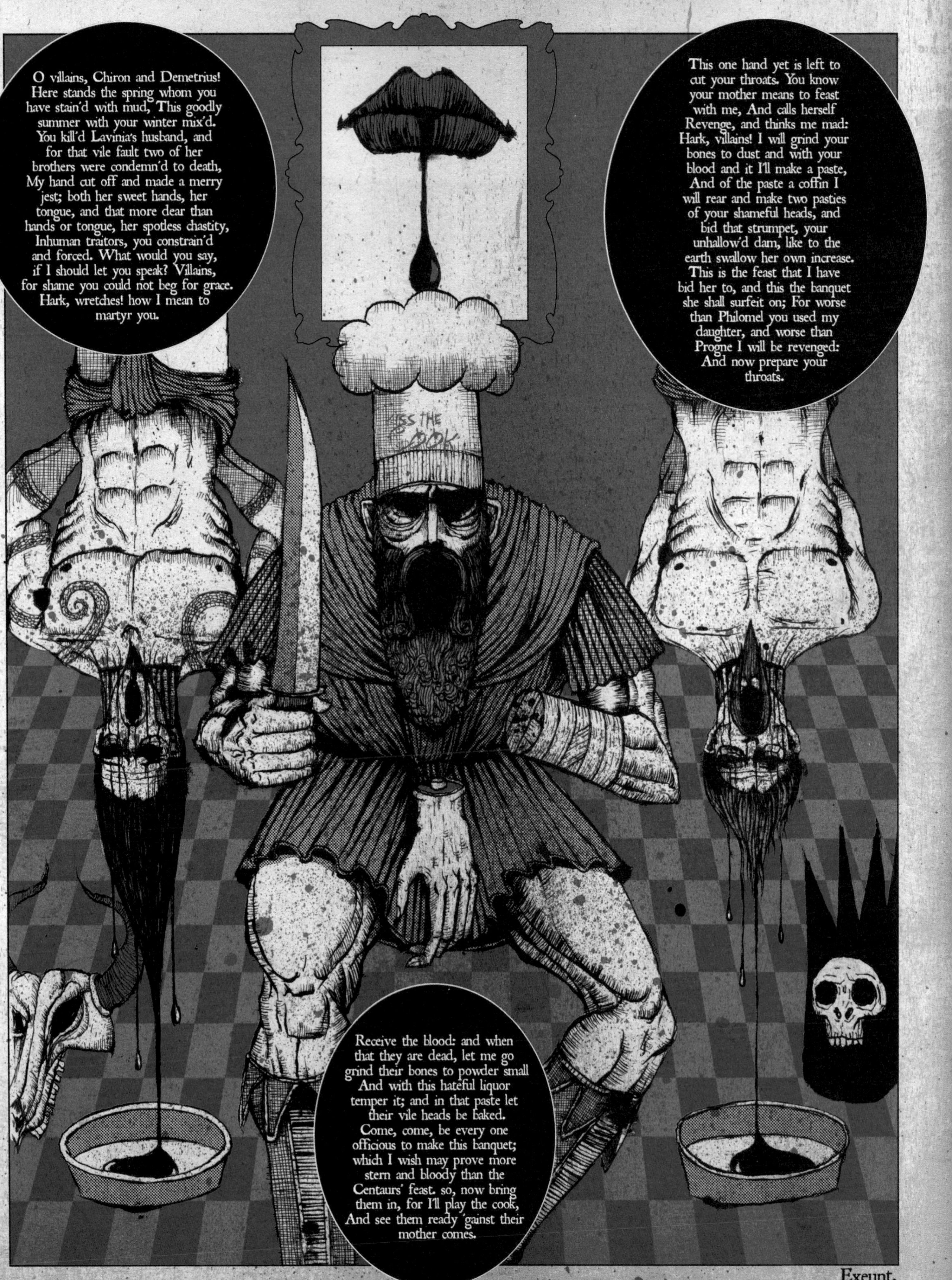
O villains, Chiron and Demetrius! Here stands the spring whom you have stain'd with mud, This goodly summer with your winter mix'd. You kill'd Lavinia's husband, and for that vile fault two of her brothers were condemn'd to death, My hand cut off and made a merry jest; both her sweet hands, her tongue, and that more dear than hands or tongue, her spotless chastity, Inhuman traitors, you constrain'd and forced. What would you say, if I should let you speak? Villains, for shame you could not beg for grace. Hark, wretches! how I mean to martyr you.
This one hand yet is left to cut your throats. You know your mother means to feast with me, And calls herself Revenge, and thinks me mad: Hark, villains! I will grind your bones to dust and with your blood and it I'll make a paste, And of the paste a coffin I will rear and make two pasties of your shameful heads, and bid that strumpet, your unhallow'd dam, like to the earth swallow her own increase. This is the feast that I have bid her to, and this the banquet she shall surfeit on; For worse than Philomel you used my daughter, and worse than Progne I will be revenged: And now prepare your throats.
Receive the blood: and when that they are dead, let me go grind their bones to powder small And with this hateful liquor temper it; and in that paste let their vile heads be baked. Come, come, be every one officious to make this banquet; which I wish may prove more stern and bloody than the Centaurs' feast. so, now bring them in, for I'll play the cook, And see them ready 'gainst their mother comes.

Exeunt.

Court of TITUS's house. A banquet set out.

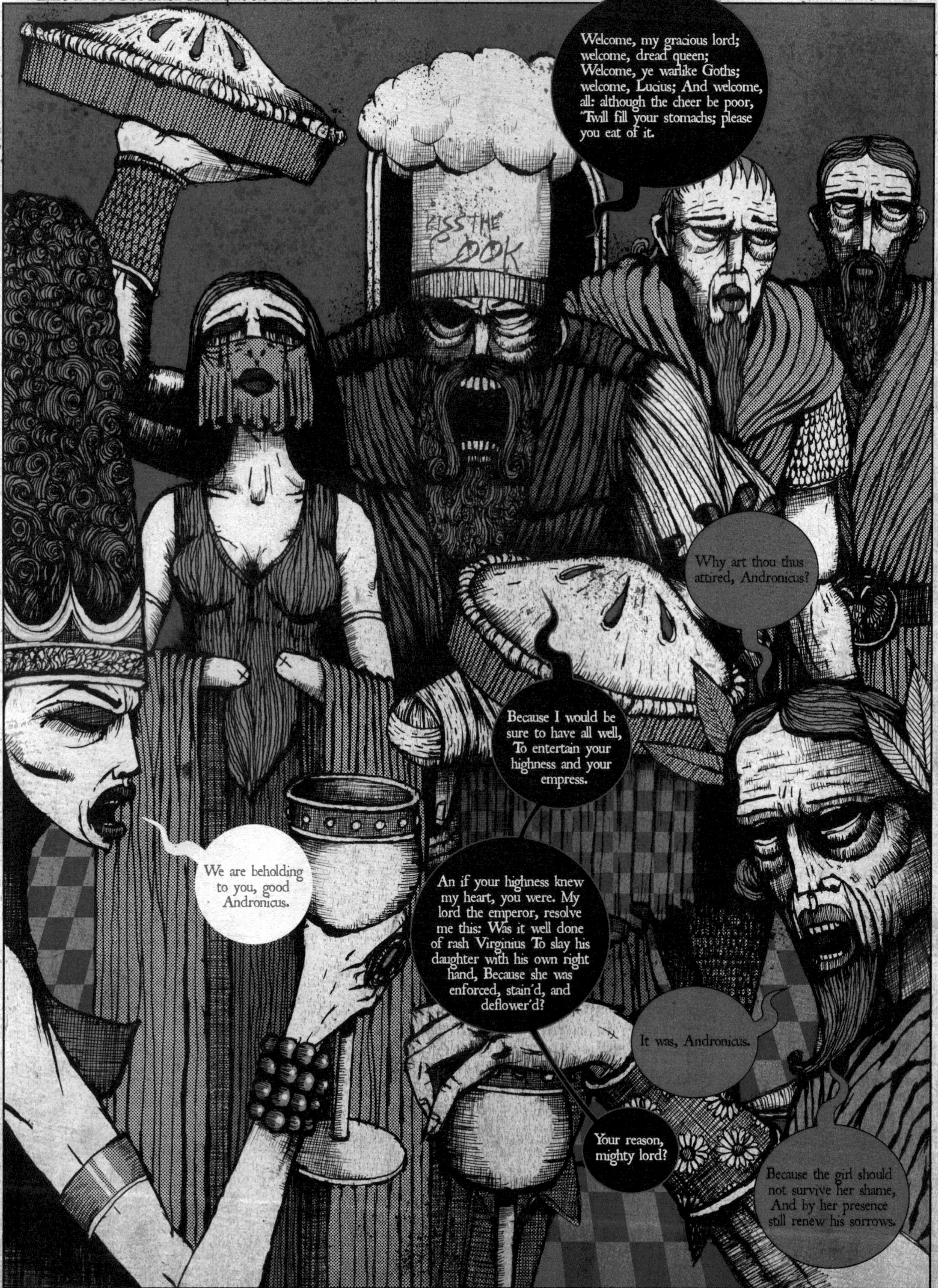

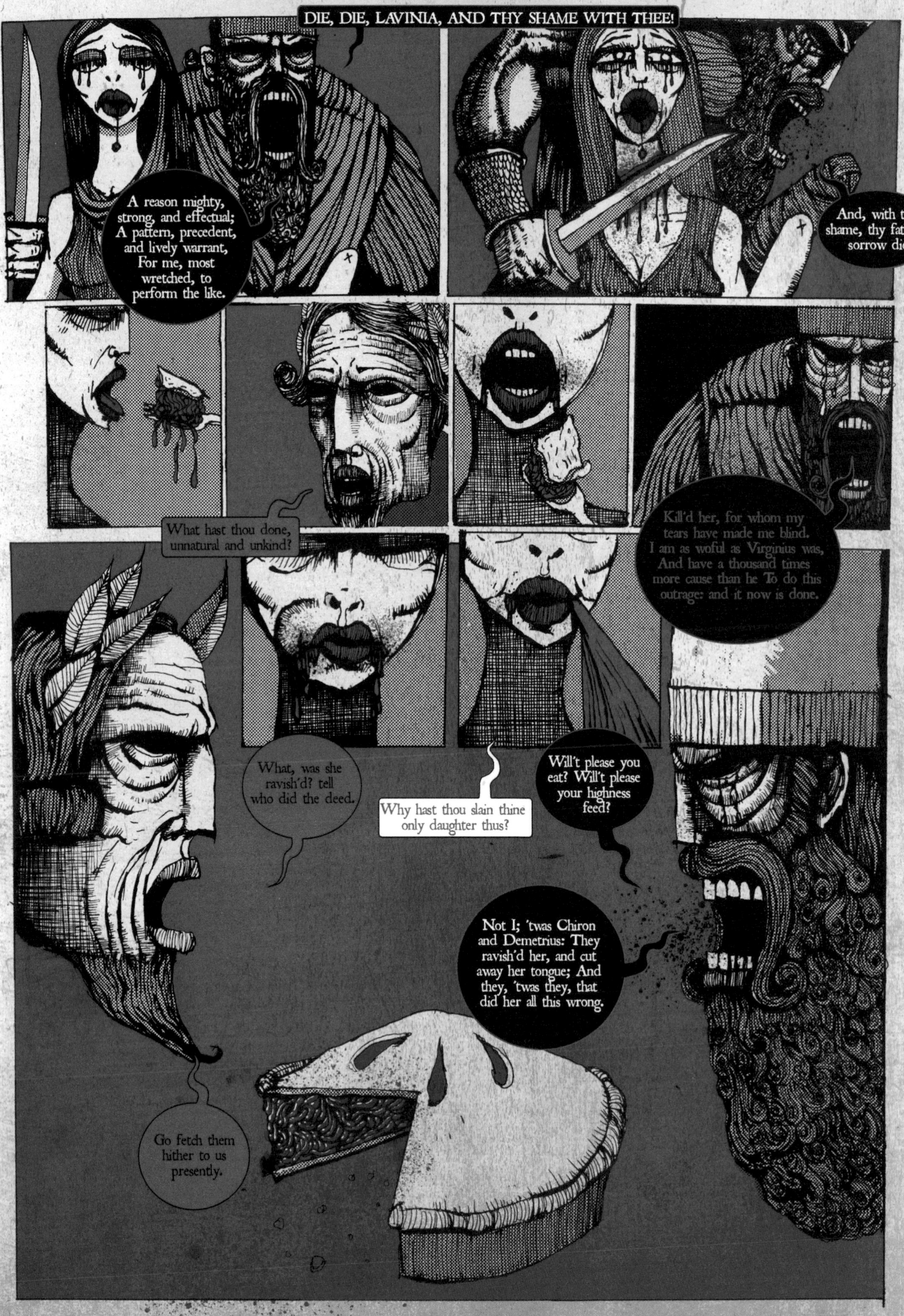
DIE, DIE, LAVINIA, AND THY SHAME WITH THEE!
A reason mighty, strong, and effectual; A pattern, precedent, and lively warrant, For me, most wretched, to perform the like.
And, with thy shame, thy father's sorrow die!
What hast thou done, unnatural and unkind?
Kill'd her, for whom my tears have made me blind. I am as woful as Virginius was, And have a thousand times more cause than he To do this outrage: and it now is done.
What, was she ravish'd? tell who did the deed.
Why hast thou slain thine only daughter thus?
Will't please you eat? Will't please your highness feed?
Not I; 'twas Chiron and Demetrius: They ravish'd her, and cut away her tongue; And they, 'twas they, that did her all this wrong.
Go fetch them hither to us presently.

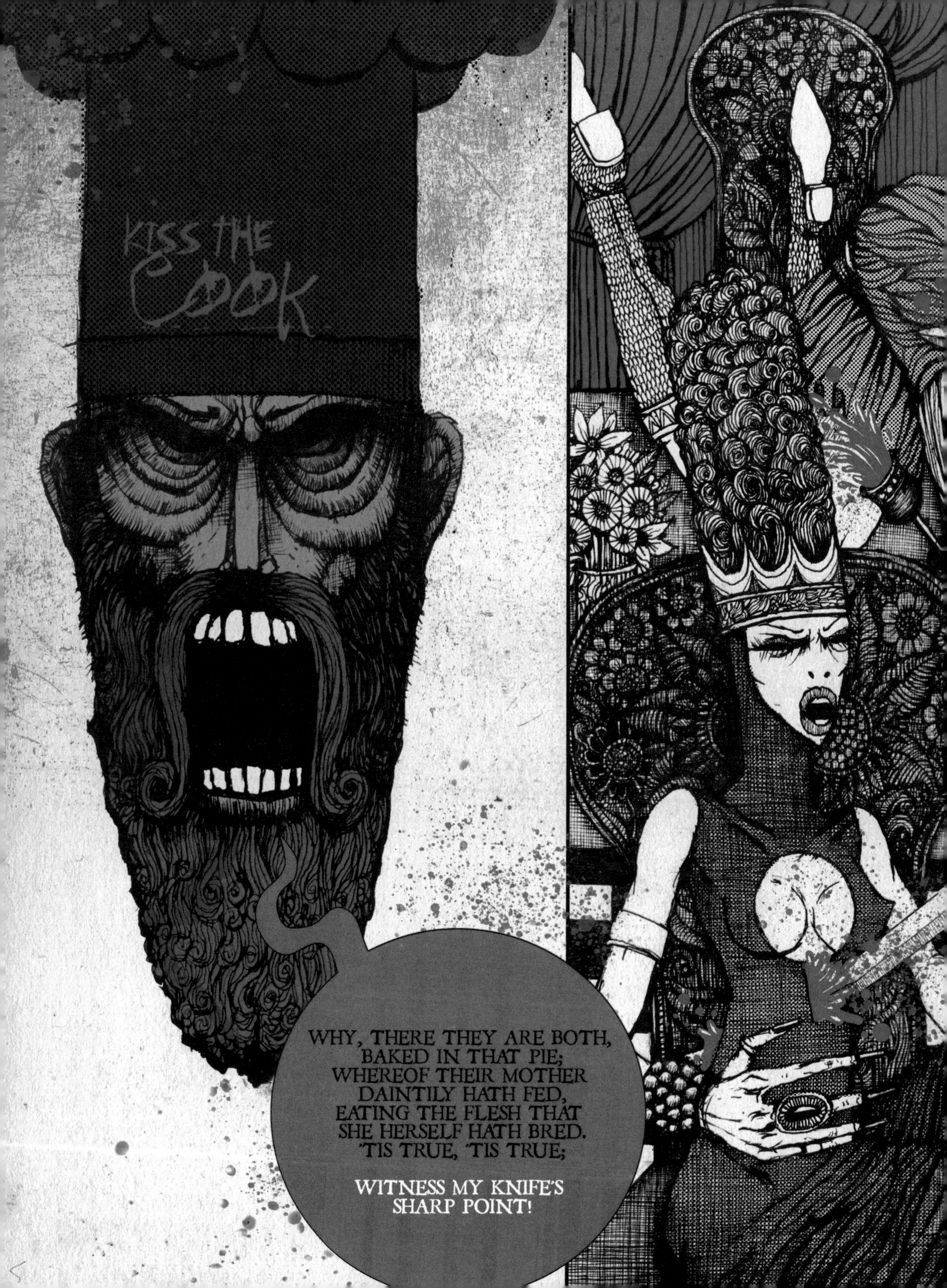
KISS THE COOK
WHY, THERE THEY ARE BOTH, BAKED IN THAT PIE; WHEREOF THEIR MOTHER DAINTILY HATH FED, EATING THE FLESH THAT SHE HERSELF HATH BRED. 'TIS TRUE, 'TIS TRUE;
WITNESS MY KNIFE'S SHARP POINT!

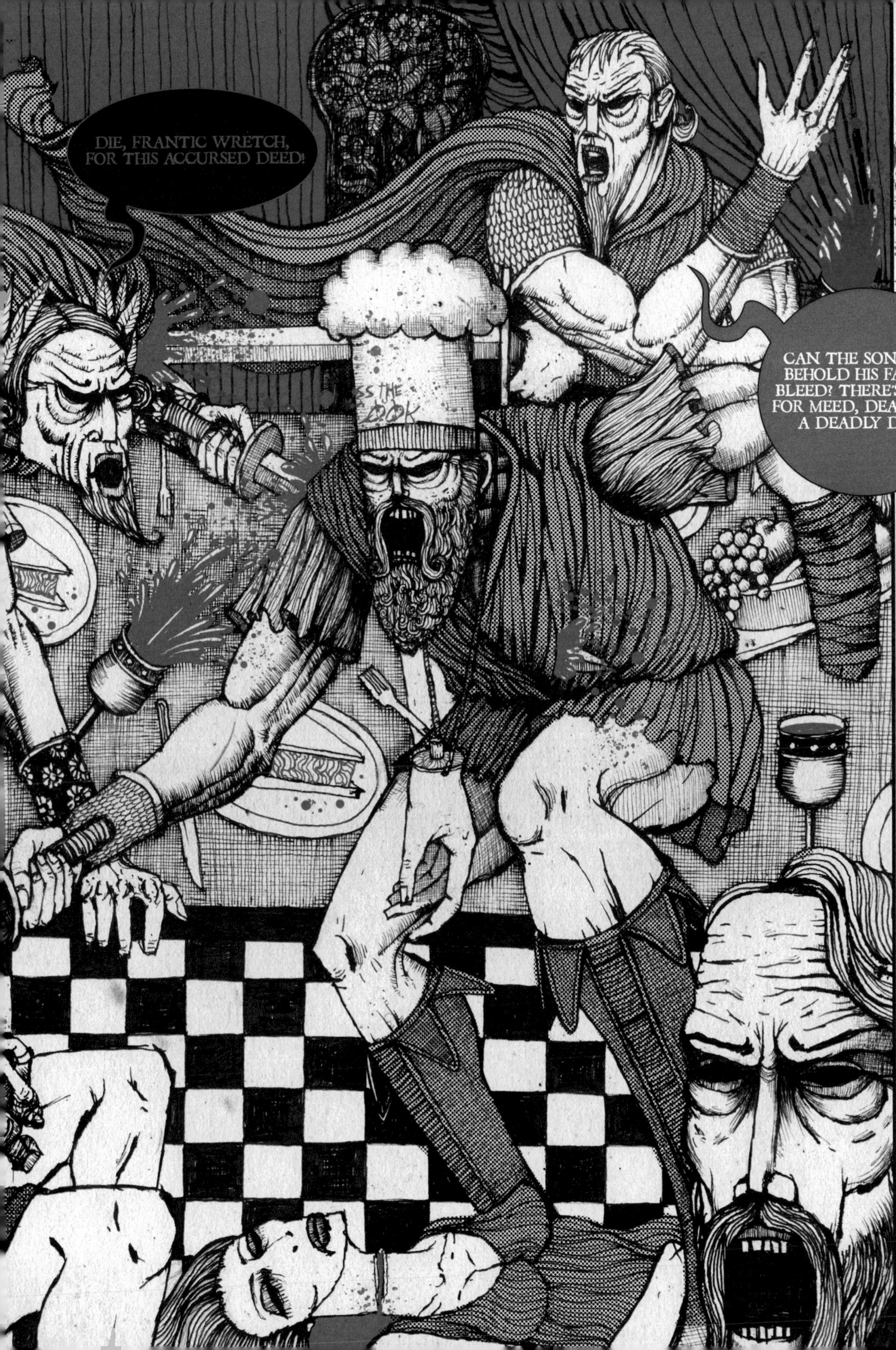
DIE, FRANTIC WRETCH, FOR THIS ACCURSED DEED!
CAN THE SON'S EYE BEHOLD HIS FATHER BLEED? THERE'S MEED FOR MEED, DEATH FOR A DEADLY DEED!

You sad-faced men, people and sons of Rome,
By uproar sever'd, like a flight of fowl
Scatter'd by winds and high tempestuous gusts,
O, let me teach you how to knit again
This scatter'd corn into one mutual sheaf,
These broken limbs again into one body;
Lest Rome herself be bane unto herself,
And she whom mighty kingdoms court'sy to,
Like a forlorn and desperate castaway,
Do shameful execution on herself.

Some loving friends convey the emperor hence,
And give him burial in his father's grave:
Titus and Lavinia shall forthwith
Be closed in their household's monument.
As for that heinous tiger, Tamora,
No funeral rite, nor man in mourning weeds,
No mournful bell shall ring her burial;
But throw her forth to beasts and birds of prey:
Her life was beast-like, and devoid of pity;
And, being so, shall have like want of pity.

the
End.

Rebecca

Daphne du Maurier

ART/ADAPTATION BY **Emily Rose Dixon**

REBECCA (1938), THE FILM, IS ABOUT THE psychological haunting of a widower's second wife by his first wife. It's also a mystery novel because, well, how did Rebecca de Winter die anyway? Daphne du Maurier used the adjectives *gloomy* and *grim* to describe her fifth, most successful novel, and others have chimed in with *bleak* and "the relentlessness of a vivid nightmare." It's also complex and ambiguous: There are elements of androgyny, and the name of the narrator—the second wife of Rebecca's widower—is never revealed. It was made into a classic film by Alfred Hitchcock, who also adapted du Maurier's novel *Jamaica Inn* and short story "The Birds."

Emily Lambert is a full-time designer/ illustrator of greeting cards, and she formed a comics collective with her two sisters (shades of the Brontës). The delicacy of her style aptly reflects the fragile state of mind of the unnamed narrator, the unworldy second Mrs. de Winter, who isn't prepared for the life she's jumped into.

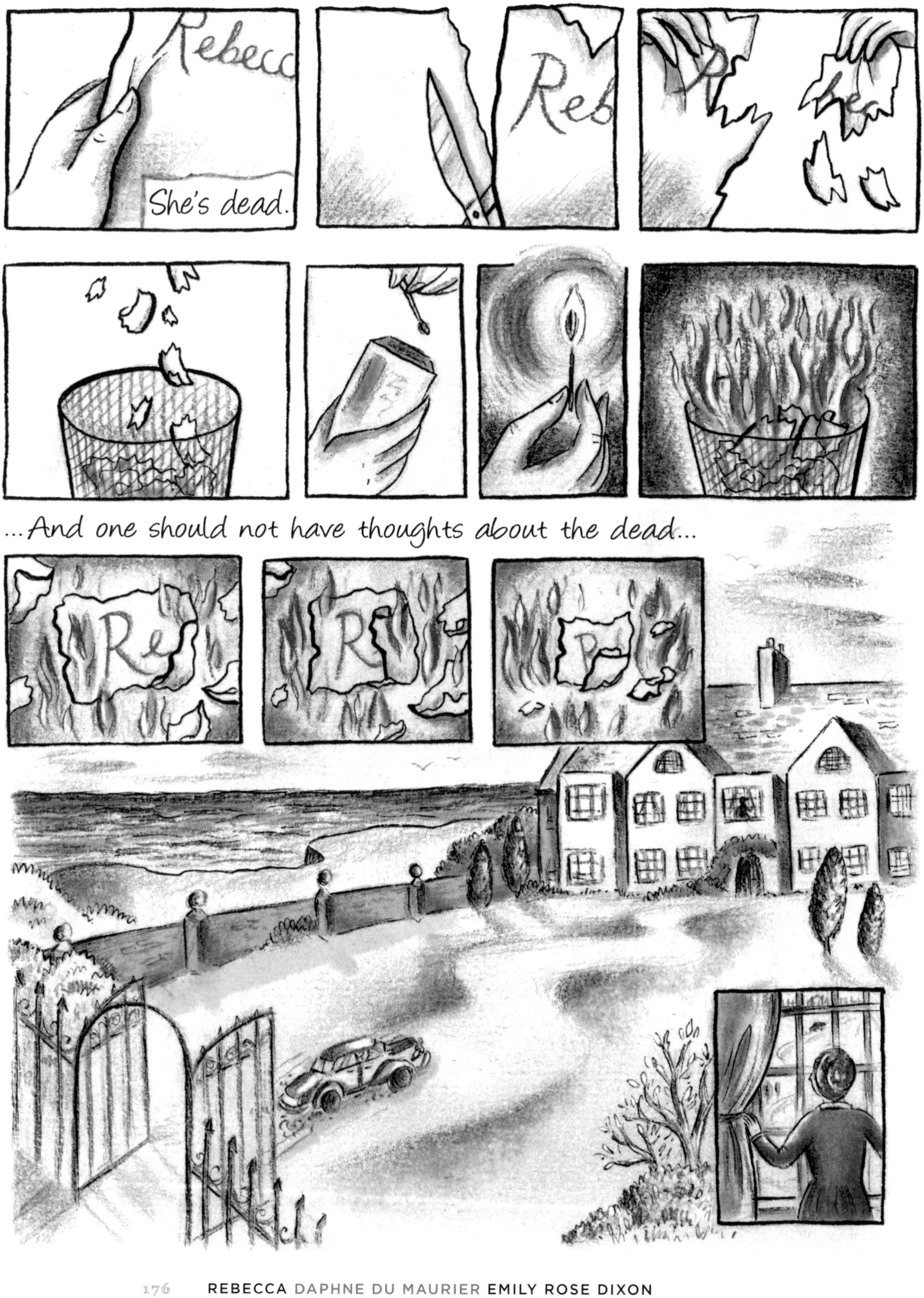
Rebecca
She's dead.
Reb
...And one should not have thoughts about the dead...
Re
R

All the pictures in the gallery would make good costumes.

Especially that one of the young lady in white...

What the hell are you doing?

Get changed at once!

The picture you copied. It was what Rebecca wore at the last fancy dress ball. Identical. The same picture, the same dress...

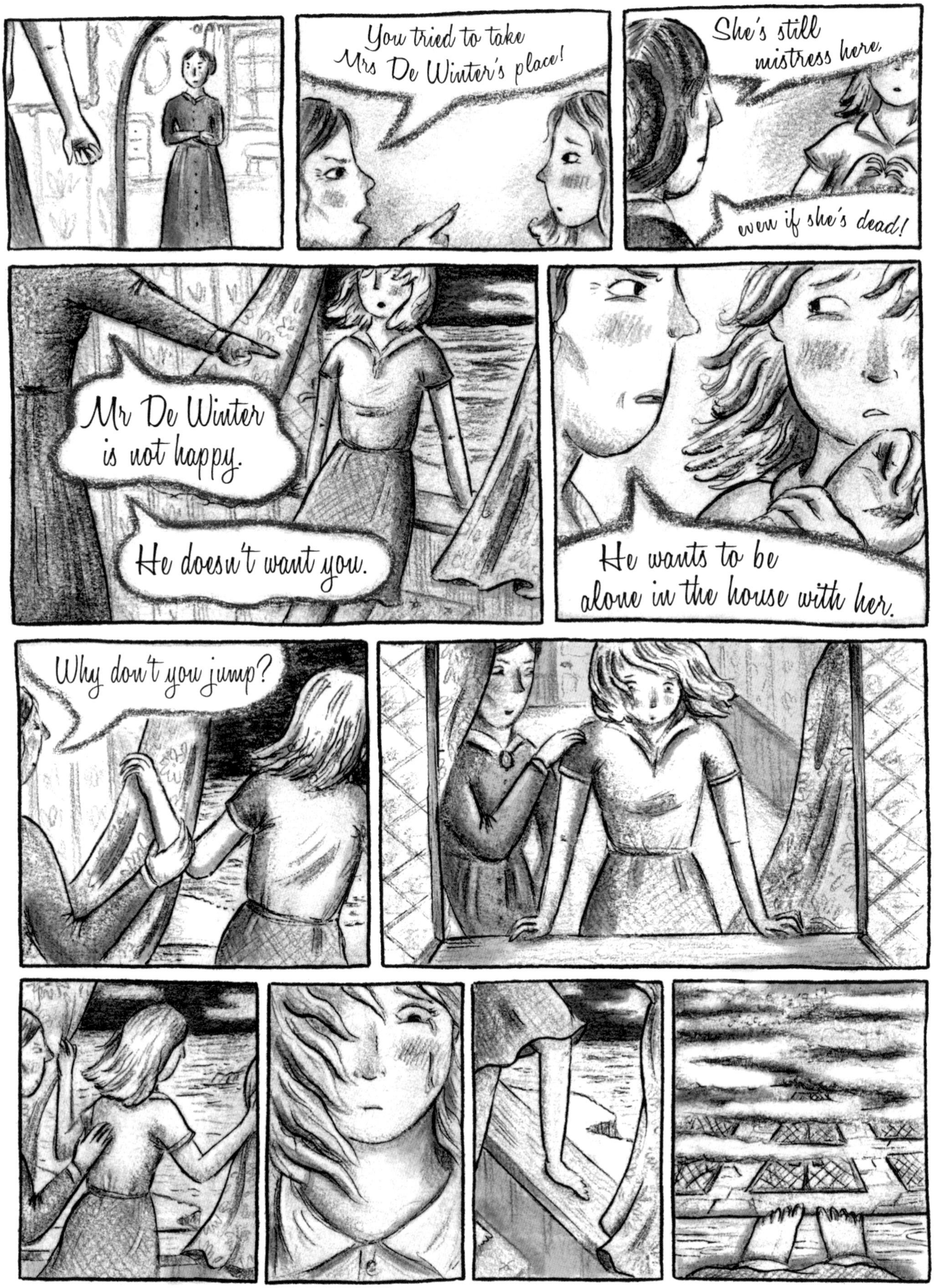
You tried to take Mrs De Winter's place!
She's still mistress here,
even if she's dead!
Mr De Winter is not happy.
He doesn't want you.
He wants to be alone in the house with her.
Why don't you jump?

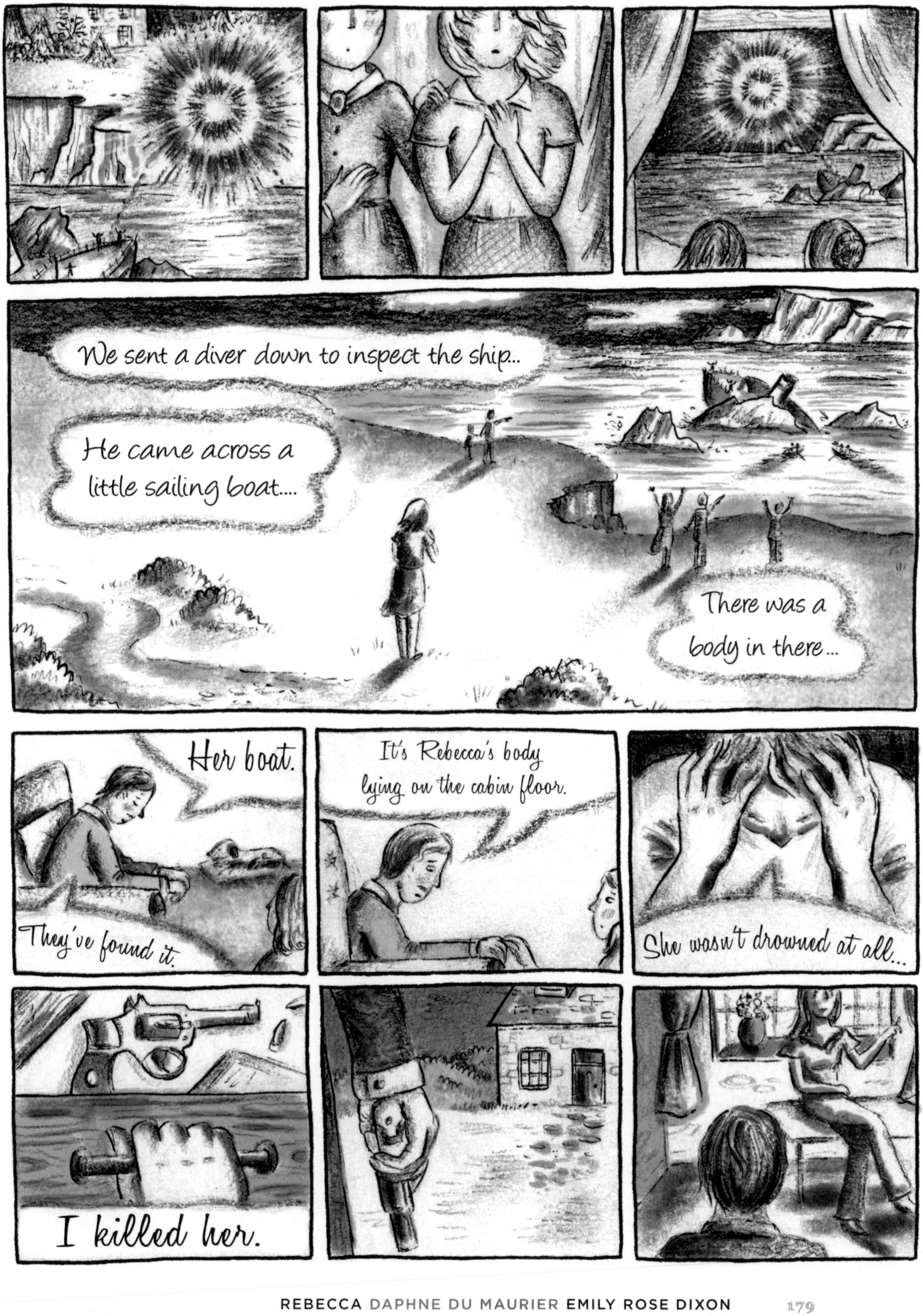
We sent a diver down to inspect the ship...
He came across a little sailing boat....
There was a body in there...
Her boat.
They've found it.
It's Rebecca's body lying on the cabin floor.
She wasn't drowned at all...
I killed her.

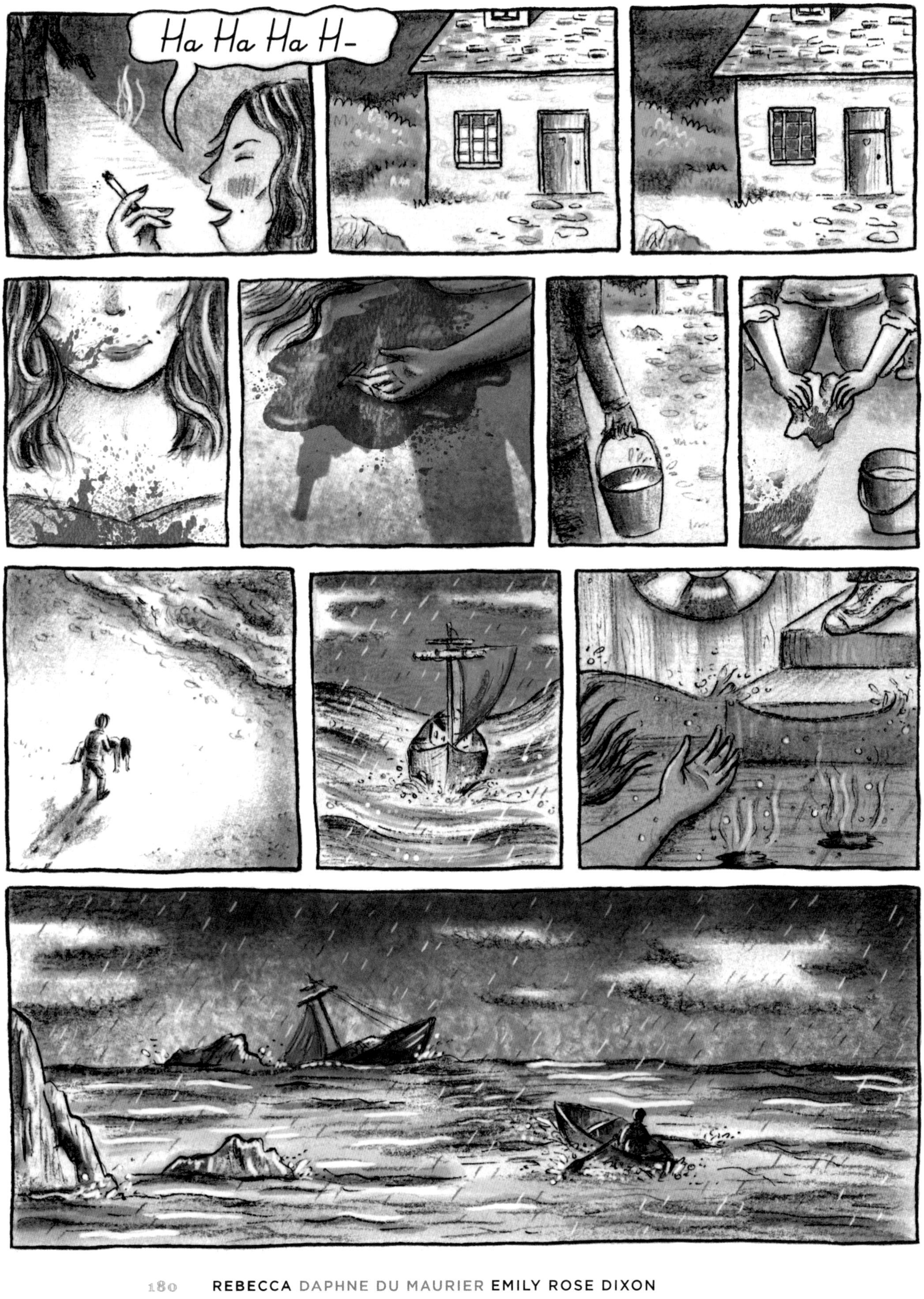
Ha Ha Ha H-

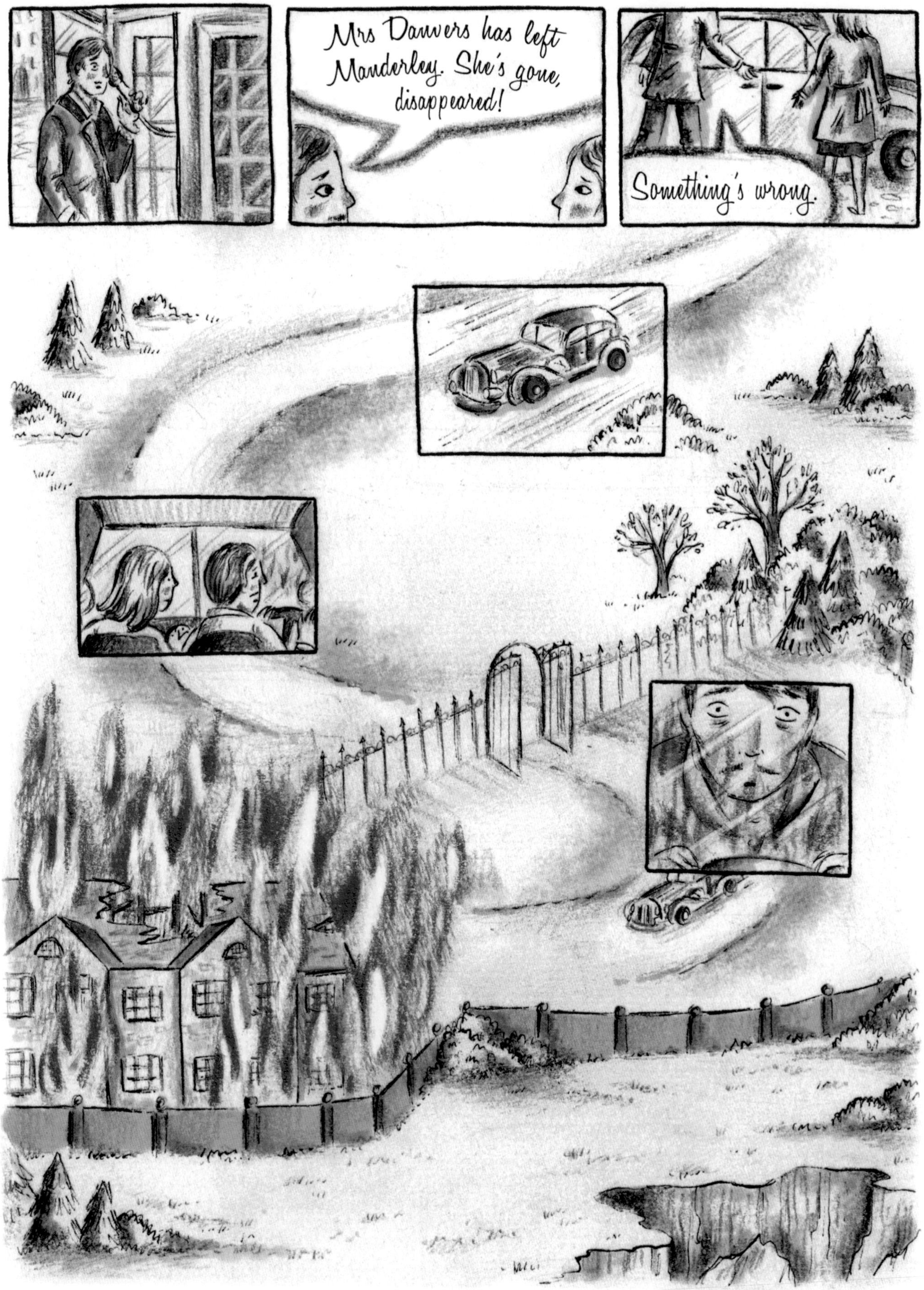
Mrs Danvers has left Manderley. She's gone, disappeared!
Something's wrong.

The Godfather

Mario Puzo

ART/ADAPTATION BY **Rachel Smythe**

LIKE *PSYCHO* AND *SILENCE OF THE LAMBS*, Mario Puzo's 1969 Mafia novel *The Godfather* is ingrained in our cultural consciousness as a movie adaptation. Rachel Smythe is reclaiming it through an intense moment between two sons of patriarch Vito Corleone—Sonny and Michael. James Caan and Al Pacino are nowhere to be seen.

Rachel's other work ranges from labels for craft beer to an epic, ongoing comics adaptation of the Persephone myth, *Lore Olympus*. Here she works on a small scale, creating an almost claustrophobic take on sibling conflict, mob-style, that feels ready to boil over.

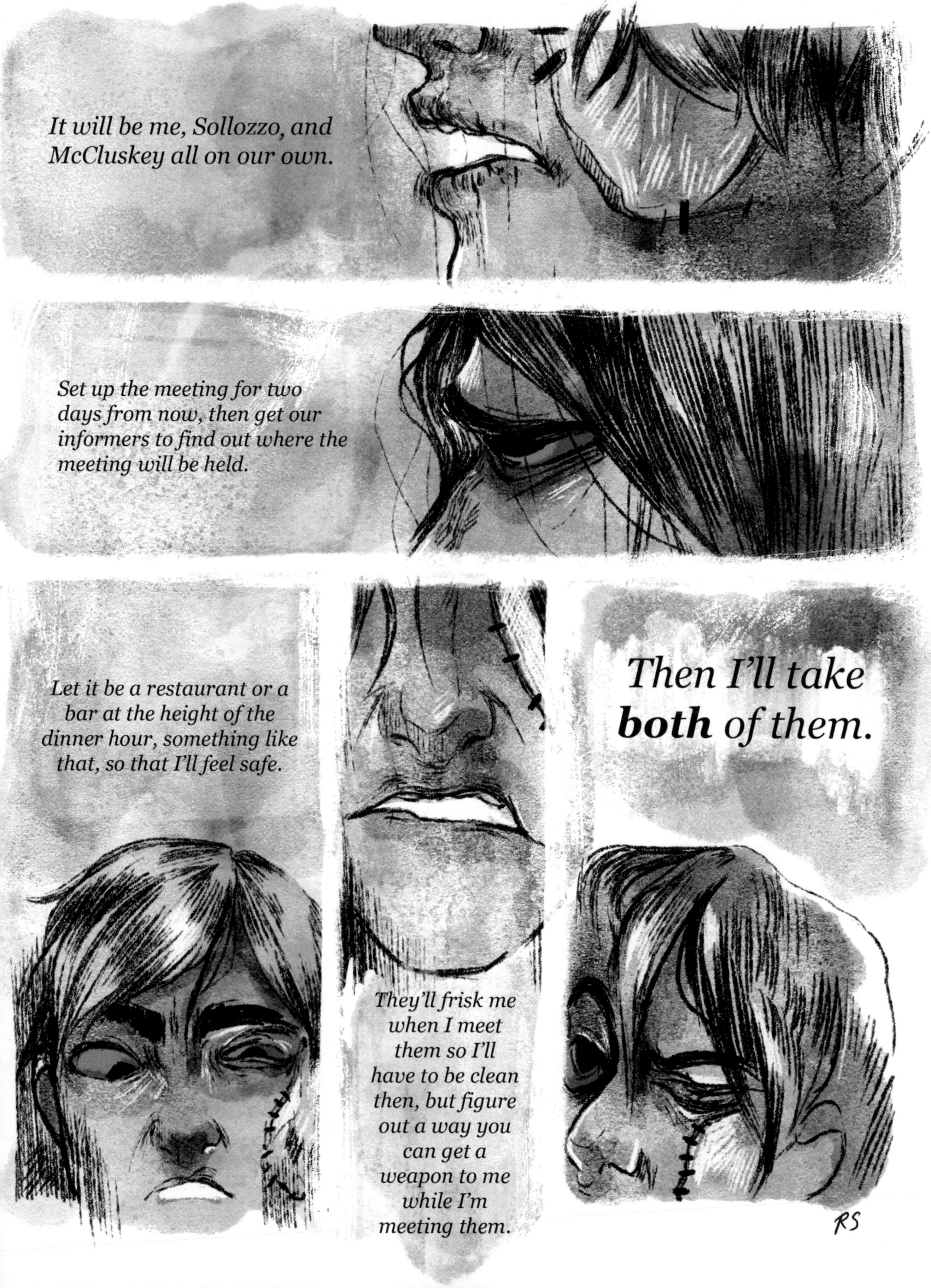
It will be me, Sollozzo, and McCluskey all on our own.
Set up the meeting for two days from now, then get our informers to find out where the meeting will be held.
Let it be a restaurant or a bar at the height of the dinner hour, something like that, so that I'll feel safe.
They'll frisk me when I meet them so I'll have to be clean then, but figure out a way you can get a weapon to me while I'm meeting them.
Then I'll take **both** of them.
RS

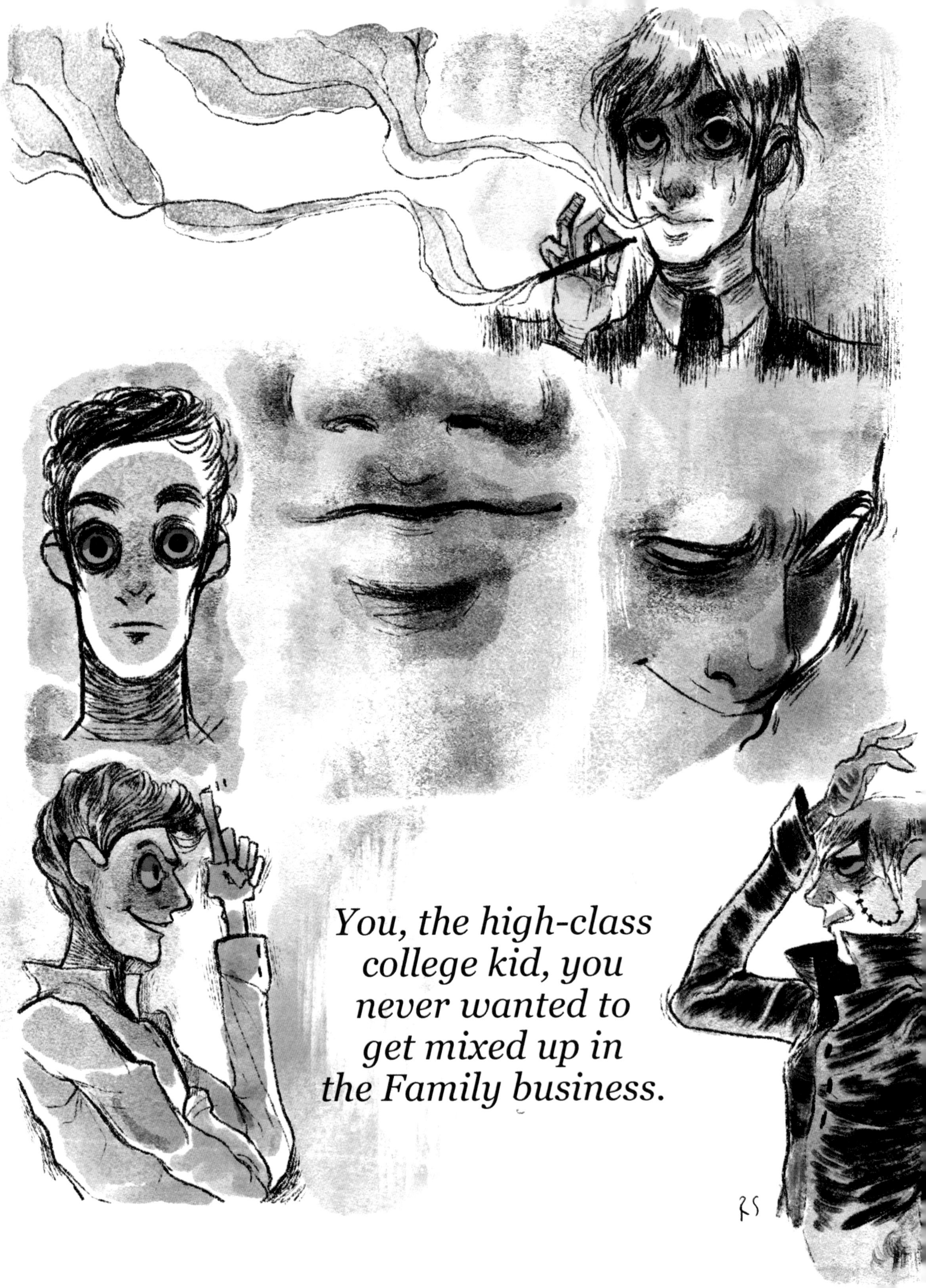
You, the high-class college kid, you never wanted to get mixed up in the Family business.

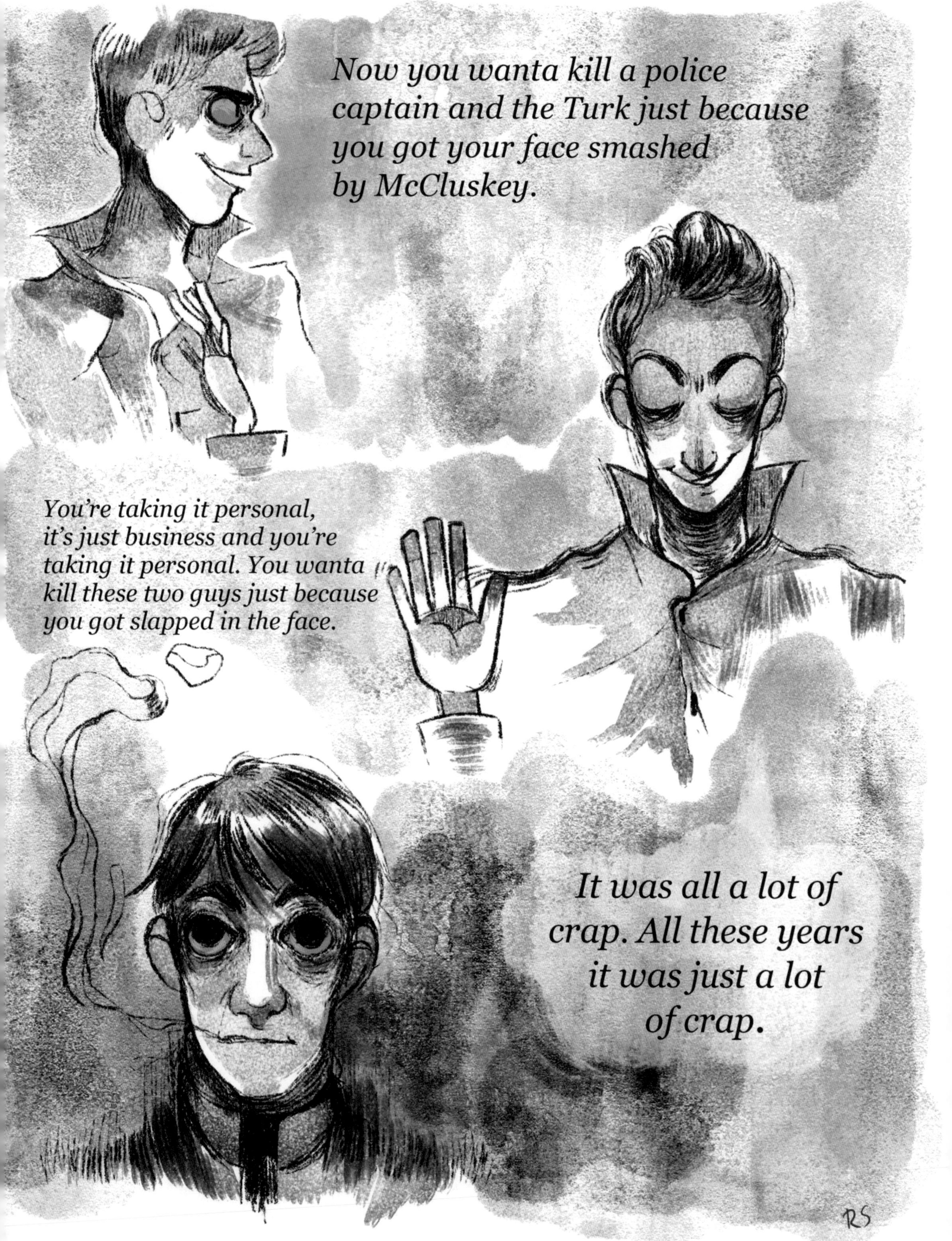
Now you wanta kill a police captain and the Turk just because you got your face smashed by McCluskey.
You're taking it personal, it's just business and you're taking it personal. You wanta kill these two guys just because you got slapped in the face.
It was all a lot of crap. All these years it was just a lot of crap.
RS

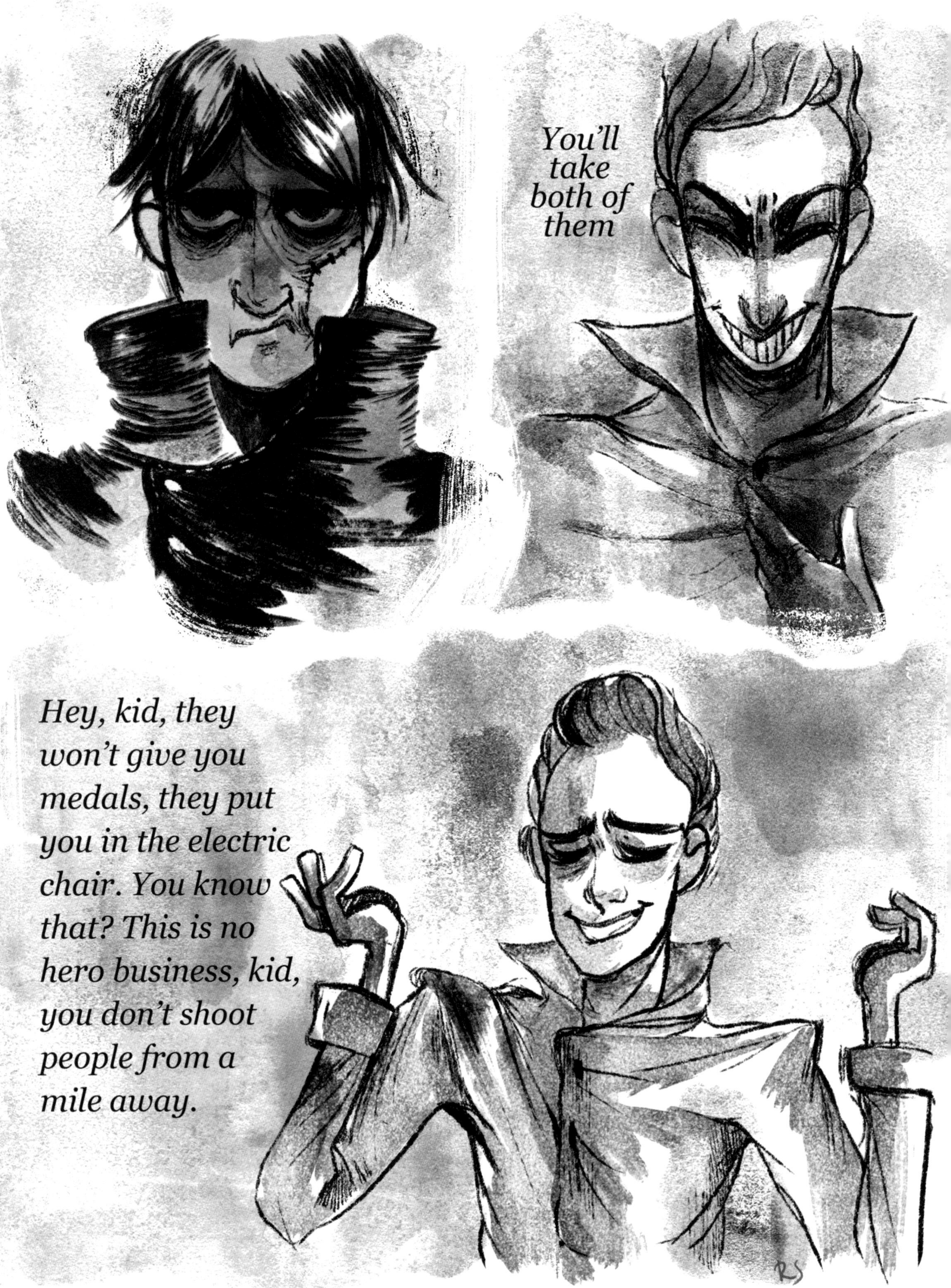
You'll take both of them
Hey, kid, they won't give you medals, they put you in the electric chair. You know that? This is no hero business, kid, you don't shoot people from a mile away.
RS

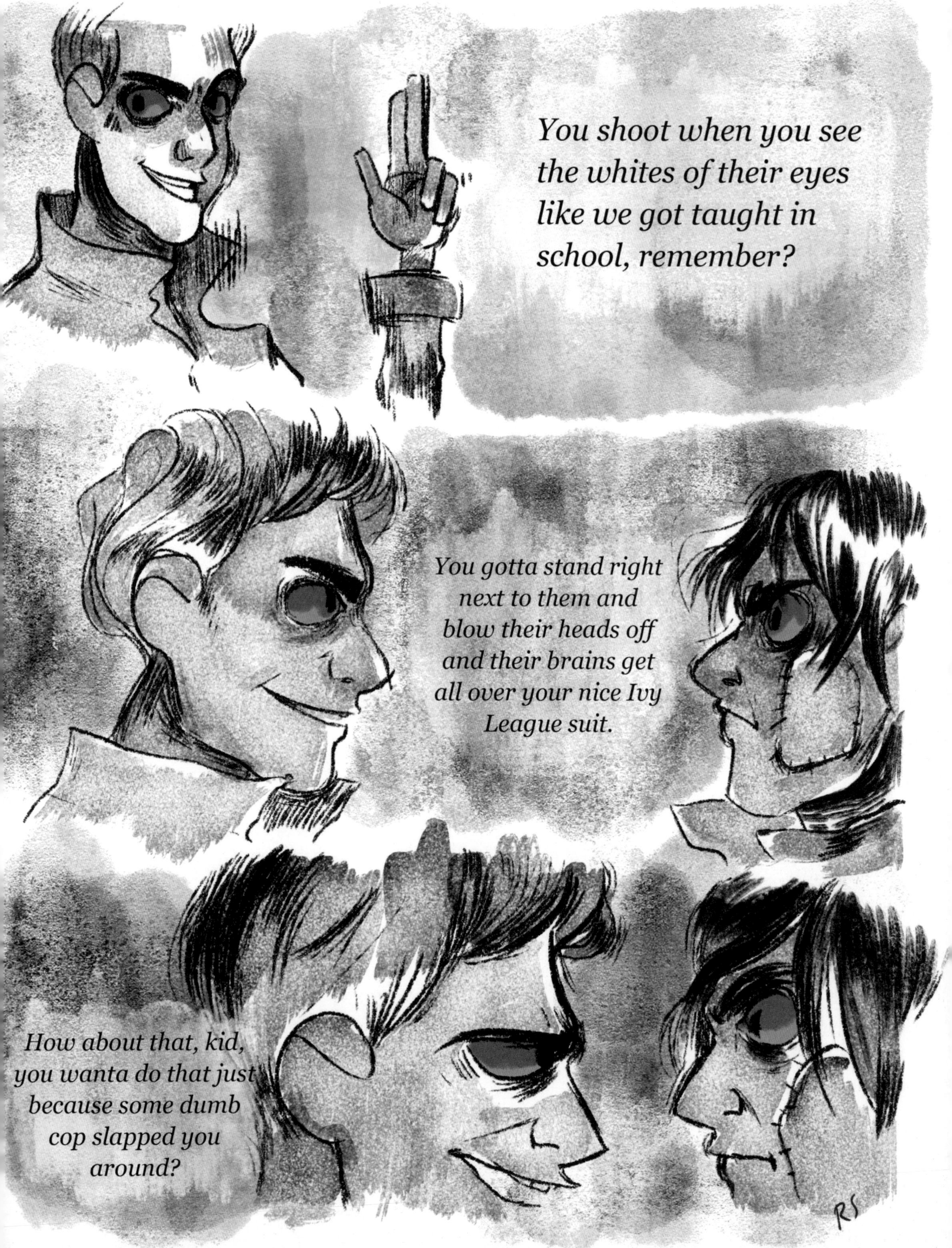
You shoot when you see the whites of their eyes like we got taught in school, remember?
You gotta stand right next to them and blow their heads off and their brains get all over your nice Ivy League suit.
How about that, kid, you wanta do that just because some dumb cop slapped you around?
RS

PART THREE
The System

gulp

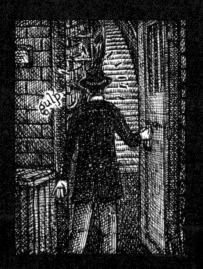

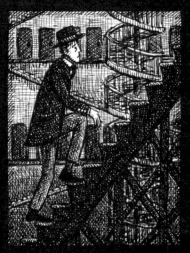

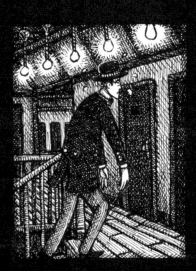

"The Lady, or the Tiger?"

Frank R. Stockton

ART/ADAPTATION BY Omer Hoffmann

FRANK R. STOCKTON WAS A BORN storyteller who earned success in the second half of the 1800s for his children's books and, to a lesser extent, tales for adults. His work is mostly forgotten now with the extreme exception of "The Lady, or the Tiger?" With its legendarily ambiguous, unknowable ending that acts as a Rorschach test for your view of human nature (particularly female nature), it went viral across the globe and is still widely anthologized. Prolific children's book author Jane Yolen writes:

> "His life was changed from the moment of its publication. . . . . It came out in the November 1882 edition of *The Century Magazine*. Within months, it

was known worldwide, being argued in debating societies and lectured on from the pulpits."

Stockton was asked incessantly about how the story ended but would only say, "If you decide which it was—the lady or the tiger—you find out what kind of person you are yourself." In which case Israeli artist Omer Hoffman has revealed himself to us. His ingeniously structured adaptation ends with his personal answer to the mystery, revealed indirectly but unmistakably. Omer's work has appeared in the *Humdrum* anthologies, the Israeli Comics and Cartoon Museum, the *New York Times*, and eight children's books.

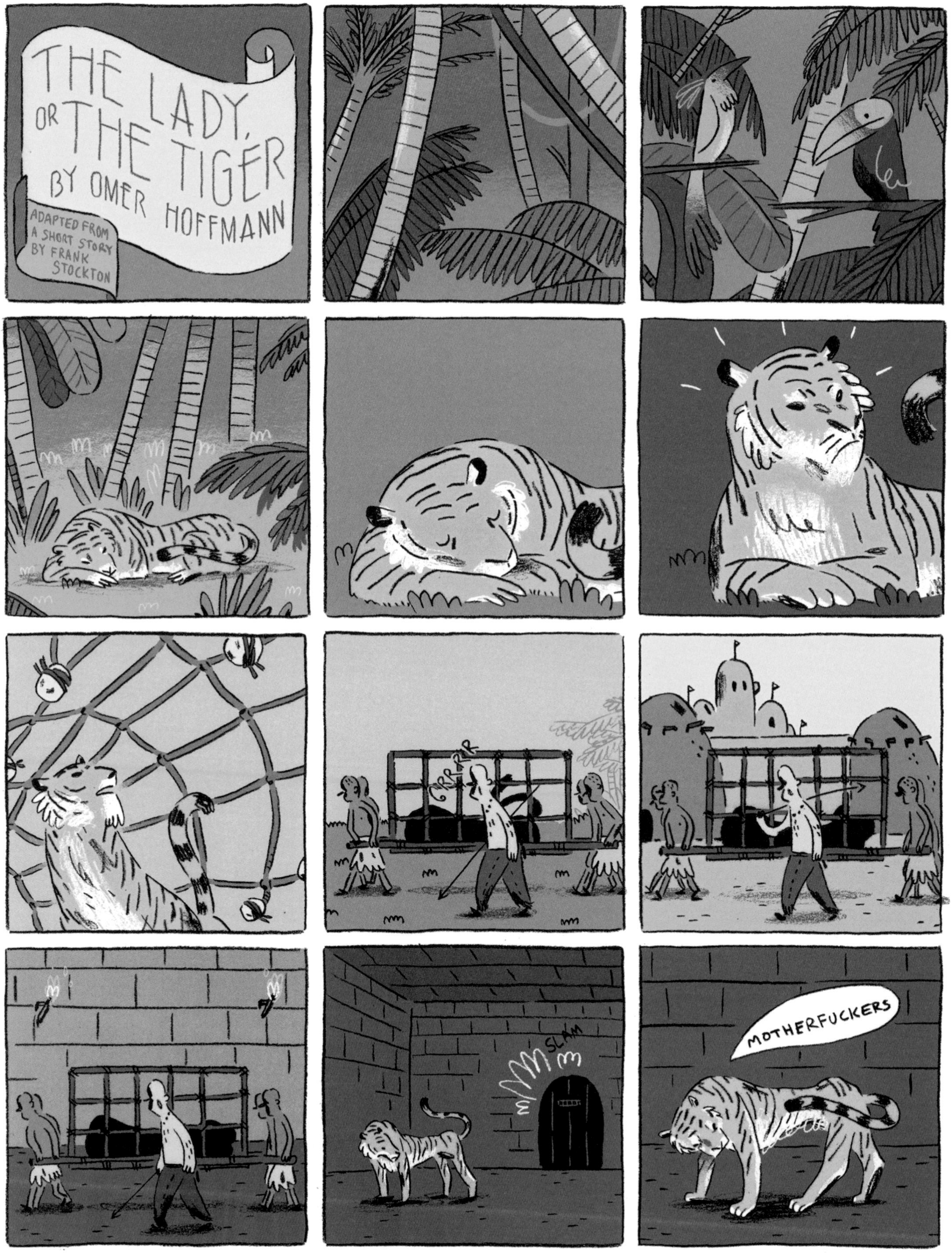
THE LADY, OR THE TIGER
BY OMER HOFFMANN
ADAPTED FROM A SHORT STORY BY FRANK STOCKTON
GRRRR
SLAM
MOTHERFUCKERS

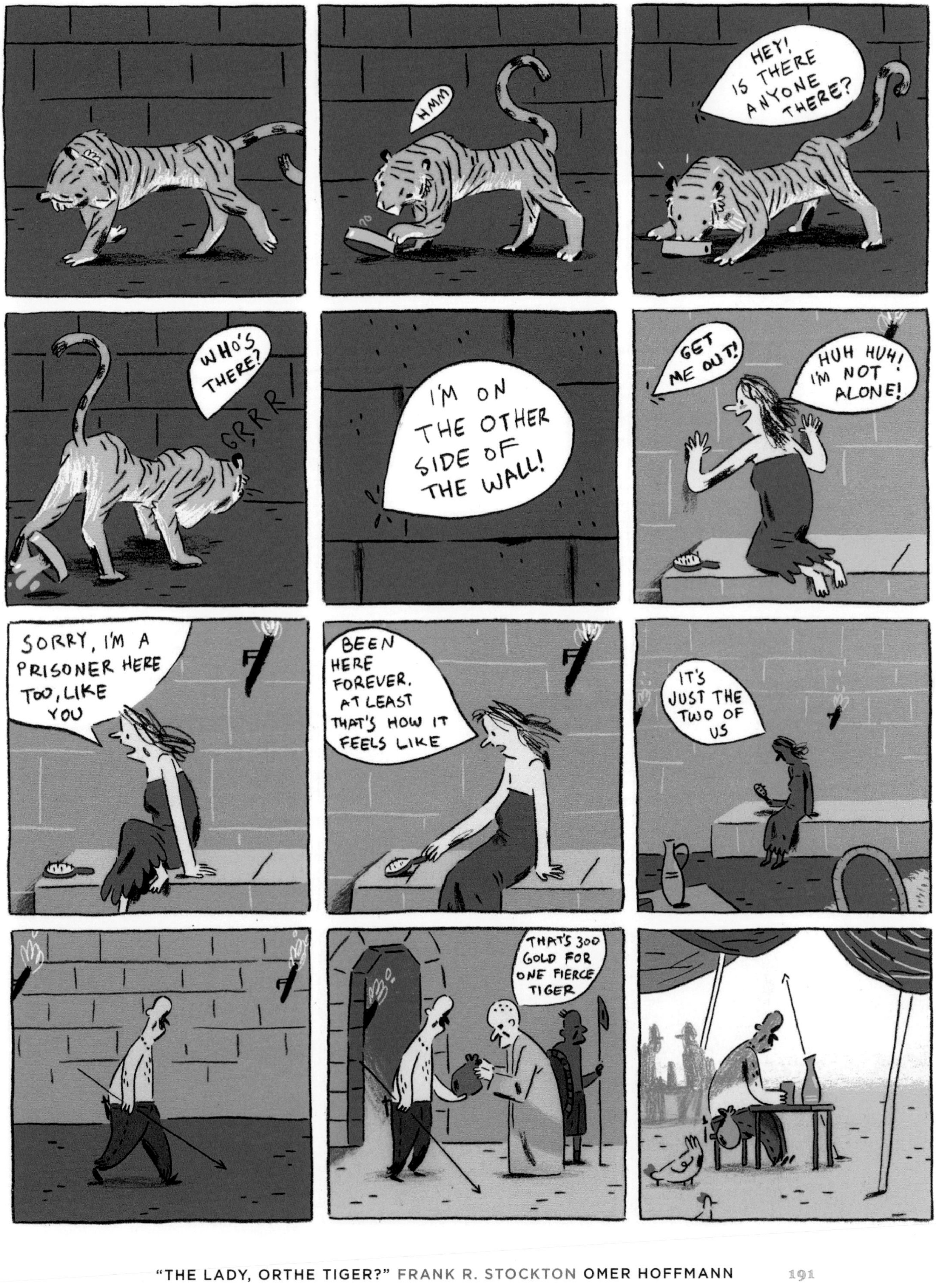
HMM
HEY! IS THERE ANYONE THERE?
WHO'S THERE?
GRRR
I'M ON THE OTHER SIDE OF THE WALL!
GET ME OUT!
HUH HUH! I'M NOT ALONE!
SORRY, I'M A PRISONER HERE TOO, LIKE YOU
BEEN HERE FOREVER. AT LEAST THAT'S HOW IT FEELS LIKE
IT'S JUST THE TWO OF US
THAT'S 300 GOLD FOR ONE FIERCE TIGER

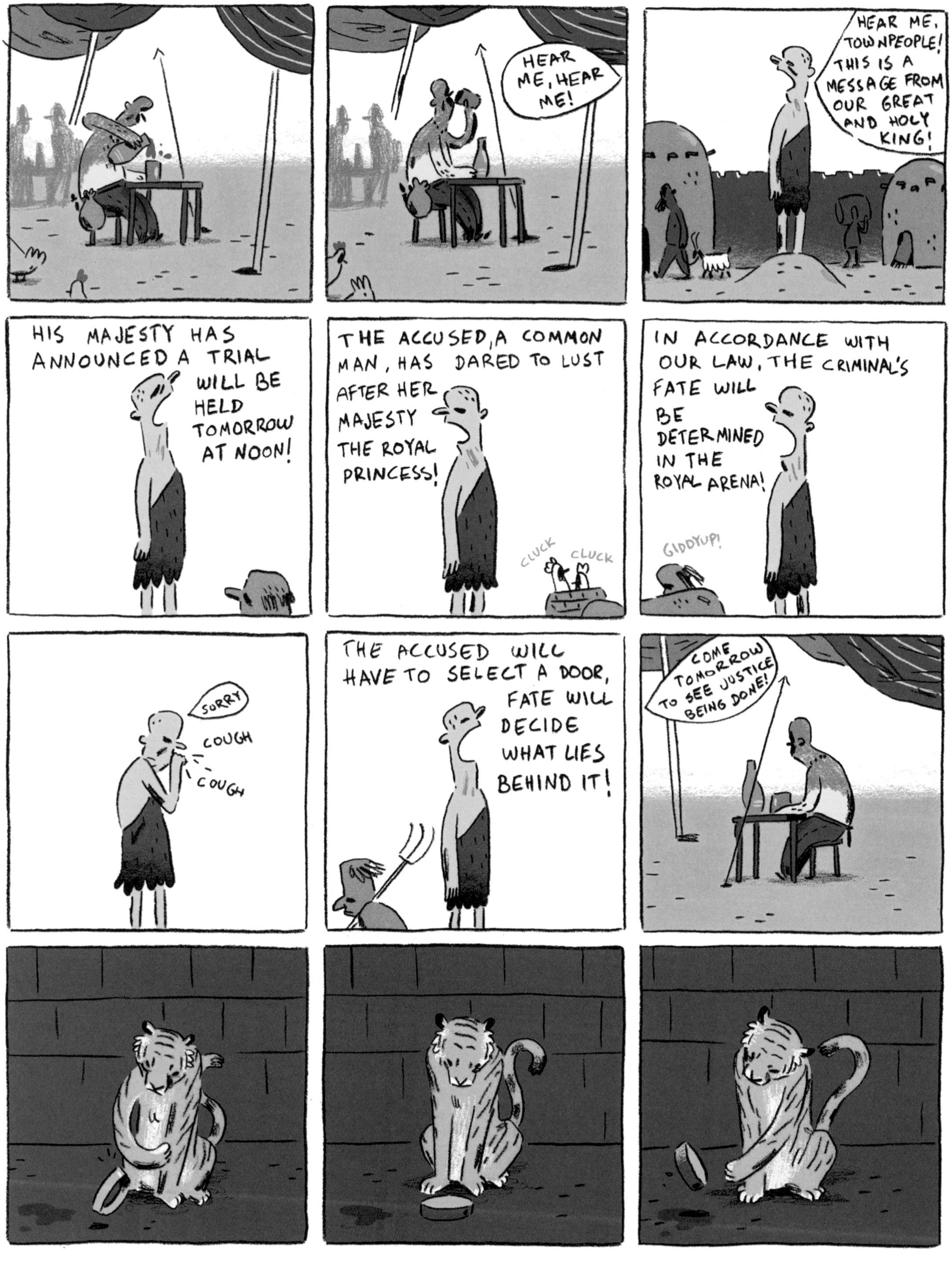
HEAR ME, HEAR ME!
HEAR ME, TOWNPEOPLE! THIS IS A MESSAGE FROM OUR GREAT AND HOLY KING!
HIS MAJESTY HAS ANNOUNCED A TRIAL WILL BE HELD TOMORROW AT NOON!
THE ACCUSED, A COMMON MAN, HAS DARED TO LUST AFTER HER MAJESTY THE ROYAL PRINCESS!
CLUCK
CLUCK
IN ACCORDANCE WITH OUR LAW, THE CRIMINAL'S FATE WILL BE DETERMINED IN THE ROYAL ARENA!
GIDDYUP!
SORRY
COUGH
COUGH
THE ACCUSED WILL HAVE TO SELECT A DOOR, FATE WILL DECIDE WHAT LIES BEHIND IT!
COME TOMORROW TO SEE JUSTICE BEING DONE!

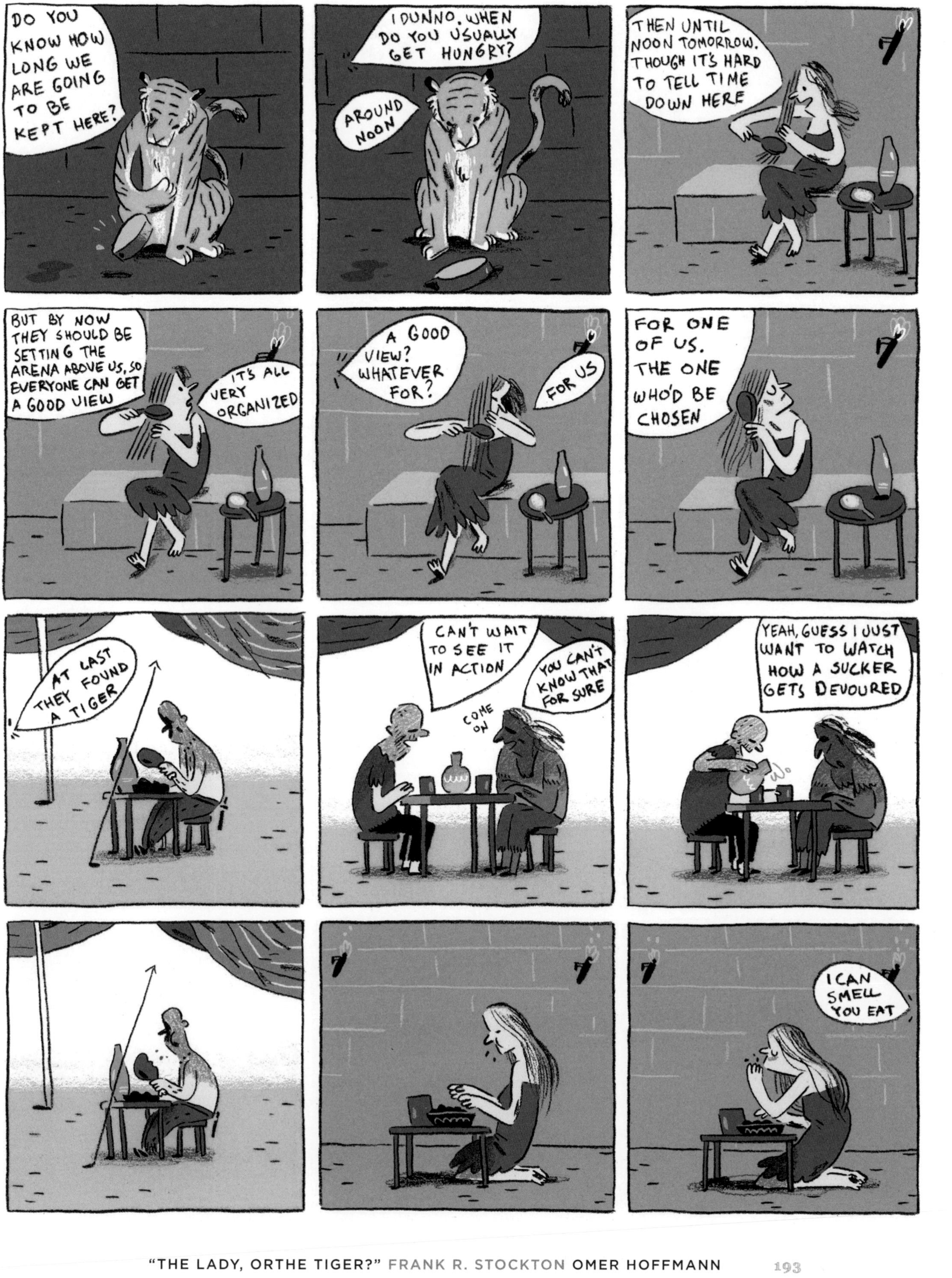
DO YOU KNOW HOW LONG WE ARE GOING TO BE KEPT HERE?
I DUNNO. WHEN DO YOU USUALLY GET HUNGRY?
AROUND NOON
THEN UNTIL NOON TOMORROW. THOUGH IT'S HARD TO TELL TIME DOWN HERE
BUT BY NOW THEY SHOULD BE SETTING THE ARENA ABOVE US, SO EVERYONE CAN GET A GOOD VIEW
IT'S ALL VERY ORGANIZED
A GOOD VIEW? WHATEVER FOR?
FOR US
FOR ONE OF US. THE ONE WHO'D BE CHOSEN
AT LAST THEY FOUND A TIGER
CAN'T WAIT TO SEE IT IN ACTION
YOU CAN'T KNOW THAT FOR SURE
COME ON
YEAH, GUESS I JUST WANT TO WATCH HOW A SUCKER GETS DEVOURED
I CAN SMELL YOU EAT

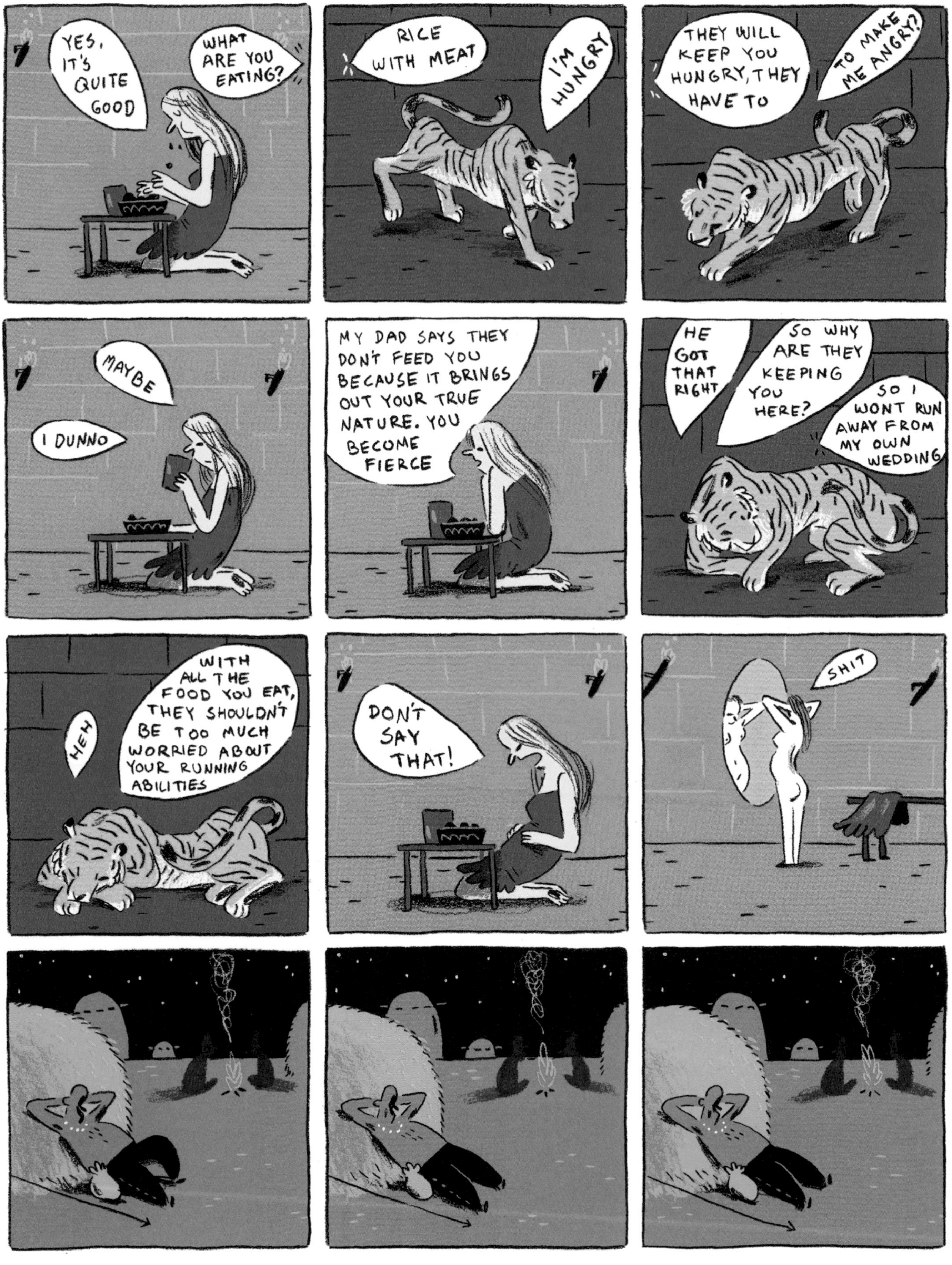
WHAT ARE YOU EATING?
YES, IT'S QUITE GOOD
RICE WITH MEAT
I'M HUNGRY
THEY WILL KEEP YOU HUNGRY, THEY HAVE TO
TO MAKE ME ANGRY?
MAYBE
I DUNNO
MY DAD SAYS THEY DON'T FEED YOU BECAUSE IT BRINGS OUT YOUR TRUE NATURE. YOU BECOME FIERCE
HE GOT THAT RIGHT
SO WHY ARE THEY KEEPING YOU HERE?
SO I WONT RUN AWAY FROM MY OWN WEDDING
HEH
WITH ALL THE FOOD YOU EAT, THEY SHOULDN'T BE TOO MUCH WORRIED ABOUT YOUR RUNNING ABILITIES
DON'T SAY THAT!
SHIT

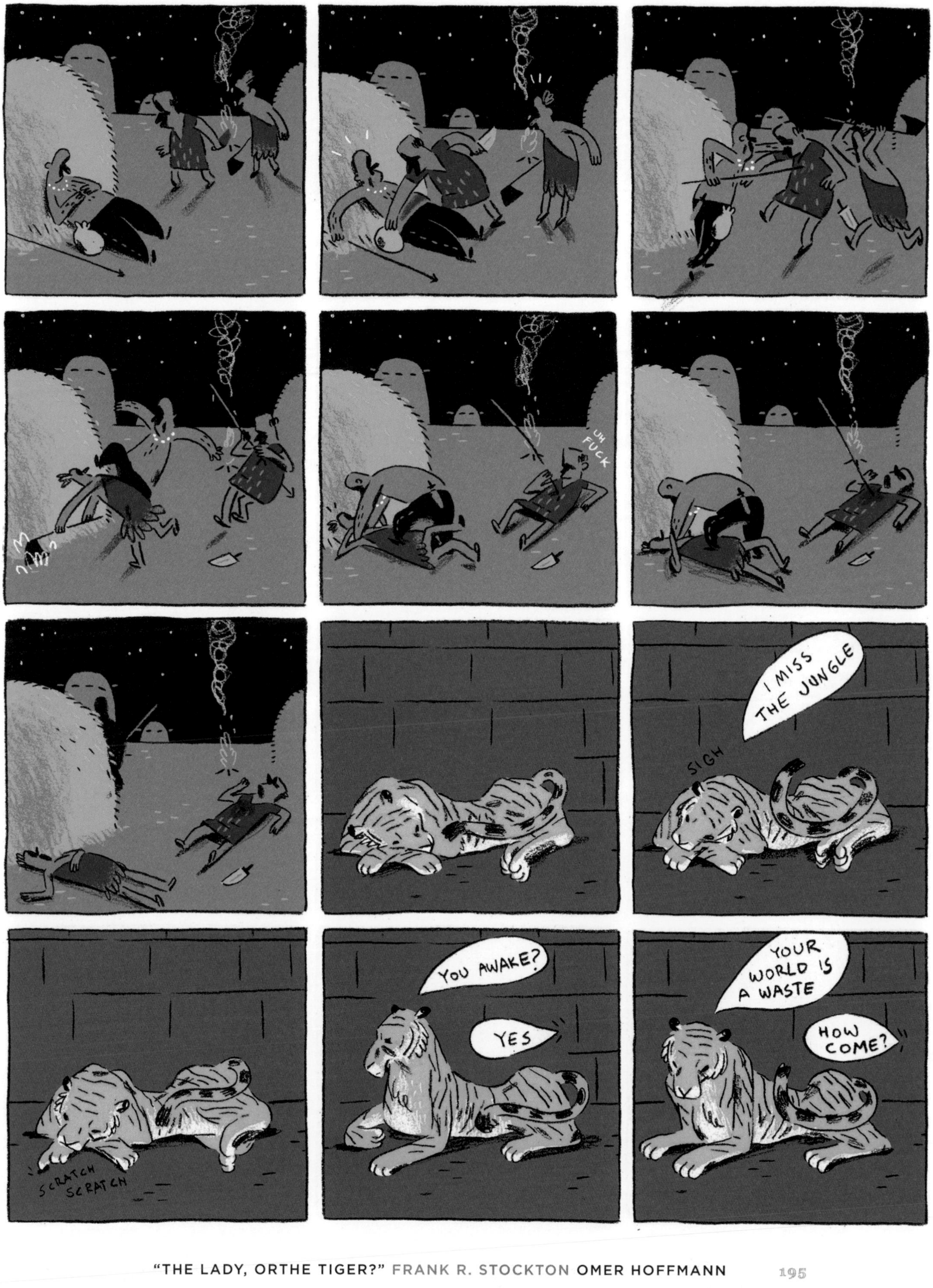
UH
FUCK
SIGH
I MISS THE JUNGLE
SCRATCH SCRATCH
YOU AWAKE?
YES
YOUR WORLD IS A WASTE
HOW COME?

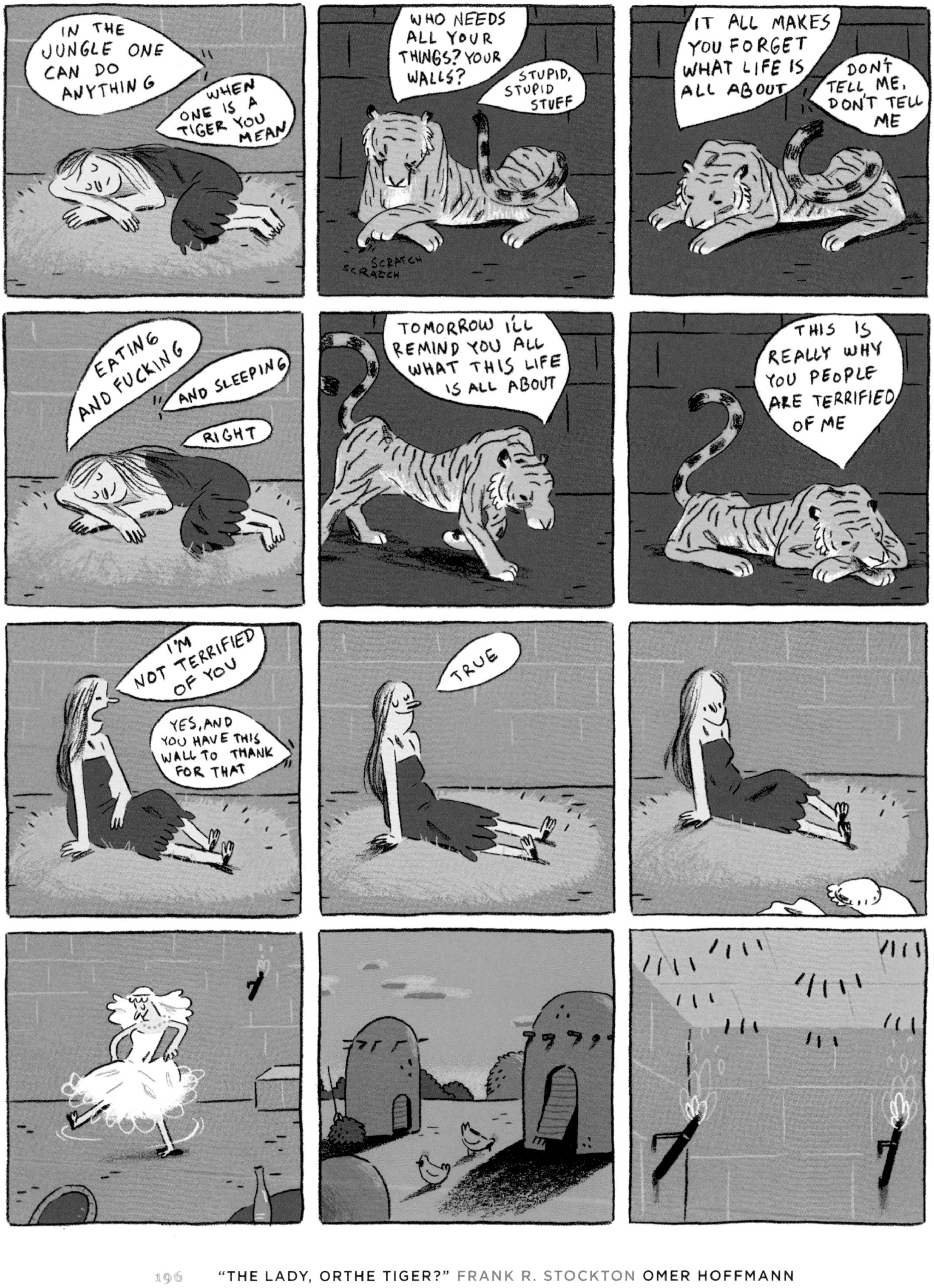
IN THE JUNGLE ONE CAN DO ANYTHING
WHEN ONE IS A TIGER YOU MEAN
WHO NEEDS ALL YOUR THINGS? YOUR WALLS?
STUPID, STUPID STUFF
SCRATCH SCRATCH
IT ALL MAKES YOU FORGET WHAT LIFE IS ALL ABOUT
DON'T TELL ME, DON'T TELL ME
EATING AND FUCKING
AND SLEEPING
RIGHT
TOMORROW I'LL REMIND YOU ALL WHAT THIS LIFE IS ALL ABOUT
THIS IS REALLY WHY YOU PEOPLE ARE TERRIFIED OF ME
I'M NOT TERRIFIED OF YOU
YES, AND YOU HAVE THIS WALL TO THANK FOR THAT
TRUE

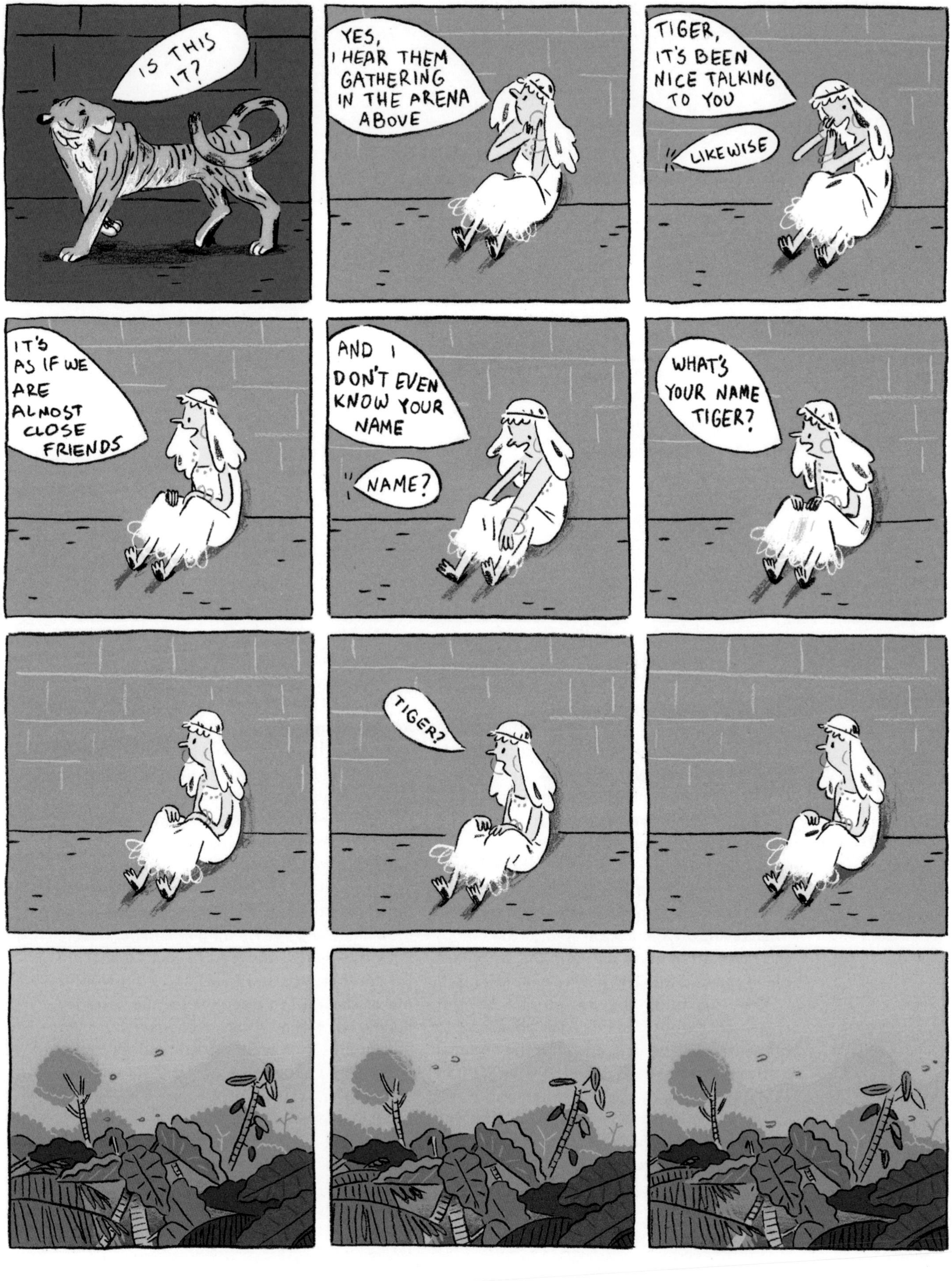
IS THIS IT?
YES, I HEAR THEM GATHERING IN THE ARENA ABOVE
TIGER, IT'S BEEN NICE TALKING TO YOU
LIKEWISE
IT'S AS IF WE ARE ALMOST CLOSE FRIENDS
AND I DON'T EVEN KNOW YOUR NAME
NAME?
WHAT'S YOUR NAME TIGER?
TIGER?

The Trial

Franz Kafka

ART/ADAPTATION BY Landis Blair

FRANZ KAFKA'S BEST-KNOWN WORKS involve people caught in terrifying, inexplicable situations in which they have no control. In "The Metamorphosis," a hapless salesman wakes up transformed into a giant bug. In *The Castle*, the protagonist unsuccessfully tries to navigate the bizarre bureaucracy that governs a village. *The Trial* opens with Joseph K. being arrested for undeclared reasons by authorities of an unknown agency. He spends the rest of the novel attempting to figure out what he's being charged with and how to defend himself.

The Trial might be literature's perfect statement about dealing with government bureaucracy in general and with the criminal justice system in particular. Kafka wrote it in 1914–1915, when the unique dread and suffocation of living in the twentieth century was becoming apparent. It definitively captures his themes of alienation, angst, and authority.

Another way of looking at *The Trial* is as a reverse mystery novel. In pretty much all whodunits, the quest is to discover the identity of the criminal and bring them to justice. In Kafka's funhouse-mirror world, Joseph K. is apprehended in the beginning and spends the rest of the novel trying to sleuth out who has arrested him, why, and what he can do about it.

Landis Blair's cross-hatching and other fine patterning give his work—which includes the graphic novels *The Hunting Accident* and *The Envious Siblings*—the feel of a much earlier era. He captures the darkness and claustrophobia of *The Trial* to a tee. As for the narrative, Landis has turned it into a choose-your-own-adventure. (Each section opens with a limerick, written by Landis, that cheekily summarizes the events.) You get to decide how Joseph K. will navigate the confusing and uncaring system that threatens him. But don't fret about making the "right" choices. This is Kafka. You can't win.

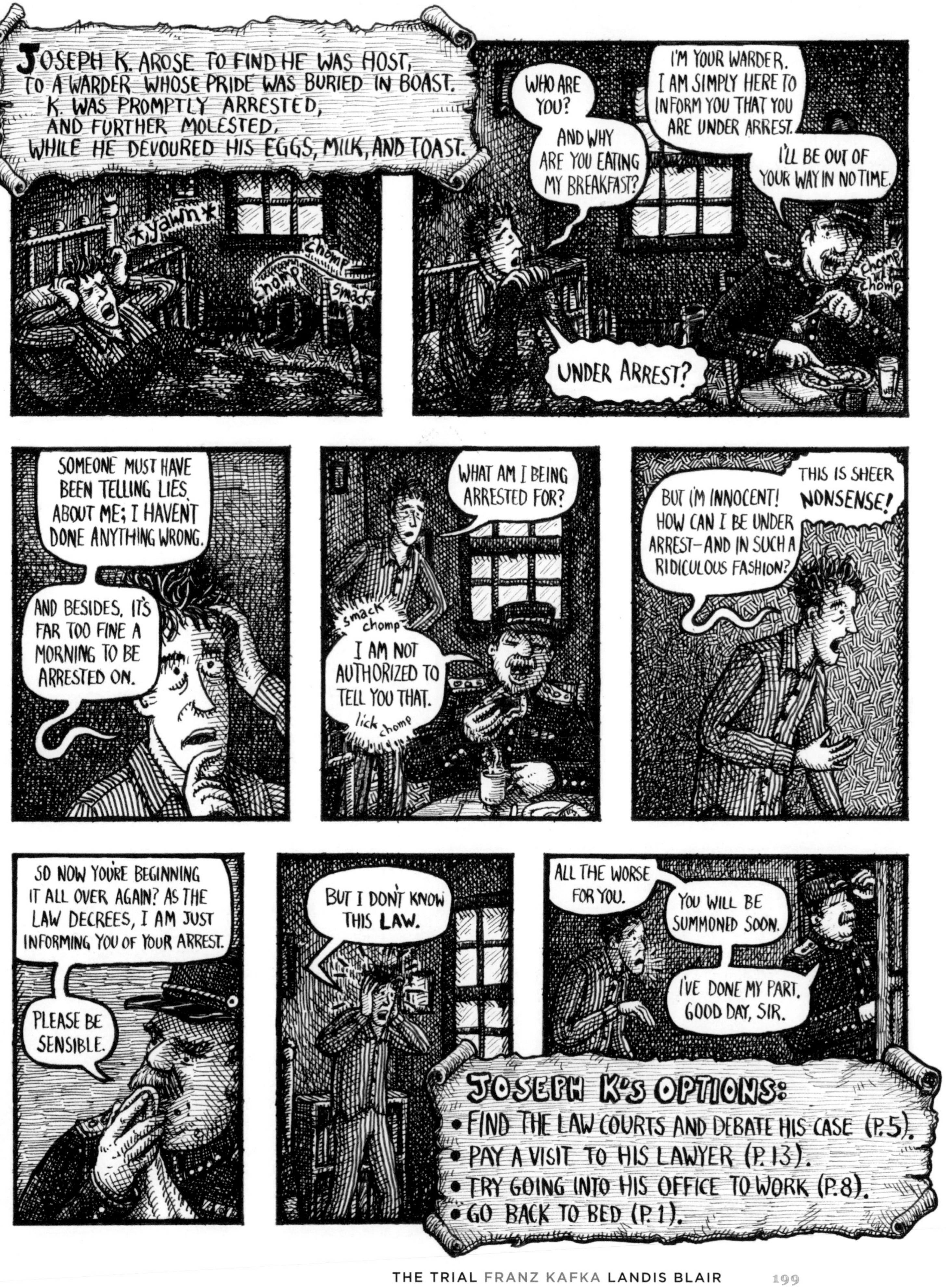
JOSEPH K. AROSE TO FIND HE WAS HOST,
TO A WARDER WHOSE PRIDE WAS BURIED IN BOAST.
K. WAS PROMPTLY ARRESTED,
AND FURTHER MOLESTED,
WHILE HE DEVOURED HIS EGGS, MILK, AND TOAST.
yawn
chomp
chomp
smack
WHO ARE YOU?
AND WHY ARE YOU EATING MY BREAKFAST?
I'M YOUR WARDER. I AM SIMPLY HERE TO INFORM YOU THAT YOU ARE UNDER ARREST.
I'LL BE OUT OF YOUR WAY IN NO TIME.
chomp
chomp
UNDER ARREST?
SOMEONE MUST HAVE BEEN TELLING LIES ABOUT ME; I HAVEN'T DONE ANYTHING WRONG.
AND BESIDES, IT'S FAR TOO FINE A MORNING TO BE ARRESTED ON.
WHAT AM I BEING ARRESTED FOR?
smack
chomp
I AM NOT AUTHORIZED TO TELL YOU THAT.
lick
chomp
BUT I'M INNOCENT! HOW CAN I BE UNDER ARREST—AND IN SUCH A RIDICULOUS FASHION?
THIS IS SHEER NONSENSE!
SO NOW YOU'RE BEGINNING IT ALL OVER AGAIN? AS THE LAW DECREES, I AM JUST INFORMING YOU OF YOUR ARREST.
PLEASE BE SENSIBLE.
BUT I DON'T KNOW THIS LAW.
ALL THE WORSE FOR YOU.
YOU WILL BE SUMMONED SOON.
I'VE DONE MY PART. GOOD DAY, SIR.
JOSEPH K'S OPTIONS:
• FIND THE LAW COURTS AND DEBATE HIS CASE (P.5).
• PAY A VISIT TO HIS LAWYER (P.13).
• TRY GOING INTO HIS OFFICE TO WORK (P.8).
• GO BACK TO BED (P.1).

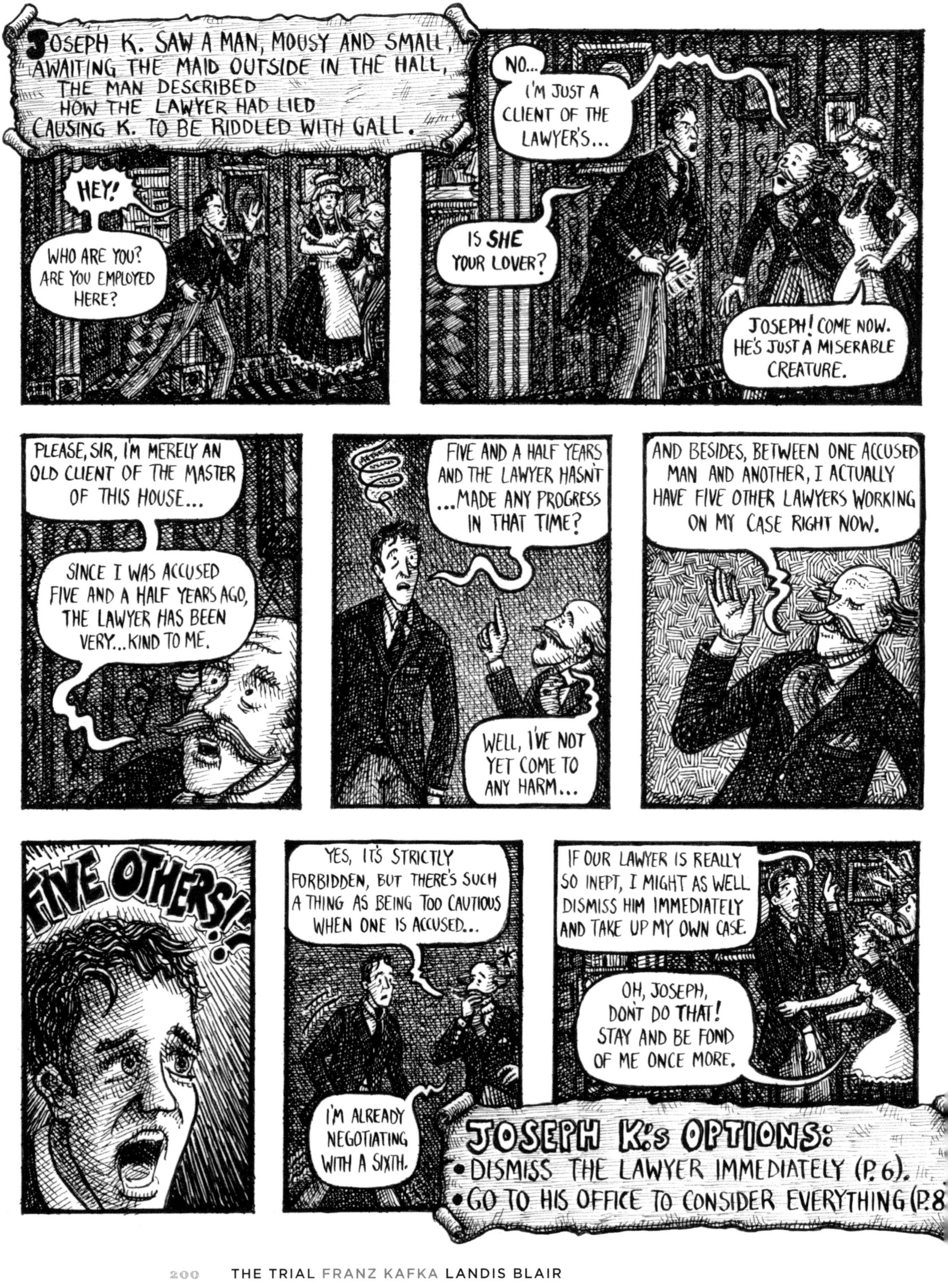
JOSEPH K. SAW A MAN, MOUSY AND SMALL,
AWAITING THE MAID OUTSIDE IN THE HALL,
THE MAN DESCRIBED
HOW THE LAWYER HAD LIED
CAUSING K. TO BE RIDDLED WITH GALL.
HEY!
WHO ARE YOU? ARE YOU EMPLOYED HERE?
NO...
I'M JUST A CLIENT OF THE LAWYER'S...
IS SHE YOUR LOVER?
JOSEPH! COME NOW. HE'S JUST A MISERABLE CREATURE.
PLEASE, SIR, I'M MERELY AN OLD CLIENT OF THE MASTER OF THIS HOUSE...
SINCE I WAS ACCUSED FIVE AND A HALF YEARS AGO, THE LAWYER HAS BEEN VERY...KIND TO ME.
FIVE AND A HALF YEARS AND THE LAWYER HASN'T ...MADE ANY PROGRESS IN THAT TIME?
WELL, I'VE NOT YET COME TO ANY HARM...
AND BESIDES, BETWEEN ONE ACCUSED MAN AND ANOTHER, I ACTUALLY HAVE FIVE OTHER LAWYERS WORKING ON MY CASE RIGHT NOW.
FIVE OTHERS!?
YES, IT'S STRICTLY FORBIDDEN, BUT THERE'S SUCH A THING AS BEING TOO CAUTIOUS WHEN ONE IS ACCUSED...
I'M ALREADY NEGOTIATING WITH A SIXTH.
IF OUR LAWYER IS REALLY SO INEPT, I MIGHT AS WELL DISMISS HIM IMMEDIATELY AND TAKE UP MY OWN CASE.
OH, JOSEPH, DON'T DO THAT! STAY AND BE FOND OF ME ONCE MORE.
JOSEPH K.'s OPTIONS:
• DISMISS THE LAWYER IMMEDIATELY (P. 6).
• GO TO HIS OFFICE TO CONSIDER EVERYTHING (P. 8

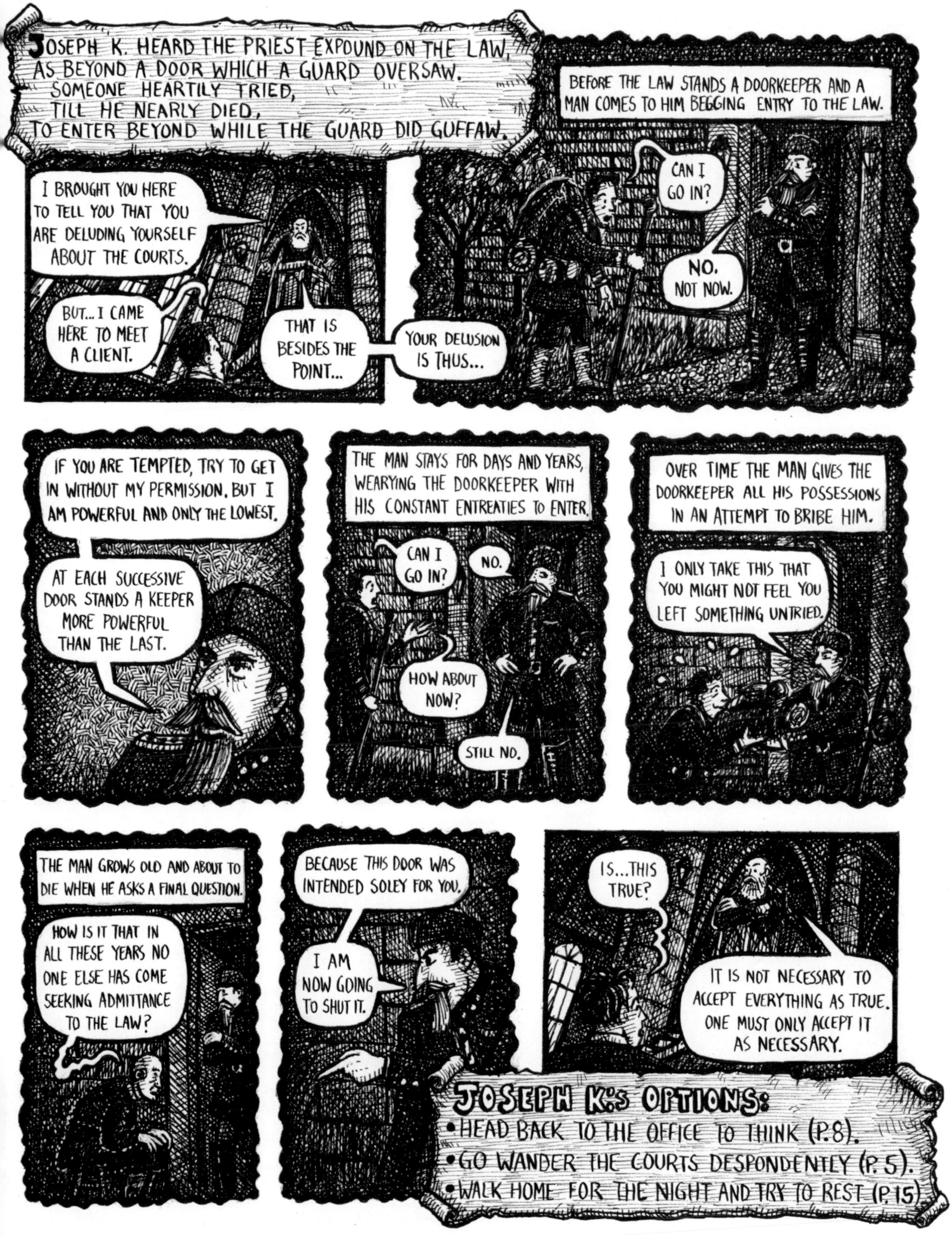
JOSEPH K. HEARD THE PRIEST EXPOUND ON THE LAW,
AS BEYOND A DOOR WHICH A GUARD OVERSAW.
SOMEONE HEARTILY TRIED,
TILL HE NEARLY DIED,
TO ENTER BEYOND WHILE THE GUARD DID GUFFAW.
I BROUGHT YOU HERE TO TELL YOU THAT YOU ARE DELUDING YOURSELF ABOUT THE COURTS.
BUT... I CAME HERE TO MEET A CLIENT.
THAT IS BESIDES THE POINT...
YOUR DELUSION IS THUS...
BEFORE THE LAW STANDS A DOORKEEPER AND A MAN COMES TO HIM BEGGING ENTRY TO THE LAW.
CAN I GO IN?
NO. NOT NOW.
IF YOU ARE TEMPTED, TRY TO GET IN WITHOUT MY PERMISSION. BUT I AM POWERFUL AND ONLY THE LOWEST.
AT EACH SUCCESSIVE DOOR STANDS A KEEPER MORE POWERFUL THAN THE LAST.
THE MAN STAYS FOR DAYS AND YEARS, WEARYING THE DOORKEEPER WITH HIS CONSTANT ENTREATIES TO ENTER.
CAN I GO IN?
NO.
HOW ABOUT NOW?
STILL NO.
OVER TIME THE MAN GIVES THE DOORKEEPER ALL HIS POSSESSIONS IN AN ATTEMPT TO BRIBE HIM.
I ONLY TAKE THIS THAT YOU MIGHT NOT FEEL YOU LEFT SOMETHING UNTRIED.
THE MAN GROWS OLD AND ABOUT TO DIE WHEN HE ASKS A FINAL QUESTION.
HOW IS IT THAT IN ALL THESE YEARS NO ONE ELSE HAS COME SEEKING ADMITTANCE TO THE LAW?
BECAUSE THIS DOOR WAS INTENDED SOLEY FOR YOU.
I AM NOW GOING TO SHUT IT.
IS...THIS TRUE?
IT IS NOT NECESSARY TO ACCEPT EVERYTHING AS TRUE. ONE MUST ONLY ACCEPT IT AS NECESSARY.
JOSEPH K.'S OPTIONS:
•HEAD BACK TO THE OFFICE TO THINK (P.8).
•GO WANDER THE COURTS DESPONDENTLY (P.5).
•WALK HOME FOR THE NIGHT AND TRY TO REST (P.15)

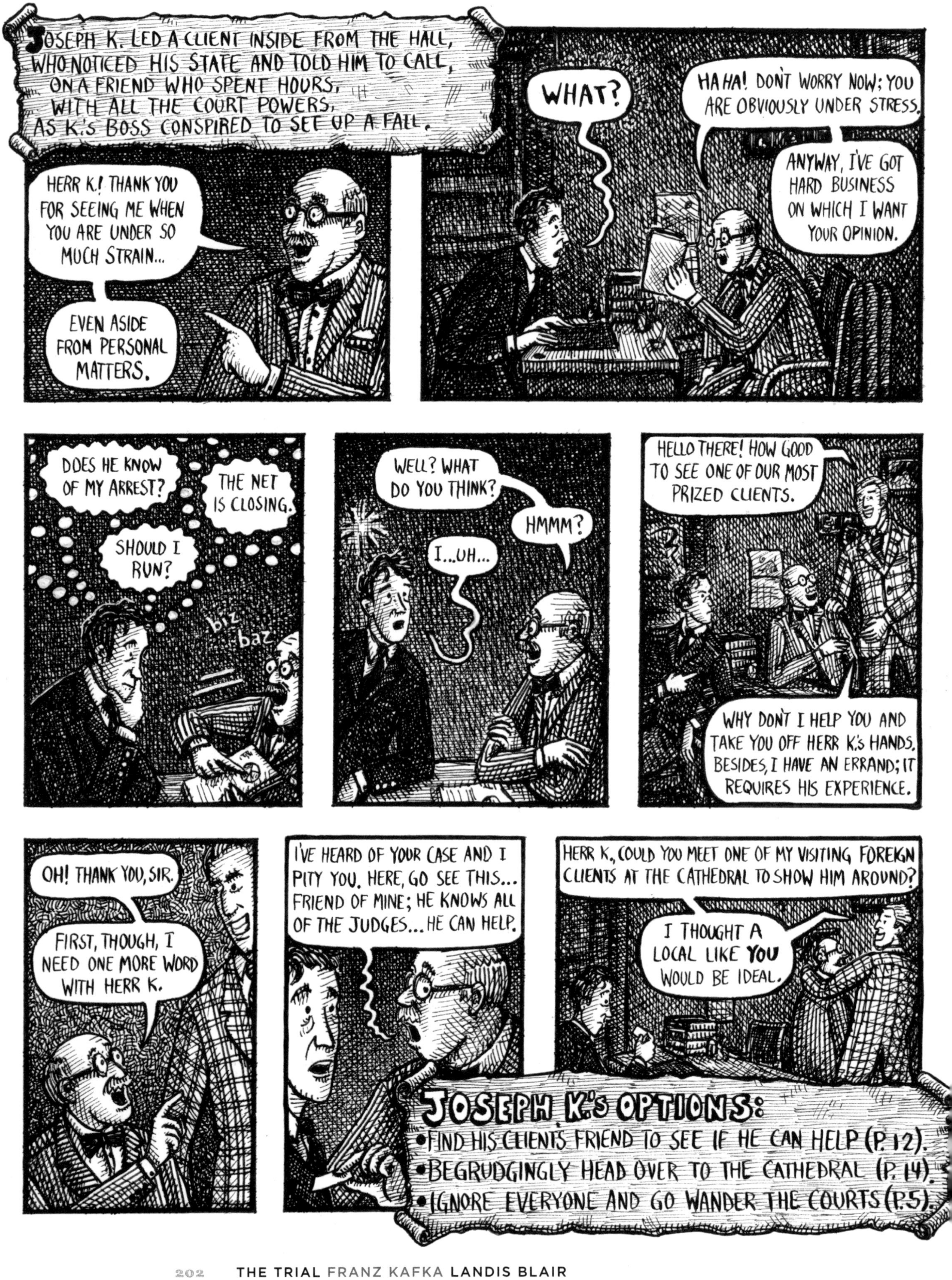
JOSEPH K. LED A CLIENT INSIDE FROM THE HALL, WHO NOTICED HIS STATE AND TOLD HIM TO CALL, ON A FRIEND WHO SPENT HOURS, WITH ALL THE COURT POWERS, AS K.'S BOSS CONSPIRED TO SET UP A FALL.
HERR K.! THANK YOU FOR SEEING ME WHEN YOU ARE UNDER SO MUCH STRAIN...
EVEN ASIDE FROM PERSONAL MATTERS.
WHAT?
HA HA! DON'T WORRY NOW; YOU ARE OBVIOUSLY UNDER STRESS.
ANYWAY, I'VE GOT HARD BUSINESS ON WHICH I WANT YOUR OPINION.
DOES HE KNOW OF MY ARREST?
THE NET IS CLOSING.
SHOULD I RUN?
biz baz
WELL? WHAT DO YOU THINK?
HMMM?
I...UH...
HELLO THERE! HOW GOOD TO SEE ONE OF OUR MOST PRIZED CLIENTS.
WHY DON'T I HELP YOU AND TAKE YOU OFF HERR K.'S HANDS. BESIDES, I HAVE AN ERRAND; IT REQUIRES HIS EXPERIENCE.
OH! THANK YOU, SIR.
FIRST, THOUGH, I NEED ONE MORE WORD WITH HERR K.
I'VE HEARD OF YOUR CASE AND I PITY YOU. HERE, GO SEE THIS... FRIEND OF MINE; HE KNOWS ALL OF THE JUDGES... HE CAN HELP.
HERR K., COULD YOU MEET ONE OF MY VISITING FOREIGN CLIENTS AT THE CATHEDRAL TO SHOW HIM AROUND?
I THOUGHT A LOCAL LIKE YOU WOULD BE IDEAL.
JOSEPH K.'s OPTIONS:
•FIND HIS CLIENT'S FRIEND TO SEE IF HE CAN HELP (P. 12).
•BEGRUDGINGLY HEAD OVER TO THE CATHEDRAL (P. 14).
•IGNORE EVERYONE AND GO WANDER THE COURTS (P. 5).

JOSEPH K. DID THEN LEAVE IN A FLURRY,
RUSHING ABOUT WITH PROFOUNDEST WORRY.
HE SOUGHT THE COURTS,
AND THEIR COHORTS,
TILL HIS VISION BECAME QUITE BLURRY.

...I THINK THESE ARE THE COURTS.

GULP

EXCUSE ME, MISS. DO YOU KNOW WHERE THE COURT OF INQUIRY IS LOCATED?

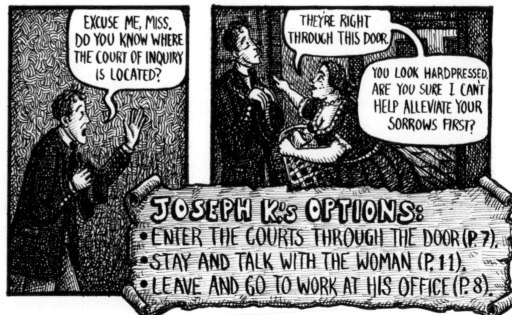

THEY'RE RIGHT THROUGH THIS DOOR.

YOU LOOK HARDPRESSED, ARE YOU SURE I CAN'T HELP ALLEVIATE YOUR SORROWS FIRST?

JOSEPH K.'s OPTIONS:
• ENTER THE COURTS THROUGH THE DOOR (P. 7).
• STAY AND TALK WITH THE WOMAN (P. 11).
• LEAVE AND GO TO WORK AT HIS OFFICE (P. 8).

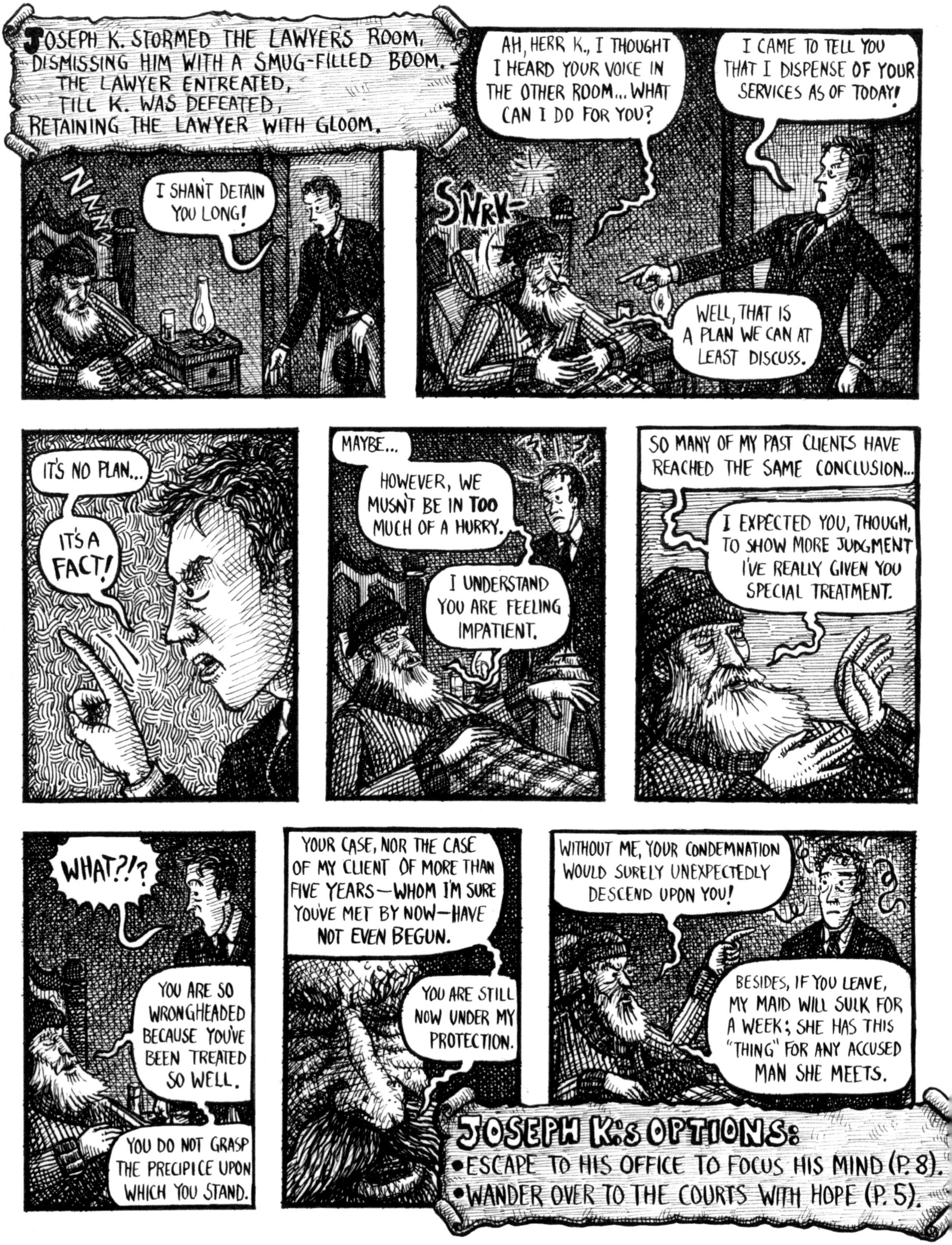
JOSEPH K. STORMED THE LAWYER'S ROOM, DISMISSING HIM WITH A SMUG-FILLED BOOM. THE LAWYER ENTREATED, TILL K. WAS DEFEATED, RETAINING THE LAWYER WITH GLOOM.
ZZZZ
I SHAN'T DETAIN YOU LONG!
SNRK-
AH, HERR K., I THOUGHT I HEARD YOUR VOICE IN THE OTHER ROOM... WHAT CAN I DO FOR YOU?
I CAME TO TELL YOU THAT I DISPENSE OF YOUR SERVICES AS OF TODAY!
WELL, THAT IS A PLAN WE CAN AT LEAST DISCUSS.
IT'S NO PLAN...
IT'S A FACT!
MAYBE...
HOWEVER, WE MUSN'T BE IN TOO MUCH OF A HURRY.
I UNDERSTAND YOU ARE FEELING IMPATIENT.
SO MANY OF MY PAST CLIENTS HAVE REACHED THE SAME CONCLUSION...
I EXPECTED YOU, THOUGH, TO SHOW MORE JUDGMENT I'VE REALLY GIVEN YOU SPECIAL TREATMENT.
WHAT?!?
YOU ARE SO WRONGHEADED BECAUSE YOU'VE BEEN TREATED SO WELL.
YOU DO NOT GRASP THE PRECIPICE UPON WHICH YOU STAND.
YOUR CASE, NOR THE CASE OF MY CLIENT OF MORE THAN FIVE YEARS—WHOM I'M SURE YOU'VE MET BY NOW—HAVE NOT EVEN BEGUN.
YOU ARE STILL NOW UNDER MY PROTECTION.
WITHOUT ME, YOUR CONDEMNATION WOULD SURELY UNEXPECTEDLY DESCEND UPON YOU!
BESIDES, IF YOU LEAVE, MY MAID WILL SULK FOR A WEEK; SHE HAS THIS "THING" FOR ANY ACCUSED MAN SHE MEETS.
JOSEPH K.'s OPTIONS:
•ESCAPE TO HIS OFFICE TO FOCUS HIS MIND (P. 8).
•WANDER OVER TO THE COURTS WITH HOPE (P. 5).

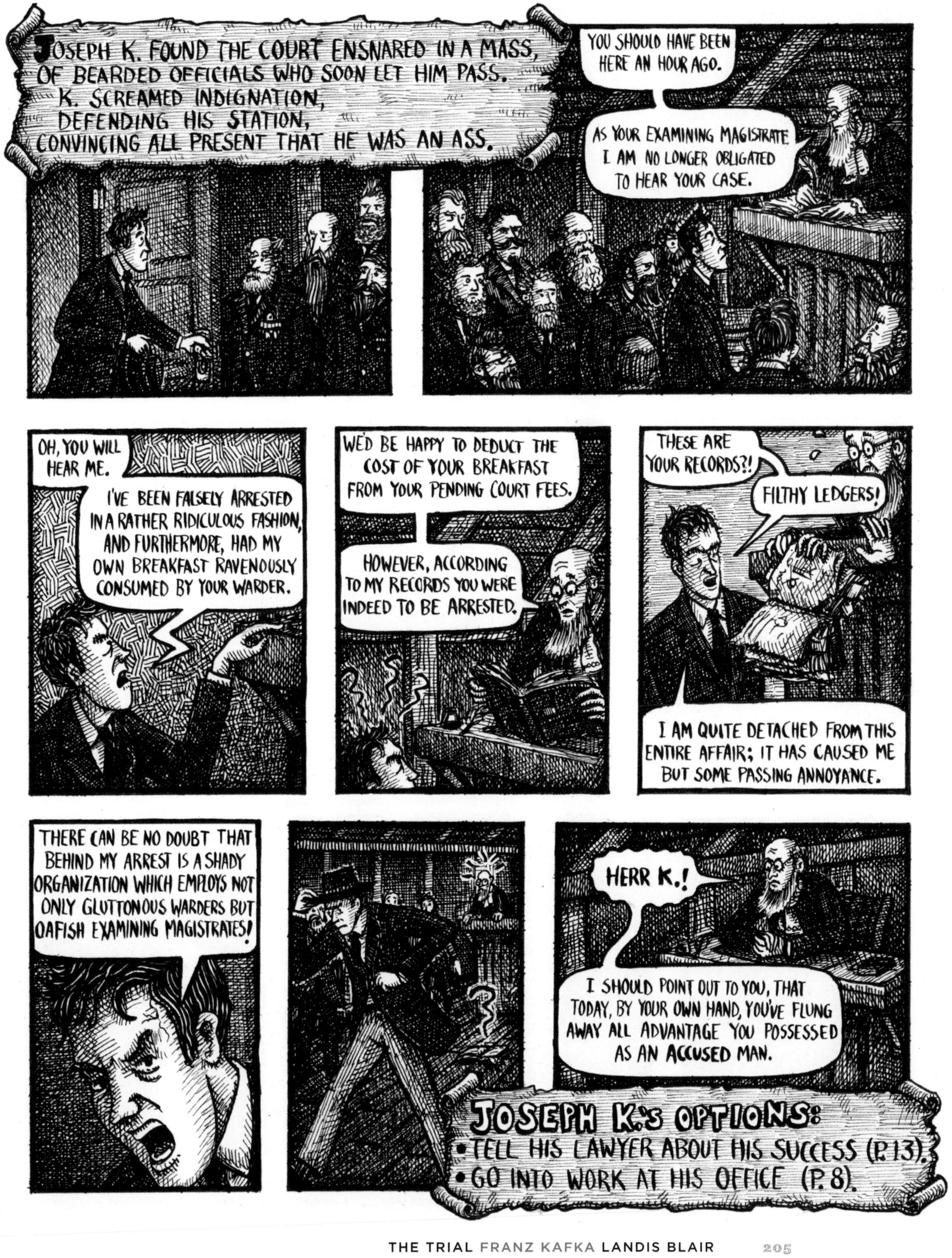
JOSEPH K. FOUND THE COURT ENSNARED IN A MASS,
OF BEARDED OFFICIALS WHO SOON LET HIM PASS.
K. SCREAMED INDIGNATION,
DEFENDING HIS STATION,
CONVINCING ALL PRESENT THAT HE WAS AN ASS.
YOU SHOULD HAVE BEEN HERE AN HOUR AGO.
AS YOUR EXAMINING MAGISTRATE I AM NO LONGER OBLIGATED TO HEAR YOUR CASE.
OH, YOU WILL HEAR ME.
I'VE BEEN FALSELY ARRESTED IN A RATHER RIDICULOUS FASHION, AND FURTHERMORE, HAD MY OWN BREAKFAST RAVENOUSLY CONSUMED BY YOUR WARDER.
WE'D BE HAPPY TO DEDUCT THE COST OF YOUR BREAKFAST FROM YOUR PENDING COURT FEES.
HOWEVER, ACCORDING TO MY RECORDS YOU WERE INDEED TO BE ARRESTED.
THESE ARE YOUR RECORDS?!
FILTHY LEDGERS!
I AM QUITE DETACHED FROM THIS ENTIRE AFFAIR; IT HAS CAUSED ME BUT SOME PASSING ANNOYANCE.
THERE CAN BE NO DOUBT THAT BEHIND MY ARREST IS A SHADY ORGANIZATION WHICH EMPLOYS NOT ONLY GLUTTONOUS WARDERS BUT OAFISH EXAMINING MAGISTRATES!
HERR K.!
I SHOULD POINT OUT TO YOU, THAT TODAY, BY YOUR OWN HAND, YOU'VE FLUNG AWAY ALL ADVANTAGE YOU POSSESSED AS AN ACCUSED MAN.
JOSEPH K.'s OPTIONS:
• TELL HIS LAWYER ABOUT HIS SUCCESS (P. 13).
• GO INTO WORK AT HIS OFFICE (P. 8).

JOSEPH K. ENTERED HIS OFFICE AND SWORE, GREETING HIS BOSS FULL OF FAKE RAPPORT. WHILE CLIENTS WERE WAITING, AND BOSS BERATING, A DEEP SIGH EMERGED FROM UNDER A DOOR.

JOLLY MORNING...ER... AFTERNOON, K.!

COME NOW, YOU LOOK FURTHER FROM PERFECTION THAN USUAL. HA HA!

SIR...THAT'S MY DESK.

I WAS JUST LOOKING FOR SOME PAPERS TO ASSIST ONE OF YOUR MANY WAITING CLIENTS.

JUDGING BY YOUR FACE, AND THE CLOCK'S, I THINK I MIGHT ALLEVIATE SOME OF YOUR CURRENT...TROUBLES.

WHATEVER DO YOU MEAN BY THAT?

MAYBE YOU NEED A DAY OFF TO CLEAR YOUR HEAD, EH? I CAN EASILY MANAGE YOUR AFFAIRS HERE...

PROVIDED YOU GIVE ME YOUR DESK KEY.

SIGHHH

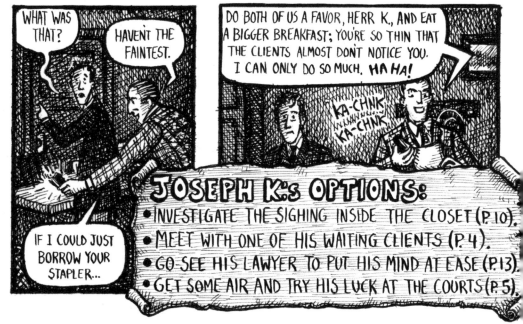

WHAT WAS THAT?

HAVEN'T THE FAINTEST.

IF I COULD JUST BORROW YOUR STAPLER...

DO BOTH OF US A FAVOR, HERR K., AND EAT A BIGGER BREAKFAST; YOU'RE SO THIN THAT THE CLIENTS ALMOST DON'T NOTICE YOU. I CAN ONLY DO SO MUCH. HA HA!

KA-CHNK KA-CHNK

JOSEPH K.'s OPTIONS:
• INVESTIGATE THE SIGHING INSIDE THE CLOSET (P. 10).
• MEET WITH ONE OF HIS WAITING CLIENTS (P. 4).
• GO SEE HIS LAWYER TO PUT HIS MIND AT EASE (P. 13).
• GET SOME AIR AND TRY HIS LUCK AT THE COURTS (P. 5).

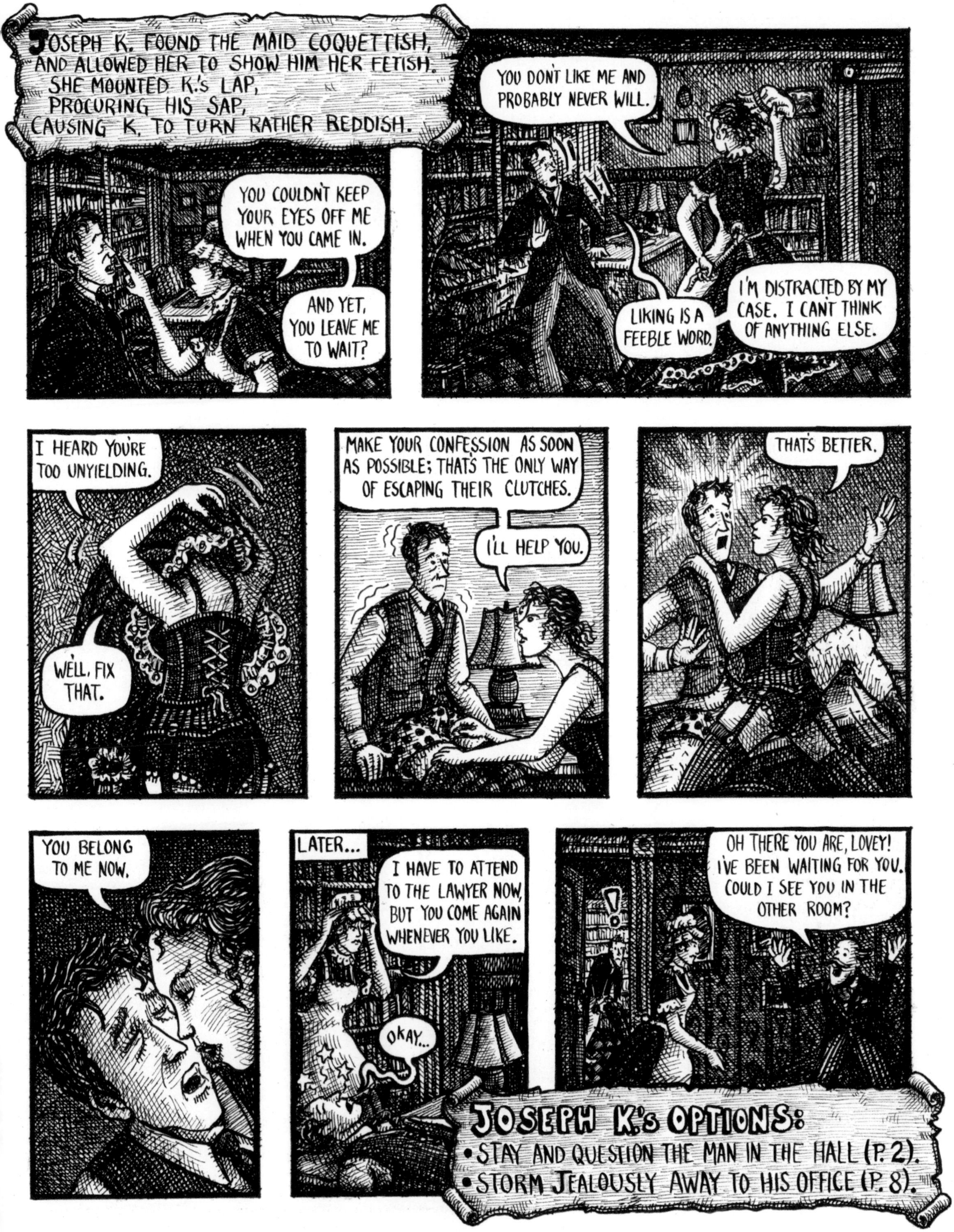
JOSEPH K. FOUND THE MAID COQUETTISH,
AND ALLOWED HER TO SHOW HIM HER FETISH.
SHE MOUNTED K.'s LAP,
PROCURING HIS SAP,
CAUSING K. TO TURN RATHER REDDISH.
YOU COULDN'T KEEP YOUR EYES OFF ME WHEN YOU CAME IN.
AND YET, YOU LEAVE ME TO WAIT?
YOU DON'T LIKE ME AND PROBABLY NEVER WILL.
LIKING IS A FEEBLE WORD.
I'M DISTRACTED BY MY CASE. I CAN'T THINK OF ANYTHING ELSE.
I HEARD YOU'RE TOO UNYIELDING.
WELL, FIX THAT.
MAKE YOUR CONFESSION AS SOON AS POSSIBLE; THAT'S THE ONLY WAY OF ESCAPING THEIR CLUTCHES.
I'LL HELP YOU.
THAT'S BETTER.
YOU BELONG TO ME NOW.
LATER...
I HAVE TO ATTEND TO THE LAWYER NOW, BUT YOU COME AGAIN WHENEVER YOU LIKE.
OKAY...
OH THERE YOU ARE, LOVEY! I'VE BEEN WAITING FOR YOU. COULD I SEE YOU IN THE OTHER ROOM?
JOSEPH K.'s OPTIONS:
• STAY AND QUESTION THE MAN IN THE HALL (P. 2).
• STORM JEALOUSLY AWAY TO HIS OFFICE (P. 8).

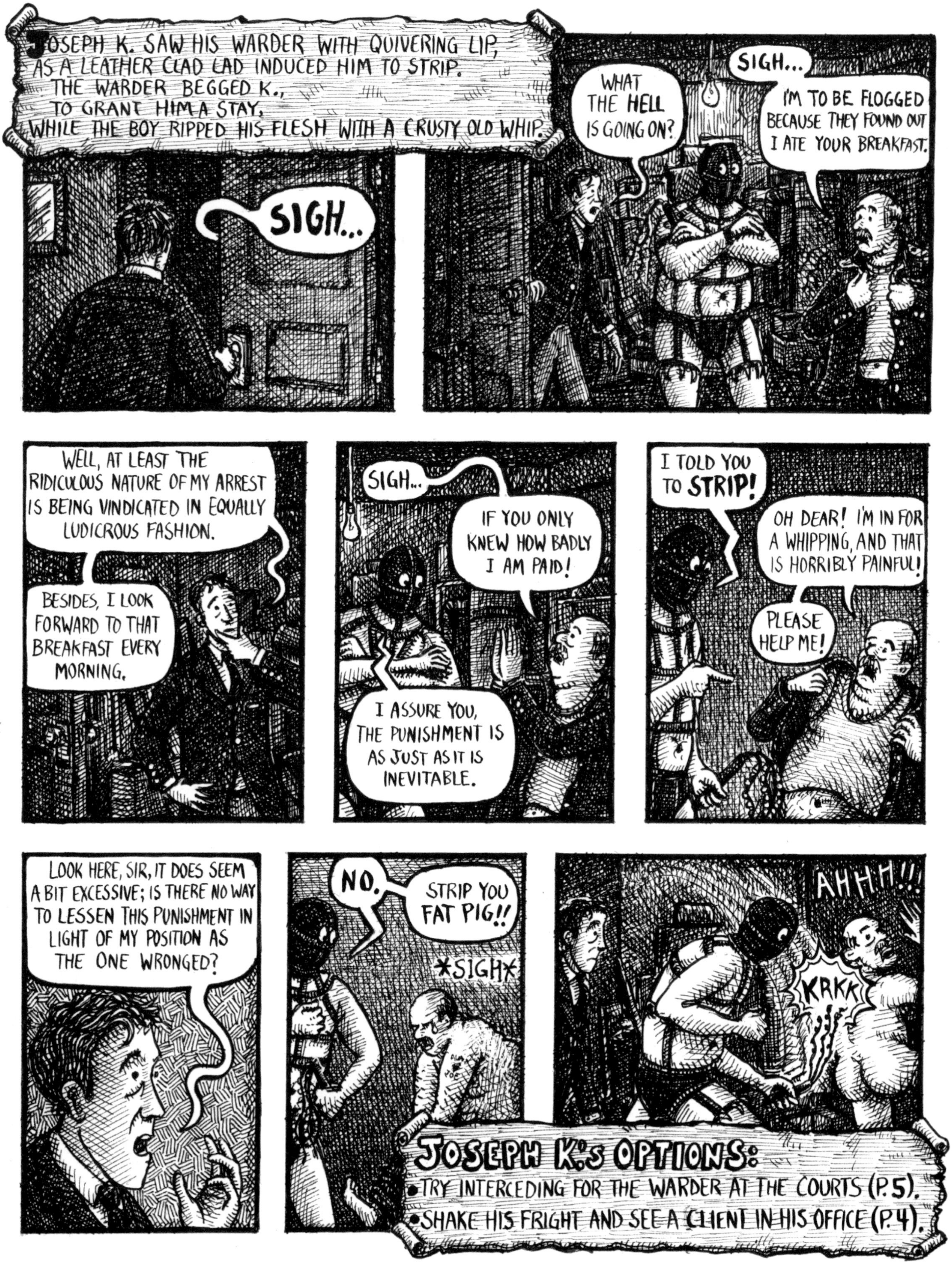
JOSEPH K. SAW HIS WARDER WITH QUIVERING LIP,
AS A LEATHER CLAD LAD INDUCED HIM TO STRIP.
THE WARDER BEGGED K.,
TO GRANT HIM A STAY,
WHILE THE BOY RIPPED HIS FLESH WITH A CRUSTY OLD WHIP.
SIGH...
WHAT THE HELL IS GOING ON?
SIGH...
I'M TO BE FLOGGED BECAUSE THEY FOUND OUT I ATE YOUR BREAKFAST.
WELL, AT LEAST THE RIDICULOUS NATURE OF MY ARREST IS BEING VINDICATED IN EQUALLY LUDICROUS FASHION.
BESIDES, I LOOK FORWARD TO THAT BREAKFAST EVERY MORNING.
SIGH...
IF YOU ONLY KNEW HOW BADLY I AM PAID!
I ASSURE YOU, THE PUNISHMENT IS AS JUST AS IT IS INEVITABLE.
I TOLD YOU TO STRIP!
OH DEAR! I'M IN FOR A WHIPPING, AND THAT IS HORRIBLY PAINFUL!
PLEASE HELP ME!
LOOK HERE, SIR, IT DOES SEEM A BIT EXCESSIVE; IS THERE NO WAY TO LESSEN THIS PUNISHMENT IN LIGHT OF MY POSITION AS THE ONE WRONGED?
NO.
STRIP YOU FAT PIG!!
SIGH
AHHH!!!
KRKK
JOSEPH K.'s OPTIONS:
• TRY INTERCEDING FOR THE WARDER AT THE COURTS (P. 5).
• SHAKE HIS FRIGHT AND SEE A CLIENT IN HIS OFFICE (P. 4).

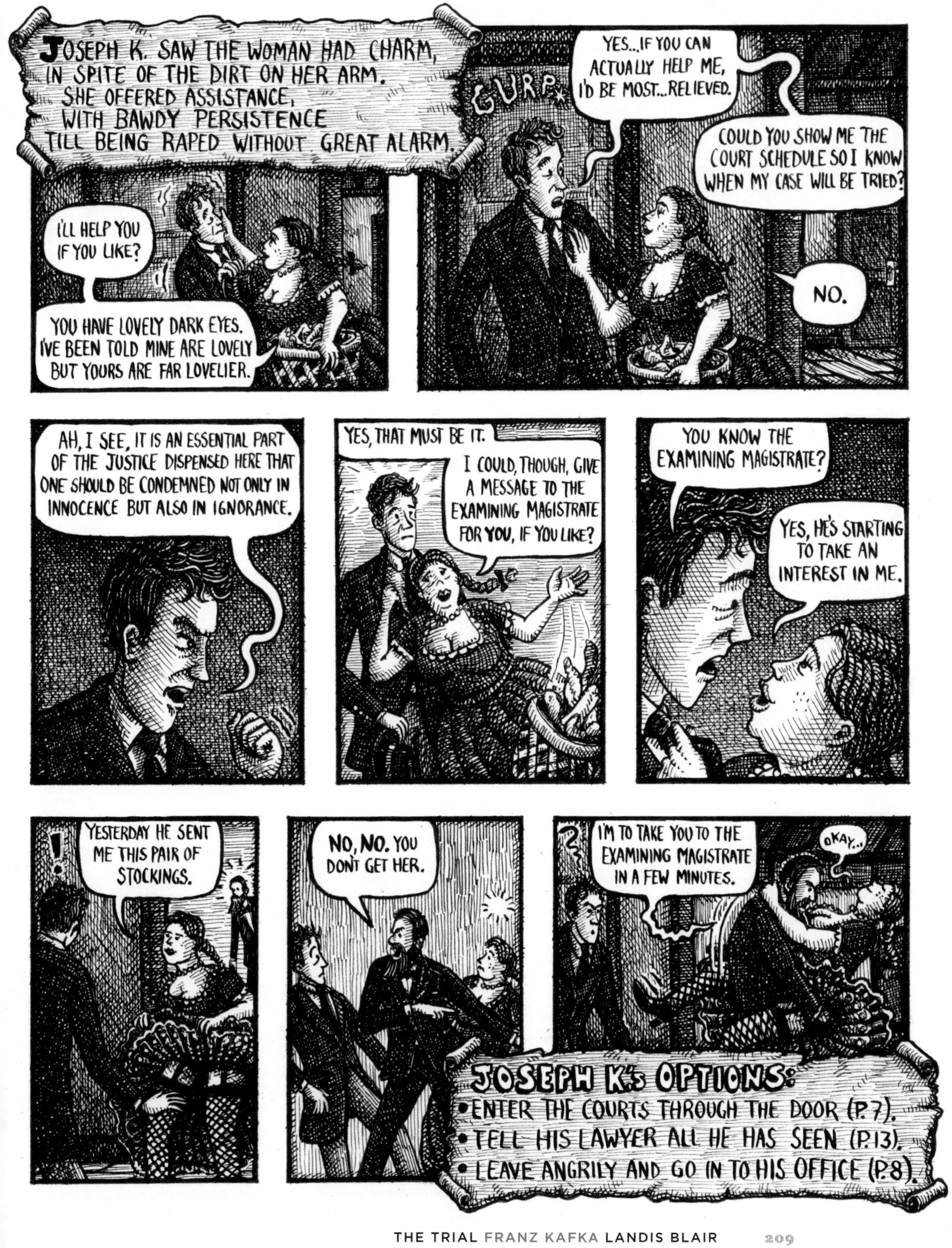

JOSEPH K. SAW THE WOMAN HAD CHARM, IN SPITE OF THE DIRT ON HER ARM. SHE OFFERED ASSISTANCE, WITH BAWDY PERSISTENCE TILL BEING RAPED WITHOUT GREAT ALARM.
I'LL HELP YOU IF YOU LIKE?
YOU HAVE LOVELY DARK EYES. I'VE BEEN TOLD MINE ARE LOVELY BUT YOURS ARE FAR LOVELIER.
GURP
YES... IF YOU CAN ACTUALLY HELP ME, I'D BE MOST... RELIEVED.
COULD YOU SHOW ME THE COURT SCHEDULE SO I KNOW WHEN MY CASE WILL BE TRIED?
NO.
AH, I SEE, IT IS AN ESSENTIAL PART OF THE JUSTICE DISPENSED HERE THAT ONE SHOULD BE CONDEMNED NOT ONLY IN INNOCENCE BUT ALSO IN IGNORANCE.
YES, THAT MUST BE IT.
I COULD, THOUGH, GIVE A MESSAGE TO THE EXAMINING MAGISTRATE FOR YOU, IF YOU LIKE?
YOU KNOW THE EXAMINING MAGISTRATE?
YES, HE'S STARTING TO TAKE AN INTEREST IN ME.
YESTERDAY HE SENT ME THIS PAIR OF STOCKINGS.
NO, NO. YOU DON'T GET HER.
I'M TO TAKE YOU TO THE EXAMINING MAGISTRATE IN A FEW MINUTES.
OKAY...
JOSEPH K.'s OPTIONS:
• ENTER THE COURTS THROUGH THE DOOR (P. 7).
• TELL HIS LAWYER ALL HE HAS SEEN (P. 13).
• LEAVE ANGRILY AND GO IN TO HIS OFFICE (P. 8).

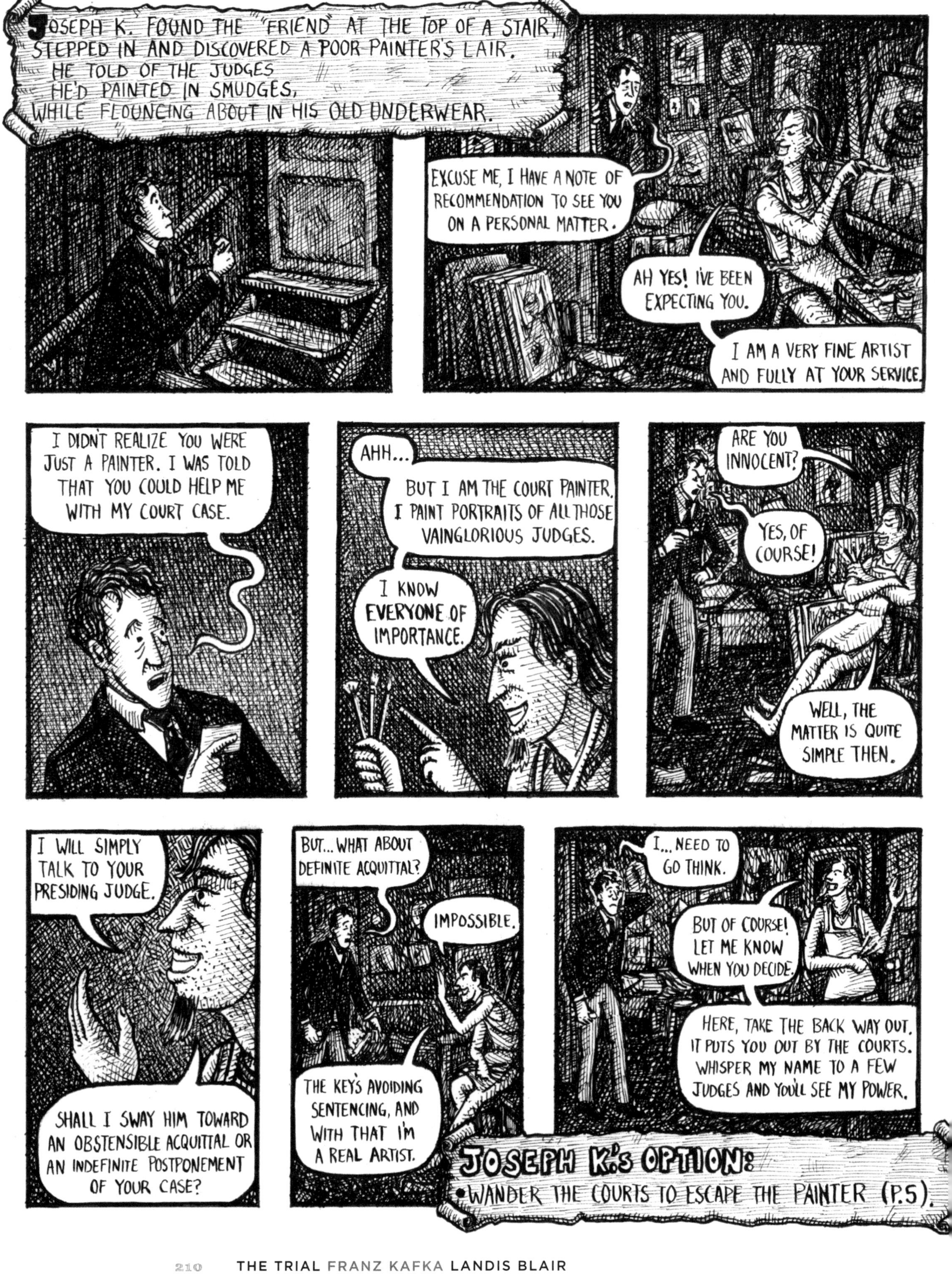

JOSEPH K. FOUND THE "FRIEND" AT THE TOP OF A STAIR,
STEPPED IN AND DISCOVERED A POOR PAINTER'S LAIR.
HE TOLD OF THE JUDGES
HE'D PAINTED IN SMUDGES,
WHILE FLOUNCING ABOUT IN HIS OLD UNDERWEAR.
EXCUSE ME, I HAVE A NOTE OF RECOMMENDATION TO SEE YOU ON A PERSONAL MATTER.
AH YES! I'VE BEEN EXPECTING YOU.
I AM A VERY FINE ARTIST AND FULLY AT YOUR SERVICE.
I DIDN'T REALIZE YOU WERE JUST A PAINTER. I WAS TOLD THAT YOU COULD HELP ME WITH MY COURT CASE.
AHH...
BUT I AM THE COURT PAINTER. I PAINT PORTRAITS OF ALL THOSE VAINGLORIOUS JUDGES.
I KNOW EVERYONE OF IMPORTANCE.
ARE YOU INNOCENT?
YES, OF COURSE!
WELL, THE MATTER IS QUITE SIMPLE THEN.
I WILL SIMPLY TALK TO YOUR PRESIDING JUDGE.
SHALL I SWAY HIM TOWARD AN OBSTENSIBLE ACQUITTAL OR AN INDEFINITE POSTPONEMENT OF YOUR CASE?
BUT... WHAT ABOUT DEFINITE ACQUITTAL?
IMPOSSIBLE.
THE KEY'S AVOIDING SENTENCING, AND WITH THAT I'M A REAL ARTIST.
I... NEED TO GO THINK.
BUT OF COURSE! LET ME KNOW WHEN YOU DECIDE.
HERE, TAKE THE BACK WAY OUT. IT PUTS YOU OUT BY THE COURTS. WHISPER MY NAME TO A FEW JUDGES AND YOU'LL SEE MY POWER.
JOSEPH K.'s OPTION:
• WANDER THE COURTS TO ESCAPE THE PAINTER (P.5).

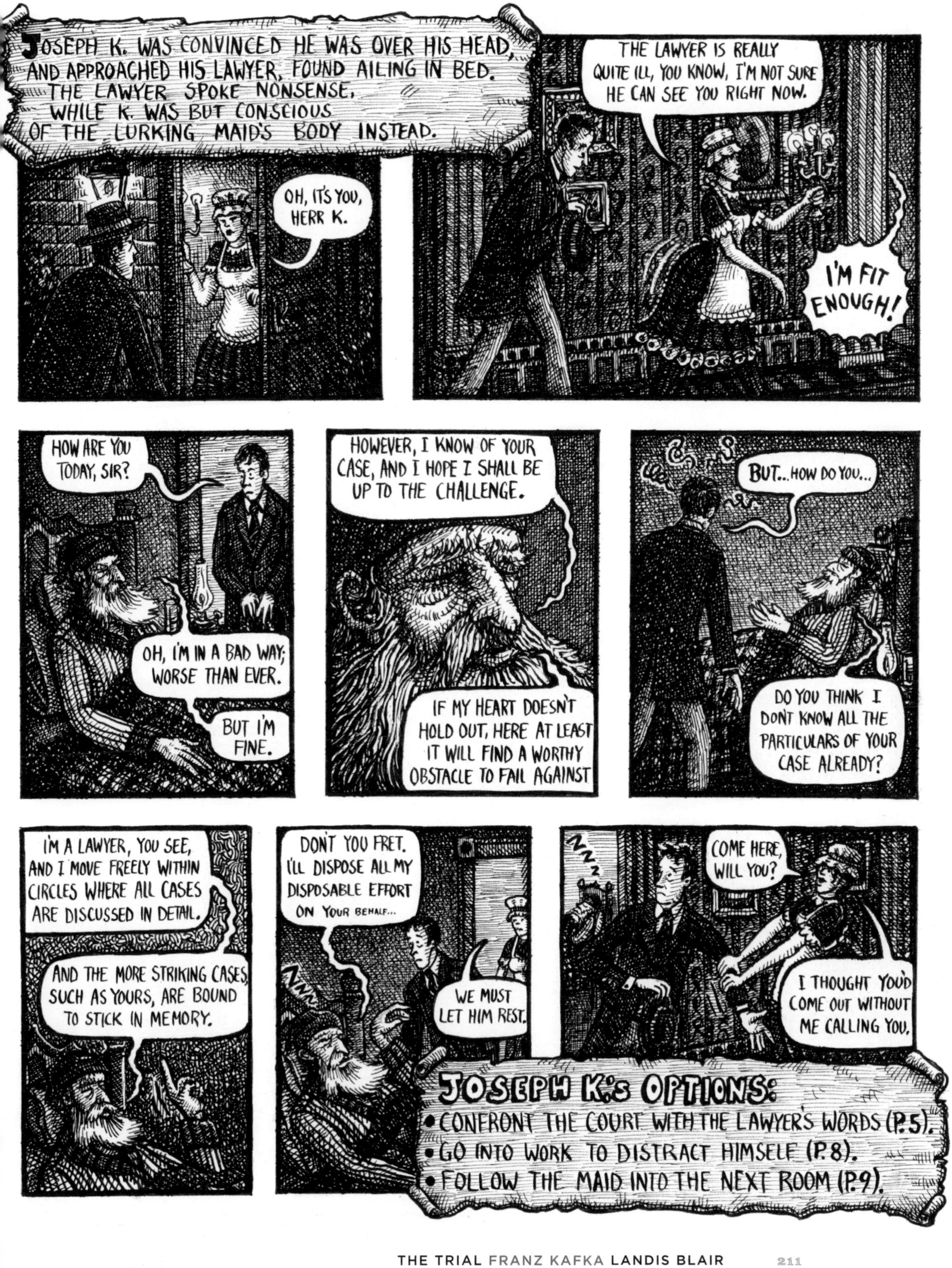
JOSEPH K. WAS CONVINCED HE WAS OVER HIS HEAD, AND APPROACHED HIS LAWYER, FOUND AILING IN BED. THE LAWYER SPOKE NONSENSE, WHILE K. WAS BUT CONSCIOUS OF THE LURKING MAID'S BODY INSTEAD.
OH, IT'S YOU, HERR K.
THE LAWYER IS REALLY QUITE ILL, YOU KNOW, I'M NOT SURE HE CAN SEE YOU RIGHT NOW.
I'M FIT ENOUGH!
HOW ARE YOU TODAY, SIR?
OH, I'M IN A BAD WAY; WORSE THAN EVER.
BUT I'M FINE.
HOWEVER, I KNOW OF YOUR CASE, AND I HOPE I SHALL BE UP TO THE CHALLENGE.
IF MY HEART DOESN'T HOLD OUT, HERE AT LEAST IT WILL FIND A WORTHY OBSTACLE TO FAIL AGAINST
BUT... HOW DO YOU...
DO YOU THINK I DON'T KNOW ALL THE PARTICULARS OF YOUR CASE ALREADY?
I'M A LAWYER, YOU SEE, AND I MOVE FREELY WITHIN CIRCLES WHERE ALL CASES ARE DISCUSSED IN DETAIL.
AND THE MORE STRIKING CASES, SUCH AS YOURS, ARE BOUND TO STICK IN MEMORY.
DON'T YOU FRET. I'LL DISPOSE ALL MY DISPOSABLE EFFORT ON YOUR BEHALF...
WE MUST LET HIM REST.
ZZZ
COME HERE, WILL YOU?
I THOUGHT YOU'D COME OUT WITHOUT ME CALLING YOU.
JOSEPH K.'s OPTIONS:
• CONFRONT THE COURT WITH THE LAWYER'S WORDS (P.5).
• GO INTO WORK TO DISTRACT HIMSELF (P.8).
• FOLLOW THE MAID INTO THE NEXT ROOM (P.9).

JOSEPH K. WALKED AROUND THE CATHEDRAL IN VAIN,
NO SIGN OF THE CLIENT, K. CHOSE TO REMAIN,
HE TROD IN THE DARK,
TILL HE HEARD A BARK,
FROM A PRIEST WHO BELLOWED HIS NAME.

35 MINUTES LATER...

I'M SUCH A FOOL!

THERE GOES ANOTHER COMMISSION.

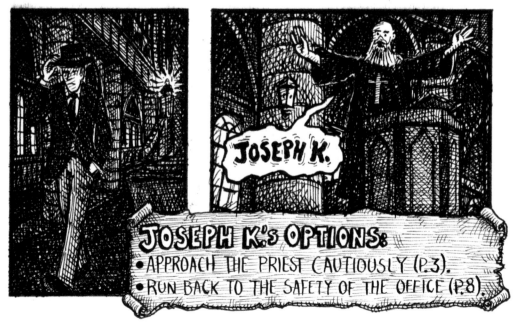

JOSEPH K.

JOSEPH K.'S OPTIONS:
• APPROACH THE PRIEST CAUTIOUSLY (P.3).
• RUN BACK TO THE SAFETY OF THE OFFICE (P.8).

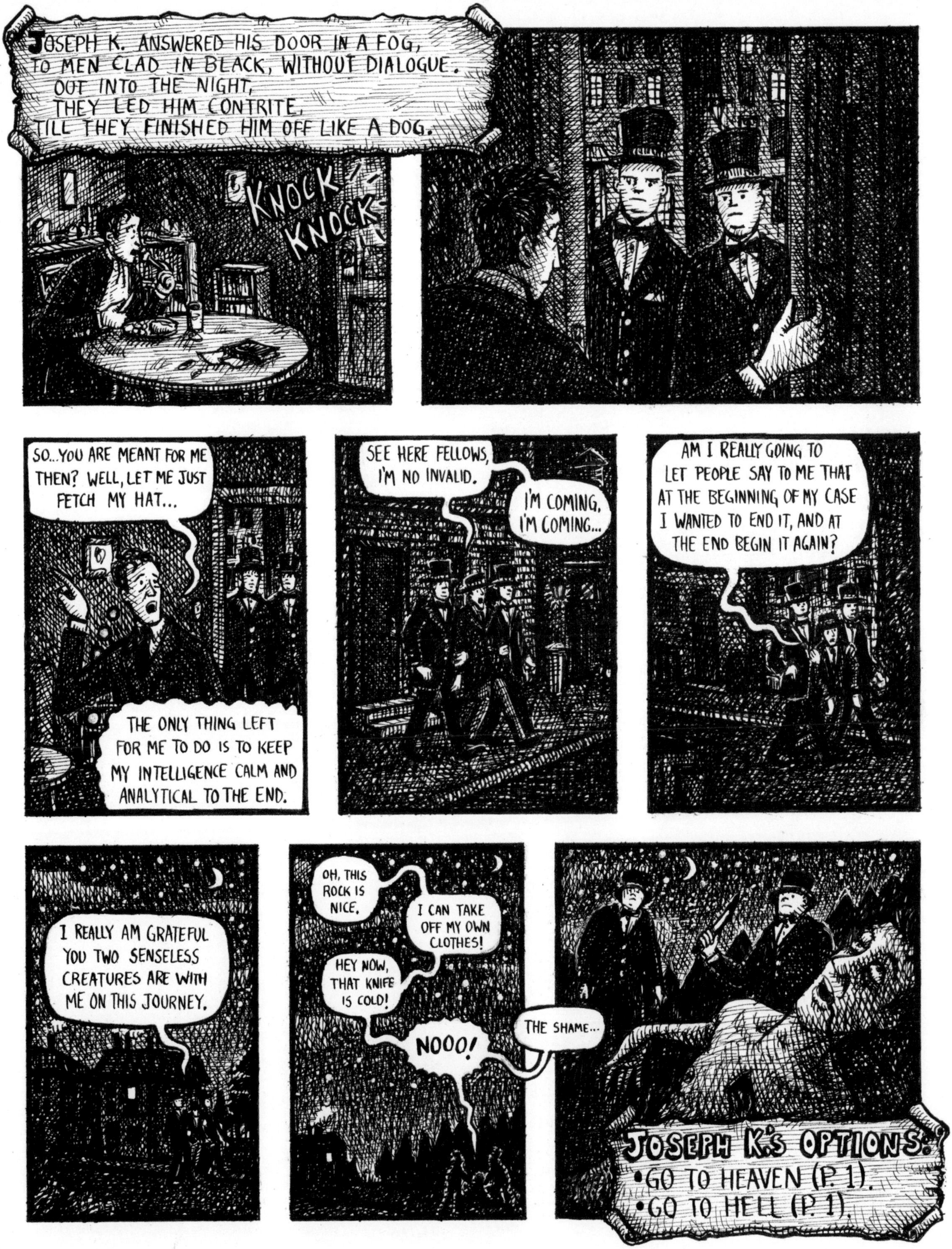
JOSEPH K. ANSWERED HIS DOOR IN A FOG,
TO MEN CLAD IN BLACK, WITHOUT DIALOGUE.
OUT INTO THE NIGHT,
THEY LED HIM CONTRITE,
TILL THEY FINISHED HIM OFF LIKE A DOG.
KNOCK! KNOCK!
SO... YOU ARE MEANT FOR ME THEN? WELL, LET ME JUST FETCH MY HAT...
THE ONLY THING LEFT FOR ME TO DO IS TO KEEP MY INTELLIGENCE CALM AND ANALYTICAL TO THE END.
SEE HERE FELLOWS, I'M NO INVALID.
I'M COMING, I'M COMING...
AM I REALLY GOING TO LET PEOPLE SAY TO ME THAT AT THE BEGINNING OF MY CASE I WANTED TO END IT, AND AT THE END BEGIN IT AGAIN?
I REALLY AM GRATEFUL YOU TWO SENSELESS CREATURES ARE WITH ME ON THIS JOURNEY.
OH, THIS ROCK IS NICE.
I CAN TAKE OFF MY OWN CLOTHES!
HEY NOW, THAT KNIFE IS COLD!
NOOO!
THE SHAME...
JOSEPH K.'S OPTIONS:
•GO TO HEAVEN (P. 1).
•GO TO HELL (P. 1).

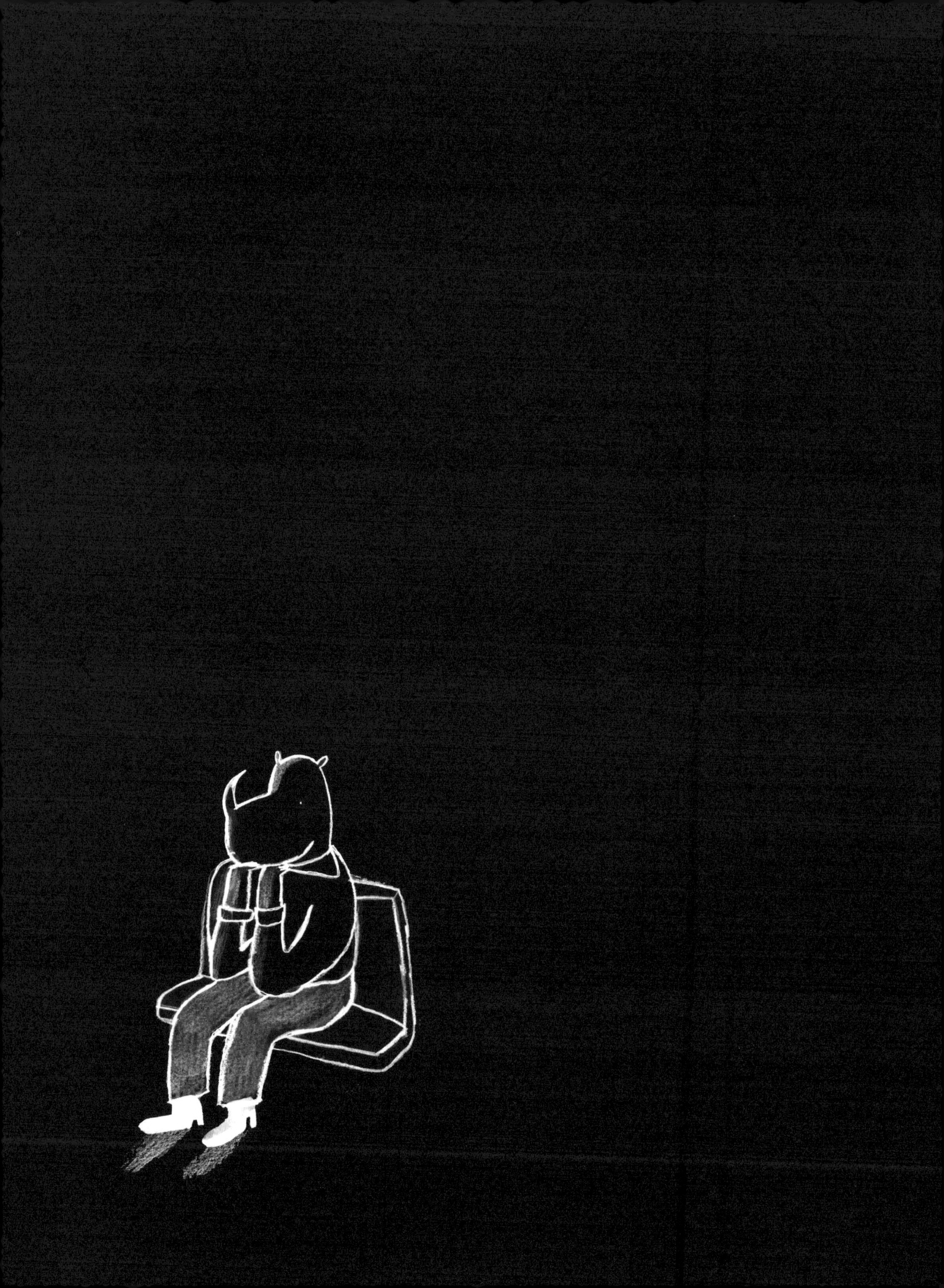

PART FOUR
Elementary

"The Case of the Wild Cat and the Crown Prince"

(a Justice Bao mystery)

ART/ADAPTATION BY **Sonia Leong**

BAO ZHENG WAS A CIVIL SERVANT IN China's Song Dynasty in the eleventh century. He held many positions, but he achieved legendary status for his work as a magistrate. Justice Bao was wise, fair, and absolutely unafraid to root out corruption and force accountability on even the most powerful. Like another great magistrate from long ago, the Israelite King Solomon, Bao was a cross between a judge and a detective, often using genius tactics to trick or force the guilty into revealing themselves.

As with many popular figures from centuries and millennia ago, his deeds have been embellished, and it's hard to know where the man ends and the myth begins. Tales of Bao's feats of justice are a part of Chinese legend and literature, and manga/anime artist Sonia Leong read them as a child. Sonia's work spans comics, children's books, art instruction books, magazine work, TV and film production, ads for Toyota, and more. I'm pleased she gave us a rare (in the West) adaptation of one of Justice Bao's most famous cases.

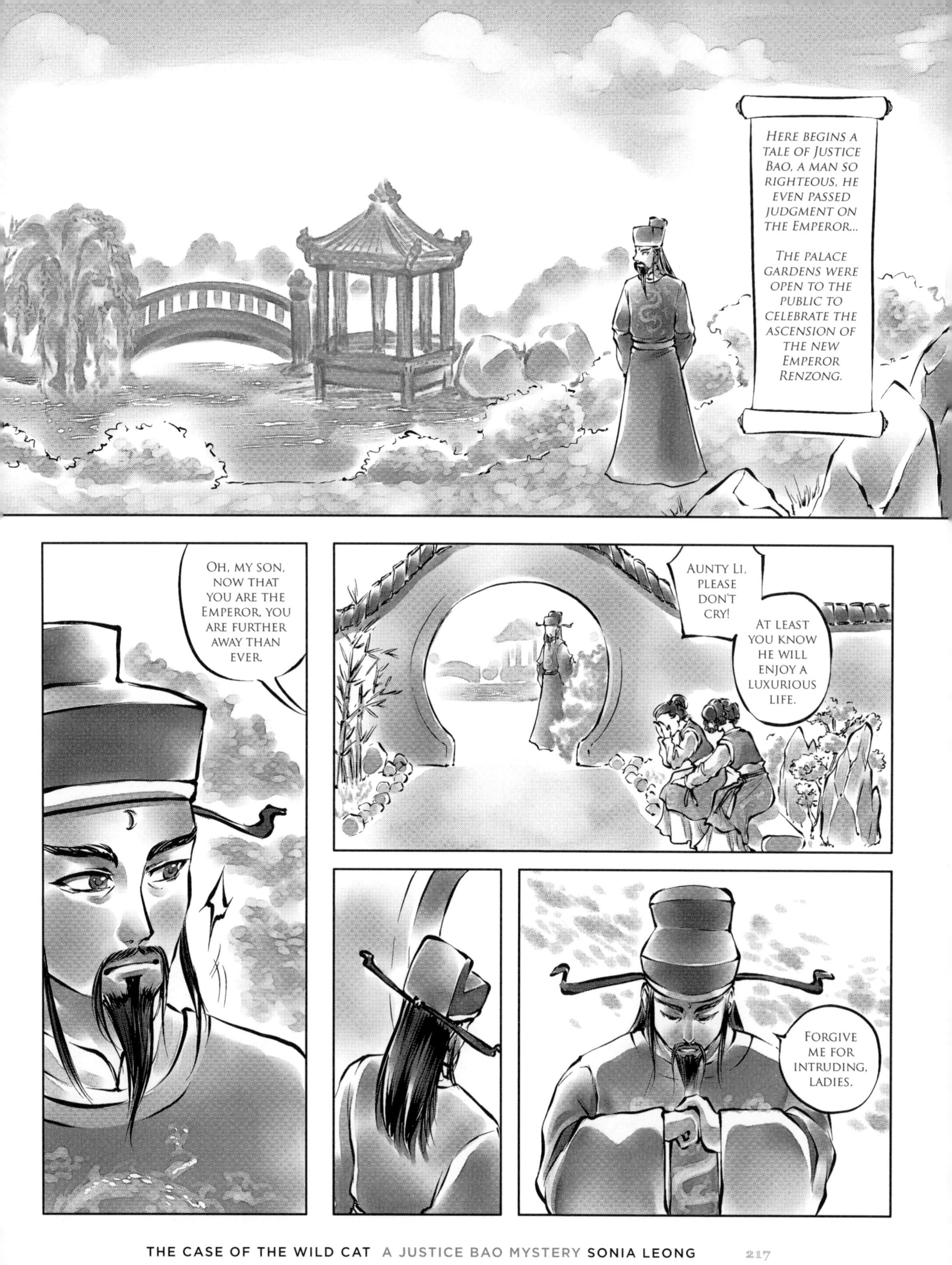
Here begins a tale of Justice Bao, a man so righteous, he even passed judgment on the Emperor...
The palace gardens were open to the public to celebrate the ascension of the new Emperor Renzong.
Oh, my son, now that you are the Emperor, you are further away than ever.
Aunty Li, please don't cry!
At least you know he will enjoy a luxurious life.
Forgive me for intruding, ladies.

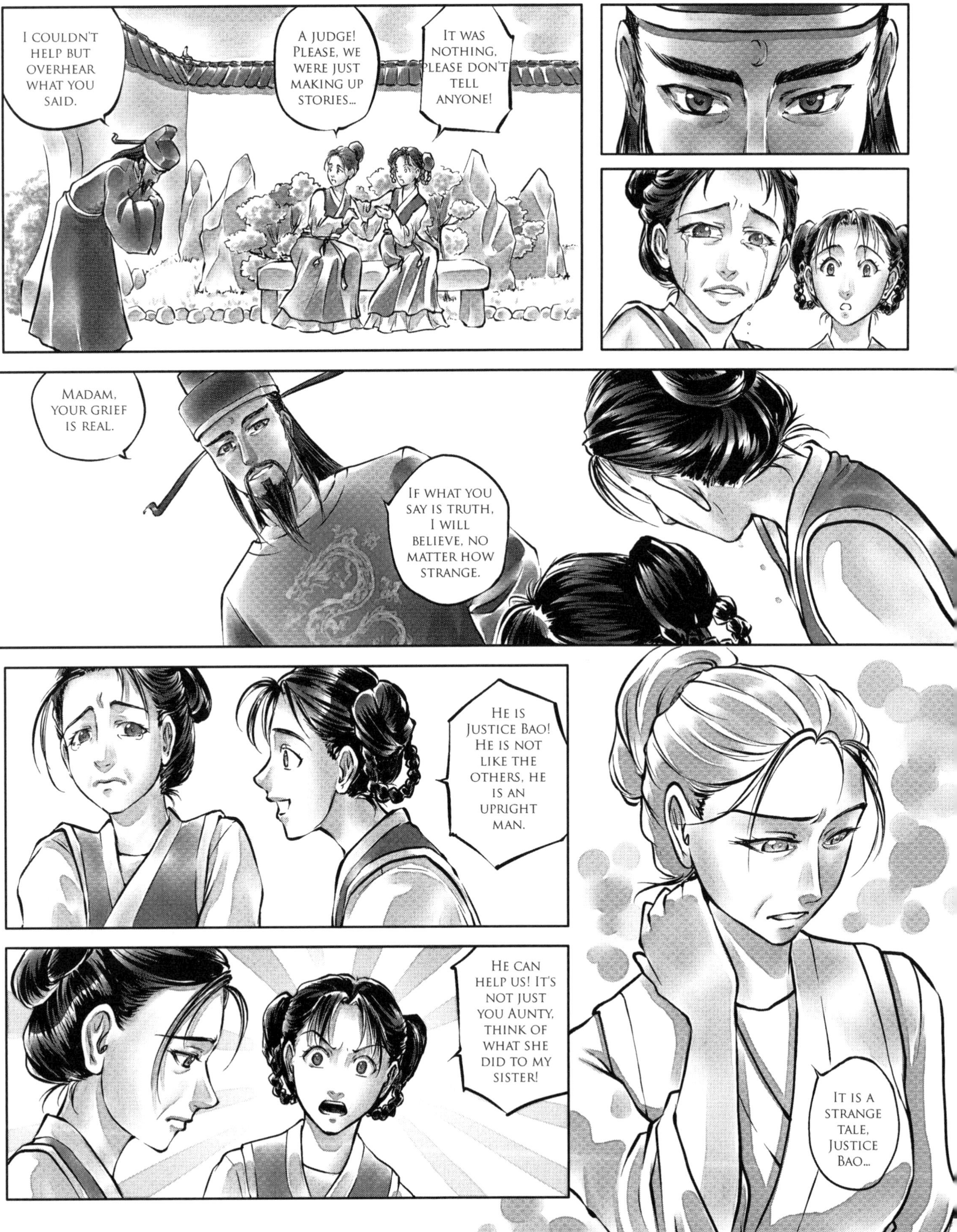

I couldn't help but overhear what you said.
A judge! Please, we were just making up stories...
It was nothing, please don't tell anyone!
Madam, your grief is real.
If what you say is truth, I will believe, no matter how strange.
He is Justice Bao! He is not like the others, he is an upright man.
He can help us! It's not just you Aunty, think of what she did to my sister!
It is a strange tale, Justice Bao...

MANY YEARS AGO, I WAS ONCE A CONSORT OF FORMER EMPEROR ZHENZONG, ALONG WITH CONSORT LIU, WHO IS NOW THE EMPRESS DOWAGER.

SHE WAS HIS FAVORITE, BUT I BECAME PREGNANT WITH HIS CHILD.

SHE WAS JEALOUS, OF COURSE. BUT I HAD NO IDEA TO WHAT LENGTHS SHE WOULD GO TO MAINTAIN HER STATUS.

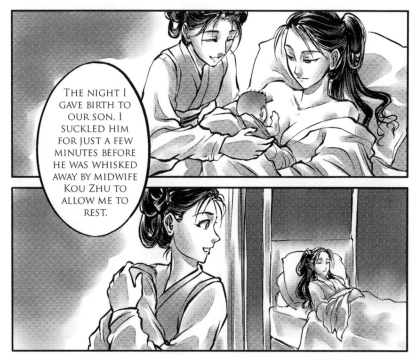

THE NIGHT I GAVE BIRTH TO OUR SON, I SUCKLED HIM FOR JUST A FEW MINUTES BEFORE HE WAS WHISKED AWAY BY MIDWIFE KOU ZHU TO ALLOW ME TO REST.

A FEW HOURS LATER, I WAS ROUSED BY CONSORT LIU, EUNUCH GUO AND THE EMPEROR HIMSELF.

THE CASE OF THE WILD CAT A JUSTICE BAO MYSTERY SONIA LEONG

THEY STORMED INTO MY ROOM, HOLDING... A DEAD WILDCAT!

THEY SAID THEY HAD TO KILL IT AS MY BABY HAD TRANSFORMED AND IT WAS AN ILL OMEN.

I WAS BANISHED TO THE WINTER PALACE AS SOON AS I COULD WALK AGAIN, AND WAS TOLD TO WORK AS A MAID.

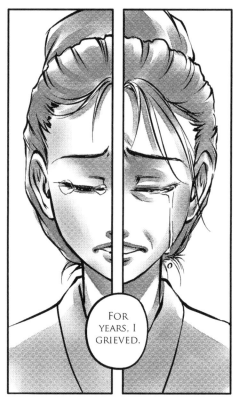

FOR YEARS, I GRIEVED.

BUT THEN I HEARD THAT KOU ZHU WAS ARRESTED, TORTURED AND HANGED.

THE EMPEROR NEVER HAD A SON IN THE END. DID THEY PLACE THE BLAME ON HER? I BECAME FEARFUL FOR MY LIFE.

THEN, KOU ZHI CAME TO WORK AT THE PALACE WITH ME. THAT WAS WHEN I FOUND OUT WHAT REALLY HAPPENED.

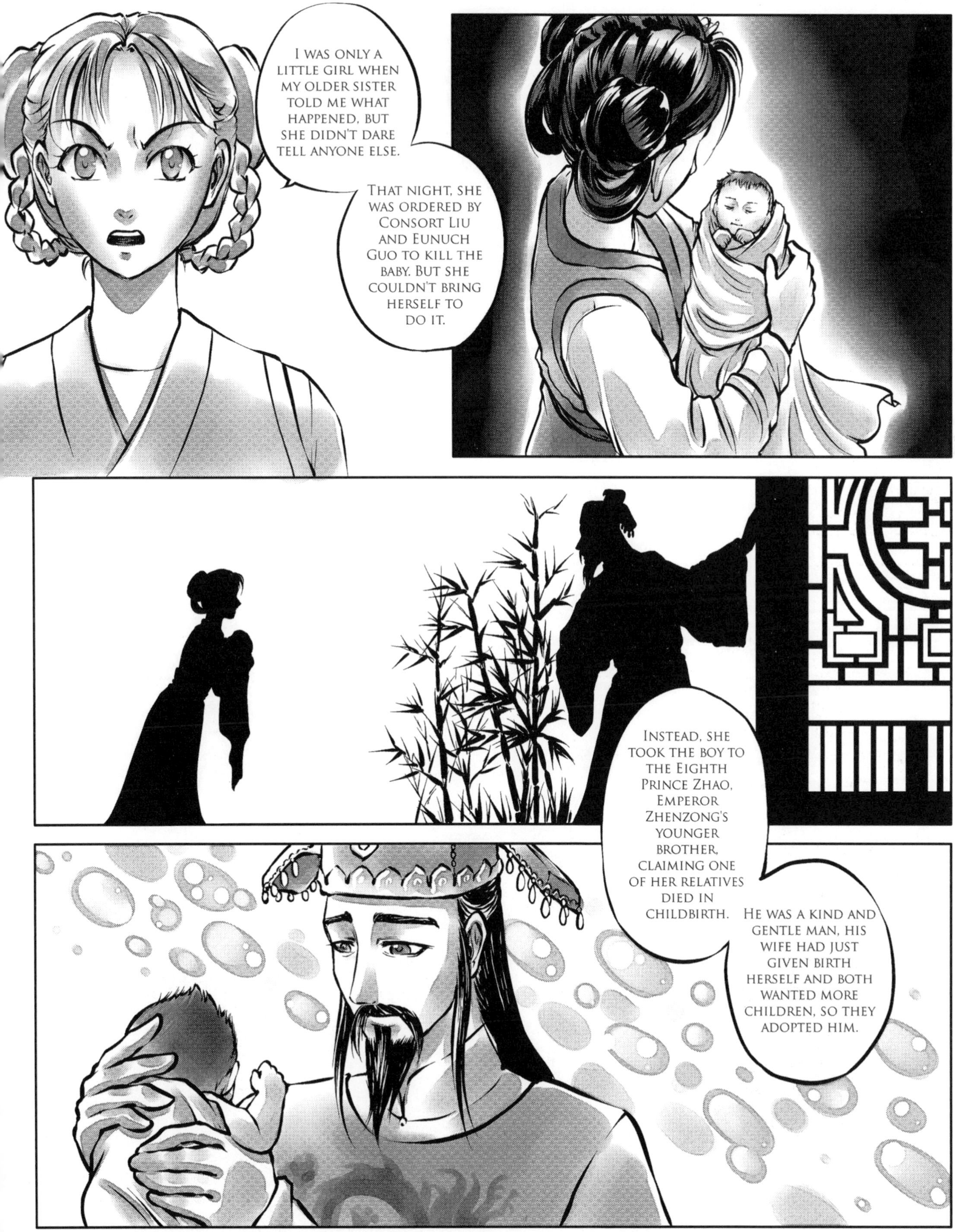
I was only a little girl when my older sister told me what happened, but she didn't dare tell anyone else.
That night, she was ordered by Consort Liu and Eunuch Guo to kill the baby. But she couldn't bring herself to do it.
Instead, she took the boy to the Eighth Prince Zhao, Emperor Zhenzong's younger brother, claiming one of her relatives died in childbirth.
He was a kind and gentle man, his wife had just given birth herself and both wanted more children, so they adopted him.

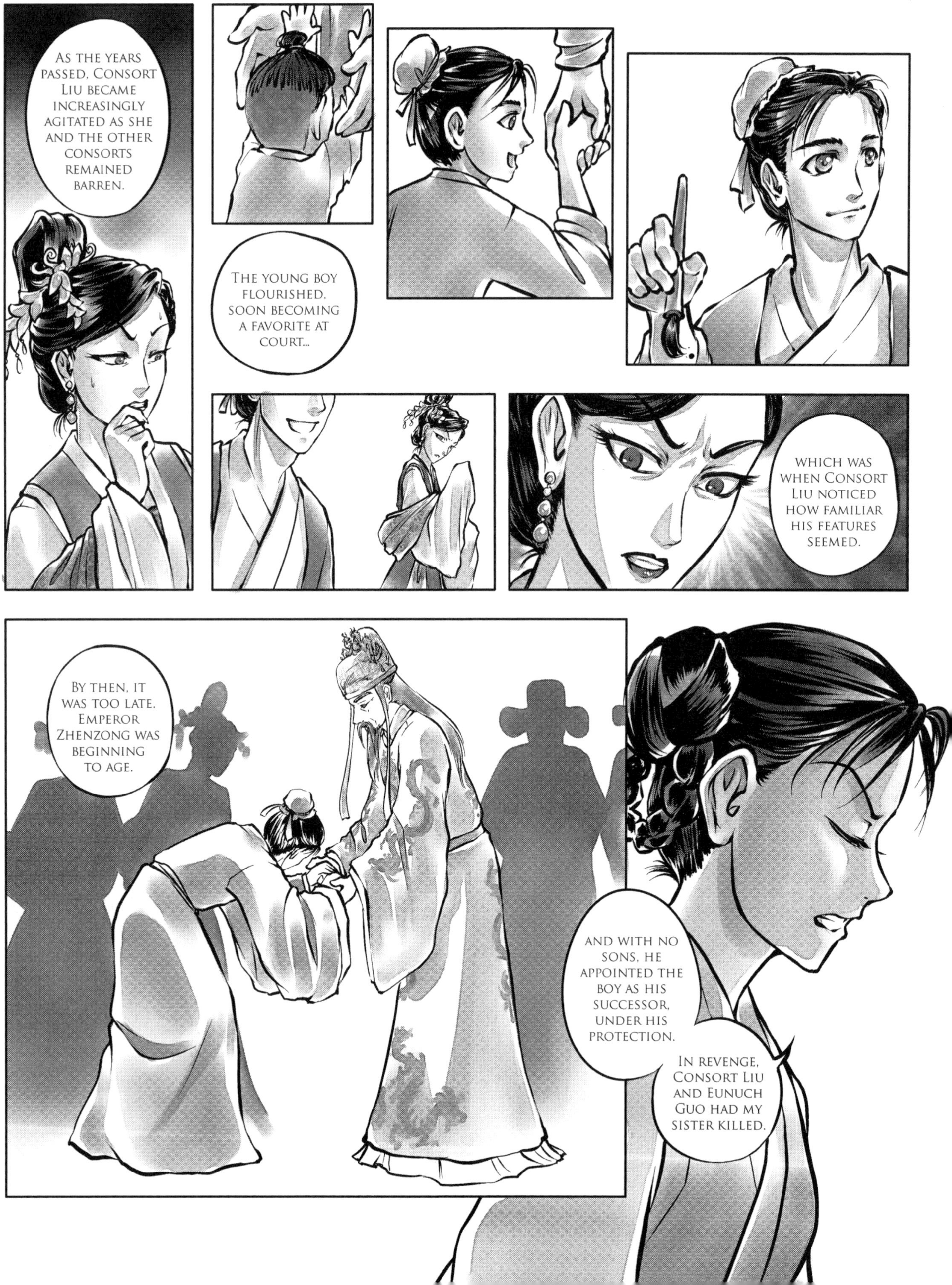

As the years passed, Consort Liu became increasingly agitated as she and the other consorts remained barren.
The young boy flourished, soon becoming a favorite at court...
which was when Consort Liu noticed how familiar his features seemed.
By then, it was too late. Emperor Zhenzong was beginning to age.
And with no sons, he appointed the boy as his successor, under his protection.
In revenge, Consort Liu and Eunuch Guo had my sister killed.

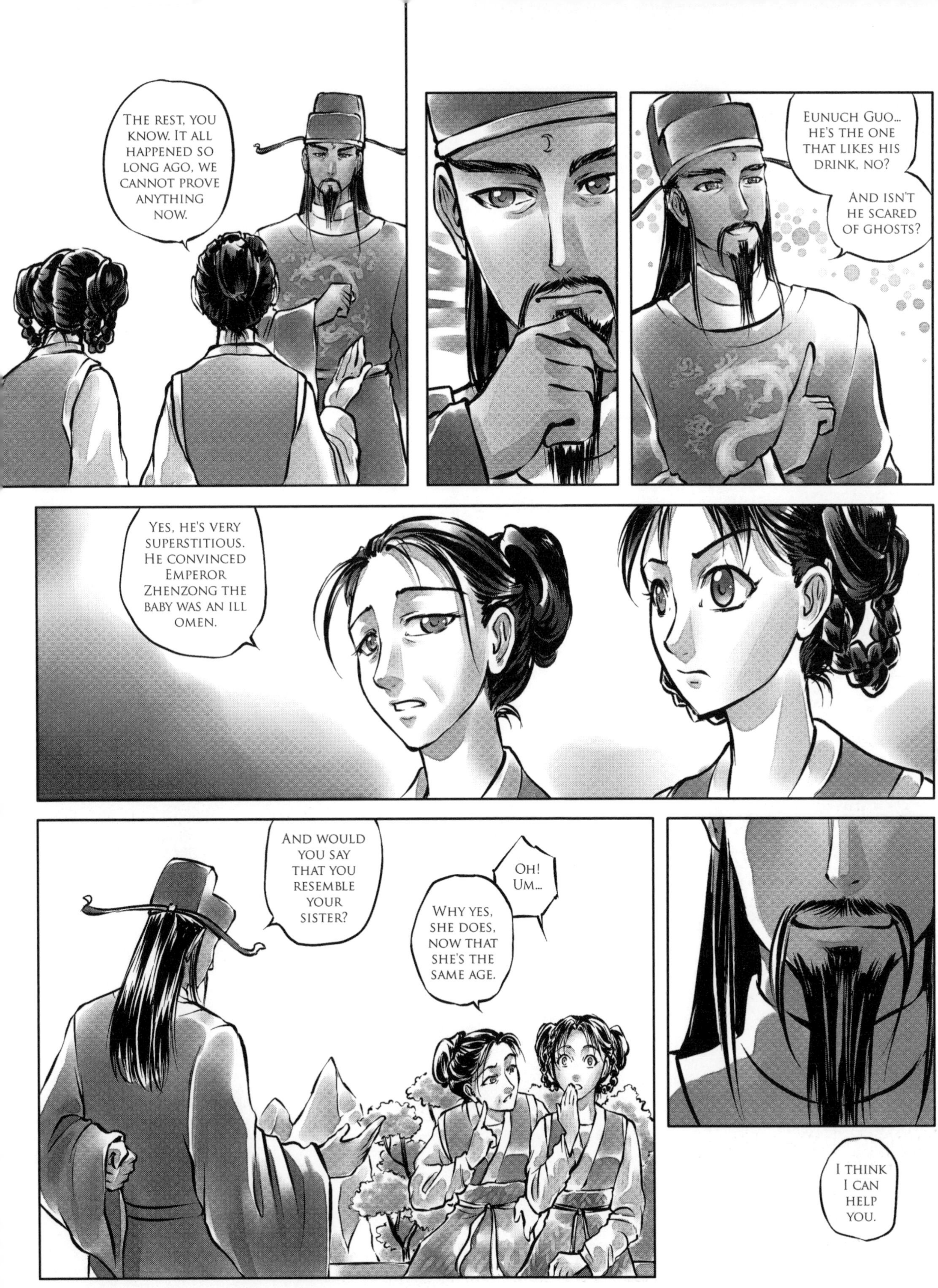
The rest, you know. It all happened so long ago, we cannot prove anything now.
Eunuch Guo... he's the one that likes his drink, no?
And isn't he scared of ghosts?
Yes, he's very superstitious. He convinced Emperor Zhenzong the baby was an ill omen.
And would you say that you resemble your sister?
Oh! Um...
Why yes, she does, now that she's the same age.
I think I can help you.

IN THE MIDDLE OF THE NIGHT, THE PARTIES AT THE PALACE ARE STILL ONGOING...

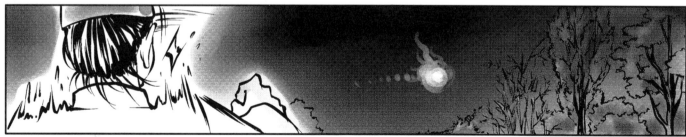

HELLO? WHO'S THERE?

WHA-!

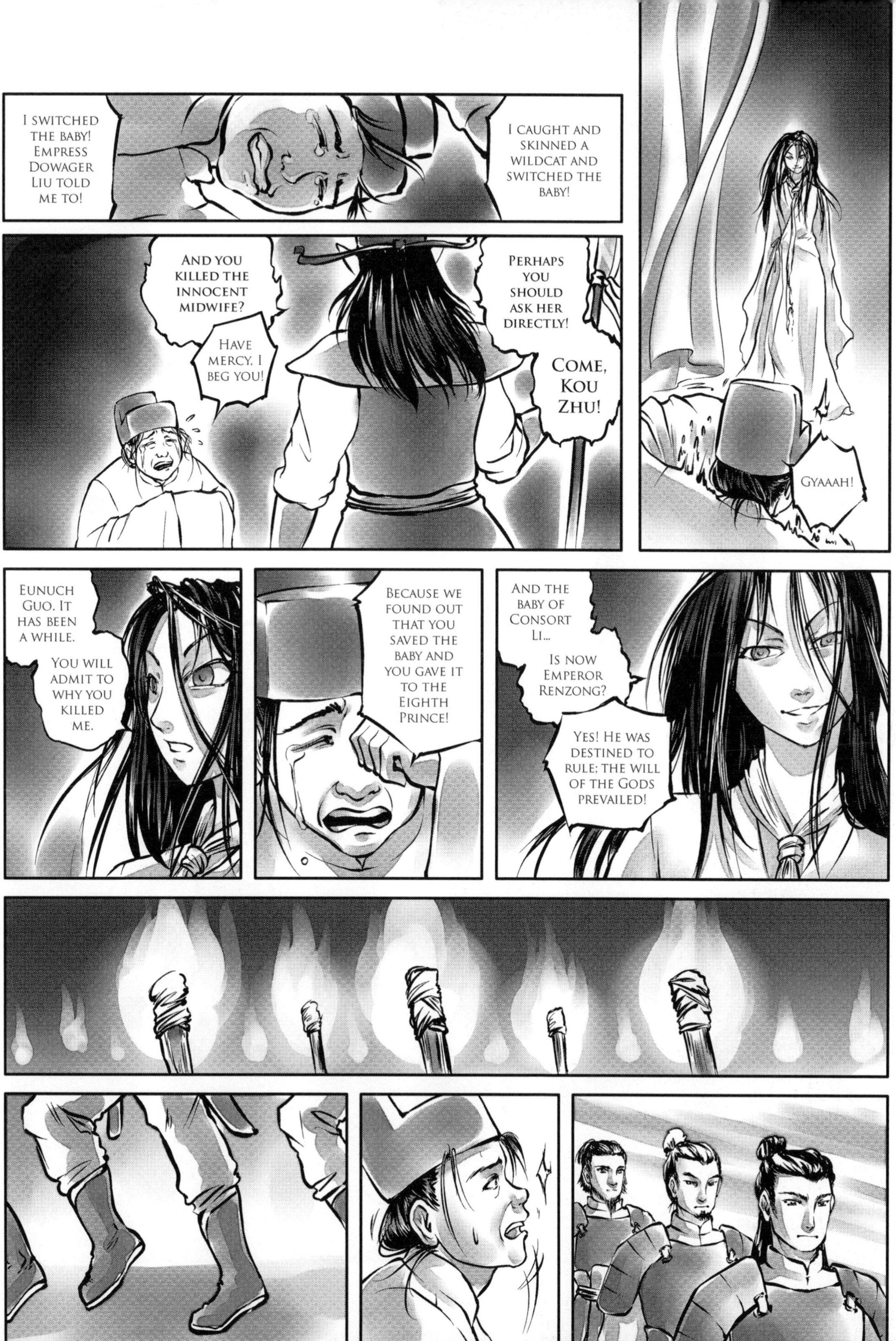
I switched the baby! Empress Dowager Liu told me to!
I caught and skinned a wildcat and switched the baby!
And you killed the innocent midwife?
Perhaps you should ask her directly!
Have mercy, I beg you!
Come, Kou Zhu!
Gyaaah!
Eunuch Guo. It has been a while.
You will admit to why you killed me.
Because we found out that you saved the baby and you gave it to the Eighth Prince!
And the baby of Consort Li...
Is now Emperor Renzong?
Yes! He was destined to rule; the will of the Gods prevailed!

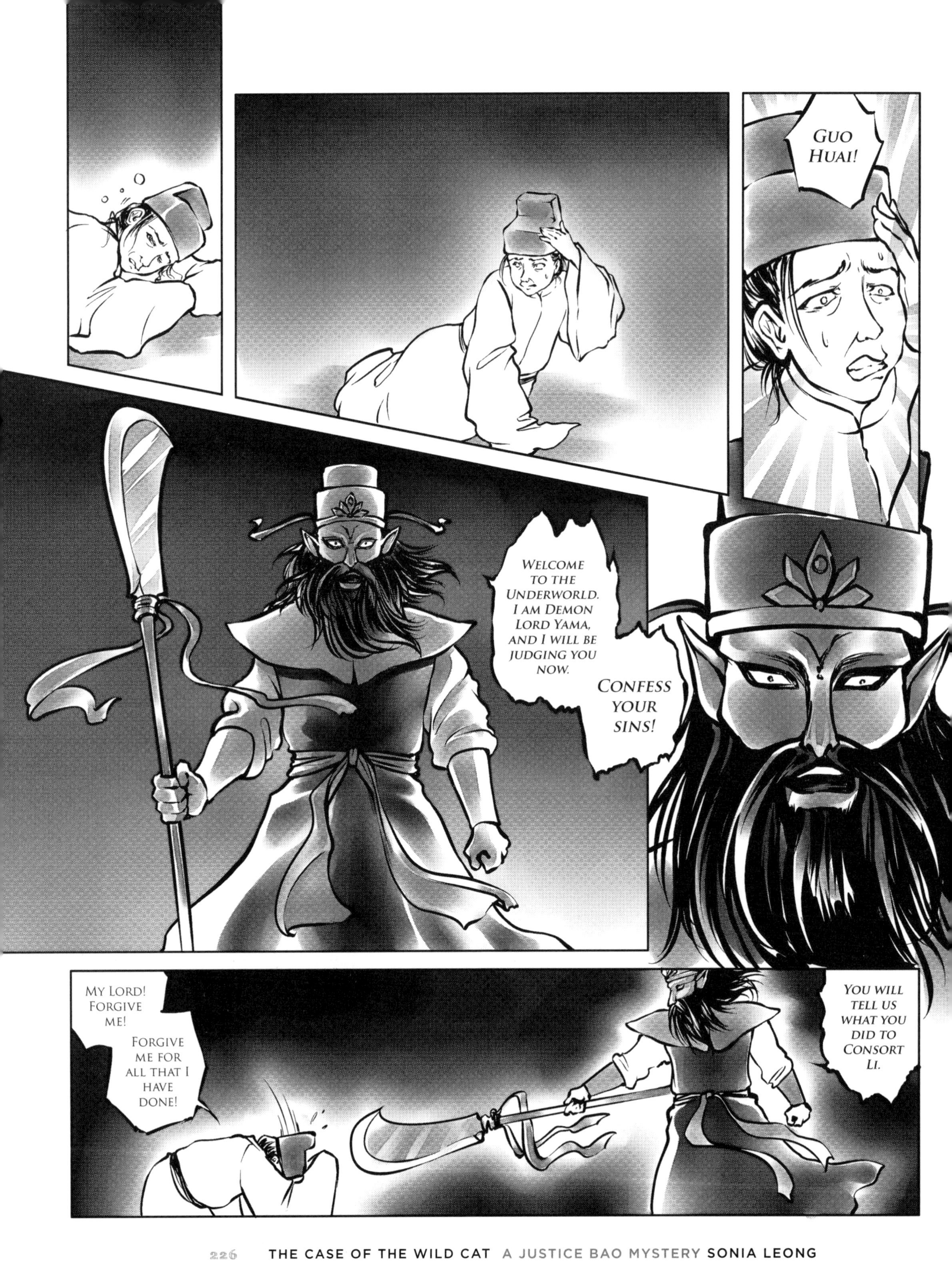
GUO HUAI!
WELCOME TO THE UNDERWORLD. I AM DEMON LORD YAMA, AND I WILL BE JUDGING YOU NOW.
CONFESS YOUR SINS!
MY LORD! FORGIVE ME!
FORGIVE ME FOR ALL THAT I HAVE DONE!
YOU WILL TELL US WHAT YOU DID TO CONSORT LI.

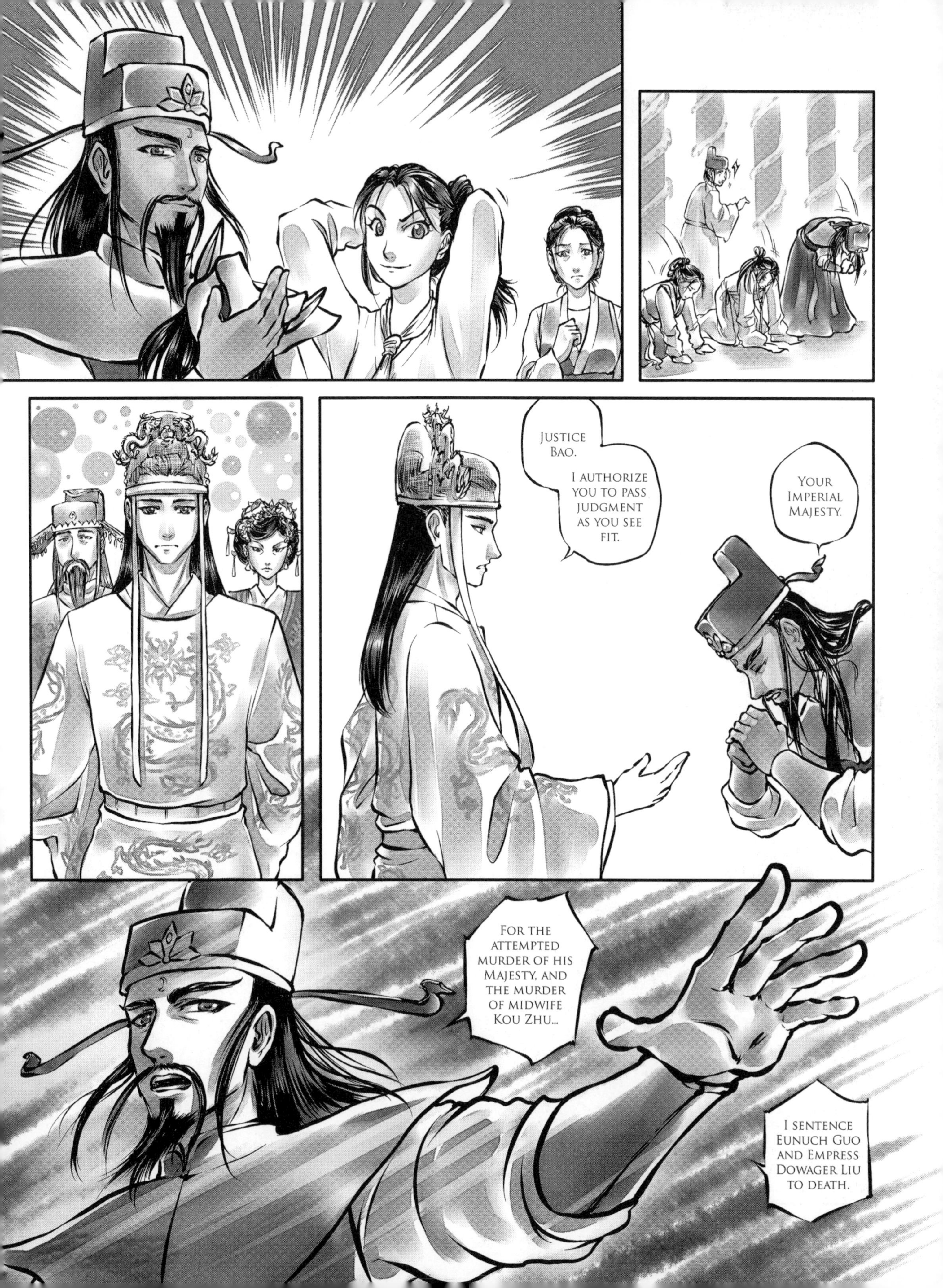
Justice Bao.
I authorize you to pass judgment as you see fit.
Your Imperial Majesty.
For the attempted murder of his Majesty, and the murder of midwife Kou Zhu...
I sentence Eunuch Guo and Empress Dowager Liu to death.

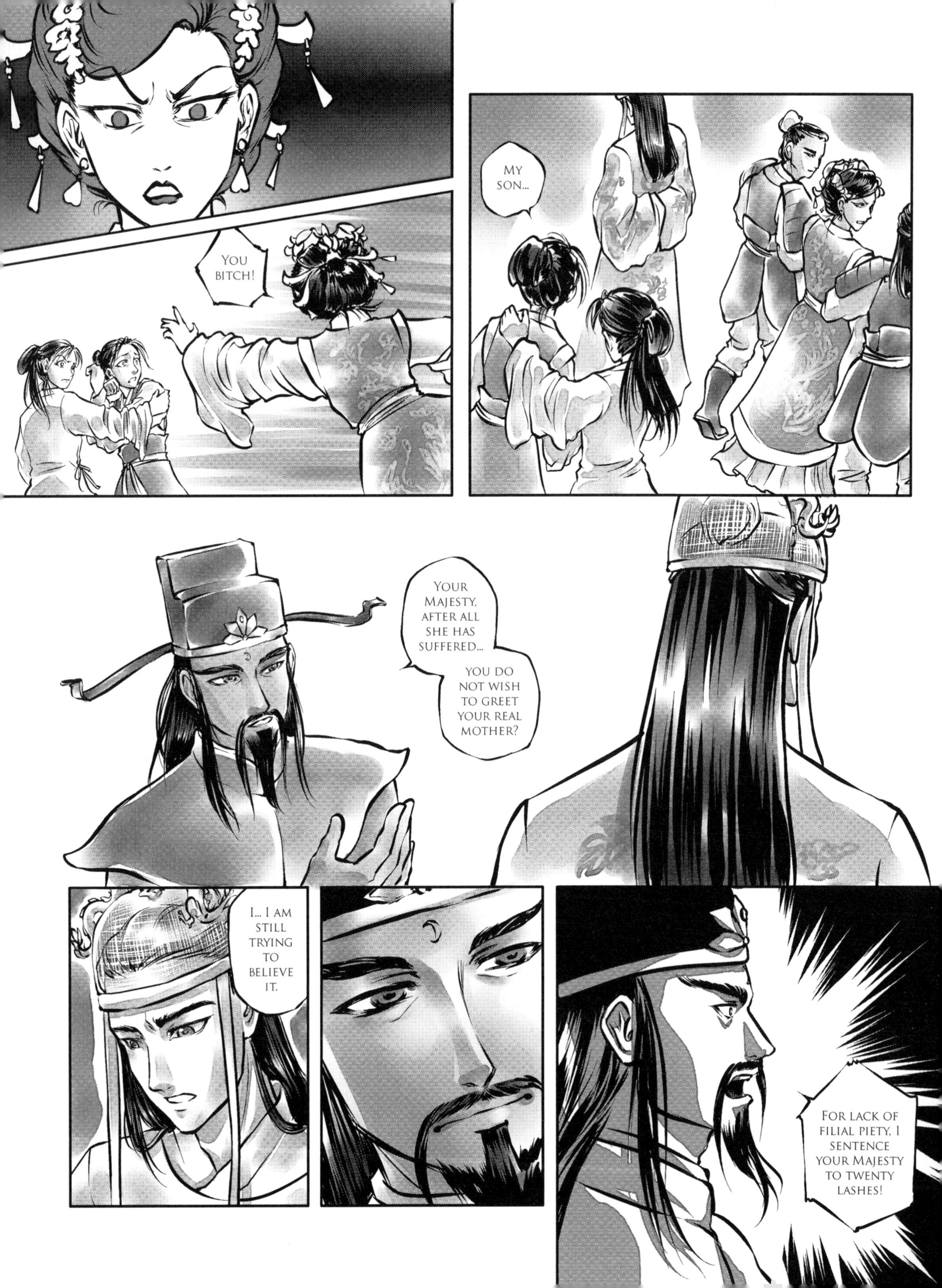

You bitch!
My son...
Your Majesty, after all she has suffered...
You do not wish to greet your real mother?
I... I am still trying to believe it.
For lack of filial piety, I sentence your Majesty to twenty lashes!

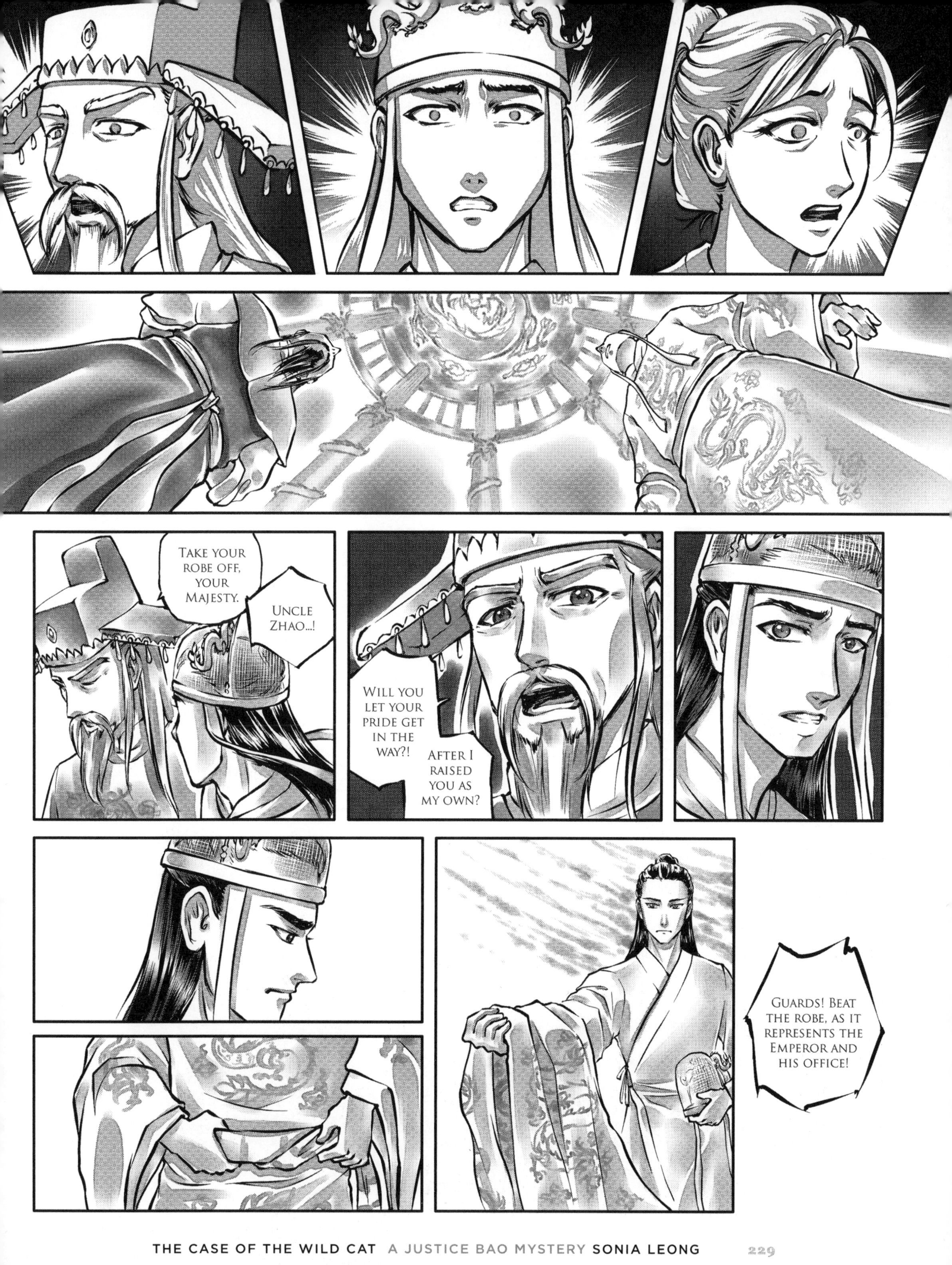
Take your robe off, your Majesty.
Uncle Zhao...!
Will you let your pride get in the way?!
After I raised you as my own?
Guards! Beat the robe, as it represents the Emperor and his office!

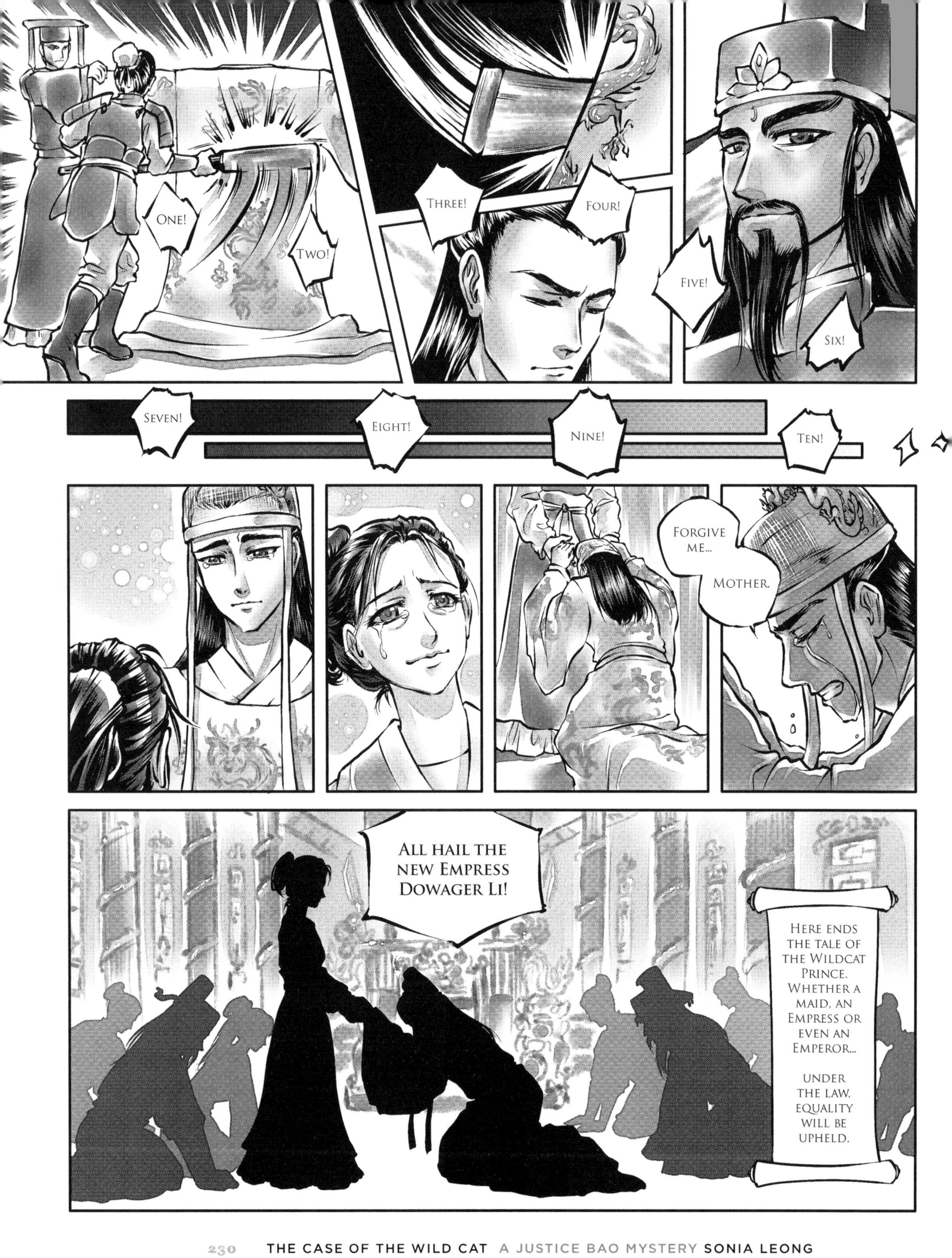
One!
Two!
Three!
Four!
Five!
Six!
Seven!
Eight!
Nine!
Ten!
Forgive me...
Mother.
All hail the new Empress Dowager Li!
Here ends the tale of the Wildcat Prince. Whether a maid, an Empress or even an Emperor...
Under the law, equality will be upheld.

"The Swedish Match"

Anton Chekhov

ART/ADAPTATION BY Hila Noam

WHEN YOU THINK OF MURDER MYSTERIES, one of the Russian titans of literature might not pop into your head, but "The Swedish Match" by Anton Chekhov gets a spot in lots of histories of the genre. Early in his career, the master of the short story wrote about two detectives who pounce on every clue as they go about reaching the inescapable conclusion and collaring all the bad guys. Except, well. . . .

Sherlock Holmes was still three years away when Chekov's story came out in 1884, but Poe and others had already established the category of detective fiction. Chekhov decided to have fun with the genre, penning a story that totally works as a suspenseful mystery yet upturns several of the conventions and comes close to being a parody.

Hila Noam of Tel Aviv has made comics for *National Geographic*, done coloring for an adaptation of Anne Frank's diary, and teaches at Bezalel Art and Design Academy in Jerusalem.

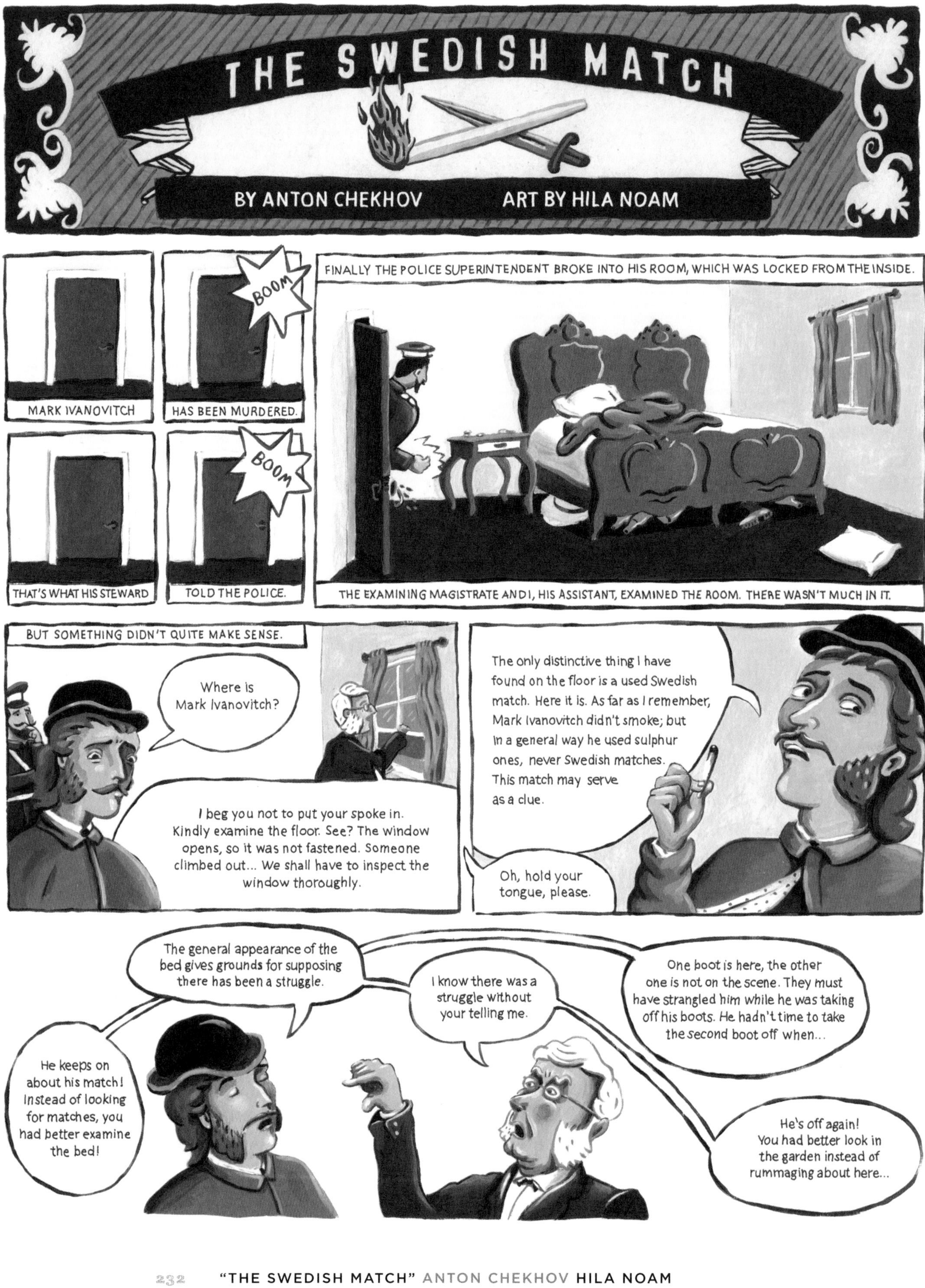
THE SWEDISH MATCH
BY ANTON CHEKHOV
ART BY HILA NOAM
MARK IVANOVITCH
BOOM
HAS BEEN MURDERED.
THAT'S WHAT HIS STEWARD
BOOM
TOLD THE POLICE.
FINALLY THE POLICE SUPERINTENDENT BROKE INTO HIS ROOM, WHICH WAS LOCKED FROM THE INSIDE.
THE EXAMINING MAGISTRATE AND I, HIS ASSISTANT, EXAMINED THE ROOM. THERE WASN'T MUCH IN IT.
BUT SOMETHING DIDN'T QUITE MAKE SENSE.
Where is Mark Ivanovitch?
I beg you not to put your spoke in. Kindly examine the floor. See? The window opens, so it was not fastened. Someone climbed out... We shall have to inspect the window thoroughly.
The only distinctive thing I have found on the floor is a used Swedish match. Here it is. As far as I remember, Mark Ivanovitch didn't smoke; but in a general way he used sulphur ones, never Swedish matches. This match may serve as a clue.
Oh, hold your tongue, please.
The general appearance of the bed gives grounds for supposing there has been a struggle.
I know there was a struggle without your telling me.
One boot is here, the other one is not on the scene. They must have strangled him while he was taking off his boots. He hadn't time to take the second boot off when...
He keeps on about his match! Instead of looking for matches, you had better examine the bed!
He's off again! You had better look in the garden instead of rummaging about here...

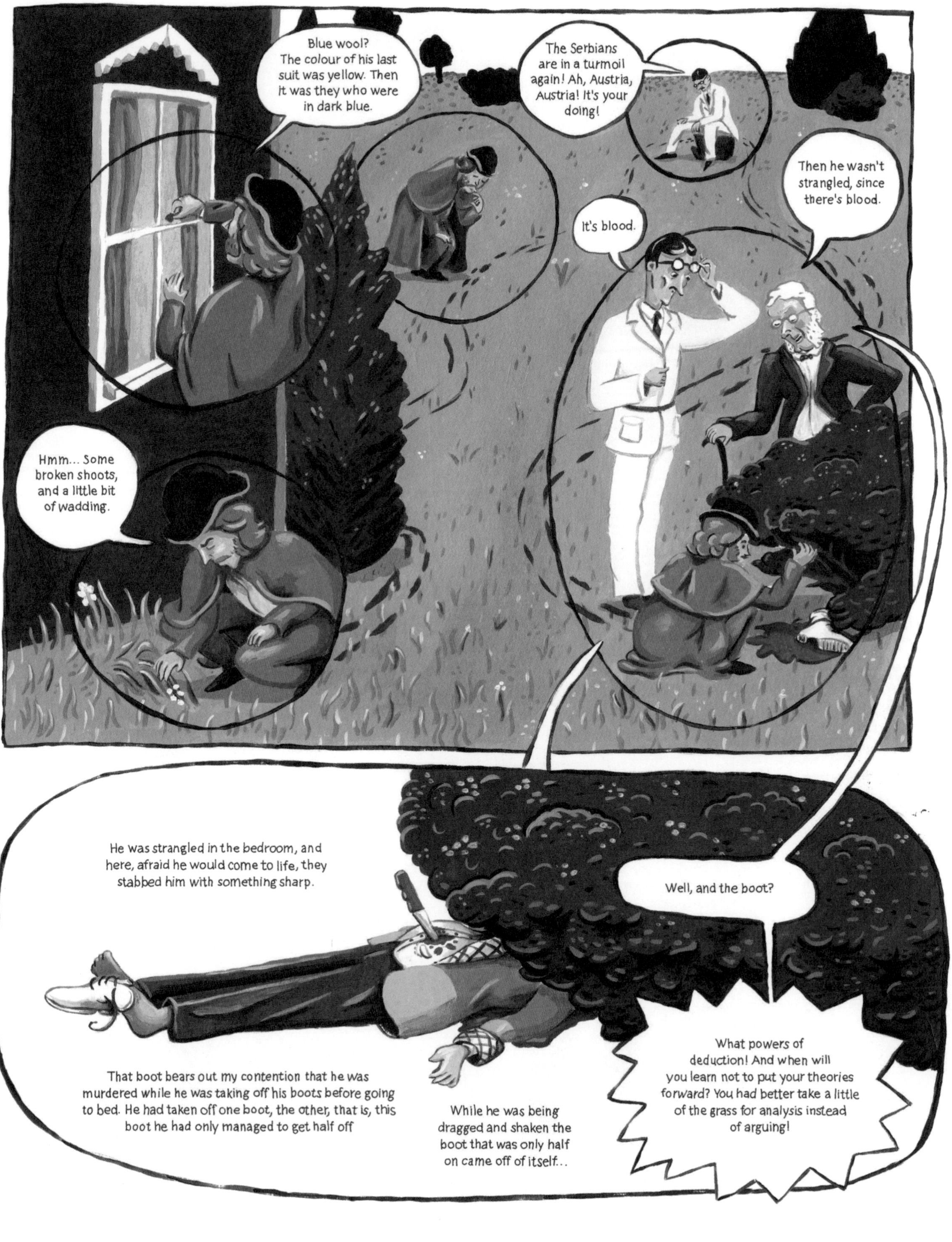
Blue wool? The colour of his last suit was yellow. Then it was they who were in dark blue.
The Serbians are in a turmoil again! Ah, Austria, Austria! It's your doing!
Hmm... Some broken shoots, and a little bit of wadding.
It's blood.
Then he wasn't strangled, since there's blood.
He was strangled in the bedroom, and here, afraid he would come to life, they stabbed him with something sharp.
Well, and the boot?
That boot bears out my contention that he was murdered while he was taking off his boots before going to bed. He had taken off one boot, the other, that is, this boot he had only managed to get half off
While he was being dragged and shaken the boot that was only half on came off of itself...
What powers of deduction! And when will you learn not to put your theories forward? You had better take a little of the grass for analysis instead of arguing!

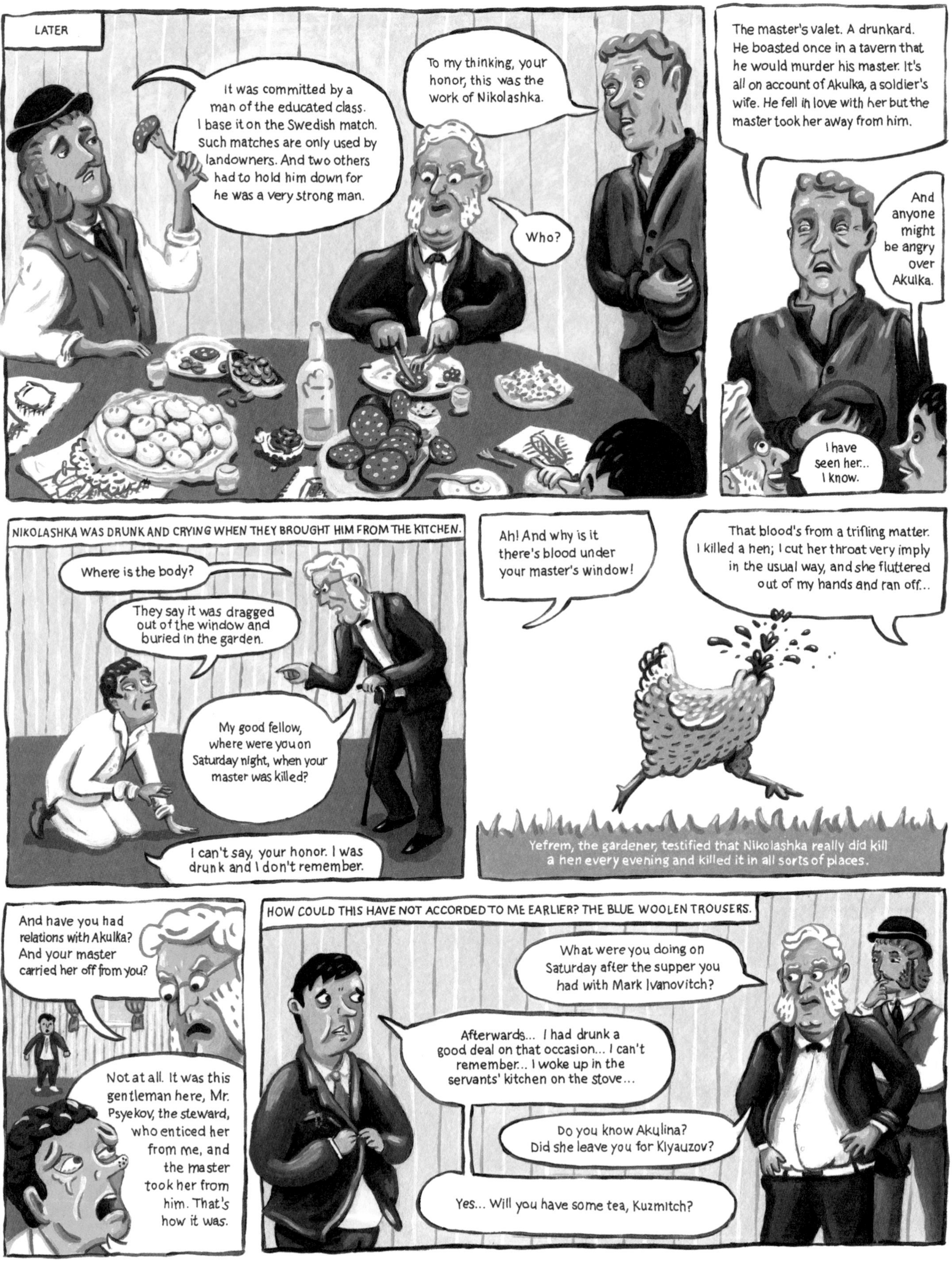
LATER
It was committed by a man of the educated class. I base it on the Swedish match. Such matches are only used by landowners. And two others had to hold him down for he was a very strong man.
To my thinking, your honor, this was the work of Nikolashka.
Who?
The master's valet. A drunkard. He boasted once in a tavern that he would murder his master. It's all on account of Akulka, a soldier's wife. He fell in love with her but the master took her away from him.
And anyone might be angry over Akulka.
I have seen her... I know.
NIKOLASHKA WAS DRUNK AND CRYING WHEN THEY BROUGHT HIM FROM THE KITCHEN.
Where is the body?
They say it was dragged out of the window and buried in the garden.
My good fellow, where were you on Saturday night, when your master was killed?
I can't say, your honor. I was drunk and I don't remember.
Ah! And why is it there's blood under your master's window!
That blood's from a trifling matter. I killed a hen; I cut her throat very imply in the usual way, and she fluttered out of my hands and ran off...
Yefrem, the gardener, testified that Nikolashka really did kill a hen every evening and killed it in all sorts of places.
And have you had relations with Akulka? And your master carried her off from you?
Not at all. It was this gentleman here, Mr. Psyekov, the steward, who enticed her from me, and the master took her from him. That's how it was.
HOW COULD THIS HAVE NOT ACCORDED TO ME EARLIER? THE BLUE WOOLEN TROUSERS.
What were you doing on Saturday after the supper you had with Mark Ivanovitch?
Afterwards... I had drunk a good deal on that occasion... I can't remember... I woke up in the servants' kitchen on the stove...
Do you know Akulina? Did she leave you for Klyauzov?
Yes... Will you have some tea, Kuzmitch?

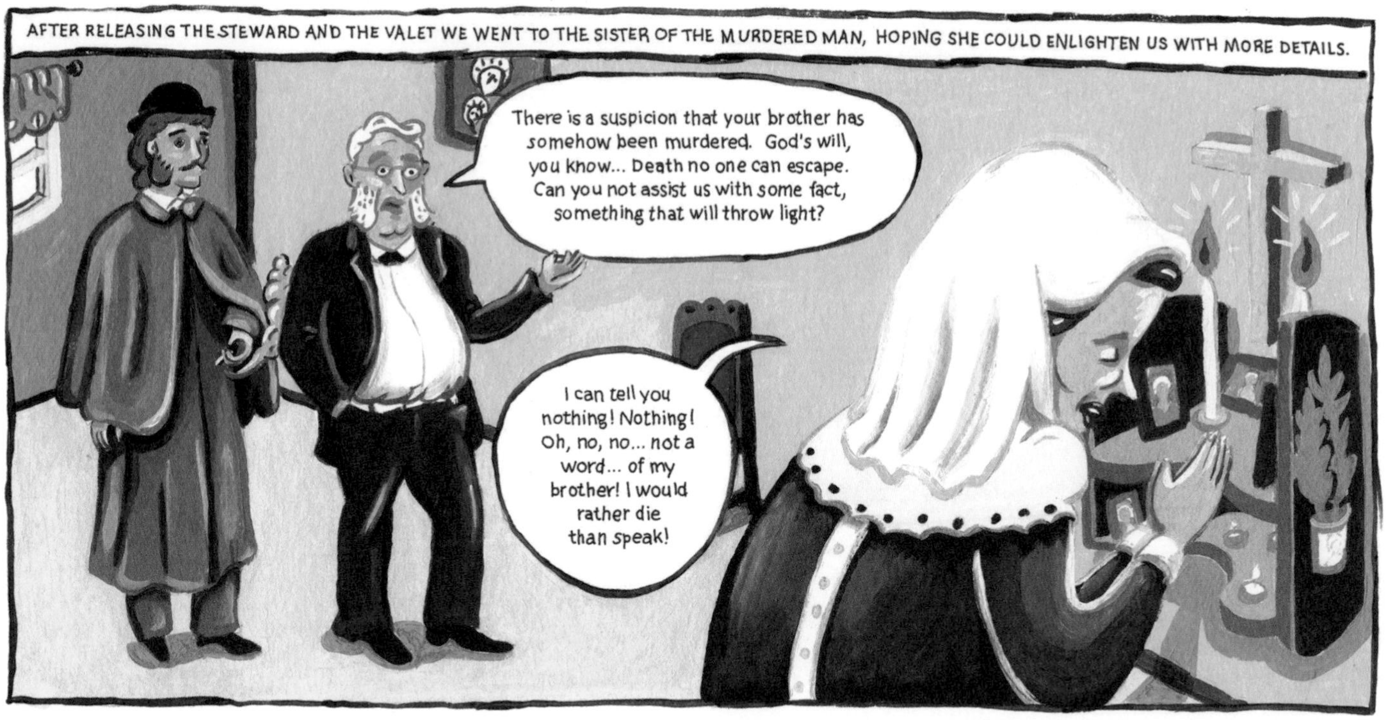
AFTER RELEASING THE STEWARD AND THE VALET WE WENT TO THE SISTER OF THE MURDERED MAN, HOPING SHE COULD ENLIGHTEN US WITH MORE DETAILS.
There is a suspicion that your brother has somehow been murdered. God's will, you know... Death no one can escape. Can you not assist us with some fact, something that will throw light?
I can tell you nothing! Nothing! Oh, no, no... not a word... of my brother! I would rather die than speak!

AT THIS POINT I SUSPECTED THREE PEOPLE. THE STEWARD AND THE VALET BOTH HAD A CLEAR ROMANTIC MOTIVE. UNLIKE THE THIRD SUSPECT – THE ASSASSINATED MAN'S SISTER. SHE WAS A RELIGIOUS FANATIC, AND HER BROTHER – A DISSIPATED DRUNK. SHE SURE DIDN'T LIKE THAT. SHE WAS ALSO A WOMAN OF THE EDUCATED CLASS, WHICH SUITS THE SWEDISH MATCH! HIS HONOUR DIDN'T BELIEVE THIS ANALYSIS AT FIRST, BUT THEN CAME THE WITNESS.

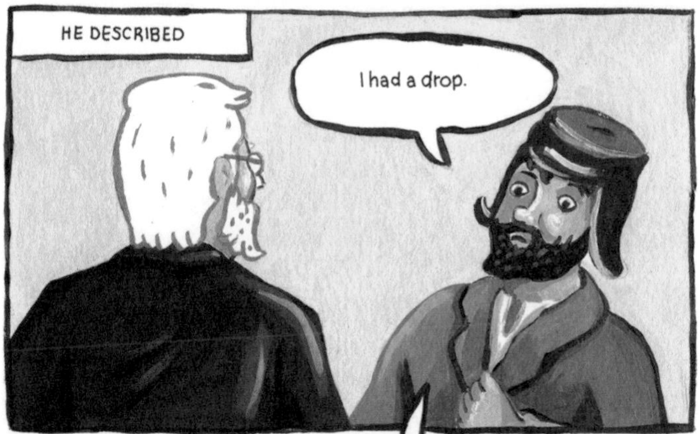
HE DESCRIBED
I had a drop.

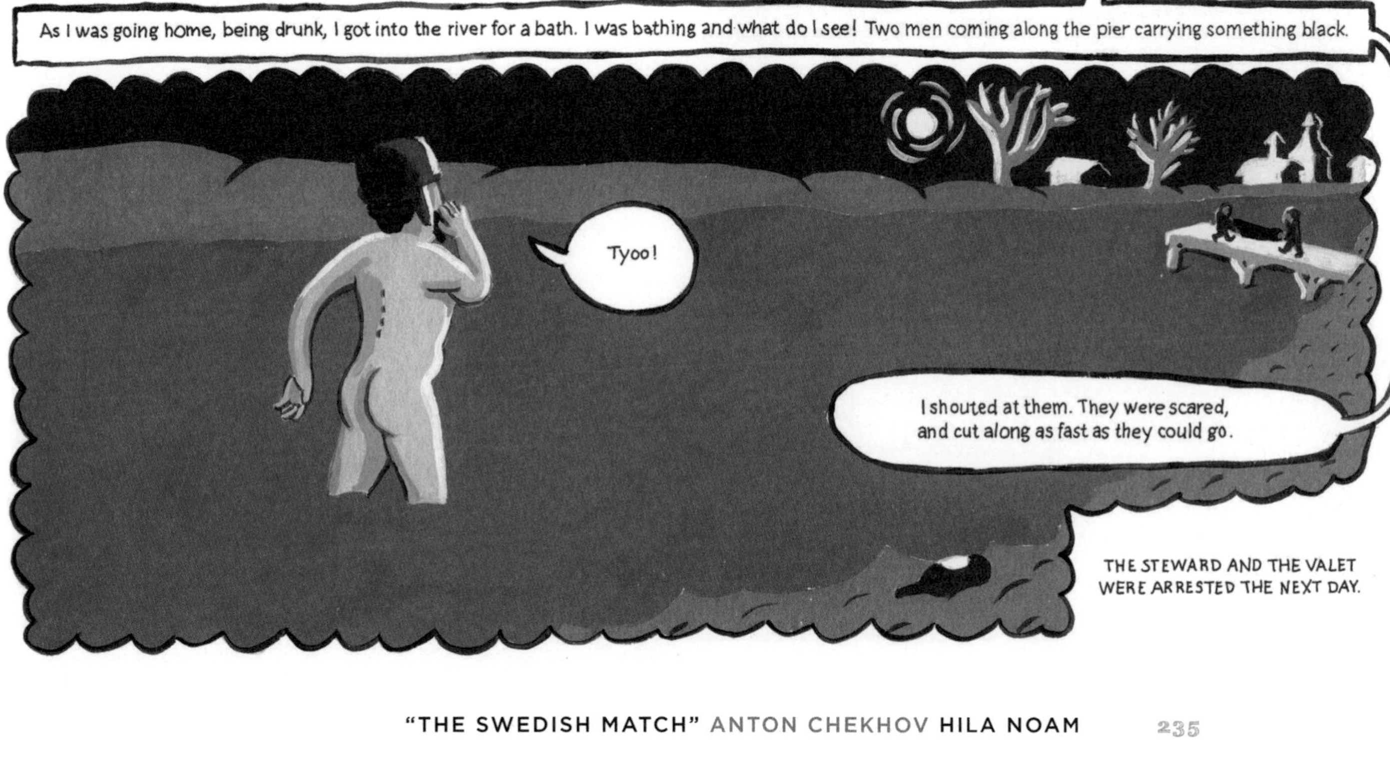
As I was going home, being drunk, I got into the river for a bath. I was bathing and what do I see! Two men coming along the pier carrying something black.
Tyoo!
I shouted at them. They were scared, and cut along as fast as they could go.

THE STEWARD AND THE VALET WERE ARRESTED THE NEXT DAY.

In 1879 you were convicted of theft and condemned to a term of imprisonment. In 1882 you were condemned for theft a second time, and a second time sent to prison... We know all about it...

I'm sorry, may I leave to go to wash, and calm myself?

Urggh... Bring in Psyekov

If you don't confess today, tomorrow it will be too late. Come, tell us...

I know nothing, and I don't know your evidence.

Well then, allow me to tell you how it happened.

You were sitting in Klyauzov's bedroom drinking vodka and beer with him. Nikolay was waiting upon you.

Between twelve and one, while Mark Ivanovitch was taking off his boots, Nikolay and you seized him. One of you sat on his feet, the other on his head.

At that moment the lady in black, you know who, came in from the passage. She picked up the pillow, and proceeded to smother him with it.

During the struggle, the light went out. The woman took a box of *Swedish* matches out of her pocket and lit the candle. Isn't that right? I see from your face that what I say is true.

Then, Nikolay and you dragged him out of the window and put him down near the burdocks. Afraid that he might regain consciousness, you struck him with something sharp. Then you carried him, and laid him under a bush.

After resting a little, you carried him... Near the pier you were frightened by a peasant. But what is the matter with you?

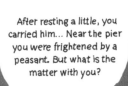

I am suffocating! Very well... So be it... Only I must go... Please.

Take him away!

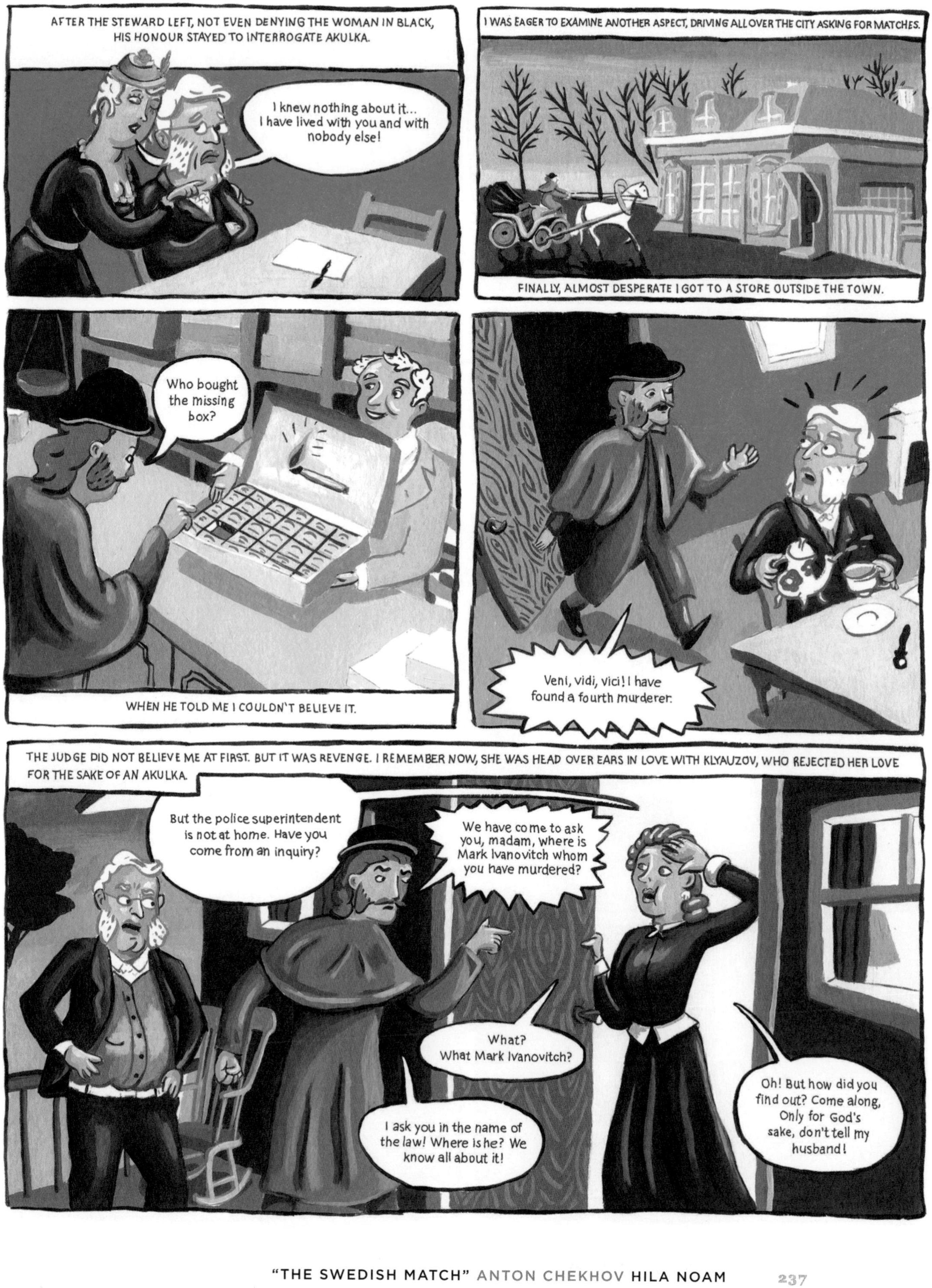
AFTER THE STEWARD LEFT, NOT EVEN DENYING THE WOMAN IN BLACK, HIS HONOUR STAYED TO INTERROGATE AKULKA.
I knew nothing about it... I have lived with you and with nobody else!
I WAS EAGER TO EXAMINE ANOTHER ASPECT, DRIVING ALL OVER THE CITY ASKING FOR MATCHES.
FINALLY, ALMOST DESPERATE I GOT TO A STORE OUTSIDE THE TOWN.
Who bought the missing box?
WHEN HE TOLD ME I COULDN'T BELIEVE IT.
Veni, vidi, vici! I have found a fourth murderer.
THE JUDGE DID NOT BELIEVE ME AT FIRST. BUT IT WAS REVENGE. I REMEMBER NOW, SHE WAS HEAD OVER EARS IN LOVE WITH KLYAUZOV, WHO REJECTED HER LOVE FOR THE SAKE OF AN AKULKA.
But the police superintendent is not at home. Have you come from an inquiry?
We have come to ask you, madam, where is Mark Ivanovitch whom you have murdered?
What? What Mark Ivanovitch?
I ask you in the name of the law! Where is he? We know all about it!
Oh! But how did you find out? Come along, Only for God's sake, don't tell my husband!

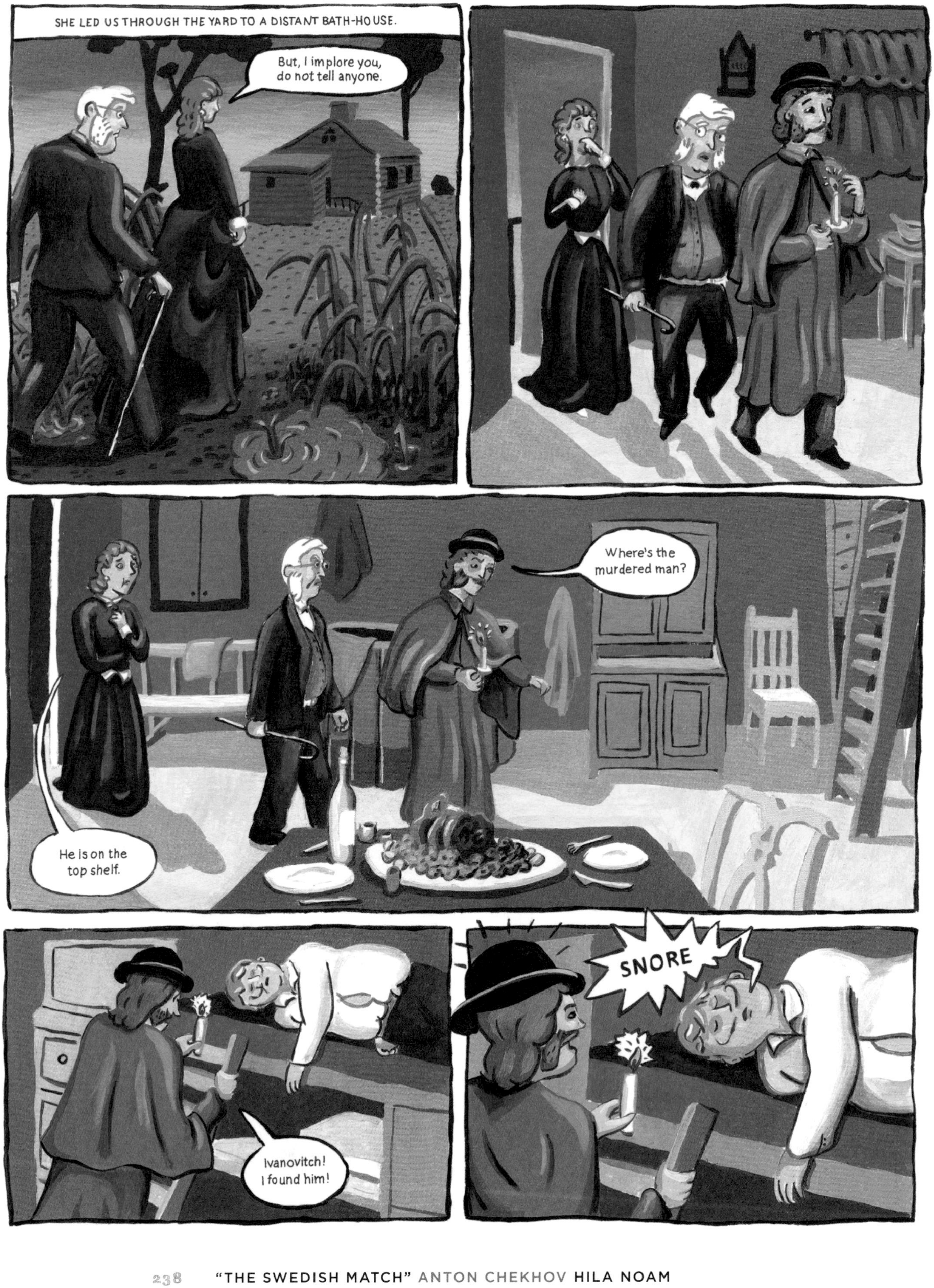
SHE LED US THROUGH THE YARD TO A DISTANT BATH-HOUSE.
But, I implore you, do not tell anyone.
Where's the murdered man?
He is on the top shelf.
Ivanovitch! I found him!
SNORE

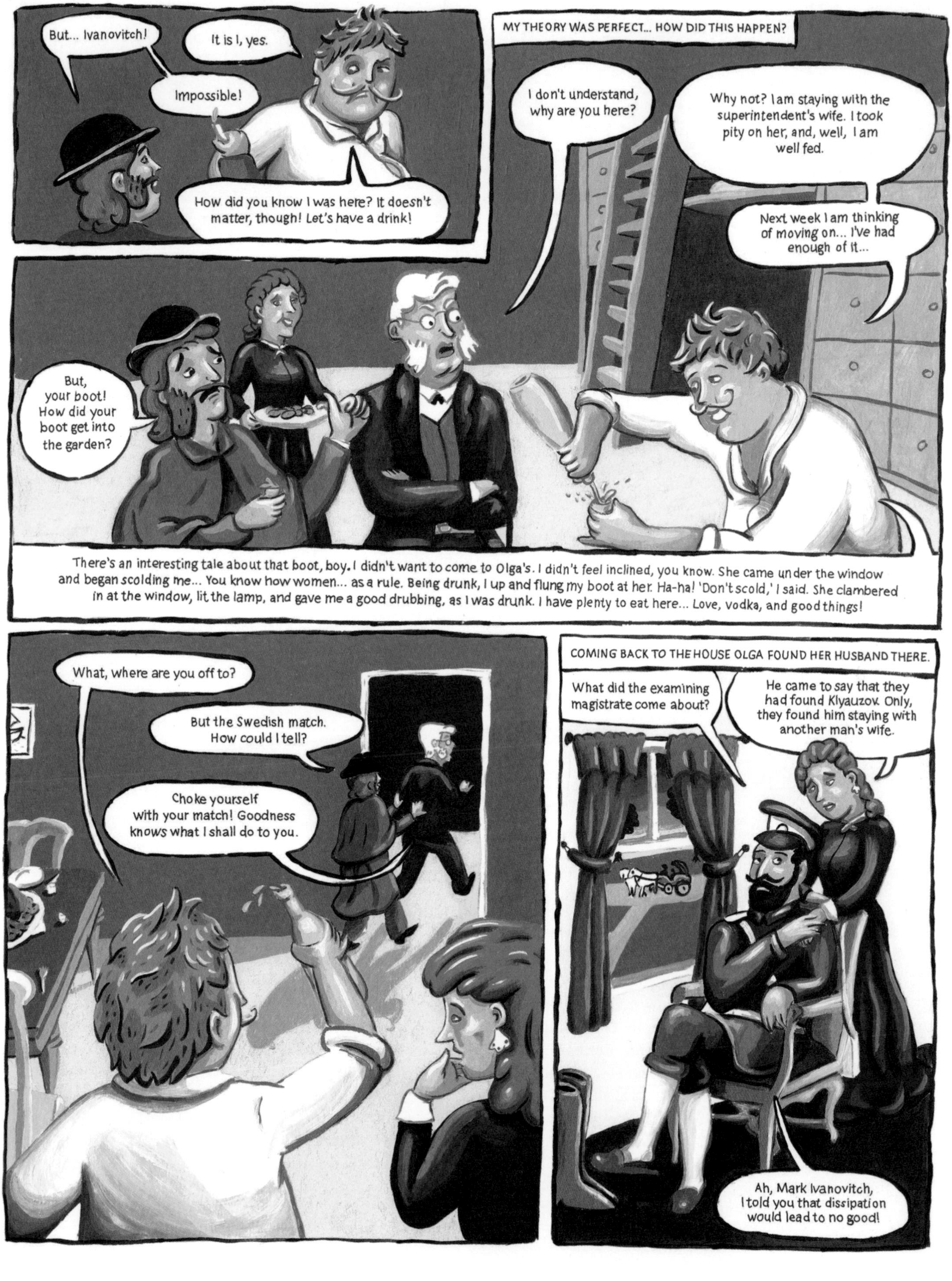

But... Ivanovitch!
It is I, yes.
Impossible!
How did you know I was here? It doesn't matter, though! Let's have a drink!
MY THEORY WAS PERFECT... HOW DID THIS HAPPEN?
I don't understand, why are you here?
Why not? I am staying with the superintendent's wife. I took pity on her, and, well, I am well fed.
Next week I am thinking of moving on... I've had enough of it...
But, your boot! How did your boot get into the garden?
There's an interesting tale about that boot, boy. I didn't want to come to Olga's. I didn't feel inclined, you know. She came under the window and began scolding me... You know how women... as a rule. Being drunk, I up and flung my boot at her. Ha-ha! 'Don't scold,' I said. She clambered in at the window, lit the lamp, and gave me a good drubbing, as I was drunk. I have plenty to eat here... Love, vodka, and good things!
What, where are you off to?
But the Swedish match. How could I tell?
Choke yourself with your match! Goodness knows what I shall do to you.
COMING BACK TO THE HOUSE OLGA FOUND HER HUSBAND THERE.
What did the examining magistrate come about?
He came to say that they had found Klyauzov. Only, they found him staying with another man's wife.
Ah, Mark Ivanovitch, I told you that dissipation would lead to no good!

"A Scandal in Bohemia"
(a Sherlock Holmes mystery)

Arthur Conan Doyle

ART/ADAPTATION BY **Lara Antal** AND **Dave Kelly**

HERE WE HAVE THE FIRST SHORT STORY to feature Sherlock Holmes. Now, this wasn't the first work starring the detective. Sir Arthur Conan Doyle had written two novels featuring Holmes, but they hadn't made much of a splash. It was the short stories appearing in the super-poplar magazine *The Strand* that launched the sleuth into the cultural stratosphere.

"A Scandal in Bohemia" has remained one of the most popular Sherlock stories, not only because of its role in lighting the fuse but also because it features the only woman to outsmart Holmes, Irene Adler. Late in life, Conan Doyle named it as one of his favorite Sherlock stories.

Besides bringing us this crisp adaptation, the team of artist Lara Antal and writer Dave Kelly also run comics publisher So What? Press, probably best known for its series *Tales of the Night Watchman*. Among other things, Lara has reinvigorated the "how to help a choking victim" posters that are required in NYC restaurants, and her part-time job must be the envy of everyone around her: archivist at Random House Children's Books.

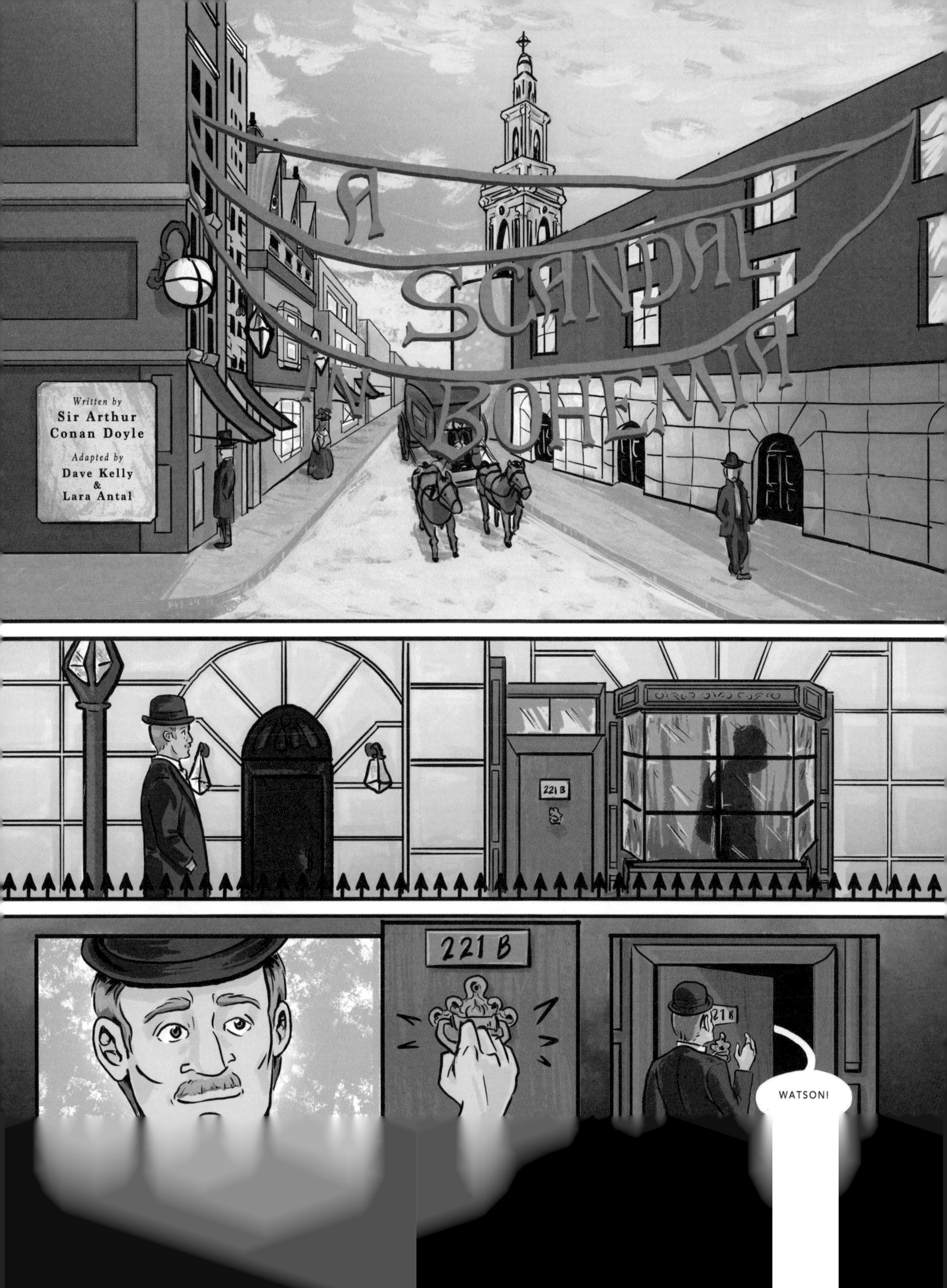
A SCANDAL IN BOHEMIA
Written by
Sir Arthur Conan Doyle
Adapted by
Dave Kelly
&
Lara Antal
221 B
221 B
221 B
WATSON!

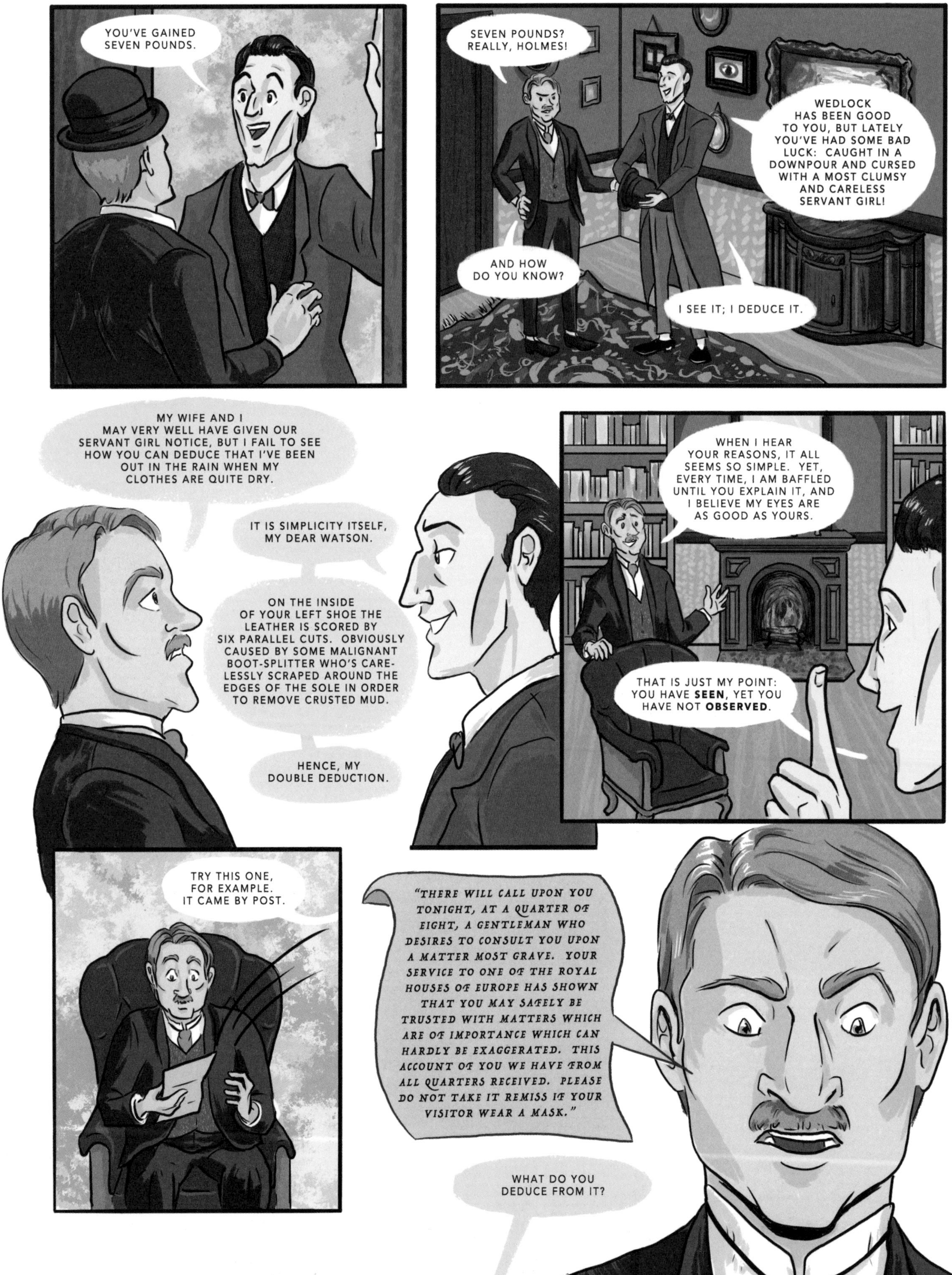

YOU'VE GAINED SEVEN POUNDS.
SEVEN POUNDS? REALLY, HOLMES!
WEDLOCK HAS BEEN GOOD TO YOU, BUT LATELY YOU'VE HAD SOME BAD LUCK: CAUGHT IN A DOWNPOUR AND CURSED WITH A MOST CLUMSY AND CARELESS SERVANT GIRL!
AND HOW DO YOU KNOW?
I SEE IT; I DEDUCE IT.
MY WIFE AND I MAY VERY WELL HAVE GIVEN OUR SERVANT GIRL NOTICE, BUT I FAIL TO SEE HOW YOU CAN DEDUCE THAT I'VE BEEN OUT IN THE RAIN WHEN MY CLOTHES ARE QUITE DRY.
IT IS SIMPLICITY ITSELF, MY DEAR WATSON.
ON THE INSIDE OF YOUR LEFT SHOE THE LEATHER IS SCORED BY SIX PARALLEL CUTS. OBVIOUSLY CAUSED BY SOME MALIGNANT BOOT-SPLITTER WHO'S CARELESSLY SCRAPED AROUND THE EDGES OF THE SOLE IN ORDER TO REMOVE CRUSTED MUD.
HENCE, MY DOUBLE DEDUCTION.
WHEN I HEAR YOUR REASONS, IT ALL SEEMS SO SIMPLE. YET, EVERY TIME, I AM BAFFLED UNTIL YOU EXPLAIN IT, AND I BELIEVE MY EYES ARE AS GOOD AS YOURS.
THAT IS JUST MY POINT: YOU HAVE **SEEN**, YET YOU HAVE NOT **OBSERVED**.
TRY THIS ONE, FOR EXAMPLE. IT CAME BY POST.
"THERE WILL CALL UPON YOU TONIGHT, AT A QUARTER OF EIGHT, A GENTLEMAN WHO DESIRES TO CONSULT YOU UPON A MATTER MOST GRAVE. YOUR SERVICE TO ONE OF THE ROYAL HOUSES OF EUROPE HAS SHOWN THAT YOU MAY SAFELY BE TRUSTED WITH MATTERS WHICH ARE OF IMPORTANCE WHICH CAN HARDLY BE EXAGGERATED. THIS ACCOUNT OF YOU WE HAVE FROM ALL QUARTERS RECEIVED. PLEASE DO NOT TAKE IT REMISS IF YOUR VISITOR WEAR A MASK."
WHAT DO YOU DEDUCE FROM IT?

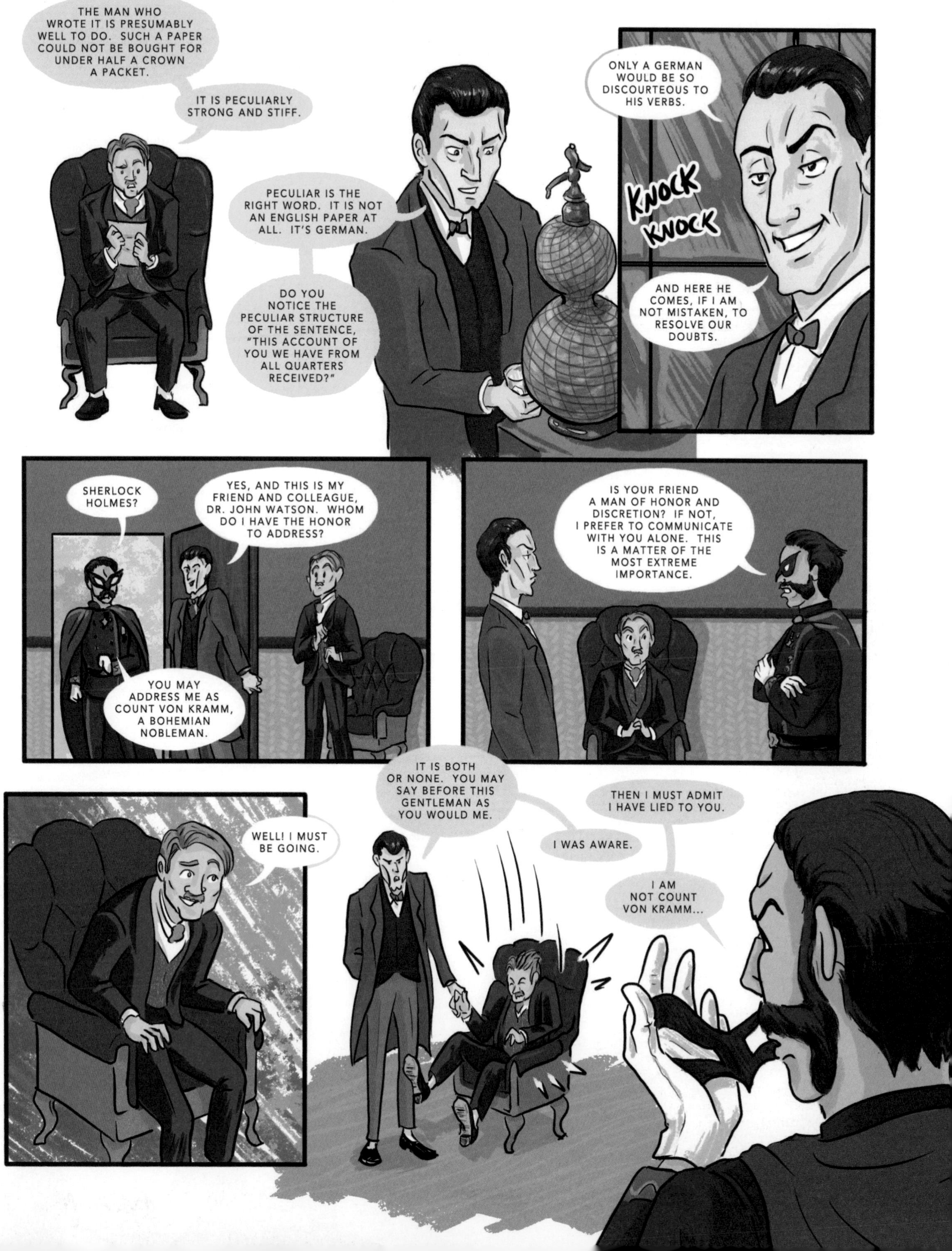
THE MAN WHO WROTE IT IS PRESUMABLY WELL TO DO. SUCH A PAPER COULD NOT BE BOUGHT FOR UNDER HALF A CROWN A PACKET.
IT IS PECULIARLY STRONG AND STIFF.
PECULIAR IS THE RIGHT WORD. IT IS NOT AN ENGLISH PAPER AT ALL. IT'S GERMAN.
DO YOU NOTICE THE PECULIAR STRUCTURE OF THE SENTENCE, "THIS ACCOUNT OF YOU WE HAVE FROM ALL QUARTERS RECEIVED?"
ONLY A GERMAN WOULD BE SO DISCOURTEOUS TO HIS VERBS.
KNOCK KNOCK
AND HERE HE COMES, IF I AM NOT MISTAKEN, TO RESOLVE OUR DOUBTS.
SHERLOCK HOLMES?
YES, AND THIS IS MY FRIEND AND COLLEAGUE, DR. JOHN WATSON. WHOM DO I HAVE THE HONOR TO ADDRESS?
YOU MAY ADDRESS ME AS COUNT VON KRAMM, A BOHEMIAN NOBLEMAN.
IS YOUR FRIEND A MAN OF HONOR AND DISCRETION? IF NOT, I PREFER TO COMMUNICATE WITH YOU ALONE. THIS IS A MATTER OF THE MOST EXTREME IMPORTANCE.
WELL! I MUST BE GOING.
IT IS BOTH OR NONE. YOU MAY SAY BEFORE THIS GENTLEMAN AS YOU WOULD ME.
THEN I MUST ADMIT I HAVE LIED TO YOU.
I WAS AWARE.
I AM NOT COUNT VON KRAMM...

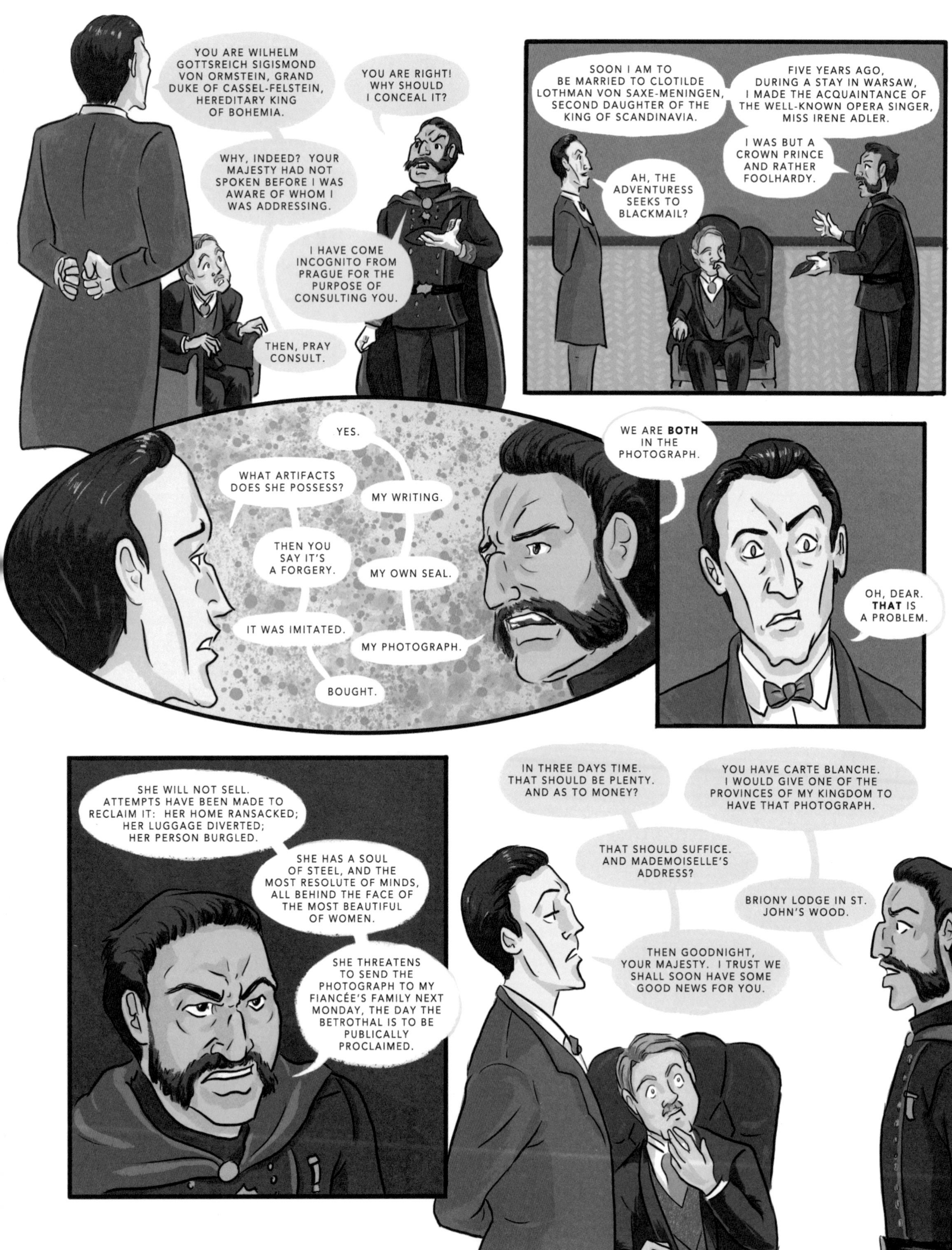

YOU ARE WILHELM GOTTSREICH SIGISMOND VON ORMSTEIN, GRAND DUKE OF CASSEL-FELSTEIN, HEREDITARY KING OF BOHEMIA.
YOU ARE RIGHT! WHY SHOULD I CONCEAL IT?
WHY, INDEED? YOUR MAJESTY HAD NOT SPOKEN BEFORE I WAS AWARE OF WHOM I WAS ADDRESSING.
I HAVE COME INCOGNITO FROM PRAGUE FOR THE PURPOSE OF CONSULTING YOU.
THEN, PRAY CONSULT.
SOON I AM TO BE MARRIED TO CLOTILDE LOTHMAN VON SAXE-MENINGEN, SECOND DAUGHTER OF THE KING OF SCANDINAVIA.
FIVE YEARS AGO, DURING A STAY IN WARSAW, I MADE THE ACQUAINTANCE OF THE WELL-KNOWN OPERA SINGER, MISS IRENE ADLER.
I WAS BUT A CROWN PRINCE AND RATHER FOOLHARDY.
AH, THE ADVENTURESS SEEKS TO BLACKMAIL?
YES.
WHAT ARTIFACTS DOES SHE POSSESS?
MY WRITING.
THEN YOU SAY IT'S A FORGERY.
MY OWN SEAL.
IT WAS IMITATED.
MY PHOTOGRAPH.
BOUGHT.
WE ARE **BOTH** IN THE PHOTOGRAPH.
OH, DEAR. **THAT** IS A PROBLEM.
SHE WILL NOT SELL. ATTEMPTS HAVE BEEN MADE TO RECLAIM IT: HER HOME RANSACKED; HER LUGGAGE DIVERTED; HER PERSON BURGLED.
SHE HAS A SOUL OF STEEL, AND THE MOST RESOLUTE OF MINDS, ALL BEHIND THE FACE OF THE MOST BEAUTIFUL OF WOMEN.
SHE THREATENS TO SEND THE PHOTOGRAPH TO MY FIANCÉE'S FAMILY NEXT MONDAY, THE DAY THE BETROTHAL IS TO BE PUBLICALLY PROCLAIMED.
IN THREE DAYS TIME. THAT SHOULD BE PLENTY. AND AS TO MONEY?
YOU HAVE CARTE BLANCHE. I WOULD GIVE ONE OF THE PROVINCES OF MY KINGDOM TO HAVE THAT PHOTOGRAPH.
THAT SHOULD SUFFICE. AND MADEMOISELLE'S ADDRESS?
BRIONY LODGE IN ST. JOHN'S WOOD.
THEN GOODNIGHT, YOUR MAJESTY. I TRUST WE SHALL SOON HAVE SOME GOOD NEWS FOR YOU.

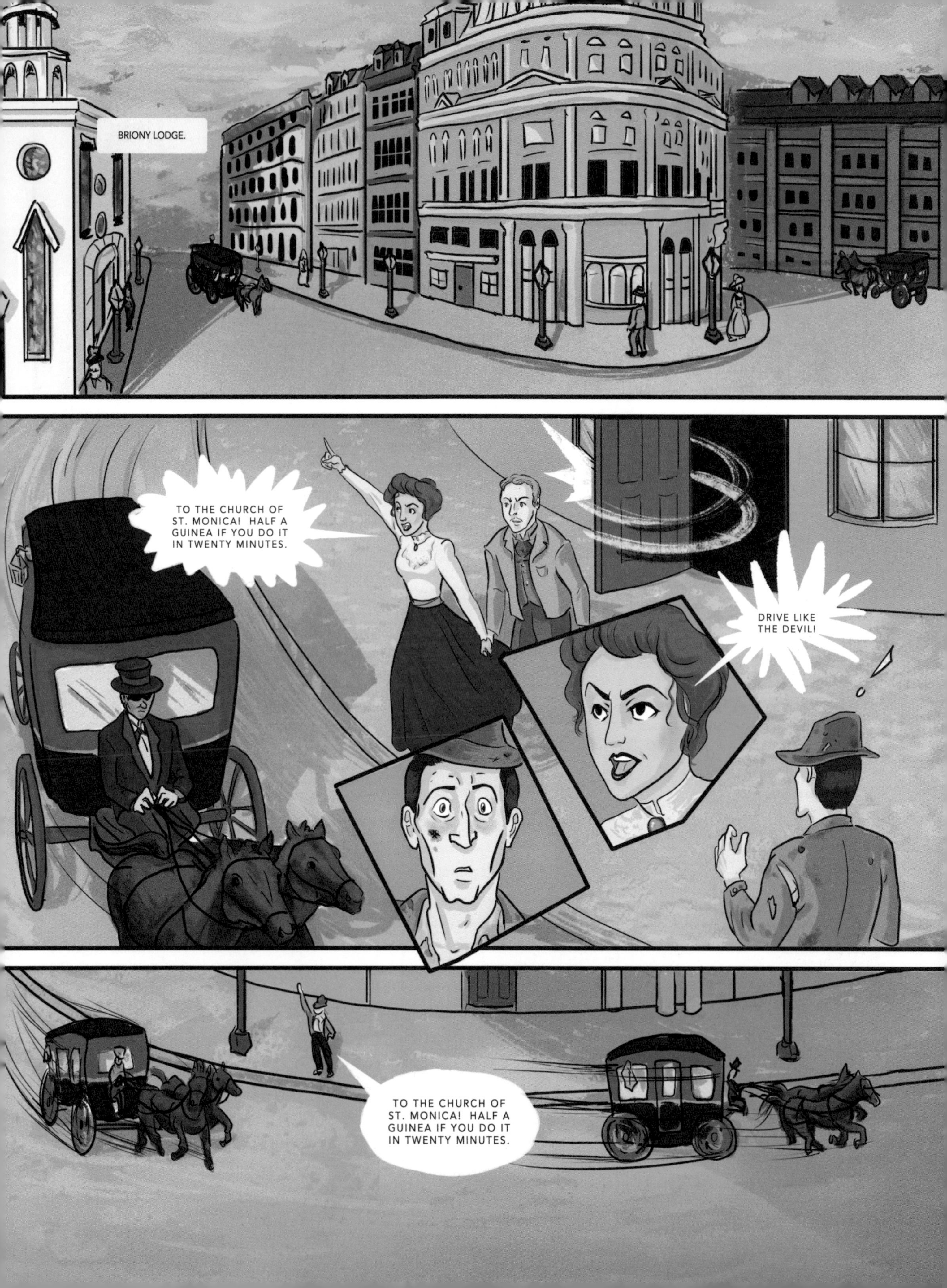
BRIONY LODGE.
TO THE CHURCH OF ST. MONICA! HALF A GUINEA IF YOU DO IT IN TWENTY MINUTES.
DRIVE LIKE THE DEVIL!
TO THE CHURCH OF ST. MONICA! HALF A GUINEA IF YOU DO IT IN TWENTY MINUTES.

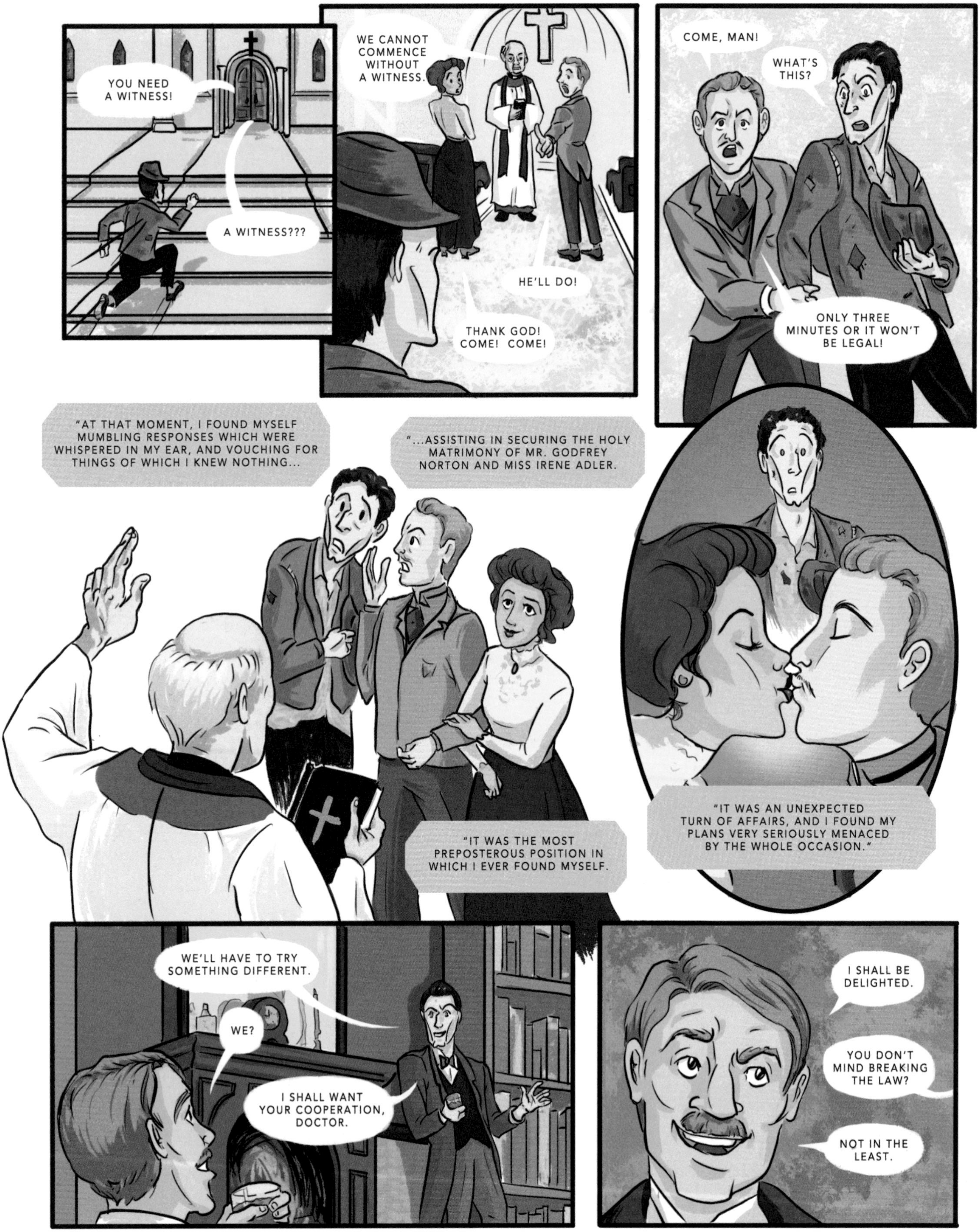
YOU NEED A WITNESS!
A WITNESS???
WE CANNOT COMMENCE WITHOUT A WITNESS.
HE'LL DO!
THANK GOD! COME! COME!
COME, MAN!
WHAT'S THIS?
ONLY THREE MINUTES OR IT WON'T BE LEGAL!
"AT THAT MOMENT, I FOUND MYSELF MUMBLING RESPONSES WHICH WERE WHISPERED IN MY EAR, AND VOUCHING FOR THINGS OF WHICH I KNEW NOTHING...
"...ASSISTING IN SECURING THE HOLY MATRIMONY OF MR. GODFREY NORTON AND MISS IRENE ADLER.
"IT WAS THE MOST PREPOSTEROUS POSITION IN WHICH I EVER FOUND MYSELF.
"IT WAS AN UNEXPECTED TURN OF AFFAIRS, AND I FOUND MY PLANS VERY SERIOUSLY MENACED BY THE WHOLE OCCASION."
WE'LL HAVE TO TRY SOMETHING DIFFERENT.
WE?
I SHALL WANT YOUR COOPERATION, DOCTOR.
I SHALL BE DELIGHTED.
YOU DON'T MIND BREAKING THE LAW?
NOT IN THE LEAST.

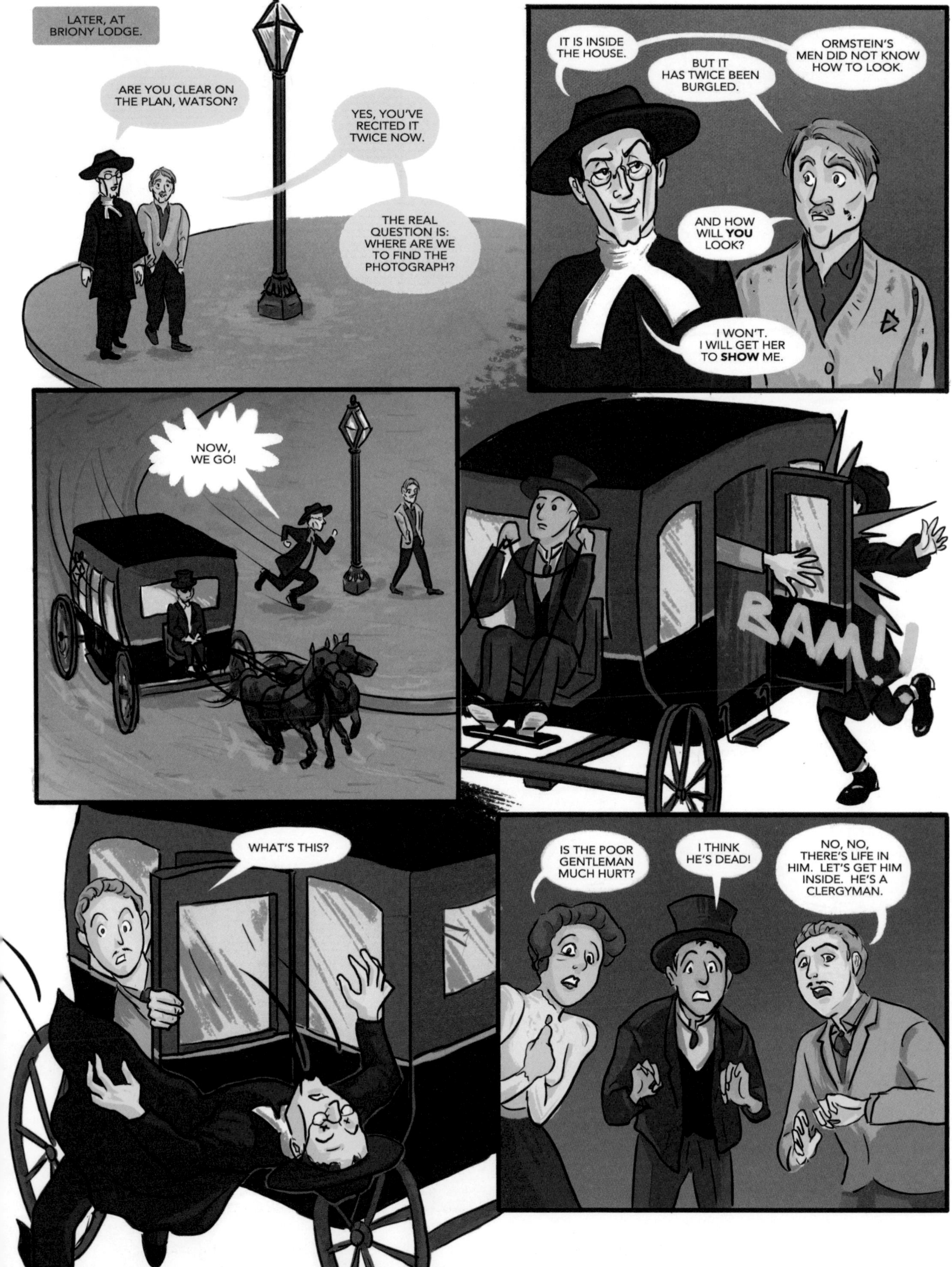
LATER, AT BRIONY LODGE.
ARE YOU CLEAR ON THE PLAN, WATSON?
YES, YOU'VE RECITED IT TWICE NOW.
THE REAL QUESTION IS: WHERE ARE WE TO FIND THE PHOTOGRAPH?
IT IS INSIDE THE HOUSE.
ORMSTEIN'S MEN DID NOT KNOW HOW TO LOOK.
BUT IT HAS TWICE BEEN BURGLED.
AND HOW WILL **YOU** LOOK?
I WON'T. I WILL GET HER TO **SHOW** ME.
NOW, WE GO!
BAM!!
WHAT'S THIS?
IS THE POOR GENTLEMAN MUCH HURT?
I THINK HE'S DEAD!
NO, NO, THERE'S LIFE IN HIM. LET'S GET HIM INSIDE. HE'S A CLERGYMAN.

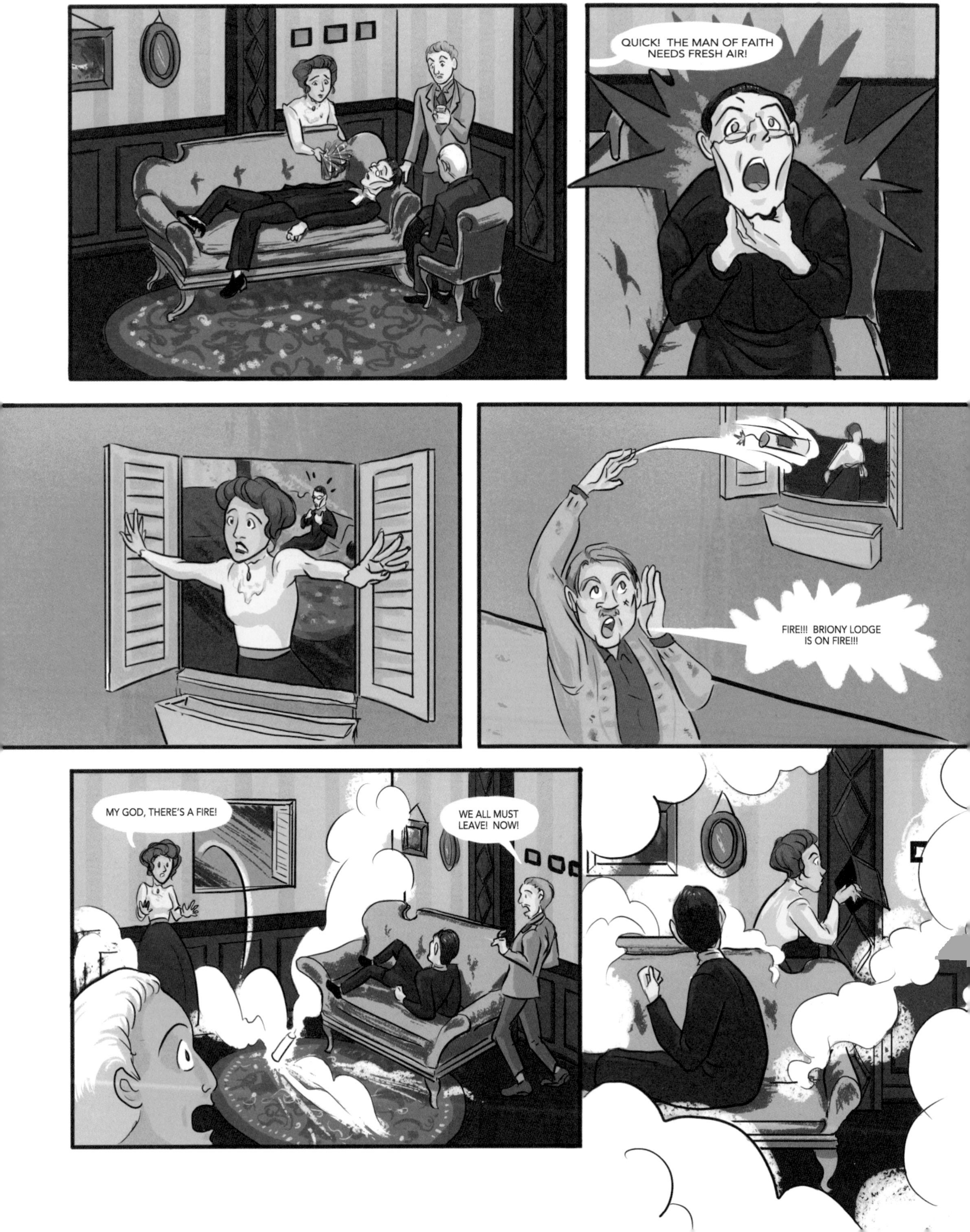
QUICK! THE MAN OF FAITH NEEDS FRESH AIR!
FIRE!!! BRIONY LODGE IS ON FIRE!!!
MY GOD, THERE'S A FIRE!
WE ALL MUST LEAVE! NOW!

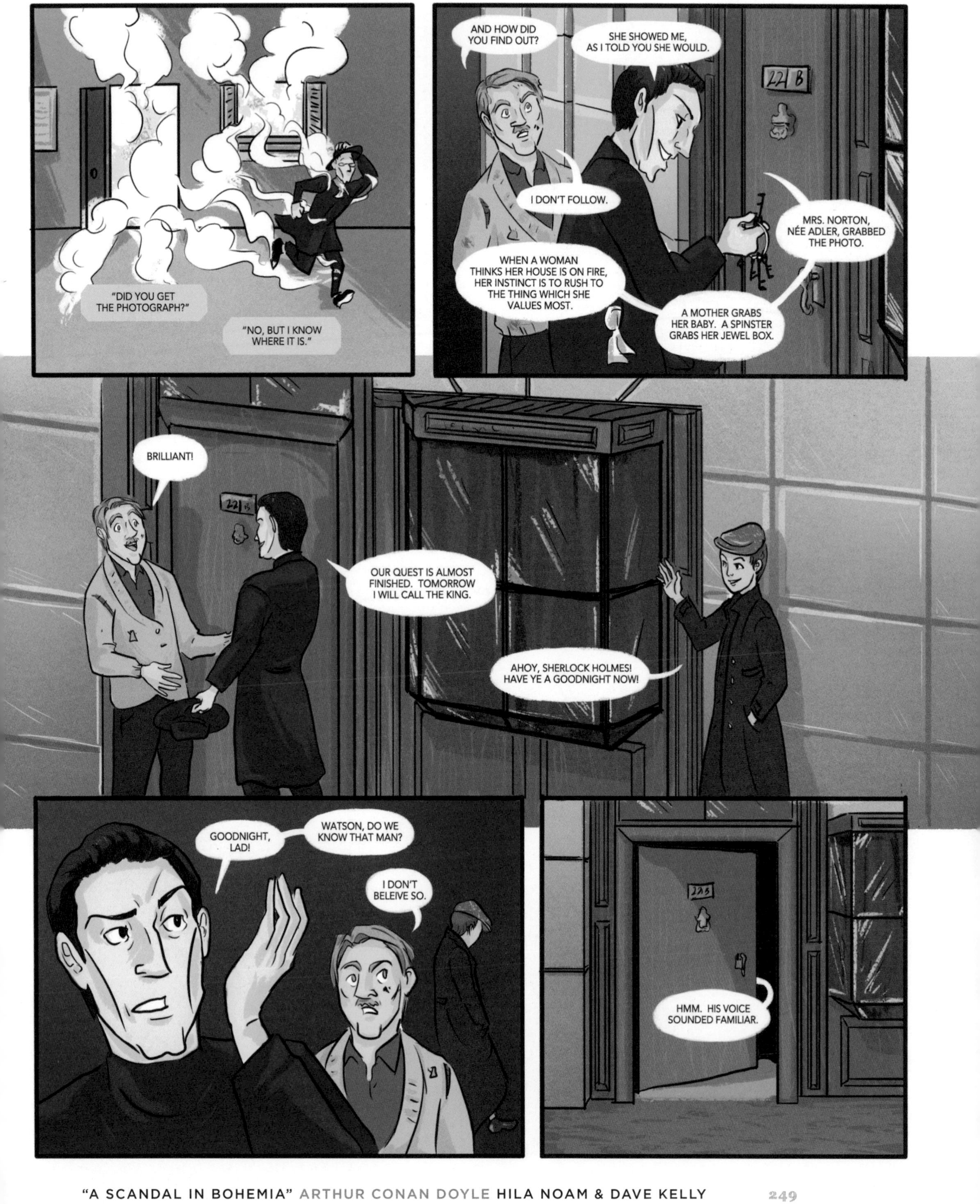
"DID YOU GET
THE PHOTOGRAPH?"
"NO, BUT I KNOW
WHERE IT IS."
AND HOW DID
YOU FIND OUT?
SHE SHOWED ME,
AS I TOLD YOU SHE WOULD.
221 B
I DON'T FOLLOW.
WHEN A WOMAN
THINKS HER HOUSE IS ON FIRE,
HER INSTINCT IS TO RUSH TO
THE THING WHICH SHE
VALUES MOST.
A MOTHER GRABS
HER BABY. A SPINSTER
GRABS HER JEWEL BOX.
MRS. NORTON,
NÉE ADLER, GRABBED
THE PHOTO.
BRILLIANT!
OUR QUEST IS ALMOST
FINISHED. TOMORROW
I WILL CALL THE KING.
AHOY, SHERLOCK HOLMES!
HAVE YE A GOODNIGHT NOW!
GOODNIGHT,
LAD!
WATSON, DO WE
KNOW THAT MAN?
I DON'T
BELEIVE SO.
HMM. HIS VOICE
SOUNDED FAMILIAR.

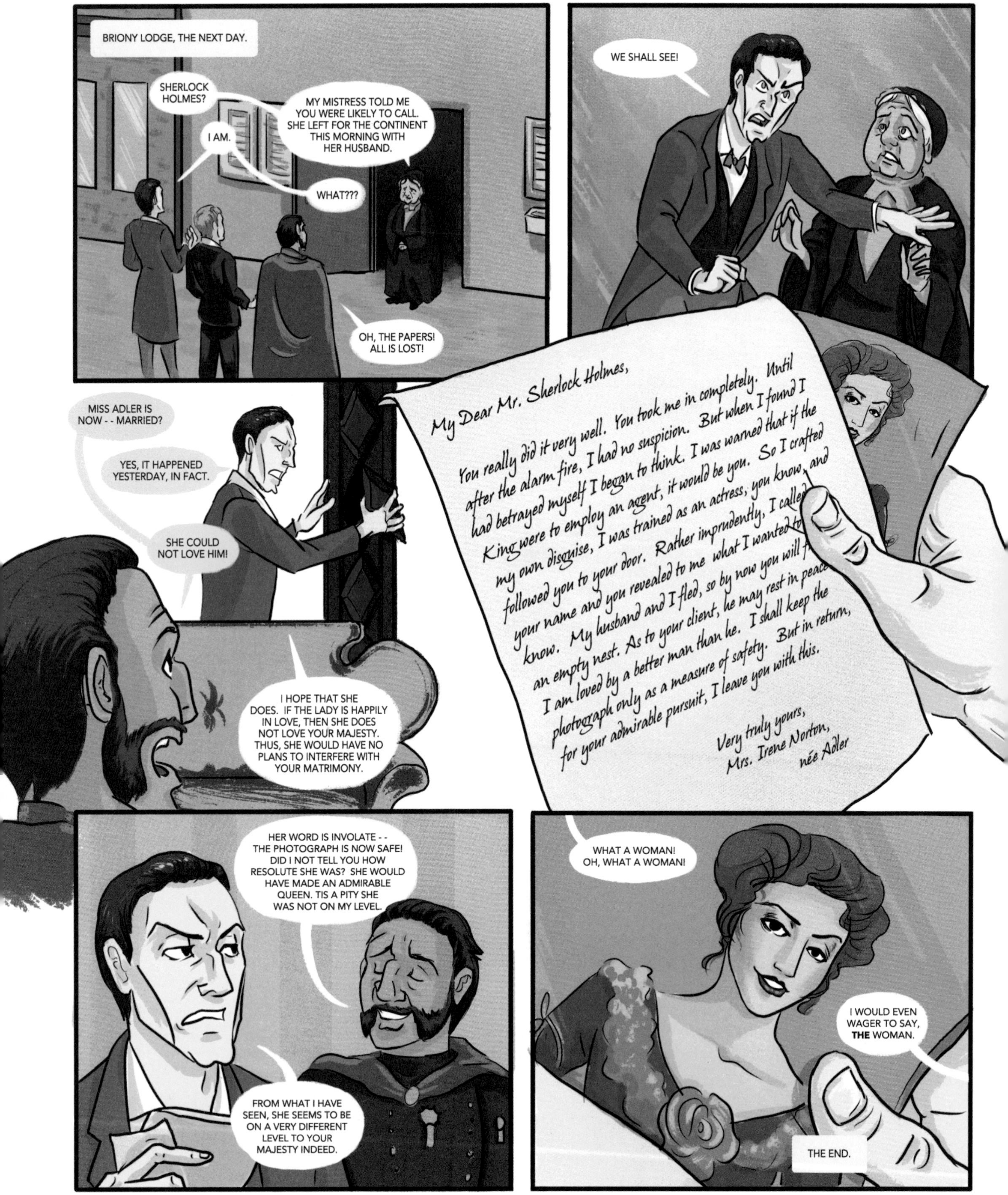
BRIONY LODGE, THE NEXT DAY.
SHERLOCK HOLMES?
I AM.
MY MISTRESS TOLD ME YOU WERE LIKELY TO CALL. SHE LEFT FOR THE CONTINENT THIS MORNING WITH HER HUSBAND.
WHAT???
OH, THE PAPERS! ALL IS LOST!
WE SHALL SEE!
MISS ADLER IS NOW - - MARRIED?
YES, IT HAPPENED YESTERDAY, IN FACT.
SHE COULD NOT LOVE HIM!
I HOPE THAT SHE DOES. IF THE LADY IS HAPPILY IN LOVE, THEN SHE DOES NOT LOVE YOUR MAJESTY. THUS, SHE WOULD HAVE NO PLANS TO INTERFERE WITH YOUR MATRIMONY.
My Dear Mr. Sherlock Holmes,
You really did it very well. You took me in completely. Until after the alarm fire, I had no suspicion. But when I found I had betrayed myself I began to think. I was warned that if the King were to employ an agent, it would be you. So I crafted my own disguise, I was trained as an actress, you know, and followed you to your door. Rather imprudently, I called your name and you revealed to me what I wanted to know. My husband and I fled, so by now you will find an empty nest. As to your client, he may rest in peace. I am loved by a better man than he. I shall keep the photograph only as a measure of safety. But in return, for your admirable pursuit, I leave you with this.
Very truly yours,
Mrs. Irene Norton,
née Adler
HER WORD IS INVOLATE - - THE PHOTOGRAPH IS NOW SAFE! DID I NOT TELL YOU HOW RESOLUTE SHE WAS? SHE WOULD HAVE MADE AN ADMIRABLE QUEEN. TIS A PITY SHE WAS NOT ON MY LEVEL.
FROM WHAT I HAVE SEEN, SHE SEEMS TO BE ON A VERY DIFFERENT LEVEL TO YOUR MAJESTY INDEED.
WHAT A WOMAN! OH, WHAT A WOMAN!
I WOULD EVEN WAGER TO SAY, THE WOMAN.
THE END.

"The Ninescore Mystery"
(a Lady Molly mystery)

Baroness Emmuska Orczy

ART/ADAPTATION BY Becky Hawkins

IT'S BEEN FORGOTTEN NOW, BUT DURING the Victorian era, which saw the birth of the mystery genre as we know it, a lot of literary detectives were women. This was so true during the middle of the 1800s that literature professor Joseph A. Kestner wrote that Poe's C. Auguste Dupin and Dickens's Inspector Bucket were more the exception than the rule. This remained the case into the Edwardian era, which saw, among others, teenage sleuth Violet Strange (a forerunner of Nancy Drew) and Lady Molly of Scotland Yard.

The Lady Molly stories were written by Emmuska Orczy, a Hungarian noblewoman who became a British writer best known for *The Scarlet Pimpernel*. Orczy wrote twelve short stories starring her female detective, but rather than appearing in magazines of the day, they were published all at once in a 1910 book.

Unlike the male detectives at Scotland Yard, who use logic and deduction, Lady Molly is repeatedly said to use "intuition," and she becomes known as the best of them. Portland cartoonist Becky Hawkins brings a pleasingly light touch to the first story in the book (and the first story chronologically), "The Ninescore Mystery." Becky says she's "mostly known for doing watercolor cartoons on postcards," although she also creates the 1940s lesbian superhero webcomic *Super-Butch* (with Barry Deutsch), posts her personal journal in comic form at frenchtoastcomix.com, and has contributed to several anthologies and *The Nib*.

THE NINE SCORE MYSTERY

A LADY MOLLY STORY

Some say she is the daughter of a duke...

Good morning.

Good morning, my lady.

'Morning, Lady Molly.

My lady.

...others that she was born in the gutter, and the title is an affectation.

I could tell you a thing or two, but my lips are sealed.

Mary!

Mary, the chief says I may go to Ninescore!

For the murder investigation?

They are becoming quite desperate about the case up at the Yard... this investig... dragged for... the public is... so I pers... Chief... on... train if we a... t... ut Ninescore... ti... he inquest. Chie... wo... hesitant... b... e him dow... e... n... fo... an ho... bu... I... he meant fo... s... t... late, and... ...n didn't u... thing, but... t possibly...

A murder case--in the hands of the Female Department!

All through her career at Scotland Yard, she honoured me with her friendship and confidence.

This is the chance I've been waiting for!

The chief suggested I take one of his men along, but I'd rather have you with me.

Yes, we always called her "my lady," from the moment that she was put at the head of our section.

Meet me at Charing Cross station at 11!

"THE NINESCORE MYSTERY" BARONESS EMMUSKA ORCZY BECKY HAWKINS

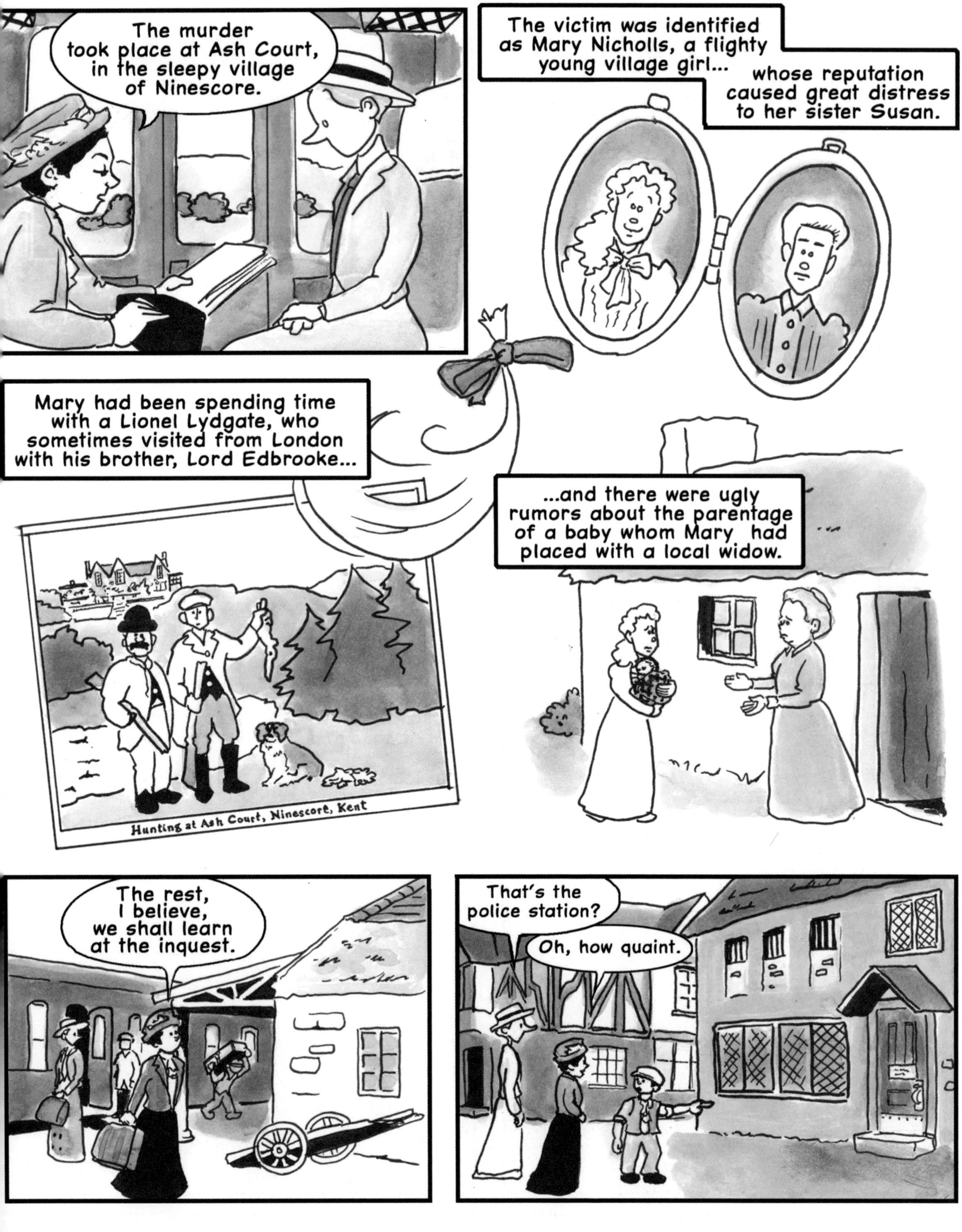
The murder took place at Ash Court, in the sleepy village of Ninescore.
The victim was identified as Mary Nicholls, a flighty young village girl...
whose reputation caused great distress to her sister Susan.
Mary had been spending time with a Lionel Lydgate, who sometimes visited from London with his brother, Lord Edbrooke...
Hunting at Ash Court, Ninescore, Kent
...and there were ugly rumors about the parentage of a baby whom Mary had placed with a local widow.
The rest, I believe, we shall learn at the inquest.
That's the police station?
Oh, how quaint.

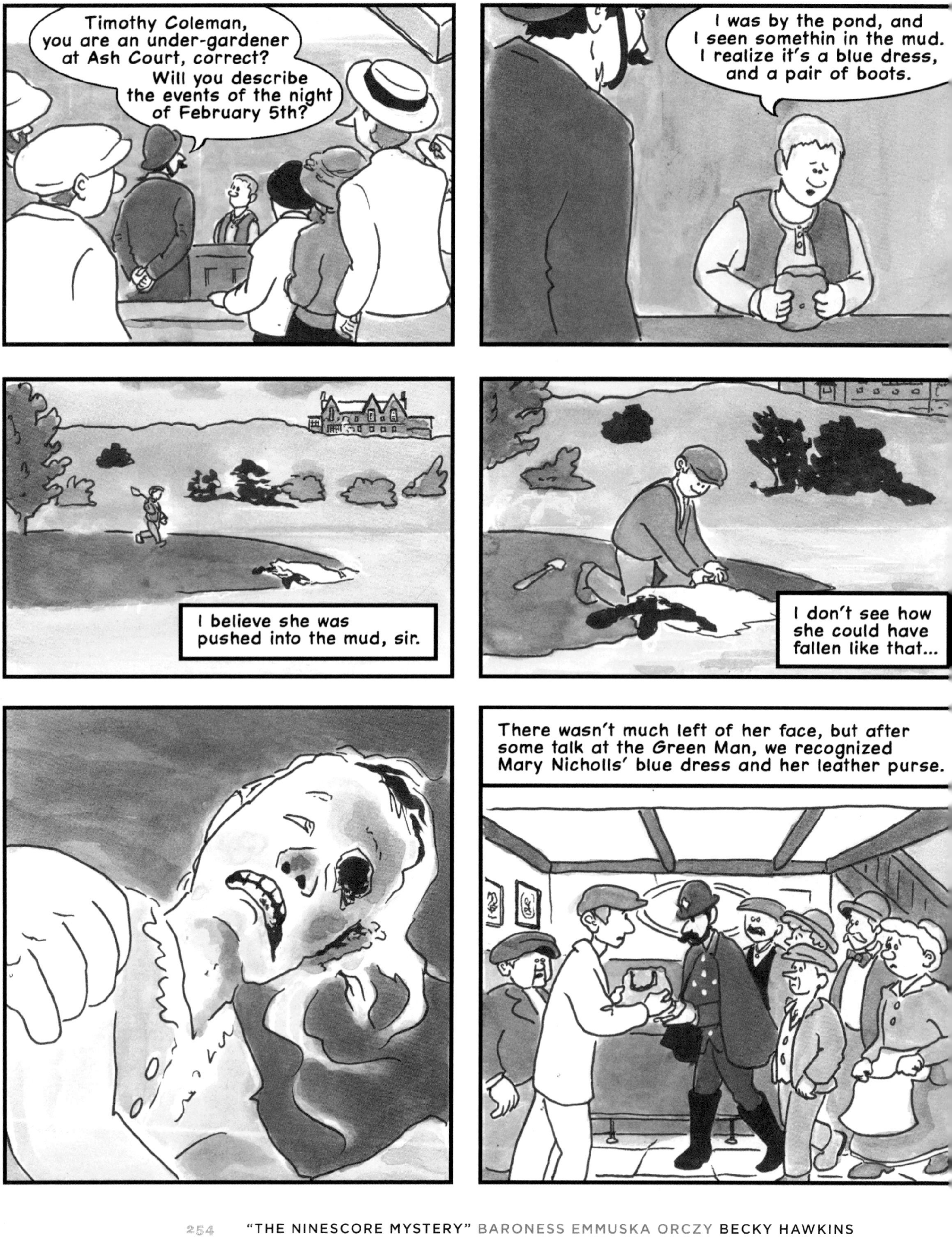
Timothy Coleman, you are an under-gardener at Ash Court, correct?
Will you describe the events of the night of February 5th?
I was by the pond, and I seen somethin in the mud. I realize it's a blue dress, and a pair of boots.
I believe she was pushed into the mud, sir.
I don't see how she could have fallen like that...
There wasn't much left of her face, but after some talk at the Green Man, we recognized Mary Nicholls' blue dress and her leather purse.

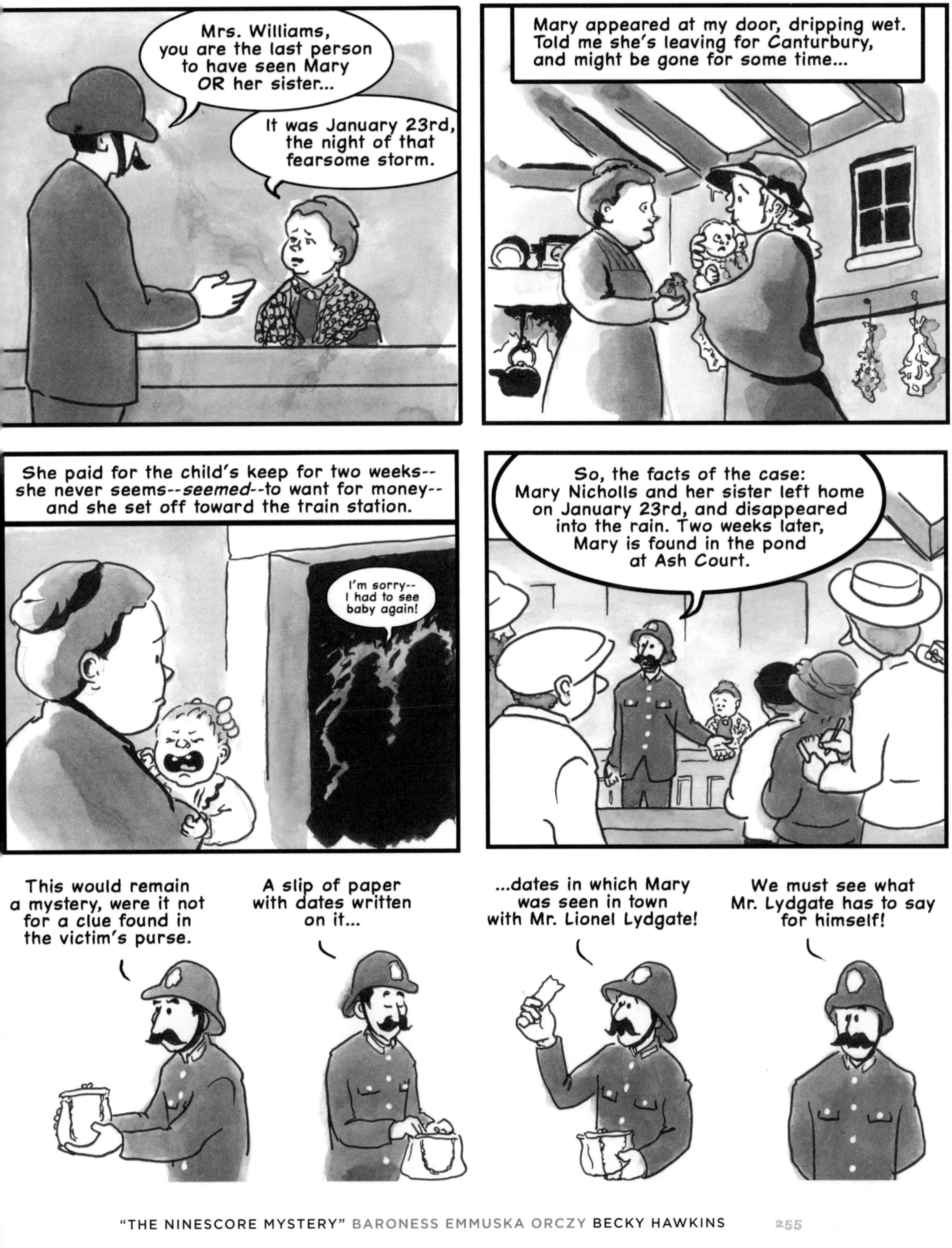
Mrs. Williams, you are the last person to have seen Mary OR her sister...
It was January 23rd, the night of that fearsome storm.
Mary appeared at my door, dripping wet. Told me she's leaving for Canturbury, and might be gone for some time...
She paid for the child's keep for two weeks-- she never seems--*seemed*--to want for money-- and she set off toward the train station.
I'm sorry-- I had to see baby again!
So, the facts of the case: Mary Nicholls and her sister left home on January 23rd, and disappeared into the rain. Two weeks later, Mary is found in the pond at Ash Court.
This would remain a mystery, were it not for a clue found in the victim's purse.
A slip of paper with dates written on it...
...dates in which Mary was seen in town with Mr. Lionel Lydgate!
We must see what Mr. Lydgate has to say for himself!

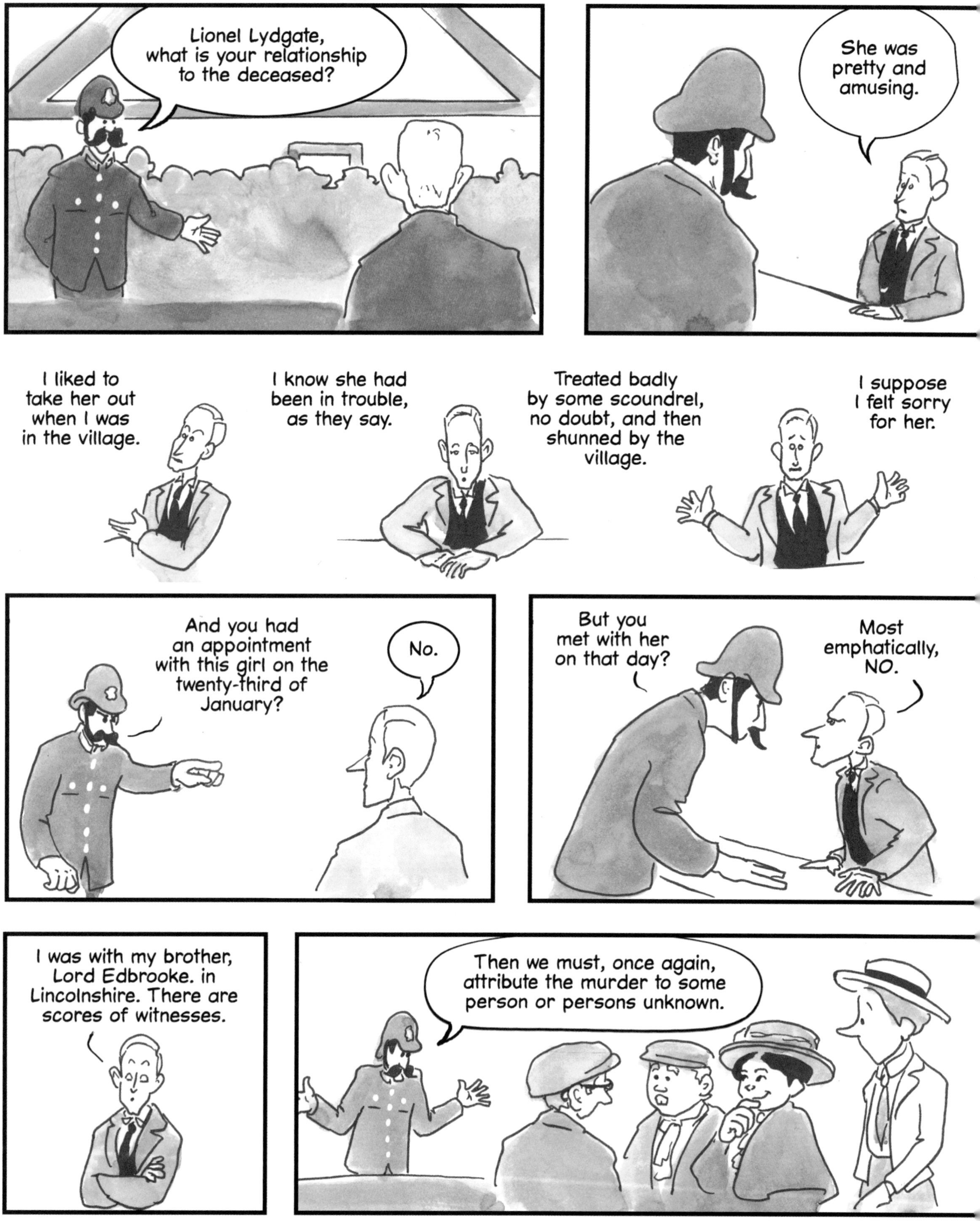
Lionel Lydgate, what is your relationship to the deceased?
She was pretty and amusing.
I liked to take her out when I was in the village.
I know she had been in trouble, as they say.
Treated badly by some scoundrel, no doubt, and then shunned by the village.
I suppose I felt sorry for her.
And you had an appointment with this girl on the twenty-third of January?
No.
But you met with her on that day?
Most emphatically, NO.
I was with my brother, Lord Edbrooke. in Lincolnshire. There are scores of witnesses.
Then we must, once again, attribute the murder to some person or persons unknown.

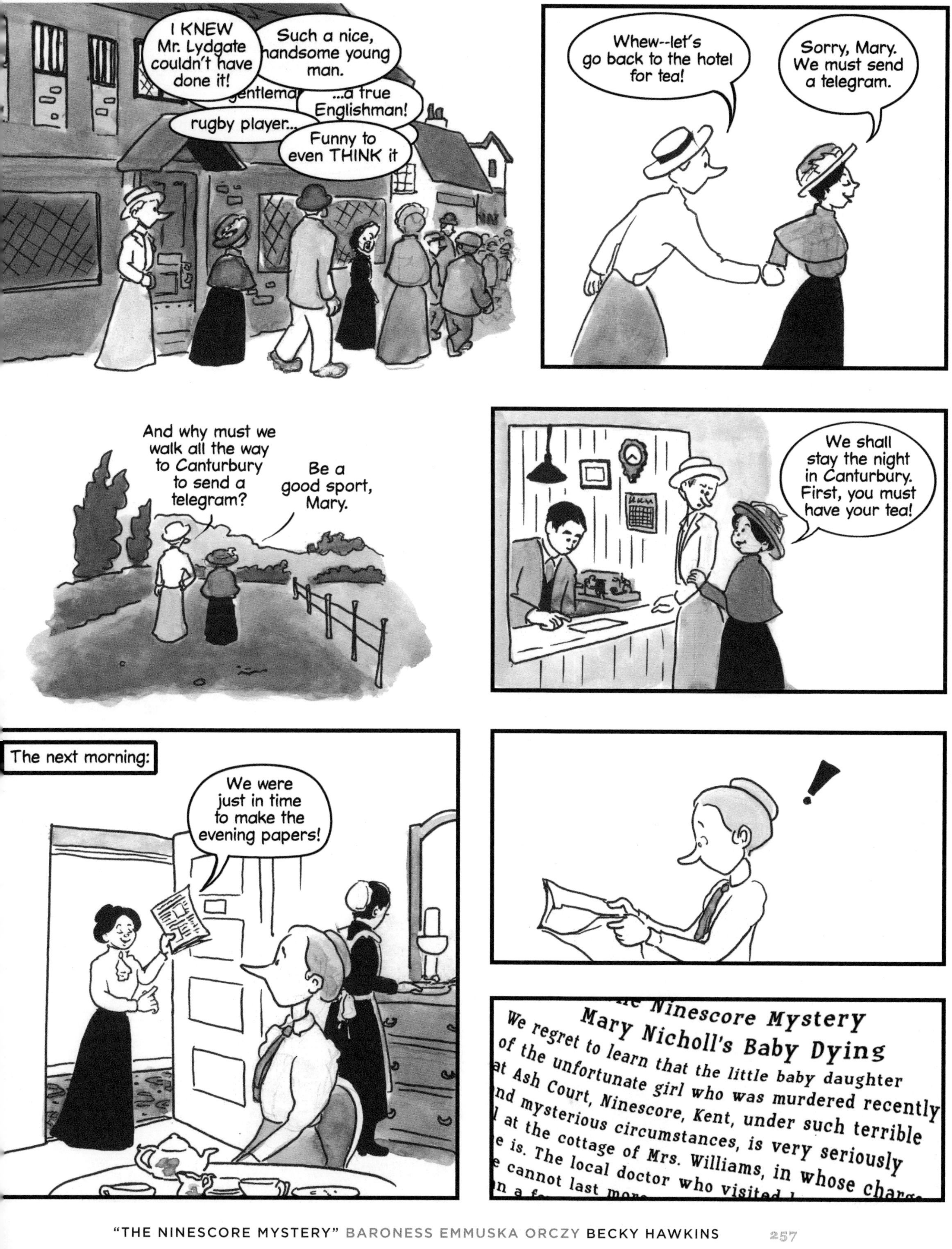
I KNEW Mr. Lydgate couldn't have done it!
Such a nice, handsome young man.
...a true Englishman!
rugby player...
Funny to even THINK it
Whew--let's go back to the hotel for tea!
Sorry, Mary. We must send a telegram.
And why must we walk all the way to Canturbury to send a telegram?
Be a good sport, Mary.
We shall stay the night in Canturbury. First, you must have your tea!
The next morning:
We were just in time to make the evening papers!
!
Ninescore Mystery
Mary Nicholl's Baby Dying
We regret to learn that the little baby daughter
of the unfortunate girl who was murdered recently
at Ash Court, Ninescore, Kent, under such terrible
nd mysterious circumstances, is very seriously
l at the cottage of Mrs. Williams, in whose charge
e is. The local doctor who visited

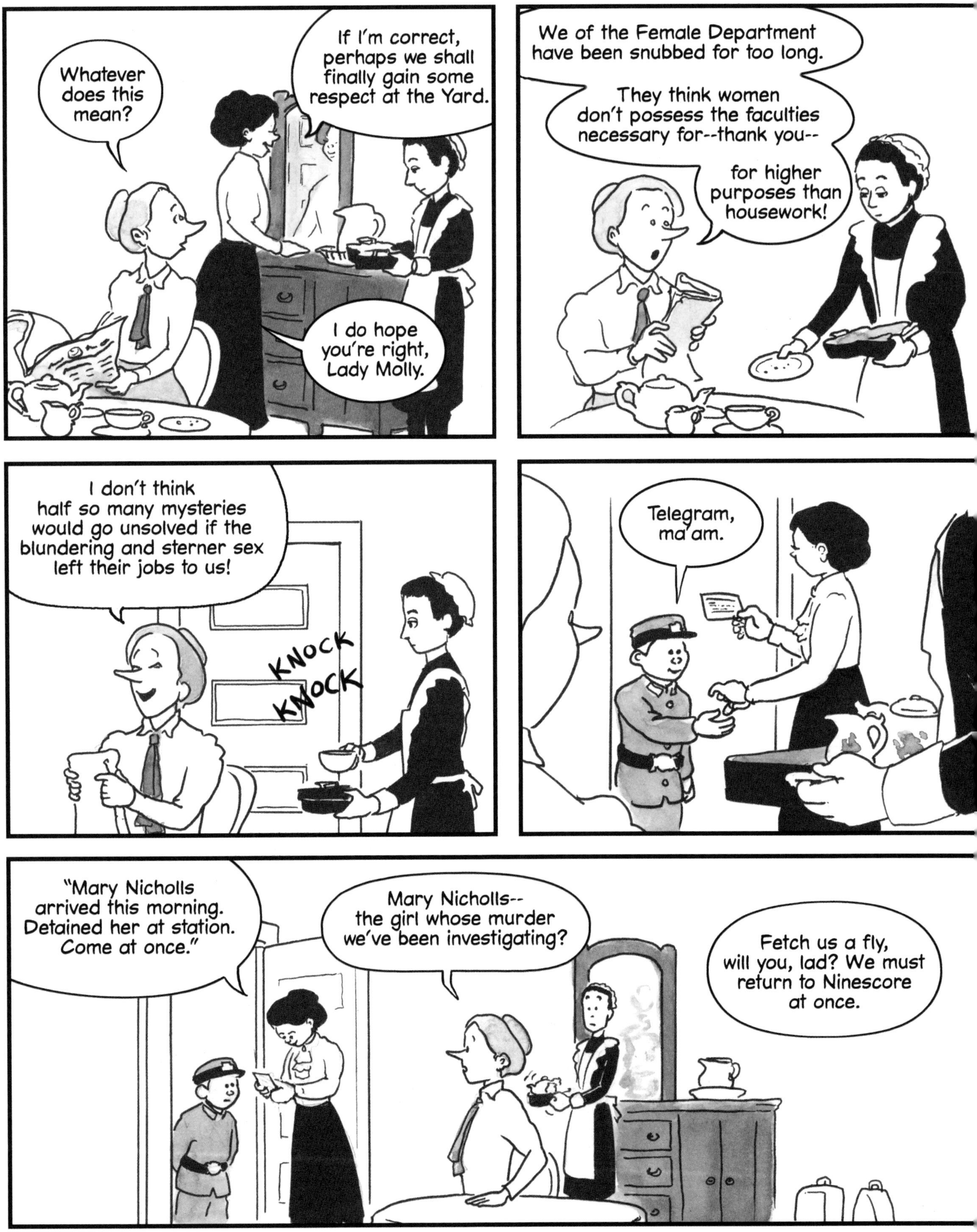
Whatever does this mean?
If I'm correct, perhaps we shall finally gain some respect at the Yard.
I do hope you're right, Lady Molly.
We of the Female Department have been snubbed for too long.
They think women don't possess the faculties necessary for--thank you--
for higher purposes than housework!
I don't think half so many mysteries would go unsolved if the blundering and sterner sex left their jobs to us!
KNOCK
KNOCK
Telegram, ma'am.
"Mary Nicholls arrived this morning. Detained her at station. Come at once."
Mary Nicholls-- the girl whose murder we've been investigating?
Fetch us a fly, will you, lad? We must return to Ninescore at once.

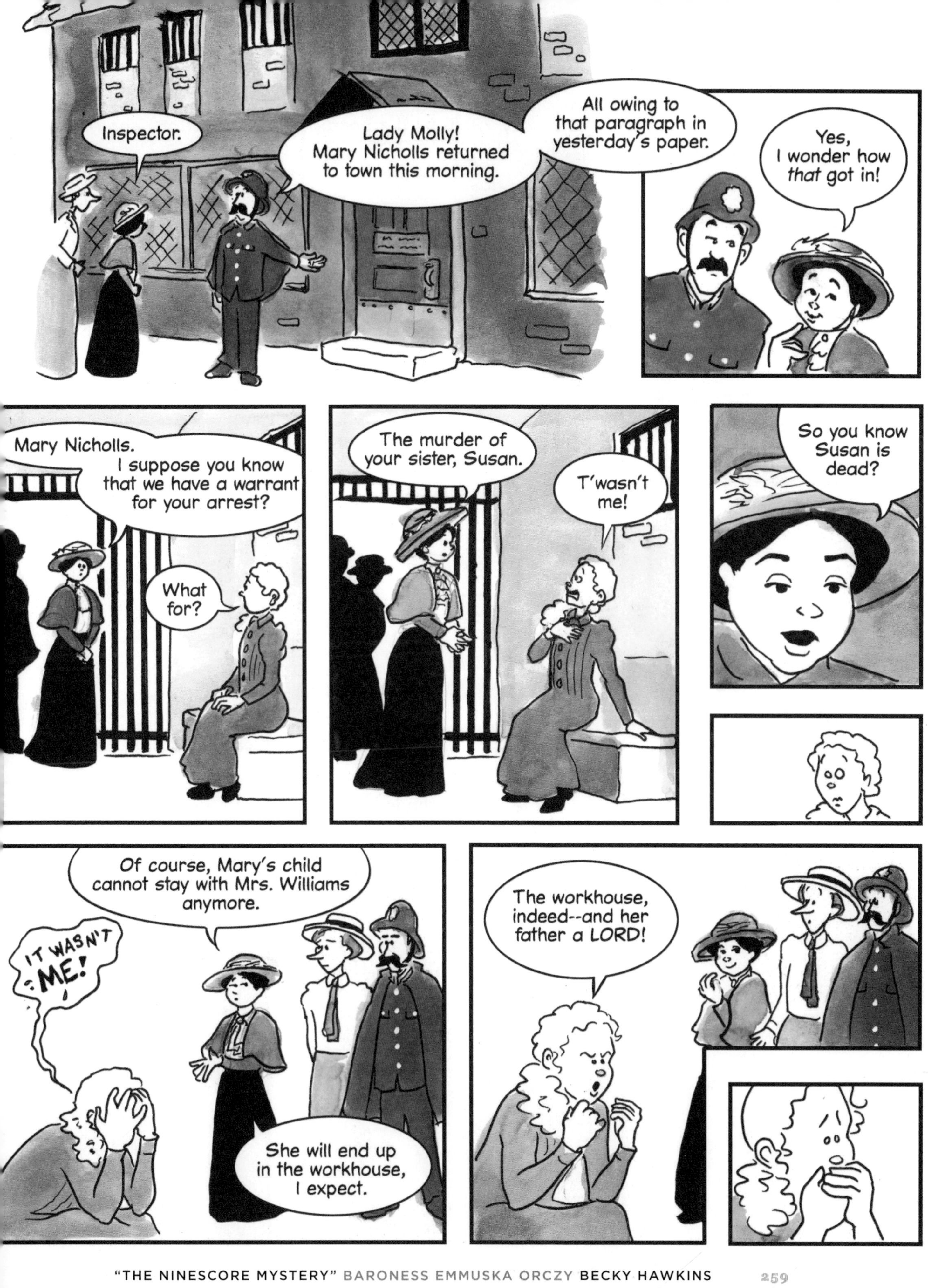
Inspector.
Lady Molly! Mary Nicholls returned to town this morning.
All owing to that paragraph in yesterday's paper.
Yes, I wonder how *that* got in!
Mary Nicholls.
I suppose you know that we have a warrant for your arrest?
What for?
The murder of your sister, Susan.
T'wasn't me!
So you know Susan is dead?
Of course, Mary's child cannot stay with Mrs. Williams anymore.
IT WASN'T ME!
She will end up in the workhouse, I expect.
The workhouse, indeed--and her father a LORD!

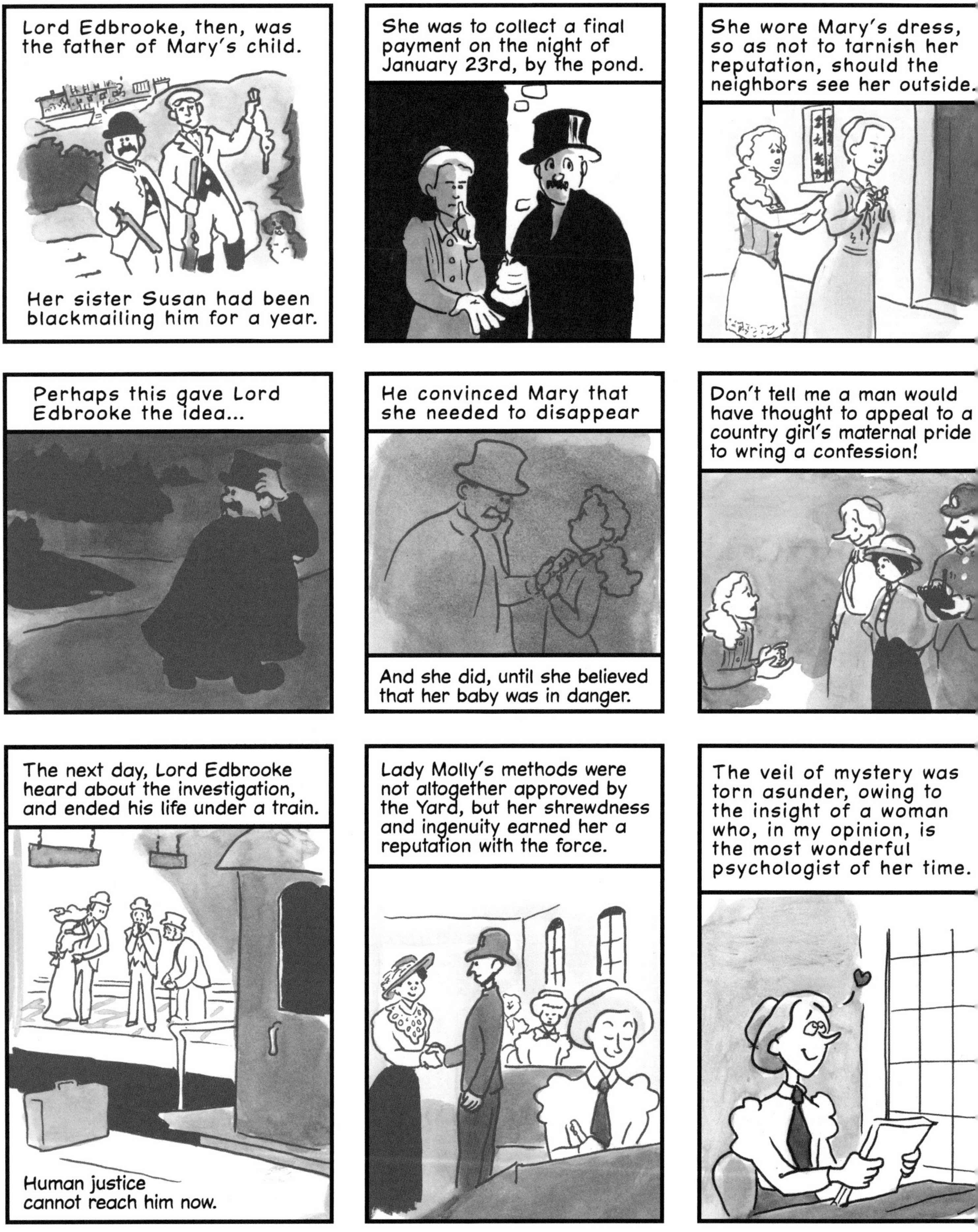

Lord Edbrooke, then, was the father of Mary's child.
Her sister Susan had been blackmailing him for a year.
She was to collect a final payment on the night of January 23rd, by the pond.
She wore Mary's dress, so as not to tarnish her reputation, should the neighbors see her outside.
Perhaps this gave Lord Edbrooke the idea...
He convinced Mary that she needed to disappear
And she did, until she believed that her baby was in danger.
Don't tell me a man would have thought to appeal to a country girl's maternal pride to wring a confession!
The next day, Lord Edbrooke heard about the investigation, and ended his life under a train.
Human justice cannot reach him now.
Lady Molly's methods were not altogether approved by the Yard, but her shrewdness and ingenuity earned her a reputation with the force.
The veil of mystery was torn asunder, owing to the insight of a woman who, in my opinion, is the most wonderful psychologist of her time.

"The Sins of Prince Saradine"
(a Father Brown mystery)

G.K. Chesterton

ART/ADAPTATION BY **Sally Madden**

CATHOLIC DETECTIVE FATHER BROWN is the intuitive, philosophizing hero of more than 50 short stories, written from 1910 to 1936 by religious man of letters G.K. Chesterton (who also had 80 books and 4,000 essays to his credit). Perennially popular, they've been made into numerous movies, radio series, and TV series, including the much-loved BBC series still in production. Comparing Brown's popular-ity to that of Sherlock Holmes, Martin Gardner wrote: "The little priest is by all odds the second most famous mystery-solver in English literature, and has always had a devoted following, not just in England, but throughout the world."

Sally Madden has previously regaled *Graphic Canon* readers with *Peter Pan* and *Lolita*. Here she brings her unmistakable color palette to an early Father Brown story from 1911.

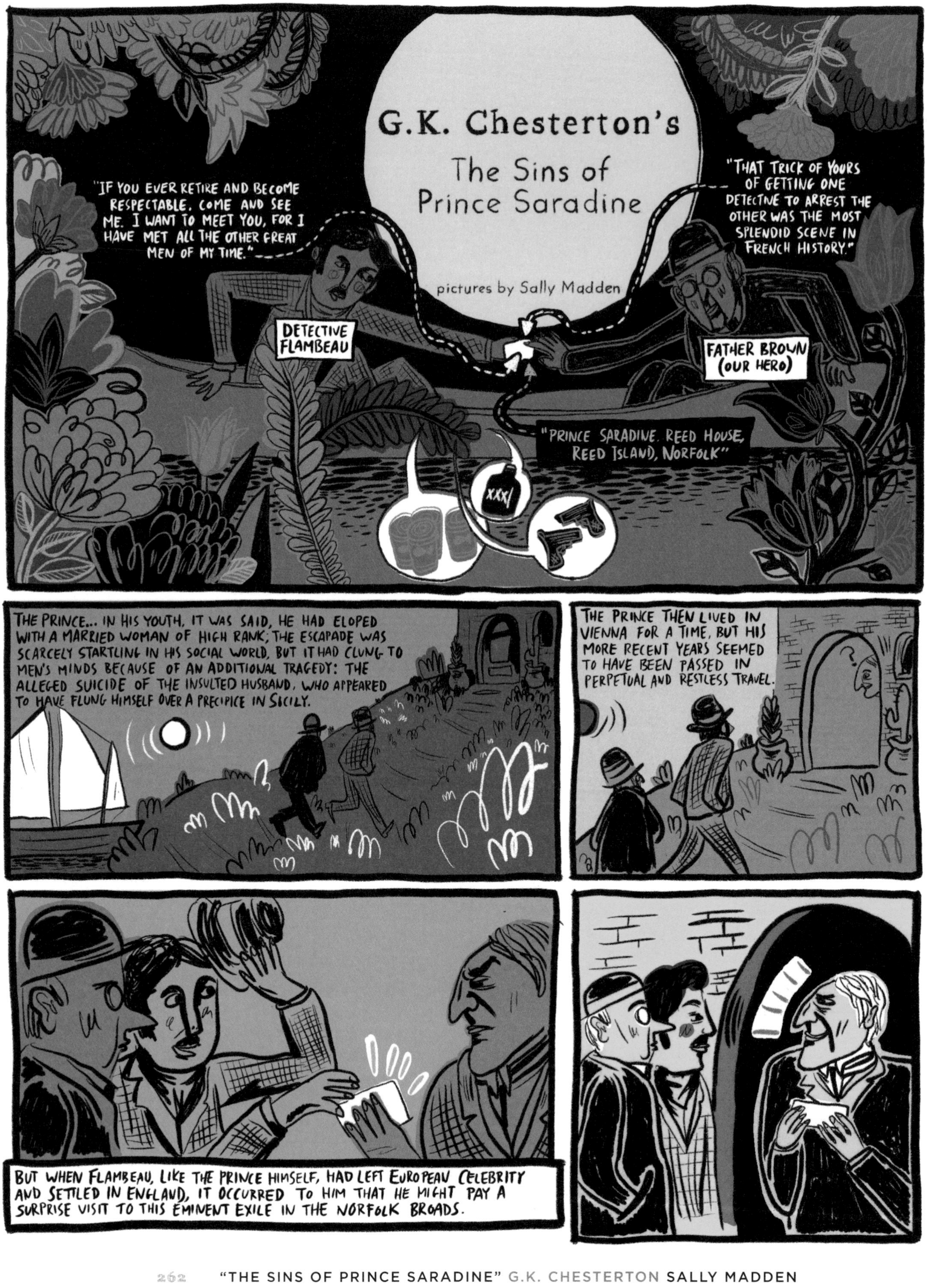
G.K. Chesterton's
The Sins of Prince Saradine
pictures by Sally Madden
"IF YOU EVER RETIRE AND BECOME RESPECTABLE, COME AND SEE ME. I WANT TO MEET YOU, FOR I HAVE MET ALL THE OTHER GREAT MEN OF MY TIME."
"THAT TRICK OF YOURS OF GETTING ONE DETECTIVE TO ARREST THE OTHER WAS THE MOST SPLENDID SCENE IN FRENCH HISTORY."
DETECTIVE FLAMBEAU
FATHER BROWN (OUR HERO)
"PRINCE SARADINE, REED HOUSE, REED ISLAND, NORFOLK"
XXX
THE PRINCE... IN HIS YOUTH, IT WAS SAID, HE HAD ELOPED WITH A MARRIED WOMAN OF HIGH RANK; THE ESCAPADE WAS SCARCELY STARTLING IN HIS SOCIAL WORLD, BUT IT HAD CLUNG TO MEN'S MINDS BECAUSE OF AN ADDITIONAL TRAGEDY: THE ALLEGED SUICIDE OF THE INSULTED HUSBAND, WHO APPEARED TO HAVE FLUNG HIMSELF OVER A PRECIPICE IN SICILY.
THE PRINCE THEN LIVED IN VIENNA FOR A TIME, BUT HIS MORE RECENT YEARS SEEMED TO HAVE BEEN PASSED IN PERPETUAL AND RESTLESS TRAVEL.
?
BUT WHEN FLAMBEAU, LIKE THE PRINCE HIMSELF, HAD LEFT EUROPEAN CELEBRITY AND SETTLED IN ENGLAND, IT OCCURRED TO HIM THAT HE MIGHT PAY A SURPRISE VISIT TO THIS EMINENT EXILE IN THE NORFOLK BROADS.

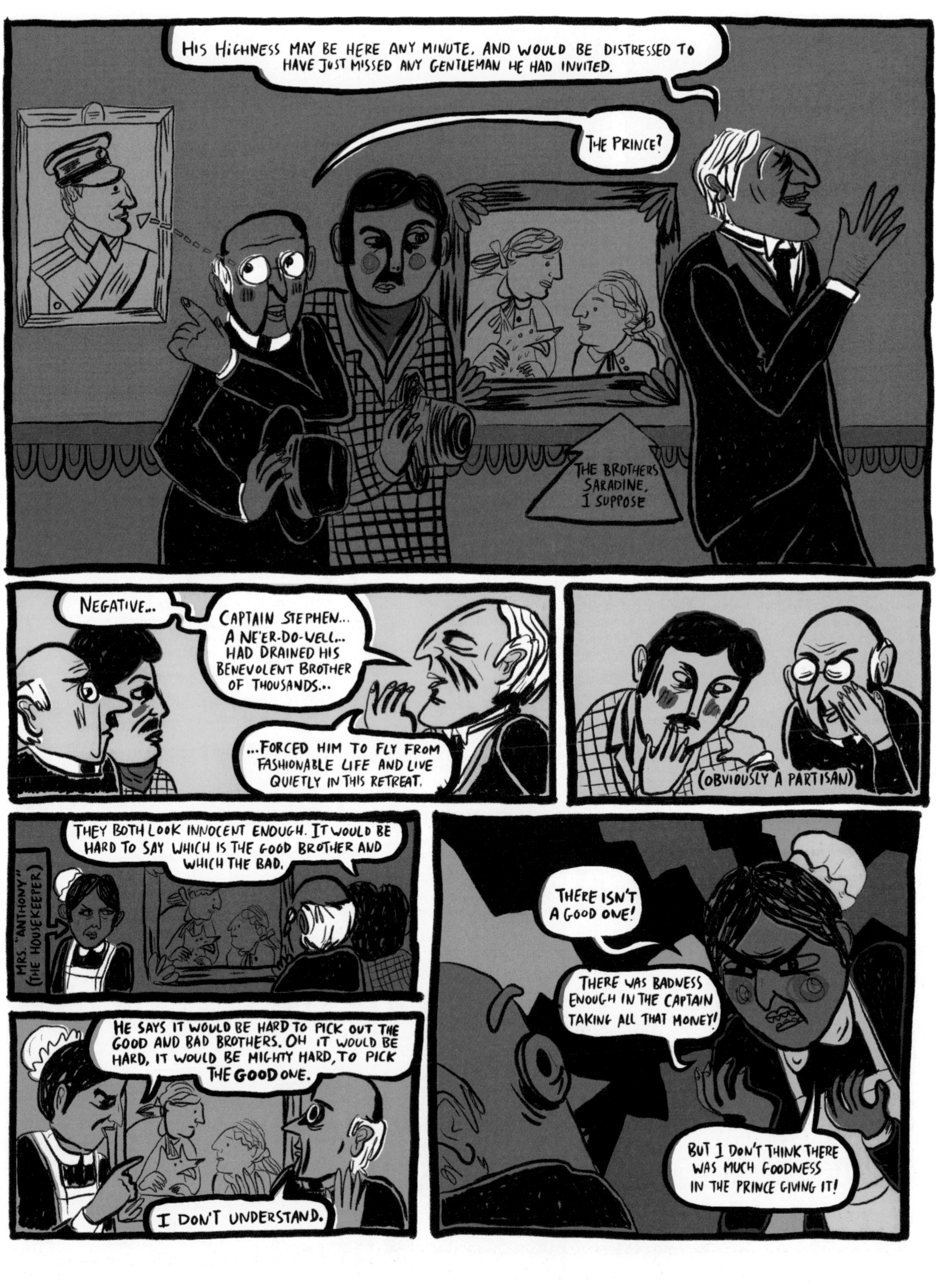

HIS HIGHNESS MAY BE HERE ANY MINUTE, AND WOULD BE DISTRESSED TO HAVE JUST MISSED ANY GENTLEMAN HE HAD INVITED.
THE PRINCE?
THE BROTHERS SARADINE, I SUPPOSE
NEGATIVE...
CAPTAIN STEPHEN... A NE'ER-DO-WELL... HAD DRAINED HIS BENEVOLENT BROTHER OF THOUSANDS...
...FORCED HIM TO FLY FROM FASHIONABLE LIFE AND LIVE QUIETLY IN THIS RETREAT.
(OBVIOUSLY A PARTISAN)
THEY BOTH LOOK INNOCENT ENOUGH. IT WOULD BE HARD TO SAY WHICH IS THE GOOD BROTHER AND WHICH THE BAD.
MRS. "ANTHONY" (THE HOUSEKEEPER)
HE SAYS IT WOULD BE HARD TO PICK OUT THE GOOD AND BAD BROTHERS. OH IT WOULD BE HARD, IT WOULD BE MIGHTY HARD, TO PICK THE **GOOD** ONE.
I DON'T UNDERSTAND.
THERE ISN'T A GOOD ONE!
THERE WAS BADNESS ENOUGH IN THE CAPTAIN TAKING ALL THAT MONEY!
BUT I DON'T THINK THERE WAS MUCH GOODNESS IN THE PRINCE GIVING IT!

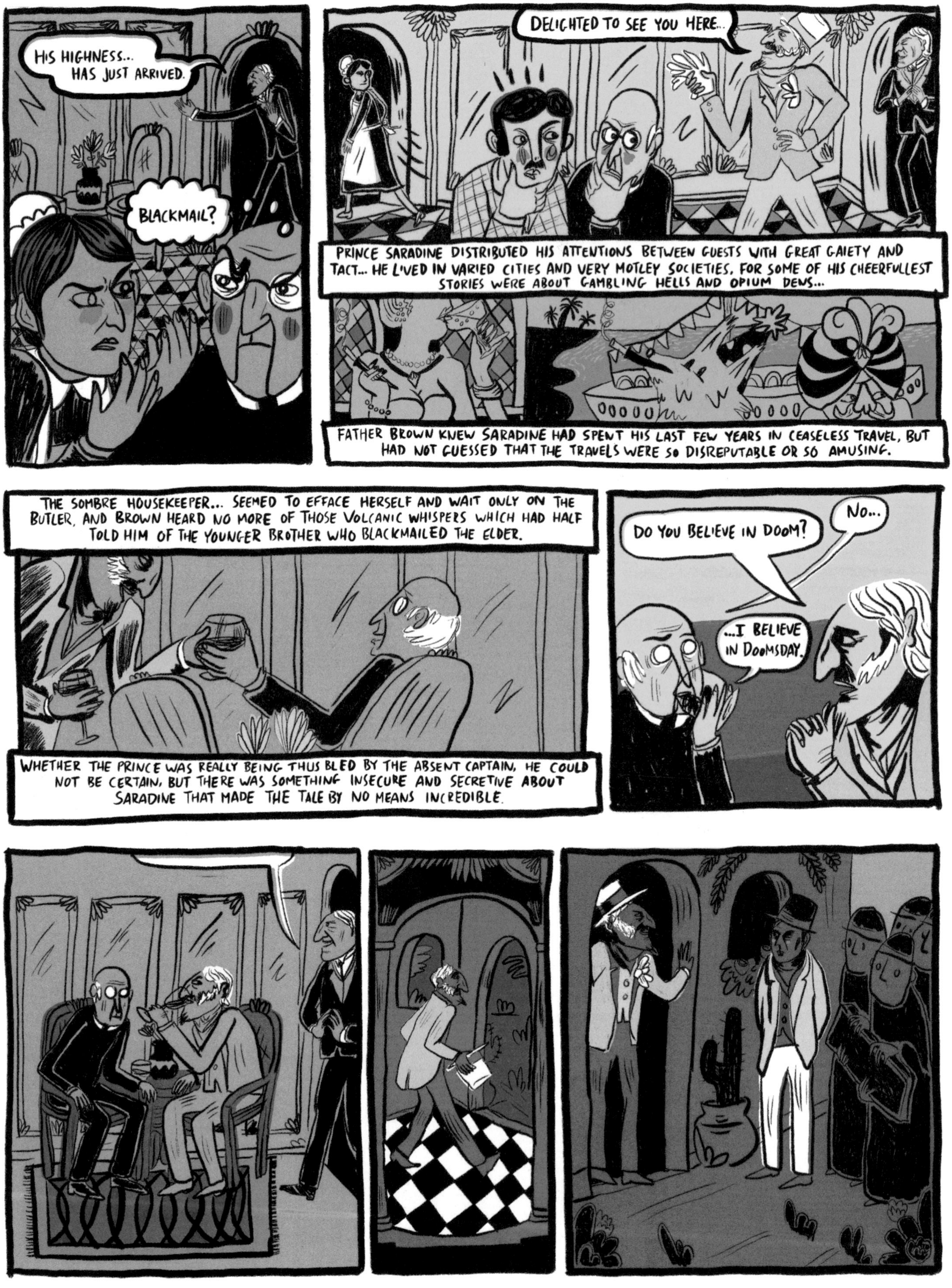
HIS HIGHNESS... HAS JUST ARRIVED.
BLACKMAIL?
DELIGHTED TO SEE YOU HERE...
PRINCE SARADINE DISTRIBUTED HIS ATTENTIONS BETWEEN GUESTS WITH GREAT GAIETY AND TACT... HE LIVED IN VARIED CITIES AND VERY MOTLEY SOCIETIES, FOR SOME OF HIS CHEERFULLEST STORIES WERE ABOUT GAMBLING HELLS AND OPIUM DENS...
FATHER BROWN KNEW SARADINE HAD SPENT HIS LAST FEW YEARS IN CEASELESS TRAVEL, BUT HAD NOT GUESSED THAT THE TRAVELS WERE SO DISREPUTABLE OR SO AMUSING.
THE SOMBRE HOUSEKEEPER... SEEMED TO EFFACE HERSELF AND WAIT ONLY ON THE BUTLER, AND BROWN HEARD NO MORE OF THOSE VOLCANIC WHISPERS WHICH HAD HALF TOLD HIM OF THE YOUNGER BROTHER WHO BLACKMAILED THE ELDER.
WHETHER THE PRINCE WAS REALLY BEING THUS BLED BY THE ABSENT CAPTAIN, HE COULD NOT BE CERTAIN, BUT THERE WAS SOMETHING INSECURE AND SECRETIVE ABOUT SARADINE THAT MADE THE TALE BY NO MEANS INCREDIBLE.
DO YOU BELIEVE IN DOOM?
NO...
...I BELIEVE IN DOOMSDAY.

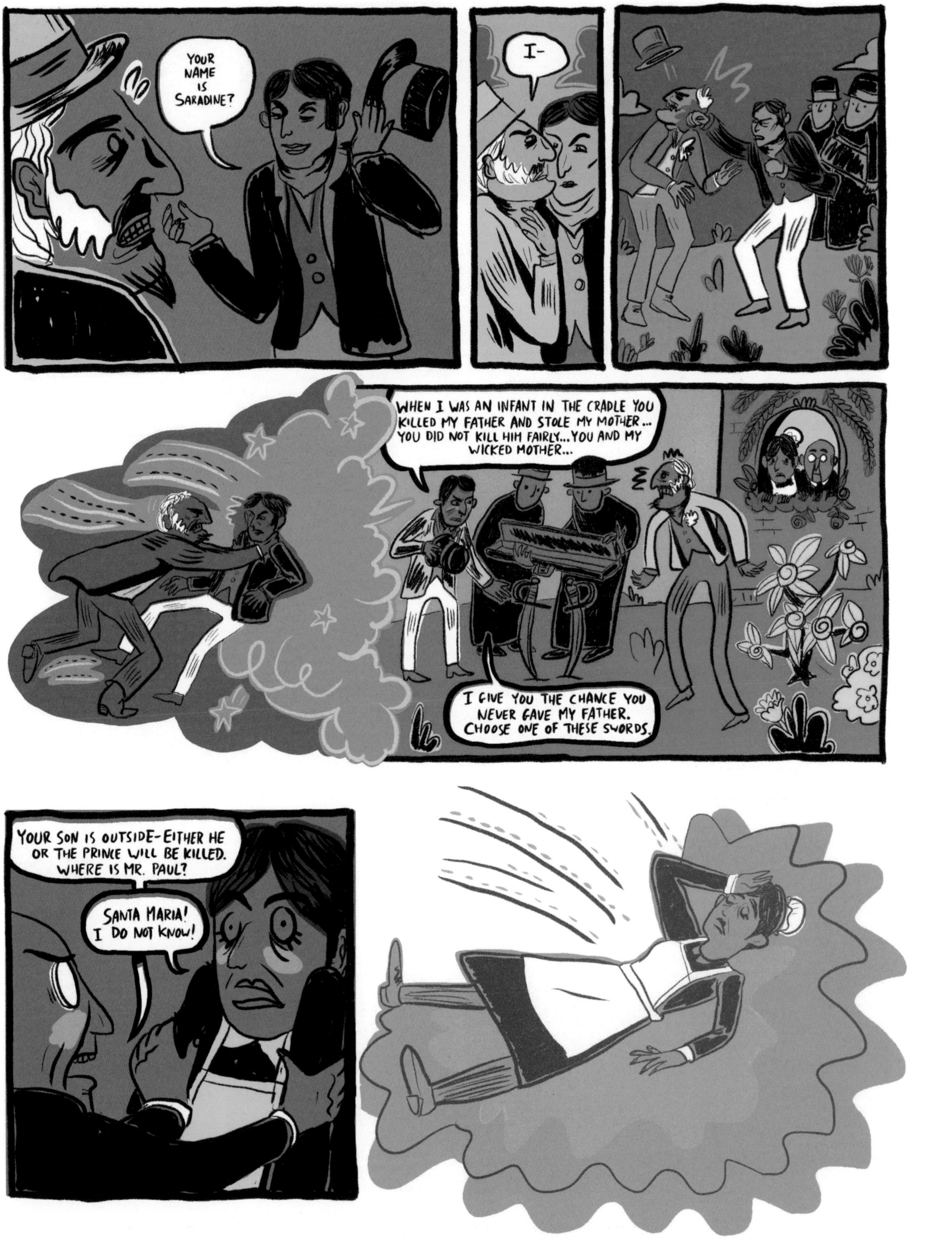
YOUR NAME IS SARADINE?
I-
WHEN I WAS AN INFANT IN THE CRADLE YOU KILLED MY FATHER AND STOLE MY MOTHER... YOU DID NOT KILL HIM FAIRLY... YOU AND MY WICKED MOTHER...
I GIVE YOU THE CHANCE YOU NEVER GAVE MY FATHER. CHOOSE ONE OF THESE SWORDS.
YOUR SON IS OUTSIDE- EITHER HE OR THE PRINCE WILL BE KILLED. WHERE IS MR. PAUL?
SANTA MARIA! I DO NOT KNOW!

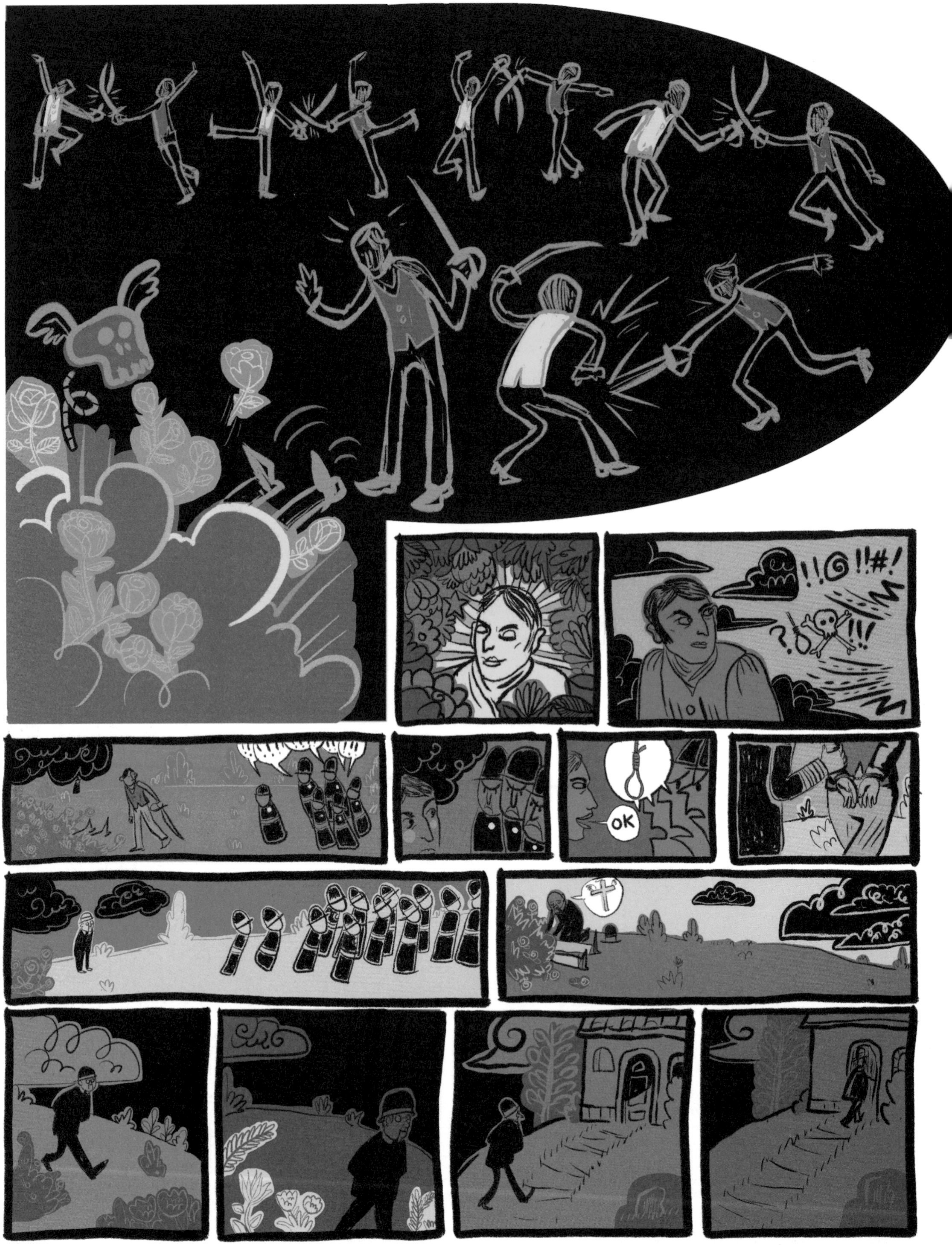
OK

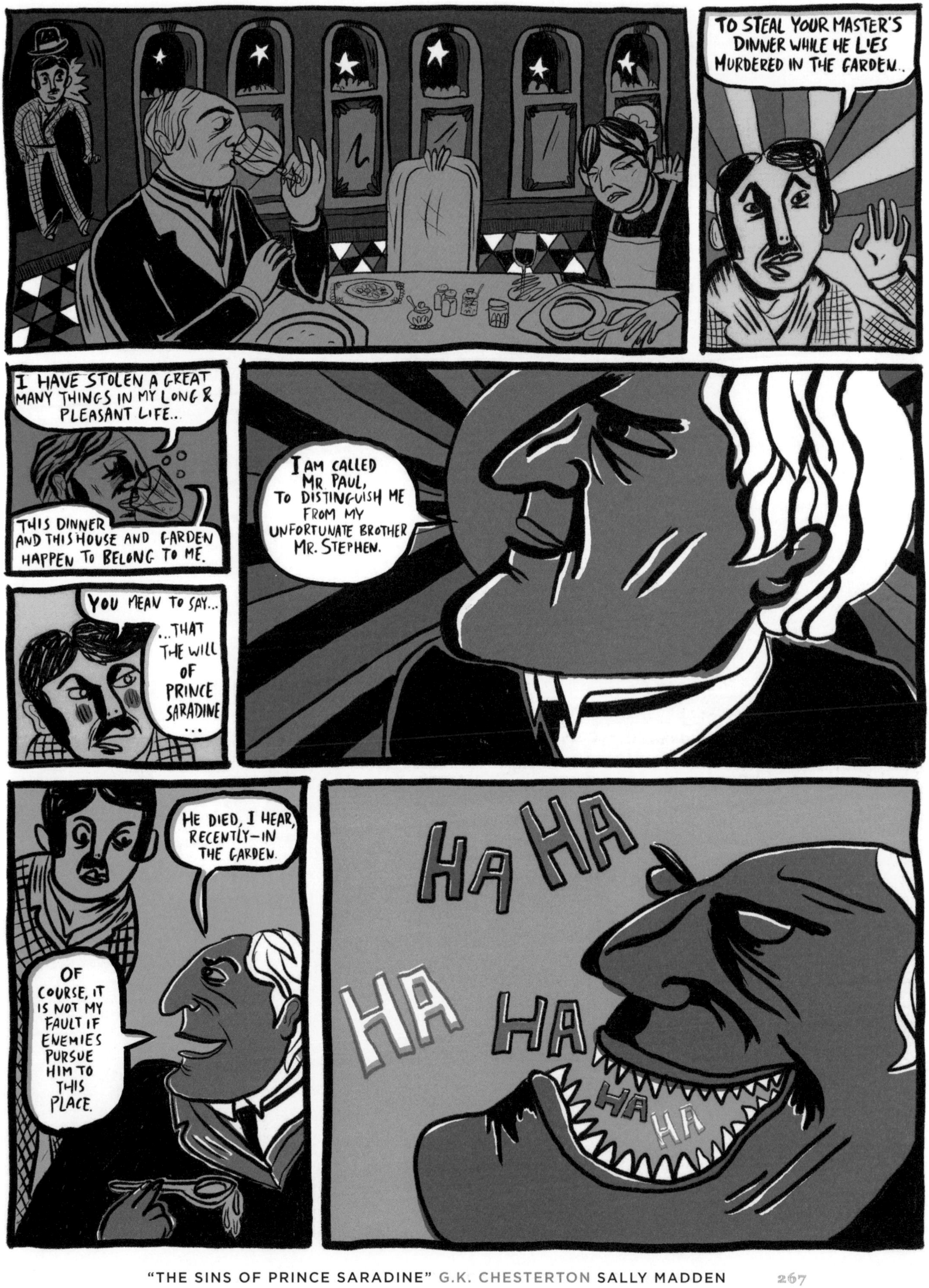
TO STEAL YOUR MASTER'S DINNER WHILE HE LIES MURDERED IN THE GARDEN...
I HAVE STOLEN A GREAT MANY THINGS IN MY LONG & PLEASANT LIFE...
THIS DINNER AND THIS HOUSE AND GARDEN HAPPEN TO BELONG TO ME.
I AM CALLED MR. PAUL, TO DISTINGUISH ME FROM MY UNFORTUNATE BROTHER MR. STEPHEN.
YOU MEAN TO SAY...
...THAT THE WILL OF PRINCE SARADINE...
HE DIED, I HEAR, RECENTLY—IN THE GARDEN.
OF COURSE, IT IS NOT MY FAULT IF ENEMIES PURSUE HIM TO THIS PLACE.
HA HA HA
HA HA HA HA

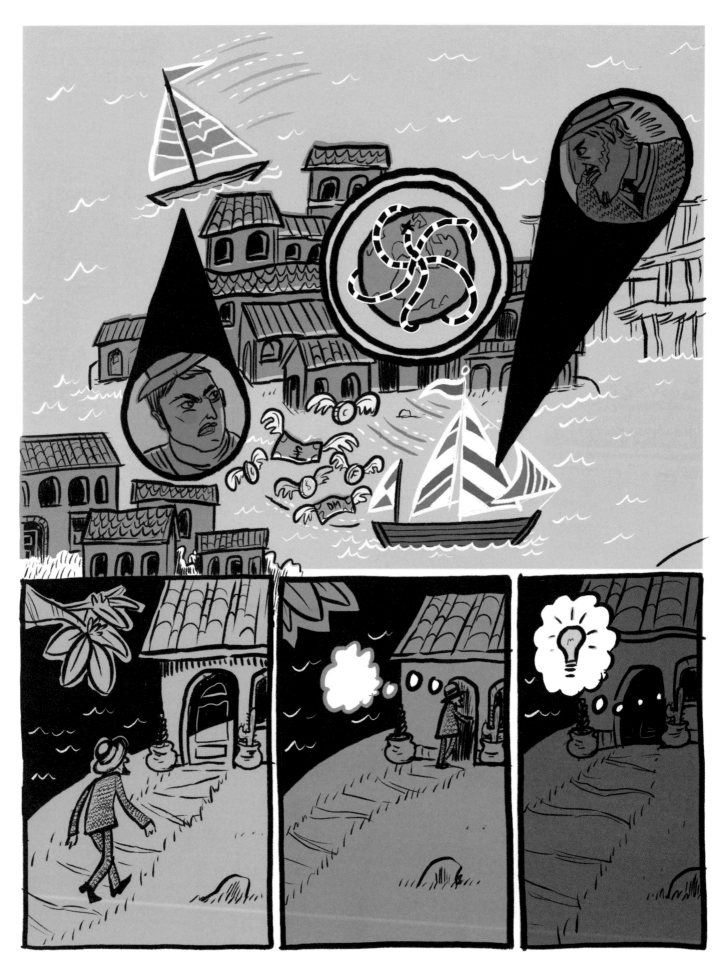

"THE SINS OF PRINCE SARADINE" G.K. CHESTERTON SALLY MADDEN

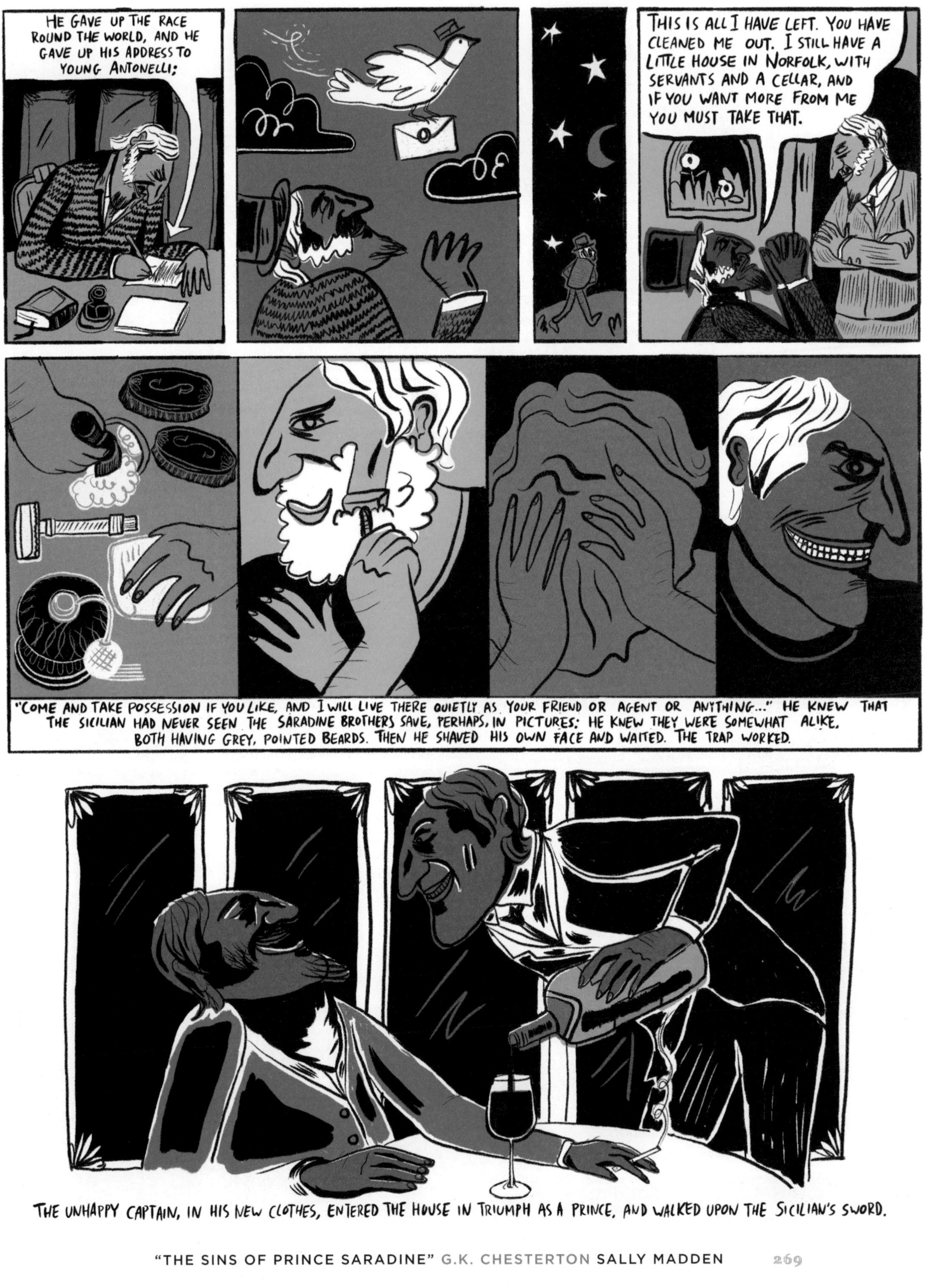
HE GAVE UP THE RACE ROUND THE WORLD, AND HE GAVE UP HIS ADDRESS TO YOUNG ANTONELLI:
THIS IS ALL I HAVE LEFT. YOU HAVE CLEANED ME OUT. I STILL HAVE A LITTLE HOUSE IN NORFOLK, WITH SERVANTS AND A CELLAR, AND IF YOU WANT MORE FROM ME YOU MUST TAKE THAT.
"COME AND TAKE POSSESSION IF YOU LIKE, AND I WILL LIVE THERE QUIETLY AS YOUR FRIEND OR AGENT OR ANYTHING..." HE KNEW THAT THE SICILIAN HAD NEVER SEEN THE SARADINE BROTHERS SAVE, PERHAPS, IN PICTURES; HE KNEW THEY WERE SOMEWHAT ALIKE, BOTH HAVING GREY, POINTED BEARDS. THEN HE SHAVED HIS OWN FACE AND WAITED. THE TRAP WORKED.
THE UNHAPPY CAPTAIN, IN HIS NEW CLOTHES, ENTERED THE HOUSE IN TRIUMPH AS A PRINCE, AND WALKED UPON THE SICILIAN'S SWORD.

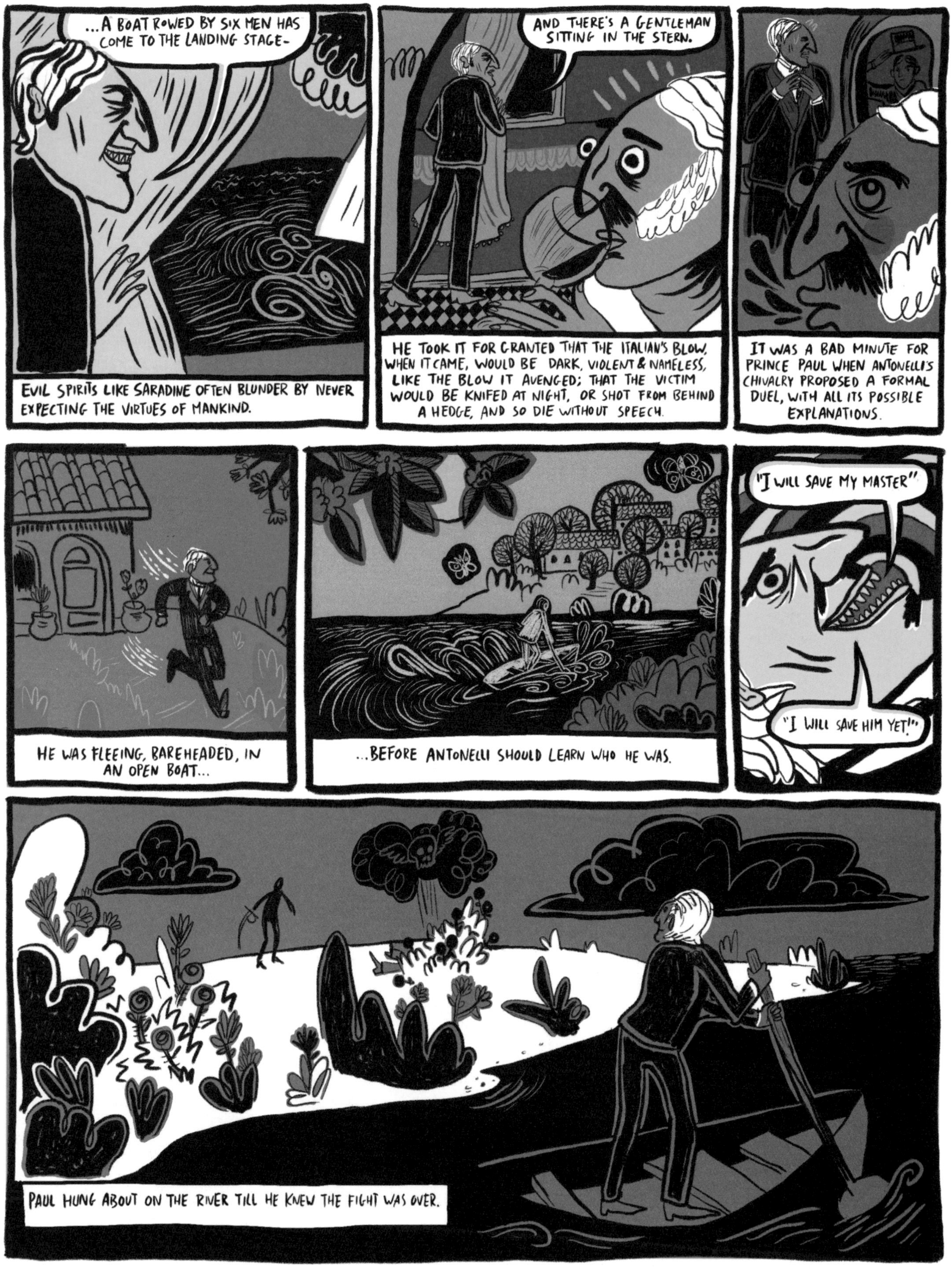
...A BOAT ROWED BY SIX MEN HAS COME TO THE LANDING STAGE-
EVIL SPIRITS LIKE SARADINE OFTEN BLUNDER BY NEVER EXPECTING THE VIRTUES OF MANKIND.
AND THERE'S A GENTLEMAN SITTING IN THE STERN.
HE TOOK IT FOR GRANTED THAT THE ITALIAN'S BLOW, WHEN IT CAME, WOULD BE DARK, VIOLENT & NAMELESS, LIKE THE BLOW IT AVENGED; THAT THE VICTIM WOULD BE KNIFED AT NIGHT, OR SHOT FROM BEHIND A HEDGE, AND SO DIE WITHOUT SPEECH.
IT WAS A BAD MINUTE FOR PRINCE PAUL WHEN ANTONELLI'S CHIVALRY PROPOSED A FORMAL DUEL, WITH ALL ITS POSSIBLE EXPLANATIONS.
HE WAS FLEEING, BAREHEADED, IN AN OPEN BOAT...
...BEFORE ANTONELLI SHOULD LEARN WHO HE WAS.
"I WILL SAVE MY MASTER"
"I WILL SAVE HIM YET!"
PAUL HUNG ABOUT ON THE RIVER TILL HE KNEW THE FIGHT WAS OVER.

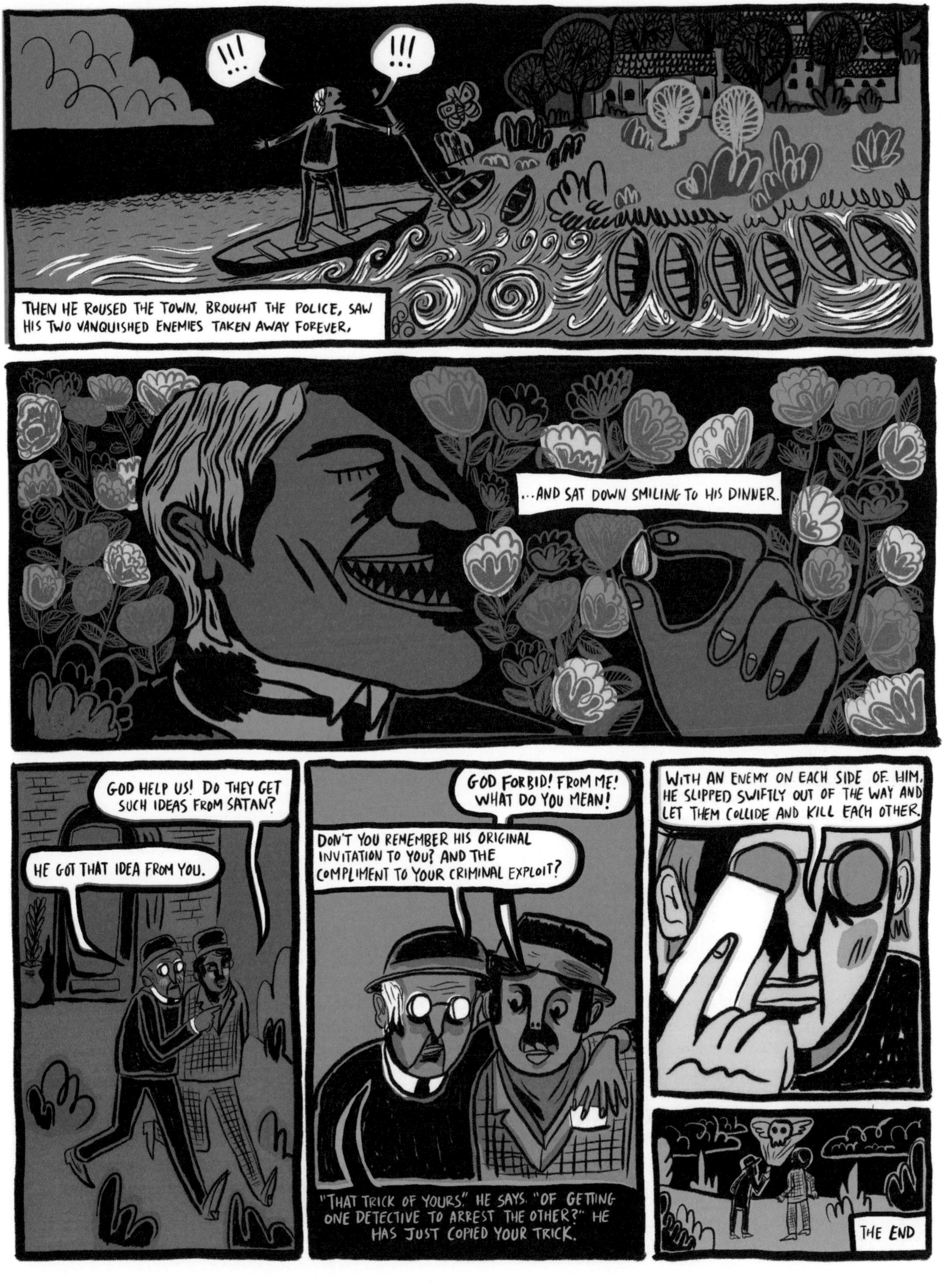
!!!
...
!!!
...
THEN HE ROUSED THE TOWN, BROUGHT THE POLICE, SAW HIS TWO VANQUISHED ENEMIES TAKEN AWAY FOREVER,
...AND SAT DOWN SMILING TO HIS DINNER.
GOD HELP US! DO THEY GET SUCH IDEAS FROM SATAN?
HE GOT THAT IDEA FROM YOU.
GOD FORBID! FROM ME! WHAT DO YOU MEAN!
DON'T YOU REMEMBER HIS ORIGINAL INVITATION TO YOU? AND THE COMPLIMENT TO YOUR CRIMINAL EXPLOIT?
"THAT TRICK OF YOURS," HE SAYS. "OF GETTING ONE DETECTIVE TO ARREST THE OTHER?" HE HAS JUST COPIED YOUR TRICK.
WITH AN ENEMY ON EACH SIDE OF HIM, HE SLIPPED SWIFTLY OUT OF THE WAY AND LET THEM COLLIDE AND KILL EACH OTHER.
THE END

The Secret Adversary
(a Tommy and Tuppence mystery)

Agatha Christie

ART/ADAPTATION BY **Kim Clements**

AGATHA CHRISTIE'S FIRST NOVEL (_THE Mysterious Affair at Styles_**)** introduced one of the genre's greatest detectives, Hercule Peroit. Wasting no time, _The Secret Adversary_, her second novel, gave the world one of the greatest detective duos, Tommy and Tuppence. (Christie would of course go on to write 66 novels that have sold around two billion copies, making her name synonymous with murder mysteries.)

Both in their early twenties, Tommy and Tuppence had been involved in World War I— he as a soldier, she as a nurse. Now broke, the childhood friends decide to start a business, The Young Adventurers Ltd., and they _immediately_ get drawn into international intrigue.

The Secret Adversary revolves around extremely sensitive government documents (right up my alley!) that have disappeared along with the young woman tasked with keeping them. A cell of Soviet revolutionaries trying to overthrow the British government wants those papers.

Illustrator Kim Clements, as you might deduce, tends to work with children's books. She brings an abstracted style and inventive, often jam-packed layouts to her anthropomorphized adaptation of Dame Agatha's sophomore effort.

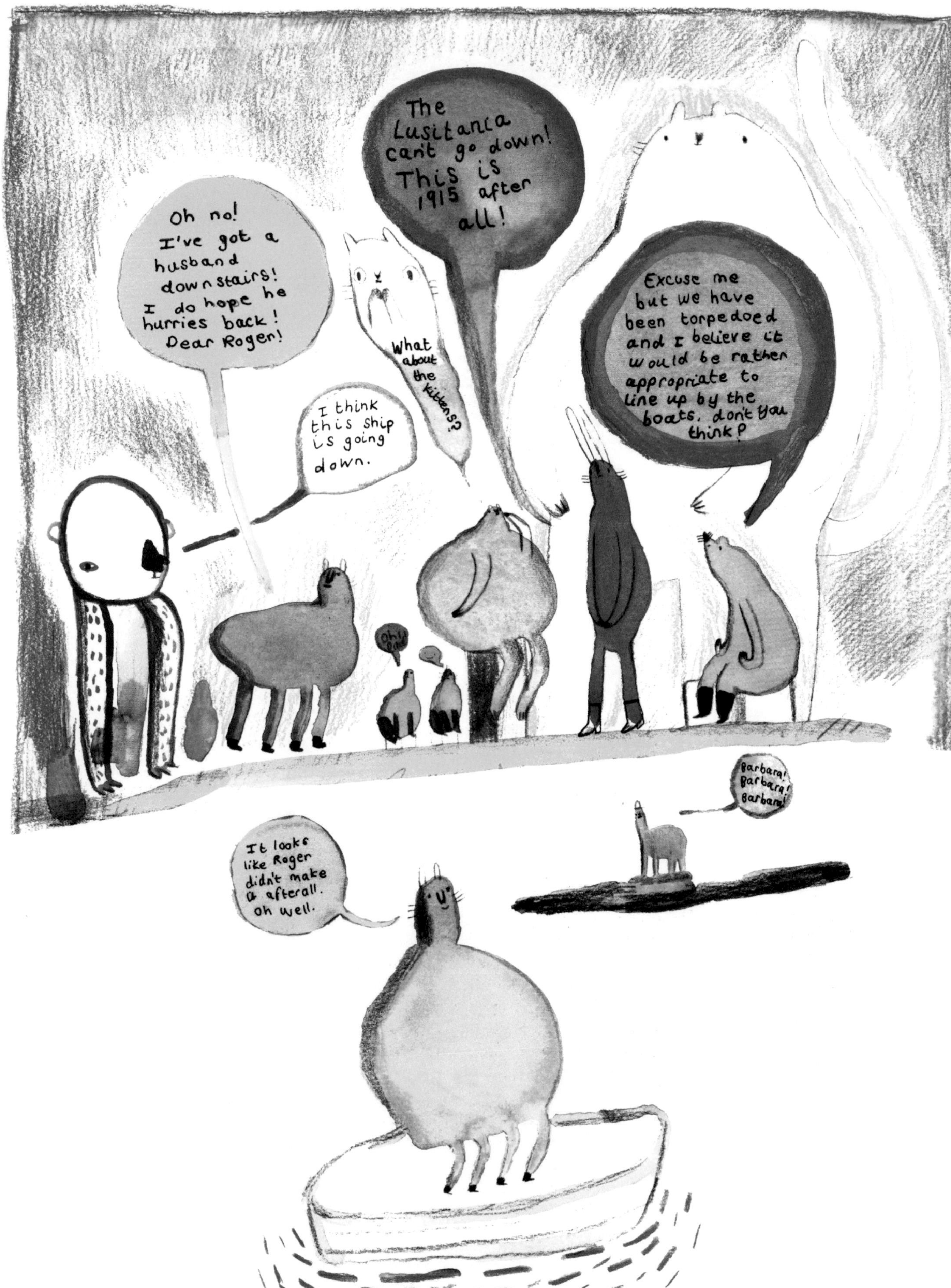
Oh no! I've got a husband downstairs! I do hope he hurries back! Dear Roger!
I think this ship is going down.
What about the kittens?
The Lusitania can't go down! This is 1915 after all!
Excuse me but we have been torpedoed and I believe it would be rather appropriate to line up by the boats, don't you think?
Barbara! Barbara! Barbara!
It looks like Roger didn't make it afterall. Oh well.

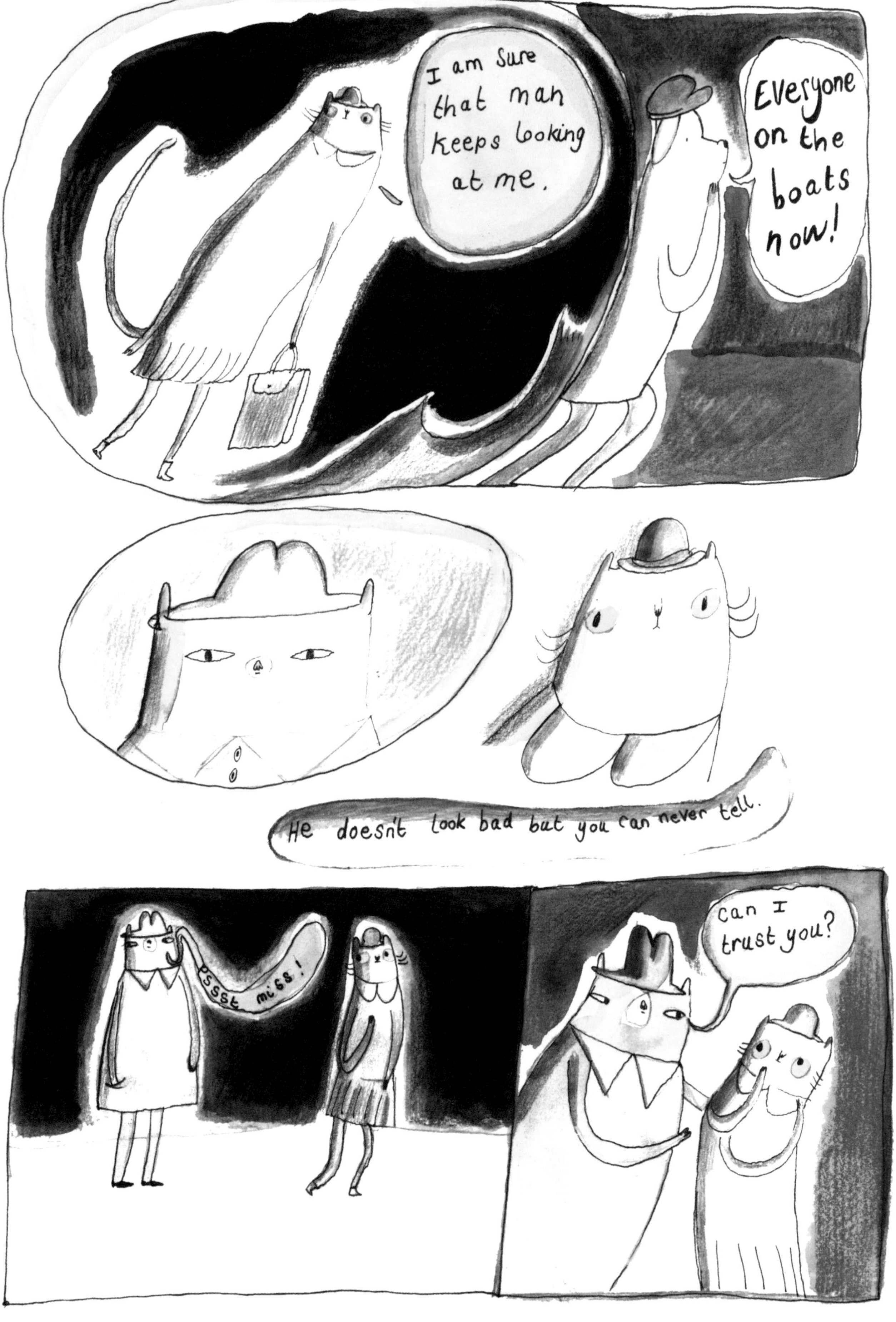
I am sure that man keeps looking at me.
Everyone on the boats now!
He doesn't look bad but you can never tell.
psssst miss!
Can I trust you?

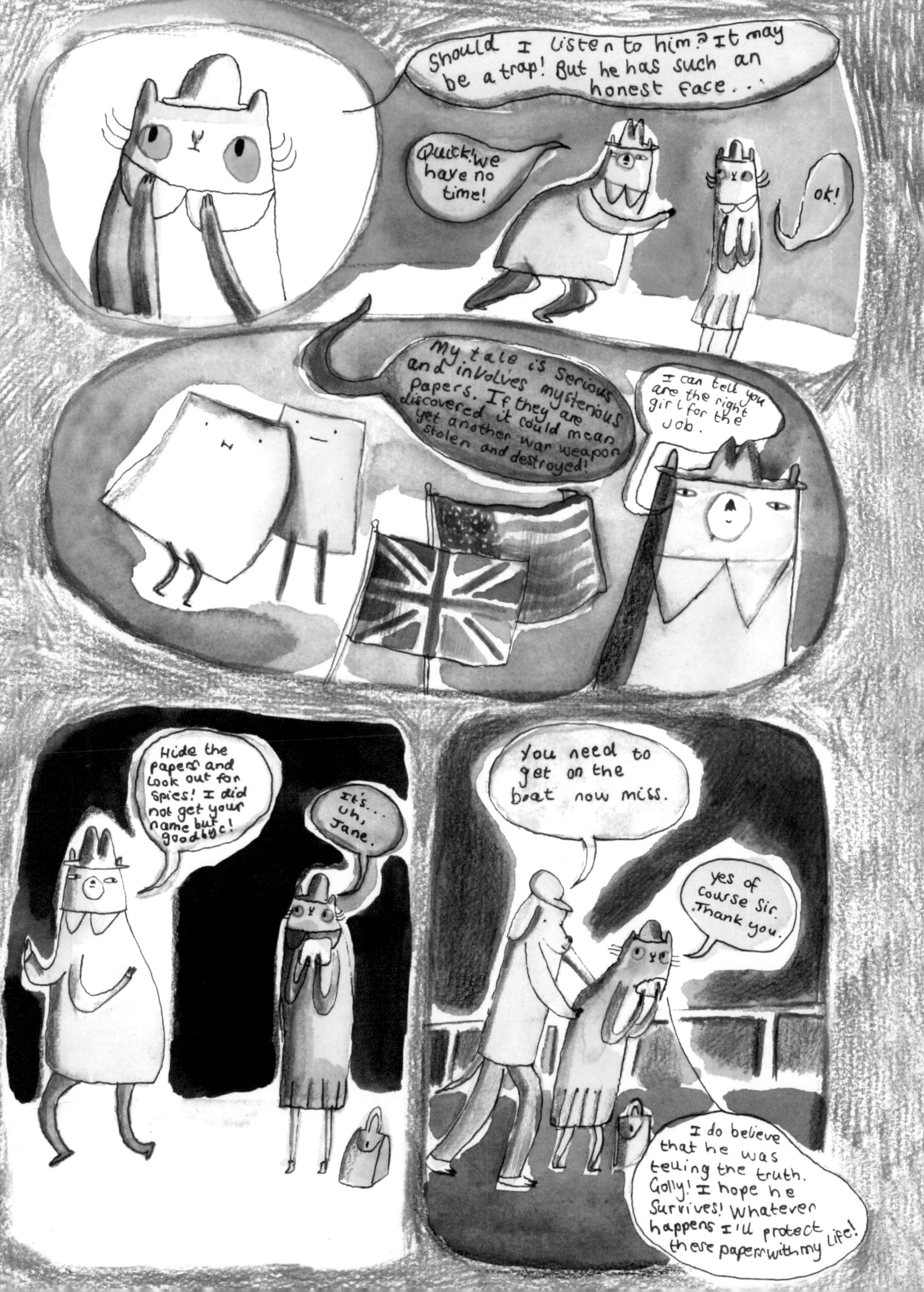
Should I listen to him? It may be a trap! But he has such an honest face...
Quick! we have no time!
ok!
My tale is serious and involves mysterious papers. If they are discovered it could mean yet another war weapon stolen and destroyed!
I can tell you are the right girl for the job.
Hide the papers and look out for spies! I did not get your name but goodbye!
It's... uh, Jane.
You need to get on the boat now miss.
yes of course sir. Thank you.
I do believe that he was telling the truth. Golly! I hope he survives! Whatever happens I'll protect these papers with my life!

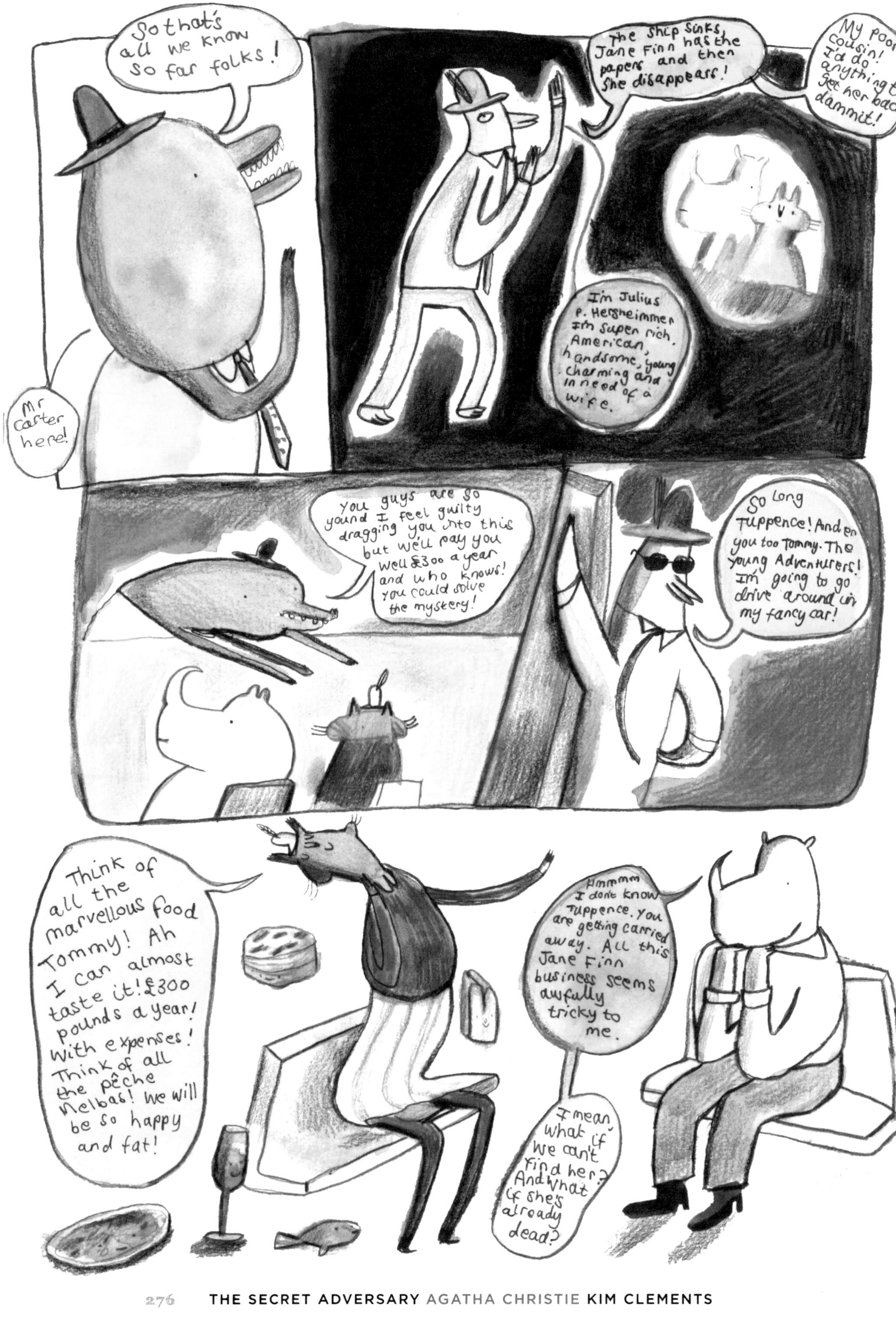

Mr Carter here!
So that's all we know so far folks!
The ship sinks, Jane Finn has the papers and then she disappears!
My poor cousin! I'd do anything to get her back dammit!
I'm Julius P. Hersheimmer I'm super rich, American, handsome, young charming and in need of a wife.
You guys are so young I feel guilty dragging you into this but we'll pay you well £300 a year and who knows! you could solve the mystery!
So long Tuppence! And er you too Tommy. The young Adventurers! I'm going to go drive around in my fancy car!
Think of all the marvellous food Tommy! Ah I can almost taste it! £300 pounds a year! with expenses! Think of all the pêche Melbas! We will be so happy and fat!
Hmmmm I don't know Tuppence. You are getting carried away. All this Jane Finn business seems awfully tricky to me.
I mean, what if we can't find her? And what if she's already dead?

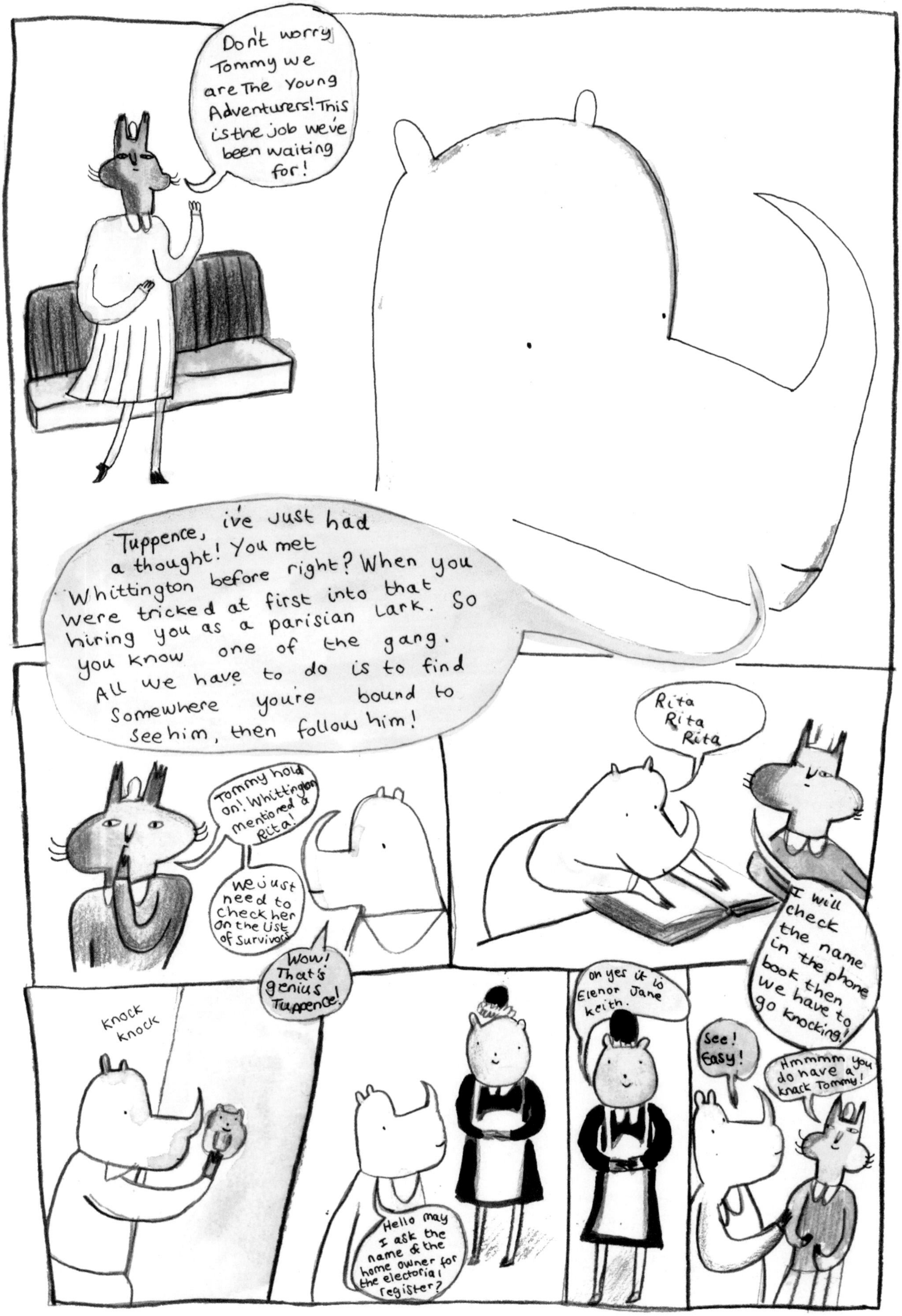
Don't worry Tommy we are The Young Adventurers! This is the job we've been waiting for!
Tuppence, i've just had a thought! You met Whittington before right? When you were tricked at first into that hiring you as a parisian lark. So you know one of the gang. All we have to do is to find somewhere you're bound to see him, then follow him!
Tommy hold on! Whittington mentioned a Rita!
We just need to check her on the list of survivors
Wow! That's genius Tuppence!
Rita Rita Rita
I will check the name in the phone book then we have to go knocking!
knock knock
Hello may I ask the name & the home owner for the electorial register?
oh yes it is Elenor Jane keith.
See! Easy!
Hmmmm you do have a knack Tommy!

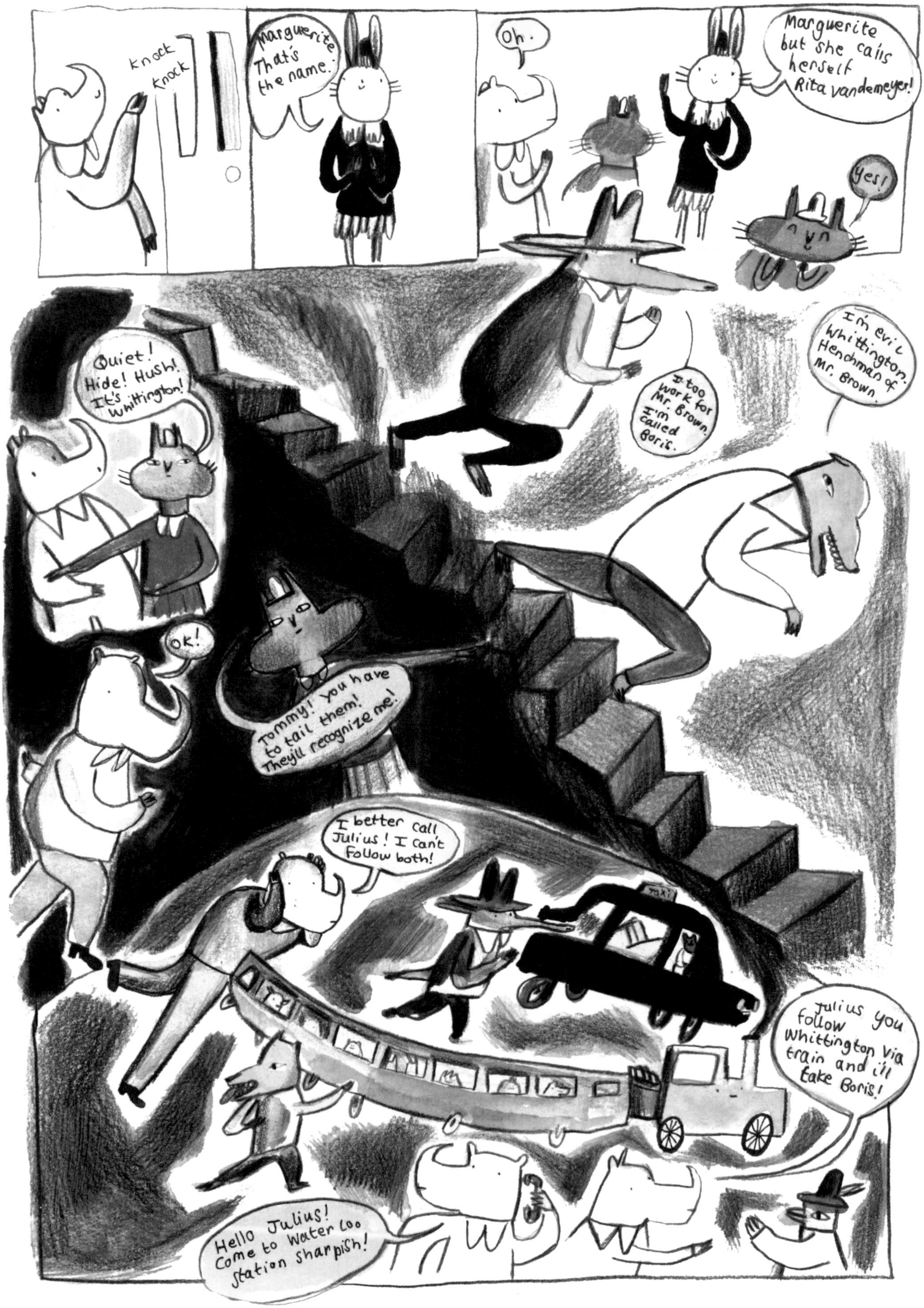
knock knock
Marguerite That's the name.
Oh.
Marguerite but she calls herself Rita Vandemeyer!
Yes!
Quiet! Hide! Hush! It's Whittington!
I'm evil Whittington. Henchman of Mr. Brown.
I too work for Mr. Brown. I'm called Boris.
OK!
Tommy! You have to tail them! They'll recognize me!
I better call Julius! I can't follow both!
TAXI
Julius you follow Whittington via train and i'll take Boris!
Hello Julius! Come to Water Loo Station sharpish!

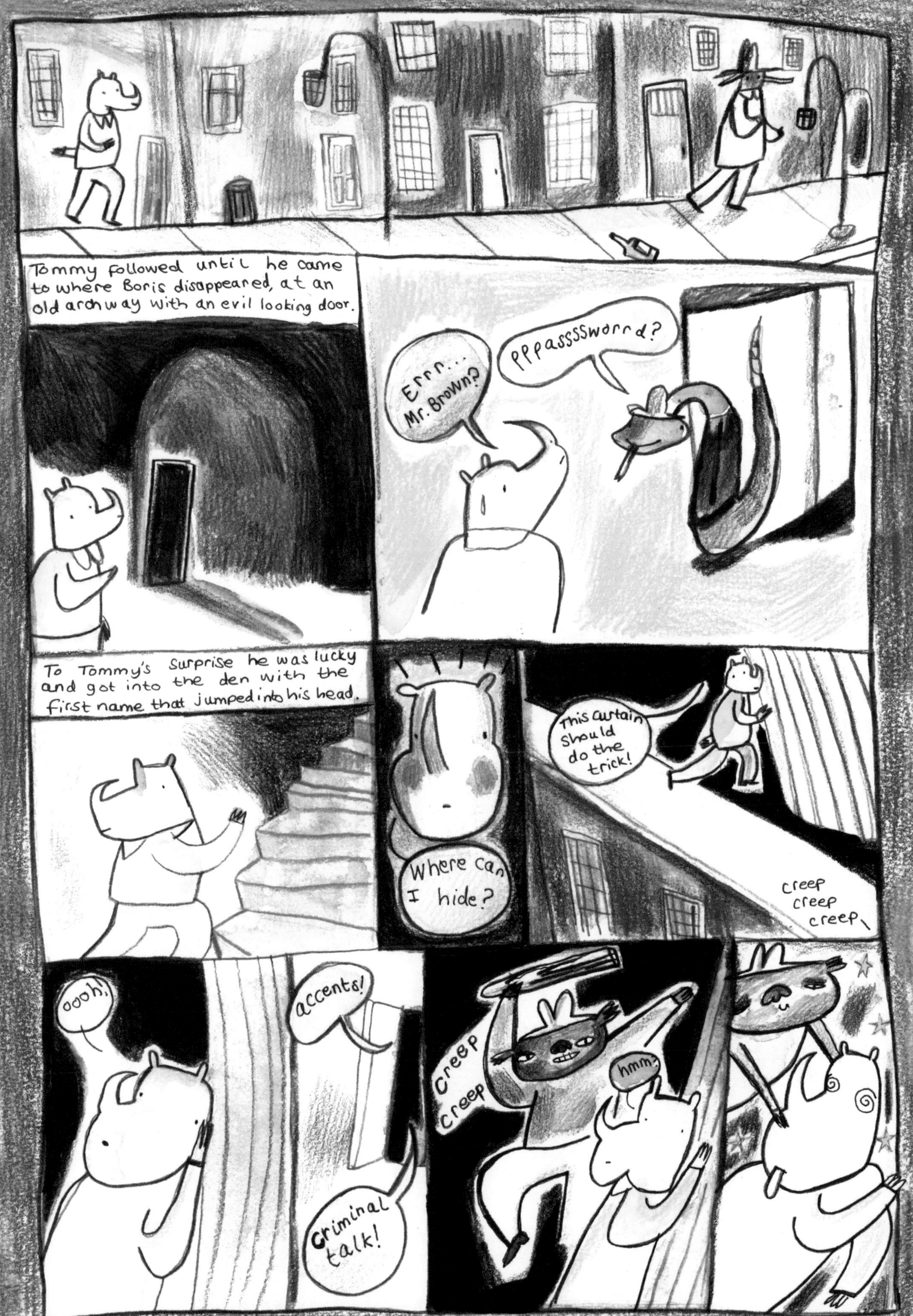

Tommy followed until he came to where Boris disappeared, at an old archway with an evil looking door.
Errr... Mr. Brown?
pppassssworrd?
To Tommy's surprise he was lucky and got into the den with the first name that jumped into his head.
Where can I hide?
This curtain should do the trick!
creep creep creep
oooh!
accents!
criminal talk!
creep creep
hmm?

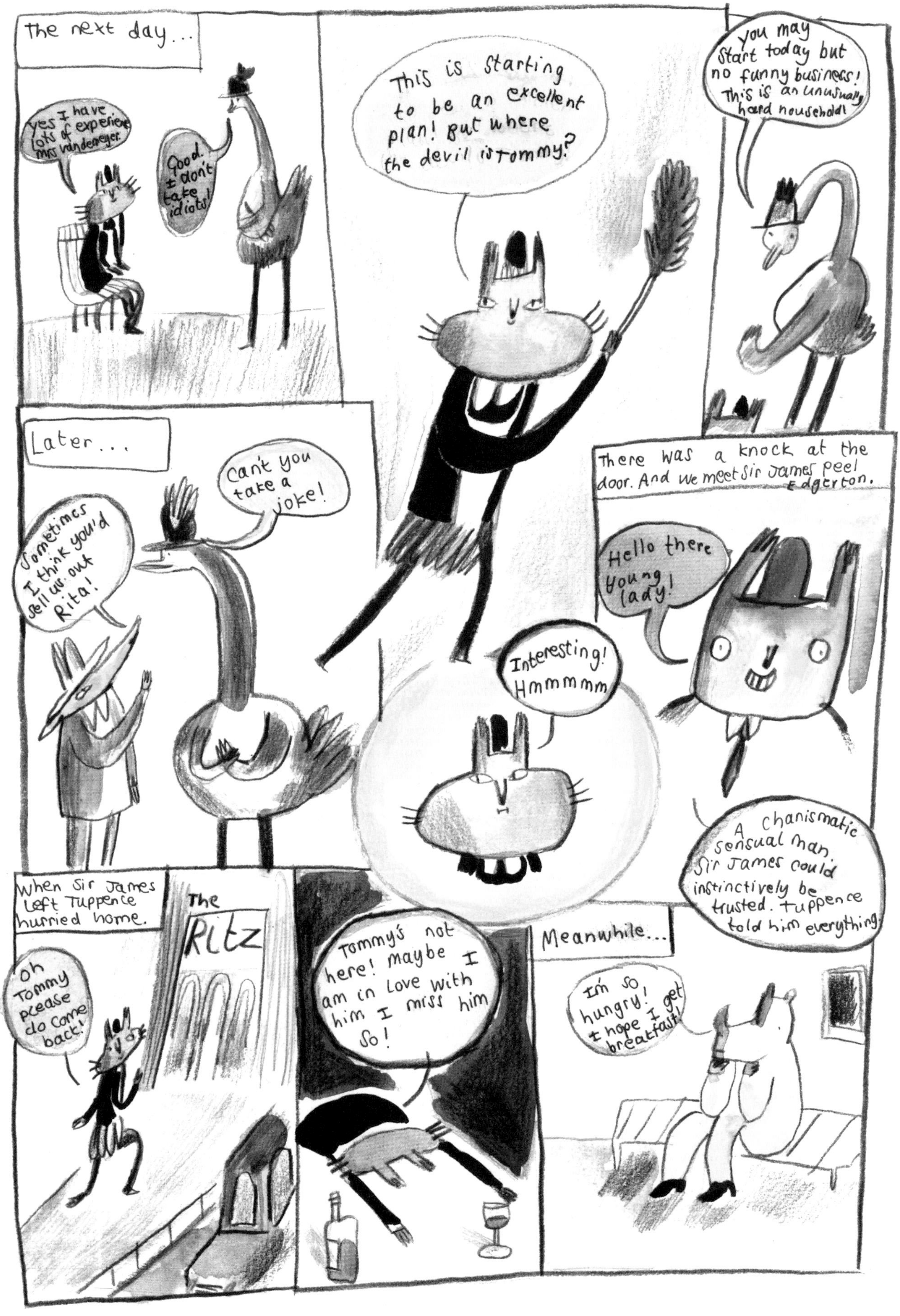

the next day...
yes I have lots of experience mrs vandemeyer.
Good. I don't take idiots!
This is starting to be an excellent plan! But where the devil is tommy?
you may start today but no funny business! This is an unusually hard household!
Later...
Sometimes I think you'd sell us out Rita!
Can't you take a joke!
There was a knock at the door. And we meet Sir James Peel Edgerton.
Hello there young lady!
Interesting! Hmmmmm
A charismatic sensual man. Sir James could instinctively be trusted. Tuppence told him everything.
When Sir James left Tuppence hurried home.
The Ritz
Oh Tommy please do come back!
Tommy's not here! maybe I am in love with him I miss him so!
Meanwhile...
I'm so hungry! I hope I get breakfast!

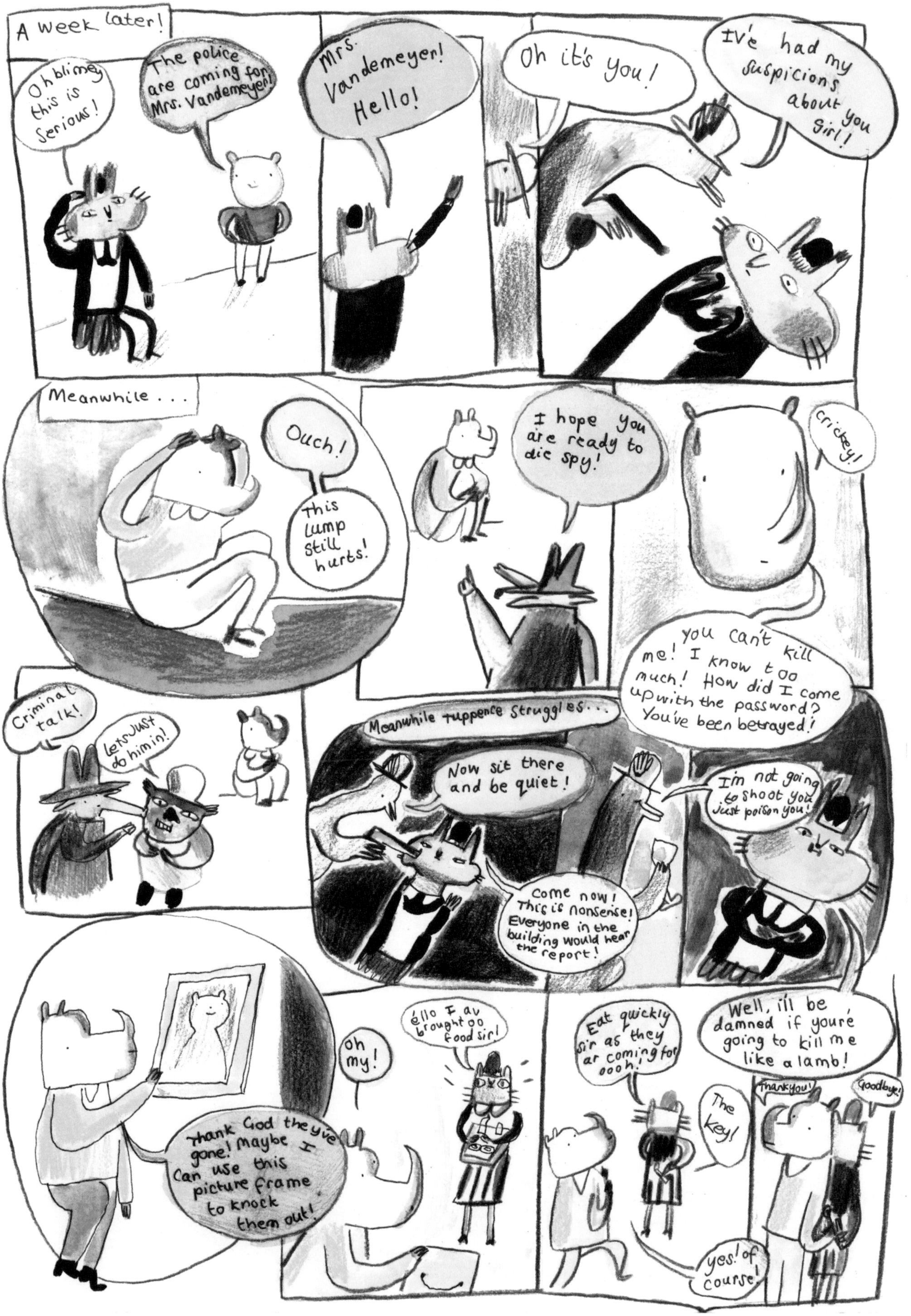
A week later!
Oh blimey this is serious!
The police are coming for Mrs. Vandemeyer!
Mrs. Vandemeyer! Hello!
Oh it's you!
I've had my suspicions about you girl!
Meanwhile . . .
Ouch!
This lump still hurts!
I hope you are ready to die spy!
crickey!
You can't kill me! I know too much! How did I come up with the password? You've been betrayed!
Criminal talk!
lets just do him in!
Meanwhile tuppence struggles . . .
Now sit there and be quiet!
I'm not going to shoot you just poison you!
Come now! This is nonsense! Everyone in the building would hear the report!
Thank God they've gone! Maybe I can use this picture frame to knock them out!
Oh my!
éllo I av brought oo food sir!
Eat quickly sir as they ar coming for oooh!
The key!
yes! of course!
Well, i'll be damned if you're going to kill me like a lamb!
Thankyou!
Goodbye!

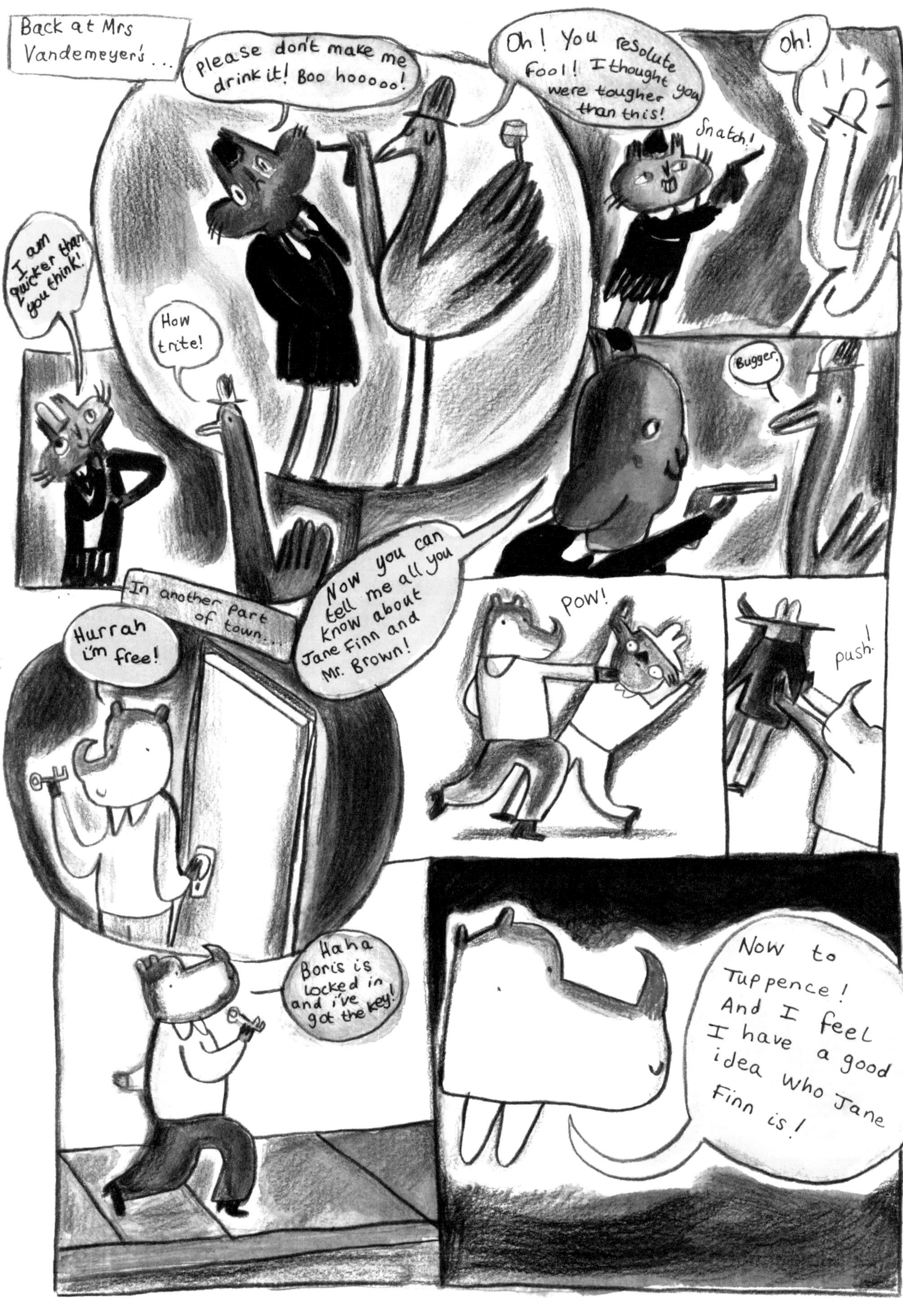

Back at Mrs Vandemeyer's . . .
Please don't make me drink it! Boo hooooo!
Oh! You resolute fool! I thought you were tougher than this!
Oh!
Snatch!
I am quicker than you think!
How trite!
Bugger.
Now you can tell me all you know about Jane Finn and Mr. Brown!
In another part of town...
Hurrah I'm free!
POW!
push!
Haha Boris is locked in and i've got the key!
Now to Tuppence! And I feel I have a good idea who Jane Finn is!

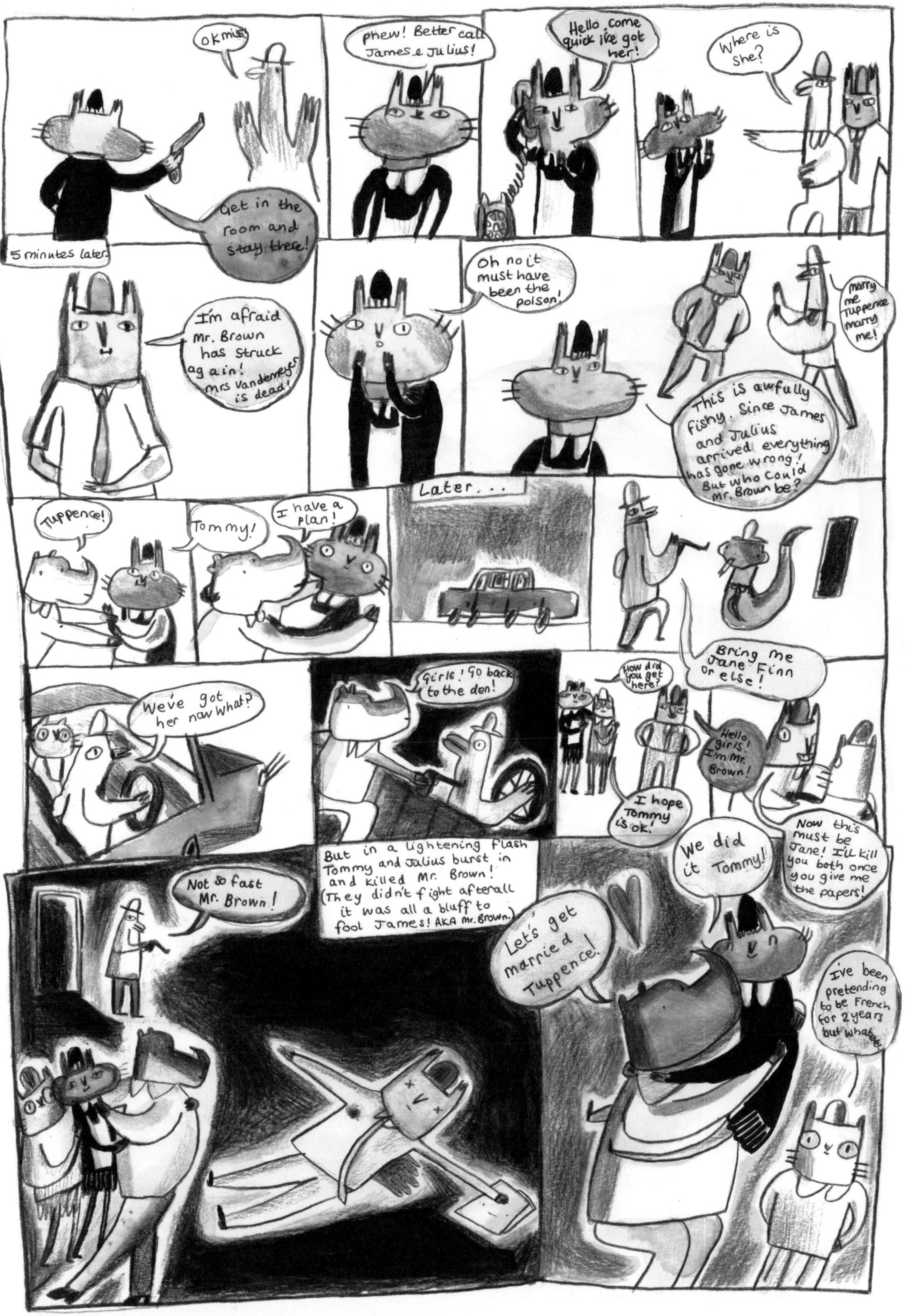
ok miss!
Get in the room and stay there!
phew! Better call James & Julius!
Hello come quick i've got her!
Where is She?
5 minutes later
I'm afraid Mr. Brown has struck again! Mrs Vandemeyer is dead!
Oh no it must have been the poison!
marry me Tuppence marry me!
This is awfully fishy. Since James and Julius arrived everything has gone wrong! But who could Mr. Brown be?
Tuppence!
Tommy!
I have a plan!
Later...
We've got her now What?
Girls! Go back to the den!
How did you get here?
Bring me Jane Finn or else!
Hello, girls! I'm Mr. Brown!
I hope Tommy is ok!
Not so fast Mr. Brown!
But in a lightening flash Tommy and Julius burst in and killed Mr. Brown! (They didn't fight afterall it was all a bluff to fool James! AKA Mr. Brown.)
We did it Tommy!
Now this must be Jane! I'll kill you both once you give me the papers!
Let's get married Tuppence!
I've been pretending to be French for 2 years but whatever!

"The Road Home"

Dashiell Hammett

ART/ADAPTATION BY Teddy Goldenberg

WHAT YOU WILL WITNESS IN THE following pages is the birth of the hard-boiled detective story. Some experts credit Dashiell Hammett's first published short story, "The Road Home," with creating the genre. As with any such literary debate, not everyone agrees, with some pointing to other stories that appeared at that point in time (end of 1922, early 1923). But no matter who got there first, Hammett was far and away the most influential, and he soon went on to pen several classic novels in his spare style, including *The Maltese Falcon* (which introduced P.I. Sam Spade) and *The Thin Man* (birthing another classic detective: the Continental Op).

A real-life private detective for several years (with the permanent scars to prove it), Hammett brought gritty reality to the mystery genre. Raymond Chandler, another, slightly later pioneer of hard-boiledism, wrote:

> Hammett gave murder back to the kind of people that commit it for reasons, not just to provide a corpse . . . He put these people down on paper as they were, and he made them talk and think in the language they customarily used for these purposes.

Apparently set on a jungle river in Burma, "The Road Home" is grim, lonely, and claustrophobic. Israeli artist Teddy Goldenberg does a perfect job visually conveying the murkiness of the story—both the dark, dense physical setting and the tantalizing ambiguity that suffuses almost every aspect of the story itself.

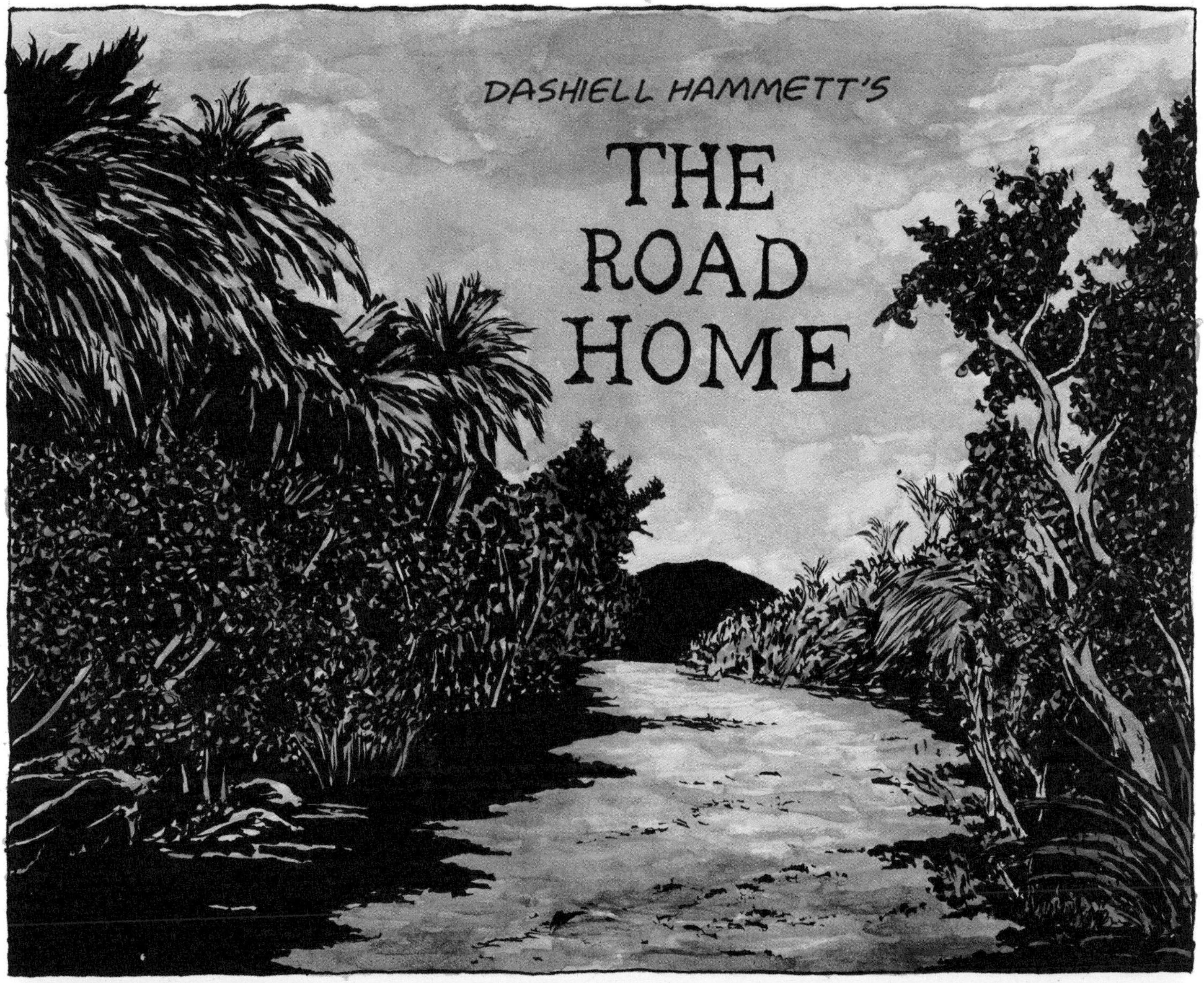
DASHIELL HAMMETT'S
THE ROAD HOME

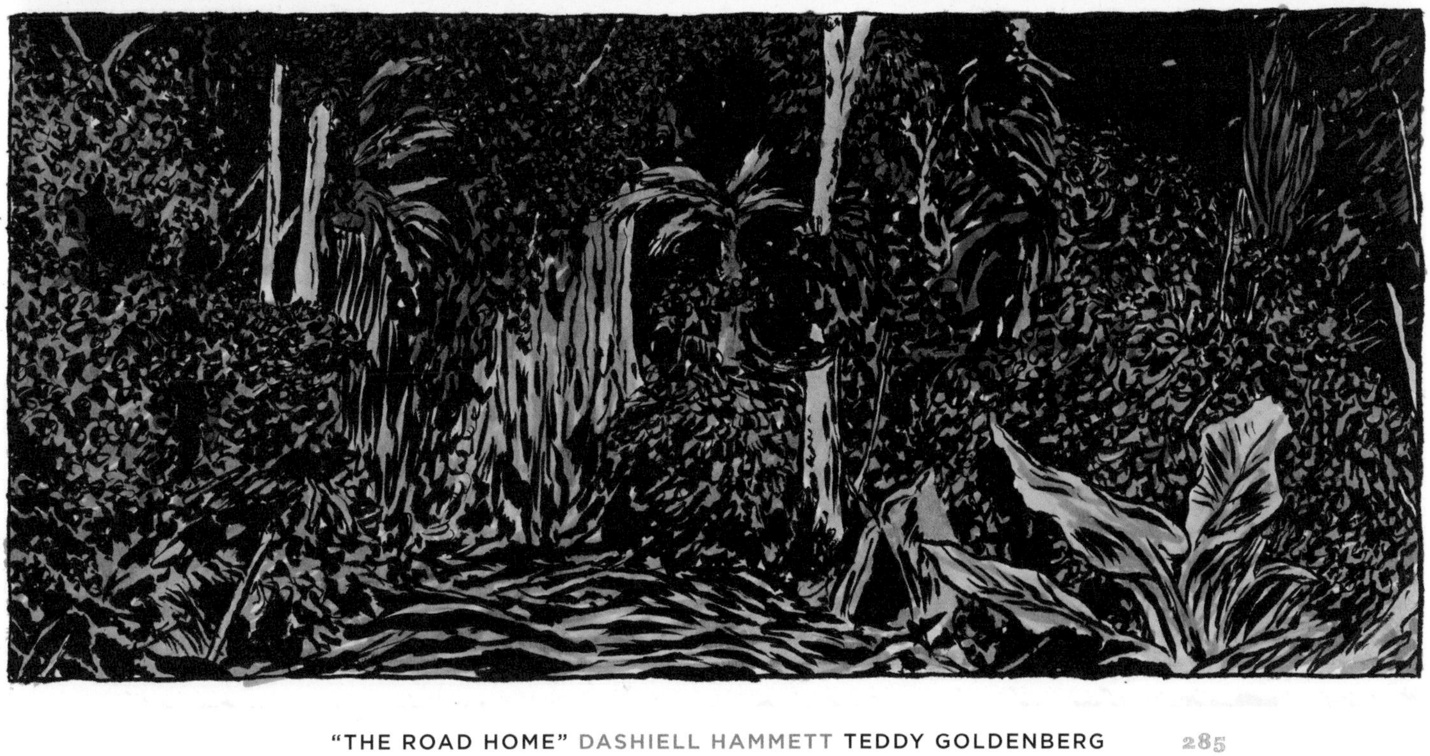

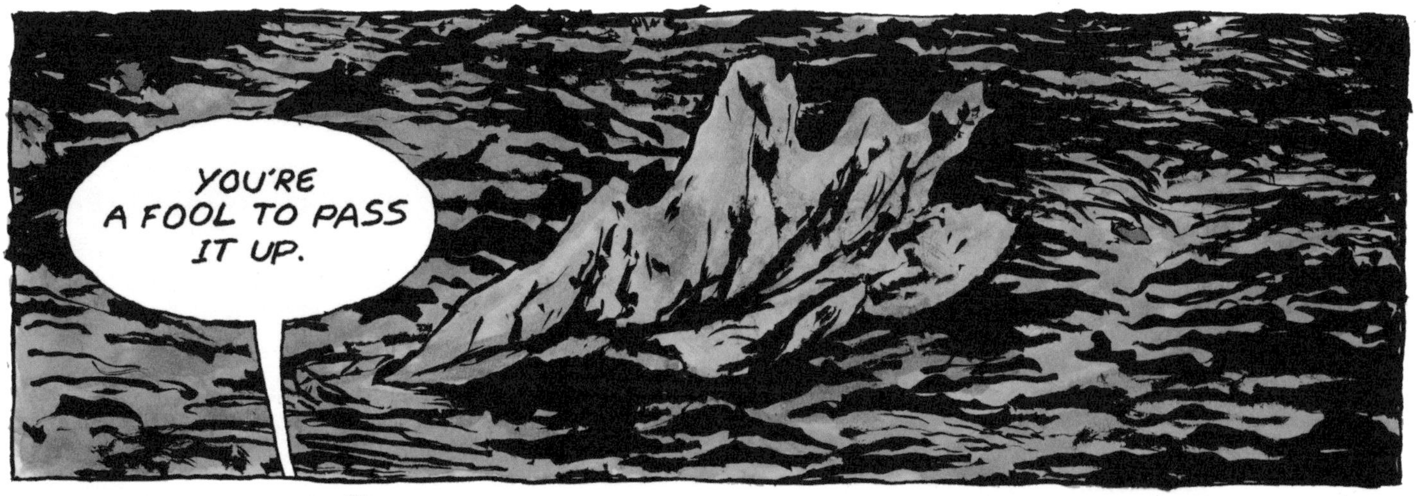
YOU'RE A FOOL TO PASS IT UP.

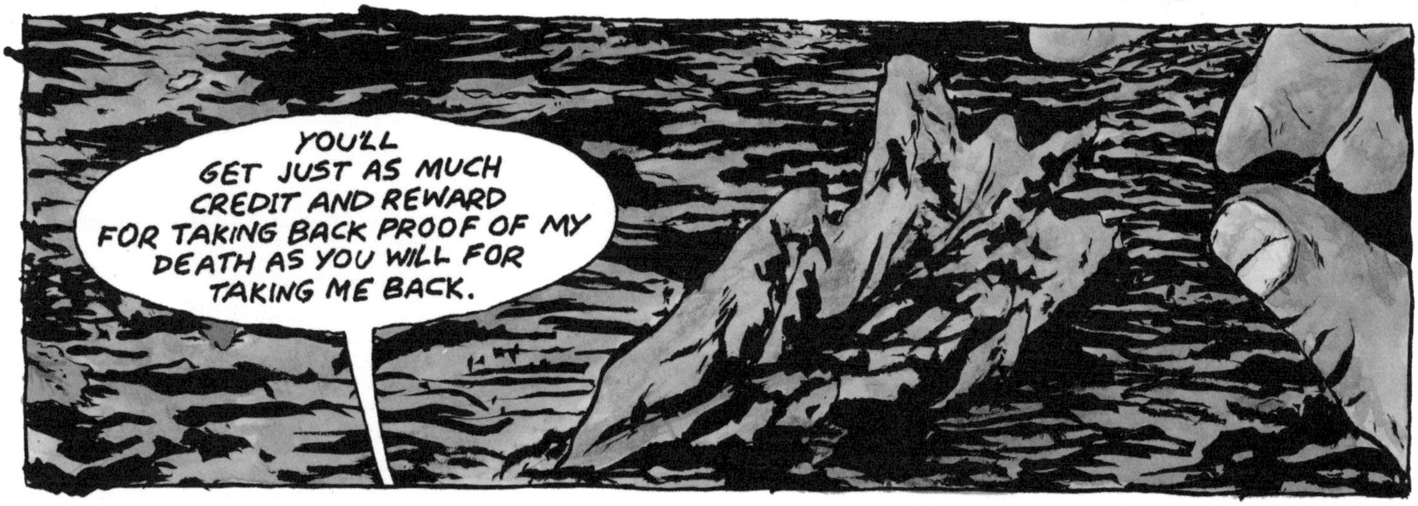
YOU'LL GET JUST AS MUCH CREDIT AND REWARD FOR TAKING BACK PROOF OF MY DEATH AS YOU WILL FOR TAKING ME BACK.

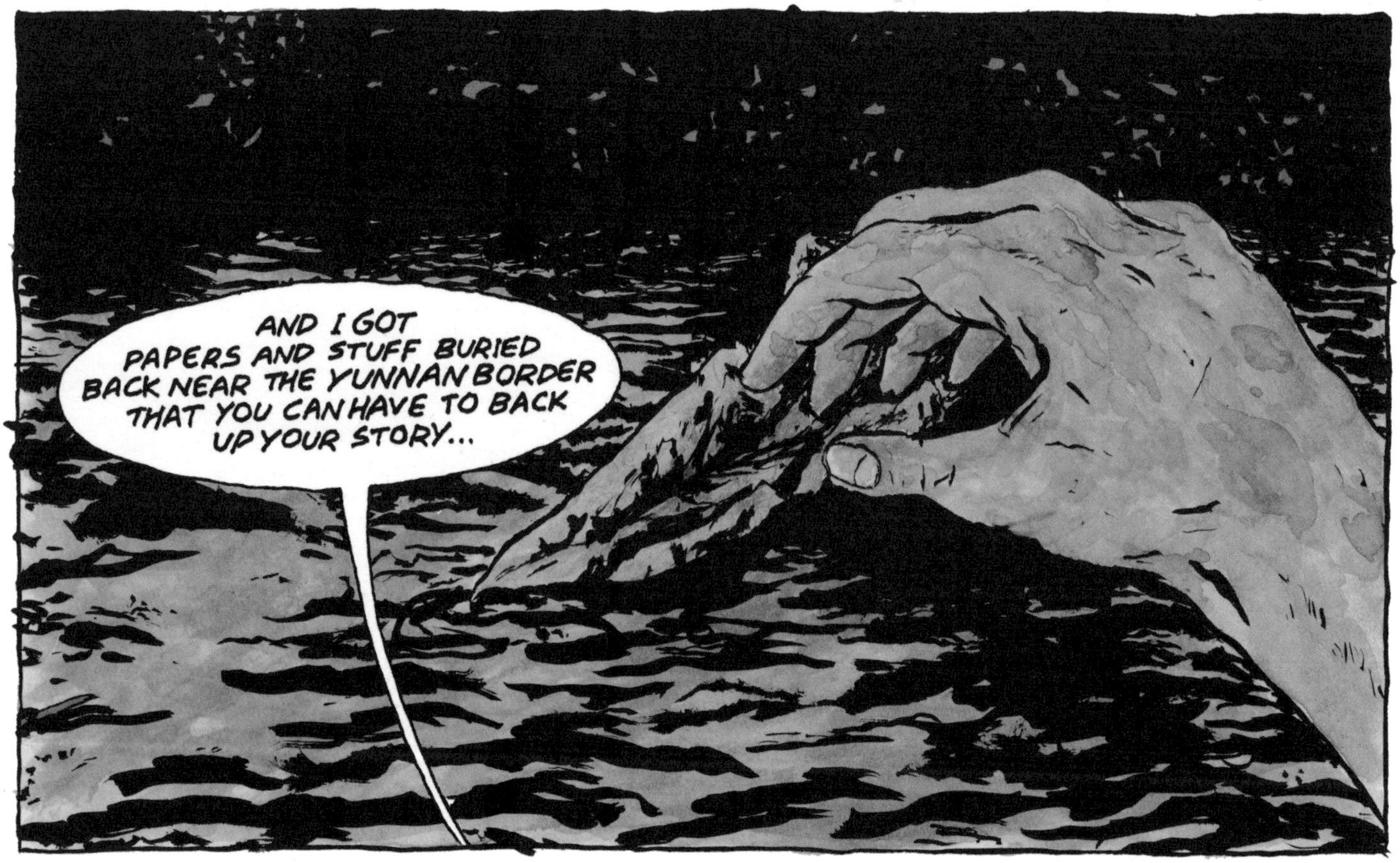
AND I GOT PAPERS AND STUFF BURIED BACK NEAR THE YUNNAN BORDER THAT YOU CAN HAVE TO BACK UP YOUR STORY...

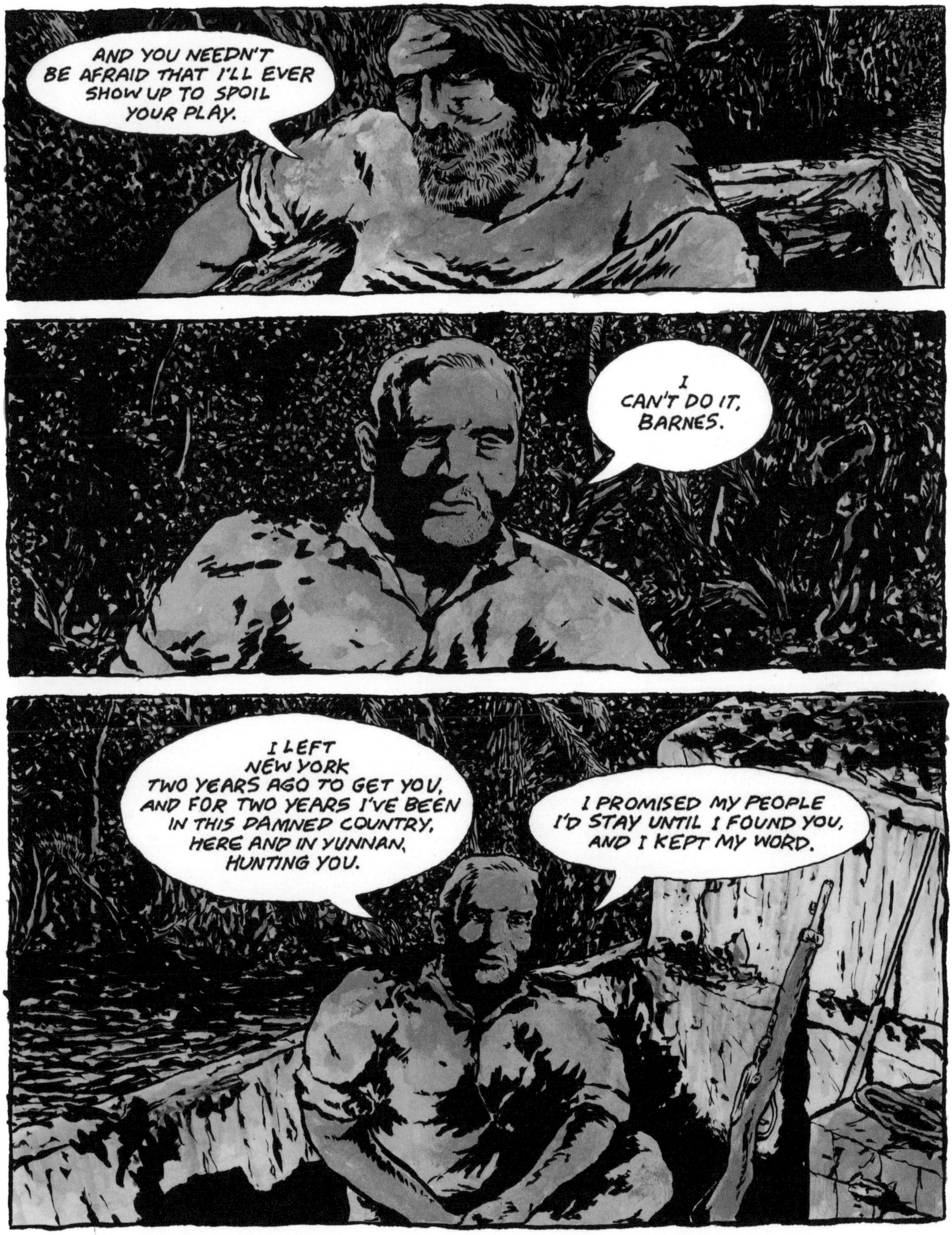
AND YOU NEEDN'T BE AFRAID THAT I'LL EVER SHOW UP TO SPOIL YOUR PLAY.
I CAN'T DO IT, BARNES.
I LEFT NEW YORK TWO YEARS AGO TO GET YOU, AND FOR TWO YEARS I'VE BEEN IN THIS DAMNED COUNTRY, HERE AND IN YUNNAN, HUNTING YOU.
I PROMISED MY PEOPLE I'D STAY UNTIL I FOUND YOU, AND I KEPT MY WORD.

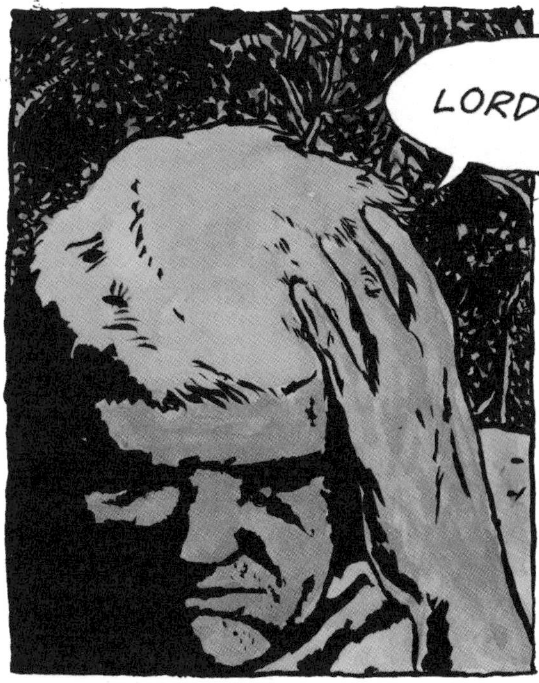
LORD. MAN.

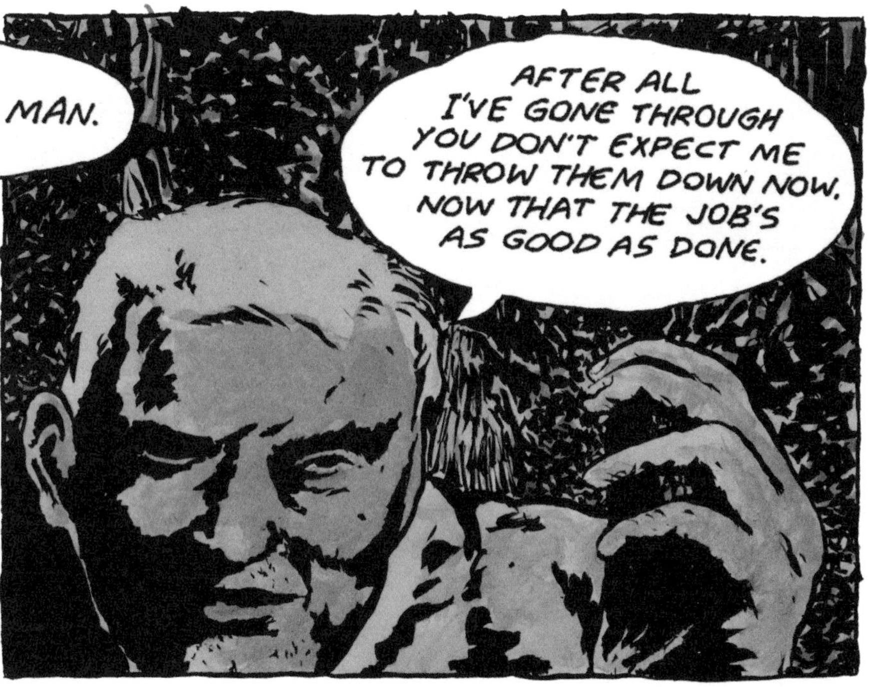
AFTER ALL I'VE GONE THROUGH YOU DON'T EXPECT ME TO THROW THEM DOWN NOW. NOW THAT THE JOB'S AS GOOD AS DONE.

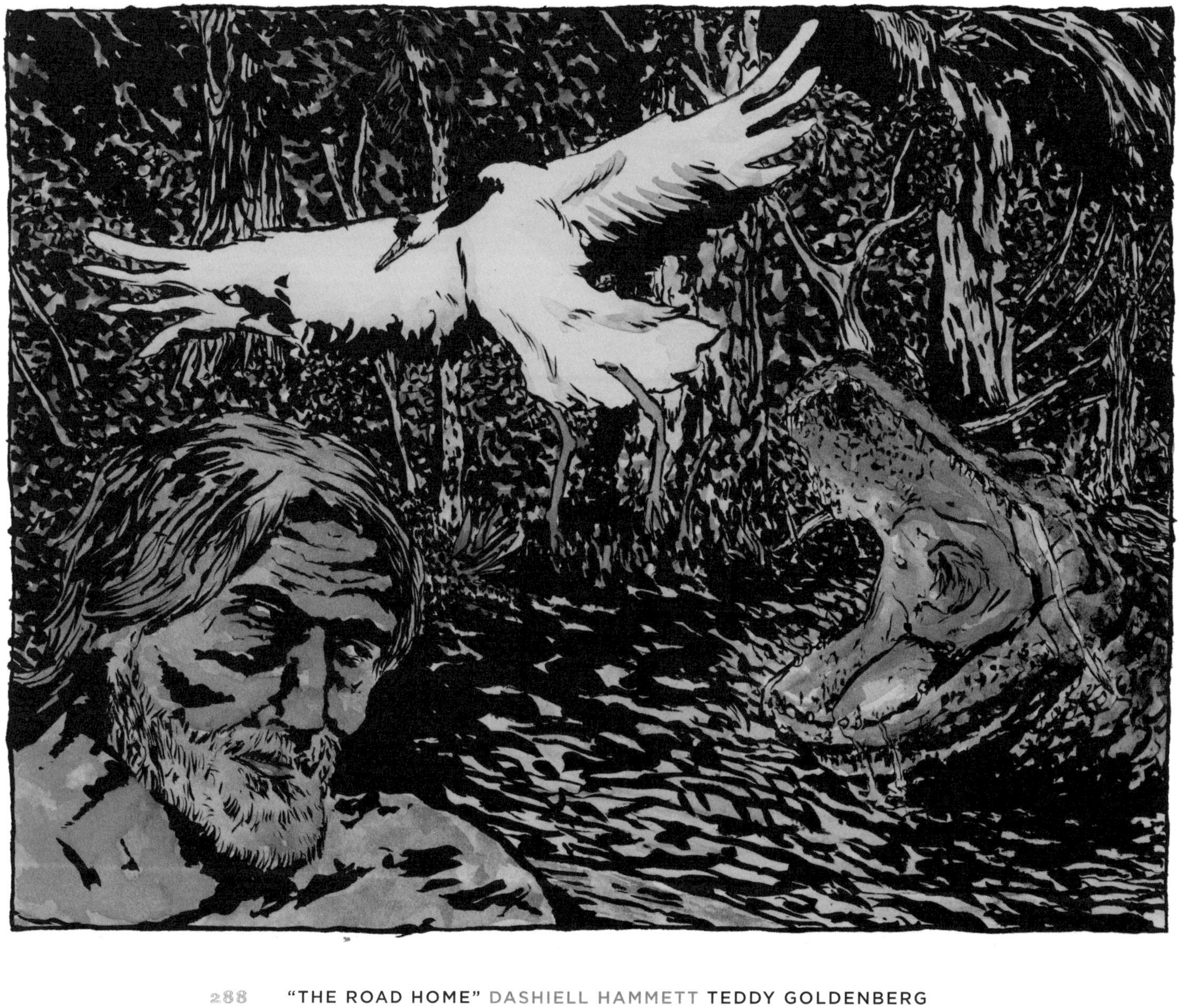

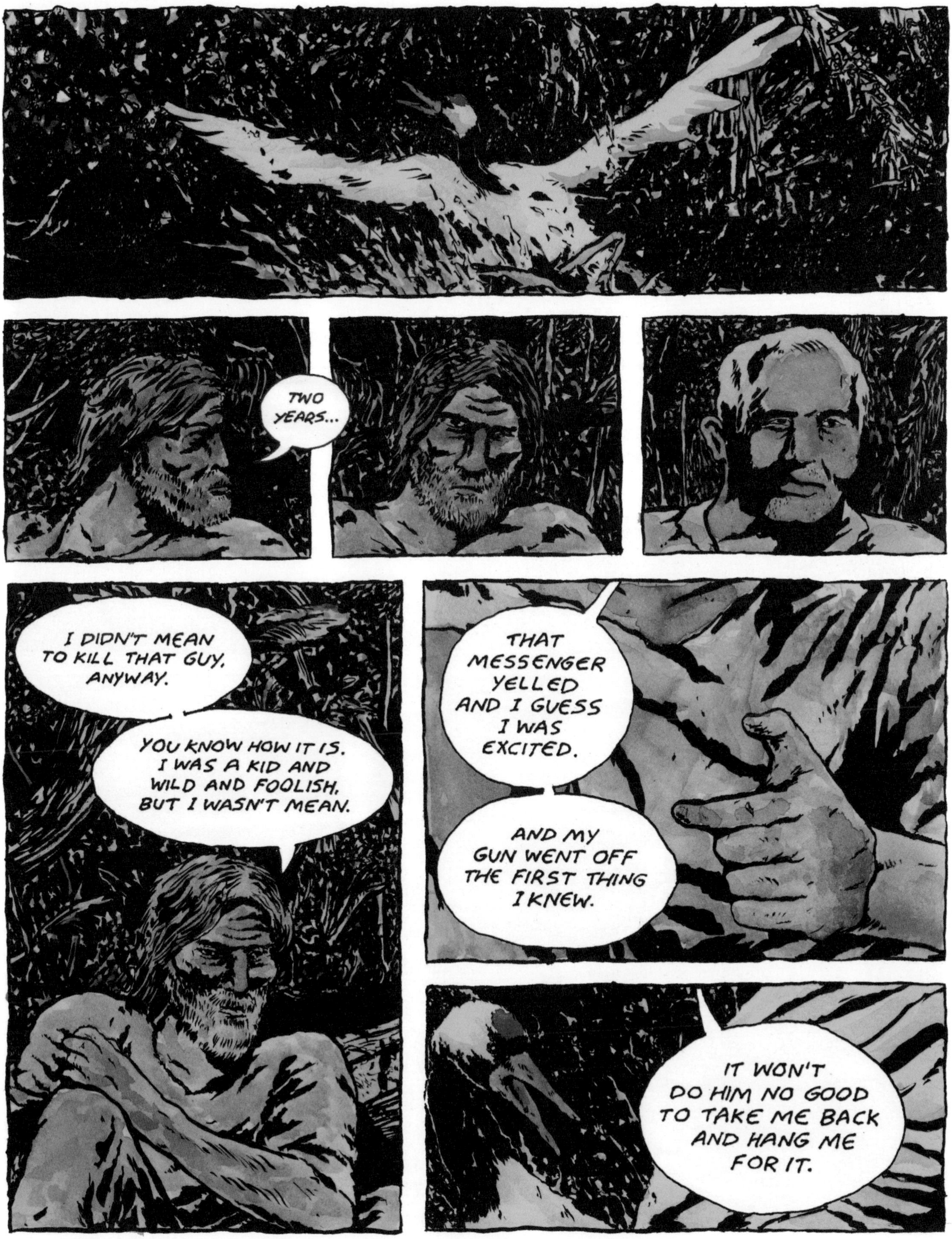
TWO YEARS...
I DIDN'T MEAN TO KILL THAT GUY, ANYWAY.
YOU KNOW HOW IT IS. I WAS A KID AND WILD AND FOOLISH, BUT I WASN'T MEAN.
THAT MESSENGER YELLED AND I GUESS I WAS EXCITED.
AND MY GUN WENT OFF THE FIRST THING I KNEW.
IT WON'T DO HIM NO GOOD TO TAKE ME BACK AND HANG ME FOR IT.

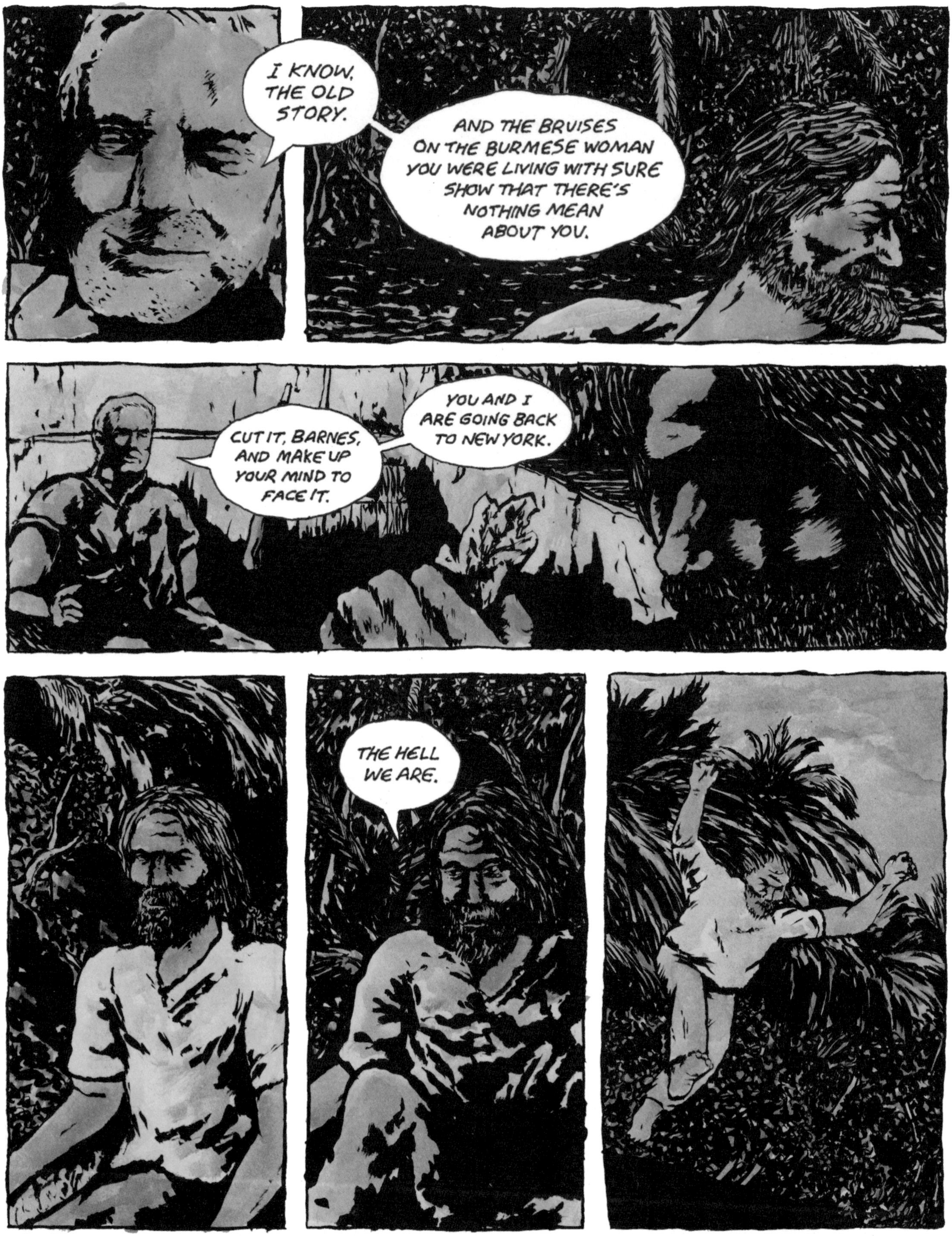
I KNOW. THE OLD STORY.
AND THE BRUISES ON THE BURMESE WOMAN YOU WERE LIVING WITH SURE SHOW THAT THERE'S NOTHING MEAN ABOUT YOU.
CUT IT, BARNES, AND MAKE UP YOUR MIND TO FACE IT.
YOU AND I ARE GOING BACK TO NEW YORK.
THE HELL WE ARE.

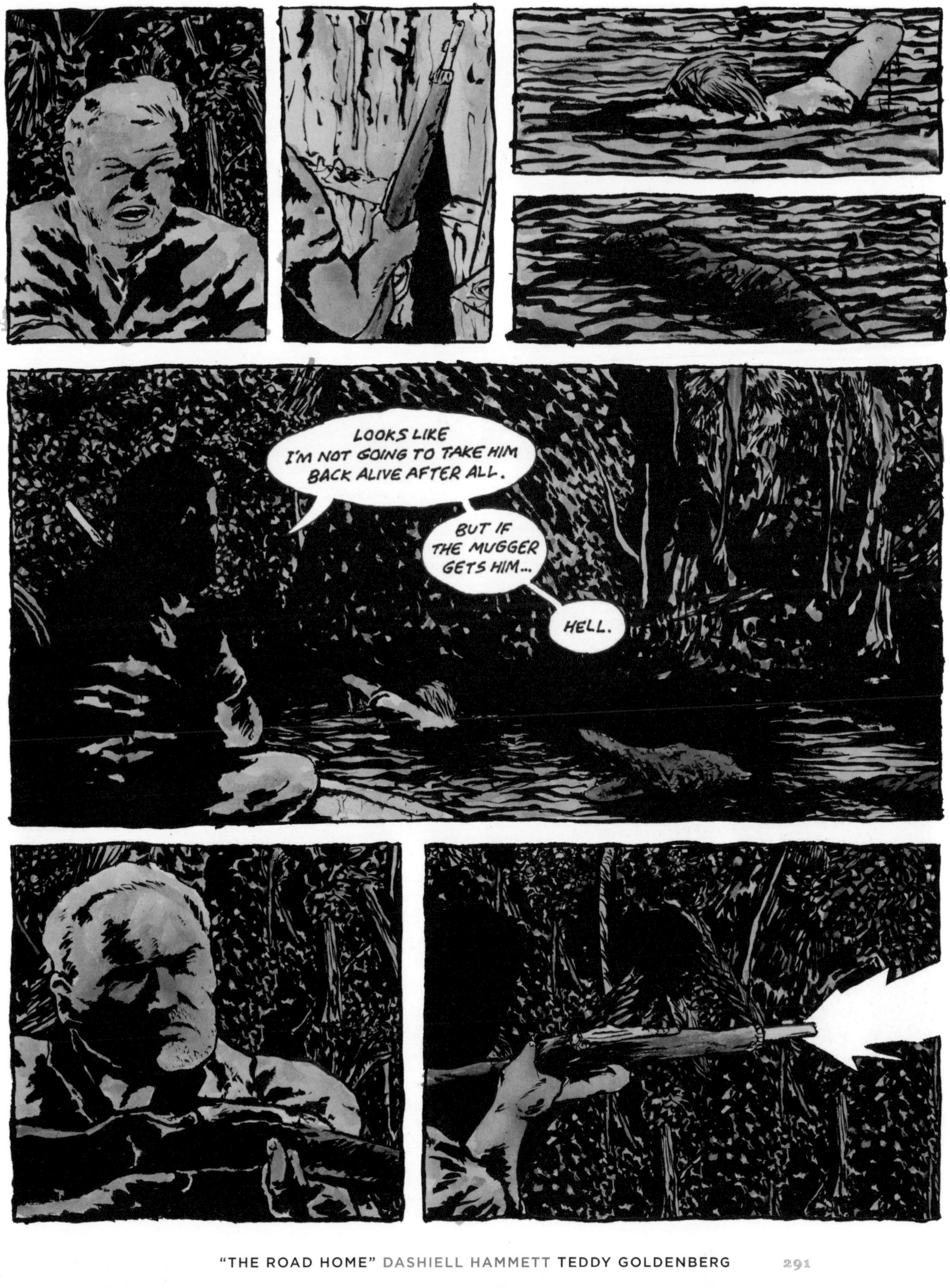
LOOKS LIKE I'M NOT GOING TO TAKE HIM BACK ALIVE AFTER ALL.
BUT IF THE MUGGER GETS HIM...
HELL.

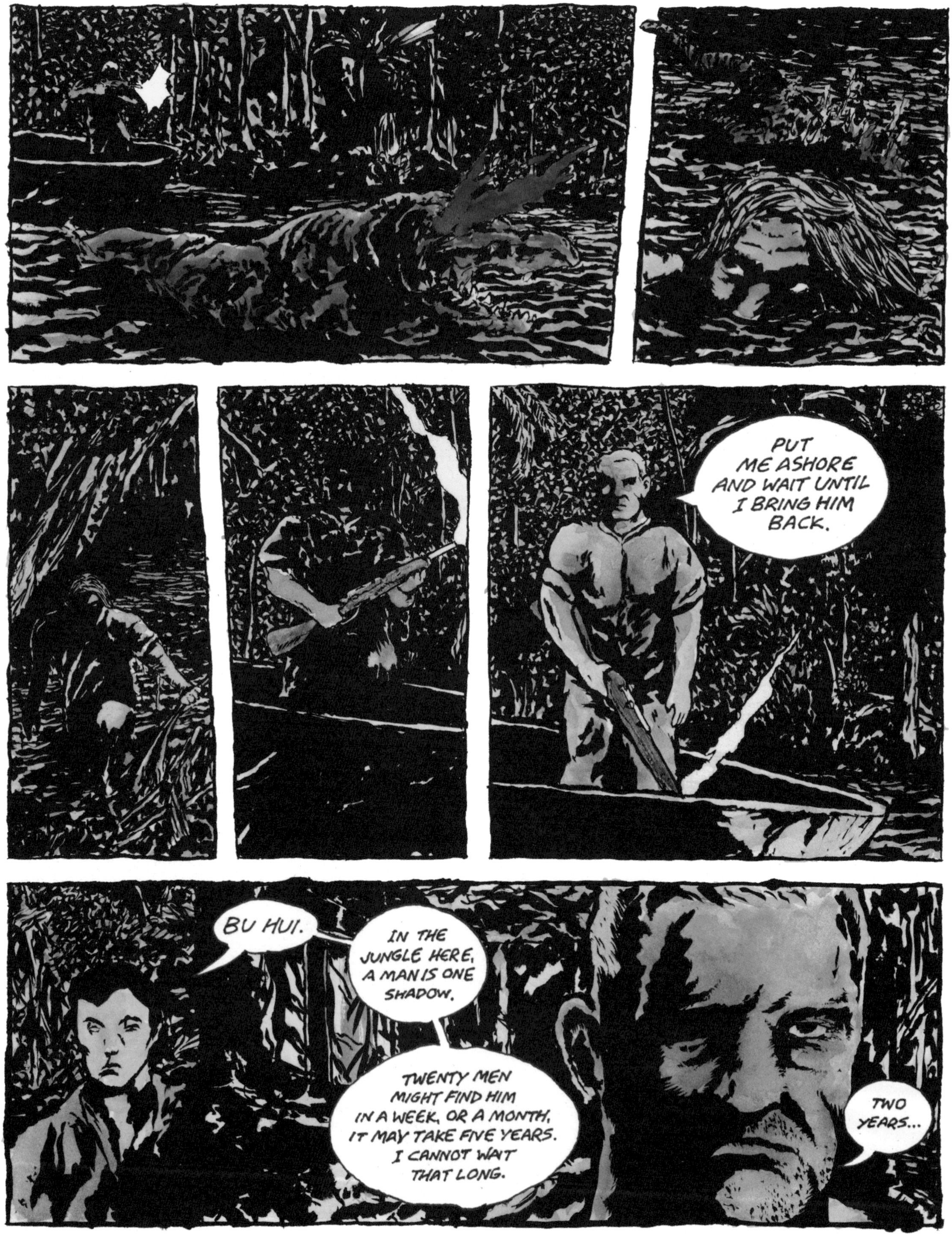
PUT ME ASHORE AND WAIT UNTIL I BRING HIM BACK.
BU HUI.
IN THE JUNGLE HERE, A MAN IS ONE SHADOW.
TWENTY MEN MIGHT FIND HIM IN A WEEK, OR A MONTH. IT MAY TAKE FIVE YEARS. I CANNOT WAIT THAT LONG.
TWO YEARS...

I GO AFTER HIM. YOU WAIT UNTIL DARK. IF I AM NOT BACK THEN DO NOT WAIT.
HUI.

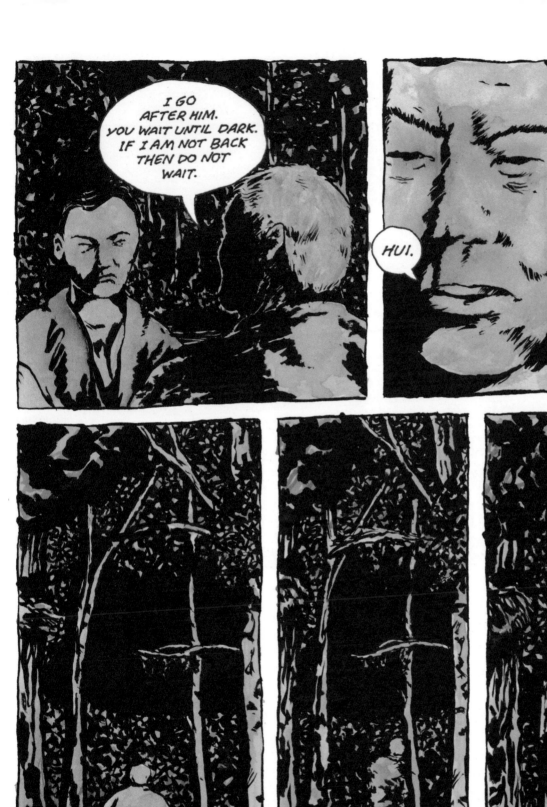

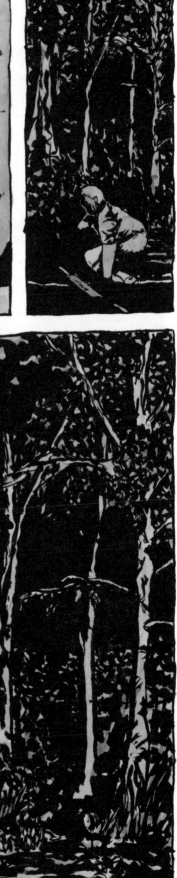

"THE ROAD HOME" DASHIELL HAMMETT TEDDY GOLDENBERG

"The Lamp of God"

Ellery Queen

ART/ADAPTATION BY Till Lukat

ELLERY QUEEN WAS ONE OF THE leading names in mystery fiction from the 1930s through the 1960s, and that name was actually a pseudonym for two cousins who produced an astonishing amount of work. Frederic Dannay and Manfred Bennington Lee wrote around 35 novels and seven short story collections featuring a crime-solver named Ellery Queen. They were also anthologists, bibliographers, and historians of crime fiction, and they produced numerous groundbreaking and lauded books along these lines. On top of that, Dannay founded *Ellery Queen's Mystery Magazine* in 1941, and it's still going strong.

The Lamp of God is a 1935 novella by and starring Queen, often considered one of the cousins' best works. It certainly contains one of the most outlandish mysteries that ever needed solving. Berlin-based artist Till Lukat brings a snappy two-color palette to the proceedings. Among other things, Till created the graphic nonfiction book *Tuff Ladies: 24 Remarkable Women of History*, and he's part of the European Research Council's effort to present cutting-edge scientific research as comics.

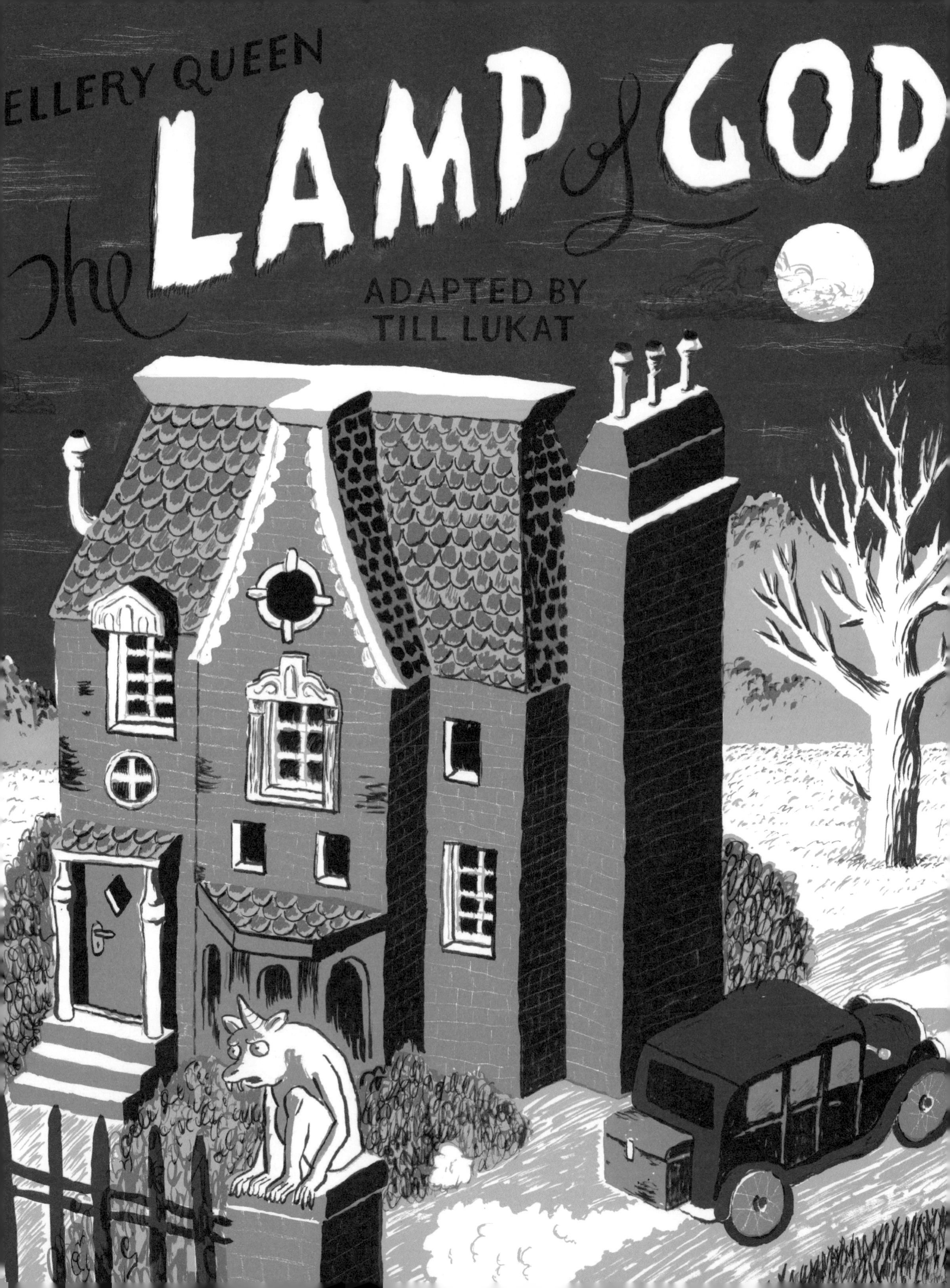
ELLERY QUEEN
The LAMP of GOD
ADAPTED BY
TILL LUKAT

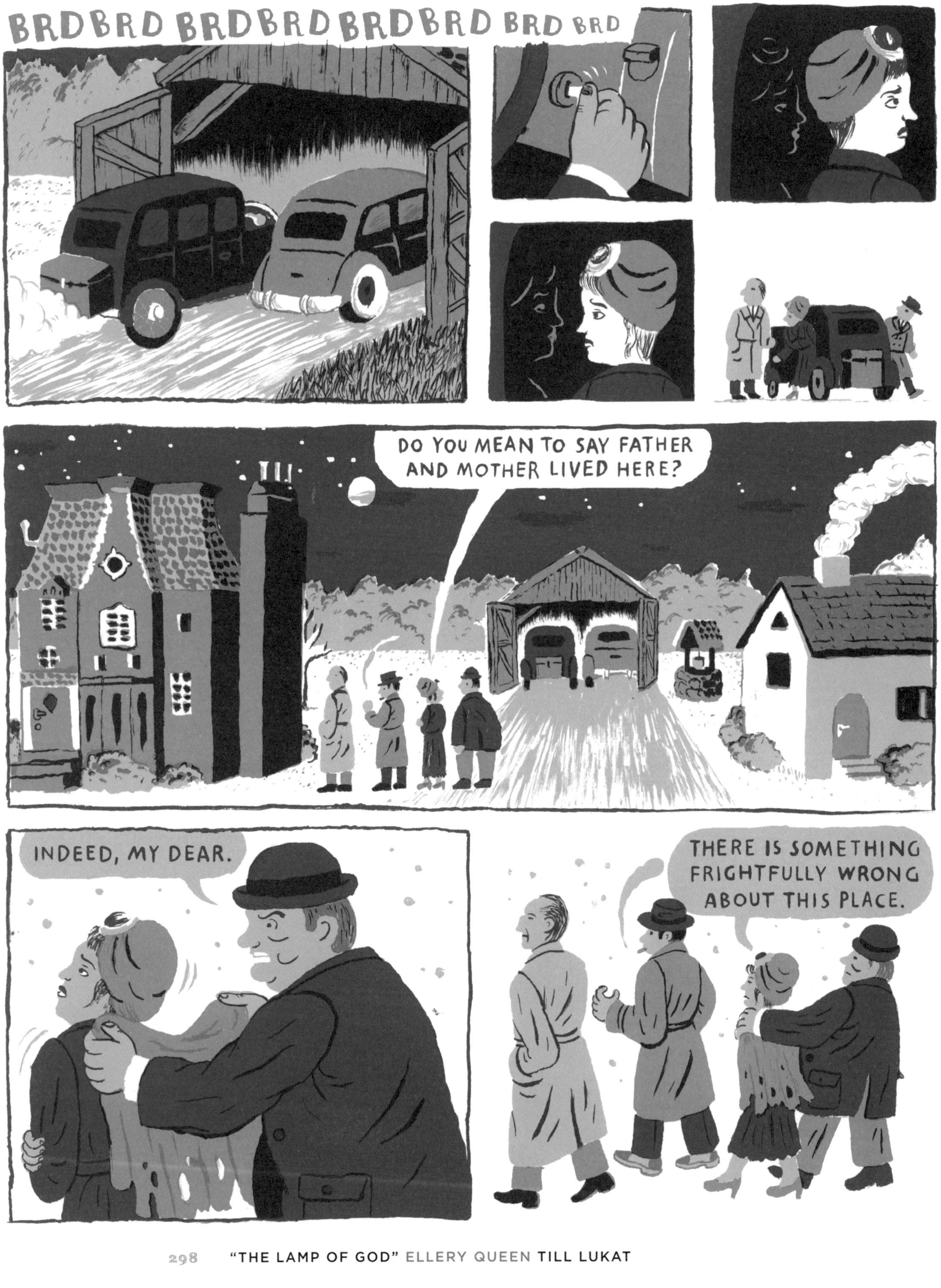
BRDBRD BRDBRD BRDBRD BRD BRD
DO YOU MEAN TO SAY FATHER AND MOTHER LIVED HERE?
INDEED, MY DEAR.
THERE IS SOMETHING FRIGHTFULLY WRONG ABOUT THIS PLACE.

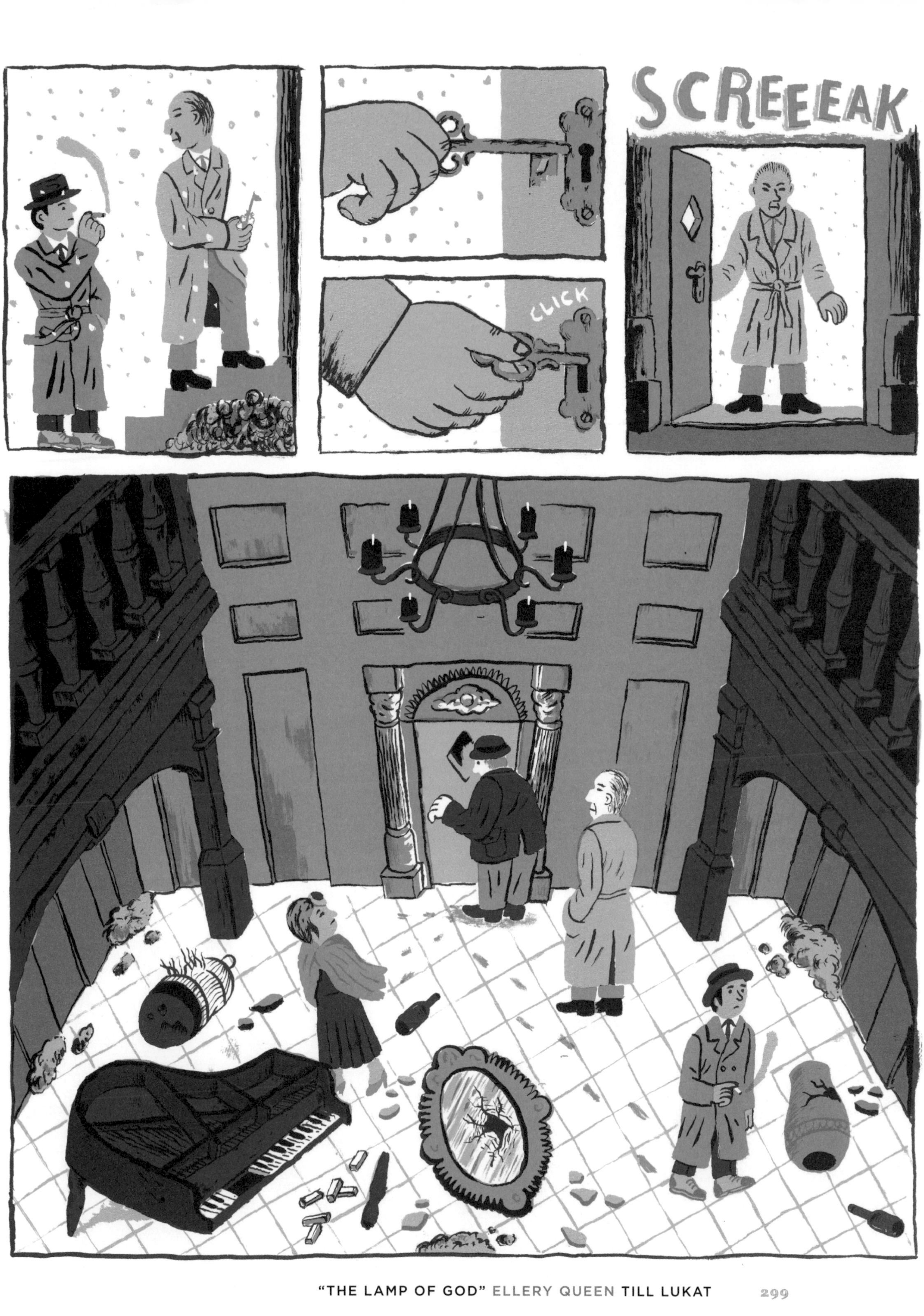
CLICK
SCREEEEAK

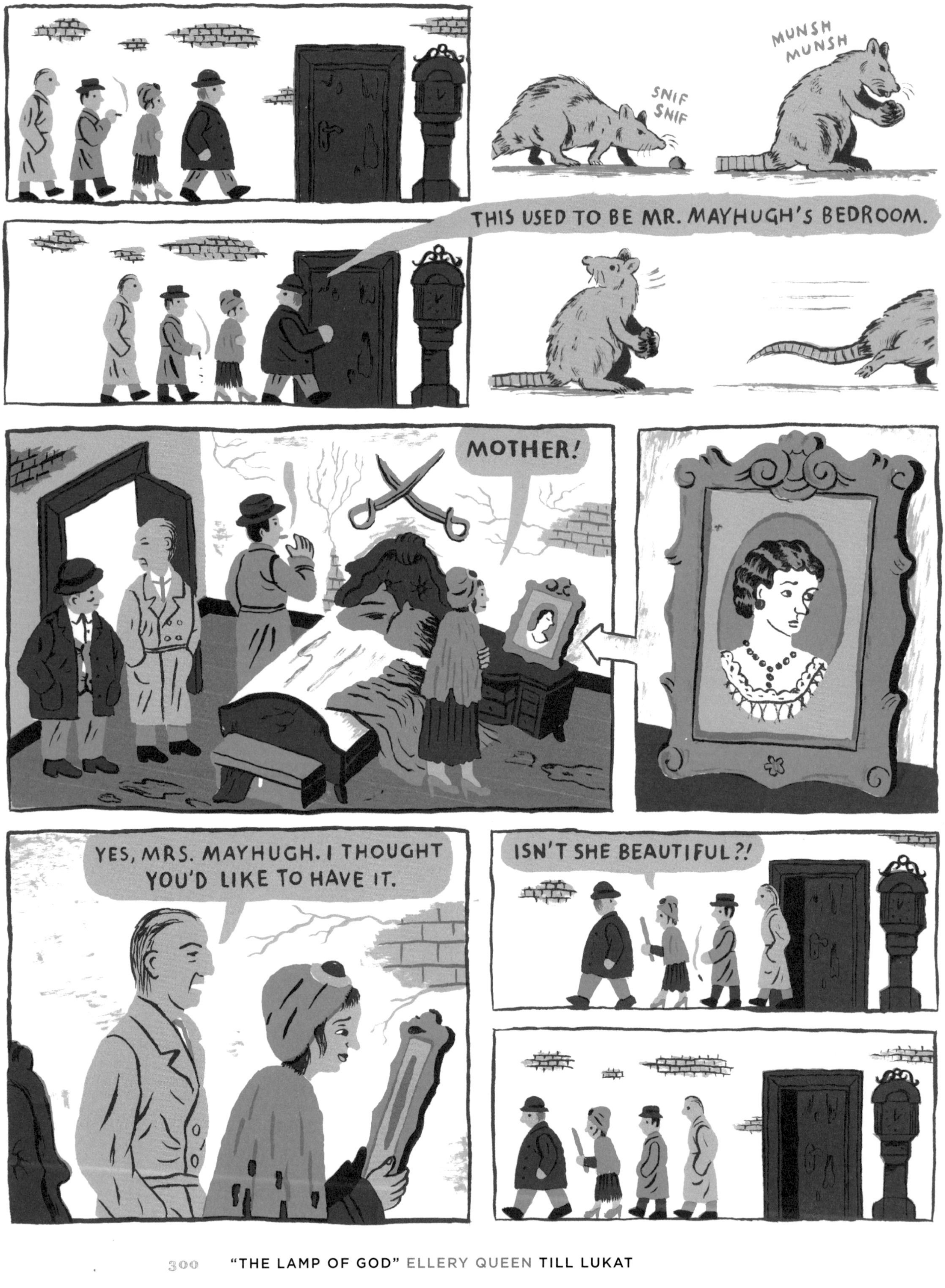
SNIF
SNIF
MUNSH
MUNSH
THIS USED TO BE MR. MAYHUGH'S BEDROOM.
MOTHER!
YES, MRS. MAYHUGH. I THOUGHT YOU'D LIKE TO HAVE IT.
ISN'T SHE BEAUTIFUL?!

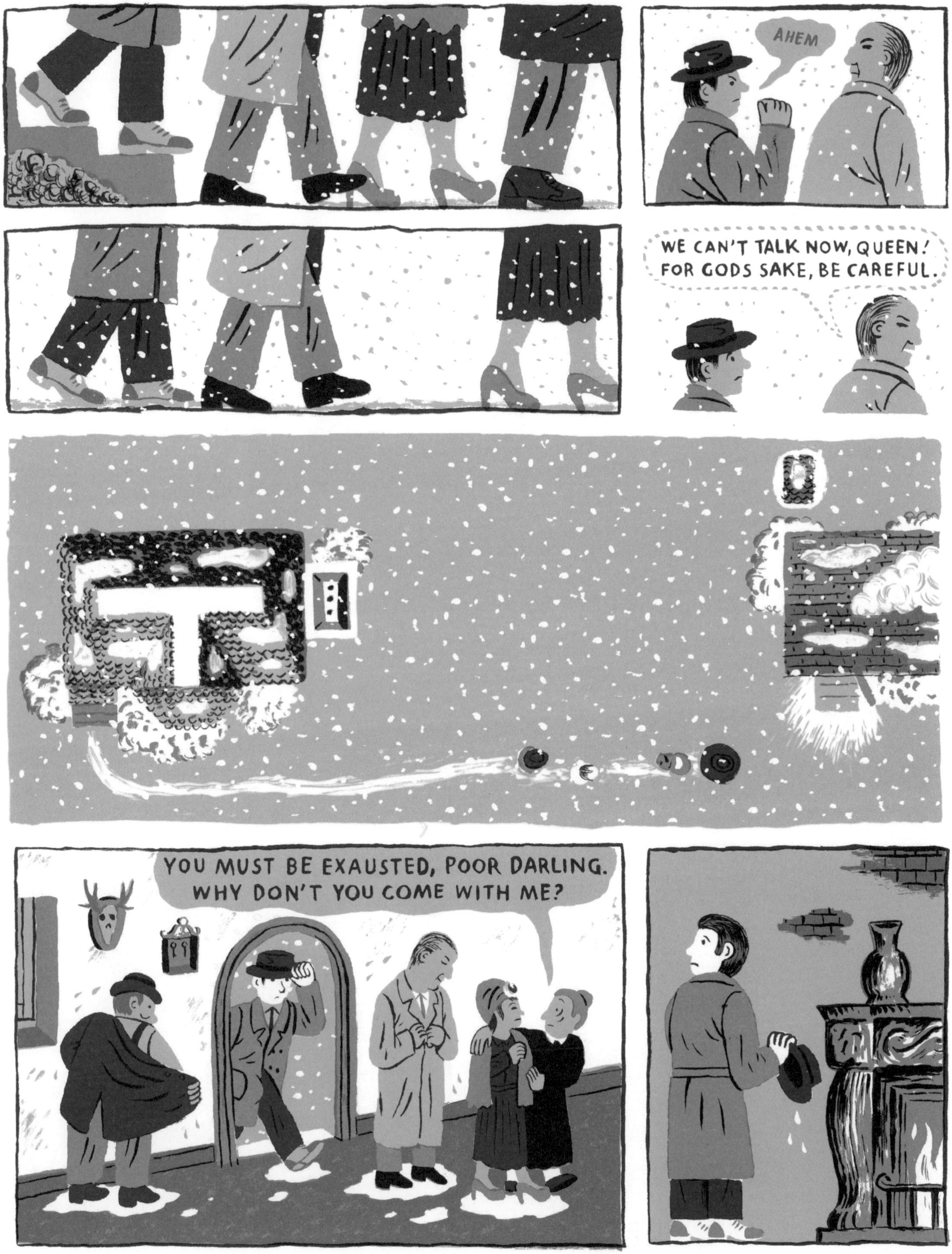
AHEM
WE CAN'T TALK NOW, QUEEN! FOR GODS SAKE, BE CAREFUL.
YOU MUST BE EXAUSTED, POOR DARLING. WHY DON'T YOU COME WITH ME?

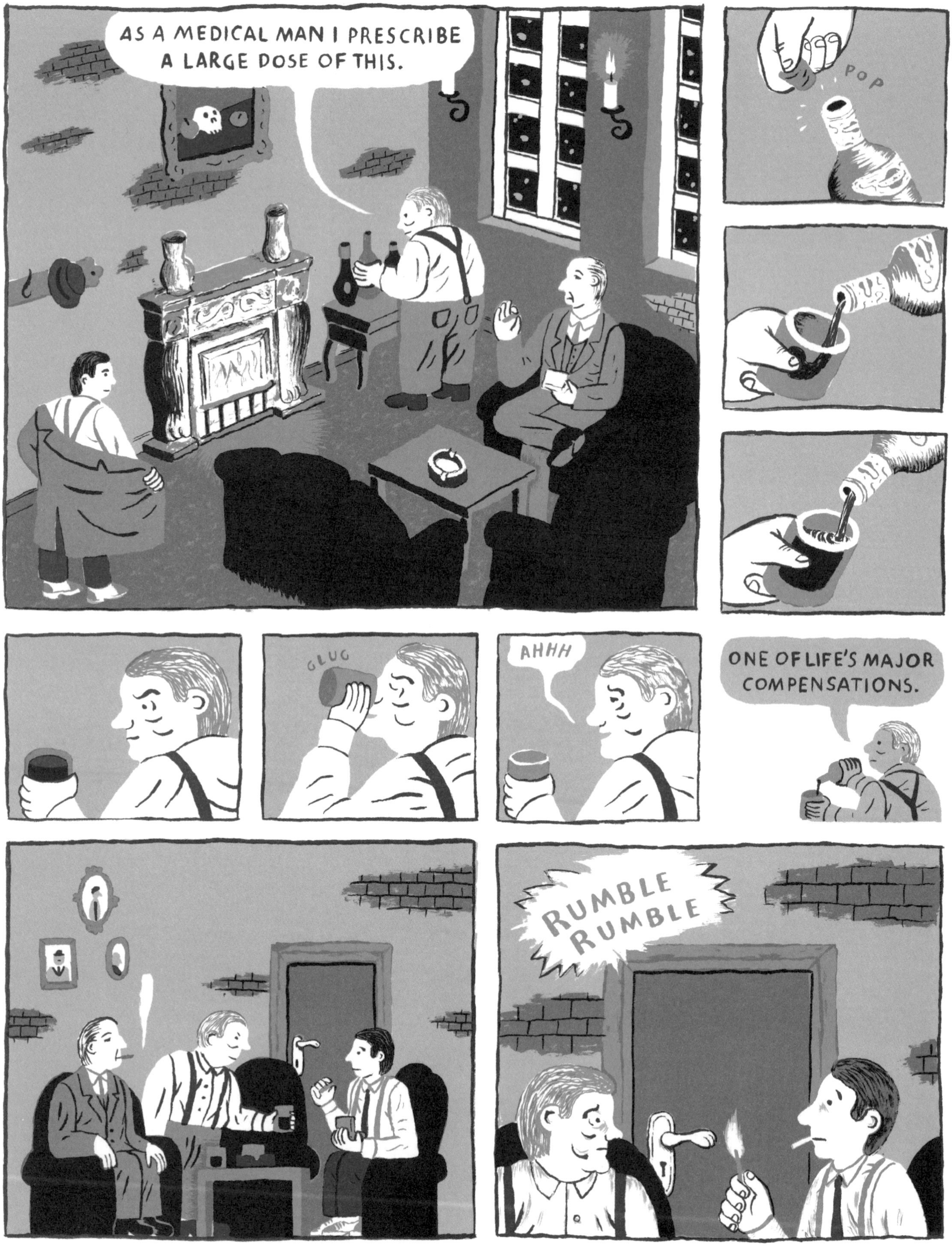
AS A MEDICAL MAN I PRESCRIBE A LARGE DOSE OF THIS.
POP
GLUG
AHHH
ONE OF LIFE'S MAJOR COMPENSATIONS.
RUMBLE RUMBLE

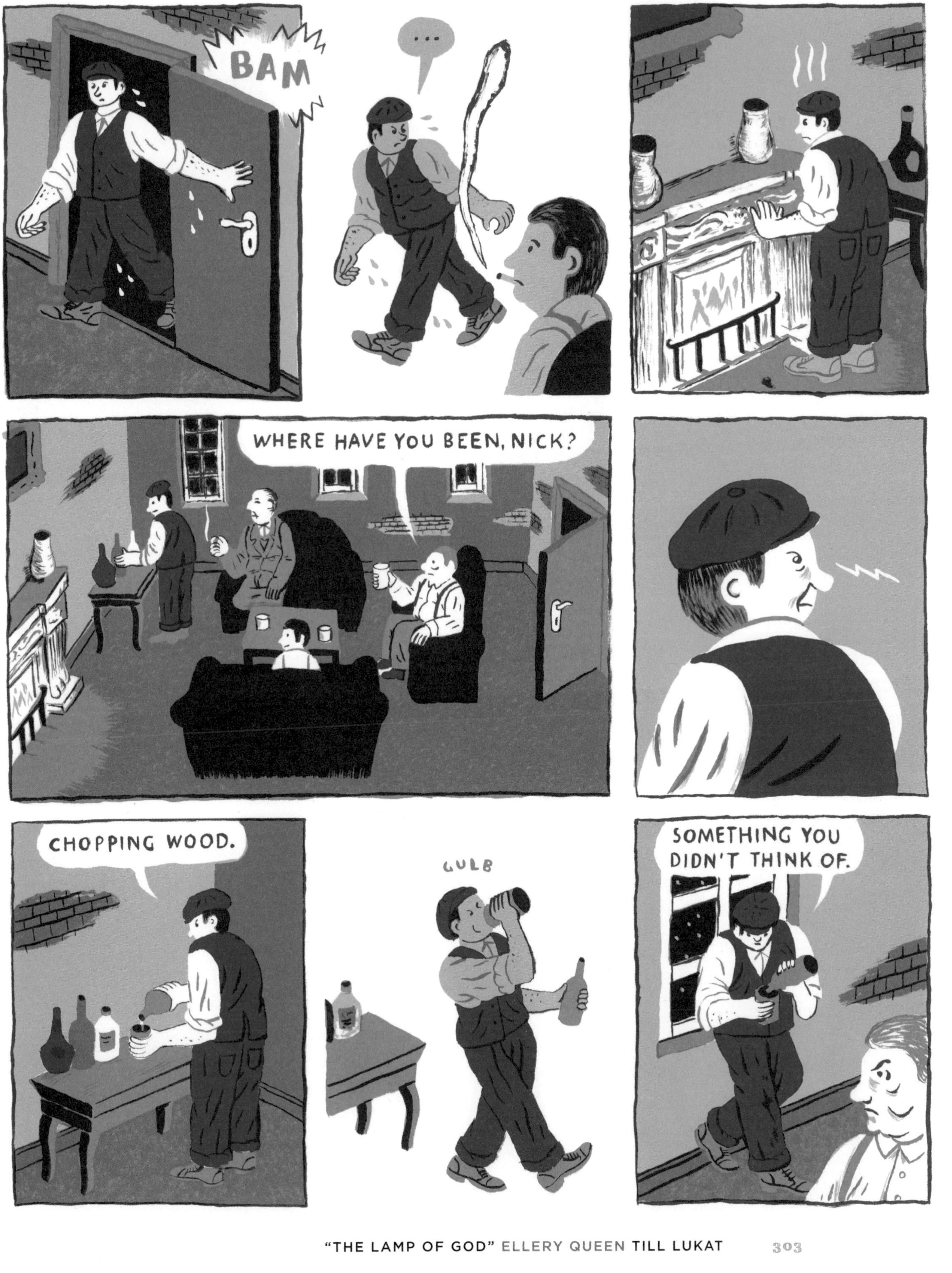
BAM
...
WHERE HAVE YOU BEEN, NICK?
CHOPPING WOOD.
GULB
SOMETHING YOU DIDN'T THINK OF.

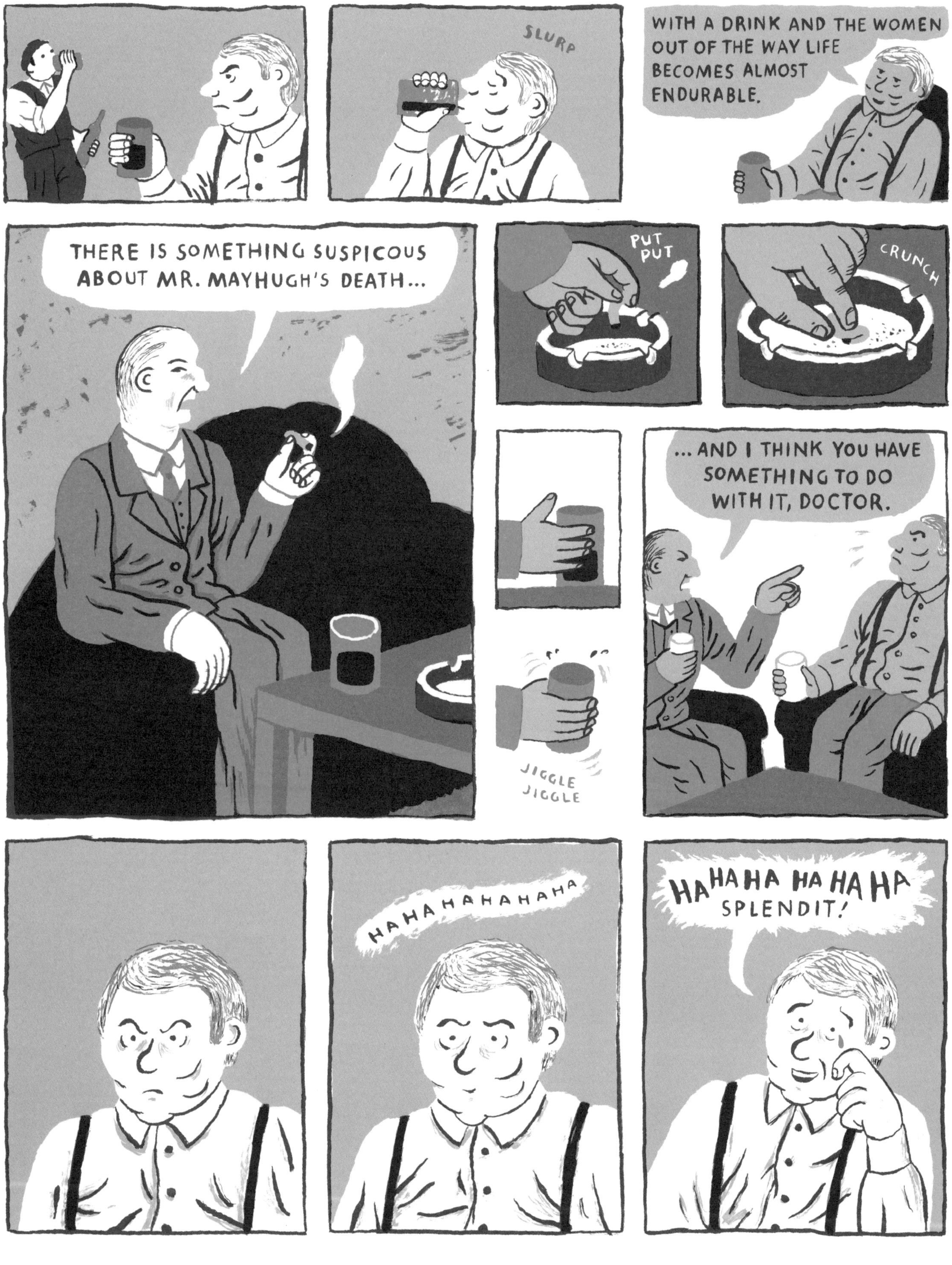
SLURP
WITH A DRINK AND THE WOMEN OUT OF THE WAY LIFE BECOMES ALMOST ENDURABLE.
THERE IS SOMETHING SUSPICOUS ABOUT MR. MAYHUGH'S DEATH...
PUT PUT
CRUNCH
...AND I THINK YOU HAVE SOMETHING TO DO WITH IT, DOCTOR.
JIGGLE JIGGLE
HAHAHAHAHAHAHA
HAHAHA HA HAHAHA
SPLENDIT!

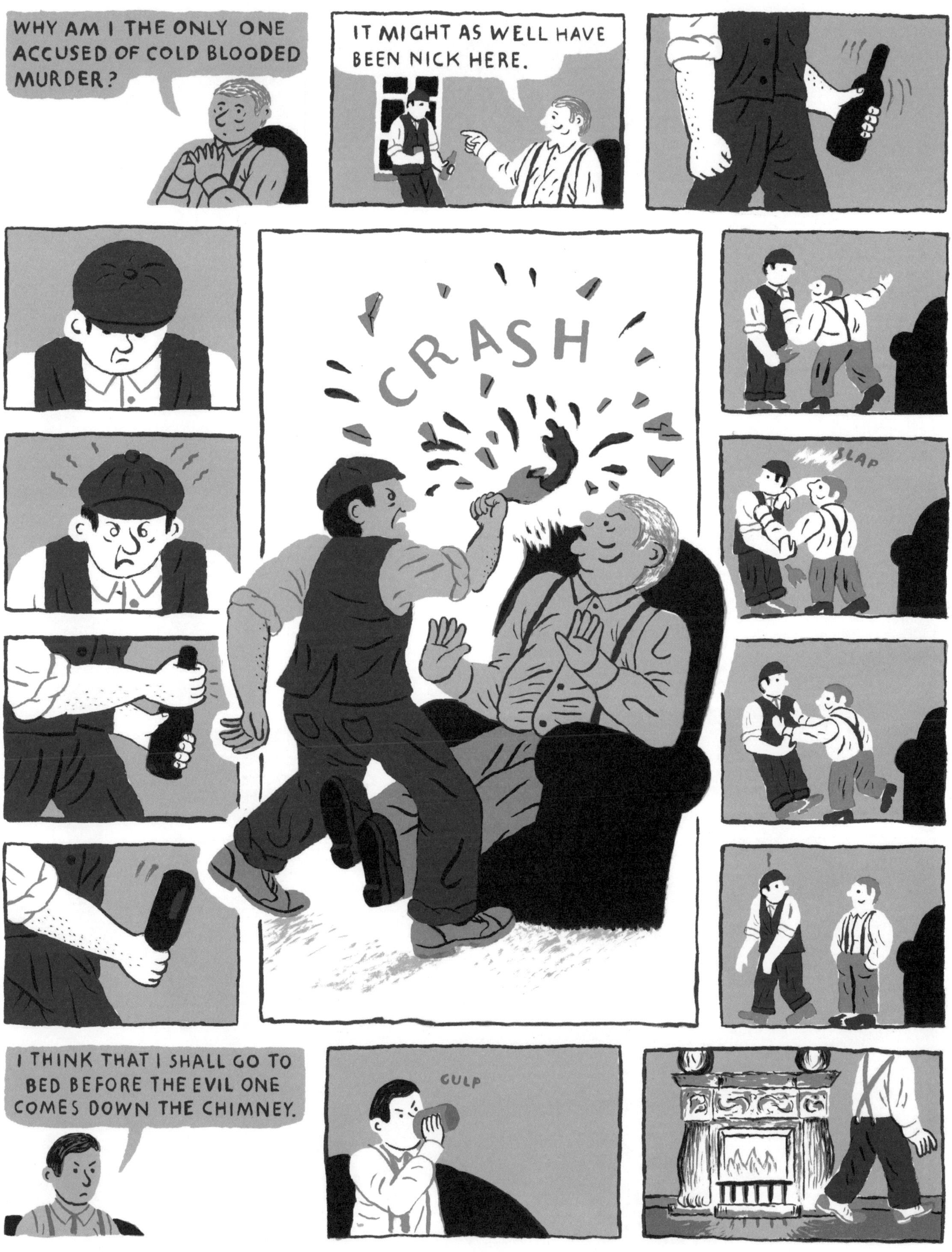
WHY AM I THE ONLY ONE ACCUSED OF COLD BLOODED MURDER?
IT MIGHT AS WELL HAVE BEEN NICK HERE.
CRASH
SLAP
I THINK THAT I SHALL GO TO BED BEFORE THE EVIL ONE COMES DOWN THE CHIMNEY.
GULP

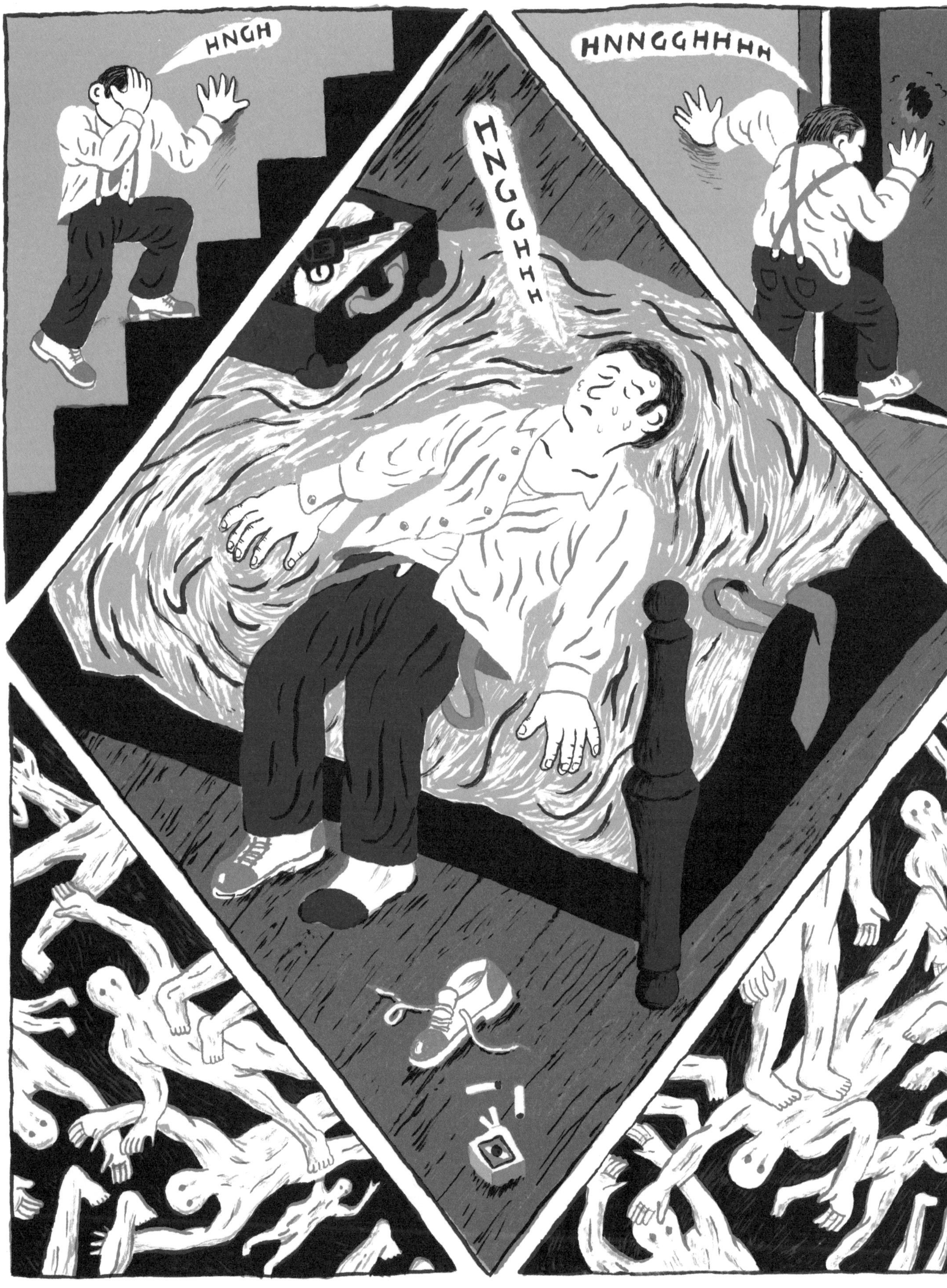
HNGH
HNNGGHHHH
HNNGGHHHH

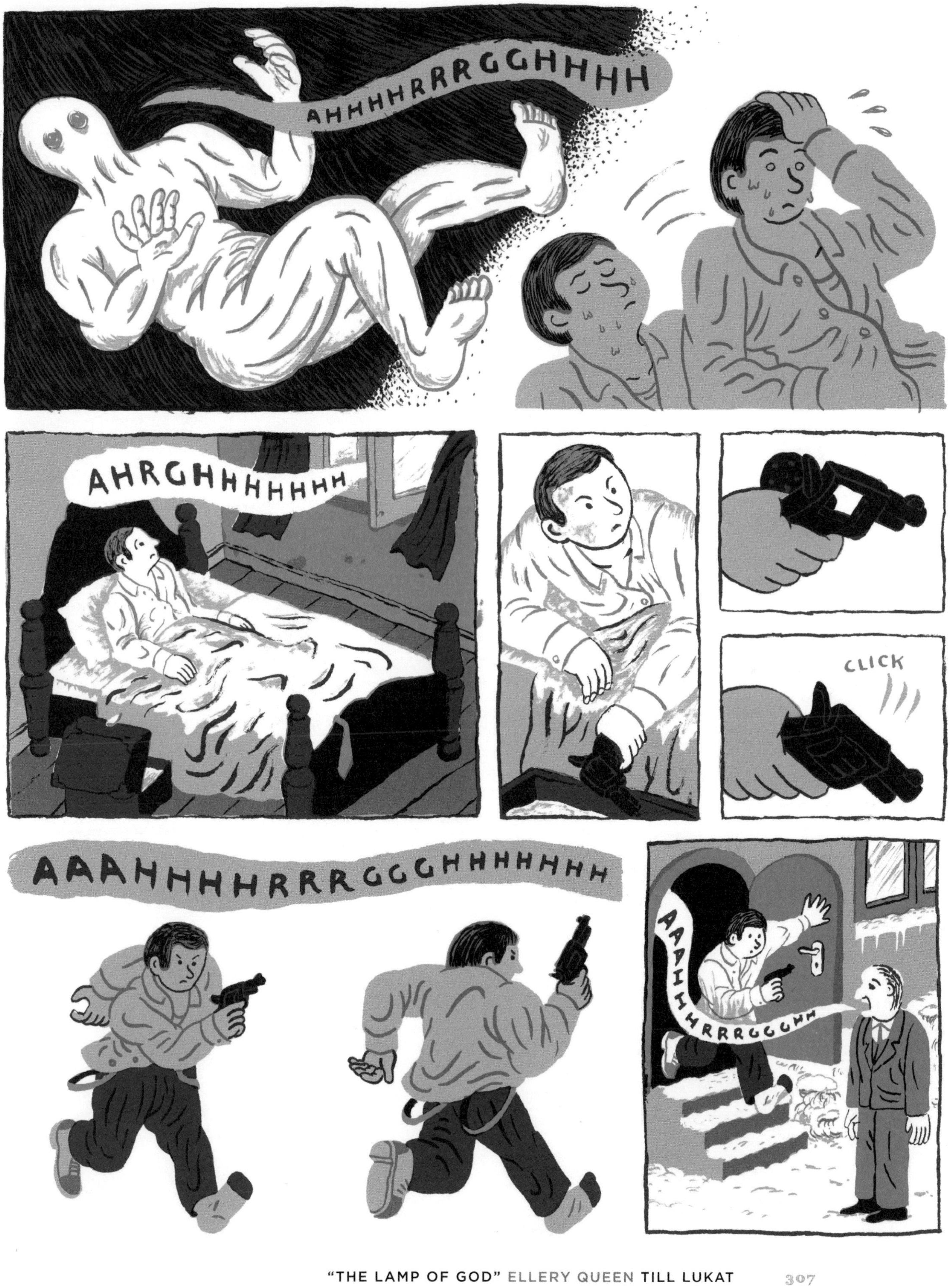
AHHHHRRRGGHHHH
AHRGHHHHHHH
CLICK
AAAHHHHHRRRGGGHHHHHHH
AAAHHHHRRRGGGHH

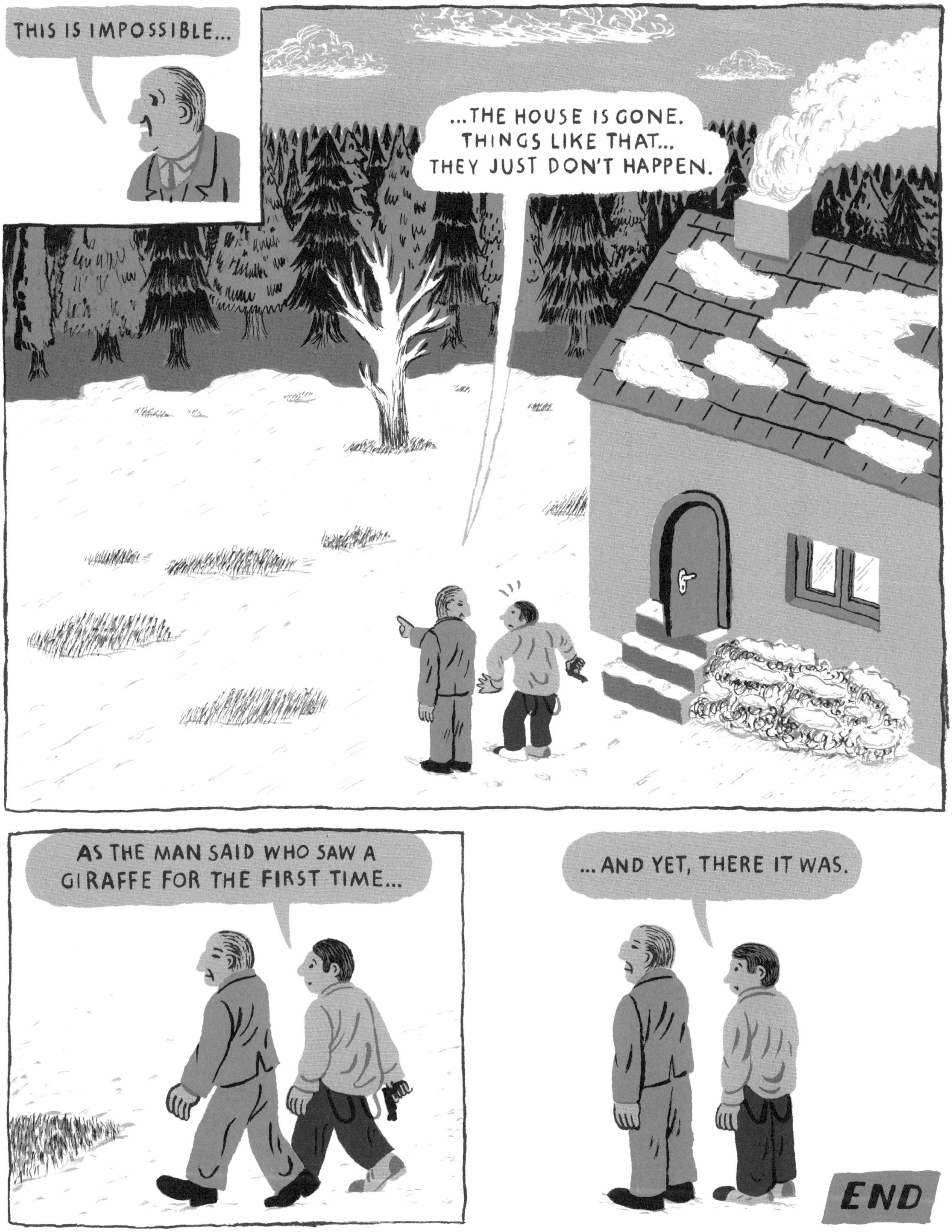
THIS IS IMPOSSIBLE...
...THE HOUSE IS GONE. THINGS LIKE THAT... THEY JUST DON'T HAPPEN.
AS THE MAN SAID WHO SAW A GIRAFFE FOR THE FIRST TIME...
...AND YET, THERE IT WAS.
END

CREATOR BIOGRAPHIES

LARA ANTAL is an illustrator and cartoonist who creates stories about magic and the mundane. If you dine in NYC you might see one of her infamous *Choking Victim* posters. Lara and her partner, Dave Kelly, run So What? Press, an award-winning comics imprint. She is also an archivist at Random House Children's Books. A Wisconsin native, she currently lives in Brooklyn. Website: lara-antal.com, Instagram: @laraantal

LANDIS BLAIR is the author and illustrator of *The Envious Siblings and Other Morbid Nursery Rhymes*, as well as the illustrator of the *New York Times* bestseller *From Here to Eternity* and the graphic novel *The Hunting Accident*, which won Best in Adult Books at the Excellence in Graphic Literature awards. He has published illustrations in the *New York Times*, *Chicago* magazine, *VQR*, and Medium. He lives in Chicago, Illinois. Website: landisblair.com, Twitter and Instagram: @landisblair

SHAWN CHENG is an artist and cartoonist working in New York City. He is a member of the comics collective Partyka and a core contributor to the all-ages fantasy anthology *Cartozia Tales*. His comics have appeared in the *SPX Anthology* and *Best American Comics*. His paintings and prints have been shown at Fredericks & Freiser Gallery (New York), Giant Robot (LA and San Francisco), as well as the Worcester Art Museum.

KIM CLEMENTS is a UK-based illustrator who focuses on children's books and zines. See more of her colorful palettes and quirky characters at kimclements.co.uk. Instagram: @kim.clements. Pinterest: Kim Clements

DAME DARCY is the creator of *Meat Cake* from Fantagrapahics, Mermaid and Queen Alice Tarot decks, coronated Coney Island Mermaid Queen, sea captain. She is also a doll-crafting witch, filmmaker, and musician. Over 100 titles of Dame Darcy's comix and graphic novels have been published internationally. She's currently working with partner Pleasant Art to create Meat Cake Manor Haunted House Hotel featuring theme rooms, zine and comix library, seance room, and witchcraft center in the most Haunted City in America: Savannah, Georgia. To find out more and become a patron, please go to patreon.com/damedarcy or damedarcy.com.

EMILY ROSE DIXON is an illustrator and comic artist based in the UK. As well as self-publishing comics, her work has appeared in numerous anthologies, including the *Broken Frontier Yearbook*, *Dirty Rotten Comics*, *Radio On*, and the *Thought Bubble* anthology. She was featured on Broken Frontier as one of "Six Small Press Creators to Watch in 2016." Emily and her sisters formed the Big Brown Eyes Collective in 2015 to help support and promote emerging comic artists. They produce themed anthologies, comics, and zines, and can often be found tabling at comic fairs around the country. Website: emilyroseillustration.co.uk. Instagram: @emilyrose_illustration @bbecollective

RACHEL LEAH GALLO is a Philadelphia-based artist and chef. She works mainly in pen and ink, watercolor, and acrylic paint. You can find her work on Instagram: @rachel_leah_gallo

TEDDY GOLDENBERG is an Israeli cartoonist and artist, born in 1985. He began creating comics in 2003. His works combine horror with humor. Teddy studied illustration at Bezalel Academy in Jerusalem. Online shop: teddy-goldenberg-comics-art.myshopify.com. Instagram: @teddygoldenberg

BECKY HAWKINS makes comics about life in Portland, Oregon, with her tiny cartoon sidekick, Shoulder Angel. She spent five years traveling the world as a cruise-ship musician and has been doing watercolor journal comics on postcard paper ever since. She also draws the 1940s lesbian superhero noir history webcomic *SuperButch*, co-created with cartoonist Barry Deutsch. Find it all at superbutchcomic.com!. Instagram: @becky_and_shoulder_angel

KATHERINE HEARST is an illustrator and artist based in London, with a body of work ranging from illustrated stories to figurative painting. Since her childhood was spent in Moscow, Russian storytelling has exerted a powerful influence over her work. Her subjects are taken primarily from folklore or children's literature. She wants to bring these timeless stories into the context of modern-day Russia.

OMER HOFFMANN is an Israel-based illustrator, cartoonist, and author. He studied illustration in Bezalel Art and Design Academy and his work is featured regularly in newspapers, commercials, animations, children's books, and graphic novels. Omer has illustrated ten picture books and is the recipient of several international awards, including the Andersen Honor List 2016 and a silver medal from the Society of Illustrators for his personal comics project *2 Years in New York City*. His latest comics story *Foreigner* has been published in Israel and Germany. He currently lives in Givatayim, Israel. You can see more work by Omer at ohoffmannn.com

DAVE KELLY runs So What? Press with his partner, Lara Antal. He is a co-creator of *Tales of the Night Watchman* and a contributor to the Eisner-nominated *Mine!* anthology. Follow him on instagram: @sowhatpress

JOY KOLITSKY started making comics after college at the encouragement of comic-loving friends and has continued to enjoy doing so to this day. She also works as an illustrator of children's books, magazines, greeting cards, and the occasional mural. Joy lives and works in Ocean City, New Jersey. Website: joykolitsky.com. Instagram: @joykolitsky

SONIA LEONG is an award-winning manga artist and member of the UK-based Sweatdrop Studios. Best known for *Manga Shakespeare: Romeo and Juliet* (SelfMadeHero), she's worked with Tokyopop, Image, *Neo Magazine*, Channel 4, HarperCollins, Hachette, Walker, and others on over eighty projects. She has taught manga the *Gaurdian*'s Hay Festival, Victoria & Albert Museum, London County Hall, and internationally with the British Council. Her art has been featured in the Kyoto International Manga Museum and London Cartoon Museum.

HILA NOAM is an Israeli comic book artist, illustrator, and author based in Tel Aviv. Her work has been published in magazines, anthologies, and childrens books worldwide (including Abrams Books, *Strapazine*, and *Kutikuti*) and has been displayed in solo and group exhibitions around the globe (Fumetto Comix Festival, Switzerland, Society of Illustrators, NY, Israeli Comics Museum, Israel). Hila is a comics columnist for *National Geographic Kids Israel*. *Rambly*, her first graphic novel for children, was recently published in French and Hebrew. Hila is an illustration lecturer at the Bezalel Academy of Art and Design in Jerusalem.

JOHN PIERARD is the offspring of a peripatetic US Air Force family. He lived in many places around the world before settling in his beloved Northern Mannahatta. Obsessed from an early age with *Mad* magazine, science fiction paperbacks, early 70's Hollywood movies, and cinema from Korea and China. Lately, John has been grinding out literally tons of material inspired by the political nightmare we've been living with the last couple of years, much of which can be seen on the Facebook page John Pierard's Art Lounge.

TILL LUKAT is an award-winning cartoonist from Berlin, Germany. He studied Illustration and Visual Communication at the University of Arts in Berlin and at the University of the West of England in Bristol. He has published two books, which have been translated into three languages, won first prize at Ligatura Pitching and second place in the *Fumetto* short story contest. His work has appeared in publications such as *Stripburger*, *Kuš!*, *Off Life*, *Beneficial Shock!* magazine, and *Strapazin*, and he worked with the European Research Council on a scientific comic about the beginning of life on this planet.

SALLY MADDEN has been voted best waitress in Philadelphia, probably. Fellow cartoonist Matt Wiegle has been changing her cat's litter box since 2010.

ANDREA MONTANO is an illustrator, comic book artist, and portrait artist. Her works are varied, from children's books and comic book titles for various clients and publishers. Her comic works are mostly centered in fun storytelling and action-adventure, as well as historical narrative. You may find her works at montanogallery.com and Instagram: @amontanoart

JSEBA MORALES is an illustrator and sequential artist from Canary Islands, Spain. He has been published in the *Financial Times*, *Alterna Comics*, and other publications. Website: josebamorales.com. Twitter: @joseba_morales. Instagram: @josebamoralesart

DOUGLAS NOBLE was raised in the Borders. His previous comics include *The Silent Choir* (part of the British Library's "Comics Unmasked" exhibition), *Horrible Folk*, and *Black Leather* (with Sean Azzopardi). He is also the editor of the award-winning anthology *Jazz Creepers*. More details can be found at his website: strip-for-me.com.

RACHEL SMYTHE's work ranges from labels for craft beer to an epic, ongoing comics adaptation of the Persephone myth, *Lore Olympus*, which was nominated for best webcomic for the 2019 Will Eisner Comic Industry Award. Follow her on instagram @usedbandaid.

ANGELLE SUNDBERG is a classically trained artist who has channeled her creative passion into the culinary arts. When she's not making comics, she's crafting cakes.

ALICE URBINO is a Bristol-based comic creator who specializes in the use of body horror to visualize emotional states and invisible illnesses. Previously a part of Ignatz-nominated collective Comic Book Slumber Party, she has also been named one of Broken Frontier's Six to Watch. To have a glimpse into her brain and to find out more, visit her personal internet experience at aliceurbino.com or follow her on Instagram: @aliceurbino

ANTHONY VENTURA is an award-winning Illustrator from Canada whose work has appeared worldwide in various publications, advertising, and multimedia. Some clients have included *Playboy*, *Rolling Stone*, Doritos, ESPN Xgames, *Phoenix* magazine, *Time* magazine (Asia), *SPIN*, *Miami New Times*, *North American Review*, and more. He currently resides in Canada. Follow him on Instagram: @anthv

ZAVKA: is an illustrator and comics artist based in Warsaw, Poland. His works are a mixture of beauty, dreams, and madness. His books include: *The Hunter*, a dreamlike comics; *The Serpent*, a bloody illustrated book based on an Italian fairy tale; and *Hungry Hansel and Gluttonous Gretel*, a psychedelic comic story. Website: zavka.webnode.com, Instagram: @_zavka_

CREDITS AND PERMISSIONS

"Cain and Abel" from the Book of Genesis was created especially for this volume. Copyright © 2020 by Zavka. Printed by permission of the artist.

"Bluebeard" by Charles Perrault was created especially for this volume. Copyright © 2020 by Shawn Cheng. Printed by permission of the artist.

"The Tell-Tale Heart" by Edgar Allan Poe was created especially for this volume. Copyright © 2020 by Dame Darcy. Printed by permission of the artist.

Lady Audley's Secret by Mary Elizabeth Braddon was created especially for this volume. Copyright © 2020 by Joy Kolitsky. Printed by permission of the artist.

"Murder Ballads" was created especially for this volume. Copyright © 2020 by John Pierard. Printed by permission of the artist.

Psycho by Robert Bloch was created especially for this volume. Copyright © 2020 by Rachel Leah Gallo. Printed by permission of the artist.

The Sailor Who Fell From Grace With the Sea by Yukio Mishima was created especially for this volume. Copyright © 2020 by Andrea Montano. Printed by permission of the artist.

The Silence of the Lambs by Thomas Harris was created especially for this volume. Copyright © 2020 by Alice Urbino. Printed by permission of the artist.

The Black Dahlia by James Ellroy was created especially for this volume. Copyright © 2020 by Josebo Morales. Printed by permission of the artist.

I Was Dora Suarez by Derek Raymond was created especially for this volume. Copyright © 2020 by Douglas Noble. Printed by permission of the artist and writer.

"Salome and John the Baptist" from the Gospel of Matthew was created especially for this volume. Copyright © 2020 by Angelle Sundberg. Printed by permission of the artist.

"The Pardoner's Tale" by Geoffrey Chaucer was created especially for this volume. Copyright © 2020 by Katherine Hearst. Printed by permission of the artist.

Titus Andronicus by William Shakespeare was created especially for this volume. Copyright © 2020 by Anthony Ventura. Printed by permission of the artist.

Rebecca by Daphne du Maurier was created especially for this volume. Copyright © 2020 by Emily Rose Dixon. Printed by permission of the artist.

The Godfather by Mario Puzo was created especially for this volume. Copyright © 2020 by Rachel Smythe. Printed by permission of the artist.

"The Lady, or the Tiger?" by Frank R. Stockton was created especially for this volume. Copyright © 2020 by Omer Hoffmann. Printed by permission of the artist.

The Trial by Franz Kafka was created especially for this volume. Copyright © 2020 by Landis Blair. Printed by permission of the artist.

"The Case of the Wild Cat and the Crown Prince" was created especially for this volume. Copyright © 2020 by Sonia Leong. Printed by permission of the artist.

"The Swedish Match" by Anton Chekhov was created especially for this volume. Copyright © 2020 by Hila Noam. Printed by permission of the artist.

"A Scandal in Bohemia" by Arthur Conan Doyle was created especially for this volume. Copyright © 2020 by Lara Antal and Dave Kelly. Printed by permission of the artist and writer.

"The Ninescore Mystery" by Baroness Emmuska Orczy was created especially for this volume. Copyright © 2020 by Becky Hawkins. Printed by permission of the artist.

"The Sins of Prince Saradine" by G.K. Chesterton was created especially for this volume. Copyright © 2020 by Sally Madden. Printed by permission of the artist.

The Secret Adversary by Agatha Christie was created especially for this volume. Copyright © 2020 by Kim Clements. Printed by permission of the artist.

"The Road Home" by Dashiell Hammett was created especially for this volume. Copyright © 2020 by Teddy Goldenberg. Printed by permission of the artist.

"The Lamp of God" by Ellery Queen was created especially for this volume. Copyright © 2020 by Till Lukat. Printed by permission of the artist.

INDEX

TITLE	AUTHOR	ARTIST/ADAPTER
The Black Dahlia 104	Robert Bloch 58	Laura Antal 240
"Bluebeard" 11	Mary Elizabeth Braddon 31	Shawn Cheng 11
Cain and Abel 4	Geoffrey Chaucer 134	Kim Clements 272
"The Case of the Wild Cat and the Crown Prince" 216	Anton Chekhov 231	Dame Darcy 20
The Godfather 182	G.K. Chesterton 261	Teddy Goldenberg 284
I Was Dora Suarez 116	Agatha Christie 272	Becky Hawkins 251
Lady Audley's Secret 31	Arthur Conan Doyle 240	Katherine Hearst 134
"The Lady, or the Tiger?" 189	James Ellroy 104	Omer Hoffmann 189
"The Lamp of God" 296	Dashiell Hammett 284	Dave Kelly 240
Murder Ballads 46	Thomas Harris 88	Joy Kolitsky 31
"The Ninescore Mystery" 251	Franz Kafka 198	Emily Rose Dixon 175
"The Pardoner's Tale" 134	Daphne du Maurier 175	Rachel Leah Gallo 58
Psycho 58	Yukio Mishima 79	Sonia Leong 216
Rebecca 175	Baroness Emmuska Orczy 251	Till Lukat 296
"The Road Home" 284	Charles Perrault 11	Sally Madden 261
The Sailor Who Fell From Grace With the Sea 79	Edgar Allen Poe 20	Andrea Montano 9
Salome and John the Baptist 124	Mario Puzo 182	Jose Morales 104
"A Scandal in Bohemia" 240	Ellery Queen 296	Hila Noam 231
The Secret Adversary 272	Derek Raymond 116	Douglas Noble 116
The Silence of the Lambs 88	William Shakespeare 147	John Pierard 46
"The Sins of Prince Sardine" 261	Frank R. Stockton 189	Rachel Smythe 182
"The Swedish Match" 231	From the Book of Genesis 4	Angelle Sundberg 124
"The Tell-Tale Heart" 20	From the Gospel of Matthew 124	Alice Urbino 88
Titus Andronicus 147		Anthony Ventura 147
The Trial 198		Zavka 4